THOMSON

NASD Stockbroker Exam

SERIES 7

PREPARATION GUIDE

Part of the COMPASS Learning System.

http://professional.swlearning.com

Welcome to the South-Western

NASD Stockbroker Exam SERIES 7

PREPARATION GUIDE

part of the COMPASS Learning System.

Congratulations! Your path to an exciting and rewarding career begins right here. By selecting one of the most innovative certification exam prep programs available, you are taking an important step toward achieving success on the NASD Series 7 exam — and launching your new career.

Not only is the **South-Western NASD Series 7 Exam Prep Guide** packed with valuable insight and information for potential stockbrokers, but it's also engineered around the identical structure of the actual Series 7 exam from NASD. Built on a highly proven test-prep model, this new guide fully prepares you both to pass the Series 7 exam and to excel in the seven critical functions of a registered representative.

Select Superior Tools

The **South-Western NASD Series 7 Exam Prep Guide** is designed specifically for those preparing to become stockbrokers — licensed registered representatives or account executives employed by brokerage firms. It is part of the new COMPASS Learning System from South-Western.

As one of the most respected providers of business learning solutions worldwide, South-Western is committed to meeting the learning needs of professionals like you, providing the tools you need to reach personal career goals and to achieve business success. Designed unlike any other program, the COMPASS system combines proven methodology with innovative technology to deliver highly targeted and streamlined instruction that quickly leads to success on the NASD Series 7 exam.

Prepare with a Proven Approach

Nationally recognized for their high success rate in preparing candidates for certification exams, the Prep Guide author team applies their unique test-prep instructional methodology to the Series 7 exam. Extensively classroom tested, this precise, streamlined approach is designed to help candidates pass the NASD Series 7 the first time. It is an ideal test-prep solution for self-paced, instructor-led, and blended learning solutions.

Just like the NASD Exam, the Prep Guide organizes material around the seven critical functions of a registered representative. This emphasis prepares candidates for success on the exam, as well as for their responsibilities after the test. In addition, South-Western's innovative technology helps candidates focus on improving their weaknesses, instead of wasting time on material they already know.

Bottom line: The South-Western NASD Series 7 Exam Prep Guide helps you quickly and precisely chart your way to Series 7 success!

Examining NASD's Series 7 Exam

The NASD General Securities Registered Representative (Series 7) examination is administered by the National Association of Securities Dealers (NASD) as a safeguard for the investing public to ensure that registered representatives (RRs) have the knowledge and skills to perform their duties. Series 7 registration allows an individual to sell all types of securities offered by the member broker-dealer (except commodities futures).

Designed to measure candidates' competence at an entry level, the Series 7 requires no prerequisite exams, but candidates must be sponsored by their firm.

Focus on 7 Critical Functions

The NASD General Securities Representative (Series 7) exam consists of 250 four-option multiple-choice questions. The six-hour test is administered in two three-hour parts (125 questions per part). A score of 70 percent or higher is required to pass.

To ensure the integrity of new test questions, candidates are also given 10 additional, unidentified questions that do not count toward their score.

The exam is organized around the seven critical functions performed by RRs and the specific job tasks related to each — ensuring that test topics are relevant to representatives' actual responsibilities. All exam questions are written and reviewed by experienced registered representatives, trainers, and supervisors.

Critical Function	No. of Exam Questions
1. Seeking Business for the Broker-Dealer	9
2. Evaluating Customers' Needs and Investment Objectives	4
3. Providing Customers With Investment Information	123
4. Managing Customer Accounts and Account Records	27
5. Explaining Various Securities	53
6. Processing Customers' Instructions	13
7. Monitoring Customers' Portfolio	21
Total	250

The questions on the actual exam do not appear in any particular order. Each test candidate receives a randomized set of 260 multiple-choice questions based on the present topic weights of the exam. (Remember, 10 of the 260 questions are "new" questions under review and do not count toward your score.)

Plan for Exam Day

On the day of your scheduled exam, you should arrive at the testing center at least 30 minutes before your appointment. You need valid picture identification (such as your driver's license, passport, or military ID). You must also agree to the rules of conduct with your signature and provide a finger imprint.

Exams are administered via PROCTOR®, a computer system specifically designed for computer-based testing and training. The PROCTOR® system is user friendly and requires no previous computer experience. An introductory lesson familiarizes you with the system before you begin the exam.

As soon as you complete the exam, the computer tallies and presents your score, detailing your performance in each area of the exam.

The Series 7 is a closed book examination. Personal possessions — books, briefcases, and notes — are not allowed in the testing/training room. Candidates are not allowed to use personal calculators. At your request, the testing center staff will provide a calculator. Scratch paper also is provided.

Streamlining Your Learning Curve

Combining an exceptional methodology with interactive technology, the South-Western's COMPASS Series 7 Learning System helps you chart a customized course to achieve personal success. It helps you evaluate exactly where you are, where you need to go, and how to get there. Fast.

And there are no surprises. This cutting-edge prep guide provides an excellent preview of the exam — and the practice to master it.

Chart the Most Direct Course with COMPASS

Built on a highly successful class-tested instructional test-prep model that has helped thousands of professionals pass certification exams, South-Western's COMPASS Learning System delivers focused instruction targeting the core content areas critical for you to pass the NASD Series 7 exam. Unlike the topical approaches of other Series 7 test-prep materials, each of the learning tools from South-Western aligns directly with the seven sections of the actual Series 7 exam.

South-Western's innovative
COMPASS Learning System for the NASD Series 7 exam includes:

- **NASD Stockbroker Series 7 Exam: Preparation Guide**
  0-324-18695-9 Organized around the seven critical functions of registered representatives (the same way the actual Series 7 exam is structured), this comprehensive resource provides a thorough review and preparation for the NASD General Securities Examination.
- **NASD Stockbroker Series 7 Exam Prep: Drill & Practice**
  CD 0-324-20333-0 This powerful study tool helps candidates check their knowledge and polish their test-taking skills through a variety of exam types and a multitude of questions.
- **NASD Stockbroker Series 7 Exam Prep: Guide & Practice**
  CD 0-324-22444-3 This includes the Preparation Guide and Drill & Practice CD packaged together.
- **NASD Stockbroker Series 7 Exam: Prescriptive SmartLink**
  CD 0-324-20181-8 Creating a customized learning path, this inventive tool helps candidates chart the most direct and efficient path to practicing for and passing the Series 7 exam. The CD features the entire prep course — including the full text of the Preparation Guide — in an interactive format.
- **NASD Stockbroker Series 7 Exam Prep: Online Course**
  0-324-20332-2 The complete innovative package is also available online.

p

preface

South-Western NASD Series 7 Exam Pre

Brief Table of Contents

Putting You in the Driver's Seat

Realizing serious candidates are already familiar with basic theory and concepts, the South-Western Prep Guide takes you beyond basic knowledge and focuses on the duties and responsibilities associated with the seven critical functions. The self-paced instructional design allows you to take charge of your exam preparation — and plot a targeted course for success based on your unique needs.

The result: more efficiency. You spend your valuable time improving knowledge and skills in your weaker areas — not re-hashing what you already know. You go into the exam well prepared and confident of success.

Here are some of guide's exceptional navigational tools to help you track your individual progress:

- ▷ **Success Tips** — Abundant tips and valuable insights to passing the Series 7 exam found throughout each chapter help you zero in on the key elements of the exam and build your confidence each step of the way.
- ▷ **Concise Coverage** — Comprehensive yet succinct, each chapter provides a quick overview and direct application of the essential knowledge and concepts you need to pass the Series 7 exam. Found in the margin, "Test Key" icons spotlight important points or explanations of complex topics to help prepare you for the exam.
- ▷ **Comprehensive Summaries & Reviews** — Each chapter ends with a detailed summary highlighting key points from the text, as well as a brief quiz. Providing an excellent review of chapter material, these tools test your comprehension and give immediate feedback on your progress chapter by chapter.
- ▷ **Chapter Key Terms & Expansive Glossary** — A list of key terms with definitions at the beginning of each chapter provides easy reference, while a extensive glossary is included at the end. The Prep Guide provides thorough definitions, equipping you with a solid understanding of industry jargon.
- ▷ **Two Practice Final Exams** — Test your mastery of the content by completing the two Practice Final Exams that mimic the NASD Series 7 exam. These practice exams include the same proportion of questions per topic established by NASD for the actual Series 7 exam.
- ▷ **Test Answer Keys & Rationale** — Check your understanding with the detailed explanations provided for each Practice Final Exam question. This valuable self-paced feature enables you to immediately determine your mastery of the exam content and provides you with insight into the logic of each answer.

Hitting the Mark with the Drill & Practice CD

Coupled with its superior instructional model, the **South-Western NASD Series 7 Exam Prep Guide** employs cutting-edge technology to enhance and accelerate your learning curve. The vigorous Drill & Practice CD challenges you to put your knowledge and skills to the test, then offers immediate feedback on how you're progressing. The CD randomizes the question sequence, so each time you take a test it's fresh, continually challenging and testing your mastery of the seven critical functions.

The CD's diversity of drills and testing tools gives you maximum variance and ultimate flexibility as you chart your personal course to successful exam preparation.

Thorough Chapter Quizzes

Seven quizzes for each chapter enable you to check your understanding of critical functions as you progress through the seven chapters.

Unique Customization Option

Streamlining your understanding of content, you can create customized exams to practice drills on the functions you choose — allowing you to spend more time on areas in which you need reinforcement and less time on areas you have mastered.

Practice Exam 1, Practice Exam 2

Once you have mastered the chapter quizzes, you can challenge your skills in an exam setting. Two Practice Final Exams consisting of 250 questions each — just like the actual NASD Series 7 exam — test your overall knowledge of the seven critical functions, providing a valuable gauge of how prepared you are for the NASD Series 7 exam and spotlighting areas that still need improvement.

Comprehensive Final Exam

Once you master the Practice Exams, you are ready for the Final. If you aren't satisfied with your scores, you can brush up on your skills based on feedback from the Final Exam and then re-take it. (We recommend scores of 90 percent or higher.) The Final Exam pulls 250 questions from a pool of many — so it's a new test every time. The Final is weighted according to NASD specifications for the Series 7 exam.

Flexible Timer & Feedback Options

The CD gives you the option to take exams timed or untimed, depending on whether you're using the exams to study or to simulate the actual Series 7 exam. Some exams give immediate feedback and some delay it until the completion of the exam. Immediate feedback provides more of a learning tool — you know at once if your response is right or wrong and why. The delayed feedback feature enables you to mirror the real testing environment.

Critical Vocabulary Drills

A significant part of the Series 7 exam is terminology. Therefore it is critical for you to know and effectively use industry terminology. Unique to the CD, Vocabulary Drills can be organized by terms or by definitions, allowing you to start with a term and match it to the appropriate definition or begin with a definition and find the correct term.

Resourceful Reporting Functions

As you work through the program, you can print progress reports of topics completed, percentage of questions answered correctly, and the time and date when you took the exam. You can use the reports as verification of your progress through the course or to document your achievement of understanding.

In addition, after taking quizzes or exams you can print questions you missed with the correct answers for additional review.

Interactive Glossary

A dictionary of all key terms provides an excellent reference and reinforces learning, enabling you to perform a quick search when you come across a word you haven't mastered.

Navigating Your Own "Learning Path"

Combining the content of the Prep Guide text with innovative software, the SmartLink™ CD delivers the entire prep course in an individualized, interactive learning experience. An ideal study aid, the SmartLink™ software helps you quickly and accurately ascertain where your trouble spots are, and then maps out a personal learning path to quickly turn them into strengths.

Available in both online and CD-ROM formats, this diagnostic electronic prep tool accelerates and streamlines your exam preparation time by helping you focus on what you don't know. Innovative SmartLink™ tools offer immediate reinforcement and a targeted roadmap for review specific to your individual study needs.

The result is the most direct and efficient "learning path" for practicing for, preparing for, and passing the NASD Series 7 exam.

Powerful Technology, Simple Operation

Extremely user friendly, SmartLink™ employs point-and-click technology, helping you focus on your studies — not the software. From the Opening Screen, you can smoothly navigate through the program and access features by using buttons and links to

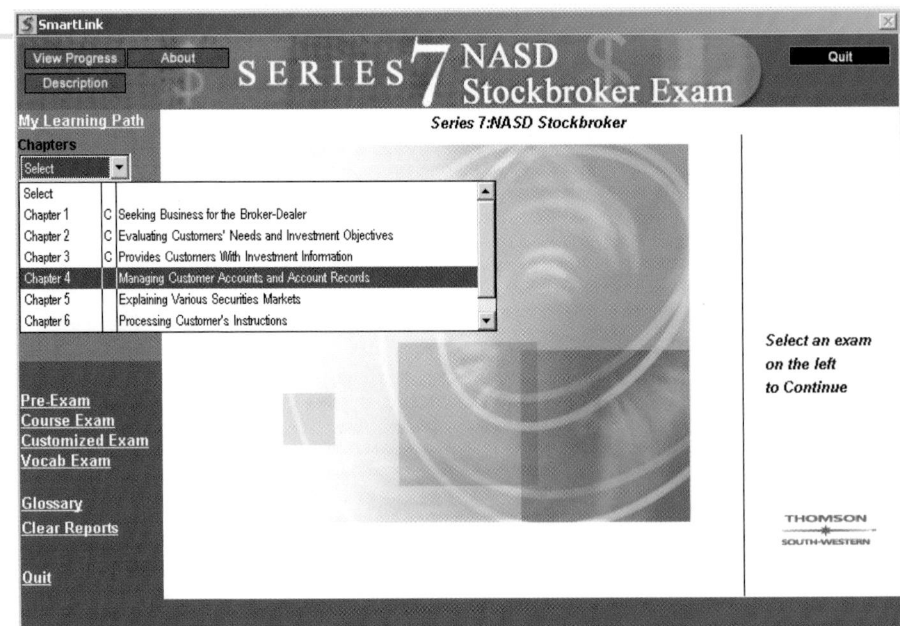

- View your progress report
- View a description of the course
- Access My Learning Path
- Access Chapter study material
- Access Chapter Exams
- Access Vocabulary Drills
- Access the Pre-Exam
- Access the Course Exam
- Access the Customized Exam
- Access Vocabulary Exams
- Access the Glossary
- Clear your progress report data
- Exit the program

Interactive Pre-Exam

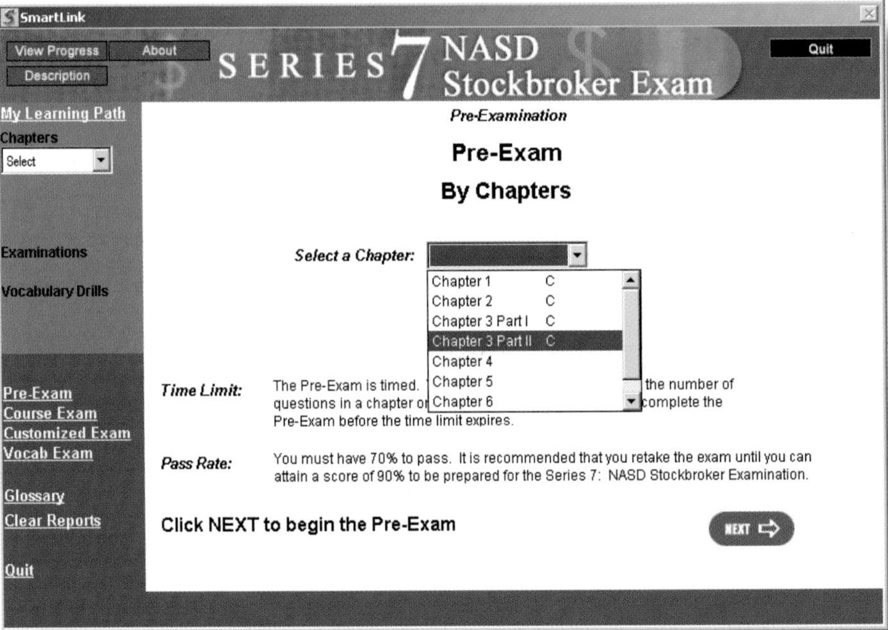

Upon initial start-up, you have the option to take the Pre-Exam, an interactive tool that assesses your specific learning needs. Providing immediate feedback, the Pre-Exam is an excellent instrument to test how much you know going into the course and as you progress. It quickly and accurately pinpoints your mastery of topics and creates a powerful, individualized learning path to improve the areas you did not master. (Scores of 90 percent and above are considered mastery level.)

A full 250-question, six-hour long exam (like the actual NASD Series 7 exam), the Pre-Test gives you the option of testing one chapter at a time (there are seven chapters) or in two parts. The test is timed.

As you progress through the program, you can take the Pre-Exam again — and again — to create a new learning path as your knowledge increases.

Personalized "My Learning Path"

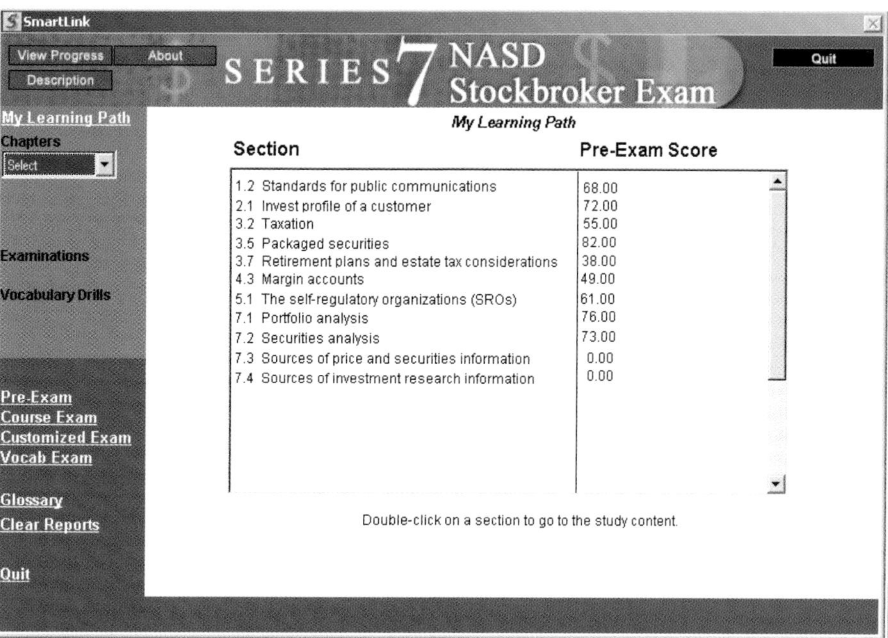

At the heart of the SmartLink™ software is a customized, prescriptive learning path based on the results and evaluation of your individual Pre-Exam scores. By using the My Learning Path option, you can easily review areas where more study is needed. Focusing only on areas you have not mastered, My Learning Path uses a variety of exams and drills to both challenge and test your understanding and, ultimately, bolster your weak spots. With this unique tool, you could cut your preparation time by as much as 20 percent!

Once the software develops your Learning Path, you simply click on the area where you want to begin. It's that easy! Even if you choose not to take the Pre-Exam, you proceed through the program by selecting your desired topics.

Diverse Chapter Study Materials

Study material for each of the seven chapters includes content, graphs, definitions, key terms, summaries, and overviews. You select the material you want to view by choosing a chapter or a section from the drop-down menus.

Self-Paced Chapter Quizzes

Based on the seven critical functions covered in the NASD Series 7 exam, the quizzes offer excellent practice in the areas you need. Completely flexible, the quizzes are not timed, and you select the number of questions you want. You can also print questions from the Chapter Quizzes for further review.

Practical Vocabulary Drills

Organized by chapter, Vocabulary Drills test your knowledge on words and terms used in the securities market — jargon essential to your success on the NASD Series 7 exam as well as in the field. The two types of drills — Words by Term or Words by Definition — offer a thorough test of your understanding. The drills can be taken timed or untimed, and you select the number of questions you want for each drill.

Rigorous Vocabulary Exams

Vocabulary Exams test your knowledge on words and terms used in the securities market. With 1,074 questions, the exams cover vocabulary from the entire Prep Guide and can be taken timed or untimed. You simply choose the number of questions you want for the exam

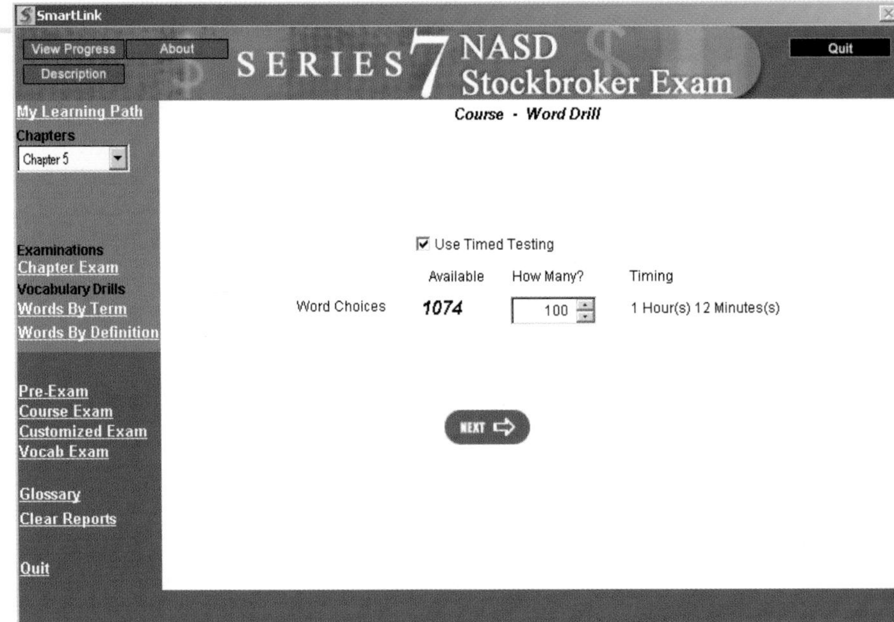

Unique Customized Exam

The Customized Exam feature allows you to create personalized tests for additional practice from over 150 available questions. You select the number of questions you want from each chapter, as well as whether the test is timed or not.

Final Course Exam

With 250 questions and a six-hour time limit, the comprehensive Final Exam simulates the actual NASD Series 7 exam. You can take the exam timed or untimed, and you can take it more than once. The questions are randomized each time you take the test.

User-Friendly Question Screen

When the Question Screen presents question and answer choices for your selected exam or drill, it displays the question, term, or definition in the question text box while multiple-choice answers are displayed in four answer selection boxes. You choose your answer by clicking on the letter to the left of the answer selection boxes. The program evaluates your answer and displays "Correct" or "Wrong" under the answer — giving immediate feedback. It also displays your correct scoring percentage after each answer.

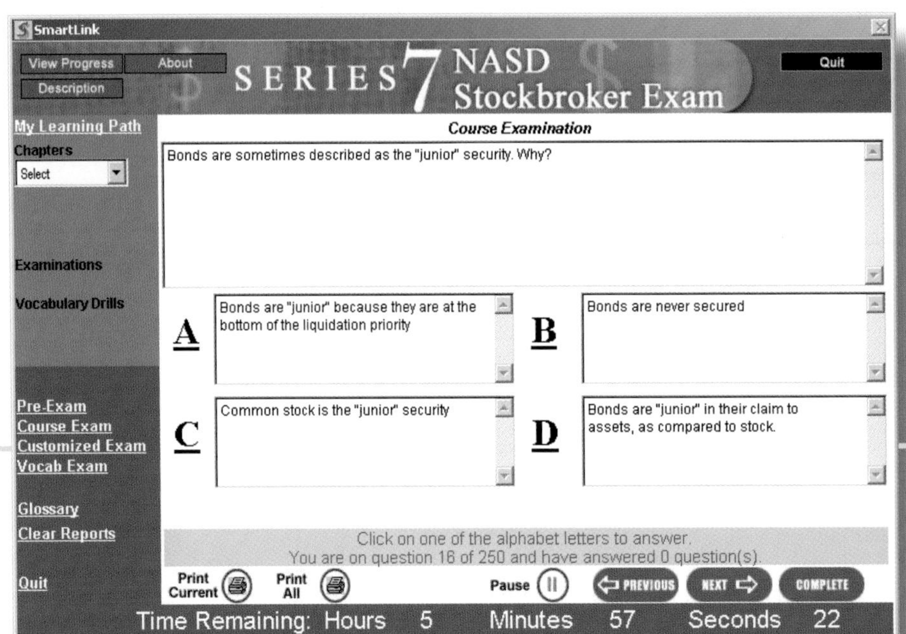

Informative Results Screen

This screen displays your final score and recommends whether you should re-take the exam or drill or if you have mastered the material. It also displays a list of all the exam or drill questions and the status of your answers — "Correct," "Wrong," or "No Answer." From here you can select a question you answered incorrectly. The program will display your incorrect answer vs. the correct answer and offer an explanation of the correct answer — helping you understand the "why" of the correct answers and, therefore, improving your understanding of key material.

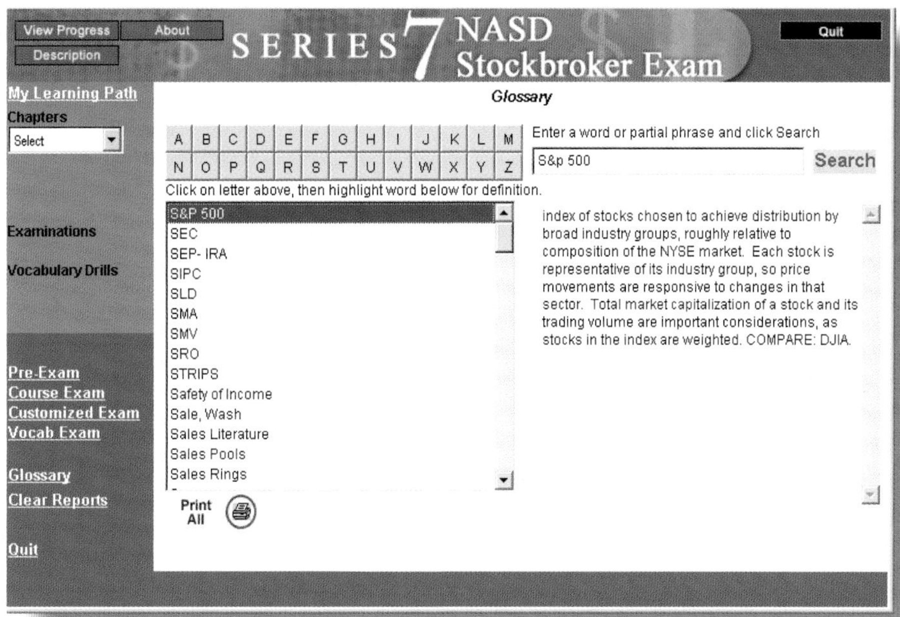

Exhaustive Glossary

This quick-reference tool defines industry words and phrases with a click of a mouse. You can look for a particular entry by typing in a word or phrase and clicking the Search button or by clicking on a letter and scrolling through all the words that begin with that letter.

Progressive Reporting Function

The resourceful "View Progress" reporting function enables you to track your progress through detailed reports each step of the way, from start to finish. The report displays or prints your exams accessed, exam date, and your score.

You also have the option to print questions from drills and exams — with or without the correct answers listed with the questions.

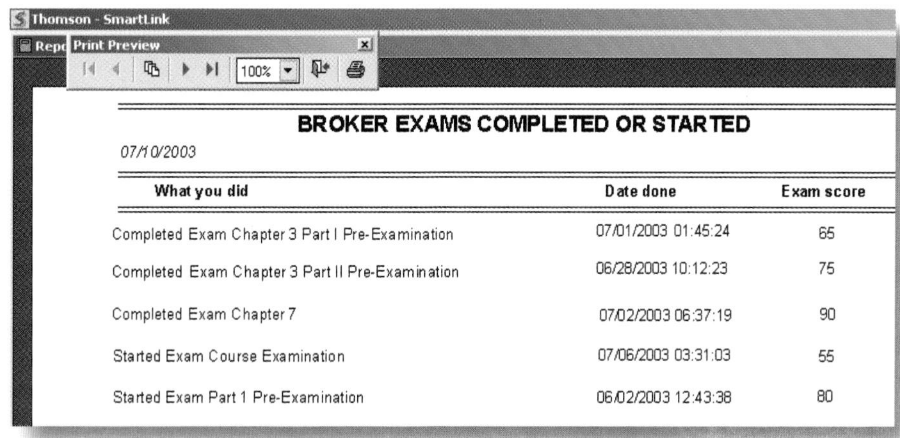

BROKER EXAMS COMPLETED OR STARTED

07/10/2003

What you did	Date done	Exam score
Completed Exam Chapter 3 Part I Pre-Examination	07/01/2003 01:45:24	65
Completed Exam Chapter 3 Part II Pre-Examination	06/28/2003 10:12:23	75
Completed Exam Chapter 7	07/02/2003 06:37:19	90
Started Exam Course Examination	07/06/2003 03:31:03	55
Started Exam Part 1 Pre-Examination	06/02/2003 12:43:38	80

p

preface

Preparing for the Exam Experience

In addition to preparing for the content of the Series 7 exam, it's also a good idea to prepare for the test-taking experience itself. If you haven't taken an exam in awhile, you may be feeling a little anxious. Good study habits and test-taking techniques can help you achieve your personal best on exam day.

PRACTICE HEALTHY STUDY HABITS

▷ **Study at a time of day that is comfortable for you.** Everyone is different, but it should be a time of day when you are alert and focused.

▷ **Minimize distractions.** This means no TV, food, children, or spouses. Try to stay off a bed or couch where you are more likely to fall asleep.

▷ **Do not cram the night before the exam.** You will retain information effectively by studying regularly.

▷ To improve your success and streamline your exam preparation schedule, **use one of South-Western's CD-ROM learning tools** to take additional computerized practice tests, identify areas you have mastered, and target specific content you may need to review further to ensure your success on the exam.

▷ **Read the exam question** at least three times before you look at the answer and then read the answers at least two times before selecting the best one. Understand what the question is asking and catch key words like EXCEPT and ONLY.

▷ **Know definitions by studying the glossary in this prep guide.** If you don't, you are doing yourself an injustice because the exam not only tests candidates' knowledge of material, but also their ability to apply it.

▷ **Sleep well the night before the exam.** Try to have your exam scheduled first thing in the morning so you are alert and refreshed.

ADOPT TRIED-AND-TRUE TEST-TAKING TIPS

▷ If you tell your friends and family when you are taking your exam, it may place pressure on you by setting up expectations. Instead of worrying about their expectations, try to keep your exam date a secret and then surprise them after you pass.

▷ Don't spend too much time on one question. If you don't know the answer to a question, mark it and come back to it later. You may think of the answer later or you might even find it in another question as you work through the exam.

▷ During the exam, you may lose your train of thought. When this happens stop, relax, and take a deep breath. Return your focus to the exam and proceed.

▷ Many times two of the four answers are not worth considering. Pick one of the two remaining answers when guessing.

- ▷ Your first answer is usually the right one, so do not change it unless you are sure.
- ▷ Answers with absolutes — such as must, always, greatest, never, and has to be — generally are not the correct answers.
- ▷ Above all, do not panic. Stop. Take a moment. Reorganize the material. You know more than you think you do. Relax and let it become clear.

Registering for the Exam

To obtain admission to the Series 7 exam, your firm will submit your application along with the processing fees. Upon receipt of valid enrollment, register immediately to take the exam at a local Prometric Testing Center.

Exam and training sessions are provided at many convenient delivery locations — more than 380 Prometric Testing Centers throughout the United States and Canada. To schedule an appointment, contact the Prometric National Call Center at (800) 578-6273 or visit www.prometric.com/nasd. Make sure you confirm the location/address when you schedule your appointment. You can also make an appointment by calling the local Prometric center of your choice directly.

The sponsoring firms of candidates who require special arrangements due to physical or learning disabilities can contact NASD Field Support Services at

(800) 999-6647 or visit http://www.nasdr.com/reg_rep/register.asp.

Information on exam and training sessions in Europe or the Pacific Rim is also available through these resources.

Reaching Your Goal

Achieving success is not by chance. It requires solid commitment, targeted strategy, and superior resources.

Passing the Series 7 exam will require a commitment on your part for serious study and diligent preparation. Our commitment is to deliver the best study tools available. South-Western's COMPASS Learning System provides the most targeted and streamlined instructional resources available.

Together, these commitments offer an excellent opportunity for success on the Series 7 exam and — as a result — a promising start to your new career as a registered representative.

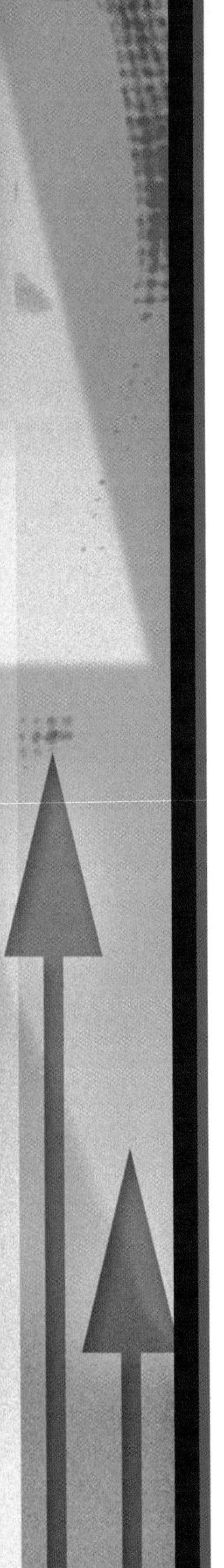

The **COMPASS Learning System** is part of the South-Western Professional Portfolio – advanced business topics in finance, management, marketing, corporate strategy and more – delivering real business solutions for real business problems. For over 100 years, South-Western has provided time-tested and market-leading learning materials for business success. South-Western, part of The Thomson Corporation, is the leading learning solutions provider of business learning materials worldwide.

NASD Series 6 –

- ▷ NASD Series 6 Exam: Preparation Guide — 0-324-18696-7
- ▷ NASD Series 6 Exam Prep: Drill & Practice — 0-324-20335-7
- ▷ NASD Series 6 Exam Prep: Online Course — 0-324-20334-9
- ▷ Success on the NASD Series 6 Exam: Prescriptive CD-ROM — 0-324-20179-6

NASD Series 7

- ▷ NASD Stockbroker Series 7 Exam: Prep Guide & CD Package — 0-324-22444-3
- ▷ NASD Stockbroker Series 7 Exam: Preparation Guide — 0-324-18695-9
- ▷ NASD Stockbroker Series 7 Exam Prep: Drill & Practice — 0-324-20333-0
- ▷ NASD Stockbroker Series 7 Exam Prep: Online Course — 0-324-20332-2
- ▷ Success on the NASD Series 7 Exam: Prescriptive CD-ROM — 0-324-20181-8

Certified Business Manager

- ▷ Part I: Core Areas
  - Volume 1 -- Theory for Core Areas — 0-324-27157-3
  - Volume 2 -- Practice for Core Areas — 0-324-27328-2
- ▷ Part II: Functional Areas
  - Volume 3 -- Theory for Functional Areas — 0-324-27327-4
  - Volume 4 -- Practice for Functional Areas — 0-324-27326-6
- ▷ Part III: Integrated Areas
  - Volume 5 -- Theory for Integrated Areas — 0-324-20011-0
  - Volume 6 -- Practice for Integrated Areas — 0-324-20121-4

Certified MBA

- ▷ Certified MBA Exam Prep Guide — 0-324-20239-3

Turn to South-Western as you continue on your path to career success in business and financial services. Call 1-800-842-3636 to order or visit http://professional.swlearning.com for a complete list of professional references, management education resources and learning solutions.

10650 Toebben Dr. Independence, KY 41051 | ISBN: 0-324-22229-7 | | Printed in the U.S.A. 9/03

NASD Stockbroker Exam

SERIES 7

PREPARATION GUIDE

Australia · Canada · Mexico · Singapore · Spain · United Kingdom · United States

NASD Stockbroker Exam, Series 7
Preparation Guide
Greensward Publications

VP/Executive Publisher:
Dave Shaut

Sr. Acquisitions Editor:
Scott Person

Developmental Editor:
Sara Froelicher

Marketing Manager:
Mark Linton

Production Editor:
Robert Dreas

Media Developmental Editor:
Rhonda Brown

Media Production Editor:
Edward Stubenrauch

Manufacturing Coordinator:
Charlene Taylor

Production House:
Shepherd Incorporated

Printer:
West
Eagan, Minnesota

Design Project Manager and Internal Designer:
Chris A. Miller

Cover Designer/Illustrator:
Chris A. Miller

Printed in the United States of America

2 3 4 5 07

ISBN-13: 978-0-324-18695-6
ISBN-10: 0-324-18695-9
Library of Congress Control Number:
2003107633

For more informationcontact
South-Western,
5191 Natorp Boulevard,
Mason, Ohio 45040.
Or you can visit our Internet site at:
http://www.swlearning.com

Contents

C

Contents

3 Providing Customers With Investment Information 38

Contents

C

Contents

Seeking Business for the Broker-Dealer

"Seeking Business for the Broker-Dealer" is the first of the seven critical functions performed by a Registered Representative. A Registered Representative (RR) is licensed, as required by law, after passing the General Securities Examination (Series 7). The tasks undertaken by the RR in seeking business for the broker-dealer include contacting customers and potential customers in person, by telephone, by mail, and through various other means. The RR may also seek business for the broker-dealer by conducting lectures, seminars and forums with current and potential customers. All of these activities are subject to strict laws set out by statute and enforced by the Securities and Exchange Commission (SEC), as well as strict industry rules and guidelines established by one or more of the various self-regulatory organizations (SRO) that oversee the securities industry.

As the text unfolds, we will discuss each of the seven critical functions of the RR in the order in which a registered representative would perform them in prospecting for and handling new customers. Be aware, though, that this does not necessarily represent the order in which these topics will be covered on the Series 7 Examination. In fact, some sections are weighed much more heavily than others.

This first critical function covered in Chapter 1 ("Seeking Business for the Broker-Dealer") represents about 4 percent of the total exam: approximately 8–10 questions of the total 250 questions on the Series 7 Exam. This is somewhat deceptive, however, as questions from other areas may refer to the rules and regulations of the securities industry, which this chapter introduces. There are lots of potential questions that can be asked on the exam about SEC rules, even though the question may not obviously state that it is asking about a specific rule. Furthermore, this material is important for compliance with applicable laws and in communications with the public. This is where many violations occur, so take note.

This chapter will be broken up into two sections:

1.1 **Requirements for Registration of Individuals.** This first section will look at the rules, regulations, and requirements for registration. This will include defining exactly who can be a registered representative and the procedure for becoming licensed, as well as the transfer and termination of licenses. Rule violations and penalties will also be examined. The first section will also look at thc role of the investment advisor, defining the term and differentiating it from that of the registered representative.

1.2 **Standards for Public Communications.** This section will examine the standards for all forms of communication between registered representatives and the public. This will include an examination of the rules for contact in person, by phone, by mail and through other means. The distinction between advertising and sales literature will be outlined, along with examples of each and the rules governing each. There are specific regulations and requirements (and in some cases pre-approval) that will be gone over in detail.

key terms

Advertising: any kind of public communication which comes from the brokerage firm, but is not specifically distributed by the firm; as such, the brokerage firm has no control over who receives the material. (e.g., TV, magazine, website)

Arbitration: an alternative means of dispute resolution whereby an impartial third party or panel of people listen to evidence presented by both sides and render a decision, thus avoiding the court system.

Investment Adviser (IA): anyone who gives investment advice for a fee.

Municipal Securities Rulemaking Board (MSRB): an SRO that is responsible for all activities related to municipal bonds and other intrastate government securities that are issued, sold, or traded.

National Association of Securities Dealers (NASD): self-regulatory organization responsible for all activities related to securities sold in the over-the-counter market; also has regulatory authority over investment banking, investment companies and limited partnerships.

New York Stock Exchange (NYSE): self-regulatory organization responsible for all activities related to securities listed and traded on the New York Stock Exchange and some regional stock exchanges (e.g., Philadelphia Stock Exchange).

Registered Representative (RR): an employee of a stock exchange member firm who acts as an account executive for clients, giving advice on which securities to buy and sell, and who collects a commission through the firm for services rendered. RRs must be licensed by the Securities and Exchange Commission (SEC), by one or more of the various self-regulatory organizations (SRO), and by the state or states in which he or she engages in securities activities.

Sales literature: any written, electronic or oral material distributed by a brokerage firm upon the request of a client, sent by the firm to a selected group of people, or disseminated in any other way such that the brokerage firm has control over who receives the material (e.g., brochure, research report, e-mail newsletter).

Securities: any investment relationship with a company. This can be equity in a company (stock), debt with a company (bond), a pooling of investment instruments (mutual fund), or any instrument transferring a future right (option).

Securities and Exchange Commission (SEC): a federal government agency created by the Securities Exchange Act of 1934 to oversee the securities industry, establish regulations governing the issuance and sale of securities, and enforce the securities laws enacted by Congress.

Self-Regulatory Organizations (SRO): created by federal securities laws to help maintain a fair and orderly trading environment, to help oversee various aspects of the securities industries, and to aid in the enforcement of securities rules and regulations. Each SRO also adopts and enforces its own "industry rules."

1.1

Requirements for Registration of Individuals

Registration is required for all employees of a member stock exchange broker-dealer, if those employees will be involved with the sale or promotion of securities. Series 7 registration allows an individual to sell all types of securities offered by the member broker-dealer (except commodities futures). Achieving registration consists of passing the General Securities Examination (Series 7) and complying with various rules and regulations.

The entities charged with oversight of the securities industry are the SEC and SROs. These will be referred to constantly throughout the text since they are the principal means through which rules and regulations in the securities industry are enforced. There will be more detail on these in Chapter 5, but for now a brief description and a few points will suffice.

SEC. The **Securities and Exchange Commission (SEC)** is a federal government agency created by the Securities Exchange Act of 1934 to oversee the securities industry, establish regulations governing the issuance and sale of securities, and enforce the securities laws enacted by Congress. For purposes of the law, securities are defined very broadly. **Securities** are any investment relationship with a company. A security can represent an equity stake in a company (stock), a debt relationship with a company (bond), a pooling of investment instruments (mutual fund), or any instrument of value that transfers a future right of investment (option). In order for the SEC to perform its oversight functions, all securities industry participants must register with the SEC. Industry participants include

▷ **exchanges** where securities are bought and sold,
▷ **companies** wishing to issue or sell securities, and
▷ **broker-dealers** in the business of securities buying, selling & advising.

Included in this last group are the employees of broker-dealer firms, when such employees interact with the public with regard to securities. Clerical personnel would not need to be registered unless their duties involved answering customer questions, but account executives who buy and sell stocks on behalf of clients would need to be registered representatives. Furthermore, fingerprinting is required of all employees who

▷ handle cash or securities,
▷ supervise people who handle cash or securities,
▷ are involved with the sale of securities to the public, or
▷ supervise people who are involved with the sale of securities to the public.

SRO. **Self-Regulatory Organizations (SRO)** were created by federal securities laws to help maintain a fair and orderly trading environment, to help oversee various aspects of the securities industries, and to aid in the enforcement of securities rules and regulations. SROs fall under the jurisdiction of the SEC and are responsible for the conduct of their own members. As such, each have adopted and enforce their own set of "industry rules" that members agree to abide by as a condition of participation in the market or exchange. This is in addition to those rules and regulations set out by the SEC and various state regulatory bodies.

Each major exchange has its own SRO charged with oversight of activity within that marketplace. The three largest SROs are the New York Stock Exchange (NYSE), the National Association of Securities Dealers (NASD) and the Municipal Securities Rulemaking Board (MSRB). Although there will be more detail on these in Chapter 5, let's look at them briefly here since they will also be referred to throughout the text.

NYSE. The **New York Stock Exchange (NYSE)** is an SRO that is responsible for all activities related to securities listed and traded on the New York Stock Exchange. To become a member firm, one of the 1366 individual "seats" must be purchased. Member firms and salesperson employees of member firms must register with the NYSE and agree to abide by its rules and regulations. The NYSE also has responsibility for some of the regional stock exchanges in the United States (e.g., Philadelphia Stock Exchange).

NASD. The **National Association of Securities Dealers (NASD)** is an SRO that is responsible for all activities related to securities that are sold in the over-the-counter market. Any broker-dealer registered and in good standing with the SEC may apply to become an NASD member. Salesperson employees of member firms must also be registered with NASD and agree to abide by its rules and regulations. The NASD also has regulatory authority over investment banking, investment companies, and limited partnerships. (All of these will be discussed later in the text.)

MSRB. The **Municipal Securities Rulemaking Board (MSRB)** is an SRO that is responsible for all activities related to municipal bonds and other intrastate government securities that are issued, sold, or traded. Firms and employees associated with those firms must be qualified in accordance with MSRB rules and agree to abide by its regulations.

Exam Topic Alert

Note that both the NYSE and the NASD have the power to enforce their regulations on registered member firms and registered representatives (RR) who work for those firms. Also note that the NYSE and the NASD do not have the power to enforce each other's rules and regulations; they may discipline only their own members. Finally, the MSRB does *not* have the power to enforce the rules it makes, but instead relies on the NASD, other SROs, and the SEC for enforcement.

1.1.1

Registered Representatives

A **registered representative (RR)** is an employee of a stock exchange member firm who acts as an account executive for clients, giving advice on which securities to buy and sell, and who collects a commission through the firm for services rendered. Being "registered" means that a person is licensed by the Securities and Exchange Commission (SEC), by one or more of the various self-regulatory organizations (SRO), and by the state or states in which he or she engages in securities activities. Registration for all SROs includes the requirement that the General Securities Examination (Series 7) be passed as per SEC regulations. Being "registered" also means that the person has agreed to observe the regulations set forth by the governing SRO, and be bound by the SRO's rules.

Each of the SROs can and do have additional varying requirements that must be met in order to be considered "registered" and able to participate in the market or exchange over which the SRO has jurisdiction. For example, the NYSE requires a 120-day apprenticeship period during which a candidate may not interact with the public nor collect a commission, but does have the chance to watch the workings of the firm in preparation for taking the Series 7 examination. The NASD requires member firms to conduct extensive background checks into a candidate's education, experience, qualifications, and character. After becoming registered, an NASD RR must complete certain continuing education requirements (detailed in Chapter 5). The MSRB requires a 90-day apprenticeship period during which a candidate may interact only with other dealer firms and may not collect a commission. The MSRB has a 180-day window within which the candidate must pass the examination.

A candidate may be disqualified from becoming a RR if he or she is, or has been, subject to disciplinary action by the SEC, an SRO, or a foreign securities governing body. Automatic, statutory disqualification is in effect if the person

- ▷ has ever been expelled or suspended by a securities industry governing body (SEC, SRO, or foreign equivalent),
- ▷ caused another person or firm to be expelled or suspended by a securities industry governing body (SEC, SRO, or foreign equivalent),
- ▷ has a felony conviction,
- ▷ has a misdemeanor conviction related to money or securities in past 10 years,
- ▷ is under an SEC order (or foreign equivalent) barring participation in the securities industry, or
- ▷ is under a court order barring participation in the securities industry.

TERMINATION AND TRANSFER. Rules covering the termination and transfer of membership status vary by SRO. The NYSE does not permit a transfer of registration by a RR. Instead, the RR must resign from one firm and reapply for registration with the new firm. Whether an RR is terminated or chooses to resign voluntarily, the NYSE still retains jurisdictional authority over that person for an additional one-year period. Likewise, the NASD does not permit registrations to be transferred. The RR must resign from one firm (using form U-5) and reapply for registration with the new firm (using form U-4). The U-4 form must be filed within two years or the RR will be required to requalify for license registration. MSRB rules also require signing on with another firm within two years to avoid the requalification process.

If an RR voluntarily leaves a member firm, registration ceases 30 days after the SRO receives written notice from the firm. Firms which terminate employees must notify the NYSE and NASD within 30 days, but firms may not terminate an employee during an investigation for securities violations or other pending SRO actions.

DISCLOSURE OF OUTSIDE BUSINESS ACTIVITIES. RRs of NYSE and NASD firms may not engage in any outside business activities without the knowledge and consent of the employing firm. The NYSE goes one step further, requiring that consent to take a second job be in writing, since the NYSE expects employees of member firms to be full-time employees. Special care is taken by the NYSE and NASD because seemingly unrelated activities, such as a speech given by an RR, could be misconstrued as a solicitation of business or misinterpreted as promoting a specific security, and thus subject to the public communication rules discussed in the next part of this chapter.

Both the NYSE and NASD require that commissions and compensation for securities transactions go through the member firm. All transactions must go through the broker-dealer firm so that the firm can monitor compliance with the law. The NASD has additional Conduct Rules governing private securities transactions, requiring prior written approval if compensation is involved, but specifically exempting transactions for immediate family members where no commission is paid.

PENALTIES AND SANCTIONS FOR RULE VIOLATIONS. The NYSE and NASD have separate but similar procedures for resolving disputes within the industry and for imposing penalties and sanctions for rule violations against member firms and their employees. The differences and nuances that make each procedure unique will be detailed in Chapter 5, but here we will focus briefly on the similarities. Both NYSE and NASD require disputes among member firms, and between member firms and their employees, to be settled by arbitration. **Arbitration** is an alternative means of dispute resolution whereby an impartial third party or panel of people listen to evidence presented by both sides and render a decision, thus avoiding the court system. Arbitration is often final and binding, although appeals to the court system may be allowed in limited circumstances. Arbitration is used primarily because of the advantages in cost and time savings the process has over the courts. Member firms and RRs agree to submit disputes to arbitration as a condition of becoming registered members.

As for rule violations by RRs, the NYSE holds a disciplinary hearing before a panel selected by the NYSE Board of Directors, whereas the NASD has a Department of Enforcement that arranges a hearing following the detailed procedures laid out in the NASD Code of Procedure. This Code of Procedure deals with NASD rules violations, as well as MSRB rules violations and federal securities laws infractions. Details will be provided in Chapter 5, but for now know that the penalties and sanctions for rule violations handed down by the NYSE and NASD, although administered independently, are very similar. Penalties may include censure, fines, suspensions, termination of membership, prohibition against association with other members or member firms, and other sanctions as deemed appropriate. Finally, be aware that penalties or sanctions for rules violations may be cumulative. For example, an RR who commits fraud could be investigated and punished by the NYSE, NASD, SEC and state securities authorities.

1.1.2

Investment Advisers

An **investment adviser (IA)** is anyone who gives investment advice for a fee. The compensation can be a flat fee or it can be a percentage of the assets managed. An IA can be part of an investment advisory service working with many companies, a consultant working one-on-one with a particular company, perhaps as the portfolio manager of an investment company, or an IA may produce a newsletter offering the same investment advice to all subscribers. In all these cases, investment advisors must register with the SEC, and are subject to the Investment Advisors Act of 1940. The purpose of the Act is to protect the public from fraud and misrepresentation. Among the provisions of the Act, for example, is a requirement that IAs disclose all potential conflicts of interest, such as the IA owning a particular stock about which he or she is making a recommendation.

FEDERAL AND STATE REGISTRATION REQUIREMENTS. Investment advisors who comply with federal registration guidelines are often referred to as Registered Investment Advisors (RIA). Federal registration includes registering with the SEC after having passed the appropriate examination. Persons who currently hold a Series 6 license would be required to pass the Series 65 exam to become an RIA; persons with a Series 7 license would be required to pass the Series 66 exam to become an RIA. The various state securities regulatory bodies often also have their own additional registration requirements for conducting business or offering investment advice as an IA within their state. This can range from simple notification and registration with the state authority to the requirement of additional testing and other compliance measures.

EXEMPTIONS. Note that the Investment Advisors Act of 1940 applies to those who receive compensation solely for their investment advice, and not to those who give investment advice which is incidental to their primary function, such as stockbrokers. To make this distinction clear, think about how a stockbroker is compensated. A stockbroker is receiving compensation primarily from the commission that the buying or selling of the stock generates, not from the investment advice itself. Likewise, anyone who sells mutual funds is not required to be a registered advisor. On the other hand, the investment advisor of a mutual fund *must* be registered under the Act, since he or she is paid a fee by the fund for investing advice and guidance.

The main exemption from registration that you should be aware of is for regular salaried employees, working exclusively for a particular company, and who give advice only to that company. An example would be an economic advisor, hired as a regular salaried employee by a bank, who gives advice and analysis only to the bank for internal purposes and does not share that information with the public.

1.2 Standards for Public Communications

Communication with the public is one area that is highly regulated by the SEC and the various SROs. This is because the potential for false or misleading statements can have a seriously devastating impact on an unsophisticated investing public. In fact, securities rules and regulations define public communications very broadly, covering everything from advertising and sales literature to seminars and lectures. Telephone solicitations, correspondence, market letters, research reports, educational materials, press releases, and all electronic communications also fall under the public communications rules.

Different rules and compliance requirements apply to different kinds of public communication. These rules are designed to ensure that the public is given a certain amount of information with which to make an informed decision. Before we examine some specific public communications regulations, it is important to note that the SEC, NYSE and NASD distinguish between sales literature and advertising.

SALES LITERATURE. **Sales literature** is any written, electronic, or oral material distributed by the brokerage firm upon the request of a client, sent by the firm to a selected group of people, or disseminated in any other way such that the brokerage firm has control over who receives the material. A brochure, research report or e-mail newsletter would all fall under the sales literature classification.

ADVERTISING. **Advertising** is any kind of public communication which comes from the brokerage firm, but is not specifically distributed by the firm; as such, the brokerage firm has no control over who receives the material. Advertising on the radio, on television, in magazines, or in newspapers would fall under this classification, as would a website put up by the brokerage firm.

1.2.1

Regulation of Telephone Solicitations

Telephone solicitations are regulated by the Telephone Consumer Protection Act of 1991. As defined by the Act, a **telephone solicitation** is any telephone call initiated to encourage a person to buy a good or service, or make an investment. When the caller does not have a prior relationship with the party being called this is referred to as **cold calling.** The Act covers all calls to telephones, fax machines and modems, but does not cover Internet solicitations. (Separate "spam" rules apply.)

Exam Topic Alert

The Act specifically requires companies who make telephone solicitations, whether by persons or recorded autodialer messages, to call only between the hours of 8 A.M. and 9 P.M. *of the time zone where the person being called is located.* Firms must state their names and the purpose of the call.

The Act also requires the maintenance of a "do-not-call" list for those who request not to be called again. Once a person's name and phone number are added to the "do-not-call" list, they may not be called for 10 years. It is the firm's responsibility to maintain the list for the 10-year period, to have a written policy regarding the "do-not-call" list, and to train telephone sales reps on use of the list.

RRs and broker-dealer firms must comply with the Telephone Consumer Protection Act. Calls exempt from the Act include those where a prior business relationship exists, where the person being called has given permission, calls to collect a debt, calls by a nonprofit organization, and personal phone calls.

COLD CALLING RULES FOR PENNY STOCKS. The SEC has adopted additional telephone solicitation regulations that cover "penny stocks." **Penny stocks** are over-the-counter (OTC, i.e., non-listed) equity securities that trade for less than $1 per share (although they may trade as high as $5–$10 per share), but are highly volatile because the companies who issue the stock usually have short and erratic operating histories. Because of their highly speculative nature, the SEC has adopted the Penny Stock Cold Calling Rules to protect unsophisticated investors. When an RR for a broker-dealer makes a cold call for a penny stock, the RR must first attempt to ascertain the prospect's suitability for the investment. In fact, a suitability statement must be signed by the prospect before any penny stock trades can be executed.

The RR for the broker-dealer is also required under SEC rules for penny stock cold calling to make certain disclosures when soliciting penny stock trades. These disclosures include the name of the stock, the number of shares being sold, the current price of the shares, and the amount of commission to be paid to the RR and to the firm. Furthermore, a monthly statement must be provided showing the number of penny stock shares a client holds and the current market value. Although current customers of the broker-dealer firm are exempt from the Penny Stock Cold Calling Rules, the disclosure requirements are still in effect. For purposes of the cold calling rules, a current customer is defined as someone who has an active account with the firm, has made any securities transaction in the prior 12 months, or has in the past made at least three separate penny stock purchases on separate occasions.

1.2.2

Requirements for Recommendations of Securities

The NASD has established additional rules which members must adhere to when recommending specific securities to clients or prospective clients. In order to protect the interests of the investing public, the NASD requires that the broker-dealer firm and the RR must determine whether or not the stock or security being recommended is an appropriate investment for the client given the client's investment objectives and experience. Furthermore, recommendation as to the appropriateness of the investment must be made with some basis in fact. This documentation must be presented to the client upon request. All recommendations to the client must disclose

- ▷ the current market value of the security,
- ▷ total transaction costs that would be incurred for the trade,
- ▷ whether or not the broker-dealer firm plans to buy or sell the recommended security for its own account, and
- ▷ any interest or relationship the broker-dealer firm may have with the company represented by the security.

This last point about any interest or relationship the broker-dealer firm may have with the company includes such things as whether or not the broker-dealer took part in a public stock offering or other securities issue for the company in the past three years, whether or not the broker-dealer is a market maker for that company's stock, if the firm or any of its employees own warrants, options or other rights in the company being recommended, and if any of the firm's employees are officers or directors of the company being recommended.

In making recommendations to clients, the broker-dealer firm must also be careful not to guarantee anything, nor make any predictions about the company or stock's future performance. In most broker-dealer advertising, the statement "past performance does not guarantee future results" is often heard as a way to show compliance with this part of the NASD regulations. If the firm chooses to give details about past performance, there are additional NASD disclosure requirements that must be made:

- ▷ availability to client of the supporting information that the firm used,
- ▷ current market conditions and the market's general direction,
- ▷ current market value of the security at the time of the recommendation,
- ▷ list of similar recommendations the firm made during the past 12 months, and
- ▷ how firm's other recommendations fared during past performance period.

The past performance period for the firm's current recommendations, as well as the firm's other recommendations, must show a consecutive block of time without skipping over any periods where the security may have had a less than stellar performance. Furthermore, the NASD stresses that the firm may not compare dissimilar securities, may not make exaggerated, fraudulent, or misleading statements about any securities, and must always balance the positive aspects of a security by stating its associated risks and potential downside. Finally, the RR must always make sure that the security being recommended is suitable for the customer given the client's financial situation, investment experience, risk tolerance, and investment objectives.

1.2.3

Definition and Approval of Public Communications

As stated previously, the SEC and SROs define public communications very broadly. Advertising, sales literature, seminars, lectures, telephone solicitations, correspondence, market letters, research reports, educational materials, press releases, and all electronic communications are just some of the items that fall under the public communications rules. These rules are designed to help ensure that the public is treated fairly and is given a certain amount of information with which to make an informed decision.

Exam Topic Alert

Remember the distinction between sales literature and advertising because this may show up on the Series 7 examination. Sales literature is distributed by the brokerage firm in a way such that the brokerage firm has control over who receives the material. Advertising, on the other hand, is not specifically distributed by the firm, and as such the brokerage firm has no control over who receives the material.

Certain types of public communication are exempt from these "advertising" and "sales literature" definitions, but they have their own rules and regulations (some of which will be discussed later in this textbook). These include individual correspondence, personal e-mail sent to only one person, tombstone ads, and prospectuses. (**Tombstone ads** are special ads placed by broker-dealer firms to draw attention to a prospectus or announce some other major business event, without the ad being a specific offer to sell or buy securities. A **prospectus** is a formal written document detailing the financial information, business plan, and operating history of a company that is selling securities.) Of course, all communication from a brokerage firm and RRs must still be true, accurate, and free from misleading statements.

APPROVAL. The NASD does not "approve" advertising or sales literature. Instead, advertising and sales literature must be approved by a registered principal of the member firm. The firm must keep all advertising and sales literature on file for a period of three years from the date of use. New firms must also file all advertising and sales literature with the NASD at least 10 days before its initial usage during the firm's first year of operation. Again, this is not for "approval," but rather allows the NASD to more easily conduct spot checks in an effort to monitor compliance. The NASD also has the authority to require any firm to file its advertising and sales literature if the NASD feels it is necessary.

OTHER POINTS. All public communications must clearly state the name of the firm that is the source of the advertising and sales literature. The only exception to this is recruitment advertising, which may be done blind to protect the identity of the firm seeking to hire new reps. Fictitious names and dba's ("Doing Business As. . .") are permitted if they are registered with the SEC and the NASD, or other appropriate SRO. Parent company names and/or divisional names are permitted if they actually exist, and the ad or sales material clearly states the relationship between the company and divisions.

Also, public communications (including business cards) must, in addition to the member's name, mention the member's affiliation with the NASD. The NASD name or logo must be the same size or smaller than the member's name and not in a more prominent position so as not to mislead the public into thinking that the NASD somehow endorses the activities of that member. Finally, all advertising must be honest, free from misleading statements, and adhere to the principles of full and fair disclosure in order to fulfill the letter and the spirit of NASD rules and regulations.

1.24

Definition and Approval of Options-Related and Other Advertisements

Options-related advertisements, sales literature, and educational materials must be approved by a Registered Options Principal (ROP) within the broker-dealer firm. This person is also sometimes referred to as a Compliance Registered Options Principal (CROP). This approval by the CROP must come before any material is permitted to be put out for public consumption. Again, the material in question is defined very broadly. The CROP must approve not only traditional ads, but also such things as general prospecting letters and seminar transcripts. Even options worksheets that go through various risk-reward scenarios are considered sales literature and must be approved by a CROP. As an additional safeguard, all research reports relating to options must also be approved by a supervisory analyst.

A good rule of thumb is that the more risky an investment is, the more regulations the NASD and other SROs put in place to ensure that investors have the best understanding possible of what they are getting themselves into. Given that, you should not be surprised to learn that the NASD also requires that all public communications related to options be filed with them 10 days in advance of first use, and kept on file for three years. Furthermore, all clients or prospective clients must be sent an Options Disclosure Document (ODD) from the Options Clearing Corporation (OCC) prior to, or along with, any options materials that are sent out.

ODD. The **Options Disclosure Document (ODD)** is a document that explains in detail how options work, various option strategies, and the risk-reward potential of trading in options. The ODD was developed by the OCC to ensure fair and full disclosure of the risks involved to all potential options traders before they actually begin trading options. (The OCC issues, clears, and guarantees options and other derivative securities. It is the largest clearing house of its kind, and is owned by the four U.S. options trading exchanges.)

1.2.5

Definition, Specific Standards, and Approval of Municipal Securities Ads

Municipal securities-related advertisements, sales literature, marketing literature, and research reports must be approved by a principal of the firm prior to any material being made available to the public. In fact, approval for municipal securities advertising must be done by the principal *in writing*. Here, market letters, offering circulars and summaries of official statements fall under the definition of advertising; however, the official statements themselves are *not* considered advertising.

Speaking engagements are also considered a form of public communication. The employing firm must give written consent prior to the event, which must be of a broad educational nature, and literature may not be handed out (although it may be left on a table for pickup). Logs of the event detailing the date, time, speaker, topic, etc. should be kept for three years. Copies of all advertising materials must also be kept for three years from date of use.

In addition to the standards set forth in MSRB rules that all ads must be truthful and not misleading, the firm must disclose if there is a "control relationship" between the firm and the municipality. This would include any contractual relationship for advice or other services in addition to the sale of the securities, or other position of influence between the firm and the municipality. This need not be disclosed in ads, but must be done no later than the settlement date if securities are purchased.

PROFESSIONAL ADVERTISEMENTS. Advertising that refers to the skills of the firm or its reps must be truthful, accurate, and not misleading with regard to the track record, research facilities, or credentials of the members. Any spokesperson chosen must be knowledgeable in the subject discussed, and any payment must be disclosed.

PRODUCT ADVERTISEMENTS. Advertising that refers to the product or products being offered for sale must be truthful, accurate, and not misleading with respect to the past performance of that product or similar products, nor can projections or opinions of future value be presented as fact.

NEW ISSUE ADVERTISEMENTS. In addition to all other rules, advertising for new issues must state the current sale price of the issue as of the date of publication of the advertising—with the date of publication clearly stated on the ad—and a notice stating that the current price may be different from that shown in the advertisement.

1.2.6 Specific Requirements for Ads of Investment Company Products

Investment company-related advertisements, sales literature, marketing literature, and research reports must be sent to the NASD no later than ten days after first being used or being made available to the public. This requirement is waived if the material has already been filed by another member firm. This is often the case with mutual funds, which are the primary type of investment company products you will likely deal with. With mutual funds, there is a sponsoring broker-dealer (also referred to as the **underwriter** or **distributor**) whose primary responsibility is to market the fund and create the collateral sales literature. As other broker-dealers begin selling the fund, they are not required to submit sales literature to the NASD if they are using the same materials already submitted by the sponsor. These rules also apply to other investment company products, such as variable annuity contracts.

Note that the requirement for investment company products is different from that for first year broker-dealers: first-year broker-dealers must submit advertising *before* first use; investment companies can submit materials *after* use. And the NASD does not "approve" materials, but collects them to perform compliance spot checks. Broker-dealers must keep all advertising and sale literature on file for three years.

USING CHARTS AND GRAPHS. The NASD requires that broker-dealers use charts and graphs with mutual fund advertising and sales literature to show the performance of the fund over the past 10 years. Longer time periods can also be used, but shorter periods should not be used as they may not indicate the fund's performance in varying market conditions. Furthermore, the charts and graphs cannot be misleading, and are not permitted to skip over time periods where the fund's performance was lagging. Finally, the advertising or sale literature must state the source of the information depicted in the charts and graphs.

SHOWING RETURNS. If mutual fund returns are advertised, they must be calculated using the SEC method, which assumes reinvestment of all dividends, capital gains, and other fund distributions and payouts. Also, when calculating return, sales charges, management fees, and other such charges are not included. The SEC calculation for fund performance must be explained if returns are advertised, and figures must show 1-year, 5-year, 10-year, or average life-of-fund returns. Finally, any mention of current yield must be based on income distributions over the past 12 months per SEC rules. (Mutual fund yield calculations will be done in Chapter 3.)

OTHER RULES. Additional NASD rules for investment company product ads are:

- ads may not state that mutual funds are safer than other investments,
- ads must show the highest possible sales charges and commissions (whether or not an investor may be at a breakpoint to pay less commission), and
- ads that state cash returns must combine dividends and capital gains.

1.2.7

Specific Requirements for Ads of Other Securities

Advertisements, sales literature, and other materials must always be truthful and not misleading. All such materials must also be kept on file by the broker-dealer for a period of three years. In addition to these rules, which apply to *all* types of public communication from a broker-dealer, we have looked at some additional SEC, NASD, and other SRO requirements. Following are a few more miscellaneous SEC, NASD, and SRO rules which may appear on the Series 7 examination.

GOVERNMENT SECURITIES. Government securities are generally exempt from SEC and NASD rules when they are issued directly by the government. This would include treasury bills, treasury notes, savings bonds, and government agency issues, like Ginnie Mae mortgage-backed securities. Still, on the test, you may have to apply a little common sense. If you are asked if the federal government must keep advertising and sales literature for a three-year period, the answer is no; but you also would not be wise to choose an answer that implies the government can be misleading in the claims it makes about its securities. And of course, member firms are not exempt if they produce and use advertising or sales literature.

Municipal government securities, though, are a separate matter. Remember, these typically have a broker-dealer as sponsor or underwriter, so they would fall under the MSRB rules for municipal securities discussed previously in Section 1.2.5.

CMOs. Collateralized Mortgage Obligations (CMOs) are securities backed by mortgages, which pass through principal and interest payments to investors. These are very similar to the Ginnie Maes referred to in the previous section; but while Ginnie Maes are government agency issues, CMOs are private sector issues backed by a pool of Fannie Mae, Freddie Mac and other mortgages. These will be explained in much greater detail in Chapter 3. For now, just know that all public communications must be filed with NASD ten days in advance of first use, and that the risks of investing CMOs must be fully disclosed to potential investors.

CDs. Certificates of Deposit (CDs) are debt securities, usually issued by a financial institution. There are actually two kinds of CDs: "standard" CDs that are offered by neighborhood banks to depositors, and "jumbo" CDs that have a minimum face value of $100,000 and are offered by commercial banks to investors as a time deposit. Standard CDs are nonnegotiable, but jumbo CDs *are* negotiable and as such they are considered a money market instrument.

NASD member broker-dealers that sell or trade in jumbo CDs must follow SEC and NASD rules just as they do for any other security. Banks have separate rules governing them when it comes to advertising CDs. One main point is that if they choose to advertise the return on the CD, they must use a standard calculation that assumes reinvestment of interest earned when figuring the annual percentage yield. Also, CD amounts over $100,000 are not FDIC insured.

1.X Summary

1.1 Registration is required for all member stock exchange broker-dealer employees involved with the sale or promotion of securities. Registration consists of passing the Series 7 exam and complying with SEC, SRO rules.

SEC is federal government agency that oversees all industry participants: exchanges, companies, broker-dealers, employees. Fingerprinting required for all who handle cash, sell stocks to public, or are supervisors of either group.

SRO created to help keep market fair & orderly, help enforce securities rules. NYSE: oversees activities of NY Stock Exchange and regional exchanges. NASD: responsible for over-the-counter, investment banking, limited partnership. MSRB: oversees activities related to municipal bonds, other intrastate government. NASD & NYSE can't enforce each other's rules; MSRB needs NASD to enforce.

1.1.1 Registered Rep is licensed by SEC, SRO, states to give advice to clients about buying, selling securities—can receive commission. Disqualified if disciplined by SEC, SRO, foreign agency; expelled, has suspended before; has felony conviction or misdemeanor for money/securities last 10 years; or is barred by SEC, foreign agency, or court order.

Transfer of registration usually not permitted. Must resign and reapply within 2 years. Registration ceases 30 days after termination, but can't terminate if under investigation. NYSE has jurisdiction 1 year afterwards.

Must disclose outside business activities. NYSE requires written approval. All transactions, commissions, compensation must go through the firm.

NYSE, NASD require arbitration for disputes. Rule violation sanctions may include censure, fine, suspension, termination. Penalties can be cumulative.

1.1.2 Investment advisors must be licensed by SEC, state. Stockbrokers exempt if commission only from stock sales. Mutual fund manager not exempt.

1.2

All public communications must comply with SEC, SRO rules. Advertising is not specifically distributed by firm, firm has no control over who sees it. Sales literature is distributed by firm, so firm can control who sees it.

1.2.1 Phone solicitation only 8 A.M.–9 P.M. of time zone of the person being called. Must maintain do-not-call list for 10 years if person asks not to be called.

Penny stock cold calling rules: RR must check suitability for investor, must disclose stock name, number of shares, current price, commissions.

1.2.2 Recommendations must disclose current market value of stock, total transaction costs for trade, broker-dealer plans to buy/sell stock, relationship of B-D firm to company. If detailing past performance, disclosures must also include supporting info, current market condition, current market value of the stock, list of similar recommendations for past 12 months, how firm's other recommendations fared. History must show a consecutive time block.

1.2.3 Distinction between advertising and sales literature is important. (See 1.2.) Tombstone ads and prospectuses are exempt, but have own rules. All ads, sales literature must be true, accurate, free from misleading statements; approved by a registered principal of the firm; kept on file for 3 years. NASD doesn't approve ads, sales literature, but new firms must file all ads and sales literature at least 10 days before first use during firm's first year.

All public communications must state name of firm, except for recruiting. Fictitious names, dba's must be filed with SEC, SRO. NASD logo may not be bigger, more prominent than member name.

1.2.4 Options-related ads, sales literatuare, educational materials must be approved by a Registered Options Principal, or CROP. Seminar transcripts and options worksheets must also be approved by a CROP. Options research reports must be approved by CROP and a supervisory analyst. NASD requires all option materials be filed 10 days before use, and Options Disclosure Document (ODD) explaining how options work must be given to client.

1.2.5 Municipal securities ads, sales, literature, etc. must be approved by a principal in writing before first use. Market letters, offering circulars, summaries of official statements also count, but the actual summaries do not. Speaking engagements also count, need written consent, cannot hand out literature, must keep logs for 3 years. All ads, sales literature must be kept for 3 years, and must disclose if there's a control relationship between firm and municipality.

Professional, product ads must be true and not mislead about track record. New issue ads must state current sale price of the issue as of the ad date, show date ad was printed, state that issue price may be different now.

1.2.6 Investment company ads, sales literature, etc. must be sent to NASD no later than 10 days after first use. Charts and graphs showing performance should go back at least 10 years, cannot skip over time periods, must show sources. If returns are shown, must be calculated using SEC method that assumes reinvestment of all payouts, must show multi-year or average life-of-fund returns; yield calculations must be based on income over past 12 months.

Other NASD rules: ads can't say mutual funds are safer than other investments, must show highest possible commission, cash returns must combine dividends and capital gains.

1.2.7 Government securities exempt from ad rules if issued directly by government. Collateralized mortgage obligations (CMO) ads must be filed 10 days in advance of first use, must fully disclose risks.

Two kinds of CDs: jumbo CDs with minimum face value of $100,000 offered by commercial banks, negotiable, money market instrument; standard CDs are nonnegotiable, must assume reinvestment of interest if advertising a calculated annual percentage yield, CDs over $100,000 aren't FDIC insured.

Chapter 1 Review Quiz

1. Which of these people would *not* need to be fingerprinted under SEC rules?
   a. registered representative
   b. broker-dealer principal
   c. clerical person who opens the mail
   d. receptionist who answers phones

2. Which of the following self-regulatory organizations does *not* have the power to enforce its own rules?
   a. New York Stock Exchange
   b. National Association of Securities Dealers
   c. Municipal Securities Rulemaking Board
   d. none of the above

3. To transfer membership status in an SRO, a registered representative must:
   a. notify the SRO of the intent to transfer.
   b. notify the SEC of the intent to transfer.
   c. resign from one firm and reapply with another.
   d. apply with a new firm then resign from the first if the new firm accepts him.

4. Which of the following is *not* a characteristic of sales literature?
   a. It is distributed in such a way the firm has control over who receives it.
   b. It is distributed in such a way the firm has no control over who receives it.
   c. It is sent out upon request of a client.
   d. It is sent by the firm to a select group of people.

5. All of the following rules apply to advertising *except:*
   a. it must be approved by a principal of the firm.
   b. it must be approved by NASD.
   c. it must clearly state the name of the firm (except recruitment ads).
   d. if mutual fund returns are used, they must be calculated using SEC method.

6. A registered representative in New York is calling a person in California about a penny stock. When could the person *not* make the call?
   a. 9:30 A.M. Pacific time
   b. 9:30 A.M. Eastern time
   c. 9:30 P.M. Eastern time
   d. Telephone solicitation rules don't apply to penny stock calls.

7. Which of the following must submit advertising to the SEC before it is used?
   a. broker-dealers in their first year
   b. issuers of municipal securities
   c. all NYSE, NASD and MSRB members
   d. investment companies

Evaluating Customers' Needs and Investment Objectives

"Evaluating Customers' Needs and Investment Objectives" is the second of the seven critical functions that are performed by a Registered Representative. When evaluating customers, it is important to do so in terms of their financial needs, current holdings, and available investment capital. The client's entire financial picture must be considered. In fact, one of the tasks undertaken by the RR in evaluating customer needs is obtaining a current financial and investment profile of the customer. The RR must listen to a customer's investment objectives, and then help her achieve those goals. The RR may assist clients in determining needs and objectives, but this can be done only after listening to the customer, assembling all the data, and applying the RR's knowledge and experience in advising the client.

Making recommendations and offering advice and guidance can be a tricky undertaking, as you can imagine. When money is at stake and can be lost, customers will want answers. Since giving advice is subjective, the SEC and the various SROs have established rules, regulations and guidelines to ensure that all investors are dealt with fairly, honestly, and ethically. Strict adherence to these standards is important for maintaining the confidence of your client base—and keeping yourself out of trouble with regulatory authorities.

This second critical function covered in Chapter 2 ("Evaluating Customers' Needs and Investment Objectives") represents about 2 percent of the total exam: approximately 4–6 questions of the total 250 questions on the Series 7 Exam. This again is deceptive, though, as SEC, NASD, and other SRO rules and regulations are a large part of the test, even though a question may not directly appear to be about a specific rule. Plus, vocabulary and terminology introduced in this chapter lay the foundation for some important concepts that will be introduced in later chapters. For example, in this chapter we will examine a sample client balance sheet and income statement, which will be a precursor to our analysis in Chapter 7 of a company's balance sheet and income statement (which is likely to appear on the Series 7 exam in some form).

This chapter will be broken up into two sections:

2.1 Investment Profile of a Customer. This first section will examine what constitutes the investment profile of a customer. This will include assembling a financial profile of the client through the use of a balance sheet and income statement, and taking into account other financial considerations. The first section will also look at nonfinancial investment considerations, as well as determine how a client's risk tolerance and investment experience figure into the evaluation.

2.2 Investment Objectives. This section will look at ten different investment objectives, as well as products and strategies that can help a client meet those goals. Some are opposing strategies where one must be chosen, while others are not mutually exclusive and can in fact peacefully coexist or even reinforce one another.

key terms

Assets: things of value that are owned or in one's possession. (e.g., cash, stock, land).

Balance sheet: a financial report that shows the financial status of an entity with regard to assets, liabilities, and net worth as of a particular date.

Equity: the difference between what has been paid on an obligation and the value of the asset. (There are additional definitions for equity—see the Glossary.)

Income statement: a financial report that summarizes an entity's income and expenses over a given period of time. Also called a **profit and loss statement.**

Know your customer: concept that says it is the responsibility of the broker-dealer and RR to have a complete and accurate understanding of a client's financial situation so as to give appropriate advice and make suitable recommendations.

Liabilities: any debt, financial obligation, or claim that another has on the ownership of an asset (e.g., credit card bill, car installment loan, home mortgage).

Liquidity: the ease with which assets can be converted into cash.

Net worth: the value that is left over after adding up all assets and subtracting all liabilities from that total.

Portfolio diversification: spreading out risk by holding investments in varying types, amounts, and asset classes.

Speculation: assuming higher risk in anticipation of higher returns.

2.1

Investment Profile of a Customer

Examining the investment profile of a customer is one of the key elements in evaluating how you as the RR can best advise your client. A customer's investment profile consists of many elements, but these can be broken down into two broad categories: the financial profile and nonfinancial investment considerations. Once you have a good understanding of your client's investment profile, you will have a solid foundation to help the client identify attainable investment objectives and give appropriate advice and recommendations.

When looking at a client's financial needs, you must also take into account his available investment capital, current investment holdings, risk tolerance, and investment experience in order to get a complete picture of your client. This is important because it's a violation of NASD rules to recommend an investment that's not suitable for the customer's financial situation. In fact, all of the major exchanges and SROs have ethical rules or guidelines that state or imply the "know your customer" maxim.

KNOW YOUR CUSTOMER. This concept says that it is the responsibility of the broker-dealers and RRs to have a complete and accurate understanding of a client's financial situation so that they are in a position to give appropriate advice and make suitable recommendations to the client. To this end, most brokerage firms have special forms that new clients must fill out as a means of gathering the necessary information to satisfy this requirement.

The NYSE "Know Your Customer" Rule 405 even goes so far as to say that it is the responsibility of the broker-dealer and RR to perform due diligence to check out the information given to them by the client to ensure that it is valid and accurate. The NASD "Know Your Customer" guidelines in the Rules of Fair Practice, Article 3, are a little less ominous in that the broker-dealer and RR just need to have reasonable grounds to believe that the trade is suitable, and this can be based on facts, if any, that are supplied by the client. In MSRB Rule G-19, "Know Your Customer" includes having the broker-dealer and RR make reasonable efforts to obtain the customer's tax status (second in importance after determining the customer's financial status, and even before the customer's investment objectives).

If a customer refuses to give financial information to the broker-dealer or RR, or if the information given turns out to be inaccurate, it is up to the individual broker-dealer firm whether or not to open or continue the account for the client. While there is no statutory prohibition against opening the account and making trades for the client, most broker-dealers would avoid making recommendations to the client in this type of situation even if they allowed the account to remain open and active.

2.1.1

Financial Profile

In examining the financial profile of a client, there are several items which must be gathered and analyzed. Most of the information needed can be obtained from a typical new account form used by most broker-dealers. It contains many questions for the client to answer about assets, liabilities, current investment holdings, income, and expenses. From this information, the RR can assemble a simple balance sheet and income statement to get a clearer picture of the client's current holdings, net worth, and cash flow. Let's take a look at some of these concepts, go through a few examples, and define some of the terms that will appear again later in this textbook (and are also likely to appear in one form or another on the Series 7 examination).

BALANCE SHEET. A **balance sheet** is a financial report that shows the financial status of an entity with regard to assets, liabilities, and net worth as of a particular date. Here we are using the balance sheet to get a clearer picture of an individual's situation, but in Chapter 7 we will use these same techniques to analyze a company's financial situation (albeit in greater detail). On one side of the page, the assets are listed. **Assets** are things of value that are owned or in one's possession. Assets would include such things as cash, stocks, or real estate. On the other side of the page, the liabilities are listed. **Liabilities** are any debt, financial obligation or claim that another has on the ownership of an asset. Liabilities would include such things as credit card bills, installment loans, home mortgages, or taxes due but unpaid.

Often, though, the claim that another has on the ownership of an asset is only a partial claim. A good example of this is when a down payment is made on a house or mortgage payments have been made for a time. In both of these cases, it is likely that the person who owns the asset has some equity. We will come to learn many definitions of equity, but here **equity** is the difference between what has been paid on an obligation, and the value of the asset. So if a home is worth $100,000, but you made a down payment of $20,000 and borrowed $80,000, then we would say that the asset is worth $100,000 but the owner has a liability of $80,000 and thus has equity of $20,000. Making additional mortgage payments could increase the owner's equity.

While we talk about the net value of a particular asset in terms of "equity," when we look at the entire financial situation of an individual or a company we use the term net worth. **Net worth** is the value that is left over after adding up all assets and subtracting all liabilities from that total. In short, assets are what you have; liabilities are what you owe; net worth is what you own. Of course, the net worth figure could be a negative number, meaning that the person or company owes out more money than it has in assets, and thus really doesn't "own" anything.

chart 2.1.1a

SIMPLE BALANCE SHEET FOR CHRIS SMITH AS OF 12-31-02

ASSETS	
House	$175,000
Car	25,000
Stocks	75,000
Checking Account	5,000
Retirement/Savings	45,000
Total Assets	**$325,000**
LIABILITIES	
Mortgage (on home)	$100,000
Installment loan (car)	20,000
Credit Cards	15,000
Total Liabilities	**$135,000**
TOTAL NET WORTH (Assets – Liabilities)	**$190,000**

Note that the balance sheet covers a specific date only. New assets may have been acquired or more debt may have been incurred since the date the statement was prepared. Also, remember that our example is a very simple one. A personal balance sheet would include more detail, and more items would be classified under assets, such as marketable securities (e.g., treasury bills, CDs close to maturity, etc.) and deferred assets (e.g., annuities, retirement accounts, etc.).

Balance sheets are most helpful when they are compared with balance sheets from prior years. This gives a better picture of the trend of the person's or company's financial situation. Is it in a better or worse position now than it was a year ago? This is a good financial profile tool, and when used together with an income statement, can be helpful in determining what types of investments are suitable for a customer, what she still needs to meet her objectives, and what she can afford.

INCOME STATEMENT. An **income statement** is a financial report that summarizes an entity's income and expenses over a given period of time. Typically, an income statement is done for a corporation (where it is also referred to as a **profit and loss statement**), but this is nevertheless a good exercise to help you understand your customer's financial situation. By creating an income statement that details a client's income and expenses, you can clearly see the amount of net spendable income that is available for investing. This **net spendable income,** arrived at by subtracting expenses from income, is sometimes referred to as **liquid net worth** because it is readily accessible. Let's look at a sample personal income statement.

chart 2.1.1b

SIMPLE INCOME STATEMENT CHRIS SMITH 12-01 THRU 12-31	
INCOME	
Salary	$55,000
Interest/Investments	8,000
Other	3,000
Total Income	**$66,000**
EXPENSES	
Housing (mortg., prop. tax)	$14,000
Other Debt (car, Visa, etc.)	9,000
Food	2,700
Utilties	1,800
Other	1,000
Total Expenses	**$28,500**
Total Tax Payments	**$20,500**
NET SPENDABLE INCOME (Income – Expenses – Tax)	**$17,000**

Note that the income statement covers a certain period of time, not just a single date like the balance sheet. Plus, you can glean more information from an income statement. By looking at different lines, you can perform different analyses of the client's financial situation. For example, by looking at the client's income before taxes and after taxes and doing some calculations, you can determine whether or not the client would benefit from investments that are tax-free or tax-deferred. Another thing that can be learned is how much income the client receives from a job versus how much income he receives from current investments. Looking at this information in conjunction with the assets listed on the balance sheet may help you recommend investments that have the potential for better returns.

Again, remember that our example is a very simple one. An income statement can have much more detail, and sometimes the information is broken down to show exactly what was received or paid out during even narrower time periods, such as monthly or quarterly. (A company's income statement has even more detail that is helpful in analyzing a company's financial situation, as we will see in Chapter 7.) Our simple example shows how analysis of a client's financial situation can reveal information to help you make suitable recommendations. But there's more to consider.

OTHER FINANCIAL CONSIDERATIONS. Net worth and net spendable income are not the only considerations when deciding what is a suitable recommendation to make to a client. The complete financial profile of a customer also includes such things as whether or not the client owns a home, has insurance, needs a tax shelter, or has credit concerns. For example, home ownership is an important objective for many. A client who does not yet own a home may be trying to save up for the down payment. You would be neglecting your duty as financial advisor if you didn't try to dissuade a young couple from gambling their down payment nest egg in a risky investment they thought might help them buy a bigger home.

Insurance is also an important component of a client's overall financial plan. Unexpected disabilities can derail retirement investment plans, so disability insurance can help offset that risk. Life insurance is needed so that loved ones can continue the lifestyle they are used to without having to sell assets, or cash in investments to pay estate taxes. Knowing the client's tax status is also important if you are to give suitable advice on what types of products would make good investments. Finally, a client's creditworthiness and credit report information would be helpful when making recommendations about investing with borrowed money, or helping the client plan to have enough cash or down payment for a desired purchase.

2.12 Nonfinancial Investment Considerations

The investment profile of a client also has several nonfinancial components that must be considered by an RR if he or she is to make suitable recommendations to the client. Most of this information is individual and family data that can be obtained from a typical new account form used by most broker-dealers. Knowing things such as the client's age, marital status, and number of dependents is important in assessing the current and future financial needs of the client. Certainly age and marital status are important for retirement planning. And, dependents require more financial assistance as they get older, and the client may also want to plan for college and/or other future expenses for those dependents. The client's goals and objectives will likely be shaped by these things and more. It is the job of the RR to understand these goals, and know the timetable for when they need to be achieved.

The employment status of the client and other family members also brings up important considerations. Does the client have a steady job with a regular paycheck that allows for periodic payment investments, or is the client self-employed and receives large but sporadic checks for consulting services? Are other family members dependent on the client, or are they employed and making additional income which could contribute to a retirement account or other investment? Each of these situations would require a different investment strategy. They might also affect the client's goals. For example, the client with the steady job may want to max out retirement contributions because he is not worried about meeting monthly expenses, while the client with the consulting business may want more liquid investments so that she has ready access to cash between consulting contracts.

Finally, the existence of a will is an important consideration for the RR. Are all of the client's assets being transferred to a spouse upon death, or are some of the investments earmarked for the client's children, who won't need the money until sometime down the road? This could change the investment strategy advice you as the RR give a client. Perhaps the client would be interested in aggressive investing with the assets that will go to the children in the future; perhaps not. You are likely not credentialed enough to replace the consultation of a good estate attorney, but you need as much information as you can get in order to give your client the best advice.

2.1.3 Risk Tolerance and Investment Experience

The final piece that makes up the investment profile of a customer is also perhaps one of the most important when considering what suitable recommendations to make to the client. The client's risk tolerance and investment experience will likely influence all investment decisions. Of course, the more risky an investment is, the greater the payoff will be if it succeeds. Yet this can be only a portion of the client's overall portfolio. Furthermore, the client must fully understand the risks and be prepared to take them. As we examine different kinds of investments in the coming chapters, we will also discuss the various risks associated with those investments. You may be surprised to learn that even within investment products and classes, there are varying degrees of risk.

It is the job of the RR to give advice on what risks may be appropriate given an investor's situation. For example, the RR should try to discourage an elderly couple that just entered retirement from gambling their entire nest egg in a risky investment. On the other hand, the RR should also try to encourage a young couple who has 100 percent of their retirement money invested in bank CDs to try and get a better return since they are far from retiring and inflation will eat up a good portion of the return from the CDs. Diversification of an investor's portfolio is one area where an RR can offer important advice. Asking clients what they have invested in before is an important gauge of their experience, but the RR should show them how to structure a well-balanced portfolio. The financial pyramid diagram, Figure 2.1.3, can help illustrate risk-reward trade-offs, and show how the client should diversify.

Examining the financial profile and other elements of the investor's investment profile is the first step in "knowing your client," but this must always be coupled with questions: What is your current situation? How much can you afford to invest? What will you do if an investment doesn't pan out? Do you have adequate cash reserves? How liquid do you want your investments to be? What are some upcoming expenses you know you will need to take care of? What are your future plans, goals, dreams?

The RR can get some idea of the client's risk tolerance and investment experience by looking at current investment holdings on the balance sheet. But situations can

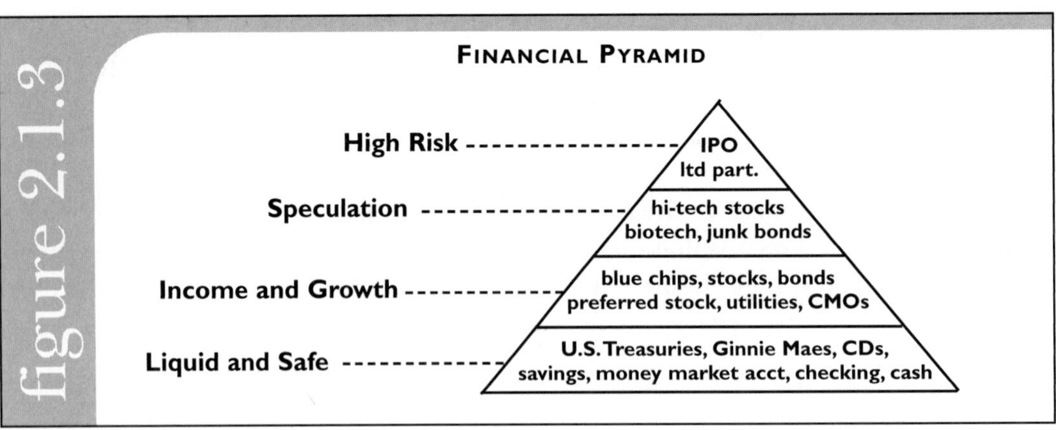

and do change, so the RR needs to continually ask questions to make sure that the client's investment objectives haven't changed.

An important point for all RRs (and this may appear on the test) is that *one cannot assume that every investor has the same objectives for his or her portfolio.*

In the next section, we will discuss what some of those objectives might be and how they can be met.

2.2 Investment Objectives

After a thorough analysis of a client's investment profile, it is time for the RR to make recommendations. These recommendations should be based on the investment objectives the client has laid out or the RR has ascertained from the information collected and analyzed thus far. The client's investment objectives may include any one of ten potential investment objective strategies, or a combination of these. As we look at each one, we will mention where they fall on the financial pyramid and also give an example or two of a type of investment that would fit the criteria for that investment objective. (Don't worry if you don't know all of the investment products mentioned as examples. They will be explained in detail in upcoming chapters.)

PRESERVATION OF CAPITAL. Preservation of capital is ensuring that the original amount of money invested is as safe as possible. No one likes to lose money, and everyone who invests hopes to make money. But clients who tell you that preservation of capital is their prime objective are a special case. They are telling you that safe investments are more important than trying to get larger returns on their money. They would want most of their money (if not all of it) in the bottom of our financial pyramid, invested in "safe" investments such as CDs, money market funds, fixed annuities, and perhaps some high grade bonds or government securities. People at or near retirement age often have this as their main investment objective.

CURRENT INCOME. **Current income** is trying to generate an immediate cash flow from a portfolio of investments. This is a common investment objective that can certainly be done through some of the "safe" investments mentioned previously, but now the client may be giving you a little more latitude. Bonds, of course, are a good source of income, but the rating of the company (or government) issuing them must be balanced against the returns offered. Investing in mortgage-backed securities can also be a relatively safe way to generate income (especially safe are the Ginnie Maes), although there are other risks associated with these that we will learn about in later chapters. Preferred stock and even some utility stocks, while slightly higher on the risk scale than bonds, can also be a source of income. Real estate investment trusts (REITs) can also pass through rental and other income with less risk than for a client actually owning and managing the piece of real estate directly.

CAPITAL GROWTH. **Capital growth** is trying to make the original amount of invested money appreciate over the long term. Here we are starting to move up in our financial pyramid as the client has defined a new objective that is less compatible with the first two. The best way for a client's money to grow over time is to have it invested in stock. Common stock in corporations is an excellent way to achieve growth, but the potential risk of principal must always be in the back of the investor's mind. Of course, this risk can be mitigated somewhat by the type of stocks chosen for the portfolio: "blue chip" stocks of well-established companies is safer but the trade-off is lower, more moderate capital growth; biotech or high-tech stocks offer the potential of high, more aggressive growth, but they are much higher on the financial pyramid in the speculation to high risk range. Mutual fund investing and other sector funds are another way to achieve growth while mitigating risk through the diversification of stocks that a fund has invested in. Still the risk of loss is there. Direct investment in real estate offers growth potential, but entails additional risk.

TOTAL RETURN. **Total return** is an investment objective that seeks capital growth with asset appreciation and interest or dividends. This is a somewhat harder goal to achieve, but can be done. Owning stock in companies with a history of dividend payouts is one way to accomplish this, but this is far from a guarantee of future income. Another way is to achieve growth with income is to buy convertible preferred stock. As we will see in the next chapter, preferred stock pays out dividends but does not allow for much appreciation in the value of the stock. The convertible feature, however, lets the client convert the preferred stock to common stock at a future date if the company's stock price begins to rise significantly. There are other routes a client could go to try and achieve his goal of total return, but these would be higher up in risk on the financial pyramid. Some types of real estate and some limited partnerships would fit into this category, offering potential income along with a chance for appreciation, but also with much higher risk.

TAX ADVANTAGES. Tax advantages are an objective whereby money is invested in structured ways or in particular kinds of investments to minimize taxes, defer taxes, or avoid taxes altogether. Clients who are looking to reduce their tax liability or offset gains in other areas have a few options at their disposal. These investment choices range from rather safe, like municipal bonds, to fairly risky, like limited partnerships. And all have different tax implications. For example, municipal bonds pay interest that is free from federal income tax; IRAs (individual retirement accounts) allow pretax contributions that lower current tax liability and defer the taxes until retirement; and limited partnerships allow write-offs of only certain kinds of losses. Indexed funds, annuities, and several other kinds of IRAs beyond the standard IRA all offer different tax advantages and incentives. We will discuss some of these in the coming chapters, not so that you can give tax advice, but so that you can understand your client's needs and goals and help him or her achieve them.

Exam Topic Alert

An important point about the Series 7 exam is *watch the tax status of customers in test questions!* You should not recommend the sale of municipal bonds or other tax advantaged investments to clients who would not benefit from the tax savings. This is considered a violation of the "know your customer" rules. For example, if a test question talks about a client in the lowest tax bracket or is low income, look for answers that *do not* include municipal bonds. You can sell these types of "low tax" clients a municipal bond only if the client already has a specific bond purchase in mind, gives you the specific purchase information, and explicit instructions to buy.

PORTFOLIO DIVERSIFICATION. Portfolio diversification is spreading out risk by holding investments in varying types and amounts. As an RR, you should explain to each client the merits of a diversified investment portfolio. This would entail spreading the client's risk over the entire financial pyramid, having most of his or her money in the bottom safety portion, and the smallest amount invested in high-risk investments at the top of the pyramid. Of course, different clients will have different risk tolerances and want more money put into different areas, depending on their investment needs. Portfolio diversification will likely be an important goal, though, for clients who have all of their money tied up in one investment or one type of investment; perhaps all in a savings account or retirement account, or for clients who recently received a large amount of money, perhaps through an inheritance. Having a diverse portfolio can be a hedge against a downturn in a particular sector of the economy, as well as being a good means of keeping pace with inflation.

LIQUIDITY. Liquidity is the ease with which assets can be converted into cash. Although much investing is done for retirement or to fill other future needs, most clients will need to get to their money at one time or another before that. How often this occurs will depend on the client's job status, family situation, and lifestyle. Clients who know that their income situation is unstable, or who know that they are close to a major purchase or expense will likely want to have a specific amount of money readily available in liquid investments. These would include regular CDs, marketable securities, money market funds, and bonds close to maturity. Stocks that trade on the major exchanges are also fairly liquid because they can be readily sold, but they carry with them some market risk because their value may be down at the time that the client needs to sell them and get his money out. Highly illiquid investments would include such things as limited partnerships (because there is no secondary market for them), real estate (because of the time and expense involved in selling it), and annuities and other retirement accounts (because of the penalties for early withdrawal of funds).

An important point about the Series 7 exam is *never ignore liquidity considerations of a client on the test!* For example, if a test question says that your client needs money soon, or your client will need money in less than six months or in some other short period of time, look for an answer that talks about you as the RR recommending money market investments, regular bank CDs, or some other short-term investment that is not speculative and is very liquid to meet your customers needs. Any other answer would be a bad recommendation not in the best interests of your customer.

SPECULATION. Speculation is assuming higher risk in anticipation of higher returns. It is not gambling with a random outcome, but rather high stakes investing made after a thorough analysis of a situation. Certainly speculation is not for everyone, but having a small portion of a portfolio invested in speculative investments can greatly enhance the overall return of the portfolio. Speculative investments might include high tech company stocks on the low end of the risk scale, and oil and gas partnerships on the high end of the risk scale. Safer ways to speculate include options, where the investor has the right, but not the obligation, to buy or sell something. Here the amount at risk is limited to the initial purchase price of the options contract, but the potential gain may be unlimited. There are a number of variations which investors can use to hedge their investments as well. We will discuss these in greater detail in the next chapter.

TRADING PROFITS. Trading profits are profits earned from short term trades. These can be highly speculative if the investor does not intend to hold the investment for any significant period of time, and higher risk because small movements in price that can have a great impact on an investment position can happen quickly. An example of a strategy to capitalize on trading profits could involve options contracts, and the like, or it can involve day trading. Both of these are somewhat speculative, and each have its own unique considerations. For example, commissions and sales charges must be an important consideration in determining whether or not day trading is a profitable strategy. And, in addition to the risky nature of trying to profit from short term trades, the investor must also consider the tax implications since all profits will be taxed as regular income. Certain types of options contracts can also put the investor in a position of unlimited risk, depending on which side of the transaction the investor is on.

LONG-TERM vs. SHORT-TERM RISK. Long-term vs. short-term risk is the attempt to balance the risk-reward ratio of investments. We will go into a detailed discussion of the different types of investment risks at the beginning of the next chapter, but a brief description is in order here. Basically, this risk analysis recognizes that ALL investments have some element of risk. Thus, one consideration and possible objective for portfolio diversification is balancing these investment risks within the portfolio. For example, investing in bank CDs and government securities may appear to be low risk, but their low risk of losing the principal capital invested must be balanced against the relatively high risk that the low returns on those investments will not keep pace with inflation over the long term. And, stocks that historically have a moderate risk of capital loss over the long term, have the short-term market risk that the overall broad market and perhaps even the individual stock value may be down at the time that the client needs to sell the stock and get money out. The more diversified a portfolio is, the less any one type of risk can impact the overall value and performance of the entire portfolio.

2.X Summary

2.1 Client profile is financial & nonfinancial. Must consider client's available capital, current holdings, risk tolerance, investment experience. Making unsuitable recommendations is violation of NASD rules.

"Know your customer" says it is responsibility of broker-dealer, RR to get complete, accurate understanding of client to give appropriate advice. NYSE rules say B-D, RR must do due diligence to verify info. NASD says must have reasonable grounds to believe trade is suitable based on client info. MSRB says tax status of client is second only to knowing financial status.

2.1.1 Most client info can be gathered from new account form. Balance sheet shows assets, liabilities, net worth as of certain date. Assets – Liabilities = Net Worth. Equity is difference between value of asset and what's owed. (many meanings) Income statement summarizes income, expenses over period of time (thus can show net spendable income—liquid net worth—available for investing).

Other financial considerations: home ownership, insurance, taxes, credit.

2.1.2 Nonfinancial considerations: age, marital status, dependents, job, will.

2.1.3 Risk tolerance: greater risk = greater reward. Diversification is important. Financial pyramid: safety at base (biggest part), high risk on top (smallest). Cannot assume every investor has same objectives for his or her portfolio.

2.2 Client's investment objectives are learned by listening, analysis of RR.

Preservation of capital requires safety: CDs, money market funds, fixed annuities, high grade bonds, government securities (people near retirement).

Current income to generate cash now: bonds (watch ratings), mortgage-backed securities (Ginnie Maes), preferred stock, utility stock, REIT (risk).

Capital growth for long term appreciation: common stock (blue chips), mutual funds (can spread risk), direct real estate investment (more risky).

Total return seeks growth and income: common stock (dividend history), convertible preferred stock, real estate or limited partnerships (more risky).

Tax advantages to minimize, defer, avoid taxes: municipal bonds, indexed-funds, annuities, IRAs, limited partnerships (passive losses, passive income). Watch tax status of clients in test questions—low tax should not buy munis.

Portfolio diversification spreads risk over entire financial pyramid.

Liquidity is ease of converting assets to cash: money market investments, CDs, short-term investments. Never ignore liquidity in test questions.

2.2+ Speculation is assuming higher risk for higher reward: high tech stocks, oil and gas partnerships (risky), options (many variations).

Trading profits earned from short-term trades: options (potential for unlimited risk if not careful), day trading (trading costs, tax implications).

Long vs. short risk, balance of risk-reward: all investments have risk. Safe short-term investments (e.g., CDs) have risk of low return. Safe long-term investments (e.g., stocks) have market risk (low price when need to sell).

Chapter 2 Review Quiz

1. Which of the following is an implication of the "Know Your Customer" maxim?
   a. RRs should know that a customer has a child ready to enter college
   b. a NYSE broker-dealer should verify information given by a customer
   c. RRs should learn clients' tax situation before suggesting tax-exempt bonds
   d. all of the above

2. Which of the following does *not* appear on a balance sheet?
   a. assets
   b. liabilities
   c. expenses
   d. net worth

3. A balance sheet:
   a. is good for one full year from the date it was prepared.
   b. covers the date it was prepared only.
   c. tells about the year preceding the date it was prepared.
   d. is good for the month or year stated only.

4. Which of the following does *not* appear on an income statement?
   a. assets
   b. debt obligations
   c. expenses
   d. liquid net worth

5. An income statement:
   a. is good for one full year from the date it was prepared.
   b. covers the date it was prepared only.
   c. tells about the future income potential.
   d. is good for the time period stated at the top only.

6. A client you have been advising has done very well with some high-tech stocks that you have been recommending. The client refers some friends to invest with you, too. You should:
   a. immediately put them in the same investments as the client who referred them.
   b. advise them to put money in cash because they look like older people who want safe investments for retirement.
   c. have them fill out a new client form and ask them questions about their investment objectives and experience.
   d. turn away the business because it is a conflict of interest.

7. When advising a client, which investment objective is the most important?
   a. preservation of capital (safety of principal)
   b. current income
   c. capital growth
   d. whichever the client tells you is most important

8. A client comes in and complains that he doesn't like to pay taxes, and does everything in his power to pay as little of his money to the government as possible. The client tells you that he is in the lowest tax bracket, then says he wants to buy Missouri dam project bonds because he is very familiar with the issue. You should:
   a. put all of the clients money into tax-exempt municipal bonds since he doesn't like to pay taxes.
   b. help the client buy the Missouri dam project bonds because he asked for them by name, but also explain to him that his tax situation does not necessarily warrant the purchase of additional municipal securities.
   c. avoid recommending Treasuries of any kind since the client doesn't like to give any of his money to the government.
   d. recommend that the client instead put his money into risky, tax-sheltered limited partnerships so he can avoid taxes.

9. A client tells you that she will begin studying for her Ph.D in six months and will need to pull her money out then, but in the meantime she wants to make her investment grow as much as possible. You should:
   a. immediately invest the client's money into high growth stocks.
   b. tell the client that she is best off keeping her money in cash.
   c. recommend that a portion of the funds go into money market funds and that some of the money should go into CDs
   d. advise the client to put the funds into long-term Treasuries because the money will be safe and she can get higher yields than with short-term securities.

Providing Customers with Investment Information

"Providing Customers with Investment Information" is the third of the seven critical functions that are performed by a registered representative (RR). Providing customers with information is key in helping clients make informed decisions about their investments. After all, you can make all the recommendations you want, but in the end it is still the client's money to do with as he or she sees fit. In order for you to make suitable recommendations and give clients the advice they need, you as the RR must have a good grasp of the various investment vehicles available, and the associated characteristics, advantages and disadvantages, risks and rewards of each.

When you have finished studying this chapter, you should be able to fully describe the characteristics, risks, and rewards of various securities. This will ensure that the customer is provided with the pertinent information for a particular investment. As the RR continues to work with and advise the customer, the RR should continue to obtain and update relevant information about the customer when making recommendations, and investigate alternative investments if this updated information warrants it. Tax implications of these investments will also be discussed so that you as RR can consider the tax implications with clients in the process of making suitable recommendations. Furthermore, mastering the information in this chapter will enable you as RR to explain how the risks and rewards of a particular investment or strategy relate to the customer's financial needs and investment objectives. (Providing the customer with information also includes informing him or her of the costs and fees associated with the transaction.)

This third critical function covered in Chapter 3 ("Providing Customers with Investment Information") represents nearly 50 percent of the total exam: approximately 125 questions of the total 250 questions on the Series 7 Exam. There is much material covered in this chapter, some of which you may already be familiar with. Key concepts will be introduced in a logical progression that will help you on the test, and later as you function as an RR in the securities industry. To facilitate learning the material, we will break down the information more so than in the other chapters.

This chapter will be broken up into seven sections:

3.1 **Investment Risk.** This first section will examine the concept of investment risk in much more detail. Ten different types of investment risk will be identified, defined, and described in relation to their importance in portfolio management. The first section will also explain some different types of investment advice that can be used to mitigate these risks. These strategies include using growth, speculative, and defensive stocks to achieve investment objectives for the portfolio.

3.2 **Taxation.** This section will look at U.S. federal taxation, and how it relates to types of income (earned, investment, passive). Tax treatment of foreign securities purchased by U.S. citizens will also be discussed, as will the important topic of tax treatment of "wash sales." (Tax information will also be included in other parts of this chapter—indeed the entire book—as it relates to specific investments and topics.)

3.3 **Equity Securities.** This section goes into considerable detail about terms, agents, and procedures associated with equity securities. It defines common stock, as well as the terms associated with types of stock, the rights of common stockholders, dividends, and stock splits. An explanation of preferred stock will not only define it and the principal kinds of preferred stock, but also explain what makes it different from common stock. Other types of equity securities will also be discussed, including rights offerings, warrants, and American Depository Receipts (ADRs). Tax treatment of equity securities transactions will deal with several important points, including defining capital gains, other types of gains and losses, holding periods, cost basis, and part position sales. Finally, direct participation

key terms

Adjusted cost basis: the original price, plus any commissions, adjustments or allowable expenses. (Used for computing tax liability.)

and interest: buyer of a security must pay the quoted price of the bond or note, plus accrued interest since last interest payment was made. Opposite: **traded flat.**

Basis point: 1/100%, or .01 of yield. A basis point is the smallest unit of measure used to quote yields. It takes 100 basis points to equal 1 percent. So if we say that the yield on a bond is 1/4 point higher, we are saying that it rose 0.25 percent, or 25 basis points.

Breakpoint selling: keeping a client's trades just below breakpoints where the investor would save on sales charges. **This is a violation of NASD rules.**

Call: 1. redeeming a bond or preferred stock before maturity by paying principal and interest owed, and often a call premium, as per terms stated in the security; 2. option that gives an investor the **right to buy** a certain number of shares of a security, at a predetermined price, before a certain date.

Commercial paper: short-term debt issued by corporations to finance inventories, accounts receivable, and other obligations. (*Not* issued by commercial banks.)

Coupon: nominal interest rate. (Term comes from old bearer bonds which had physical coupons that were detached and submitted to collect interest payments.)

Derivative security: an instrument whose value is dependent on the value of another underlying security. For example, see **option.**

Discount: the amount below par that an investor pays for a bond. Also see **OID.**

Earned income: money generated from providing labor, goods or services. Also called **active income** (e.g., salary, wages, tips, bonuses, other employee compensation, pensions, social security payments, annuity income payments). Opposite: **investment income, unearned income.** Also see **passive income.**

Forward pricing: when buy and sell orders for mutual fund shares are placed before the final price is known, and thus priced at the next **NAV** calculation.

Inflationary risk: chance that the value of assets or income will decline relative to the prices of other goods and services. Also called **purchasing power risk.**

Investment grade bonds: bonds that have one of the top four ratings from Moody's (Aaa, Aa, A, Baa) or S&P (AAA, AA, A, BBB). Also called **bank grade bonds.**

Long: a position in a stock, option, etc. when an investor **buys** it. You can also say that the investor is the **owner** or **holder** of the option, or is **long** the option. (These terms are synonymous: **buyer = owner = holder = long.**) Opposite: **short.**

OID: Original Issue Discount, bonds that are sold at a discount from par value when they are first issued.

Option: the right, but not obligation, to buy or sell something at a predetermined price and under predetermined conditions (time limit and/or other conditions).

Passive income: income derived from any business activity in which the person is not an active participant (e.g., limited partnerships or real estate). Tax law change in 1986: passive losses are deductible only against passive income.

Preemptive rights: the right of existing stockholders to buy, in proportion to their current holdings, additional shares of a new issue by the company before the stock is offered to the public. Also called an **antidilution provision.**

Premium: 1. the amount above par that an investor pays for a bond; 2. the price an investor pays to buy an option contract.

programs (DPPs) will be examined, going over the general characteristics and procedures, various types of DPPs, subscription agreements, offerings, and how to evaluate DPPs.

3.4 **Debt Instruments.** This section begins with a discussion of U.S. Treasury securities, their characteristics, interest computations, and yields. U.S. government agency securities will also be defined, along with their characteristics and some examples of specific agency securities, including government agency mortgage-backed securities. Other types of asset-backed securities will also be introduced, such as the private sector collateralized mortgage obligations (CMOs), their characteristics, and the risk-reward trade-off. Next, corporate bonds will be examined, along with their characteristics, specific types of corporate bonds (including convertibles and callables), interest and yield calculations, and corporate bond ratings. Tax treatment of debt securities and corporate taxation will be mentioned, followed by definitions of a number of money market instruments. Finally, municipal securities will be covered at length, including defining the different types of municipal bonds, investment features and marketability factors, early retirement of the debt, pricing and other calculations, and tax treatment of municipal bonds.

3.5 **Packaged Securities.** This section will outline the three basic types of packaged securities: investment companies, variable annuity contracts, and real estate investment trusts (REITs). Each will be defined along with an explanation of its main features, characteristics, and tax treatment.

3.6 **Derivative Products.** Derivative products include a number of kinds of investments, but most are related to options: options on stock, options on bonds, options on foreign currency, etc. Options are the right, but not the obligation, to buy or sell something at a predetermined price and under predetermined conditions. The characteristics of options will be explained, along with basic option strategies, and tax treatment of various types of option transactions.

3.7 **Retirement Plans and Estate Tax Considerations.** This final section will discuss individual retirement plans, such as IRAs and Keogh plans, employer-sponsored plans, such as 401(k), the Employees Retirement Income Security Act (ERISA), and federal estate and gift tax considerations.

3.1

Investment Risk

As we stated at the end of the last chapter, all investments have some element of risk. When most people hear the term "risk," though, they associate that with "risk of principal." **Risk of principal** is the chance that invested capital will decrease in value. Here one thinks of the investor who buys a stock that becomes worthless, but this is hardly the only risk that an investor faces. **Investment risk** is the chance that adverse conditions will cause the value of an investment to drop. The important difference here is that we are speaking about the investment value in relative terms. Furthermore, these "adverse conditions" may or may not be directly related to the investment itself.

Suppose your client buys a bond that is paying 6 percent interest. That may sound like a good return but there are other factors that must be considered. What if inflation were to rise to 8 percent? The investor did not lose any of the principal invested, and indeed may still collect the entire amount of interest owed. But what once may have been a "good" investment is not anymore—even if the bond is repaid in full—because the investor *did* lose money vis-à-vis inflation. And what if that same investor bought the bond because it was a tax-free municipal issue, but the tax laws change? This could effectively reduce the investor's net return on the investment. These are just two of the many investment risks that must be considered when advising clients about what investments to make when putting together a diversified portfolio.

Put: option that gives an investor the **right to sell** a certain number of shares of a security, at a predetermined price, before a certain date.

Refunding: replacing a debt obligation with another debt security that has different terms, such as a lower interest rate.

Rights offering: an offer to existing common stockholders that allows them to buy additional shares of newly issued stock before it is offered for sale to the public. This is done to honor the preemptive rights of existing common stockholders. (Term used with **standby underwriting.**)

Short: a position in a stock, option, etc. when an investor **sells** it. You can also say that the investor is the **writer** of the option, or is **short** the option. (These terms are synonymous: **seller = writer = short.**) Opposite: **long.**

Standby underwriting: when an investment banking firm guarantees the issuing company that the firm will buy all shares that are not bought as part of the new issue offering. (Term used with **rights offering.**)

Strike price: the price at which the contract holder can exercise the option. Also called **exercise price.**

Traded flat: when bonds trade at the quoted price without accrued interest. (e.g., zero coupon bonds or when issuer is in default.) Opposite: **and interest.**

Tranches: separate maturity groups. (Term used with **CMOs.**)

Warrants: an additional security offered along with the sale of another security, which allows the warrant holder to buy shares of common stock at some point in the future at a predetermined price. (These are called **sweeteners.**)

Wash sale: when the same securities (or substantially similar securities) are bought and sold simultaneously or within a short period of time. Wash sales that occur 30 days before or 30 days after a transaction are not capital losses per IRS rules.

3.1.1

Definitions of Types of Investment Risks

In the prior section, we briefly mentioned two ways that an investor can actually lose money without any adverse condition being directly attributable to the underlying investment. There are, in fact many more kinds of risks. Each must be fully understood by you as advisor and by your client as investor if suitable recommendations and investments are to be made for your client's portfolio.

INFLATIONARY RISKS. Inflationary risk is the chance that the value of assets or income will decline relative to the prices of other goods and services, thus resulting in less purchasing power (so it is also called **purchasing power risk**). Inflation is one of the most important investment risks that must be considered since it exerts great force on the markets. Inflation can be bad for current bondholders who are receiving a fixed rate of return. Long-term bondholders are hit the hardest because they are typically locked in at a lower interest rate. Retirement investments especially must be structured so as to minimize the effects of inflation.

Inflation is also bad for the stock market, not only because it can hurt the bottom-line performance of companies, but also because as inflation rises, money will move from stocks and into the bond market seeking those new higher (and safer?) returns.

CAPITAL RISKS. Capital risk is the chance that an investment will go down in value or lose money without something bad having happened to the underlying company. The best example of this is when an investor owns an option to buy stock in a company. When the option expires, the capital invested to buy that option is lost even though the company is still thriving. It just means that the stock price (for example) did not go up in value enough to make it worthwhile to use the option. In this case, the investor loses the premium paid to buy the option contract.

TIMING RISKS. Timing risk is the danger that an investor will not pick the best time to buy or sell an investment, and thus not maximize his or her gain. Timing risk actually involves four risks rolled into one: getting in, getting out, transaction costs, and tax consequences. Buy low and sell high is not as easy as it sounds. Certainly getting in and out at the right time is important, but no one truly knows which way the market is going or when a particular investment has peaked or bottomed out. Then the investor must also figure the transaction costs of continually trying to get in and out to beat the market. This is especially true for day traders. Finally, tax consequences can affect timing decisions. Selling early to move taxable gains to an earlier year can result in a sale too early; delaying a sale to have it taxed as a capital gain instead of higher tax rates could also result in missed opportunity to sell higher.

INTEREST RATE RISKS. Interest rate risk is the risk that changes in interest rates will adversely affect the value of an investment. As interest rates rise, the value of bonds falls. This is what's known as an inverse relationship. As with our discussion of inflationary risks, bonds with long-term maturities are hit the hardest. In fact, many of the same principles that apply to inflationary risks also apply to interest rate risks.

This is because interest rates typically rise as inflation rises. The effects here, though, can be more pronounced because short-term interest rates generally move in bigger swings than long-term interest rates.

As we saw with inflationary risks, the stock market is also affected by interest rate risks. As interest rates rise, money will move out of stocks and into bonds, seeking those new higher interest rates (which are perceived to be safer than stocks). Also, since utility companies are highly leveraged, utility company stocks also take a hard hit in value as interest rates rise, because as utilities devote a higher portion of their revenue to pay debt service their bottom line profitability suffers. In fact, this is true of all highly leveraged companies.

MARKET RISKS. **Market risk** is risk that is common to all investments of the same type or classification, owing more to broad market conditions or investor sentiment towards a particular sector of stocks or bonds. This is also referred to as **systematic risk** that can't be eliminated through diversification, although it can be lowered by adding more types of securities to a portfolio. The narrower the focus of investments in the portfolio (e.g. emphasis on certain sector funds), the more pronounced the risk.

CREDIT RISKS. **Credit risk** is defined as the risk that an investment will lose money because it is not repaid. This is also referred to as **repayment risk** or **financial risk.** Here, the default of the debt issuer is borne by the person holding the bond or other debt instrument. Of course, bondholders do have some recourse in a bankruptcy proceeding, but they are likely to take a loss. This type of risk can be minimized by the quality of debt instruments chosen for investment, but at the trade-off of lower returns. Federal government securities are the safest, but offer lowest returns. Some corporate bonds offer very attractive returns, but their credit ratings must be examined carefully so that the investor understands the risks.

LIQUIDITY RISKS. **Liquidity risk** is the chance that an investor may not be able to convert an investment, security, or asset into cash when needed. This can be because the asset is stock in a privately-held company, shares in a limited partnership or real estate. Even regional stocks and some thinly traded over-the-counter shares may not be able to be sold easily. And, if one of these investments is sold, the investor may have to accept less than market price because there is limited demand for it. This is an important consideration in recommendations you make to clients.

This is a good place to reiterate an important point about the Series 7 exam: ***never*** ignore liquidity considerations of a client on the test! If a test question says your client needs money soon or in less than six months or some other short period of time, look for an answer that talks about you recommending money market investments, regular bank CDs, or some other short-term investment that is very liquid.

POLITICAL RISKS AND LEGISLATIVE RISKS. These two risks are related, but slightly different. **Political risk** refers to the risk of a change in government policy that adversely affects an investment. This usually refers to a foreign country, such as when an industry is nationalized or protectionist measures are adopted that affect specific import or export products. **Legislative risk** refers to the risk of a change in the law that adversely affects an investment. This usually refers to domestic policies, such as new clean air requirements or tax law changes. Sometimes these laws can have unintended consequences beyond the scope of their original intent. For example, new clean air requirements not only affect utilities and transportation industries, but they also have ripple effects throughout other sectors that rely on them. Another example is the tax law changes of 1986, which changed the deductibility of passive losses. This certainly had a direct effect on values of limited partnerships, but it was also a contributing factor to the devaluation of some real estate investments and the Savings & Loan crisis.

CALL RISKS. **Call risk** is the chance that a bond issuer or company that has issued preferred stock may call (redeem) the security before the actual maturity date. Bonds often have such a provision so that as interest rates fall, the issuer can redeem the high interest bond and replace it with a lower interest bond. For the investor, this represents a risk because he or she may have been counting on the higher rate of return on that bond, but once it is called the investor must try to find a replacement vehicle to invest in. Since it is likely that falling interest rates generated the call, it is unlikely that the investor can replace the investment with one of a similar yield. This is also referred to as **reinvestment risk,** and is very common with mortgage-backed securities, since homeowners are likely to refinance their homes at lower interest rates when rates drop. The investor is repaid his or her investment and left with the difficult task of finding a suitable replacement investment that can match the yield of the one that was paid off.

CURRENCY RISKS. **Currency risk** is the chance of foreign exchange loss because of fluctuations in the value of foreign money vis-à-vis the dollar. This is also referred to as **exchange risk.** At first glance, this may only seem to affect speculators who trade in the foreign currency markets, or those who invest in foreign companies. In reality, though, any multinational corporation which has profits from foreign subsidiaries, companies who have manufacturing facilities in other countries, or any other entity that imports or exports goods or services is susceptible to this risk. Of course, there are ways to minimize this risk, hedging with foreign currency options and futures contracts for example, but good investment advice must consider this risk to ensure that appropriate steps are taken to protect the investor, or make sure that the companies he or she is investing in have taken steps to protect themselves.

3.1.2

Risks Related to Various Types of Investment Recommendations

As we discussed the various investment risks that an investor must consider in the previous section, we also periodically mentioned some things that could be done to offset those risks. In the end, though, the only true way to mitigate investment risks is for the investor to have a diversified portfolio. Still, within the framework of a diversified portfolio there is room for different strategies to help clients achieve other investment objectives as well. As discussed, these objectives might include safety or moderate growth through defensive investments, speculation or high growth using aggressive investments, or a combination of the two. Let's briefly look at each of these and see how a portfolio might be weighted to achieve the investor's desired goal.

SAFETY. Safety entails preservation of capital. The investor may also desire to generate some income. Safety and moderate growth are best achieved through the use of defensive investments. **Defensive investments** are stocks with prices that are more stable over time than the broad market, and high grade bonds. Some stocks that would be in a typical "defensive" portfolio would be utilities, certain blue chip stocks, and some high grade preferred stock. The blue chips would allow for some moderate growth, and may even pay a dividend, while maintaining the safety component that the investor requires. A defensive portfolio would also hold debt securities as a larger portion of the overall portfolio. These bonds would be government issued, or high grade corporate bonds from companies that have excellent debt ratings.

SPECULATION. Speculation entails greater accepted risk. Investors who want to maximize their return on investment understand that the greater the risks, the greater the potential rewards. Speculation and high growth are best achieved through the use of aggressive investments. **Aggressive investments** are stocks of rapidly growing companies that have prospects for above-average growth, but with prices that are highly volatile over time when compared with the broader market. Some stocks that would be in a typical "aggressive" portfolio would be high-tech companies and other start-ups. These stocks are generally relied upon solely for capital appreciation since they usually offer no dividend income. An aggressive portfolio would have very little in the way of investments with fixed returns, such as bonds (although zero coupon bonds are one way to speculate on interest rates because the zero coupon prices are very volatile). An aggressive portfolio would also have a portion of securities bought on margin to gain maximum leverage with its funds.

COMBINATION. In reality, most investment portfolios fall somewhere between these two extremes. This is at the heart of diversification. As we discuss different types of securities throughout the rest of this chapter and in chapters to come, you will see how these investments fit into the diversification picture. You will also learn ways to show clients that they can hedge their bets to minimize the various risks facing them. Finally, by Chapter 7, we will go through some various portfolio management scenarios that will show you how to take everything you have learned and apply it to real-life questions, decisions, and recommendations that you will encounter with clients on a daily basis. (They will certainly be important concepts for you to know for the Series 7 exam.)

3.2 Taxation

Taxation is an important consideration for any investment portfolio. Since the payment of taxes does not enhance income or growth in the portfolio, a good investment strategy includes finding ways to minimize taxes, defer taxes, or avoid taxes altogether. As we discuss various investments later in this chapter and in subsequent chapters, we will also point out some specific tax considerations and consequences that are unique to that investment. Here, though, we will give you a brief overview of some of the tax laws that all investors must deal with.

3.2.1 U.S. Federal Taxation

The U.S. federal tax system is progressive. **Progressive tax** is a system of taxation whereby people with higher incomes pay a higher percentage of their income in taxes. This is accomplished through the use of tax brackets. A **tax bracket** is a section on the tax schedule which shows what percentage of income is owed in taxes based on the income being reported. Tax brackets, though, are **marginal,** meaning that only the portion of income that falls above each bracket is taxed at that higher level. The higher a person is on the income scale, the higher the tax percentage that must be paid. The progressive system used to calculate income taxes is the opposite of the regressive tax system (where all people pay the same tax rate regardless of income, such as a sales tax).

There are three types of income—earned, investment, passive—which are treated differently for tax purposes. Even within each classification, there are rules and distinctions that affect how taxes are calculated, so let's look at some of these.

EARNED. Earned income is money generated from providing labor, goods, or services. Usually when we hear about "earnings" we think of salary, wages, tips, bonuses, or other employee compensation. Earned income, though, can also be from any business activity, such as net sales or payment for services rendered. This is why earned income is sometimes referred to as **active income.** Pensions, social security payments and annuity income are also classified as earned income.

Earned income is subject to standard income tax treatment, meaning that minimal deductions are allowed and that the remaining amount is subject to taxation based on the income tax bracket that the individual falls into.

INVESTMENT. Investment income is money generated from securities or other assets. This could mean interest from bonds, dividends from stocks, or capital gains from the sale of securities. Since this income is derived from nonbusiness activity it is sometimes referred to as **unearned income.** There are, however, some additional rules for the treatment of investment income that you must be aware of.

First, interest income is generally fully taxable as ordinary income, but there are a few exceptions. Since interest paid on U.S. government securities is free from state and local taxes, the federal government does not collect federal income tax on municipal bond interest payments. Another exception is that any interest that accrues in a tax-deferred investment, such as an individual retirement account (IRA), is not subject to income tax until the money is withdrawn from the investment. This is not the case with other investments, where interest is taxable in the year it is earned—even if the interest income is reinvested or allowed to stay in the account.

Next, dividends are fully taxable to the shareholder who receives them. They are not a deductible expense to the paying corporation, so in effect dividends are taxed twice. Like interest income, dividend income is taxed in the year that it is earned, even if the dividends are reinvested or stay in the account.

Finally, net capital gains are a taxable event when they are realized. (This goes for capital losses, too.) Generally, capital gains are realized when a security or other asset is sold or redeemed, but this is not always the case. (Mutual funds in particular have special rules that will be discussed later.) Furthermore, capital gains that are the result of an investment that was held for 12 months or more are considered long-term capital gains, and are taxed at a more favorable rate than short-term capital gains, which are taxed as ordinary income. (Again, mutual funds have some exceptions.) Net capital gain (or loss) calculations are also dependent on the type of investment when figuring the cost basis. These special rules will be explained as we discuss the various investments later in this chapter and in subsequent chapters.

PASSIVE. Passive income is derived from any business activity in which the person is not an active participant. This would include income or losses from limited partnerships or real estate. The important thing to know is that because of tax law changes in 1986, passive losses are deductible only against passive income.

3.2.2

Tax Treatment of Foreign Securities

When foreign securities are purchased by U.S. citizens, they must still pay taxes in the United States for interest from bonds, dividends from stocks, or capital gains from the sale of securities. Generally, though, the U.S. citizen is not liable for payment of taxes in the foreign country. If the foreign taxes are withheld, then the investor is entitled to a **tax credit.** A **tax credit** is an actual dollar for dollar reduction in the amount of taxes owed. (This is better than a **deduction,** which is a reduction in the amount of income that taxes are figured on.) An investor in this situation should consult with a tax advisor to obtain the latest rules in this area because the tax credit is usually only a percentage of the amount withheld in the foreign country.

3.2.3

Tax Treatment of Wash Sales

Another area where special tax rules apply has to do with wash sales. **Wash sales** are when the same securities (or substantially similar securities) are bought and sold simultaneously or within a short period of time. The Internal Revenue Service has established that wash sales which occur within 30 days before or 30 days after a transaction are not eligible for use as a capital loss. Effectively, this creates a 61 day window within which substantially similar activity may not occur, or any resulting losses are not deductible by the investor. This is to avoid the situation where an investor attempts to create a loss when a stock is down by selling it, realizing the loss, and then buying back the same security so that the investor's position did not change (i.e., the investor owns the same number of shares as before, but now also has a capital loss to claim on his or her taxes).

IRS rules also state that the investor cannot buy calls, puts, preferred stock, options, or any other security or derivative security from the same company during the 30-day window before or after the date of the trade that established the loss. The only "exception" to this is that investors may do **bond swaps.** In essence, the investor is selling a bond to create a capital loss, while buying back other bonds to replace the ones sold. To get around the wash sale rules, the investor will buy bonds from a different issuer, or buy bonds from the same issuer with two or more different characteristics (e.g., different interest rate and maturity date). We will mention the wash sale rules again when discussing the securities later on.

3.3 Equity Securities

When we discussed assets in Chapter 2, we defined *equity* as the difference between what has been paid on an obligation and the value of the asset. In other words, "equity" is that part of an asset (in that example, a home) which is actually owned by the investor. Here, **equity** is an ownership interest in a company. **Securities** are any investment relationship with a company, and the instruments that represent that investment. Thus, **equity securities** are the instruments that signify an ownership interest in a company. That was really a long-winded way to say that an equity security is **stock.**

There are actually many kinds of stock, and other instruments that represent rights to buy stock which are also referred to as equity securities. Let's run through some of these definitions, explain how they work, and show how they are related to the value of the underlying shares in the company.

3.3.1

Terms, Agents and Procedures Associated with Equity Securities

There are four broad classifications of stock: authorized, issued, outstanding, and treasury. Some are negotiable, some are not. Some can be bought and sold, some cannot. And sometimes, stock starts in one classification and moves to another.

AUTHORIZED. Authorized stock is the stock originally approved by a corporation in its Articles of Incorporation. This is the maximum number of shares that the company may create, but the company does not have to issue or sell all of the shares at once. In fact, a company will usually only sell enough shares to raise the money it needs in its initial stages, and will save shares to sell later as more expenses arise. The decision to sell shares up to the maximum number of authorized stock is made by the board of directors, but if the company wants to sell more stock than the original number of authorized shares, it must put the matter to a vote of current shareholders.

ISSUED. Issued stock is stock that has been distributed by the corporation. This can be the result of stock sold to investors, stock distributed to the founders of the company, or stock given to employees as incentives, bonuses, or for retirement plans. Stock that has been authorized, but not yet issued, is referred to as **unissued stock.** This is stock held back for future needs, and does not have voting privileges nor count when doing calculations for capitalization, earnings per share, or dividends.

OUTSTANDING. Outstanding stock is stock presently held by shareholders. Again, this could be investors, founders, or employees. The difference, though, between *issued* and *outstanding,* is that shares may have been issued but subsequently reacquired by the corporation and thus are no longer outstanding.

TREASURY. Treasury stock is stock reacquired by the corporation. It is issued, but not outstanding. Treasury stock may be held to resell at a future date, or reissued for incentives, bonuses, or retirement plans. The company can also retire the shares. Like unissued stock, treasury stock does not have voting privileges nor count when doing calculations for capitalization, earnings per share, or dividends.

There will likely be a Series 7 Exam question asking you how much stock a company has outstanding. You will likely be given several figures (perhaps even some extraneous ones) and you will need to know this formula.

Exam Topic Alert

Since a company's earnings and capitalization figures are based only on the number of outstanding shares, an important formula to remember is:

Issued Stock – Treasury Stock = Outstanding Stock

How Stock Classifications Change. It is easy to understand why companies authorize shares—they want to distribute ownership shares to founders and they want to raise money. Some of the other mechanics may be a little less clear. Once stock has been authorized in the original Articles of Incorporation or charter of the company, it is available to the company for any purpose the board of directors sees fit. It can be sold to raise money, it can be given to employees as incentives, it can be kept by the company for future use. But once stock is authorized, the stock does not become unauthorized. Instead, authorized stock either is used—and thus becomes issued stock—or it remains unused—and thus it remains unissued stock.

Issued stock is outstanding stock unless and until it is reacquired by the company. Once it has been reacquired by the company, it is treasury stock until it is retired or reissued. Treasury stock does not have voting rights and is not eligible to receive a share of any dividends declared by the company. You may wonder why the company would be interested in buying back its own stock. Here are five reasons:

1. **To increase earnings per share.** Later we'll learn about earnings per share calculations, but for now just know that this is one measure of a company's performance. Having fewer shares outstanding improves this number (since treasury stock doesn't count in the equation), so buying back shares is a plus.
2. **To use for employee benefit programs.** Companies may offer stock options as incentives or put stock in retirement plans for employees. As this is done, the stock must come from somewhere—and treasury stock is one place where the company can get it. (Note that once stock is given to employees as bonuses or "deposited" into retirement accounts, the shares are considered issued again so the stock accrues dividends and figures into earnings calculations.)
3. **To boost share price.** If a company thinks that its shares are undervalued, it may choose to repurchase some of its stock. Since stock prices are based on supply and demand, having less supply available in the market (because the company took some out of circulation) can cause the stock price to increase. Having higher earnings per share can also boost stock price.
4. **To support merger and acquisition activity.** One other use for company stock is to merge with or buy other companies. This can be done with cash, but is also commonly done with stock. In a good merger, both companies benefit because the company buying or acquiring does not have to use up cash reserve and the company being bought or acquired gets to share in the appreciation of the stock of the newly combined company. If investors like the merger, the market will react favorably and drive the stock price up.
5. **To increase management control over the company.** Since shareholders of outstanding stock have the right to vote on the board of directors and other important company matters, the management of the company may want to buy back more of its shares so that the stock owned by management represents a larger percentage of the outstanding shares. Remember, treasury stock does not have voting rights. By decreasing the number of outstanding shares, the management of the company can feel more secure that they won't be outvoted when company matters are voted upon. Buybacks may also occur to get rid of problem shareholders, or to make the public company into a private one again.

How Stock Value is Determined. There are actually three different stock values that can be talked about: **par value, book value** and **market value.** All three values are usually *very* different. It is important to note that when stock starts out as authorized but unissued it has no market value. The company may assign an arbitrary value to the stock (called **par value**), it may assign no par value to the stock, or it may give the stock a stated value. This value may or may not appear on the stock certificates, but is largely irrelevant (except with preferred stock, as we shall see). The difference between the initial par value and the actual money the corporation receives for selling the stock is referred to as paid-in capital. **Paid-in capital** is money received from investors, as opposed to money actually earned by the company. Paid-in capital is an asset to the company.

A company that is a going concern regularly acquires assets and incurs liabilities. Remember our important formula: Assets – Liabilities = Net Worth? Although it is a simplified version, if we take the net worth figure for a company, and divide it by the number of shares outstanding we would get the **book value** of the company. This value represents an estimate of what the company would be worth in a liquidation sale. It is useful to analyze the company and make comparisons with other companies in its sector, but not for much else.

Stock acquires a true value only when it has been issued. At that point, *the stock price is driven by supply and demand,* based on what investors will pay for it in the marketplace. This is referred to as **market value.** This is the price (minus commissions, etc.) at which an investor could expect to buy or sell the stock. For most purposes, this is the most relevant value.

How Stock is Transferred. Stock certificates are instruments that represent equity ownership in the company. The actual certificates are used to transfer ownership of the securities when they are bought and sold. Stock certificates are what makes the asset easily transferable, since the stock certificate is a negotiable instrument once it has been properly endorsed. The endorsements must be signed exactly as they appear on the face of the certificate, with two exceptions. The word "and" may be signed as an ampersand (&), and "company" may be abbreviated "co." Anything else (e.g., middle initial appears on the face, but not in the signature) and it is not valid. Proper endorsement begins the stock transfer procedure.

Proper endorsement entails not only that the stock certificate or a valid stock power is signed by the stock owner, but also that the signature is guaranteed by a bank or a registered broker-dealer. A **stock power** is a document, separate from the stock certificate, granting another party power of attorney to transfer the stock. This type of document is often given to a broker-dealer when the securities are held in the firm's account for the owner. The broker-dealer needs the sale order and the stock power so that the transfer agent will acknowledge that the transfer is legitimate and the broker-dealer has authority to sell the stock when the owner orders it sold.

The **transfer agent** is appointed by the corporation to maintain ownership records, to issue and cancel certificates, and to resolve problems of lost, stolen, or destroyed stock certificates. The transfer agent is the final arbiter in disputes of stock certificate authenticity. The transfer agent may be a separate entity, such as a bank or trust company, or a corporation may serve as its own transfer agent. Watching over this function is the **registrar.**

The **registrar** is appointed by the corporation to oversee the issuance of stock certificates, to make sure that no more than the total number of authorized shares of stock are in circulation, and to certify the authenticity of corporate bonds. The registrar is concerned with the "big picture" and keeps an eye on the entire system of stocks and bonds for the corporation. By law, the registrar must be an entity separate from the company, and the same entity cannot act as both registrar and transfer agent for the same corporation.

Other Important Points about Stock. Remember, only stock that is issued *and* outstanding can convey rights to the shareholder. These include the right to vote for the board of directors and to vote on other issues of major importance, and the right to receive a proportionate share of any declared dividends.

Note that *shareholders do not vote on dividends, nor do they vote on whether or not to buy back stock.* Both of these are decisions made by the company's board of directors.

Also, we said that issued and outstanding shares of stock *can* convey rights, but this is not always the case. It depends on what type of stock is held, and even within these types there can be different subclasses of stock (e.g., Class A, Class B) that convey different stockholder rights.

For the Series 7 exam, you should know that *the two primary types of equity securities are **common stock** and **preferred stock**.* In the next few sections we will examine each of these more closely.

3.3.2

Common Stock

Common stock is an ownership interest in a corporation that conveys to the holder certain rights, including the right to vote for the board of directors and certain other issues, and the right to receive a proportionate share of any declared dividend. Common stockholders enjoy the benefits of company ownership, without the potential liability that could befall owners of a business that was not incorporated. This limited liability is a big advantage. The investor is insulated from being responsible for the company's debts or other obligations (although there are some exceptions for closely held corporations). The most that a typical common stockholder can lose is the amount he or she invested to buy the stock. The other two main advantages to common stock ownership are the potential for unlimited capital appreciation and the possibility of income from dividends.

RIGHTS OF COMMON STOCKHOLDERS. In addition to the benefits of limited liability and unlimited potential appreciation, the investor who holds common stock enjoys other rights and privileges that come with ownership. These include

1. **Preemptive Rights. Preemptive rights** are the right of existing stockholders to buy, in proportion to their current holdings, additional shares of a new issue by the company before the stock is offered to the public. This is often referred to as an **antidilution provision** because it allows current shareholders the right to maintain their present proportionate control over the company in voting matters, and their present share of declared dividends.

   Remember that this is a right, not a requirement. The current stock holders get a first right of refusal to buy new shares up to their present proportion, but they may choose not to do so. Also note that these rights vary based on state law or corporate charter provisions, and either of these may also permit the corporation to pay existing shareholders in lieu of offering them stock from the new issue.

2. ***Pro Rata* Share of Dividends.** *Pro rata* is a method of proportionate allocation, meaning that each gets a percentage share based on the percentage of stock owned. **Dividends** are a distribution of company earnings to stockholders as voted on by the board of directors. We will discuss these in more depth shortly, but for now note one important thing: the shareholder does not have the right to receive a dividend unless it is declared by the board of directors. In fact, there are companies (particularly high growth companies) which choose not to declare a dividend, and instead invest the money in research and development.

3. **Access to Corporate Books.** All stockholders have the right to inspect the books of the corporation in which they hold stock. This is usually interpreted to mean that stockholders have the right to receive all financial statements of the company, annual statements, list of stockholders, and other corporate communications. This is not meant to include detailed financial records, internal memos or other confidential documents. Notes and minutes from the board of directors meetings are also off-limits. Of course, shareholders who own a substantial position in the company's stock may be afforded more access. Requests for information must be made during normal business hours.

4. **Voting Power.** Voting is one of the most important rights that a common stockholder has, because it is one of the few ways that the investor can exert some measure of control over what happens at the corporation. There are four main areas where the common stockholder is permitted to vote:

   ▷ election of the board of directors

   ▷ dilution issues (e.g., authorizing stock, issuing convertible bonds)

   ▷ changes in business direction of the company (e.g., mergers, buyouts)

   ▷ stock splits

   Note that stockholders do *not* vote on dividends, pay increases, new product introductions, or other day-to-day management items. Here are some other important key terms and points you need to know about voting:

   a. **statutory:** This is a type of voting that follows the one share, one vote rule, whereby stockholders get a single vote on each issue or each board member.

   b. **cumulative:** This is a type of voting whereby a stockholder receives a total number of votes equal to her total number of shares of stock, then may place all of those votes for a single board member, or divide the vote any way she wants. (This gives minority shareholders more influence when voting.)

c. **proxy:** This is a kind of absentee ballot, whereby the stockholder can vote on matters without having to attend the annual stockholder's meeting. Proxy solicitations must be sent to the SEC for approval before the company can send them to stockholders. Proxy fights, which attempt to alter control of a company, must have all parties register with the SEC or risk criminal penalties.

d. **nonvoting:** Corporations may decide to issue subclasses of common stock (e.g., Class A, Class B) that do not carry voting rights. Although unusual, this can be done to raise capital without fear of losing management control.

5. **Residual Claim on Corporate Assets.** In a bankruptcy, the common stockholders are the last in line to recoup any money. After all creditors and lien holders have been satisfied, though, the common stockholders do have a claim on whatever assets, if any, are left.

chart 3.3.2

ORDER OF PAYOUT IF A COMPANY LIQUIDATES

(This may be on Series 7 exam.)

Highest Claim, Paid First- - - -	1. wages
	2. taxes
	3. secured debt (bonds)
(Remember: **WTSeGSuPC**)	4. general creditors (includes debenture holders)
1 2 3 4 5 6 7	5. subordinated debt (junior debentures)
	6. preferred stockholders
Lowest Claim, Paid Last- - - -	7. common stockholders

TERMS ASSOCIATED WITH TYPES OF STOCK. There are several terms that you will often hear associated with common stocks. These refer to the different features or characteristics of the companies those stocks represent. These are all still common stocks that we are talking about. But as we go through these terms you will see that it is the profiles of the companies or the industries that cause these stocks to be categorized a certain way.

Blue Chip. These are common stocks from well-known companies who have a long history of growth and a reputation for good management. Dividends are also paid out on a fairly consistent basis. They are usually nationally known corporations, and their products or services are familiar to many people. The common stock of these companies is considered relatively safe and stable, and thus it commands a higher price in the marketplace even with low yields.

Growth. These are common stocks from companies that have shown faster-than-average increases in earnings over the past several years, even though they are likely not paying dividends. Some may be familiar names, others may be up-and-coming companies. Their growth, though, is expected to continue for years to come, so the common stock is priced with a higher price-earnings ratio, making it a more risky investment that other average priced stocks or blue chip stocks.

Emerging Growth. These are common stocks from companies that have very little history of growth, but are expected to become growth stocks either because of their brief history, because of the industry they are in, or because of their management team. These are likely not familiar names yet, except to those who follow the industry. As such, their stock price may be a little better than other growth companies, but the stock is riskier. The potential for increased earnings is there, but with no history to go on the stock is more of a gamble.

Income. These are common stocks that regularly pay good dividends to stockholders, and are in industries where companies are expected to continue doing so. These may or may not be regional companies. Utilities, banks, and insurance company stocks are good examples of income stocks.

Cyclical/Counter Cyclical. Cyclical stocks are common stocks that generally rise and fall quickly in response to economic conditions. Some examples of cyclical stocks are automobile stocks and housing-related stocks. Counter cyclical stocks are common stocks that generally rise when economic conditions worsen. The best example of a counter cyclical stock is the food sector (because demand is constant regardless of economic conditions).

Defensive. These are common stocks with prices that are more stable over time than the broad market. Some examples of defensive stocks would be utility stocks, counter cyclical stocks, and certain blue chip stocks. These stocks are more conservative than average, and thus may experience slower growth during economic expansions, but should fare better during recessions because the underlying products are necessities of everyday life. (A defensive portfolio would also hold preferred stock and debt securities as a larger portion of the overall portfolio.)

Speculative. These are common stocks of rapidly growing companies that have prospects for above-average growth, but with prices that are highly volatile. Some examples of speculative stocks would be high-tech companies and other start-ups. These stocks are more aggressive, and are generally relied upon solely for capital appreciation since they usually offer no dividends. (An aggressive portfolio, with an emphasis on speculative stocks, may also buy on margin to gain maximum leverage.)

Special Situation. These are common stocks that are undervalued for a short period of time, but are about to rise significantly because of an upcoming event. This could be a pending merger or acquisition, a new management team or new product introduction. Usually these special situations are short-lived since it is difficult to get in early, and many investors reacting to the news drive the stock price up in the marketplace. Special situation stocks can also be risky as the news could drive the stock price down if it is received unfavorably by investors or the event doesn't occur.

DIVIDENDS. **Dividends** are a distribution of company earnings to stockholders as voted on by the board of directors. Dividends are paid out to shareholders on a *pro rata* basis, based on the percentage of stock ownership in the company. The dividends are usually paid in cash, but they can also be paid out in stock or even sometimes with company products (this is rare, but actually anything of value can be distributed as a dividend). Each stockholder of record as of a certain date (more on this in a future chapter) is sent a check, or the check is sent to the brokerage house for deposit into the brokerage account if stocks are held in the firm's name. Dividend payments are made quarterly, and create a taxable event that must be declared as ordinary income in the year they are received (even if the money is reinvested).

STOCK SPLITS. A **stock split** is an attempt to adjust the price of a stock downward by increasing the number of outstanding shares without changing the percentage of company ownership held by each stockholder, and without changing the total market value of all outstanding shares. In other words, as of the date of the stock split the stockholders all own the same proportionate share of the company as they did before, and the total value of their stock holdings is also the same. Let's look at an example.

Example 1

Pat owns 1,000 shares of ABC, value is $100 each before the split. Pat's total stock value is 1,000 × $100 = $100,000. ABC Corp. announces a 2 for 1 stock split, so every one share of stock Pat owns is now split into two shares. Pat owns 2,000 shares of ABC, value is $50 each after the split. Pat's total stock value is 2,000 × $50 = $100,000

A company usually does this when it feels that its share price is too high. Investors like to see high prices, but that can also keep the stock out of the hands of smaller investors and result in less trading activity. If the company worries that its stock price is too low, it may do a **reverse split.**

A **reverse split** is an attempt to adjust the price of a stock upward by decreasing the number of outstanding shares without changing the percentage of company ownership held by each stockholder, and without changing the total market value of all outstanding shares. Companies worry that low share prices will not attract institutional investors or "sophisticated" investors because the stock price makes the company look like a "penny stock." Furthermore, if the share price drops too low for an extended period of time some exchanges will de-list the stock. Let's take a look:

Example 2

Pat owns 1,000 shares of ABC, value is $1 each before the split. Pat's total stock value is 1,000 × $1 = $1,000. ABC Corp. announces a 1 for 4 stock split, so every four shares of stock Pat owns now becomes only one share. Pat owns 250 shares of ABC, value is $4 each after the split. Pat's total stock value is 250 × $4 = $1,000

Just remember that share price and number of shares move in opposite directions for either split, and that total ownership *percentage* and total stock *value* don't change. Also, if a split would increase the authorized shares, the shareholders must vote.

3.3.3

Preferred Stock

Preferred stock is an ownership interest in a corporation that pays a specified dividend rate. Like common stock, owners of preferred stock have limited liability when it comes to corporate obligations—the most the preferred stockholder can lose is his or her original investment. Preferred stock has two advantages over common stock: preferred stockholders get paid dividends before common stockholders, and preferred stockholders can recoup assets in a liquidation, after all creditors and lien holders have been satisfied, but before the common stockholders. Because of this, common stock is a *junior security* vis-à-vis preferred stock, which here is a *senior security*. But preferred stock is a junior security vis-à-vis lienholders—it's all relative.

Preferred stock, though, has some disadvantages when compared with common stock. One disadvantage is that preferred stockholders usually do not receive the voting rights that common stockholders have. Preferred stock usually does not have preemptive rights either. Another important disadvantage is that preferred stockholders do not get to share in the capital appreciation of the company like common stockholders do. This is because preferred stockholders are guaranteed a certain rate of return on their investment. Since they have less risk, they get less reward.

PRINCIPAL KINDS OF PREFERRED STOCK. To add some incentive and make preferred stock more attractive to investors, companies have created a number of different preferred stock variations. These include

1. **Cumulative. Cumulative preferred stock** allows dividends to accrue so that in the event that dividends cannot be paid, the unpaid dividends become a liability that must be paid in full before any regular dividends can be paid to common stockholders. This is a typical feature of preferred stock today.
2. **Noncumulative. Noncumulative preferred stock** does not have dividends which accrue, so any unpaid dividends will likely never be paid. This type of straight preferred stock is rather unusual today, since most issue cumulative.
3. **Participating. Participating preferred stock** pays its stated dividends and allows preferred stockholders the chance to receive certain extra bonus payments which may be made to all common *and* preferred shareholders after regular dividends are paid. It's rare for preferred stock to have this provision.
4. **Nonparticipating. Nonparticipating preferred stock** pays only its stated dividends and does not have any provisions for extra payments. It is typical for preferred stock issued today to be nonparticipating.
5. **Convertible. Convertible preferred stock** has the added feature that the stockholders can trade in the convertible preferred stock for common stock in the company at a preset price. This allows preferred stockholders to have a chance to share in the capital appreciation of the underlying company's stock. Because of this feature, the price of convertible preferred stock may fluctuate in line with the common stock. The dividend paid on convertible preferred stock is usually *lower* since investors will accept this in exchange for a chance to convert to common stock and enjoy capital appreciation at a future date.
6. **Callable. Callable preferred stock** is redeemable by a company at a preset price. Usually there is an initial period during which the company cannot exercise this right, but after that date it can be done at any time the company feels it is advantageous to do so. This may be because interest rates have fallen and so the preferred stock can be replaced with cheaper debt, or the company wants to change its debt to equity ratio. The dividend paid out on callable preferred stock is usually *higher* since investors expect to be compensated for the added risk that their source of income could be terminated at any time.
7. **Sinking Fund. Sinking fund preferred stock** is preferred stock with a special provision stating that the issuer will regularly pay money into a separate account, thus giving investors some assurance that dividends will be paid in a timely fashion.

that dividend payments are more secure. The dividend paid on sinking fund preferred stock is usually *lower* since investors feel

8. **Adjustable-rate. Adjustable-rate preferred stock** has the dividend rate adjusted to mirror market conditions based on some index. The adjustments usually occur quarterly, and the rate is pegged to a widely-used index, such as the Treasury Bill rate. The price for this type of preferred stock is less volatile than it would otherwise be, because having the rate adjust to match market conditions has a stabilizing effect.

Exam Topic Alert

For the Series 7 exam, it is important to remember the differences between common stock and preferred stock. Like common stock, preferred stock represents ownership in the company and affords the investor the protection of limited liability. Unlike common stock, preferred stock usually does *not* confer voting rights or preemptive rights on the stockholder. Also, with preferred stock, the investor does not have the opportunity to share in capital appreciation of the company (unless the preferred stock is convertible).

The two main advantages preferred stock has over common stock are that preferred stockholders are paid dividends before common stockholders, and preferred stockholders get preference over common stockholders upon corporate dissolution.

3.3.4

Other Types of Equity Securities

Although common and preferred are the two main types of stock, there are other securities that can be bought and sold. Some of these other securities are referred to as derivative securities. A **derivative security** is an instrument whose value is dependent on the value of another underlying security. By itself, the derivative security is worthless; but it derives its value from the fact that it gives the holder the right to buy (or sell) another security or investment. Since they are a security, derivative securities may be traded in the secondary market (although their value is largely determined by the value of the underlying security on which they are based).

Let's use options as an example. Suppose you own an option contract giving you the right to buy IBM stock for $100 per share. The value of the option is derived from the underlying security—IBM stock in this example. When IBM stock is selling for under $100, your option has little value. But if IBM stock rises above $100, your option to buy IBM stock for "only" $100 has value. Thus, the value of your option depends on the value of the underlying security, but by itself has little or no value.

3.3.4.1 Rights Offering

A rights offering is an offer to existing common stockholders that allows them to buy additional shares of newly issued stock before it is offered for sale to the general public. This is done to honor the preemptive rights that the existing common stockholders have. Current shareholders get one right for each share of stock owned, as do new investors who quickly buy stock "cum" rights (with the rights still attached—because after the ex-date, no rights transfer with the stock). This gives stockholders the opportunity to buy enough shares to maintain their present proportionate ownership in the company.

When current stockholders are given notice of a rights offering, they have three choices. They can either exercise their rights offering and opt to buy more stock, they can sell their rights offering to other interested parties since it is a derivative security, or they can do nothing and allow the rights offering option to expire. Typically, rights offerings have a very short window—usually 30–45 days. Within that time frame, the current stockholder must choose one of the three courses of action we just described. Usually the price at which the rights holder can buy the new issue is less than the current market price of the stock. The price for the rights offering is referred to as the **subscription price,** and must be lower than the market price to absorb the new shares into the marketplace. If the price was the same as the current market price, there would be no incentive for investors to buy the new shares. Furthermore, the price that is offered to existing stockholders in the rights offering is even lower than the anticipated offering price of the new issue.

A more favorable price is offered to existing shareholders as an incentive to get them to make a quick buying decision. The investment banking firm that is selling the new issue for the company wants to ensure that as much of the new issue as possible is sold (or pre-sold) because typically the investment banking firm does the new issue as a standby underwriting. A **standby underwriting** means that the investment banking firm guarantees the issuing company that the firm will buy all shares that are not bought as part of the rights offering.

This definition will likely appear somewhere on the Series 7 exam. Remember, *when you see "rights offering" in a question, look for "standby underwriting" in the answer (and vice versa).*

3.3.4.2 Warrants

Warrants are an additional security offered along with the sale of another security. Warrants usually allow the warrant holder to buy shares of common stock at some point in the future at a predetermined price. Warrants are typically offered with bonds and preferred stock as an incentive, or sweetener. A warrant can entice investors to buy the underlying bond or stock when it is less attractive for some reason, or adding a warrant as a sweetener may allow a company to offer a lower interest rate for the bond or preferred stock, or a warrant may be offered to an investment banking firm if it agrees to do an offering for the company.

Like rights offerings, warrants are a derivative security. But warrants may or may not be sold separately. If the warrants are **detachable,** then the investor may sell them separately to anyone. If the warrants are **nondetachable,** then they can be transferred only with the bond, preferred stock, or security they were sold with.

When investors are given a warrant, they have two or three choices. They can exercise their warrant and buy the stock at the predetermined price, if the warrants are detachable they can sell their warrants to other interested parties since it is a derivative security, or they can do nothing and allow the warrants to expire. Typically, warrants have a very long window—usually at least five years, and sometimes they do not expire. Within that time frame, the warrant holder must choose one of the courses of action we just described.

Unlike rights offerings, the price at which the warrant holder can buy stock in the future is usually much higher than the current market price of the stock. This is because the company does not want the warrants exercised right away. In fact, if the market value of the stock does not get above the price in the warrant, the warrant will likely never be exercised. Given that fact, you can see that the warrant becomes more valuable as the market value of the stock gets closer to the price in the warrant, and becomes more and more valuable as the stock price continues to rise beyond the that price offered by the warrant.

One consideration, though, that the company must take into account is the dilutive effect that the exercise of the warrants may have on the company and the other shareholders. The company will likely "pay" for the exercised warrants with treasury stock or authorized but unissued company stock. If additional shares must be authorized, it may require the vote of current shareholders. And if the company has any kind of antidilution agreements in place, these must be considered as well.

A question about warrants will likely appear somewhere on the Series 7 exam. Remember, *when you see "warrants" in a question, look for "sweetener" in the answer (and vice versa).*

3.3.4.3 ADRs

American Depository Receipts (ADRs) are a United States substitute for foreign common stock. Investors can hold ADRs rather than having to deal with trying to obtain stock in a foreign country. And with ADRs, foreign companies can sell shares to U.S. investors without having to go through the lengthy and expensive SEC registration process. ADRs allow investors in the United States to collect dividends and enjoy the capital gains of the foreign stock, but do not usually come with voting rights or preemptive rights.

Although ADRs trade in the secondary market, they are not money market instruments because they are not liquid enough. Furthermore, ADRs may be less liquid than the underlying foreign stock because the ADRs have less trading volume than the underlying stock in the foreign country. At any time, the investor can demand actual delivery of the foreign stock, which is typically held in the vault of a commercial bank. There is an advantage to the bank holding the foreign stock, though, because the bank will take care of collecting dividend payments in the foreign currency and converting them into U.S. dollars. In either case, whether the investor owns ADRs or the actual foreign stock, there must also be consideration for the risk of fluctuations in the value of the foreign currency from the company's home country. It is in that currency that dividends will be calculated, as will earnings, stock price, capital appreciation, etc.

3.3.5

Tax Treatment of Equity Securities Transactions

Equity securities transactions are subject to a number of different rules and regulations for tax purposes. For example, capital gains from increases in the value of securities are taxed at different rates, depending on how long the investment is held before it is sold. Dividends are taxed in the year that they are received and treated as ordinary income (except for some IRA contributions). And corporations in the United States are permitted a **dividend exclusion,** whereby they do not have to pay corporate income tax on 70 percent of the dividend income they receive from other U.S. corporations. Let's look at some of these securities tax rules in more detail.

3.3.5.1 Capital Gains and Losses

Normally, you would think that a gain or loss would be calculated by comparing the prices at which you bought something and then sold it. Technically, though, the original purchase price does not form the basis for determining whether an investor gained or lost money. Instead, IRS rules use an adjusted cost basis. For stocks, the adjusted cost basis is the original price, plus any commissions or allowable expenses, with a further adjustment made if the stock has split since the original purchase. Thus, a capital gain is the increase in value above the adjusted cost basis that is realized by an investor when an asset is sold. A capital loss is the decrease in value below the adjusted cost basis that is realized by an investor when an asset is sold.

Tax treatment of capital gains and losses varies depending on how long the asset was held before it was sold. If the asset was held for less than 12 months, then any gain is treated as ordinary income and taxed at the investor's marginal tax rate. If the asset was held for at least 12 months, the gain is treated as a long-term capital gain and taxed at a lower rate. Capital losses are a bit more complicated, and will be discussed in the next section. Also note that buying puts (which give you the right to sell the stock at a predetermined price) can restart the 12-month holding period for determining whether an asset sold is a long-term or short-term gain (if the 12 months had not already elapsed before the put was purchased).

In general, cash dividend distributions are taxed in the year that they are received and treated as ordinary income. This is true even if the investor reinvests the dividends by buying more stock in the company. There are two exceptions that may come up on the Series 7 exam, so read the questions closely. First, if the stocks are in an individual retirement account (IRA), depending on the type of IRA, the tax consequences of the dividend distribution may be deferred. These will be dealt with in greater detail at the end of this chapter when we discuss IRAs and retirement plans. Second, remember that U.S. corporations are permitted a **dividend exclusion,** whereby they do not have to pay corporate income tax on 70 percent of the dividend income they receive from other U.S. corporations. Individual investors are not permitted any such exclusion. Also note that stock dividend distributions by a company are not an immediate taxable event, but rather incur tax consequences when the stock is actually sold.

3.3.5.2 Determination of Net Gains and Losses

To determine net capital gains and losses, the investor must first separate out all taxable events as being a short-term gain or long-term gain, short-term loss or long-term loss. As stated above, if the asset was held for less than 12 months, any resulting gain or loss is considered short term; if the asset was held for at least 12 months, any resulting gain or loss is considered long term. (There are exceptions that will be discussed as we encounter them.)

Short-term gains are taxed as ordinary income at the investor's marginal tax rate; long-term gain are taxed at the lower capital gains rate. Capital losses are deducted first against capital gains, and if there is any additional loss, then up to $3,000 of the capital loss may be deducted against ordinary income. Capital losses over the $3,000 limit may be carried forward indefinitely to subsequent years, but the maximum capital loss that may be claimed is still $3,000 per year. Also note that short-term losses are offset against short-term gains; long-term losses are offset against long-term gains.

Holding Periods. In addition to the standard rules noted above for determining whether securities qualify for long-term or short-term capital gains treatment, there are three more special situations that may appear on the Series 7 exam. First, there is the case of "when issued" securities. **"When issued"** is a security that has been authorized, but not officially issued yet. As such, the official settlement date may not yet be known (NASD's Uniform Practices Committee decides the final settlement date). Still, though, the shares are tradeable.

For tax purposes, the holding period begins at the trade date (when you authorize the trade), not the settlement date (when you pay for the trade).

Second, we need to look at securities acquired through conversion. For tax purposes, securities acquired through conversion are treated much the same as were stock dividends. If the current security was held as a capital asset, the holding period for the new stock received from the preferred stock conversion or the stock dividend will include the holding period of the shareholder's original position. So, if the investor has already held the preferred stock for six months, then upon conversion the common stock received needs to be held only for an additional six months to be given favorable tax treatment as a long term capital gain. If the investor acquired the original securities at various times, those various times also apply to the newly received shares. Finally, like stock dividends, the conversion from preferred stock to common stock is not a taxable event, so all tax consequences occur when it is sold.

Third, there are securities received as a gift or inheritance. If the securities are received as a gift, the start of the holding period depends on the intent of the giver. If the person giving the securities is donating them in exchange for a tax write-off (as when securities are given to charity), the holding period starts on the day after the gift was given. If, on the other hand, the person is giving the securities as a personal gift and not seeking a tax deduction, the holding period is considered to have started on the same day the donor's holding period started. For inherited securities, any future gain or loss is treated as a long-term capital gain—regardless of how long the recipient actually owns the asset. Holding periods don't come into effect, since all inheritances are treated as if the one year period has already elapsed.

Cost Basis. Questions regarding determination of the cost basis for securities are also likely to appear on the Series 7 exam. For purchases, we have already discussed that the cost basis is the purchase price, plus commissions and other allowable expenses. For exchanges involving conversions for common shares, the cost basis of the stock received is generally the same as the basis of the old securities that were originally purchased. IRS rules do not view the conversion as a taxable event, but the investor's cost basis must be adjusted by any gain realized from the exchange, and for the value of any money or other property received.

For stock dividends, stock rights and stock splits, the total cost basis that the investor has remains the same, but that amount is now divided by the new number of shares. In effect, this reduces the cost basis of each share so the investor will incur a greater tax liability when any of the shares are finally sold. Furthermore, the cost basis of the old shares must be allocated to the old and new shares in proportion to the fair market value of each on the date of the distribution of the new shares of stock. Usually, the company will report these percentages to the shareholders. The result of applying these percentages to the shares of stock gives the investor the new cost basis per share of stock. If the old shares were purchased in separate lots for differing amounts of money, the adjusted basis of the old stock must be allocated between the old and new stock on a lot by lot basis.

Finally, if stocks are received as an inheritance, the cost basis is stepped up to the fair market value (FMV) of the securities on the date the deceased passed away. On the other hand, if the securities are passed on during the person's lifetime they are considered a gift and different rules apply. The gift recipient's cost basis for tax purposes will be determined according to the following rules:

If the FMV of the stock is *less* than the donor's basis at the time of the gift:
Your cost basis for gain is the same as the donor's adjusted basis.
Your cost basis for loss is the FMV at the time of the gift.

If the FMV of the stock is *more* than the donor's basis at the time of the gift:
Your cost basis is the same as the donor's adjusted basis.

Also, if the donor was required to pay gift tax, the recipient's cost basis is increased by the amount of gift tax paid that is attributable to that gift of securities.

chart 3.3.5.2

COST BASIS

Security Transaction	Cost Basis
Purchase	purchase price + commissions + expenses
Conversion	same as original security
Stock Dividend, Rights Split	same as original but divided by new # of shares
Inheritance	stepped up to Fair Market Value on date of death
Gift	if FMV < donor's basis, gain is same as donor
	if FMV < donor's basis, loss is FMV at gift time
	if FMV > donor's basis, gain/loss is donor's basis

Selling Part of a Position. If an investor does not sell all of his or her shares in a particular stock, then there may need to be some analysis to determine which shares to sell first to minimize tax consequences. Of course, if the investor bought all of the shares at the same time, for the same price, and did not receive any additional shares for stock splits or any other reason, the cost basis for all shares would be the same. In reality, however, this is rarely the case. There are actually several different methods for selling part of a position and figuring the cost basis.

First in, first out (FIFO) is an accounting method whereby it is assumed that the shares of stock being sold are the earliest ones that were purchased by the investor. With the FIFO method, the investor will likely incur the greatest amount of tax liability because the earliest shares purchased are most likely to have the lowest cost basis. For this reason, if no accounting method is chosen by the investor, the IRS applies the FIFO method to all sales of stock.

Last in, first out (LIFO) is an accounting method whereby the last shares of stock purchased are the ones being sold. With the LIFO method, the investor will likely incur the least amount of tax liability because the latest shares purchased are likely close to the current market value at which they are being sold.

Identified shares is the best of both worlds for the investor. By keeping good records, the investor can keep records of what was paid for each lot of shares purchased and can thus use the most favorable cost basis for the his or her current tax situation. The investor can identify which shares are being sold when filing taxes with the IRS, and might be able to show losses when needed or take a larger tax hit in years when it would not result in being bumped into a higher marginal tax bracket.

Direct Participation Programs (DPPs)

Direct participation programs (DPPs) are a type of limited partnership investment that allows investors to receive the cash flow, capital gains, losses, and tax benefits of the underlying partnership business activity, without the liability that would be incurred with a general partnership. Limited partnerships such as these were popular in the 1970's and early 1980's because rules at that time permitted partnership losses to offset ordinary income. This changed with the Tax Reform Act of 1986, when tax law changes allowed only passive losses from such limited partnerships (where the investor was not actively involved in the business) to offset passive income. This tax change has caused DPPs and limited partnerships to lose some of their appeal for the average investor, but DPPs still offer an attractive alternative means for some investors to achieve certain investment goals.

3.3.6.1 Limited Partnership Procedures

One of the big advantages enjoyed by a limited partnership is its favorable tax treatment. A standard "C" corporation must pay taxes on its income, and then may pass on dividends to shareholders, who again pay taxes on the amount received. This double taxation is avoided in a limited partnership because all income and expenses are allowed to flow through directly to the investors. To gain this advantage, a limited partnership must be set up correctly or it will be disallowed by the IRS (and the favorable tax treatment nullified). This entails meeting certain IRS requirements, preparing and executing the appropriate documentation, and observing other rules and procedures for limited partnerships.

Requirements. In forming the limited partnership, the business must be structured and operated within parameters established by the IRS. Since the limited partnership receives much more favorable tax status, IRS rules state that the limited partnership must prove it is not a corporation which is calling itself a limited partnership in name only as a means of getting the favorable tax treatment. As proof, the IRS has created a test by identifying the six typical traits of a corporation. The limited partnership can have no more than four of these traits, or else the IRS will rule that it is really just a disguised corporation. The six traits are:

1. associates of the business
2. profit motive
3. central management structure
4. limited liability
5. continuity of existence
6. freely transferable shares

The IRS has ruled that the first two criteria are traits that all businesses must have. Limited partnerships by their very nature involve more than one person because they have a managing general partner who runs the business, and one or more limited partners who invest money. Just think partners = associates. As far as trying to make money, this is where some partnerships run into trouble. Even if they initially create losses, the limited partnership must be conducted as a real business that has a plan to try to make money. If the IRS determines that the partnership was established solely to generate losses for the investors, then the IRS can disallow the partnership, make the investors liable for back taxes, interest and penalties, and could even choose to pursue criminal charges of fraud.

Centralized management structure is a trait of most well-run businesses, so it would be hard for the limited partnership not to have this. In fact, the very structure of the limited partnership has a general partner who runs the business. Just think general partner = manager.

If a question on the Series 7 exam asks you which trait a limited partnership is most likely to have (or which one is hardest to avoid), remember the limited partnership structure and choose "centralized management."

Limited liability is also a trait that limited partnerships share with C corporations, but one which the limited partnership is unlikely to give up because it is one of the advantages an investor looks for in an investment. Here again, the limited liability means that in most cases a limited partner can lose no more than his or her original investment amount.

Thus, since the limited partnership can have no more than four of these traits of a corporation, the last two are the ones where a limited partnership is most likely to deviate. In fact, in the original partnership documents, there is often a provision that says that the partnership will cease to exist or dissolve after a certain number of years (avoiding #5). The documents also usually include a clause that limits the transferability of the partnership shares (avoiding #6).

Documents. The three documents that are necessary to form a limited partnership are the certificate of limited partnership, partnership agreement, and the subscription agreement. The **certificate of limited partnership** must include the partnership's name, address, business purpose, length of time partnership will exist, size of limited partners' investments, profit participation of limited partners, conditions for transfer of interests, and rules for continuation after the general partner passes on. This information is important because although the limited partners enjoy limited liability, the general partner has unlimited liability for all of the debts and other obligations of the limited partnership.

The certificate of limited partnership is the most important document because *the partnership does not exist until the certification is filed at the state level in the partnership's home state.*

The **partnership agreement** outlines the duties, responsibilities, and rights of the general partner and limited partners. Usually this limits the limited partners to monetary contributions only, and discourages their active participation in the day-to-day management of the partnership. It also states the operating guidelines for what the general partner can and can't do in the limited partnership. Usually this includes allowing the general partner to make binding decisions for the partnership, enter contracts on behalf of the partnership, and decide the amount of profits that will be shared with the partners, if any. It also gives the general partner final say over whether or not a particular limited partner may join the partnership.

The **subscription agreement** is the document that the general partner uses to decide whether or not a particular limited partner may join. The subscription agreement is signed by the potential investor, and includes his or her name, income, risk acknowledgment, and consent to having the general partner act on behalf of the partnership. At this point, though, the investor is still not a limited partner. In fact, this may be on the Series 7 exam. An investor is not a limited partner after signing the subscription agreement.

An investor becomes a limited partner only after the general partner signs the subscription agreement, accepting the investor into the limited partnership.

Only the general partner knows when the partnership has been sold out and can no longer accept more money or partners, and the general partner may also decide that the investor is not suitable for some reason.

Liability. Limited liability of partners is one of the advantages an investor looks for because it means that in most cases a limited partner can lose no more than his or her original investment amount. There are a few exceptions that we should point out. First, if a limited partner becomes too involved with the management of the limited partnership, it is possible that he or she could be considered a *de facto* general partner, and thus liable for the partnership's debts. Second, the limited partners may be responsible for certain recourse loans as a condition for their being admitted into the partnership. This responsibility is usually shared, based on the percentage of ownership held by the investor. Furthermore, the limited partners are responsible for nonrecourse loans in a real estate partnership. Finally, the limited partners may incur additional liability if the limited partnership engages in fraud.

Flow-Through. As long as the limited partnership is held to be valid by the IRS, certain income and expense flow-through rules apply. These allow the income to pass through directly to the investors, and avoid the double taxation of a corporation. As for expenses, most direct costs are deductions which may be taken by the limited partners. They may be deducted, though, only against income generated by the limited partnership or other passive investment income—not to offset ordinary income gains. Furthermore, different types of expenses are treated different ways. As stated, direct expenses become a direct write-off. Equipment or real estate, however, must be depreciated over its useful life, and likewise depletion allowances for using up natural resources must also be spread out and not taken immediately. Exceptions to these rules are allowed for intangible drilling costs, which may be deducted immediately with oil and gas partnerships, and expenses incurred for the rehabilitation of low-income or historic housing, which may be eligible for tax credits.

Restrictions. In order to retain the benefits of a limited partnership, there are certain restrictions on what the limited partners may do. By not adhering to these restrictions, the limited partners risk losing their liability shield and may even cause the entire limited partnership to be reevaluated by the IRS. Limited partners may not participate in day-to-day management of the partnership, nor act on behalf of the partnership, nor bind it to any contracts. They may make decisions only by voting, and even then they are limited to voting on such things as sale of the partnership, financing of partnership activities, change in partnership direction or focus, adding or changing powers of the general partner, and replacing the general partner. The limited partners may also inspect the partnership books and sue the general partner.

Dissolution. When the partnership reaches its natural end as stated in the original limited partnership certificate, or the partnership ends because of a sale or majority vote of the partners, any remaining assets are liquidated and obligations are paid in the following order: *secured creditors, unsecured creditors, limited partners, and general partners.*

A question may appear on the Series 7 exam asking the order of payout with the dissolution of a limited partnership.

Also know that when the limited partners are paid, they first receive their share of profits, then if money is left over they can lay claim to any capital that they originally invested. Likewise, after all limited partners have been paid, if there is money left over the general partners are paid first for fees, then for their share of profits, then for any capital they may have originally invested. General partners, though, typically invest very little capital (maybe 1 percent of the total). Instead, general partners rely on charging management fees for their services during the operation of the limited partnership.

3.3.6.2 Various Types of DPPs

As stated, DPPs are a type of limited partnership investment that allows investors to receive the cash flow, capital gains, losses, and tax benefits of the underlying partnership business activity, without the liability that would be incurred with a general partnership. With the various types of DPPs, however, there are different advantages, unique risks, and special tax implications that apply to each one. Any kind of project that requires funding could take advantage of the limited partnership structure, but the three types of DPPs you will encounter the most are those specializing in real estate investing, oil and gas programs, and equipment leasing. Let's look at each of these.

Real Estate. Real estate investing can take on many forms, from buying and holding raw land to rehabilitating existing buildings. Both of these extremes are somewhat risky, but they do offer other advantages. **Raw land** is purely speculative and does not offer tax advantages, but it has the potential to offer the greatest return. **Rehabbing property** is also risky because it is not always possible to tell if future resale value will be enough to cover rehab costs, plus there is the outlay for repairs while no income is coming in, but tax credits are a possibility, along with the usual deductions and depreciation allowances. Also, if the rehab project involves low-income housing there is potential for government assistance, and the risks are less than with historical buildings.

In between these two extremes are real estate partnerships that focus on existing properties or new construction. **New construction** is the more risky of the two, but nowhere near the risk that raw land is. And although like rehab properties you do not have income during the building stage, you have lots of tax write-offs from the initial planning and site expenses even before starting to build. Working with **existing properties** is the least risky of all real estate partnerships. Of course, the partnership could always get stuck with a property that needs more maintenance than expected, but in general the income and expenses are easier to project. Not only do you have the potential for immediate income, but it is easier to create a plan that would increase the value of the property through increased occupancy, enhanced rental income, or reduced expenses.

Oil and Gas. Oil and gas limited partnerships are set up to find, extract and market viable quantities of oil and natural gas. Although one partnership could pursue all of these goals, there are actually partnerships that specialize in each of these areas. **Wildcat drilling programs** try to find oil and gas by exploring in unproven areas. This type of exploratory program entails the highest risk because of the generally low success rate. When oil is found in commercial quantities, however, the rewards can be substantial. There is also the advantage of first-year tax write-offs for intangible drilling costs (IDC) and other direct expenses of exploration.

Developmental drilling programs try to extract oil and gas from fields already known to have oil and gas reserves, but by digging in new places in a field or to new depths trying to locate additional pockets of oil and gas. This type of program is less risky than wildcat drilling, but still involves considerable risk. The new wells are expensive and often do not produce enough oil or gas to recoup the investment. Still, potential rewards are substantial, and there's still the write-offs for IDCs.

Completion programs try to market more oil and gas by trying to increase the output of existing producing wells. This type of program entails the least risk because oil is already known to exist there, so the rewards are also much smaller than with wildcat drilling or developmental drilling. Still, there are risks from price fluctuations with oil, demand for natural gas, or the remaining commercial quantities of natural resources still in the ground. Income does flow readily from an existing well and there is the tax advantage of depletion deductions, however, there is no chance for IDC deductions with completion programs.

There are a few other points about oil and gas partnerships that may appear on the Series 7 exam. First, the term **sharing agreement** or **sharing arrangement** may show up. This is simply a way of describing how income and expenses are allocated in oil and gas partnerships. There are two main ways these are structured:

1. **Reversionary Work Interest:** limited partners pay all expenses and recoup their investment before the general partner receives any money.

2. **Functional Allocation:** limited partners pay most expenses, but income is shared; limited partners get IDC deductions, general partner gets depreciation deductions. (Most common sharing agreement.)

Also note that there is an important distinction between the accounting concepts of **depreciation** and **depletion** which form the basis for tax deductions from investments. **Depreciation** is amortization of a *man-made* asset so as to allocate the loss in value of the asset over its expected useful life. Examples of a depreciable asset are buildings, vehicles, and equipment. **Depletion** is amortization of a *natural* asset so as to allocate the loss in value of the asset over its expected useful life. Examples of a depletable asset are oil, minerals, and timber.

Equipment Leasing. Equipment leasing limited partnerships buy expensive hard assets (e.g., shipping containers or jets) and lease them to businesses. This is the least risky of the partnerships discussed thus far, but the general partner may steer the partnership into areas where demand is falling for the assets that the partnership has purchased. The advantages of equipment leasing include an income stream from collecting lease payments, depreciation write-offs for the assets, and sheltering of income to future time periods when the partnership is dissolved. In addition to the risk of acquiring unpopular assets, there is also not much chance for capital appreciation for the investment since the rental assets will likely lose value.

3.3.6.3 Subscription Agreements

In limited partnerships, the most important document to the investor—and hence to you as the RR—is the subscription agreement. This is because that document is the one that binds the investor to the group as a limited partner, and gives authority to the general partner to act on behalf of the limited partner. As an RR for the firm selling the limited partnership, it is your responsibility to advise the client on suitability of the investment. You should never sell limited partnerships solely on the basis of tax benefits. Instead, they should be sold primarily on their economic viability. Furthermore, one of the big disadvantages of limited partnerships is their illiquidity. You should be sure to point this out to your clients as well. In fact, one important part of the subscription agreement is an acknowledgment that the investor understands the risks involved with the limited partnership. Be careful, too, because the subscription agreement may also be an acknowledgment that the investor will become responsible for certain recourse loans once he or she is accepted as a limited partner.

Remember, though, that the general partner always has final say on whether or not a particular investor may join as a limited partner. You as RR collect the investor's check and signed subscription agreement, and forward both to the general partner. But your client is not a limited partner yet. Maybe the partnership is already sold out, or maybe the general partner decides that your client is not a suitable investor. *Investors become limited partners only after the general partner signs the subscription agreement, accepting the investor into the limited partnership.*

3.3.6.4 Offerings of DPPs

There are two types of offerings that can be used to sell investments in limited partnerships: private and public. Private offerings are done with a document known as a **private placement memorandum,** which discloses details of the limited partnership investment, business plan, financial information, and information on the general partners. Since private offerings are done to a small group of accredited investors, the SEC does not require registration for the deal. **Accredited investors** are defined as people who have at least $1 million of net worth or an annual income of at least $200,000, and meet certain other criteria. Still, there are legal documents which must be signed, and other state rules are in effect.

The SEC is much more concerned about publicly offered limited partnerships, where the deal is syndicated through several broker-dealer firms and designed to have broad appeal. Public deals are done with a **public offering prospectus** which explains the limited partnership investment, business plan, financial information, and information on the general partners. The prospectus must be filed with the SEC. The SEC has strict rules for these deals because it does not want the deal targeted to unsophisticated investors. In addition, responsibility falls to the RR to make appropriate recommendations to investors regarding limited partnership investments. Not only must the risks be explained, but other factors must be considered.

3.3.6.5 Evaluating DPPs

When evaluating limited partnerships with a client, it is important to consider all of the pros and cons. Although many people think about the tax advantages first when it comes to various DPPs, it is important that you as the RR do not sell limited partnerships solely for their tax benefits. The most important aspects of a partnership investment should be the economic soundness of the deal, the expertise of the general partner, and the objectives of the program. Does the deal make sense for your client? Is it a suitable investment given your client's cash flow objectives, tax needs, liquidity concerns, risk tolerance, and investment experience?

The biggest advantage to limited partnership investments is the expertise of the general manager, who can provide professional management in an industry where the investor may have limited expertise. A good example of this is the real estate market, where professional management can often be the difference between a property making money or losing money. There are other considerations as well, such as the initial start-up costs of the limited partnership project, and the ability of the project to find additional sources of revenue. Of course, the investor must always consider if a rate of return, similar to the potential offered by the limited partnership, could be attained in a less risky way for the same investment dollars.

The main problem area for investors is the illiquidity of limited partnership investments because, with rare exceptions (like master limited partnerships), they cannot be traded in the secondary market. Another point to consider is the fact that many investors are not able to benefit from the tax advantages of the limited partnership, because they do not have enough passive income against which to claim losses from the partnership investment.

3.4 Debt Instruments

When we talk about debt instruments, we are usually talking about bonds. A **bond** is a security that pays interest, and returns the principal investment amount upon maturity. Originally, all bonds were **bearer bonds,** meaning the person who held the bond was the owner. The bond had coupons that were detached and submitted to collect interest payments. To this day, the interest rate is still often referred to as the **coupon** rate, even though most bonds now are **registered bonds** where the name of the owner is recorded with the registrar and interest payments are sent out automatically or paid electronically.

Because the interest rate paid by a bond provides a fixed rate of return, another name for a bond is a **fixed-income security.** But even though bonds are a "security," most bonds are unsecured debt. Another name for an unsecured bond is a **debenture.** A debenture does not have any collateral backing up the debt. Instead, the holder relies on the full faith and credit of the issuer. The terms *bond* and *fixed-income security* are interchangeable; the terms *bond* and *debenture* are also often used interchangeably, even though they sometimes may not be the same thing.

Watch for nuances as we define terms. A debenture is a bond, but a bond does not have to be a debenture. Only a bearer bond has physical coupons, but both a bearer bond and a registered bond have coupon rates. Many of the terms in this section are likely to appear on the Series 7 exam. And as we look at bonds, note that they can be issued by corporations, the U.S. government, and municipal governments. As you might guess, each have their own unique characteristics and features. We'll discuss these different kinds of debt instruments and explain how they work.

U.S. Treasury Securities

U.S. Treasury securities are debt obligations of the U.S. government. They are sometimes referred to as **Treasuries.** Treasuries are debentures, backed by the full faith and credit of the U.S. government—but nothing else. Still, they are considered the most risk-free investment that money can buy. Because of this, though, they have lower yields than corporate bonds. Investors are willing to accept this because of the safety of principal they afford, and because the interest is free from state income tax (but not federal income tax).

There are four types of U.S. Treasury securities: U.S. Treasury bills (T-bills), U.S. Treasury notes (T-notes), U.S. Treasury bonds (T-bonds), and U.S. Treasury receipts (and STRIPS). We will discuss characteristics, interest, and yields of each.

3.4.1.1 Characteristics: Maturities, Denominations, Issue Form, Quotations, Pricing

Treasury bills

- ▷ maturities are short-term, 1 year or less (3 mo., 6 mo., 1 yr.)
- ▷ denominations are $10,000 minimum face value
- ▷ issue form is book entry registration of owner's name
- ▷ quotations have "bid" and "ask" numbers that are a discount from par, so if the Bid is 3.00 and Ask is 2.75 for $100,000, $100,000 – 3% = $97,000 bid; $100,000 – 2.75% = $97,250 ask (these calculations are probably not on the test, but know that the *bid is higher than ask here*—opposite of most!)
- ▷ pricing is done at a discount from par, and written as a decimal bid/ask discount from face value (see example above)

Treasury notes

- ▷ maturities are intermediate-term, 1–10 years (but are callable)
- ▷ denominations are $1,000 minimum face value
- ▷ issue form is book entry registration of owner's name
- ▷ quotations are done as a percentage of par, and written as 97.01 or 97-01, where 01 = 1/32 of a percentage point, so a quoted spread might be Bid 97.04, Ask 97.26, meaning that the Bid is 97 4/32 percent, and Ask is 97 26/32 percent
- ▷ pricing is done as a percentage of par in 1/32 increments, with the numbers after the point signifying the number of 32nd increments—not a decimal! Here's an example: Bid 97.04 = 97 4/32% × $1,000 (face value), so Bid = $971.25

Treasury bonds

▷ maturities are long-term, 10 years or more (but are callable)
▷ denominations are $1,000 minimum face value
▷ issue form is book entry registration of owner's name
▷ quotations are same as Treasury notes
▷ pricing is same as Treasury notes
▷ some Treasury bonds are callable (with 4 months notice)
▷ T-bonds are *not* the same as government Savings bonds

Treasury receipts and STRIPS are special securities. Treasury receipts are actually created by broker-dealer firms, and do not represent direct obligations of the U.S. government. The B-D buys T-notes and T-bonds, and separates out the interest payments and the final principal payment. The B-D then sells "receipts" to investors, allowing them to buy, at a discount, any particular future payment they choose. The investor can choose to buy only one future interest payment, a series of future interest payments, or the future principal payment. Again, all of these trade at a discount based on the time value of money paid now for payments in the future. That, in effect, represents the interest rate return on the investment. (This will be explained more in the next few sections.)

STRIPS stands for **S**eparate **T**rading of **R**egistered **I**nterest and **P**rincipal of **S**ecurities. They are essentially a zero coupon bond. STRIPS are a product of the U.S. Treasury that mirrors what the broker-dealers do with Treasury receipts. *STRIPS are backed by full faith and credit of U.S. government, but T-receipts are not.* Instead, with T-receipts, investors are relying on the B-D who has stripped the Treasury securities, and the bank or other entity holding the Treasury securities in a trust account until payments are due.

3.4.1.2 Interest

There are a few important points to note about interest payments as they relate to Treasury securities. First, Treasury bills trade without any interest. Instead, they are discounted from their face value, and the entire face value is paid upon maturity. The reason that T-bills do not pay interest is because it would be lots of extra bookkeeping to pay interest on so many notes when they have such short maturities (one year or less). At the other end of the spectrum, Treasury receipts and STRIPS also do not pay interest. They're more like zero coupon bonds, which trade at deep discounts because no interest is paid, but the full face value is paid at maturity.

In the middle of these two extremes are the T-notes and T-bonds. Both of these pay interest on a semiannual basis. Calculations are made and checks are sent out by the Treasury to owners of the securities as recorded in the book entry registration. Because interest payments are made every six months, what happens when the security is sold or transferred between interest payment dates? What happens is that the price of the securities is always quoted and traded at the stated price **"and interest."** This means that the buyer of the security must pay the quoted price of the bond or note, plus interest that has accrued since the last interest payment was made. The seller receives the quoted price plus the accrued interest. In essence, the interest is prorated because the buyer and seller are entitled to the interest only for the days that they actually hold the security.

To compute accrued interest, you must calculate the number of days that have elapsed since the last interest rate payment and then plug that into a simple formula. For U.S. government securities, an actual **365-day year** is used to calculate accrued interest. Interest accrues up to but *not* including the settlement date. So if securities are bought with cash, the settlement date is the same day the trade is made, but if securities are settled the regular way, then the settlement day is **one business day** after the trade. This is often shortened to "Trade + 1" or "T + 1."

For U.S. government securities, our accrued interest formula is:

bond face amount × interest rate × time ÷ 365 = accrued interest

EXAMPLE

An investor is buying a U.S. Treasury bond for $1,000. The bond has a coupon rate of 5 percent. The bond last paid interest January 1, the trade took place Monday, March 1. How much interest accrued?

As we analyze the problem, we are looking for the bond face amount, interest rate, and time. Regardless of how much the investor paid for the bond, the bond face amount is always $1,000. (To make our example simple, the investor bought the bond at par, but don't get tricked on the Series 7 exam.) We know the face amount is $1,000 and the interest rate is the coupon rate, so that is 5 percent. All we need to do is calculate the number of days. Since the bond is a U.S. government bond, this tells us some important things:

1. **use 365-day year (months use actual # of days)**
2. **settlement is T+1**

So, we count 31 days for January, 28 days for February (no leap years), and for March we need to count 2 days. (Remember, it's business days so if the trade occurred on Friday or before a holiday, etc., this would affect your count). We have a total of 61 days. We plug our numbers into our formula:

$1,000 bond × 5% interest × 61 days ÷ 365 year = $8.36 accrued interest

BOND FORMULA VARIABLES

chart 3.4.1.2

Variables for Bonds	U.S. Government
Cash Settlement	same day
Regular Way Settlement	T + 1
Year used	365 days
Months Used	actual

On the Series 7 exam, you will probably not have to do the interest calculations, but you may be asked to figure how many days of accrued interest must be paid for a particular trade. Be alert for a trick, though. *If a test question asks you for the number of days of accrued interest due on a T-bill trade (or a T-receipts trade or a STRIPS trade), the answer is **zero**.*

If the securities are bought with cash, the settlement date is the same day the trade is made. If securities are settled the regular way (where the buyer delivers the money the following day), the settlement day is the next business day following the trade. Since these U.S. government securities trade at a discount instead of making periodic interest payments, they trade flat. **Traded flat** means that the bond trades at the quoted price without accrued interest. Accrued interest cannot be figured for bonds that do not pay interest, such as these. The buyer of a bond that is traded flat simply pays the quoted price.

3.4.1.3 Yields

When discussing bonds, there are actually several different ways that you can calculate yield. **Yield** is the rate of return earned on an investment. The typical yield curve says that the longer you are willing to tie up your money in an investment, the more interest you should be able to earn as a return on investment to compensate for future unknown inflation, and increased risk of potential default. Yield is expressed as a percentage. Yield is higher than the stated interest rate of the security if it is bought at a discount; yield is lower if it is bought at a premium. We will graph this shortly to illustrate the relationship between yield and price. There are a few other terms you should know.

Coupon is the nominal interest rate that the issuer will pay on a security, expressed as a percentage, and often printed right on the bond. This is a fixed percentage amount that does not change.

Current yield is the coupon rate of the bond divided by the purchase price paid:

$$\textbf{Current Yield (CY)} = \textbf{coupon} \div \textbf{price}$$

CY is a relative price that depends on the price you actually pay to acquire the bond. Let's assume you buy a bond with a face value of $1,000 and a coupon rate of 10 percent. If you paid $1,000 for the bond, your coupon rate is 10 percent and your current yield is 10 percent. But if you could buy the bond at a discount for $500, now you current yield is 20 percent.

Yield-to-maturity is the total rate of return that an investor will receive by holding a bond to maturity. YTM gives the discounted price the bond should trade at, so that the present value of all future payments equals the current price of the bond. In other words, YTM considers the time value of money and calculates the present value of receiving the future interest payments and future principal payment. YTM is an annualized rate that assumes all interest payments are not taken out, but reinvested.

$$\textbf{Discount:}\quad \textbf{YTM} = \frac{\textbf{Yearly Interest} \div \left(\textbf{Discount} \div \textbf{Years Left}\right)}{\left(\textbf{Bond Price} + \textbf{Face Value}\right) \div 2}$$

$$\textbf{Premium:}\quad \textbf{YTM} = \frac{\textbf{Yearly Interest} - \left(\textbf{Premium} \div \textbf{Years Left}\right)}{\left(\textbf{Bond Price} + \textbf{Face Value}\right) \div 2}$$

The calculation is not that important for the exam, but the concept is. Here's a graph:

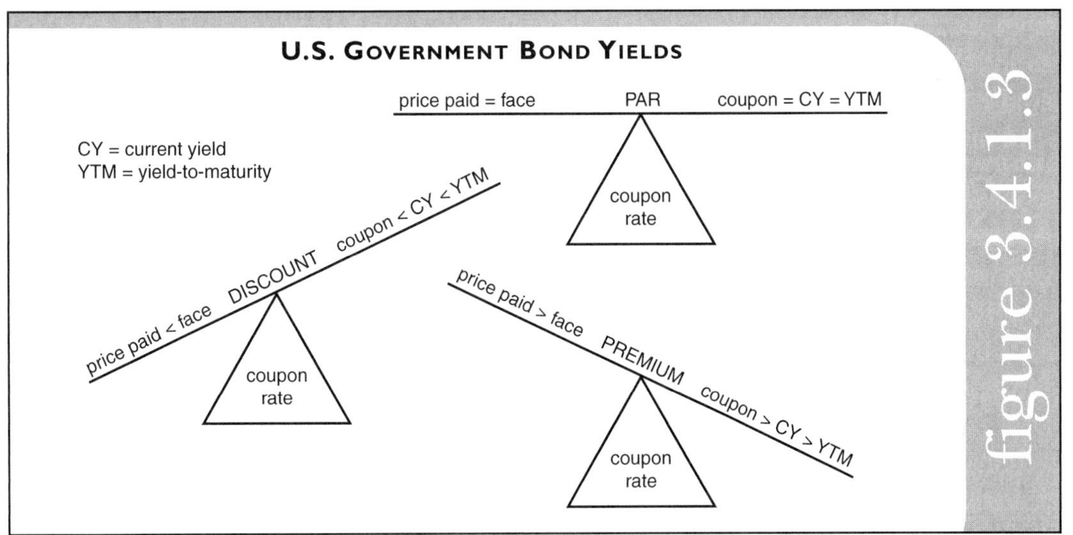

figure 3.4.1.3

Remember: CY and YTM have an inverse relationship with bond price. When price is high, CY&YTM are low. When price is low, CY&YTM are high.

Discount yield is a way to figure yield on T-bills, whereby you divide the discount by the face value of the bond, and multiply that by 360 divided by days to maturity.

$$\textbf{Discount Yield} = \frac{\textbf{Discount Amount}}{\textbf{Face Value}} \times \frac{\textbf{360}}{\textbf{Days to Maturity}}$$

Again, this calculation is not that important for the Series 7 exam. You *may* see one or two questions that ask you to calculate a YTM or discount yield, but it is not enough to decide your fate on the test. Instead, focus on the concept and understand the relationship between the values. Know that as the discount goes up, so too the discount yield goes up. This may seem to be different than the CY and YTM calculations, but it is not. Remember, T-bills are quoted differently—they are quoted at a discount from par. So as the discount goes up, the price of the bond goes down. That means that as the price of the bond goes down, discount yield goes up. This is the same inverse relationship between bond price and yield that we saw with CY and YTM. You just have to think about it a little more because T-bills are quoted at a discount from par.

A few more points to remember about Treasuries for the Series 7 exam. If you are asked which U.S. securities trade without accrued interest, the answer is T-bills. You can also recognize that a question is talking about T-bills if the bid price is higher than the ask price. Another point is that Treasury receipts are *not* backed by the full faith and credit of the U.S. government; STRIPS issued by the U.S. Treasury are. Also, for U.S. government securities, use a 365-day year to figure accrued interest, and do *not* include settlement date. (Cash sales have trade and settlement on same day; regular way settlement is T + 1 business day for government securities.)

U.S. Government Agency Securities

U.S. government agency securities are debt issued by U.S. government sponsored entities and other federally related institutions. U.S. government agency securities are exempt from SEC registration. There are several agencies involved with the issuance of U.S. government agency securities. Let's take a look at these.

3.4.2.1 Definition, Characteristics, Agencies

Government sponsored entities (GSEs) are privately owned, but publicly chartered entities which were created by the government to help out farmers, students, homeowners, and others by lowering borrowing costs. The GSEs sell securities to investors, then take the money from the investors and provide low interest loans to people in those targeted groups who meet certain criteria, or use the funds to buy mortgages in the secondary market. Some GSEs include Federal Farm Credit Consolidated Bank, Federal Home Loan Bank, Student Loan Marketing Association (Sallie Mae), Federal National Mortgage Association (FNMA or Fannie Mae), and Federal Home Loan Mortgage Corporation (FHLMC or Freddie Mac). Most GSE securities are backed by the agency issuing them, and are *not* backed by the full faith and credit of the U.S. government.

Federally related institutions are arms of the U.S. government which have the authority to issue securities for the needs of their agency. These include the Government National Mortgage Association (GNMA or Ginnie Mae), Small Business Administration, General Services Administration, and many others. In reality, though, few of these institutions issue their own securities today because the Federal Financing Bank, which is owned by the U.S. government, coordinates and consolidates all borrowing activities in an effort to reduce borrowing costs. Most federally related securities are backed by the full faith and credit of the U.S. government. Our discussion of federally related institutions will focus only on GNMA.

3.4.2.2 Specific Agency Securities: Maturities, Denomination, Ownership, Interest

Federal Farm Credit Consolidated Systemwide Bank

- maturities are short-term, less than 1 year (usually 6 or 9 mos.)
- denominations are sold in $5,000 increments
- forms of ownership are book entry registration
- interest rates are initially set by Federal Farm Credit Bank, notes sell at a discount and have active secondary market
- purpose is to provide credit services and loanable funds for farmers and farm-related entities

Federal Home Loan Bank

▷ maturities are short-term notes, less than 1 yr. (30–270 days) and long-term bonds (1–20 years)

▷ denominations are various amounts

▷ forms of ownership are book entry registration

▷ interest-bearing notes for short-term, semiannual interest payments for long-term bonds

▷ purpose is to supply credit reserves for savings & loans and other mortgage lenders by loaning them money againstthe collateral they have

Student Loan Marketing Association (Sallie Mae)

▷ maturities are short-term and medium-term (up to 5 years)

▷ denominations are various amounts

▷ forms of ownership are book entry registration

▷ interest can be fixed or variable; **floating rate notes** have interest rates that are adjusted every 6 months based on a money-market index (i.e., T-bills); floaters protect against inflation, so yields are lower than fixed-rate note

▷ purpose is to increase availability of student loans by buying old student loans from banks (so banks can make new loans) and lending money to state student loan agencies

3.4.2.3 Government Agency Mortgage-Backed Securities: Characteristics of Each, Maturities, Denominations, Risks, Payment of Principal and Interest

Government National Mortgage Association (GNMA or Ginnie Mae)

▷ characteristics:

1. securities are based on a pool of insured mortgages (FHA, VA, etc.)
2. security is *not* a bond—it's a pass-through certificate
3. backed by full faith and credit of U.S. government
4. interest is fully taxable (all government levels—federal, state, local)

▷ maturities: based on a quoted 12-year planned repayment, but often mature early as homeowners refinance loans

▷ denominations: minimum $25,000 face value

▷ risks: 1. interest rate risk (if rates go higher, you're locked in)

2. reinvestment risk (if rates go lower, get paid off early so need to find other investment with similar return)
3. almost *no* repayment risk—guaranteed by U.S. government

▷ principal and interest payments: paid monthly

Federal National Mortgage Association (FNMA or Fannie Mae)

▷ characteristics:

1. securities are based on pool of insured and uninsured mortgages (FHA, VA, and conventional loans)
2. securities *not* pass-through—FNMA is notes, bonds

3. shares of Fannie Mae trade on NYSE
4. *not* backed by U.S. government, only by FNMA credit
5. interest is fully taxable (all government levels—federal, state, local)

▷ maturities: short-term notes, 3–25 years for bonds—not callable

▷ denominations

for notes—$5,000, $25,000, $100,000, $500,000, $1 million

for bonds—minimum $10,000 (and up, $5,000 increments)

▷ risks: 1. interest rate risk (if rates go higher, you're locked in)

2. reinvestment risk (if rates go lower, get paid off early so need to find other investment with similar return)
3. repayment risk—*not* guaranteed by U.S. government

▷ interest payments: paid semiannually

Federal Home Loan Mortgage Corporation (FHLMC or Freddie Mac)

▷ characteristics:

1. securities are based on pool of insured and uninsured mortgages (FHA, VA, and conventional loans)
2. security is *not* a bond—it is a pass-through certificate two types: Participation Certificate (PC) and the Guaranteed Mortgage Certificate (GMC)
3. shares of Freddie Mac trade on NYSE
4. *not* backed by U.S. government, only by FHLMC
5. interest is fully taxable (all government levels—federal, state, local)

▷ maturities: based on a quoted planned repayment schedule, but often mature early as homeowners refinance loans

▷ denominations: issued in various face amounts

▷ risks: 1. interest rate risk (if rates go higher, you're locked in)

2. reinvestment risk (if rates go lower, get paid off early so need to find other investment with similar return)
3. repayment risk—*not* guaranteed by U.S. government

▷ principal and interest payments: PCs pay monthly (like GNMA) GMCs pay principal annually and interest semiannually

Exam Topic Alert

Here are a few more points to remember for the Series 7 exam. Securitized mortgages and pass-through certificates like those we have discussed in this section are for the investor who wants an income stream, but isn't concerned with capital appreciation. Yields on government agency securities are higher than yields on Treasuries because there is slightly more risk of repayment. Interest rate risk can also be a factor, but *reinvestment risk is single greatest risk for mortgage-backed securities.*

Exam Topic Alert

There are often more Ginnie Mae questions than other agencies. Ginnie Maes are not bonds, but are *pass-through certificates;* they are the only mortgage-backed security that is *backed by the full faith and credit of the U.S. government;* and when the monthly principal and interest payments are received, the interest portion of the payment is an immediate taxable event—fully taxable at all levels of government.

Asset-Backed Securities

Asset-backed securities are bonds, notes, or other securities which have a pool of loans behind them to give them underlying value. Asset-backed securities can be issued with any kind of debt backing them, but one of the most common is the mortgage-backed security that we discussed in the previous section. In addition to those mortgage-backed securities offered by government agencies, there are a number of similar securities available in the private sector. An example of a private mortgage-backed security vehicle is the REMIC. The other, more common mortgage-backed security vehicle is the CMO, which can be offered by either the public sector or private sector. Let's take a look at these.

REMIC. A **Real Estate Mortgage Investment Conduit (REMIC)** is a vehicle for issuing mortgage-backed securities, with the flexibility to issue the securities into different groups based on the maturity and the risk level of the pool of mortgages which back the securities. Because REMICs have varying risk levels, they have a lower bond rating, higher risk of default, and offer a higher rate of return than CMOs.

CMO. A **Collateralized Mortgage Obligation (CMO)** is a vehicle for issuing mortgage-backed securities, separated into different groups based on maturity dates. Because CMOs invest only in government-backed mortgages or other high grade mortgages, they have a higher bond rating than REMICs, but offer a lower return. Still, CMOs offer a better rate of return than the Ginnie Maes because CMOs are not government guaranteed. CMOs will probably come up a few times on the Series 7 exam, so let's take a closer look.

3.4.3.1 Characteristics, Types, and Structure

CMOs are similar to the other government agency pass-through securities that we discussed before. CMOs are backed by a pool of mortgages, payments are made monthly, and interest payments are taxable at all government levels (federal, state, local). There are, however, a few important differences from—and a few advantages to—CMOs. As stated, CMOs are separated into different groups based on their maturity. These maturity groups are called **tranches.**

Each CMO has various tranches with staggered maturities from a few months up to 20 years, and pays varying rates of interest depending on when the tranche matures. Tranches with the shortest term receive the lowest interest rate return on the money invested; the longest term tranches receive the highest rate of return. One important point to note about CMOs (and other mortgage-backed securities). If you have a CMO valued at $100,000, and receive $10,000 in payments, you are not getting a 10 percent return on your money. This is because not all of that $10,000 you received is interest; some is principal.

As mortgage payments are made by homeowners, the money is collected into the CMO and then redistributed to the investors through various payout methods, depending on the CMO structure. The separation into tranches leads to much more flexibility, allowing different types of CMOs to be structured to meet investors' needs and to help protect the investors' payment stream.

Standard CMOs. With a standard CMO, everyone receives interest payments, but after those payments the remaining money is pooled and used to pay off the principal obligation to the first short-term tranche group only. Once the first group has received its principal back in full, only then does the second group begin to receive principal payments. This continues until the last group is repaid all of its principal and interest, or until all mortgages in the pool have been repaid. If the mortgages in the pool are paid off early, it is more likely that this will affect the longer-term tranches.

Interest Only CMOs. Interest only CMOs have the investor receiving only the interest portion of the payments from the underlying mortgages. (Principal payments go to separate investors who bought a principal only CMO.) As with how a regular mortgage balance is paid down, interest only CMO payments are large at the beginning and get smaller over time as the mortgage balance declines. If the underlying mortgage loan is repaid early, the holder of the interest only CMO stops receiving payments. Thus, when interest rates rise, the value of the interest only CMO also goes up because it is anticipated that the homeowner is less likely to refinance the underlying mortgage and therefore the interest only payments are likely to continue for a longer period of time. Interest only CMOs are sold at a discount from par.

Principal Only CMOs. Principal only CMOs have the investor receiving only the principal portion of the payments from the underlying mortgages. (Interest payments go to separate investors who bought an interest only CMO.) As with how a regular mortgage balance is paid down, principal only CMO payments are small at the beginning and get larger over time as the mortgage balance declines. If the underlying mortgage loan is repaid early, the holder of the principal only CMO receives a final lump sum payment, because the CMOs are sold at a discount and eventually redeemed at par. Thus, when interest rates go down, the value of the principal only CMO goes up because it is anticipated that the homeowner is more likely to take advantage of the lower rates, refinance the underlying mortgage, and return the principal to the investor sooner.

TACs. Targeted amortization class CMOs (TACs) utilize a sinking fund to ensure that investors receive principal and interest payments. TAC obligations are paid first, and prepayments are shifted to other companion tranches. This works as long as the prepayment rate of the underlying mortgages follows the schedule planned for when the TAC was set up. If too many people pay off their mortgages too early, or if too many people default on their loans, then the TAC will not meet its payout schedule. TACs offer more stability to investors than standard CMOs, which distribute only whatever payments come in and do not have any other source from which to obtain funds. Thus, TACs trade at a premium over standard CMOs.

PACs. Planned amortization class CMOs (PACs) utilize a sinking fund to ensure that investors receive their principal and interest payments. Also, the PAC obligations are repaid first. PACs are set up similar to TACs. PACs use companion tranches to shift prepayments, and they also use companion tranches to obtain funds to maintain payments if the underlying mortgages do not pay on time. The PAC structure offers more stability to investors than the TAC or standard CMO, and thus PACs trade at a premium over TACs and CMOs.

3.4.3.2 Risks and Rewards

CMOs are a good alternative to other mortgage-backed securities because their tranche structure offers more assurance to investors that their investment will run its full course. The mortgages are packaged together to offer protection for the investor. Still, CMOs are not suitable investments for everyone. There are four risks associated with CMOs.

1. **Interest rate risk** can cause changes in value of a CMO. Interest only CMOs are hurt the most by falling rates because lower rates will cause more people to refinance their mortgages and thus cut off interest payments to investors; principal only CMOs are hurt most by rising interest rates because this will cause people to hold onto lower mortgage rate loans stretching out repayment.
2. **Prepayment risk** can cause CMO investments to halt interest payments and return principal sooner than expected. This can also lead to reinvestment risk, since the investor must now look for another investment that pays a comparable return to what he or she was getting from the CMO investment. TACs and PACs are structured with companion tranches to lessen this risk. TACs and PACs are paid first, prepayments are shifted to the other tranches.
3. **Extension risk** is the chance that homeowners will be late making payments on their mortgages, which could in turn affect payouts to investors. Only PACs are structured so that the companion tranches cover both the prepayment and extension risk that are inherent risks with mortgage-backed securities, since missed payments are shifted to companion tranches.
4. **Repayment risk** is the chance that homeowners will default on the mortgage loans. Since CMOs are privately issued, they're not backed by U.S. government; but relatively safe since CMO mortgage pools are higher quality than REMICs.

The potential rewards of CMO investments are a relatively safe investment, backed by high grade mortgages, that offer a potential monthly income stream. CMOs can offer better rates of return than some other investments, including Treasuries. And even though they are susceptible to prepayment risks, the tranche structure of CMOs offer additional stability not found with other mortgage-backed securities. Finally, interest rate risks can actually be turned into an opportunity, since some CMO variations offer a hedge against certain interest rate movements.

Interest only CMOs have the potential reward of acting as a hedge against rising interest rates, because rising interest rates make interest only CMOs more valuable. Interest only CMOs also offer investors a source for an immediate income stream. Principal only CMOs have the potential reward of acting as a hedge against declining interest rates, because falling rates make principal only CMOs more valuable. Principal only CMOs also offer investors a source of increasing cash flow over time. Finally TACs and PACs offer even more investment protection than standard CMOs.

You should see at least a few questions on the Series 7 exam about CMOs, so here are a few points to remember. CMOs are pass-through certificates, backed by a pool of mortgages, which offer investors a monthly income stream. Interest payments received are an immediate taxable event, which are fully taxable at all levels of government—federal, state and local. CMOs are not backed by the U.S. government, so their yields are higher than Treasuries or other government agency mortgage-backed securities. Risks include interest rate, prepayment, and extension. TACs and PACs are structured with a sinking fund and companion tranches to reduce prepayment risks. PACs also protect against extension risk.

Exam Topic Alert

Remember, *when you see "tranches" in a question, look for "CMOs" in the answer (and vice versa).*

3.4.4

Corporate Bonds

Corporate bonds are debt obligations of a private corporation. They are sometimes referred to as **corporates.** Remember, a **bond** is a security that pays interest, and returns the principal investment amount upon maturity. Corporate bonds are backed by the issuer, and may or may not have collateral associated with them. The bond, though, is merely a promise by the issuer to repay a fixed sum of money with interest—it does not confer any rights of ownership in the corporation like stock does. Bondholders are creditors of the corporation; stockholders are owners of the corporation. Like stocks, bonds are actively traded in the secondary market. Any interest and capital gains from corporate bonds are fully taxable at all levels of government.

3.4.4.1 General Characteristics

Corporate bonds have several unique characteristics which distinguish them from government bonds. First and foremost, corporate bonds are issued by corporations, which must comply with all SEC rules and regulations when issuing debt. Government securities are exempt from SEC rules, and from the Trust Indenture Act of 1939. The Act requires corporate bonds to have an indenture agreement. The **indenture agreement** provides for appointment of a qualified, independent trustee; protective clauses for, and list of promises to, bondholders; semiannual financial reports to bondholders; and periodic SEC filings to show compliance.

Exam Topic Alert

*Note that although the indenture agreement is designed to protect bondholders, it is a contract between the corporation and trustee—*not *between the company and bondholder.* This may be a trick question on the Series 7 exam.

Since bondholders are creditors of the corporation that issued the debt, bondholders have a claim on the assets of a corporation should the company be liquidated. There is no such right with government debt. Corporate bonds have a par value of $1,000. This amount is used for figuring interest, calculating quotes, and is the amount paid out at maturity to the holder of the bond.

Maturities. Corporate bonds are issued for anywhere from 1–20 years, and have what are called term maturities. A **term maturity** means that the bonds all come due at once. This is much different from the staggered **(serial)** maturities that government issued securities have. Because corporations must repay a significant amount of debt in one big chunk, they establish a sinking fund that they pay into regularly so that the bonds' principal amounts can be paid when the bonds come due.

Forms of Ownership. Unlike government bonds, which are typically issued as registered bonds in book entry form, corporate bonds are issued in one of four forms:

1. **Bearer bonds**—the person who holds the bond is the owner; coupons must be submitted to collect interest payments.
2. **Registered bonds**—the name of the bond owner is recorded on the face of the bond and with the registrar of the issuing company; semiannual interest payments and final principal payment are automatically sent to person of record; transfer by endorsement
3. **Registered coupon bonds** or **registered as to principal only**— the name of the bond owner is recorded on the face of the bond and with the registrar of issuing company, and final principal payment is automatically sent to person of record; but coupons must be presented to collect interest payments.
4. **Book entry bonds**—same as registered bonds, except *no* certificate.

Interest Payment Periods. Corporate bonds pay interest semiannually. The final interest payment is paid by the issuer with the return of the principal on the date that the bond matures. The buyer of a bond pays the bond price "and interest" that has accrued since the last interest payment was made.

Redeemability at Par at Maturity. On the date that the bond matures, the holder of the bond is entitled to turn in (redeem) the bond for the face value (par value) printed on the bond. For registered bonds, the holder of record is sent the final payment. Regardless of what discount or premium the bond may have traded for in the past, the day that the bond comes due the corporate issuer of the bond is liable for payment of the par value of the bond.

May Be Subject to Call. Corporate bonds often have a call feature that allows the issuer to redeem the bond early before its stated maturity date. The terms and conditions under which a call can be exercised are spelled out when the bonds are originally issued. The corporation may also have to offer a **call premium** to the bondholder if the bonds are called early. The only other protection that a bondholder has is that some bonds are issued with a **call protection** period during which time the bond may not be called early. It can be a big advantage for the issuer to be able to call bonds early if interest rates fall significantly, because then the corporation can issue new debt at the lower interest rates. Calling bonds also allows the corporation to change the terms of its debt, change its debt repayment schedule, or change its debt-to-equity ratio in its financial statements.

3.4.4.2 Specific Types of Bonds

There are many types of corporate bonds. Some are secured, some are unsecured. Different types have different claim priorities as well. Let's look at a few of the more common bond types, and some of their features.

Mortgage bonds

▷ type of collateral: mortgage issued on the corporation's real property

▷ priority of claim: first mortgage bonds are paid first, then lien order

▷ unique characteristics: mortgage bonds can be issued as open-end (meaning more bonds may be issued) or closed-end (meaning no more bonds may be issued below the mortgage bondholders); if sale of real estate does not satisfy all mortgage bond claims, then mortgage bondholders are general creditors of company

Equipment trust certificates

▷ type of collateral: equipment bought with proceeds of bond sale

▷ priority of claim: first right to seize equipment if bond is not paid

▷ unique characteristics: often used by transportation companies; equipment is held in trustee's name until bond is repaid

Debentures

▷ type of collateral: none—unsecured debt; full faith and credit of issuer

▷ priority of claim: paid after secured bonds, but before stockholders

▷ unique characteristics: debentures are backed by full faith and credit of the issuer only; if more debentures are issued at a later date, they would be subordinate to (put under, paid after) prior issued debentures; debenture holders are general creditors of a corporation

Income bonds (adjustment bonds)

▷ type of collateral: none—unsecured debt

▷ priority of claim: paid after secured bonds, but before stockholders

▷ unique characteristics: interest payment is contingent on earnings of the company; often used when company faces bankruptcy; adjustment bonds are traded for other bonds; trade flat, meaning no accrued interest is figured since it may not be paid

Guaranteed bonds

▷ type of collateral: none—unsecured debt; full faith and credit of issuer and also guaranteed by full faith and credit of another company

▷ priority of claim: paid after secured bonds, but before stockholders

▷ unique characteristics: the other company guaranteeing the bond is usually related to the issuing company, such as parent company guaranteeing a bond for a subsidiary; this may be needed to improve bond's credit rating; guarantee could be interest only

3.4.4.3 Convertible Bonds

Convertible bonds are corporate debt securities that may be traded in for common stock in the company at a predetermined price. This gives the bondholder the safety of guaranteed interest payments and status as a creditor, with a chance to share in the capital appreciation of the underlying company's stock if it goes above the conversion price.

The price for convertible bonds is usually *higher* and the interest paid is usually *lower* than standard bonds issued by the company, but investors will accept this in exchange for a chance to convert to common stock and enjoy capital appreciation at a future date.

Companies issue convertible bonds because they can be sold for more money and pay out a lower interest rate. Sometimes the conversion option is a necessary feature to attract investors to buy the issue. Of course, there are downsides to convertible bonds: if too many investors convert then the company can face lower earnings per share as the amount of outstanding stock increases, greater dividend payouts which are not tax deductible like interest payments, and the potential for a less management control as dilution occurs.

Conversion Privilege. Since convertible bonds may be exchanged for a fixed number of common stock shares, this is referred to as a **conversion privilege.** If the bondholder elects to convert to common stock, this can be done for a fixed number of shares, or for a variable number of shares based on a specific ratio or formula. The method for deciding the conversion amount is determined when the bond was originally issued. This conversion number is usually adjusted for stock splits, stock dividends, or new issues. This would depend on the terms that were spelled out in the bond's trust indenture.

Conversion Ratio or Price. The conversion price tells you at what price the stock should trade before the bondholder considers conversion. If the issuer has established a conversion price of $100, once the stock reaches $100 or above it would be advantageous to do the conversion. The conversion ratio tells you how many shares the bondholder would receive for converting. Take the par face value of the bond and divide by the conversion price to calculate the number of shares. In our example here:

face value ÷ conversion price = # of shares

$1,000 (face value) ÷ $100 (conversion price) = 10 shares

The bondholder would receive 10 shares of stock when converting the bond.

Calculation of Parity. Although the convertible bond price often fluctuates in line with the common stock price, they do not always move in tandem. Upward movements tend to go together, but when the company's stock falls the bond will usually not fall as much since the bond payments are fixed. At times when the value of the convertible bond and the stock intersect, this is referred to as **parity** because the convertible bond can be exchanged for stock of equal value. Let's go back to our example:

$1,000 (face value) ÷ $100 (conversion price) = 10 shares

Thus, if the bondholder bought the bond at par (face value), conversion parity would be $100. So if the stock price is above $100, it makes sense to convert the bond because the stock is worth more at any price above $100. (For purposes of this discussion, we'll ignore other risk factors of stock ownership, such as falling prices.)

Remember we said earlier, though, that convertible bonds often trade at a premium because of their conversion feature. This means that the parity price will have to be higher than if the bond had been purchased at face value. Let's suppose that the bond was purchased at a premium for $1,100. The conversion price is still $100 and we can still only get 10 shares of stock because the conversion ratio is still the same. But since we paid more for the bond, our conversion parity price is more.

\$1,100 (bond price) ÷ 10 shares = \$110 (conversion parity price)

Because the bondholder paid a premium for the bond, but still would receive only 10 shares of stock when converting the bond, the conversion parity price of the underlying stock must go above \$110 for conversion to benefit the bondholder.

Let's do another example where the bond was purchased at a discount.

EXAMPLE

We have a bond with a face value of \$1,000 and a conversion price of \$50. First, we need to find how many shares we're entitled to exchange for the bond if we convert:

\$1,000 (face value) ÷ \$50 (conversion price) = 20 shares

Our bond is selling at a discount, so we need to find its current market value (CMV). Suppose that the CMV of the bond is quoted in the newspaper at 90. When we see a quote like that for a bond, that price is quoted as a percentage of par, so:

\$1,000 (par) × 90% (quote) = \$900 (current bond price)

Now we have the two numbers we need to solve our problem. Our formula is the same as before, bond price ÷ shares = conversion parity price, so:

\$900 (bond price) ÷ 20 shares = \$45 (conversion parity price)

Remember, even though the bondholder bought the bond at a discount, he or she would still receive 20 shares of stock when converting the bond. But because of the bond's discounted price, the stock has to get to only \$45 for the bond and the stock to be at conversion parity price. This means that if the stock is trading at \$45, the bond and the stock have equal value—even though the conversion price stated on the certificate is \$50. That number is used only for figuring the number of shares the bondholder is entitled to. The conversion parity price moves up and down with the actual price of the bond. The conversion parity price must be calculated with the four steps we used here:

1. find par (always \$1,000 for bonds)
2. calculate how many shares you get:

   face value ÷ conversion price = # of shares

3. get the current bond price (CMV):

   par × quote = current bond price (CMV)

4. figure the conversion parity:

   bond price ÷ # of shares = conversion parity price

That's all there is to it.

Exam Topic Alert

The Series 7 exam may also ask you to reverse the logic. For example, a question might say: If the stock price increases by 20 percent, what happens to the bond price? In this situation, look for an answer that states the bond price also rises 20 percent because the theory is that these two should move in tandem. *If the question asks about a falling stock price, though, be careful.* If the stock falls only a little the bond price would probably fall by an equal amount; but if the stock drops dramatically, then theoretically the bond price should not drop as much because it still has the guaranteed interest payments to help support its price in line with other debt securities offering a similar return. Read all the possible answers and choose wisely.

Factors Influencing Conversion. There are several things that a bondholder must consider when deciding whether or not to convert a bond into common stock. First is the prospects of the company. Even if the stock price rises above the parity price, if there is no substantive reason for the movement it is possible the stock price might come back down. Second, if the company is about to be acquired or merged, the conversion option may be erased. Third, a company may do a **forced conversion** by calling the bond so that it is more advantageous for the bondholder to convert than to surrender the bond. Finally, the bondholder may decide to take advantage of the price differential between the trading price of the convertible bond and the stock, convert, and then sell the stock and profit from this **arbitrage** transaction.

3.4.4.4 Retirement of Bonds

Corporate bonds are retired in one of three ways. The bonds can be redeemed by paying them off, refunded by calling them early and replacing them with lower yielding bonds, or converted by the bondholder into common stock (if they are convertible). Let's look at each of these.

Redemption. Redemption is repayment of a debt obligation at maturity, or earlier. If done at maturity, the final interest and principal payment are made to the bondholder or holder of record and the debt is thus retired. If bonds are redeemed before they mature, they must have a call provision allowing the issuing company to redeem the bonds early in exchange for payment of principal, interest owed, and often a call premium. If an entire issue is not called, the trustee randomly chooses the bonds that will be redeemed.

If there are no call provisions in a bond, the corporation can approach current bondholders and offer to buy their bonds. This **tender offer** may be at current market value or it may be at a premium. It is the bondholder's option whether or not to accept a tender offer. The company can also go into the secondary market and buy back its bonds to retire the debt. This is referred to as **tendering.**

Refunding. Refunding is replacing a debt obligation with another debt security that has different terms, such as a lower interest rate. Bonds must have a call provision allowing the issuing company to refund the bonds early in exchange for other bonds. Usually the newly issued bonds will have a lower rate, but refunding also may occur if the company wants to restructure its debt to pay it off more quickly or over a longer period of time than the original issue. The call provision may require payment of a call premium by the company for the right to refund the debt. If the company is in financial trouble, bondholders may allow refunding even without a call provision in the bonds as a way to help the company avoid bankruptcy.

Conversion. Conversion is exchanging bonds for a fixed number of shares of common stock. This is usually done by bondholders who own convertible bonds when the parity price makes it more lucrative to own stock than to own bonds in the company. A company may also do a forced conversion by calling a bond, and leaving the bondholder with little choice but to convert the bond or surrender it.

3.4.4.5 Calculating Accrued Interest

When an investor buys a bond, he or she pays the bond price "and interest" that has accrued since the last interest payment was made. This is similar to how some government issues are traded, but there are a few important differences. Like government bonds, interest accrues up to, but does *not* include the settlement date. If securities are bought with cash, the settlement date is the same day the trade is made—so far corporate and government bonds are the same. But if securities are settled the regular way, then the settlement day is **three business days** following the trade. This is often shortened to "Trade + 3" or "T + 3." (Remember, for U.S. government securities, we use T + 1.) The other important difference is that for corporate bonds, a **360-day year** is used to calculate accrued interest, so that each month has an even 30 days. (Remember, for U.S. government securities, an actual 365-day calendar year is used.)

For corporate securities, our accrued interest formula is

bond face amount × interest rate × time ÷ 360 = accrued interest

EXAMPLE

An investor is buying the XYZ bond for $1,100. The bond has a coupon rate of 6 percent and a conversion price of $50. The bond last paid interest January 1, the trade took place Monday, March 1. How much interest accrued?

As we analyze the problem, we are looking for the bond face amount, interest rate, and time. The bond face amount is always $1,000. Don't let the price of the bond fool you. It is used only if you need to figure the total amount the investor needs to pay for the trade. Also, the conversion price is not important. So we know the face amount is $1,000 and the interest rate is the coupon rate, so that is 6 percent. All we need to do is calculate the number of days. *Since the bond has a three-letter designation, we know it is a corporate bond.* This tells us three important things:

1. **use 360-day year**
2. **all months have 30 days**
3. **settlement is T+3**

So, we count 30 days for January, 30 days for February (watch this!), and for March we need to count 4 days. (Remember, it's business days so, if the trade occurred on Friday or before a holiday, this would affect your count). We have a total of 64 days. We plug our numbers into our formula:

$1,000 bond × 6% interest × 64 days ÷ 360 year = $10.67 accrued interest

chart 3.4.4.5

BOND FORMULA VARIABLES

Variables for Bonds	Corporate	U.S. Government
Cash Settlement	same day	same day
Regular Way Settlement	T + 3	T + 1
Year Used	360 days	365 days
Months Used	30 day	actual

Let's do another example of accrued interest, and this time introduce some shorthand notation that B-D and RR use when trading securities.

Example

Client's trade is: 5 ABC 8¼% F+A callable 102 after '06. The trade took place Friday, December 7. How much interest accrued?

First, we need to decipher the trade: 5 ABC 8¼% F+A callable 102 after '06.

The trade is for 5 bonds of the ABC company, at 8¼ percent. F+A tells us that interest is paid in February and August, the bond is callable at 102 after 2006.

Corp. bond, so use 360-day year, all months have 30 days, settlement is T+3.

So, we count 30 days for August, 30 days for September, 30 days for October, 30 days for November, and for December we need to count 11 days. (Remember, it's business days, so since the trade occurred on Friday, the settle day is Wednesday, December 12). We have a total of 131 days. Using our formula:

$5,000 bond × 8¼% interest × 131 days ÷ 360 year = $150.10 interest

WATCH THIS! Trade was for 5 bonds. Either use $5,000 as face amount, or use $1,000 in formula and multiply your accrued interest total × 5 at the end.

Traded Flat. Bonds that are traded flat are the opposite of bonds that are traded "and interest." **Traded flat** means that the bond trades at the quoted price without accrued interest. Accrued interest is not figured in situations where it is uncertain whether or not the interest will actually be paid. As we saw earlier, income bonds and adjustment bonds are usually traded flat, as are other issues where the company is in default on bond payments. The buyer of a bond that is traded flat simply pays the quoted price. If the interest is actually paid on a future date as scheduled, the buyer is entitled to receive the interest with no obligation to the previous holder.

3.4.4.6 Calculating Yields

Let's review some of the yield concepts we discussed when discussing government bonds, as most of those apply to corporate bonds also.

Yield is the rate of return earned on an investment, expressed as a percentage.

Coupon is the nominal interest rate that the issuer will pay on a security, expressed as a percentage. This is a fixed percentage amount that does not change.

Current yield is a relative price that depends on the price you actually pay to acquire the bond. It is the coupon rate of the bond divided by the purchase price paid:

Current Yield (CY) = coupon ÷ price

Yield-to-maturity is the total rate of return that an investor will receive by holding a bond to maturity. YTM gives the discounted price the bond should trade at, so that the present value of all future payments equals the current price of the bond.

Now let's look at a new yield concept. Since we have been talking about callable bonds, it would be helpful for an investor to know what kind of yield can be expected on a bond assuming the worst case scenario—that the bond is called as soon as possible by the company, and replaced with a lower-yielding bond that has a lower interest rate. To figure the yield under this scenario we use a new formula: **yield-to-call.**

Yield-to-call is the total rate of return that an investor will receive by holding a bond until it is called by the issuer, assuming the call is made at the first opportunity. YTC gives the discounted price the bond should trade at, so that the present value of future payments up to the first call date equals the current price of the bond. YTC formulas are the same as the YTM formulas with two changes.

First, instead of using the "Years Left" to maturity in the formula, we use "Years Left to Call," which is until the first possible year that the issuer could call the bond. Second, instead of using "Face Value" of the bond, we use "Call Value." Let's compare:

Discount: $$\text{YTC} = \frac{\text{Yearly Interest} + \left(\text{Discount} \div \text{Years Left to Call}\right)}{\left(\text{Bond Price} + \text{Call Value}\right) \div 2}$$

Discount: $$\text{YTM} = \frac{\text{Yearly Interest} + \left(\text{Discount} \div \text{Years Left}\right)}{\left(\text{Bond Price} + \text{Face Value}\right) \div 2}$$

Premium: $$\text{YTC} = \frac{\text{Yearly Interest} - \left(\text{Premium} \div \text{Years Left to Call}\right)}{\left(\text{Bond Price} + \text{Call Value}\right) \div 2}$$

Premium: $$\text{YTM} = \frac{\text{Yearly Interest} - \left(\text{Premium} \div \text{Years Left}\right)}{\left(\text{Bond Price} + \text{Face Value}\right) \div 2}$$

Again, actual calculations are not that important for the exam, but the concept is. Let's add YTC to our graph:

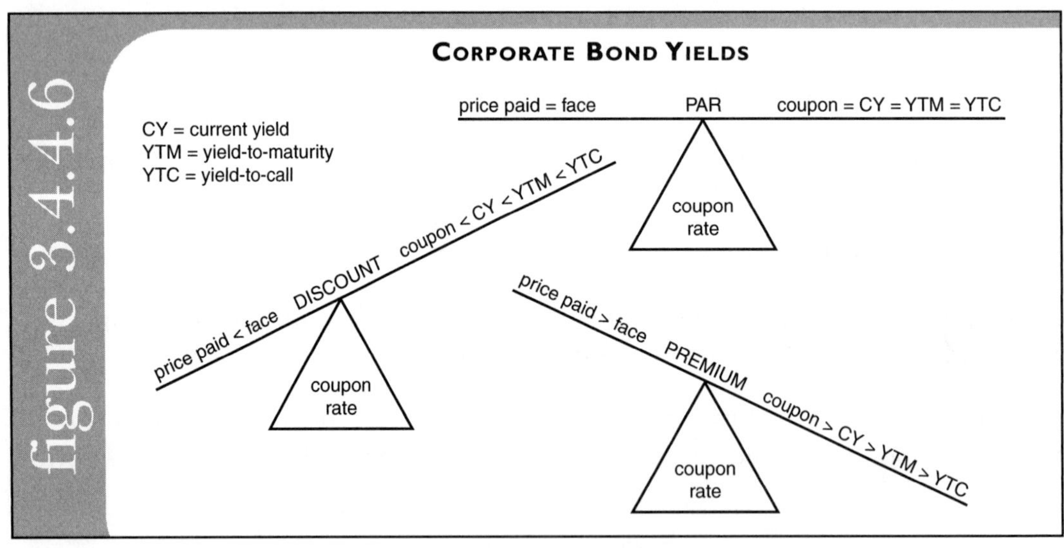

Remember: CY, YTM, YTC all have an inverse relationship with bond price. When price is high, CY, YTM, YTC are low. When price is low, CY, YTM, YTC are high.

Yield is higher than the stated interest rate of the security if it is bought at a discount; yield is lower if it is bought at a premium. You *may* see one or two questions that ask you to calculate a YTC or YTM, but it is not enough to decide your fate on the test. You decide where you want to spend your study energy. Make sure, though, that you focus on the concept and understand the relationship between the different yield values.

3.4.4.7 Corporate Bond Ratings

Bond ratings are values on a point scale that represent the likelihood that the issuer will default on a debt obligation. They are, in essence, the credit rating of an entity issuing debt securities. The ratings are done by one of several rating agencies who assign these values to companies (and to municipal governments) after considering a number of factors about the issuer. These factors include previous debt repayment history, current debt load, and prospects for future revenue stability and growth.

Rating Agencies. Of the various agencies which rate corporations, the two that you should be most familiar with are Moody's and Standard & Poor's. Moody's Investor Service, a subsidiary of Dun & Bradstreet, rates many kinds of stocks, bonds and commercial paper. Standard & Poor's (S&P) also rates stocks, bonds and commercial paper. Both companies provide additional research and analysis to help investors make informed investment decisions.

Types of Ratings. Moody's and S&P use different, but similar, scales to rate the quality of bonds. Moody's highest bond rating is "Aaa" while S&P's is "AAA". Both of these ratings indicate that the issuer is highly unlikely to default on the debt obligation. You can remember which rating agency uses which rating scale rather easily: *S&P is in all capital letters, and their ratings are in all capital letters; Moody's uses upper- and lowercase letters, as does their name.*

Moody's top four bond ratings are "Aaa," "Aa," "A," and "Baa." S&P's top four bond ratings are "AAA," "AA," "A," and "BBB." These top four bond ratings by both agencies are considered **investment grade bonds.** To further distinguish bonds within a rating group, Moody's may assign a "1," "2," or "3" to modify a rating, such as "Baa3" to indicate the lowest of that group. S&P uses "+" or "–" to modify some ratings. Although lower-grade bonds often have higher yields, they are generally referred to as **junk bonds.** Bonds with a rating of "D" are in default.

Ratings are very important for the issuing company. Many institutional investors, such as insurance companies and pension plans, will buy only investment grade bonds. Some states even mandate that fiduciaries who invest money on behalf of other people cannot buy bonds that are below investment grade. Banks can buy only investment grade bonds with reserves, per Federal Reserve and FDIC rules. (This is why investment grade bonds are sometimes called **bank grade bonds.**)

Bond Rating Table

chart 3.4.4.7

Rating Explanation	Moody's	S&P
Investment Grade	Aaa, Aa, A, Baa	AAA, AA, A, BBB
Medium Grade	Ba, B	BB, B
Highly Speculative	Caa, Ca, C	CCC, CC, C
In Default	D	DDD, DD, D

Remember, S&P uses all capital letters. Moody's is upper- and lowercase.

A few more points to remember about Corporate bonds for the Series 7 exam. If you are asked which corporate securities trade without accrued interest, the answer is income bonds or adjustment bonds. Also, for corporate securities, use a 360-day year to figure accrued interest, and do *not* include settlement date. (Cash sales have trade and settlement on same day; regular way settlement is Trade + 3 business days for corporate securities.)

3.4.5

Tax Treatment of Debt Securities

When discussing the tax treatment of corporate debt securities, there are several different things that we need to consider: When was the bond purchased? Was the bond bought at a premium or at a discount? What is the cost basis and timing of the bond's disposition (sale or redemption)? All of these questions will affect the tax liability that is incurred by the bond investor. There are also additional tax considerations for bonds that are put into IRAs or other tax-deferred investments, but we will not deal with these in any depth during our tax discussion in this section.

On the Series 7 exam, you should *never assume that a bond has gone into an IRA* or similar account unless the test question specifically states that that is the case.

INTEREST. Interest payments received from corporate bonds are an immediate taxable event. They are fully taxable at all levels of government (federal, state, local) on 100 percent of the money received. Furthermore, interest is taxed as ordinary income at the tax bracket of the investor.

Zero coupon bonds are bonds sold at a deep discount from par because they do not make periodic interest payments, but instead pay the full face amount at maturity. The investor receives a rate of return by the gradual appreciation of the bond from the purchase date until maturity. Nevertheless, the IRS views zero coupons as paying **imputed interest** to the bondholder. Thus, taxes must be paid on interest that has accrued in the investment each year, even though the bondholder does not actually receive any money until the bond matures. (For this reason, zero coupons are often held in retirement accounts.)

Also note that accrued interest paid when a bond is traded "and interest" is a taxable event to the seller who receives the accrued interest, and a deduction against interest earned for the buyer who pays the accrued interest.

The accrued interest does *not* figure into the cost basis of the bond. (*Watch for this on the Series 7 exam!*)

PRINCIPAL. When the final principal payment of a bond is received, or when the principal is returned to the investor through a sale or redemption, this also creates a taxable event. The investor owes tax on any capital gain made, or can take a deduction if a capital loss was incurred. Capital gains are taxed at a more favorable rate if the investment was held for one year or more; otherwise the capital gain is treated as ordinary income. Capital gains or losses are figured using the adjusted cost basis for the original investment. The cost basis is not adjusted for a bond that is bought at par, but may be altered for bonds bought at a premium or at a discount.

PREMIUMS. If a corporate bond is purchased at a premium (above par value), the investor has a choice of either **amortizing** the premium amount over the life of the bond until maturity, or simply keeping the premium amount as part of the cost basis used to figure any loss or gain when the bond is sold or redeemed. **Amortization** is the process of reducing an amount by dividing it into smaller equal payments over a period of time. You can amortize costs or depreciation or losses.

From the investor's perspective, paying a premium for a bond is no different from losing money because you are paying more for something than it is really worth. The IRS, however, does not allow the entire loss to be taken immediately if the investor is not selling the bond. Instead, only a portion of the "loss" can be deducted each year. The investor could choose this option to offset other current income.

If the investor chooses to amortize the premium, this also reduces the cost basis of the bond each year. By amortizing the premium over the life of the bond, this gets the cost basis back to par by the maturity date, so no capital loss is incurred. In fact, because the cost basis is reduced each year by amortizing the premium, selling the bond before maturity may actually mean that the capital gain is more than you might think. That is because you need to consider the fact that the investor has already taken a portion of the premium loss as a deduction in prior years. There is a simple calculation used to figure out the cost basis adjustment that must be done.

purchase price – face value = premium

premium ÷ years to maturity = loss per year

This loss per year figure is subtracted from the bond purchase price each year to figure out the cost basis for that year. Thus, as we said before, the adjusted cost basis will equal the par value of the bond at maturity. But if the bond is sold earlier, the adjusted cost basis will cause the investor to have a larger capital gain than simply the purchase price of the bond minus the sale price. Let's look at an example:

EXAMPLE

An investor buys a corporate bond with a 10-year maturity for $1,100, and chooses to amortize the premium. Four years later, the bond is sold for $1,160. How much of a capital gain or loss does the investor have?

First, we use our formulas:

purchase price – face value = premium

$1,100 – $1,000 = $100

premium ÷ years to maturity = loss per year

$100 ÷ 10 = $10

Next, we need to find the cost basis for the year the bond was sold:

loss per year × years held = tax loss

$10 × 4 = $40

purchase price – tax loss = adjusted cost basis

$1,100 – $40 = $1,060

Finally, we figure the gain or loss:

selling price – adjusted cost basis = gain (or loss)

$1,160 – $,1060 = $100 gain

At first glance, it might appear that the investor's gain was $60 ($1,160 – $1,100). This would be the case if the investor did not amortize, but since the investor chose to amortize we must do the calculations to adjust the cost basis to exclude the deductions the investor took in prior years for the premium.

DISCOUNTS. If a corporate bond is purchased at a discount (below par value), the IRS considers this to be a benefit to the investor and is thus a taxable event. The entire discount amount, however, is not taxed all at once. Instead the discount amount is accreted. **Accretion** is amortizing the beneficial amount over the remaining life of the bond, and adjusting the cost basis accordingly. This adjusted cost basis is then used to figure any loss or gain when the bond is sold or redeemed. The adjustment amount is a taxable event each year, treated as interest income.

From the IRS's perspective, buying a bond at a discount is no different than earning interest on the investment, because that is why the bond is discounted in the first place—to offer investors a more attractive yield. This accretion increases the cost basis of the bond each year. By accreting the discount over the life of the bond, this gets the cost basis back to par by the maturity date, so no capital gain is incurred. Here is the calculation used to figure out the cost basis adjustment that must be done.

face value – purchase price = discount

discount ÷ years to maturity = gain per year

In addition to being taxed as ordinary interest income, this gain per year figure is added to the bond purchase price each year to figure out the cost basis for that year. Thus, as we said before, the adjusted cost basis will equal the par value of the bond at maturity. But if the bond is sold earlier, the adjusted cost basis will cause the investor to have a smaller capital gain than simply the sale price of the bond minus the purchase price. That's because the investor has already paid taxes on a portion of the gain in prior years. Let's look at an example:

EXAMPLE

An investor buys a corporate bond with a 10 year maturity for $900. Four years later, the bond is sold for $1,100. How much of a capital gain or loss does the investor have?

First, we use our formulas to accrete the discount:

face value – purchase price = discount

$1,000 – $900 = $100

discount ÷ years to maturity = gain per year
\$100 ÷ 10 = \$10

Next, we need to find the cost basis for the year the bond was sold:

gain per year × years held = taxable gain
\$10 × 4 = \$40

purchase price + tax loss = adjusted cost basis
\$900 + \$40 = \$940

Finally, we figure the gain or loss:

selling price – adjusted cost basis = gain (or loss)
\$1,100 – \$940 = \$160 gain

At first glance, it might appear that the investor's gain was \$200 (\$1,100 – \$900). But since the investor had to accrete the discount and adjust the cost basis, the investor gets "credit" for taxes paid in prior years for a portion of the discount.

3.4.6

Federal Taxation of Corporations

Federal taxation of corporations in the U.S. is similar in some respects, and different in others, when compared to taxation of individuals. Both are subject to marginal tax rates for additional income earned, although the rate scales are different. Let's briefly look at corporate tax rates and treatment of dividends.

CORPORATE TAX RATES. As of the 2002 tax year, corporate tax rates have eight different brackets at the federal level, ranging from 15 percent to 38 percent. Compare this with six different marginal tax brackets for individuals, ranging from 10 percent to 38.6 percent. Corporations, though, have additional rules to contend with, which can cause them to incur additional taxes. For example, the accumulated earnings rules can subject corporations to a tax of 38.6 percent on those earnings. Personal service corporations are taxed at a rate of 35 percent regardless of income level.

Alternative minimum tax (AMT) is another area of consideration for corporations. (Individuals can also be subject to AMT, but the rules are different.) AMT is designed to ensure that wealthy individuals, corporations, and others pay at least some tax, even if they have large deductions to offset income. After all deductions are taken, certain tax preference items (such as tax-exempt interest or accelerated depreciation) are added back to adjusted gross income. After certain allowable exemptions, 20 percent of that new adjusted gross income total is taken, and the corporation pays the lower of their regular tax obligation or the AMT.

TREATMENT OF DIVIDENDS. Corporations pay income tax on interest income and dividend income received. Corporate income is treated the same as it is for individuals. With the exception of tax-exempt bonds, interest income is an immediate taxable event at all levels of government (federal, state, local), and is treated as ordinary income. Dividend income, though, is a much different situation.

U.S. corporations are permitted a **dividend exclusion,** whereby they do not have to pay corporate income tax on 70 percent of the dividend income they receive from other U.S. corporations. Individuals are not permitted any such exclusion. Corporations are given this break as an incentive to invest their capital in other U.S. corporations. Of course, the company paying the dividend has already paid tax on the money earned. The dividend exclusion rule eliminates only the double taxation that normally occurs with dividend distributions.

3.4.7

Definition and Characteristics of Money Market Instruments

Money market instruments are short-term debt obligations that are due and payable in 12 months or less. Money market instruments can be only debt securities with short term maturities. They are highly liquid and generally considered safe. Let's look at a few of these instruments and some of their characteristics.

3.4.7.1 Repurchase Agreements (REPOs)

Repurchase agreements are an arrangement between buyer and seller to sell an asset now, and then buy it back for a fixed price, and usually within a stated timeframe. It is very similar to a loan, but it is actually the sale of an asset with a locked-in agreement to buy it back. The assets involved in these types of transactions are often U.S. government securities, but they can be anything of value that is agreed upon by the parties. This arrangement is more attractive than other alternatives because the parties have more flexibility to negotiate terms that fit their particular situation. Repos are a way to park funds and make interest, or can be used by corporations, banks, and governments to cover shortfalls in inventory positions, reserve requirements, or balance sheet items. The Federal Reserve also uses repo agreements to buy and sell securities when implementing monetary policy. (We will discuss this in greater detail in Chapter 5.)

3.4.7.2 Federal Funds

Federal Funds are the monies used by commercial banks to cover reserve requirements with the Federal Reserve Banks. As such, when banks have excess reserves, these funds are often loaned to other member banks to help them meet their requirements. Most loans are overnight, and are made at the Fed Funds rate. Money can also be wired among banks to be debited or credited on a same day basis for transactions where there is no float. (Adjusting the Fed Funds rate is one of the ways that the Federal Reserve implements monetary policy objectives. We'll examine this in more detail in Chapter 5.)

3.4.7.3 Commercial Paper

Commercial paper is short-term debt that is issued by corporations to finance inventories, accounts receivable, and other obligations. Maturities range from 2–270 days to avoid registration requirements. Commercial paper issued by corporations is typically unsecured, although it is often backed by bank lines of credit. Corporations prefer commercial paper because they can get better rates than using their bank lines, plus the repayment terms can be negotiated so they're more flexible. Such debt is rated by the rating agencies discussed before, but some money market managers will not buy commercial paper since it's unsecured.

For the Series 7 exam, *if you see an answer to a question stating that commercial banks issue commercial paper, it is most likely a trick and probably the wrong answer.*

3.4.7.4 Certificates of Deposit (CDs)

Certificates of Deposit (CDs) are debt securities, usually issued by a financial institution. Negotiable CDs have a minimum face value of $100,000 and are offered by commercial banks to investors as a time deposit. Since these so-called "jumbo" CDs are negotiable, they are considered a money market instrument. (These negotiable CDs should not be confused with the "standard" CDs that are offered by neighborhood banks to depositors. Standard CDs are available in much smaller face amounts, and are not negotiable so they are not considered money market instruments.)

3.4.7.5 Eurodollars

Eurodollars are U.S. dollars that are held in foreign banks. The banks can be anywhere outside of the United States. Although many of these banks are in Europe (hence the name), they do not have to be there. These funds are available for settling transactions between companies on an international scale. **Eurodollar bonds** are debt securities that pay interest and principal in Eurodollars. These are usually traded at lower interest rates than U.S. bonds and have fewer regulatory concerns, so they are a popular money market security—especially for dealing with international transactions. (Eurodollars and Eurodollar bonds should not be confused with the new Euro currency that is being implemented as a pan-European currency. There is no connection between the two.)

3.4.7.6 Bankers' Acceptances (BAs)

Bankers' acceptances (BAs) are a time draft drawn on a particular bank, whereby the bank accepts responsibility for payment. The **time draft** designates the date on which payment will be made. BAs are a tool for handling the extension of credit. Essentially, BAs work like a letter of credit, and are often used for import-export financing or the purchase of goods and services when doing international business. Because of the bank's backing, BAs are often used as money market instruments.

For the Series 7 exam remember that *when you see "time draft" in a question, look for "banker's acceptances" in the answer (and vice versa).*

Municipal Securities

Municipal securities are debt obligations of state and local governments. They are sometimes referred to as **municipals** or **munis.** Although there are many types of municipal securities, they can be divided into two broad categories: public purpose bonds and private purpose bonds. **Public purpose bonds** benefit the general public and are afforded **tax-exempt** status. **Private purpose bonds** are those that are more than 10 percent beneficial to private parties, and as such are generally **taxable.** Most of our focus in this section will be on tax-exempt bonds.

Much of the material in this section about municipal bonds will parallel our discussion of corporate bonds. Nevertheless, municipal securities are a very big part of the Series 7 exam (as much as 20 percent of the questions), so we will revisit all important topics again. Furthermore, there are some key differences between municipal bonds and corporate bonds which we will point out as we go along because they are popular exam question material. Finally, we will look at the two main types of municipal bonds: revenue bonds and general obligation bonds.

3.4.8.1 General Characteristics

Municipal bonds have several unique characteristics which distinguish them from other bonds. Municipal securities issuers are exempt from SEC rules, but are *not exempt from the antifraud* portions of the law. (Broker-dealers who participate in municipal bond underwritings or trade in municipal securities are not exempt from SEC, NASD, MSRB or other SRO rules.)

Although many municipal bonds have an indenture agreement to make them more marketable, *it is* not *a requirement for a municipal bond to have an indenture agreement.* This may be a question on the Series 7 exam.

Generally, the interest paid on municipal bonds is tax free at the federal level. This allows municipal bonds to offer lower interest rates and still be an attractive investment. Bonds issued within the client's state of residence, and territorial bonds (Puerto Rico, Guam, U.S. Virgin Islands), normally offer tax-free interest income at the state and local level as well. Of course, capital gains made when selling municipal bonds for a profit are still fully taxable at all levels of government. Like corporate bonds, municipal bonds are rated by the rating agencies we discussed. This indicates to investors the credit quality of the bond issuer. Also, municipal bonds are usually unsecured so there is no claim on assets. Let's look at a few more key points.

Price Quotations. Municipal bond prices move freely in the open market, up or down depending on market conditions, issuer stability, and other factors (e.g., tax laws). Municipal bond prices are quoted one of two ways, **basis price** or **dollar price,** depending on the maturity structure established when the bonds were issued.

A **basis price** is an investor's yield-to-maturity at a particular bond price. The price is quoted as a percentage number. Remember, we looked at YTM calculations when we studied corporate bond yields. We said then that the theory for YTM was more important than the math on the Series 7 exam. Here's our chance to use the theory again. YTM has an inverse relationship with bond price, so if the YTM is higher than the coupon rate, the bond price must be lower than the face value and the bond is trading at a discount. If the YTM is lower than the coupon rate, the bond price must be higher than face value so the bond is trading at a premium.

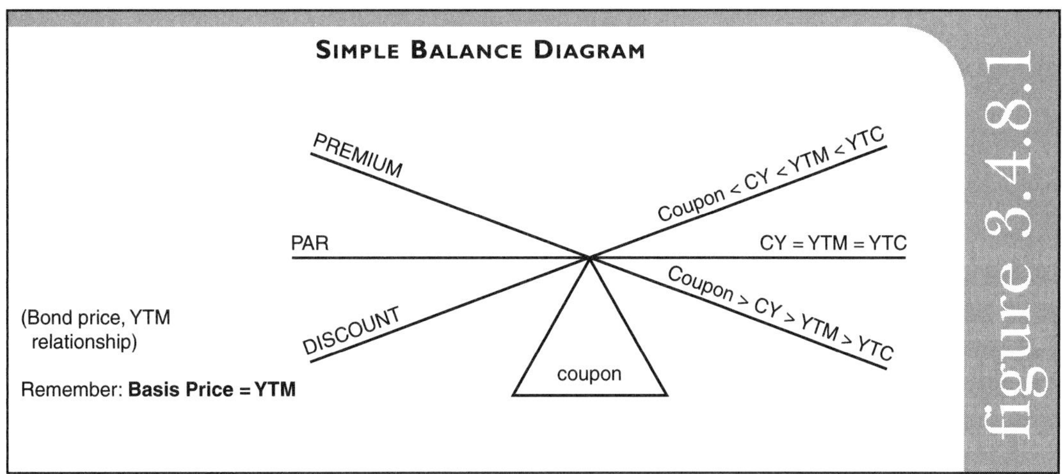

figure 3.4.8.1

This is probably the extent of what you might be asked about basis pricing on the Series 7 exam. For example, you may be given a bond with a coupon price of 5 percent that is quoted with a basis price of 5.75 percent, and you need to say whether the bond is trading at a discount or a premium. If you can remember the little diagram, you can easily answer this question because you will know that this bond is trading at a discount.

Municipal bonds that are issued as serial bonds (with staggered maturities) or as series bonds (with multiple issue dates) are quoted using the basis price method. (Do not confuse this with cost basis, which is used to determine a capital gain or loss, nor should you confuse this with basis point, which is .01% or 1/100th of a percent.)

A **dollar price** is expressed as a percentage of face value of the bond. The number is usually expressed without the percentage sign, though, just like we saw with corporate bonds. So, if we have a municipal bond with a par value of $1,000 that is quoted at 95, then the price of the bond is $950, because $1,000 × 95% = $950. If we have a muni with a par of $5,000 quoted at 110, the price is $5,500 ($5,000 × 110%). Municipal bonds that are issued as term bonds (bonds that come due all at once) are quoted using the dollar price method. This should be easy to remember, because corporate bonds are always term bonds quoted with the dollar price method, and municipal bonds that are term bonds are also quoted with the dollar price method. Municipal bonds that have different maturities (serial or series) are quoted a different way (basis price).

Forms of Ownership. Although more and more municipal bonds are being issued in book entry form to cut down on time, expense, and paperwork, municipal bonds, like corporate bonds, are issued in one of four forms. Let's review.

1. **Bearer bonds**—the person who holds the bond is the owner; coupons must be submitted to collect interest payments.
2. **Registered bonds**—the name of the bond owner is recorded on the face of the bond and with the registrar of issuing municipality; semiannual interest payments and final principal payment are automatically sent to person of record; transfer by endorsement.
3. **Registered coupon bonds** or **registered as to principal only**— the name of the bond owner is recorded on the face of the bond and with registrar of issuing municipality, and final principal payment is automatically sent to person of record; but coupons must be presented to collect interest payments.
4. **Book entry bonds**—same as registered bonds, except *no* certificate.

Interest Rate. Initially, interest rates for municipal bonds are set by the underwriter based on market conditions, strength of the issuer, and other factors. After that, the market takes over. Some bonds do offer adjustable interest rates, which tend to make the bond prices more stable, but for our purposes we will treat all municipal bonds as if they have fixed coupon rates to simplify our discussion.

Municipal bonds with interest that is tax free at the federal level can offer lower interest rates to investors because the tax advantages will offset the lower rate. At the end of this section, we will go over calculations to derive the taxable equivalent yield for tax free bond interest rates. For now, just know that if the bonds qualify for tax exempt status, they will offer lower coupon rates than other debt instruments.

Some municipal bonds also offer tax-free interest income at the state or local level (e.g., for bonds purchased by local residents), but this generally has less impact on the coupon rate of the security. Still, investors do accept lower interest rates on municipal securities than they would on corporate bonds because of these tax advantages, and also because municipalities with their taxing authority are perceived to have a lower risk of default than corporations.

Municipal bond interest payment periods are semiannual. The final interest payment is paid by the issuer with return of the principal on the date a bond matures. The buyer of a bond pays the bond price "and interest" that has accrued since the last interest payment was made, unless the bond is trading flat (without accrued interest) because the issuer has defaulted on payments or it's a zero coupon bond.

Denominations. Municipal bonds can be offered in any denomination chosen by the issuer. Generally, though, most municipal bonds are offered in $1,000 and $5,000 face values, with $5,000 being the most common amount chosen. Even though the denominations are generally $5,000, however, round lots for municipal bonds are often considered to be bonds with $100,000 of total face value.

Diversity of Maturities. Municipal bonds are issued a number of different ways, with different maturity structures to meet the needs of the issuer. The most common maturity structures are **serial, term, balloon,** and **series.**

Serial maturity issues have all bonds issued at the same time, but with staggered redemption dates. The maturity dates are scheduled at regular intervals to retire the debt over a period of time. This can help the municipality because cash flows from tax revenues can help retire debt when it comes due. Also, interest charges decrease over time as the debt is retired.

Term maturity issues have all the bonds come due at once. Because municipalities must repay a significant amount of debt in one big chunk, they usually establish a sinking fund which they pay into regularly so that the bonds' principal amounts can be paid when the bonds come due. (This is also the method used for most corporate bonds.)

Balloon maturity issues have some bonds with staggered redemption dates, but a larger number of bonds coming due on the last maturity date. This method combines the serial and term maturity methods into a hybrid. Perhaps you could think about this as being similar in concept to an interest-only loan that then requires a final lump sum payment to pay off the balance. Of course, here each bond has both an interest and a principal component that is paid off to each individual investor as each bond is retired.

Series maturity issues occur when all bonds are *not* issued at the same time. Even though an issuer may have the authority to issue a large bond offering (perhaps because of a vote of the people), debt is issued only incrementally over a period of time, or the bonds may be issued only on an as-needed basis when funds are required.

Legal Opinion. The purpose of a legal opinion with municipal bond issues is to ensure that the bonds are eligible for their tax exempt status. The issuer hires an independent attorney to examine all state and local laws, relevant legislation, and court opinions with regard to the bond issue. The attorney then issues an unqualified or qualified legal opinion. An **unqualified legal opinion** states that the attorney has thoroughly researched the contemplated bond issue, and that the municipality has the legal authority to issue the bonds. If the bonds are eligible for tax exempt status, this will also be stated in the legal opinion. If the attorney finds some problem with the issue, a **qualified legal opinion** may be issued, stating that the attorney has found that the bond issue is valid only with certain qualifications (such as the inability to confirm some essential fact, or because of pending litigation).

The legal opinion is made part of the official statement for the bond issue. The legal opinion is also distributed with the bonds, and may actually be printed right on the face of the bond. Smaller issuers may choose not to have a legal opinion done to save the expense, and thus "**ex-legal**" is stamped on all of the bond documents. This is acceptable if agreed to by the buyer prior to making any purchase of bonds.

3.4.8.2 Specific Types of Bonds

There are many types of municipal bonds. Some are backed by specific tax revenue, others by the faith and credit of the issuer. Different types have different characteristics also. Let's look at the two more common bond types first, then some other bond types you may see on Series 7 exam.

GOs. General obligation bonds (GOs) are bonds paid for out of the general revenue of the municipality, which may also use additional tax revenues or borrow funds to cover any shortfall. Tax-backed bonds offer the highest level of safety to investors. Taxes can be levied on income, on property, as sales tax, or many other user fees. In fact, the more sources of tax revenue the issuer has, the safer the issue.

GO bonds are backed by the full faith and credit of the issuer. Most GO bond issues, however, require voter approval to be enacted, especially if the bond issue will raise taxes. Some jurisdictions also have laws in place that restrict the amount of debt that a municipality can incur, or may have limitations on the tax rates that can be imposed on its citizens.

With GO bonds, it's possible that multiple taxing authorities will have jurisdiction over the same group of people, and both might issue debt that taps the same taxpayer. An example is a county and city that share the same boundaries, both issuing bonds. This debt situation is referred to as **overlapping** or **coterminous.**

Another requirement for GO bonds is that the underwriting be done by a competitive bid process. This will be explained in detail in Chapter 5. For now, let's review some of the key points to remember about GO bonds:

- type of backing: full faith and credit of issuer; issuer's taxing authority
- requirements: voter approval; competitive bid for underwriting
- unique characteristics: municipality may have legal limits on the amount of debt it can incur or the level of taxation it can impose

Revenue Bonds. **Revenue bonds** are bonds paid for from the income (revenue) generated by a specific project. These are usually used for public works projects, such as roads or water treatment plants. The revenue bonds are backed by the tolls or user fees from the project. Revenue-backed bonds are less secure than GO bonds, so yields are generally higher here. Unless specifically stated, revenue bondholders do not have a claim to other revenue sources or general tax collections to pay the debt.

Because revenue bond issues do not use tax revenue, they usually do not require voter approval. Furthermore, there are usually no restrictions on the amount of debt that a municipality can incur because revenue bonds are supposed to be self-supporting. In fact, municipalities will conduct a **feasibility study** to demonstrate to investors the economic soundness of the proposal. This will give investors the information necessary to make an informed decision, and hopefully entice them to buy the issue. Municipalities will often offer an indenture agreement as well. This is not a legal requirement, but is often a market condition for acceptance of the bonds.

The indenture agreement used with revenue bonds will often include repayment provisions in it. One such statement may be a **flow of funds** resolution that details the order in which revenues will be used. For example, the indenture may have a **net revenue pledge** that promises that after operating expenses and maintenance costs have been paid, a sinking fund will be established to ensure timely payments now, and act as a holding place for excess revenues for future payments, before any money is spent on expanding the facility. Conversely, a **gross revenue pledge** would say that debt service on the bonds is paid as a first priority—even before operational expenses.

For the Series 7 exam remember that *when you see "flow of funds" in a question, look for "revenue bond" in the answer (and vice versa).*

Revenue bonds often use what is called a negotiated underwriting to bring the issue to market. This will be explained in detail in Chapter 5. For now, let's review some of the key points to remember about revenue bonds:

- ▷ type of backing: income generated from a specific project—no taxes
- ▷ requirements: feasibility study; negotiated underwriting
- ▷ unique characteristics: may also have an indenture agreement to show flow of funds; net revenue pledge or gross revenue pledge

IDBs. Industrial revenue bonds or **industrial development bonds (IDBs)** are bonds used to finance fixed assets, which are then leased to private corporations. These are a type of revenue bond, but are usually *not* tax exempt because they are designed to help private parties, so an investor must read the official statement carefully. These are the most risky of the municipal bonds because repayment is dependent on lease payments from the corporate tenants. IDBs can be used to help revive an area, such as through the financing of an industrial park that the municipality hopes will bring high-paying jobs to the area.

- ▷ type of backing: lease payments from companies only—no taxes
- ▷ requirements: feasibility study; negotiated underwriting
- ▷ unique characteristics: may also have an indenture agreement to show flow of funds; most risky of muni bonds; *not* tax exempt

Let's take a brief look at some short-term municipal obligations.

Tax anticipation notes (TANs)

- ▷ type of backing: general obligation; full faith and credit of issuer
- ▷ unique characteristics: short-term note issued while municipality waits for anticipated tax revenue (e.g., income taxes)

Bond anticipation notes (BANs)

- ▷ type of backing: general obligation; full faith and credit of issuer
- ▷ unique characteristics: short-term note issued while municipality waits for bond issue to be complete; notes will be replaced with long-term funding once the bond issue proceeds are received

Revenue anticipation notes (RANs)

- ▷ type of backing: general obligation; full faith and credit of issuer
- ▷ unique characteristics: short-term note issued while municipality waits for anticipated revenue (e.g., sales tax) or other (e.g., aid)

Project notes (PNs)

- ▷ type of backing: **full faith and credit of U.S. government;** money through HUD
- ▷ unique characteristics: short-term note issued to finance public housing projects or urban renewal, repaid with permanent long-term bonds (called either **New Housing Authority [NHA] bonds** or **Public Housing Authority [PHA] bonds**) when the project is complete; bonds trade flat

Construction loan notes (CLNs)

- ▷ type of backing: general obligation; full faith and credit of issuer
- ▷ unique characteristics: short-term note issued while municipality waits for long-term financing upon project completion

Demand notes (variable rate)

▷ type of backing: general obligation; full faith and credit of issuer

▷ unique characteristics: short-term note; pays variable interest rate tied to another index (e.g. T-bills); principal price is more stable

Tax exempt commercial paper

▷ type of backing: general obligation; full faith and credit of issuer

▷ unique characteristics: short-term note issued while municipality waits for other revenue; maturities of 2–270 days; more flexible

There are also many special types of municipal bonds.

Special tax bonds are revenue bonds that are paid from special tax collections only. These are long-term bonds issued by a municipality to finance a specific project. Some special taxes include excise taxes on liquor, hotel bed taxes, and other use taxes. The municipality may decide to issue a special tax bond if a project will only benefit a certain segment of the public. For example, the municipality may impose a car rental surcharge tax when it wants to issue special tax bonds to improve the airport. Thus, those who will benefit from the project most will also bear most of the burden for the special tax. Note, though, that special taxes don't have to be related to the project that the special tax bonds will finance.

Special assessment bonds are revenue bonds that are paid from special assessment collections only. Special assessment bonds are long-term bonds issued by a municipality to finance a specific project. These are very similar to special tax bonds, except that here only those specific individuals benefitting from the project must pay the assessment. For example, the municipality may impose a special assessment and issue special assessment bonds when it needs to put in a new sewer for everyone on the block. Remember, special assessments are collected *only* from those who will benefit from the project.

Moral obligation bonds are revenue bonds issued by a municipality, but also backed by moral obligation of the state. This usually occurs in situations when a long-term bond is issued by a municipality, but the state legislature indicates it intends to pay on the debt if issuer defaults. Such an action, though, is not binding because future legislatures can't be bound by the actions of another legislature. Thus, the state's willingness to pay on the debt is a moral obligation only, not a legal one.

Advance refunded bonds are new bonds sold in anticipation of replacing ones that are coming to maturity, or replacing bonds that are callable. Usually this is done when interest rates are more favorable to the issuer, and may be done well in advance of the original bonds actually becoming due. If the issuer is not able to immediately replace the existing bonds (perhaps because of a call protection period), then the advance refunding proceeds are invested in a safe place, such as T-bills, until needed.

Double barreled bonds are revenue bonds which are guaranteed by an additional (usually larger) entity than just the issuer. For example, if a revenue bond was issued for a water treatment plant, the municipality might also guarantee the bond as a general obligation, in addition to the revenue from the water treatment plant. Thus the investor has two sources from which to collect the interest and principal. If the water treatment plant cannot make the payments, the municipality will step in to pay, thus making this a much safer investment than the plain revenue bond.

Taxable bonds are long-term bonds issued by a municipality for private purpose projects. An example of this might be a bond issued to build a stadium for a sports team. Because of the private purpose rules, the interest income on this type of bond is not exempt from federal taxation. Taxable bonds need to offer higher yields than other revenue bonds because they do not offer the same tax advantages.

Original issue discount (OIDs) are bonds that are sold at a discount from par value when they are first issued. The discounted amount must be **accreted** over the life of the bond. That is, the discount amount is divided by the number of years to maturity and that amount is added to the cost basis each year. This yearly addition is a taxable event with a taxable bond, but with tax exempt municipal bonds it is a tax free event. Semiannual interest payments are also tax free with tax exempt munis. And because the cost basis is adjusted each year, at maturity the cost basis will equal the face value of the bond. This means that when the bond is redeemed at maturity, there is no realized capital gain. Of course, if the bond is sold prior to maturity, any gain or loss is a taxable event. (These calculations appear earlier in section 3.4.5, and later in section 3.4.8.5.)

Zero coupons are bonds that are sold at a deep discount from par because they pay no periodic interest, but instead pay the full face value at maturity. The investor receives a rate of return by the gradual appreciation of the bond from the purchase date until maturity. Nevertheless, the IRS views zero coupons as paying **imputed interest** to the bondholder. If the bond were a taxable issue, taxes would need to be paid on interest that has accrued in the investment each year. But with tax exempt municipal zero coupon bonds, the investor does not have to worry about paying taxes on imputed interest.

Alternative Minimum Tax (AMT) bonds are municipal bonds which provide tax-free interest income to the holder for regular income tax purposes, but which are considered tax preference items and must be added back in when figuring out an investor's AMT calculation for federal income tax purposes. The alternative minimum tax is designed to ensure that all wealthy individuals and corporations pay at least some tax, by also figuring the tax obligation without the inclusion of excessive deductions to which the entity may legally be entitled. By computing tax liability with and without those items, and making certain allowances, there is a minimum tax amount that must be paid.

An AMT bond is one which has the interest income ruled tax exempt as a qualified private activity bond because of the usage, but the benefit is still for too few people (e.g., less than 10 percent) to bypass the tax preference rules of AMT. Thus, the tax exempt interest amount must be added back in to the investor's AMT calculations. This is true whether or not the investor was the beneficiary of the bond proceeds or bond project. This happens sometimes with IDBs (industrial development bonds) where they may finance an improvement project that is bringing business to the area to provide jobs. Although the bond is declared tax exempt because it is providing needed jobs to the area, since only one or two businesses are benefitting from the bond the tax-exempt interest is declared a tax preference item. With AMT bonds, it is helpful to have a professional legal opinion and/or a tax opinion.

3.4.8.3 Investment Features

There are many features which must be considered before making an investment decision with municipal bonds. Beyond the different types of municipal offerings, there are other factors that affect the marketability of municipal bonds. Furthermore, an important consideration for a portfolio is diversification across different types of municipal investments, including different types of bonds and bonds from different regions of the country. Let's look at these.

Factors Affecting Marketability. When analyzing a municipal bond investment there are numerous ways to compare the relative strengths and weaknesses of the issue. Of course, of primary consideration should be the financial condition of the issuer, including past payment history, current debt loads, and future tax prospects. All factors must be considered not only among the different types of investments available on the market, but also within the different municipal bond categories themselves. For example, a revenue bond from New York City is not necessarily equal to a revenue bond from Billings, Montana. Even when looking at two revenue bonds from the same issuer for a similar project, there are still variables to consider.

Quality or **rating** of the bond can be researched by using one of the independent rating agencies. Both Moody's and S&P rate municipal bonds with the same scale as corporate bonds, with Moody's also rating short term municipal notes. Notes with a rating of MIG-1 thru MIG-4 are considered investment grade. Like corporates, municipal bond ratings signify the likelihood that the issuer will default on a debt obligation. The higher the bond rating, the more marketable the bond is. Of course, some bonds are not rated because of the size of the issue, so this should be considered.

Maturity of the issue is important in the marketability of a bond. Bonds that will mature far into the future are generally less desirable, because interest rate risks make investors less willing to tie up their money for long periods of time. Bonds that are close to maturity are much more marketable, and can be sold more quickly.

Call features of the issue are important because the uncertainty of when a bond may be called makes it less marketable due to the call risk and reinvestment risk that come with all call features. The official statement will detail any call provisions the bond may have. Bonds that aren't subject to call are worth more and more marketable.

Interest rate or **coupon** of the bond is important because it has an impact on the cost basis of the issue if it was originally purchased at a premium or at a discount. This can affect marketability for OIDs as the accreted gain becomes taxable if sold before maturity. Other interest calculations, such as yield, YTM, YTC, and tax equivalent yield are also important in determining the marketability of municipal bonds.

Block size is an important consideration in the marketability of municipal bonds because the minimum denomination is usually $5,000 (compared to $1,000 for corporates). Also, some municipal bond issues require large block purchases, and for many a round lot is $100,000 of face value. This can be a barrier for some investors. How large is the pool of investors who can afford to buy out the bond position?

Liquidity of a bond is closely related to marketability. Secondary market size for the issue and the presence or absence of an indenture agreement are just two factors that can affect how easy it will be to sell the bond for cash quickly at a good price.

Dollar price bonds have term maturities, and usually have call features that allow them to be called early. This can affect their marketability.

Issuer name can affect marketability. Local or national reputation can give the issue broader appeal. Some local issues are attractive only to local investors familiar with the issuer or the project, and who can benefit from state and local tax breaks.

Bonds in default or **trading flat** can also hamper marketability since investors may be wary of their ability to collect future interest payments, and even the principal balance when the bond matures. (Zero coupons trading flat aren't a concern.)

Sinking funds can enhance the marketability of bonds since this gives investors more assurance that the issuer will have the money ready to make payments when they come due. The official statement should address the existence of a sinking fund.

Form of ownership of the bond issue can also affect marketability. There is a trade-off between ease of transfer and security of payments. Bearer bonds may be the easiest to transfer, but entail additional risk and responsibility for the owner. Book-entry bonds take the most effort to transfer because of the notifications involved, but they offer automatic payment of interest and principal. Registered bonds fall in the middle, with ease of transfer by simple endorsement, but with automatic payments.

Safety of principal is always an important consideration in the marketability of bonds. Although credit ratings, issuer name, and sinking funds can help increase the safety of principal, bond insurance can also be purchased from private companies to guarantee payments in the event of default. Bond insurance can be purchased by the issuer or the investor, but the trade-off is lower rates and yields on the investment.

Diversification of Municipal Investments. Another consideration when investing in municipal bonds is to diversify the range and types of investments in the portfolio. This can be done by purchasing bonds from different geographical regions, which should lessen the impact if there is an economic downturn in one area of the country. Different maturity dates can also help improve the diversity of a portfolio, since this should also provide for different rates and yields for those investments, as well as for reinvesting the funds once those original bonds mature. Finally, different purpose bonds are a good idea. General obligation bonds usually offer a slightly lower return than revenue bonds, but are safer. Revenue bonds typically offer higher returns, and also offer a wide range of projects to choose from. You probably wouldn't want all of your municipal bond money invested in an IDB in one area because you could get stuck with lots of unperforming bonds. Instead, buying bonds in several types of public works projects would offer better diversification.

3.4.8.4 Early Retirement of Debt

Retiring debt early can save a municipality money because it incurs less interest costs. Municipalities may also want to retire debt before its scheduled maturity to change the terms of its debt, or to change its debt repayment schedule. There are several ways that this can be accomplished.

Call Features. **Call features** are part of the indenture agreement put forth by the bond issuer, which spells out the schedule and price for redemptions prior to maturity. Many municipal bonds have a **call protection** period during which time the bond may not be called early. A typical call protection period is 10 years, and assures the investor of receiving interest payments for at least that period of time.

Call features listed in the indenture agreement will spell out whether the bonds can be called at par, or if the issuer must pay a **call premium** for the privilege of calling the bonds early. It will also state if the call is mandatory or optional for the issuer and the investor. If a mandatory call is made, the investor stops receiving interest payments, and must surrender the bond to collect the principal sum owed.

As stated before, the call is advantageous to the issuer because it can help save interest costs, restructure debt terms, or reschedule payments. The only real disadvantage to the issuer is that it might have to pay a call premium. A mandatory call would also be a disadvantage to the issuer if the funds were not available, but this is rarely the case. Calls are generally optional for the issuer.

From the investor's perspective, a call has more disadvantages than advantages. When a bond is called, it usually means that current rates are lower now than in the investment being called. And if rates aren't lower, then it must mean that the terms are not as favorable. The issuer calls bonds only when it is to the issuer's advantage. And even if the investor receives a call premium, this is usually not enough to compensate for the lost interest that will result from having to reinvest the money at a lower rate. The only advantage is if the investor had some doubt about the issuer's ability to repay the debt, the bond issue was not widely traded, or the investor needed to get the money out but did not want to sell the bond at a discount.

The issuer could also institute a partial call. This would entail calling the oldest issues first with a serial bond (in reverse numerical order), or doing a random call for term issued bonds. This can offer some of the same advantages to the issuer, without the municipality having to come up with as much money all at one time.

Put or Tender. A **put option** is a bondholder's right to turn in a bond for payment before its maturity date. A **put bond** has this right stated in its terms, and allows the holder to redeem the bond at full face value. Sometimes the put option must be exercised on a specific date, or is offered at a specific interval of time, or can be done at any one time during the life of the bond. This is advantageous to the bondholder because it gives the investor flexibility to redeem the bond when interest rates are more favorable in other investments. It is advantageous to the issuer because put bonds can be issued at a lower rate than standard municipal bonds.

If there are no call provisions in a bond, the issuer can approach current bondholders and offer to buy their bonds. This **tender offer** may be at current market value or it may be at a premium. It is the bondholder's option whether or not to accept a tender offer. The issuer can also go into the secondary market and buy back its bonds to retire the debt. This is referred to as **tendering.**

Redemption of Bonds. **Redemption** is repayment of a debt obligation at maturity, or earlier. If done at maturity, the final interest and principal payment are made to the bondholder or holder of record and the debt is thus retired. If bonds are redeemed before they mature, they must have the call features clearly spelled out.

When redeeming the bonds early, the municipality must give prior notice of its intentions. This is normally done in the newspaper. The issuer will advertise that it is calling its bonds per the stated call features, or it will list the terms and prices of a proposed tender offer. Bondholders then contact the company to surrender or tender their bonds. If the call is mandatory, interest payments cease to accrue as of the announced date. The municipality then begins its call procedures.

The method used for the call redemption depends on the way the bonds were issued. With serial bonds, the oldest issues are paid off first (in reverse numerical order). With term bonds, the issues are paid off randomly. A municipality may call all bonds at the same time if it has completed a new issue, or has accumulated enough in a sinking fund to pay off the issue. Even then, bonds are usually called and paid as funds become available. This is sometimes called a **sinking fund redemption.**

The municipality may also institute an **extraordinary call,** repaying debt early if the source of revenue to repay the bonds no longer exists. For example, this could be because a planned toll bridge could not be built for some reason, or a trash burning power plant burned down and can no longer generate electricity—or revenue.

Refunding Methods. When bonds are "refunded" it simply means that a new issue is replacing an old one. This is different from "redeeming" bonds by paying them off. When bonds are refunded, the old ones are paid off but only because new debt has been incurred. There are several ways that refunding can be accomplished.

A **direct exchange** would be when the municipality issues new bonds, and rather than selling them and paying off the old bonds with the proceeds, exchanges the new bonds directly with current bondholders. This may be done when the source of revenue is in peril and a direct exchange is preferable to default. The call features may allow for the direct exchange, or the bondholders may do it voluntarily as a better alternative than holding bonds that are in default.

If the direct exchange is not feasible, the municipality can simply **sell a new issue** and use the proceeds to pay off the existing debt. The existing debt can be paid off as it matures, refunded at call dates, or advance refunded. **Advance refunding** is when new bonds are sold in anticipation of replacing ones that are coming to maturity, or replacing bonds that are callable. The municipality would then **refund at call dates** as soon as the bonds can be called, according to the terms of the call feature. If the issuer is not able to immediately replace the existing bonds (perhaps because of a call protection period), then the proceeds are **escrowed to maturity.** This entails investing the funds in a safe place, such as T-bills, until needed.

3.4.8.5 Pricing Municipal Securities

When pricing municipal securities, there are several mathematical calculations that are used. Some of these are the same ones you learned for U.S. government and corporate bonds, others are unique to municipal securities. We will review some of the ones we did before, and learn a few new ones.

Dollar Price. Municipal bonds with term maturities are quoted as dollar price bonds. A **dollar price** is expressed as a percentage of face value of the bond, like corporate bonds. If a municipal bond with a par value of $1,000 is quoted at 96½, then the price of the bond is $965, because $1,000 × 96½% = $1,000 × 96.5% = $965.

Yield. Yield is an important consideration when pricing any investment. **Yield** is the rate of return earned on an investment, expressed as a percentage. There are several yield calculations that we have learned thus far. The most important of these for pricing municipal securities is the yield-to-maturity. Remember, **yield-to-maturity** is the total rate of return that an investor will receive by holding a bond to maturity. YTM gives the discounted price the bond should trade at, so that the present value of all future payments equals the current price of the bond. Municipal bonds with serial or series maturities are quoted using the basis price method, which relies on YTM. A **basis price** is an investor's yield-to-maturity at a particular bond price. The price is quoted as a percentage number, and you need to be able to tell from the basis price whether the bond is trading at a premium or at a discount.

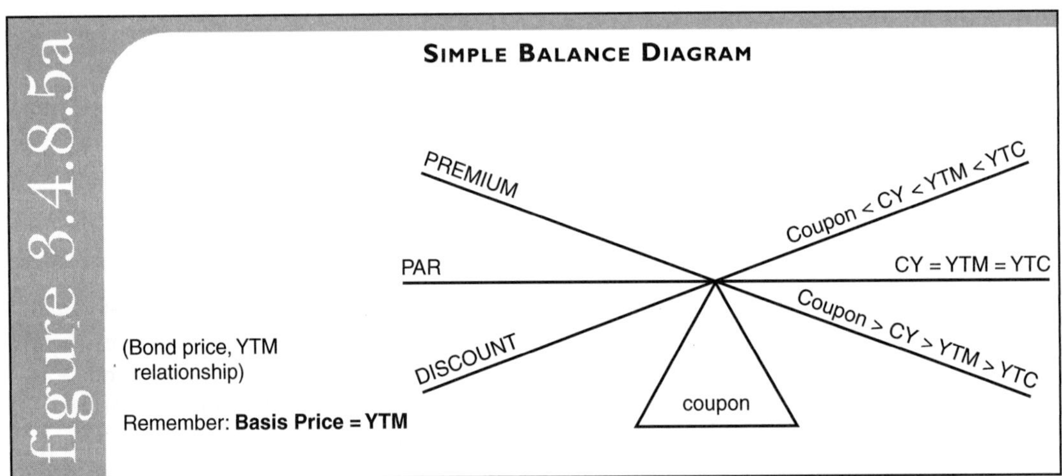

figure 3.4.8.5a

Accrued Interest. When an investor buys a bond, he or she pays the bond price "and interest" that has accrued since the last interest payment was made. Municipal bonds handle accrued interest the same way that corporate bonds do:

1. interest accrues up to, but does **not** include the settlement date;
2. cash settlement is same day a trade is made, regular way settlement is **T + 3;**
3. a **360-day year** is used to calculate accrued interest, each month has 30 days.

So for municipal securities, our accrued interest formula is:

bond face amount × interest rate × time ÷ 360 = accrued interest

Up to this point, we've always discussed accrued interest from the perspective of a buyer purchasing a bond in the secondary market and paying accrued interest to the seller. There is another instance where accrued interest can come into play (with municipal or corporate bonds). We know that bond issuers make fixed interest payments semiannually. You might think that means the issuer and original bond holder never have to worry about accrued interest, but there is an exception to this.

When a bond is first issued, the interest schedule is set by the issuer. But the first interest payment date is not always set for six months from the date of the issue. There usually is some additional time (presumably so the issue has time to sell out). So, for example, if the issue date of the bonds is January 16, the first interest payment may not be scheduled until September 1. Thus the issue has an **odd first coupon.**

An **odd first coupon** is a first bond interest payment that is for more than six months worth of interest. In this situation, the buyer of the original issue pays the price of the bond "and interest" from the **dated date** (date the bonds were issued) to the settlement date (T + 3). Then when the first interest payment is made, this amount is reimbursed to the buyer.

EXAMPLE

An investor is buying the NY muni bond at par for $1,000. The bond is a new issue with a coupon rate of 7 percent. The bond has a dated date of January 16, the trade took place Monday, March 1. How much interest accrued?

We need three numbers for our formula. The face amount is $1,000 and the interest rate is 7 percent. All we need to do is calculate the number of days.

Remember, muni computations for accrued interest use day counts of 30 days per month and 360 days per year. We count 15 days for January (the morning of the issue counts as the first day), 30 days for February (watch this!), and for March we need to count 4 days. (Remember, T + 3 is business days so if the trade occurred on Friday or before a holiday, etc., this would affect your count). We have a total of 49 days. Using our formula:

$1,000 bond × 7% interest × 49 days ÷ 360 year = $9.53 accrued interest

The question could also ask what total price did the investor paid for the bond. That would be $1,000 (purchase price) + $9.53 (accrued interest) = $1,009.53. And if the questions got really tricky (which they probably won't for accrued interest), the test might ask how much the investor's first interest payment would be. That, too, is not difficult if you remember that accrued interest the investor paid gets added back to the first payment. At 7 percent interest, one year's interest is $70, so 6 months interest is $35, plus $9.53 accrued: total is $44.53.

Amortization of Premium. If a municipal bond is bought at a premium, the premium amount (above par value) must be **amortized** over the life of the bond. That is, the premium amount is divided by the number of years to maturity, and that amount is subtracted from the cost basis each year. Because the cost basis is adjusted each year, at maturity the cost basis will equal the face value of the bond. This means that when

All municipal bonds bought at a premium must be amortized. *There is* no *choice for municipal bonds like there is for corporate bonds.*

Exam Topic Alert

the bond is redeemed at maturity, there is no realized capital loss. This is true whether the bond is an original issue or purchased in the secondary market.

This yearly subtraction would generate a loss with a taxable bond, but *not* with tax exempt municipal bonds. Since you are already earning tax-exempt income, you would be getting a double benefit if you could deduct the premium you paid for it. A taxable event is generated only if the bond is sold prior to maturity for a gain or a loss based on your adjusted cost basis. Let's review calculations for amortizing a premium:

purchase price – face value = premium

premium ÷ years to maturity = loss per year

Remember, amortizing the premium will cause our adjusted cost basis to equal par value at maturity, so we will not have any capital loss. If the bond is sold early, then we need to adjust our cost basis to determine if we have a gain or loss on the sale:

loss per year × years held = amortized loss

purchase price – amortized loss = adjusted cost basis

When the adjusted cost basis is used, the investor's gain or loss is different from simply the sale price of the bond minus the purchase price. Here's an example:

EXAMPLE

An investor buys a municipal bond with a 20 year maturity for $1,100 and sells it 4 years later for $1,200. How much is the capital gain or loss?

purchase price – face value = premium
$1,100 – $1,000 = $100
premium ÷ years to maturity = loss per year
$100 ÷ 20 = $5
loss per year × years held = amortized loss
$5 × 4 = $20
purchase price – amortized loss = adjusted cost basis
$1,100 – $20 = $1,080
selling price – adjusted cost basis = gain (or loss)
$1,200 – $1,080 = $120 gain

At first, it might look as if the investor's gain was $100 ($1200 – $1100), but since we had to amortize the premium the real, adjusted gain is $120.

Accretion of Discount. If a municipal bond is bought at a discount, it matters whether the bond is an original issue (OID) or was purchased in the secondary market. If the bond was purchased in the secondary market, you don't need to calculate anything until the bond is sold or redeemed. At the time of the sale you have a taxable event, and the sale price minus the purchase price tells you whether you had a gain or loss **(sale price – purchase price = gain or loss).**

For all muni bonds that are an original issue discount (OID), however, the discount amount (below par value) must be **accreted** over the life of the bond. That is, the discount amount is divided by the number of years to maturity, and that amount is added to the cost basis each year. This yearly addition is a taxable event with a taxable bond, but with tax exempt municipal bonds no tax is due. Because the cost basis is adjusted each year, at maturity the cost basis will equal the face value of the bond. This means that when the discounted bond is redeemed at maturity, there is no realized capital gain. But if the bond is sold before maturity, the adjusted cost basis must be calculated in order to figure out if the investor has a gain or a loss. Let's review calculations for accreting a discount:

face value – purchase price = discount

discount ÷ years to maturity = gain per year

Remember, accreting the discount will cause our adjusted cost basis to equal par value at maturity, so we will not have any capital gain. If the bond is sold early, we need to adjust our cost basis to determine if we have a gain or loss on the sale:

gain per year × years held = accreted gain

purchase price + accreted gain = adjusted cost basis

When the adjusted cost basis is used, the investor's gain or loss is different from simply the sale price of the bond minus the purchase price. Here's an example:

Example

An investor buys an OID muni bond with a 20 year maturity for $800 and sells it 4 years later for $1,100. How much is the capital gain or loss?

face value – purchase price = discount
$1,000 – $800 = $200
discount ÷ years to maturity = gain per year
$200 ÷ 20 = $10
gain per year × years held = accreted gain
$10 × 4 = $40
purchase price + accreted gain = adjusted cost basis
$800 + $40 = $840
selling price – adjusted cost basis = gain (or loss)
$1,100 – $840 = $260 gain

At first, it might look as if the investor's gain was $300 ($1,100 – $800), but since we had to accrete the discount the real gain is $260.

Bond Price Relationships. Bond price relationships are the same for U.S. government bonds, corporate bonds, and municipal bonds. Bond price has an inverse relationship with yield. Remember, yield is expressed as a percentage. If a bond is bought at a discount, the yield is higher than the coupon rate of the security. If a bond is bought at a premium, the yield is lower than the coupon rate. This is true for CY, YTM, and YTC. The best way to illustrate this is to review our balance diagrams:

Taxable Equivalent Yield. As we've stated before, investors are willing to accept a lower yield on municipal securities because they are considered safer than corporate bonds and because of the tax advantages. It's difficult to quantify the safety aspect, but there are calculations that can be done to figure the tax advantages.

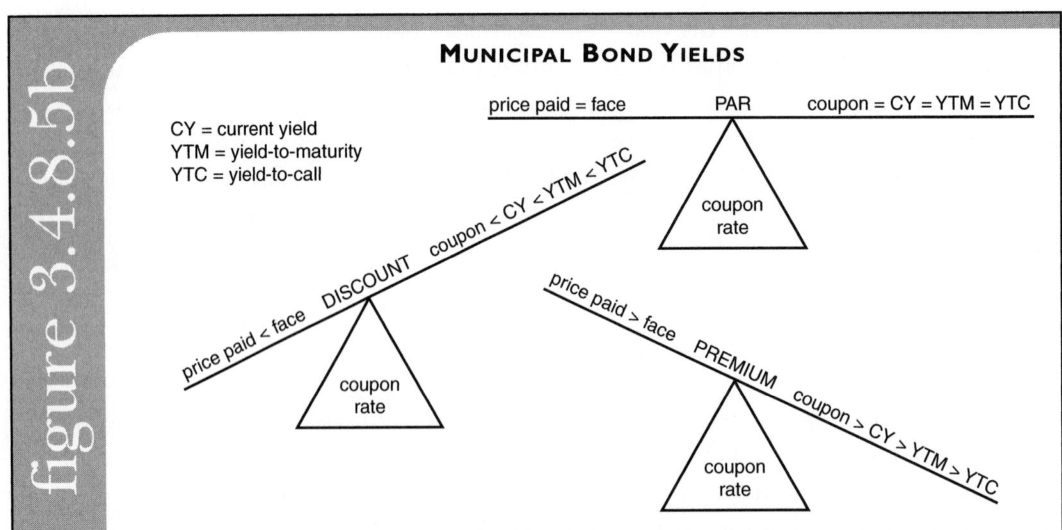

Remember: CY, YTM, YTC all have an inverse relationship with bond price.
This concept is extremely important for the Series 7 exam!
Be aware that the coupon rate is always the fulcrum on which the balance hinges.
The coupon rate stays constant as the CY, YTM, YTC and bond price move up and down.

Taxable equivalent yield is the yield that would have to be paid out on a taxable bond in order for it to equal the yield paid out on a tax-free bond. In other words, what yield on a corporate bond would give an investor the same yield as a tax-free municipal bond. The muni bond will usually have a lower yield. This formula tells the investor how much less of a yield is acceptable on the municipal bond.

municipal bond yield ÷ (1 – investor's tax bracket) = taxable equivalent yield

The number will be different for different investors because it is dependent on the investor's tax bracket. Let's do an example.

EXAMPLE

An investor is considering a municipal bond that pays 4 percent. If the investor is in a 36 percent tax bracket, what is the equivalent corporate bond yield?

municipal bond yield ÷ (1 – investor's tax bracket) = taxable equivalent yield

4 ÷ (1 – .36) = 6.25

So for our investor, a muni bond paying 4 percent is equal to a corporate bond paying 6.25 percent.

Net Yield After Tax. For most bonds, this is an important consideration. Investors count only money that they keep when deciding if something is a good investment. For taxable bonds, you would need to subtract from the return a percentage equal to the investor's tax bracket in order to find the net yield after tax. For example, if a taxable bond is earning 10 percent, but the investor is in the 36 percent tax bracket, then 36 percent of that 10 percent return must also be paid out in taxes. That means that a 10 percent yield is really only a 6.4 percent net yield after tax. For long-term capital gains, it would be only a 20 percent tax bite, but that amount must come out to figure net yield.

With municipal bonds, though, this is not an issue for OID bonds held to maturity. Since premiums are amortized and discounts are accreted, the cost basis at maturity is equal to par so there is no gain or loss to consider. The yield of the bond is the net yield after tax as well. If muni bonds are sold before maturity, then the net gain or loss, after using the adjusted cost basis, is treated the same as taxable bonds.

Current Yield. As we saw before, **current yield** is the coupon rate of the bond divided by the purchase price paid: **Current Yield (CY) = coupon ÷ price.** CY is a relative price that depends on the price you actually pay to acquire the bond. Let's assume you buy a bond with a face value of $1,000 and a coupon rate of 10 percent. If you paid $1,000 for the bond, your coupon rate is 10 percent and your current yield is 10 percent. But if you could buy the bond at a discount for $500, now your current yield is 20 percent.

Yield-to-Call. As we saw before, **yield-to-call (YTC)** is the total rate of return that an investor will receive by holding a bond until it is called by the issuer, assuming the call is made at the first opportunity. YTC gives the discounted price the bond should trade at, so that the present value of future payments up to the first call date equals the current price of the bond. Like YTM, YTC has an inverse relationship with bond price, so if the YTC is higher than the coupon rate, the bond price must be lower than the face value and the bond is trading at a discount. If the YTC is lower than the coupon rate, the bond price must be higher than face value so the bond is trading at a premium. Again, the theory for YTC is more important than the math on the Series 7 exam. (If you want to review the calculations, see section 3.4.4.6.)

In reviewing the balance diagrams, note that we have added YTC. There are two relationships you need to know. First, remember CY, YTM, and YTC all have an inverse relationship with bond price. And second, in the diagram you can see that YTC is always "more extreme" than CY or YTM. So:

if the bond was purchased at a premium, then coupon > CY > YTM > YTC
if the bond was purchased at a discount, then coupon < CY < YTM < YTC

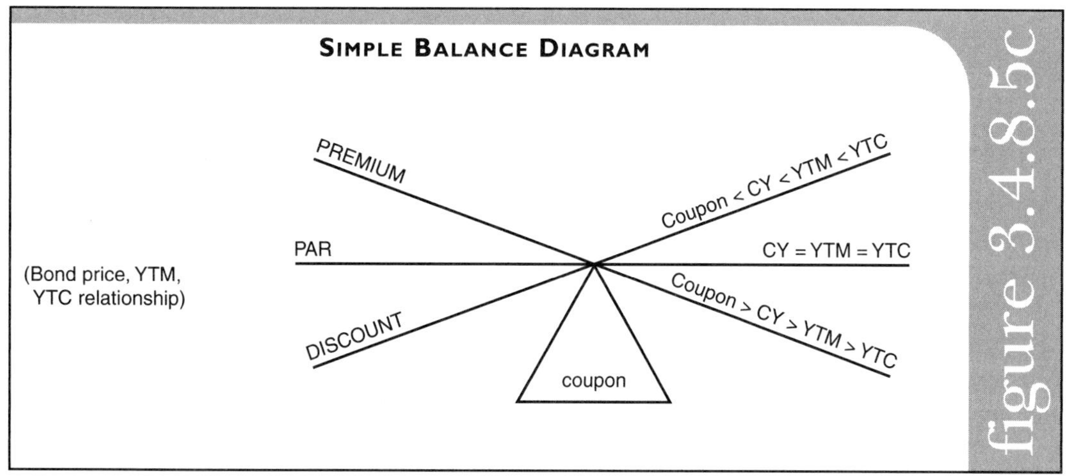

figure 3.4.8.5c

Remember: CY, YTM, YTC all have an **inverse** relationship with bond price.

Points and Fractions. When discussing bond prices, we often talk about points and fractions of points. Bond yields are also talked about this way. A **point** is equal to one percent change in the value of a bond. When we start talking about fractions of a point, we use **basis points.** A **basis point** is 1/100 percent, or .01 of yield. A basis point is the smallest unit of measure used to quote yields. It takes 100 basis points to equal 1 percent. So if we say that the yield on a bond is 1/4 point higher, we are saying that it rose 0.25 percent, or 25 basis points.

Traded Flat. Bonds that are traded flat are the opposite of bonds that are traded "and interest." **Traded flat** means that the bond trades at the quoted price without accrued interest. Accrued interest is not figured in situations where no interest is paid (e.g., zero coupons), or where it is uncertain whether or not the interest will actually be paid (e.g., the issuer is in default). The buyer of a bond that is traded flat simply pays the quoted price. If the interest in default is actually paid on a future date, the buyer has no obligation to reimburse the previous holder.

3.4.8.6 Tax Treatment of Municipal Securities

We have touched on some of the tax considerations with municipal securities as they related to other points. Here we will review and summarize some of the more important ones.

Discounts and Premiums in the Secondary Market. If a municipal bond is purchased in the secondary market at a discount, then the purchase price is the cost basis until it is sold. At the time of the sale you have a taxable event, and the sale price minus the purchase price tells you whether the investor had a gain or loss.

If a municipal bond is purchased in the secondary market at a premium, the premium amount must be **amortized** over the life of the bond, and subtracted from the cost basis each year. Thus, at maturity the cost basis will equal the face value of the bond. This means that when the bond is redeemed at maturity, there is no realized capital loss. A taxable event is generated only if the bond is sold prior to maturity for a gain or loss, based on the investor's adjusted cost basis.

OID. For all muni bonds that are an original issue discount (OID), the discount amount must be **accreted** over the life of the bond, and added to the cost basis each year. This yearly addition is considered interest income, but with tax exempt municipal bonds no tax is due. At maturity the cost basis will equal the face value of the bond. This means that when the discounted bond is redeemed at maturity, there is no realized capital gain. A taxable event is generated only if the bond is sold prior to maturity for a gain or loss, based on the investor's adjusted cost basis.

Margin Purchases. If municipal bonds are purchased on margin, the investor may *not* also take a tax deduction for any interest expenses.

Federal Income Tax Status. Municipal bonds that qualify as tax exempt are not subject to federal income tax for any interest earned. Capital gains rules still apply, though, if the bond is sold for a gain.

State and Local Tax Status. Municipal bonds issued by the state or locality where an investor is a resident may also qualify as tax exempt from state and local income tax for any interest earned. Capital gains rules still apply, though, if the bond is sold for a gain. (Nonresidents are still subject to state income taxes.)

Taxable Equivalent Yield. This formula is used to calculate what yield on a corporate bond would give an investor the same yield as a tax-free municipal bond. The muni bond will usually have a lower yield. This formula tells the investor how much less of a yield is acceptable on the municipal bond.

municipal bond yield ÷ (1 – investor's tax bracket) = taxable equivalent yield

The number will be different for different investors because it is dependent on the investor's tax bracket. Know, too, that we could start with the taxable bond rate, and figure the net yield after tax, to allow us to compare the taxable bond to the tax exempt muni bonds. For example, if a taxable bond is earning 10 percent, and the investor is in the 36 percent tax bracket, then 36 percent of that 10 percent return must also be paid out in taxes. Thus, a 10 percent yield is really only a 6.4 percent net yield after tax. For long-term capital gains, it would only be a 20 percent tax bite, but that amount must come out to figure net yield.

Accrued Interest. Accrued interest that is paid when purchasing a municipal bond is added to the investor's cost basis.

AMT. **AMT bonds** are municipal bonds which provide tax free interest income to the holder for regular income tax purposes, but which are considered tax preference items and must be added back in when figuring out an investor's AMT calculation. An AMT bond is one which is for a qualified private activity, but too few people benefit from the project to bypass the tax preference rules of AMT. Thus, the tax exempt interest amount must be added back in to the investor's AMT calculations when figuring the investor's federal income tax liability.

3.5 Packaged Securities

When we talk about packaged securities, there are actually a number of investment products that fall into this category. **Packaged securities** are investments which are created by combining several other investments. Those of you who already have your Series 6 securities license are probably very familiar with these. And many of you may have already invested in one of the more popular packaged securities—mutual funds. Just as there are many different kinds of mutual funds, there are many more kinds of other packaged securities available: unit trusts, life policies, variable annuities, and REITs. We will examine some of the packaged securities you are likely to see on the Series 7 exam and in your career as an RR.

3.5.1

Characteristics of Investment Companies, Variable Annuities, REITs

Packaged securities can readily be divided into three categories based on the players involved with assembling and managing the packaged securities. **Investment companies** are separate corporations set up for the sole purpose of packaging securities, collecting funds, investing funds, and managing the portfolio. **Variable annuities** are packaged securities often put together by insurance companies, who are responsible for managing the funds in the investment portfolio. **Real estate investment trusts (REITs)** are separate trusts that specialize in real estate investment, collect funds to control real estate, and manage the portfolio.

All of these packaged securities are offered as a way for small investors to pool their money and benefit from a larger, more diversified, and professionally managed portfolio. There are some important differences, however. Investment companies are set up to offer direct returns to investors, allowing them to share in the gains and losses of the portfolio. Variable annuities, at the other extreme, offer guaranteed payments to the investor for life, although the amount is not guaranteed. REITs allow investors to share in the gains, but they cannot deduct any losses. Let's examine each of these packaged security entities more closely.

3.5.2

Investment Companies

Investment companies are firms that assemble a pool of funds from small investors, invest those funds for the group, and collect a management fee for services. Investment companies are formed like any other corporation, with shares available to investors. Investors who own shares in the investment company also own part of the large joint investment account created by the pool of money from all the investors.

Investment companies can be conveniently divided into two groups: management companies and nonmanagement companies. Management companies are the more common of the two, and we will spend a good deal of time analyzing these in the next few sections. The main distinguishing feature, as the name implies, is that the management companies have a manager responsible for actively managing the company's investment portfolio. Mutual funds fall into this group. Nonmanagement companies, on the other hand, have a fixed portfolio that investors put their money into, so there is no need for a portfolio manager. Unit trusts are an example of these.

3.5.2.1 Management Companies

Management companies are in the business of managing money for other people. As such, they're under the jurisdiction of the SEC. To qualify for SEC registration, all management companies are required to have at least 100 investors and $100,000 in assets prior to, or within 90 days of, registration. The management company is also required to file its stated investment objectives, and other information depending on what type of management company it will be. There are two basic kinds of management companies: **closed end** and **open end.**

Closed End. Closed end management companies are investment companies that offer a fixed number of shares to investors, and use the funds raised to operate a packaged security. Shares of the closed end fund trade on an exchange, and this serves as the vehicle for investors to buy and sell their positions after the initial offering. Closed end investment companies operate just like any other company, except that the company's business is to make money through investments rather than products or services. The company issues stock to raise capital, and then hires a money manager to manage the company's investments.

The company is "closed end" because after the initial offering of shares to the public, the fund is closed out and no further investments are accepted. Investors who want to invest in the company do so by buying shares of stock in the open market; investors who want to cash out their positions do so by selling their shares in the open market. Only full shares may be bought and sold. This is all very different from open end management companies, as we will see in the next section. Also, a closed end company may issue additional common stock, preferred stock, or bonds at some point in the future, but it must go through the SEC registration process again. By contrast, open end investment companies have only one kind of stock, which is part of a continuous stock offering.

Open End. Open end management companies are investment companies that continually offer shares to investors, and use the funds raised to operate a packaged security, such as a mutual fund. Shares of the open end fund can only be sold and redeemed by the particular fund that issued them.

The goals of an open end company are similar to those of a closed end company: raise capital through an offering, hire a money manager to manage the company's investments, make money through investments. By offering shares continuously, though, some of the dynamics change. For example, the open end company must always use a prospectus when selling shares, whereas the closed end fund shares trade in the secondary market with no prospectus. Furthermore, the open end structure allows for investors to buy partial shares, since they are offered only by the fund itself. And since the open end company is the only outlet for selling the shares, it must, by law, redeem shares within seven calendar days after they are tendered.

Another important difference is that because the open end company does a continuous offering, the fund can continue to grow over time. As the fund sells more shares, it absorbs this new money and puts it to work to buy more assets for the benefit of everyone in the fund. This can best be seen by exploring the structure and characteristics of a common open end investment company vehicle: the mutual fund.

chart 3.5.2.1

COMPARISON OF CLOSED END VS. OPEN END MANAGEMENT COMPANIES

Closed End	Open End
• fixed # of shares	• variable # of shares (no limit)
• can issue more stock, bonds, etc. but need to reregister with SEC	• only one type of stock permitted because it's a continuous primary offer
• give out prospectus only at initial offering	• must always give out prospectus
• buy and sell on exchange (after offering)	• can buy from, and redeem thru, issuer only
• can purchase only whole shares	• partial shares can be purchased
• price is supply & demand (after offering)	• public offering price (NAV + sales charge)

Mutual funds are a pooled investment, managed by an investment company, offering an undivided interest in the portfolio to holders of shares in the fund. In fact, this "undivided interest" is where the name "mutual" fund comes from. Mutual funds, like mutual insurance and other mutual companies, have shared ownership with profits distributed among the members.

The three main advantages to a mutual fund are liquidity, diversification, and professional management. Liquidity comes from the fact that even though the fund itself is the only "market" for the shares, by law it must redeem shares within seven calendar days. Diversification is maintained by an investor because even after selling some mutual fund shares, the remaining shares held still have the same balance of portfolio investments. This would not be possible with a small individual portfolio because selling off part of one's holdings would entail sacrificing one part or one sector of the portfolio. Finally, professional management offers small investors access to money managers and experts specializing in different types of investments. Let's explore the mutual fund management structure and operation a little more.

The **structure and operation** of a mutual fund is a collage of different persons, groups, and organizations interacting in their respective roles to make the open end investment company operate successfully. There is a Board of Directors, Investment Advisor, Underwriter, and Custodian. Other important role players are the transfer agent, accounting firm, and legal advisors. All of these groups work together towards reaching the fund's objectives, balanced by shareholder rights in the mutual fund.

- ▷ **Board of Directors** has the primary responsibility of engaging the services of the investment advisor, as well as deciding who to use as custodian and transfer agent. The Board of Directors can enter into contractual arrangements with the underwriter who will act as sponsor and distributor for the mutual fund. The Board is also responsible for choosing the direction of the fund, specifying the type of fund it will be, and the objectives the fund is trying attain.
- ▷ **Investment Advisor** is the one who is responsible for carrying out the goals and objectives of the fund on a daily basis. The investment advisor can also be referred to as the portfolio manager. This individual or firm (as is usually the case) is charged with carrying out the investment policies described in the fund's prospectus and reg-

istration letter filed with the SEC. The investment advisor tries to make the fund's investments grow. The investment advisor

1. may not delegate or subcontract any duties without the fund's okay
2. needs to be keenly aware of what is and is not permitted for investing
3. has a two year contract, then renewed annually by shareholder vote
4. is paid a percentage of the assets under management

▷ **Underwriters** have the job of marketing the mutual fund to retail broker dealers and to the investing public. The underwriter is also referred to as the sponsor, distributor or wholesaler because he acts in these capacities at various times in the process. The retail broker-dealers enter into a selling agreement with the wholesale sponsor to resell shares to the investing public. Unless it is a no-load fund (explained later), the fund may not act as its own underwriter or distributor.

Although the underwriter may not buy excess shares to keep in his inventory, the underwriter may act as a distributor and sell shares directly to the public. The customer always pays the public offering price no matter who the shares are purchased from. The underwriter receives a percentage of the total sales charge as a fee for selling and marketing the fund. The underwriter is also responsible for developing the fund's sales literature, which must be filed with the NASD within 10 days of first use.

▷ **Custodian's** primary job is the safekeeping of the securities owned by the mutual fund. The custodian cannot be owned by or controlled by the mutual fund. It must be an independent trust organization, whose duties include

1. physically securing (locking up) securities owned by the mutual fund
2. maintaining a restricted admissions list so that not just anyone can show up and enter the place where the securities are held
3. only allowing authorized access and withdrawal of the securities
4. admitting independent auditors authorized to check on the securities
5. keeping a records handling system that is approved by the NYSE

Rights of shareholders hold the structure and operation of the mutual fund in check. Certainly the largest power the shareholders have is to vote with their money—if they don't like what the fund is doing, they will redeem their shares and invest elsewhere. Some power is wielded by shareholders within the mutual fund structure, however, since they vote for the board of directors and are permitted by law to have final say (by majority vote) of any changes in direction or objectives for the mutual fund.

Mutual fund objectives can range from very aggressive growth funds to income funds to more conservative funds that have capital preservation as their main objective. Let's look at a few of these.

▷ **Growth funds** invest a greater portion of their assets in higher risk company stocks, such as high-tech, or in other industries that appear poised for growth. As we learned before, growth companies often do not pay dividends because they reinvest profits in research and development to fuel their growth. Growth funds are also sometimes referred to as diversified common stock funds because of their emphasis on stocks to achieve the fund's primary objective of capital growth. This type of fund is best suited for money that will not be used for retirement or other expenses until well into the future so that the money has time to grow.

▷ **Income funds** invest primarily in preferred stocks and bonds. Generally, if income potential is preferred by an investor, then there is less potential for growth of capital. By looking to acquire high yielding stocks and bonds, utility company stocks, and blue chips that consistently pay dividends, the fund can meet its objectives of providing

income. This type of fund is best suited for investors who need cash flow or near term funds, perhaps for retirement.

- **Capital preservation funds** invest in safe securities, such as U.S. government securities, Ginnie Maes, and only the highest-rated bonds and stocks. This is a very conservative investment vehicle for the investor who does not want to take any risks with equity stocks or non-investment grade corporate bonds. *(Remember, Ginnie Maes are pass-through certificates;* not *bonds.)*
- **Balanced funds** seek to have all areas covered by investing in common stock, preferred stock, bonds, and cash in order to achieve the highest returns with high stability. A typical structure would be about half stock and half bonds, with perhaps 5 percent of the assets in cash. This allocation would be adjusted as market conditions change. These funds try to balance growth and income by diversifying the portfolio not only with different investment vehicles, but also across different industries, and throughout various regions of the country.

  Balanced funds that have multiple asset classes are usually referred to as **asset allocation funds.** This type of fund not only invests in different kinds of stocks (e.g., small cap, large cap), but also will tilt its asset balance between stocks, bonds, and cash much more heavily (perhaps as high as 80 percent stock at one time, 80 percent bonds another) depending on market conditions.

Mutual fund types can also be segregated by portfolio composition. Sometimes the composition of the portfolio is set up to mirror an objective. Other times, maintaining the unique composition of the portfolio *is* the objective. Here are a few examples.

- **Bond funds** invest in various types of bonds and with different maturities to meet the objectives of the fund. Certainly income is one objective, but there can be others. Funds that invest in municipal bonds can offer tax-free income, because tax advantages flow through to the investors. Funds investing in U.S. government bonds exclusively can offer even safer income, whereas funds investing in corporate bonds can seek different yields based on bond quality.
- **Money market funds** invest in money market instruments, such as short-term notes, commercial paper, banker's acceptance, repurchase agreements, government securities close to maturity, and T-bills trading in the secondary market. Money market funds serve as a good way to preserve capital while providing liquidity. Often fund holders can write checks against their money market fund accounts (but usually with restrictions as to number or amount). To meet the liquidity needs, the SEC imposes certain requirements:

  1. must be all debt securities, short-term maturities (average < 90 days)
  2. must be no load, low expense ratios (usually 0.5%), NAV=$1 per share

  (We will explain some of these terms in the next few sections on fund costs.)
- **Sector funds** invest in companies that are in a particular industry or "sector" of the economy. The sector could be chosen because it is seen as one that has high growth potential (e.g., high tech), or the sector may be chosen because it is a cyclical or counter-cyclical sector (e.g., energy, gold).

Although sector funds offer the potential of high returns or can act as a hedge for other investments, *on the Series 7 exam, do not put beginning investors in a sector fund.*

- **Index funds** are designed to track a particular recognized index, and match its portfolio composition and movements. Thus, rather than trying to "beat" the market, the index fund follows along and shares the same capital growth over time. Some recognized indices include the Standard & Poor's 500, the Wilshire 5000, Shearson-Lehman

Long-Bond Index, and the Morgan-Stanley Europe-Asia-Far East Index. There are three advantages to indexed funds:

1. less capital gains tax than other funds, because there's less buying and selling of shares (indices don't change components too often)
2. lower portfolio management costs, because there are fewer trades
3. manager name does not need to be revealed (because following index)

For the Series 7 exam, make sure you know that with an index fund, the *portfolio manager is only trying to* match *the index, not beat it.* Also know that *lower capital gains taxes* are an advantage to an index fund investor. On the Series 7 exam, always assume your client is a taxable investor and concerned about tax consequences unless you are specifically told otherwise.

Marketing of mutual funds is an involved process. As we saw before, in addition to the fund itself, there is usually a distributor and a broker-dealer involved in the transaction. But we also saw that no matter where the customer ultimately purchased the mutual fund shares, the investor was always charged the public offering price (POP). This is, in fact, an NASD rule. Only NASD members may buy fund shares at a discount.

The POP that the customer pays is actually a combination of the net asset value (NAV) of the fund plus the sales charges. When a customer sells shares back to the fund, the redemption price is always the NAV. We will discuss sales charges in greater detail in the next section. Here we will discuss the NAV, POP and others.

▷ **Net asset value (NAV)** is calculated as follows:

(Fund Assets – Fund Liabilities) ÷ # Outstanding Shares = NAV per share

Unlike a stock which is actively traded in the secondary market and can have different prices from minute to minute, mutual funds are priced once a day (usually at the end of the day). After stocks stop trading, the fund adds up the value of all its stocks and other assets, and calculates its NAV. This figure is then used to fill buy or sell orders that have been received. Since the buy and sell orders for mutual fund shares are placed before the final price is known, this is called **forward pricing.** In fact, investors buying mutual fund shares don't even know how many shares they will get until the end of the day when the NAV is calculated.

A popular test topic is what affects NAV. Lots of money going in and out of the fund to buy shares or redeem them does *not* change the NAV because they offset each other: more money coming in to buy shares equals more outstanding shares to divide the total by; money going out to redeem shares equals fewer shares to divide the total by. The primary effect on NAV is the market value of the stocks owned by the fund. Corporate dividends paid into the fund from stocks in the portfolio and reinvestment of dividends can also affect NAV. This is because these actions affect the asset value in the fund without changing the number of shares. Interest rates can also affect NAV if bonds are part of the fund.

Understand that **POP is the same as the "ask" price** when we talk about other securities and **NAV is the same as the "bid" price.** Thus, the difference between the POP and the NAV represents the sales charge, or **spread** or **load,** of the fund.

This formula may appear on the test: **POP – NAV = Sales Charge**

▷ **Public offering price (POP)** is computed by adding the NAV plus the sales charges. Sales charges may not exceed 8.5 percent per NASD rules. We will discuss sales charge calculations in depth in the next section.

▷ **Reinvestment of dividends and/or capital gains** may be done by the investor at less than the POP price, provided that certain conditions are met:

1. provisions for reinvestment of dividends and/or capital gains must be in the fund's prospectus
2. fund holders all have an equal opportunity to do a reinvestment
3. fund holders are notified annually of their right to reinvestment
4. reinvestment programs must not place a financial burden on the fund

Note that the fund may still impose a handling charge for providing the reinvestment service, but it must be reasonable and cannot equal the regular sales charge. Also, even if dividends or capital gains are reinvested, they still are a taxable event to the investor. Taxes are due and payable on the reinvestment, and the investor adds that amount to the adjusted cost basis.

Exam Topic Alert

For the Series 7 exam, know that reinvested dividends and capital gains are taxable.

▷ **Dollar cost averaging (DCA)** is an investment method whereby a set dollar amount is invested at regular intervals. Even though the investor buys fewer shares when the price is high, since he or she can buy more shares when the price is low this produces a lower average price per share and a lower total investment cost than could be achieved by buying a set number of shares at those same intervals. Furthermore, this average price per share is lower than the average share price. Let's look at a quick example to illustrate this.

Using Dollar Cost Averaging to invest the same amount at each interval:

INTERVAL	$ INVESTED	$ PER SHARE	# SHARES BOUGHT
March 31	$300	$10	30
June 30	$300	$ 7.5	40
Sept. 30	$300	$10	30
Dec. 31	$300	$15	20
	total $1200	**avg. $10.63**	**total 120**

So average cost to investor was only $1,200 ÷ 120 shares = $10 per share.

Without using Dollar Cost Averaging, buying same # of shares at each interval:

INTERVAL	$ INVESTED	$ PER SHARE	# SHARES BOUGHT
March 31	$300	$10	30
June 30	$225	$ 7.5	30
Sept. 30	$300	$10	30
Dec. 31	$450	$15	30
	total $1275	**avg. $10.63**	**total 120**

Without using dollar cost averaging, the investor must spend more money to get get the same number of shares, and pays a higher average cost per share ($10.63).

Of course, if the market keeps heading in one direction, DCA really doesn't help. And this method certainly does not guarantee profits or a certain rate of return. It is merely a method to help investors maximize their investment dollars. DCA lends itself well to mutual funds because investors can buy full or fractional shares, whereas with regular stocks an investor would be forced to buy round lots (or at least full shares) so it's unlikely the same amount of money can be invested each time.

- ▷ **Exchange privileges** within families of funds are generally permitted without sales charges. This allows investors to move their investments back and forth between growth and income, depending on their needs and perception of current market conditions. This is often a selling point when mutual funds are being marketed. The more variety that is offered the more flexibility the investor has. Keep in mind, though, that even though exchanging within a family of funds does not incur sales charges, it is *still a taxable event* that may generate a capital gain or loss for the investor.

Mutual fund sales charges can come in a variety of forms. Even so-called "no load" funds that don't have sales charges can charge "marketing fees." Let's sort out some of the different fees and expenses that are associated with open end mutual funds, explain some computations, and look at some ways that those sales charges and fees can be reduced. (Keep in mind, though, that these sales charges and fees apply only to open end mutual funds. Closed end funds are purchased OTC so they have brokerage commissions or markups instead.)

- ▷ **No load** means that there are no sales charges to fund holders for buying the mutual funds. No load funds are usually purchased directly from the fund company. For no load funds, the POP, NAV and market price are all the same, since no sales charges are added to the NAV (as is the case with load funds).
- ▷ **Load** is the sales charge added to the price of an investment. A load fund is sold by a broker-dealer or registered representative to investors. With that added sales charge comes investment advice on what to buy, when to buy, and when to sell. There are two kinds of load charges: front end and back end.

  Front end loads are taken out of the investor's proceeds right when the investment is purchased, so the investor is actually purchasing a net amount of shares. For example, if someone is investing $10,000 in a mutual fund, and there is a front end load of 3 percent, then the investor is actually only getting $9,700 worth of shares. $10,000 – $300 = $9,700. *Watch for this type of calculation on the Series 7 exam. It is likely to be part of a question that includes break point pricing (discussed shortly).*

  Back end loads are taken out when the investor sells the shares after holding them for a certain period of time. With back end loads, 100 percent of the money invested actually buys shares. The length of time shares are held determines the sales charge percentage that is charged at the time of sale, and often drops to nothing if the fund shares are held long enough. The back end load scale must be disclosed in the prospectus.
- ▷ **Distribution fees** are the compensation paid to the distributor (wholesaler, sponsor, underwriter) from the sales charges. This percentage of the sales charge is referred to as the **underwriter's concession.** The broker-dealer receives the other part of the sales charge. This is referred to as the **dealer's concession.** By NASD rule, the sales charges cannot exceed 8.5 percent, and this 8.5 percent maximum can only be charged if three conditions are met:

  1. break point pricing is offered
  2. automatic reinvestment of distributions is allowed
  3. rights of accumulation are permitted

These will be explained shortly, but essentially they are ways for investors to save sales charges later. If these three conditions are not met, the maximum sales charge permitted is 6.25 percent. The NASD does not want firms charging clients excessive fees, then adding more fees at every opportunity. In reality, though, most sales charges are much lower because of competition.

Exam Topic Alert

Note that out of all the mutual fund players—Board of Directors, Financial Advisor, Custodian, etc.—only the distributor/wholesaler/sponsor/underwriter gets paid from the sales charges. The rest are paid from the fund's net assets.

- ▷ **Management fees** are compensation to the Financial Advisor and others responsible for managing the mutual fund portfolio, paid as a percentage of the fund's net asset value. Management fees are also paid for administration and other functions within the fund. Management fees are usually an annual amount deducted from the gross assets. Typical management fees are in the 0.5 percent–2.0 percent range, but may be higher, and often have performance incentives built in. The total amount of management fees and expenses is usually limited to a certain figure. All fees must be disclosed in the prospectus.
- ▷ **12b-1 fees** are special assessments that allow mutual funds to collect money to reimburse marketing and distribution expenses. This was originally done as a way for no-load mutual funds to raise money to promote their fund, but load funds also have ways to collect these charges. The fee is figured on an annual basis, but charged quarterly to each customer's account. The fee can be no more than 0.75 percent for load funds and no more than 0.25 percent for no-load funds. The fee is not paid for investment advice, but is only for distributing and promoting the fund. A 12b-1 fee must be approved annually by:
  1. a majority vote of fund shareholders, *and*
  2. a majority vote of the Board of Directors, *and*
  3. a majority vote of the non-interested Board members.

  Termination of the 12b-1 fee can be done by a majority vote of either #1 or #3.
- ▷ **Computing sales charges** involves a few simple calculations. You will likely see one or more variations of this on the Series 7 exam, so let's take a look at some different formulas. The one you need to use will depend on what figures you are given in the question, and which number you need to solve for.

Net Asset Value + Sales Charge = Public Offering Price

POP – NAV = Sales Charge

$ Sales Charge ÷ POP = Sales Charge %

NAV ÷ (1 – Sales Charge %) = POP

These problems are not really difficult. Let's do an example to illustrate.

EXAMPLE

A mutual fund has a per share net asset value of 19 and a sales charge of 5 percent. What is the public offering price?

Since we are given the NAV and sales charge percent, the best formula to use is:

NAV ÷ (1 – Sales Charge %) = POP

19 ÷ (1 – 5 %) = POP

19 ÷ (1 – .05) = 20

So, the public offering price is $20 per share.

▷ **Sales charge reductions** are often offered to clients for quantity purchases. In fact, this is the only way investors can reduce the cost of a mutual fund since investors must always pay the POP. (Remember, only NASD member broker-dealers are permitted to buy mutual funds at a discount.) Let's look at three methods of sales charge reduction.

Breakpoints are the investment dollar levels at which investors are eligible for a reduced sales charge. Breakpoints can be achieved by combining the investment amounts of married couples, or parents and their minor children, but not for adult children, unrelated people, etc.

The RR must do what he or she can to help clients reduce sales charges. Some funds allow investments across their family of funds to count towards breakpoints, others do not. **Breakpoint selling,** so that clients' trades are always kept just below breakpoints where they would save on sales charges, **is a violation of NASD rules.**

Letters of intent is a commitment by an investor to invest a certain amount of money within 13 months, in exchange for being entitled to receive breakpoint sales charge rates now. The letter may be back-dated up to 90 days to encompass previous investments by that person. Reinvestment of dividends and capital gains do not count towards the investor's total investment commitment.

Funds are not required to offer this to clients, but it is usually done because it encourages more investment. If the client can't follow through later, the sales charge reductions must be repaid in cash or an equivalent amount of shares can be cashed in to cover the money due.

Rights of accumulation are breakpoint sales offered at a future time once the total amount of money invested has reached the breakpoint. From that point forward, all newly invested money qualifies for the reduced sales charges.

Rights of accumulation do not count the initial investment, nor are they retroactive, but they do accumulate indefinitely until the goal is reached. Also, appreciation of fund shares and reinvestment of dividends or capital gains count toward the accumulation total (unlike the letter of intent, which does not allow these to count towards the total).

Remember that for no load funds, the POP and NAV are the same. And for all calculations, *POP is always greater than or equal to NAV, never less than.*

Redemption of mutual fund shares must take place within seven calendar days in order to comply with the Investment Company Act of 1940. This is designed to protect investors since the fund itself is the only market for the fund shares. There are very few conditions under which the fund may not have to redeem the shares within seven days. This would include such things as trade restrictions on the NYSE, a redemption suspension ordered by the SEC, or other emergency.

It is important to note that when mutual fund shares are redeemed, no one else gets them. Unlike company shares of stock which trade hands, mutual fund shares are cancelled when redeemed. When clients invest money, they are always getting newly issued shares—that's why mutual funds are considered open end investment companies. They must always use a prospectus because they are always doing a primary offering.

▷ **Redemption price** for mutual fund shares is the NAV. Usually, this is only calculated once at the end of the trading day. Since the sell orders for mutual fund shares are placed before a final price is known, this is **forward pricing.** The investor will not know exactly how much money will be received until after the fund has calculated its NAV. Remember, our NAV formula is

(Fund Assets – Fund Liabilities) ÷ # Outstanding Shares = NAV per share

Some mutual funds also impose a redemption fee, primarily when shares are not held long enough. This fee combined with all others still can't exceed 8.5 percent.

- **Pay out or withdrawal plans** are a means of mutual fund redemption where the investor can receive fixed payments on a regular basis. The payments can be interest only, dividends only, or a portion of the investor's shares can be liquidated on a regular schedule. The fixed payments can be a specific dollar amount or a percentage. Usually payments are made monthly or quarterly.

  This type of plan is not designed to guarantee a lifetime of income, and the RR needs to stress this to the client. Market fluctuations can reduce the payout and funds can be exhausted. (Never show clients payout projections!) Clients should also understand that once they start to take money out, they should not put any back in because they would be wasting sales charges.
- **Conversion privilege** is the redemption of shares from one family and using the proceeds to buy another mutual fund within the same families of funds. Often there is a time limit within which the exchange must be completed in order to qualify for waived, or reduced, sales charges. Keep in mind, too, that an exchange or conversion within a family of funds is always a taxable event, so the client must be alerted to any possible tax consequences.
- **Restrictions** on redemption of shares may be imposed by the fund as long as they do not violate the Investment Company Act of 1940, and such restrictions are detailed in the fund prospectus. Some such restrictions may include a requirement that redemption of shares must be done in writing, or that shares for redemption be submitted with a guaranteed signature. Setting floor limits on how large a telephone redemption request can be is also fairly standard. Finally, many redemption restrictions involve minimum holding periods for shares in order to avoid redemption fees or qualify for reduced back end loads.

Special tax considerations are given to regulated investment companies. Under Regulation M of the IRS code, these special mutual fund companies can avoid double taxation by distributing at least 90 percent of the dividends they receive, and at least 90 percent of net income from capital gains. This is referred to as the **conduit theory, Subchapter M theory** or **pipeline theory.**

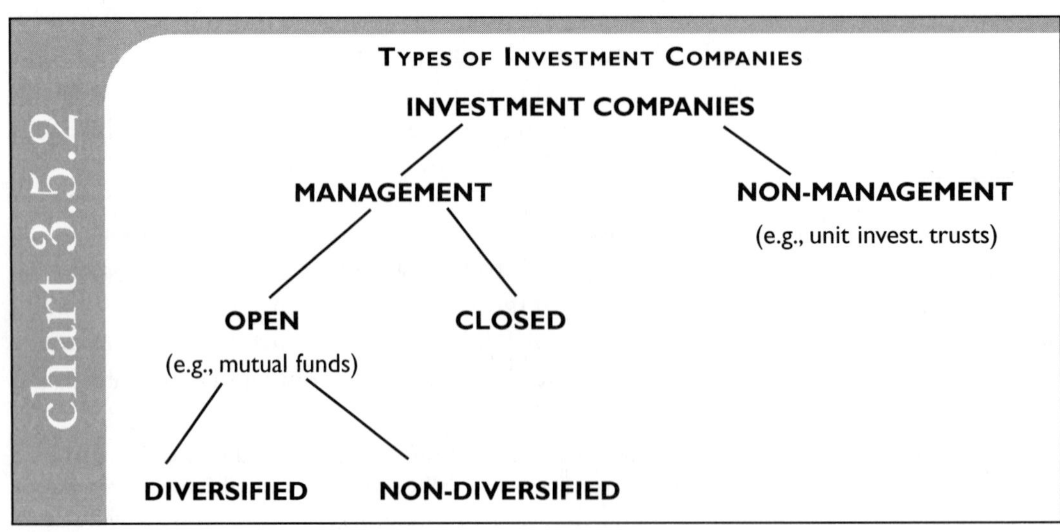

Conduit theory says that the regulated investment company that meets the IRS guidelines is merely a conduit for passing through capital gains, dividends, and interest directly to fund holders. This allows those taxes to be paid only once at the personal level. If the fund doesn't pass through the 90 percent as required, then the fund must pay tax, so in essence the fund is virtually forced to pass through the dividends and other gains to the fund holders. The tax consequences for fund holders of these pass-throughs will be discussed shortly in section 3.5.2.3.

3.5.2.2 Unit Investment Trusts

A **unit investment trust (UIT)** is a non-management investment company that invests in a fixed portfolio of securities. If the securities are bonds, then usually the UIT will dissolve when the bond matures. If the securities are stocks, then the UIT dissolves on a specified date. Like mutual funds, holders of UIT own an undivided interest in the investment portfolio of the company. And like a mutual fund, the UIT is required by the Investment Act of 1940 to redeem shares from investors since there is no secondary market trading of UIT. In fact, UITs make good vehicles for investors who want to use a periodic payment plan to withdraw funds on a regular schedule.

But there are a few important differences between the nonmanagement UIT and management companies, such as mutual funds. UITs do not have a Board of Directors. Instead matters are voted on by shareholders. And since UITs are non-management investment companies, they do not actively trade the securities in their portfolio. Thus, UITs do not have a need for Investment Advisors either. Because of this, UITs have no management fees and low sales charges.

3.5.2.3 Tax Treatment of Investment Company Securities

As we discussed before, dividends and capital gains distributions are taxable events to fund holders. But it is important to understand that only gains that are distributed to fund holders are actually subject to taxation. If a gain is realized by the portfolio and passed through to shareholders, then it is a taxable event. But, if stock prices (and hence stock values) rise, there are no tax consequences to fund holders unless and until the shares are sold by the fund and the gain is realized by the fund.

Distributions. An important point about distributions to shareholders is that the determination of whether or not a capital gain is long term or short term depends on how long the fund held the investment—not how long the shareholder held the mutual fund shares. If the fund held a certain company's shares for 18 months before selling them, but the investor just got into the fund last month, any capital gains on the sale is still considered a long term capital gain for the investor. Conversely, if the investor has held a mutual fund for three years, but the fund keeps buying and selling stocks after holding them for only six months, the capital gains from those sales are all considered short term.

Although dividends may be paid out by a mutual fund as often as the fund chooses, capital gains distributions are made no more than once per year. The fund manager at the end of the year sends a statement to each shareholder detailing how much of the distributions made were considered portfolio income, how much were investment income, and how much were capital gains. An IRS form 1099 sent by the fund details the tax liability for the investor.

Reinvestment. Reinvestment of capital gains or dividends is still a taxable event for the investor. Once the gain is realized, the taxes are owed. If the money is reinvested, that adjusts the cost basis upward for the investor. That is, once the investor has paid taxes on the money (e.g., realized capital gains from the mutual fund), taxes are not paid on it a second time down the road when the shares are redeemed. So the investor's adjusted cost basis would be equal to the original amount invested, plus any fees, plus any reinvested dividends or capital gains. In fact, investors should keep their annual statements from the mutual fund for as long as they own the fund and beyond, because this can help the investor figure out the cost basis for the investment.

Exchanges. Exchanges within a family of funds are a taxable event for the investor, which may generate a capital gain or loss. The gain or loss is reportable in the year of the exchange and the tax is due, even if the investor complied with all fund rules and made a successful exchange that avoided sales charges. Investors need to be aware of this when deciding whether or not to move investments back and forth between funds to take advantage of market conditions or fulfill their changing needs.

One final note: If there is a question on the Series 7 exam that suggests mutual funds are a good investment because of their tax advantages, that is usually a trick question or an incorrect answer. The mutual fund itself, because of the conduit theory, benefits by not having to pay taxes, and instead passes the tax liability directly to individual shareholders. For investors, mutual funds have the advantages of liquidity, diversification, and professional management.

Exam Topic Alert

Although many investors may put mutual fund shares into IRAs or other retirement plans that shelter or defer taxes, *mutual funds in and of themselves are* not *tax shelters.* Mutual funds can be good investments, but investors should not enter them to try to gain any tax advantages.

3.5.3

Variable Annuity Contracts

Annuities are simply a series of equal payments, often set up as insurance contracts because they are for the life of the holder. These annuity contracts can be set up as either fixed or variable. With a fixed annuity contract, the payments are a fixed monthly amount. This is good on the one hand because the insurance company is bearing the market risk for how well the underlying investments will perform. Even if the investments do poorly, the annuity amount is guaranteed. On the other had, it can be bad because annuity contract holders bear the inflationary risks (a.k.a. purchasing power risks) so that in the future their payments may not buy as much.

The answer to this situation was the development of the variable annuity contract. In exchange for the annuity contract holder assuming some of the market risks of the investments, the insurance company shares some of the capital appreciation of the investments to help offset the annuity holder's inflationary risk.

3.5.3.1 Insurance Aspects

A **variable annuity contract** is an annuity contract which makes payments to the holder that vary based on the value of the underlying investments. The variable annuity contract sees its value rise and fall with the value of the underlying securities, thus the annuity payments made and the return on the investment both depend on the performance of the portfolio.

Insurance companies figure into the equation because they are guaranteeing that the payments will continue for the life of the annuity contract holder. Unlike a fixed annuity contract, though, with a variable annuity contract the insurance company does *not* guarantee how much those payments will be.

It is important to note also that insurance companies which offer variable annuity contracts are regulated under the Investment Act of 1940. This is because the variable annuity contract is considered a security under the Act's definitions, and the insurance company is acting as an investment advisor in managing the funds. (Insurance companies which offer only fixed annuity contracts are regulated under insurance laws only.)

3.5.3.2 Investment Considerations

As with any investment, there are various considerations and risks which must be analyzed by the investor before an informed decision can be made. Investors need to feel that the money they are investing with the insurance company will be invested wisely. They need to learn as much as possible about the safety, stability and track record of the insurance company. Whether it is a fixed contract where all money is dumped into a general account, or a variable annuity where investor money is put into a separate account, the investor must still rely on the investment capabilities and management experience of the insurance company. A fixed annuity contract is worthless if the insurance company folds; a variable annuity contract can keep pace with inflation only through savvy investing. This is where risk assessment comes in.

As we have outlined, the main risk involved with annuity contracts is market risk. But whereas with a fixed annuity contract that risk is borne by the insurance company, with the variable annuity contract that risk is shifted to the investor. And there is always some inflationary risk, even though that is mitigated with a variable annuity contract. Certainly the ability to share in the capital appreciation of the investments afforded by a variable annuity contract is a plus, but that is far from a guarantee that the funds will be invested wisely in investments which will appreciate in value at a rate at least equal to the rate of inflation. Remember, with a variable annuity contract, the payments to the investor go up and down with the value of the underlying securities in the portfolio. (We'll explain this shortly.)

3.5.3.3 Separate Accounts

One of the things we've touched on, but which needs more explanation, is the separate accounts aspect of variable annuity contracts. With a fixed annuity contract, all investor payments that the insurance company receives are dumped into a general account. This general account is owned and controlled by the insurance company. Since the insurance company is bearing the market risk, if the account does well then the insurance company makes more money. If the general account does poorly, the insurance company must still make the fixed annuity payments to all contract holders. With a variable annuity contract, investor money is put into a separate account.

Purpose. A separate account is used with variable annuity contracts because the money in it is invested a little more aggressively to achieve some growth. Whereas general account funds are usually invested in bonds and other "safe" investments, the funds that go into a separate account buy a mix of stocks, bonds and other securities. The general account must be more conservative because it is used to pay the insurance company's claims and other obligations. The separate account, on the other hand, can be more aggressive because it is used only to pay out on the variable annuity contracts, and a higher return is what the investor expects. Furthermore, the gains in this account directly benefit those who put this money in, because the amount of payments received is tied to the performance of this account.

Portfolio Management. When investors begin making payments into an annuity account, they relinquish control of the funds to the insurance company. Insurance companies have two choices as to how portfolios will be managed with these separate accounts. This choice affects how the variable annuity contract is regulated, although both choices fall under the purview of the Investment Act of 1940. The insurance company can have its own investment advisor manage the funds that are in the separate accounts. If the insurance company employs the investment advisor, the separate account is said to be **directly managed,** and the insurance company is **regulated like a mutual fund.** The insurance company can also choose to delegate this responsibility to an outside investment advisor. If the insurance company contracts with an outside firm, then the separate account is said to be **indirectly managed,** and the insurance company is **regulated like a unit investment trust.**

Investment Policies. The investment policies of the insurance companies with regard to these separate accounts are detailed in the prospectus for the variable annuity contract. Although they are generally more aggressive with separate account investments than they are with general account investments, one of the objectives for the separate account is still conservation of capital. So although the separate accounts invest in stocks, they are still likely buying more conservative stocks, such as blue chips, rather than speculative stocks, like IPOs. Along with this conservatism, though, the separate accounts are also invested with an eye towards long-term growth and capital accumulation. Again, reading the prospectus for the variable annuity contract is the best way for the investor to understand these goals.

Another item to consider under investment policies is the rights of the variable contract owners. We said earlier that the investor relinquishes control of the invested funds to the insurance company, but the investor does still retain some measure of control as outlined in the prospectus. The primary means for exercising this control is voting. The variable annuity contract owner can vote on such things as the selection of investment advisors and money managers, changes in investment policy or strategy, and other proxies.

Performance of Account. The performance of the account can be measured several ways. Certainly the investor will look at how well the investment has met its objectives of producing payments that keep up with inflation and capital growth. Fluctuating payments can also indicate the performance of the annuity as improving or declining. The most measurable criterion, though, is the valuation of the variable annuity contract.

3.5.3.4 Valuation of Variable Annuity Contract

There are several differences with how variable annuity contracts are valued compared with other managed investments. There are no "shares" to speak of, instead variable annuity contracts are sold in **units.** The value of a unit is calculated based on the value of the investments in the separate account. Like the NAV of a mutual fund, the value of a variable annuity contract share must be calculated at least once per day, usually at the close of trading. There are accumulation units and annuity units.

Accumulation Units. **Accumulation units** are the measure of how much of an interest the investor owns in the separate account, based on the amount of payments the investor makes into the separate account during the accumulation stage. The **accumulation stage** is the time when the investor is making regular payments into the separate account as an investment. After all sales charges and other fees are deducted from these payments, the investor has a net investment amount which is applied towards the purchase of more accumulation units. At the end of each trading day, the value of an individual unit is calculated. The value of the investor's units can then be calculated as the individual unit price times the number of units owned. This number, minus any fees and early withdrawal penalties, is the surrender value of the accumulation units.

Annuity Units. **Annuity units** are the measure of how much of an interest the investor owns in the separate account, based on the amount of payments the investor is entitled to receive during the annuity stage. The **annuity stage** is the time when the investor is receiving payments from the separate account. At the time that the variable annuity contract is converted from the accumulation stage to the annuity stage, a calculation is done. This calculation is based on the assumed interest rate (AIR), and also considers other factors, such as the projected mortality risk of the individual investor. The result is that a certain number of accumulation units converts into a certain number of annuity units.

The value of these annuity units is directly related to the value of the underlying portfolio. At the end of each trading day, the value of an individual unit is calculated. The investor redeems a set number of annuity units each month, but the value of the annuity units that are cashed in fluctuates with the value of the underlying separate account. So the investor is guaranteed to receive payments for life, but the amount of that payment is dependent on the value of the separate account portfolio.

Assumed Interest Rate. The **assumed interest rate (AIR)** is an estimated interest rate that the insurance company uses when calculating the projected pay out on a variable annuity contract. This is not a guaranteed rate of return, but rather a means to calculate the conversion from accumulation units to annuity units. Once the conversion from accumulation units to annuity units has taken place, the annuity units become a set amount and no further calculations done. The AIR is then used as the benchmark for measuring performance of the separate account, and thus determining payout amounts.

Each month, the AIR is compared to the actual rate of return on investment that the separate account achieves. If the actual rate of return is the same as the AIR, then the payment for that month is the same as the previous month. If the actual rate of return for the separate account is more than the AIR, then the monthly payment increases. If the actual rate of return for the separate account is less than the AIR, then the monthly payment decreases. It is important to note that the increase or decrease in the payment amount is not equal to the AIR or the actual rate of return. Instead, a separate formula is used as detailed in the prospectus. Just know that the payment moves up or down in tandem with the up and down movements of the actual rate of return relative to the AIR. Here is an example.

Example

The investor has entered the annuity stage. The AIR is 5 percent, and the first payment is $638. Here is a sample payout schedule:

MONTH	RATE OF RETURN FOR PRIOR MONTH	AIR (ASSUMED INTEREST RATE)	PAYMENT
1	—n/a—	5%	$638
2	6%	5%	$642
3	24%	5%	$670
4	5%	5%	$670
5	–3%	5%	$656
6	2%	5%	$648

Note that the AIR is always constant—it is set once the annuity stage begins. Also note in the fourth payment in our example that the high payment stayed the same, even though the rate of return dropped from 24 percent down to 5 percent, because the rate of return did not drop below the relative AIR. And, even though the fifth month saw a dramatic drop in the rate of return, the decrease in payment was based on the prior month's payment only, so that payment was still higher than the first or second payments. Finally, the payment went down between the fifth and sixth month because, even though the rate of return for the separate account went up from the previous month, that rate was still below the AIR, so the payment declined.

3.5.3.5 Purchasing Variable Annuities

Variable annuities can be purchased with a single lump sum payment or purchased over time. Our discussion of variable annuity contracts up to this point has been geared towards the investor who went through an accumulation stage by investing money over a period of time, and then picked a date in the future to begin the annuity stage. This is the way most investors buy these contracts because they do not have enough money to make a large lump sum payment. Even with a large lump sum payment, though, the investor could still choose between starting the annuity stage at some point in the future—a **deferred annuity,** or starting the annuity stage immediately—an **immediate annuity.**

Immediate Annuity. An **immediate annuity** is an annuity contract that is purchased with a lump sum payments, with the annuity stage scheduled to begin immediately (usually no longer than two months out). Annuity pay outs may be set up so they are received for a set period of time, or for the life of the contract holder.

Deferred Annuity. A **deferred annuity** is an annuity contract that has an accumulation period for a certain amount of time, followed by an annuity stage scheduled to begin at a future date chosen by the contract holder. Payments during the accumulation stage can be paid with a lump sum, or spread out over time. Pay outs during the annuity stage may be received for a set period of time or for the life of the contract holder, depending on how it is set up.

Charges, Fees, Penalties. During the accumulation stage of a deferred annuity, payments are usually made monthly. The sales charge paid to the insurance company usually is the same each month. The maximum sales charge allowed by law is 8.5 percent (like mutual funds). The prospectus contains information on how the sales charges, mortality expenses, and operating expenses are calculated, and the maximum amounts that they will be for the variable annuity contract. Any penalties for missing investment payments during this stage must be detailed in the prospectus.

Tax penalties for early withdrawal are 10 percent tax penalty on the interest portion of any annuity payment withdrawn before age 59½. Lump sum withdrawals for any amount above the investor's cost basis is taxed as ordinary income.

Rights of Accumulation. Buying accumulation units is like buying shares in a mutual fund. As the investor puts more money in, the number of accumulation units increases. During the accumulation stage, the number of accumulation units usually does not decline, but the *value* of the units can decline.

Watch for something like this on the Series 7 exam. *Remember, number of units can't decline, value of units can.*

And don't forget that during the accumulation stage, the investor has the right to vote on such things as the selection of investment advisors and money managers, changes in investment policy or strategy, and other proxies.

Waiver of Premium. This type of clause is in many insurance contracts, including some annuities, but sometimes requires the payment of an additional fee. A **waiver of premium** clause states that if the investor becomes disabled and unable to make the required payments, the payments will be suspended but the benefits will remain in force. The waiver of payments will stay in force until it is determined that the investor is no longer incapacitated.

3.5.3.6 Electing to Annuitize

Thus far we have discussed annuities as if there were only two choices available to the contract holder: take the pay out over time or take a lump sum payment out when needed. In reality, though, there are actually at least six different choices, and some variations exist within those six. First, though, we should explain what it means to "annuitize." **Annuitize** means to convert an annuity contract from the accumulation stage to the annuity stage, so that the investor can begin to collect payments from the value that has built up in the annuity.

Believe it or not, this does not always happen. There are two reasons for this. First, the investor has ways to take money out of the variable annuity contract without making the conversion, or "annuitizing," the contract. And second, once the decision is made to annuitize, then the investor no longer has accumulation units and thus can no longer accumulate value in the annuity, but rather the investor is locked into the fixed number of annuity units assigned at conversion.

As we look at the six ways an investor can take money out of an annuity, we'll break them down into two ways that don't require annuitization and the four that do.

> Choice #1: **Lump sum withdrawal.** The investor can elect to take a lump sum payment equal to all of the annuity investment value built up, or only a partial amount. Taking only a partial amount does not require annuitization, and would leave open the option to annuitize in the future. Of course, there are tax consequences with this approach. As we saw before, tax penalties for early withdrawal are 10 percent tax penalty on the interest portion of any annuity payment withdrawn before age 59½. Lump sum withdrawals for any amount above the investor's cost basis are taxed as ordinary income.
>
> Choice #2: **Systematic withdrawal.** The investor can elect to take payments for a certain amount of money or for a certain period of time, until the contract value is exhausted. Here the entire pay out is treated as ordinary income for tax purposes. Again, this choice does not require annuitization.

The next four choices we will discuss do require annuitization. These are the ones you are most likely to see on the test. In fact, *the Series 7 exam always assumes that annuitization happens.*

Types of Election. When the investor elects to annuitize, there are only two things that are important (besides how many units the investor has): the age and sex of the investor, and what type of pay out choice the investor will elect. The age and sex of the investor are important for the insurance company's calculations because the annuity needs to pay out for the rest of the investor's life. Upon annuitization, the investor can choose a payout method by making one of four types of elections.

Choice #1: **Life annuity.** The annuity will pay out for as long as the contract holder lives, but payments end upon his or her death. This results in the largest monthly payments (still based on the value of the separate account), but is the biggest gamble because there is no guaranteed payout amount. The contract holder could die early, before the principal and interest have been returned on the annuity investment, and the beneficiaries receive nothing. This option is also called **straight life** or **life only.**

Choice #2: **Life annuity with period certain.** The annuity will pay out for as long as the contract holder lives, but upon his or her death if payments have not been made for a certain, predetermined amount of time, then the beneficiaries would continue to receive those payments until the time is over.

Choice #3: **Life annuity with amount certain.** The annuity will pay out for as long as the contract holder lives, but upon his or her death if a certain, predetermined number of annuity units have not been paid out, then the beneficiaries would continue to receive those payments until those annuity units have been paid. This option is also called refund life annuity.

Choice #4: **Life annuity with joint and last survivor.** The annuity will pay out for as long as the contract holder lives, and then upon his or her death payments will continue to be made to the contract holder's spouse until the death of the spouse. Since payments are made until both parties die, the insurance company also needs the age and sex of the contract holder's spouse to do its calculations. Payments cease upon the death of both parties, and nothing is paid to beneficiaries regardless of how little may have been paid out. This option is also called **joint and last survivor or survivor annuity.**

The Variable Payout. All of the annuitized choices use the variable payout schedule that we discussed before. Let's review it here briefly. In addition to the age and sex of the contract holder, and the payout type the investor elects, the insurance company also needs to know how many annuity units the investor has after conversion and the assumed interest rate (AIR).

Remember, AIR is used to measure performance of the separate account, and determine payout amounts. Each month, the AIR is compared to the actual rate of return that the separate account achieves. If the actual rate of return is the same as the AIR, the payment for that month is the same as the previous month. If the actual rate of return for the separate account is more than the AIR, the monthly payment rises. If the actual rate of return for the separate account is less than the AIR, the monthly payment falls. Payments move up or down each month in tandem with the up and down movements of the actual rate of return relative to the AIR. (If you need to review an example, go back to section 3.5.3.4.)

It is important that you understand that *the AIR is constant, the number of annuity units is constant, but the value of the annuity units can change and the payment amounts can change.*

3.5.3.7 Tax Treatment

Unlike mutual funds, variable annuities are a good way to defer taxes. Not only does the invested money grow tax deferred until it is drawn out at retirement age, but all dividends, capital gains and other distributions are also tax deferred. This is because these distributions are automatically reinvested into the separate account, rather than being paid directly to the investor (which is the case with mutual funds). In fact, this is a double bonus because in addition to the tax deferral, such reinvested distributions also increase the value of the investor's units.

One other distinction that we must make when considering taxes is the status of the annuity. We have not discussed it much because it comes into play only when figuring tax liability. There are actually two kinds of variable annuity contracts: **qualified** and **nonqualified. Qualified** variable annuities have the invested amount paid for with pre-tax dollars. (An example would be an annuity in an IRA account, or one that was paid for by an employer.) This means that although the money is allowed to grow tax deferred, all money that is taken out is fully taxable as ordinary income. This makes sense, since pre-tax dollars have never paid taxes, so the investor has no cost basis. Furthermore, if an investor withdraws money before age 59½, the entire amount is subject to a 10 percent tax penalty.

Nonqualified variable annuities have the invested amount paid with after-tax dollars. This allows them to have a cost basis so that only a portion of the withdrawal amount is subject to taxation.

For the Series 7 exam, you should always assume that a variable annuity contract is non-qualified for tax purposes, unless a question specifically tells you otherwise.

Let's look at taxes with non-qualified annuities.

Accumulation Period. During the accumulation period, invested money is allowed to grow tax deferred. Dividends, capital gains and other distributions also remain tax deferred until payouts begin on the contract, investor withdrawals are made, or the annuity contract is surrendered. If the investor takes money out with any of these scenarios before age 59½, the IRS charges a 10 percent tax penalty on the interest portion of the withdrawal. All withdrawals are taxed LIFO (last in, first out) so the amounts that accrued tax-deferred (e.g., interest) are all considered to be withdrawn first and taxed, before the investor can consider a withdrawal to be part of the cost basis. The investor must pay ordinary income tax for any amount above the cost basis. (*There are no capital gains with annuities.*)

Annuity Period. During the annuity period, the cost basis is adjusted to take into account the investor's life expectancy. (The IRS has tables to help compute this.) This new cost basis is then spread over the investor's expected life, such that each year the payments received are allocated with a portion being considered a return of principal, and a portion being considered interest on the investment. The amount that is considered interest is taxable to the investor as ordinary income in that year.

Taxation at Surrender. If the investor chooses to surrender the variable annuity contract prior to annuitization, the value of the contract is treated as a withdrawal, and ordinary income tax is due on any amount the investor receives over the investment in the annuity. The investor may also be subject to the 10 percent penalty if he or she is not yet age 59½ at the time of surrender.

Death Benefits. During the accumulation period, if the contract holder dies, death benefits from the contract are transferred to a beneficiary. The beneficiary may take the amount as a withdrawal and pay ordinary income tax on any amount over the investment in the annuity, or the beneficiary may elect (within 60 days of owner's death) to take a payout option and pay tax the same as other annuity payouts.

Just a few variable annuity contract reminders. First, although regulations between mutual funds and variable annuity contracts are similar, an important difference is that variable annuity contract earnings grow tax deferred. Furthermore, all payouts or withdrawals are always considered return of principal or ordinary income. There are no capital gains with variable annuity contracts. Also remember that the test assumes investors annuitize their variable annuity contracts. If a contract is annuitized, the investor will have guaranteed income for life.

3.5.4

Real Estate Investment Trusts (REITs)

Real estate investment trusts (REITs) specialize in real estate investment, collect funds to control real estate, and manage the portfolio. REITs can be organized as trusts or corporations. They offer only a set amount of shares, which are then publicly traded on various exchanges.

3.5.4.1 Characteristics

REITs are a vehicle for providing investment capital for real estate projects. They pool investor capital to finance large or long-term projects. They earn a return for shareholders in a number of different ways, using various capital structures. Equity REITs take ownership interest in properties, then distribute the rents as income to shareholders, and pass through capital gains when buildings are sold at a profit. Mortgage REITs lend money to real estate developers, then pass through interest income to shareholders.

To qualify for favorable tax treatment, 75 percent of the REITs income must come from real estate activities—rents, gains on sale of real estate, mortgage interest, etc.—and the REIT must pass through to shareholders at least 95 percent of its taxable income (this is only 90 percent for tax years after 2000, but the test will still likely use 95 percent as the correct answer for awhile). The REIT must also have 75 percent of its total assets in real estate assets, cash, and government securities at the end of each quarter of its tax year. In addition, REITs must meet six more general requirements in the IRS code (but those are beyond the scope of this textbook—and won't appear on the Series 7 exam).

3.5.4.2 Tax Treatment

REITs allow investors to share in the gains, but investors are not permitted to deduct any of the REIT's losses. Provided that the REIT meets the pass-through requirements and other IRS rules to qualify for favorable tax treatment, the REIT does not pay any tax. Instead, the shareholders pay tax on the distribution of original income and capital gains that are passed through. If the REIT does not make the minimum pass-through to shareholders, the REIT must pay tax on any undistributed income and gains that it retain. Furthermore, the IRS imposes an additional tax on REIT shareholders later when they ultimately receive the income or capital gains distribution that was retained by the REIT.

3.6 Derivative Products

When we talk about derivative products, the term is synonymous with derivative securities. A **derivative security** is an instrument whose value is dependent on the value of another underlying security. By itself, the derivative security is worthless; but it derives its value from the fact that it gives the holder the right to buy or sell another security or investment. Since they are securities, derivative securities may be traded in the secondary market (although, as stated, their value is largely determined by the value of the underlying security on which they are based).

Options are the best example of a derivative security. **Options** are the right, but not the obligation, to buy or sell something at a predetermined price and under predetermined conditions (usually conditioned by a time limit, but could have other conditions as well). The advantage of options is leverage. They allow an investor to control a large block of securities for a relatively small investment. The disadvantage of options is that they expire. They are a wasting asset because if they are not exercised the investor loses the premium amount paid to buy the option contract.

Options are the main derivative security you will encounter in your career as an RR. Options are also a very big part of the Series 7 exam—up to 20 percent of the questions. Much of the material in this section is simply learning new terminology. There will also be some options strategies and relationships that you will need to understand, which will be explained in this section as well.

3.6.1 Listed Options

There are actually two types of options: over-the-counter options and exchange-traded options. **Over-the-counter options** are distinguished by the fact that they do not trade on an exchange, and thus are nonnegotiable. This also makes them illiquid, and hence not very popular with investors. They are useful in some situations, with terms negotiated between the parties. But when most people talk about options, they are talking about exchange-traded options.

Exchange-traded options, also called **listed options,** are options that are freely tradeable on a given market exchange. There are actually listed options for stocks, commodities, and many other securities and instruments. The exchange sets the terms for acceptable options, and the Options Clearing Corporation (OCC) issues the options and is their guarantor. This is a good place to start with our definitions.

3.6.1.1 Basic Definitions

These terms all have special meanings related to options, which are important for you to know if you are to understand how options work.

OCC. Options Clearing Corporation (OCC) issues, guarantees, and clears options contracts for stocks, Treasuries, and other securities that are traded on the various exchanges. As the largest clearing organization for derivative securities, OCC is what makes the options markets work. Without OCC, you would not have any guarantee that you could exercise an option, or close out an options contract position. For example, if an investor bought an options contract agreeing to sell a certain stock at a certain price at a certain date, this obligation would be binding on the investor until that date—regardless of the stock's current price. But because of OCC, the investor has a guarantee of closing out the position by buying an offsetting option to buy the same stock. There is no guarantee of price (the investor may lose money), but at least the investor can close out the position and eliminate the uncertainty.

Call, Put. There are two basic types of options: call options and put options. (See Chart 3.6.1.A.) A **call** is the right to buy a certain number of shares of a security, at a predetermined price, before a certain date. The person who buys the call has the *option* to buy the stock; the person who sells the call has the *obligation* to sell the stock at that price if the buyer exercises the option. A **put** is the right to sell a certain number of shares of a security, at a predetermined price, before a certain date. The person who buys the put has the *option* to sell the stock; the person who sells the put has the *obligation* to buy the stock at that price if the buyer exercises the option.

Aside from these **types** (calls and puts), options can still be broken down even further. Options of the same type (e.g., all calls) with the same underlying security are a **class.** A class with all the same price and date are a series. (See Chart 3.6.1.B.)

Price, Date. Thus far when we have mentioned an options contract, we have talked about a "predetermined price" and a "certain date." The terms for these are strike price and expiration date. The **strike price** is the price at which the contract holder can exercise the option. (It is also referred to as the **exercise price.**) The option must be exercised before the **expiration date,** which is 3, 6, or 9 months from the date of issue (with one exception we'll discuss later). The actual expiration is always on Saturday after the third Friday of the expiration month, so the last possible trade or exercise day is that third Friday (assuming no holiday).

chart 3.6.1

OPTIONS CHARTS: A, B, C.

A.

BUY CALL	**SELL CALL**
option to buy stock pays money has debit	obligation to sell stock gets money has credit
BUY PUT	**SELL PUT**
option to sell stock pays money has debit	obligation to buy stock gets money has credit

B.

IBM CLASS e.g.	**IBM SERIES, e.g.**
IBM May 60 put at 5	IBM May 60 put at 5
IBM May 58 put at 6	IBM May 60 put at 5
IBM May 63 put at 7	IBM May 60 put at 5
IBM Jun 60 put at 6	IBM May 60 put at 5
IBM Jul 60 put at 7	IBM May 60 put at 5

C. **LEDGER CHART**
(Investor's acct. with broker)

DR (debit) (paid)	**CR** (credit) (rec'd)
if buying call, call $ amount	
	if selling call, call $ amount
if buying put, put $ amount	
	if selling put, put $ amount
totals	

Exercise means that the contract holder will make use of his or her rights to buy or sell securities under the contract. For example, the buyer of a call option would exercise the option by informing the seller of the option that he or she wants to buy the underlying security at the agreed upon price—the strike price. The buyer of a put option would exercise the option by informing the seller of the option that he or she wants to sell shares to the seller at the strike price. Note: *only the person who has the right to do something can exercise the option, because exercising the option obligates the other person to perform as specified in the option contract.*

In reality, when the holder of an options contract wants to exercise the option, he or she does not actually go to the seller of the option. Instead, the broker gives an **exercise notice** to OCC detailing the option holder's desire to exercise the option. It is OCC's responsibility to contact option sellers and make sure that everything is in order for the trade. The OCC does a **random assignment of exercise notice,** choosing one of the many brokers who sold that series of option to make sure that the trade will go through as directed, according to the terms of the options contract.

Premium. Investors buy an option because they think a stock (or other underlying security) will move up or down past the strike price. Of course, that means that the person selling the option thinks that the stock won't move past the strike price, but there is another reason that a person sells an option. The seller of an option is looking to collect the premium and increase portfolio income. The **premium** is the price an investor pays to buy an option contract. The price of the premium is determined by supply and demand, and market conditions. (We will examine some of the factors that influence the premium amount in a few sections.)

The seller of the option contract collects the premium—and then hopes that the stock doesn't move past the strike price. If it doesn't, then the contract will expire and the buyer will do nothing, but the seller of the option still gets to keep the premium.

If the stock does move past the strike price and the option is exercised, the seller gets to offset part of any loss by the premium amount already collected.

In-the-Money, Out-of-the-Money. These terms have to do with the status of the option contract, when comparing the strike price to the actual market price of the underlying security. The option contract is always looked at from the option holder's point of view. Thus, when the market price of a stock is *above the strike price of a call option,* the option contract is said to be **in-the-money.** Let's look at this logically. If the stock price is above the strike price of a call option, the option holder could make money by buying (calling) the stock from someone else at the lower strike price that was agreed to in the option contract. When the market price is *below the strike price of a put option,* the option contract would also be in-the-money. If the stock price is below the strike price of a put option, the option holder could make money by selling (putting) the stock to someone else at the higher strike price that was agreed to in the option contract. In other words, the holder of the option contract (the buyer) usually makes money by exercising an option that is in-the-money.

Note that the determination of whether or not an option contract is in-the-money considers only the strike price and the price of the underlying security. There is no consideration given to the price of the option, sales commissions, or any other carrying costs. This is because all investors could have paid a different amount for each of these items, even to buy the same option contract. Just be aware that an option contract that is in-the-money might not result in a profit for the contract holder if the market price of the stock is too close to the strike price.

Out-of-the-money means that the option holder would not make money by exercising the option contract. In fact, new option contracts are purchased "out-of-the-money" so the buyer hopes that the stock will move favorably and the contract will move "in-the-money." The closer an option contract is to being in-the-money, the more expensive the premium is for the option contract. Once the option contract is in-the-money, it can be cashed in by the holder or sold to another investor. Of course, options can be bought and sold when they're out-of-the-money as well. They still have some value, but that value is dependent upon the current market price of the underlying security and the time value until the option contract expires.

Intrinsic Value, Time Value. Intrinsic value is the difference between the strike price of the option and the market value of the underlying security. Intrinsic value is equal to the in-the-money option amount. An out-of-the-money option does not have any intrinsic value; it merely has a speculative value. When an option contract trades at its intrinsic value, with no time value component added to the price, it is said that the option contract is trading at **parity.**

Time value is that part of the option that reflects the amount of time remaining until expiration of the option. The closer the option is to the expiration date, the less value it has. This is true even if the strike price is very close to the current market price of the stock because if the expiration is too soon, the stock may not have time to move above the strike price in the short window of time afforded by the option. If an option is trading in the secondary market, one way to calculate the premium is to take the intrinsic value and add a factor for the time value.

Opening and Closing Transactions. Options trading is not for every investor because of the level of knowledge required and the level of risk involved. Some options contracts actually put an investor in a position of unlimited risk. Thus, before a client can begin options trading and make a first opening transaction, the broker-dealer must determine whether or not the client is suitable for options trading. The investor must receive a disclosure document (similar to a prospectus) on options trading before the first trade and must sign the OCC options agreement within 15 days of approval.

Opening transactions establish a position in an option. If an investor **buys** an option, he or she is the **owner** of the option. You can also say that the investor is the **holder** of the option, or is **long** the option. So all of these terms are synonymous: **buyer = owner = holder = long.** Actually, these terms are used with stock ownership as well as with options. Thus, if your client places an opening buy order, you need to know if the order is a long call or a long put. This is one way to open a position.

A client could also open a position if he or she **sells** an option. You can also say that the investor is the **writer** of the option, or is **short** the option. (Note that this is *not* the same as selling stock short.) So all of these terms are synonymous: **seller = writer = short.** Thus, if your client places an opening sell order, you need to know if the order is a short call or a short put. This is another way to open a position.

Closing transactions liquidate a position in an option. We said before that without OCC giving an investor a way to close out an option contract there would not be an orderly market. Let's explain why. If an investor establishes a short call position, he or she is in a position of unlimited risk if the investor does not already own the stock that the option was sold on. The options contract is an agreement to sell that stock at a particular price before a certain date, and this obligation is binding on the investor until that date—no matter what the price of the stock. So if the investor is in a short call position for stock that he or she does not own, because the stock has no limit to how high it can go, the investor's potential risk is also unlimited.

Closing transactions are a means to liquidate a position by buying an offsetting option with the same terms. If the investor has a long call or a long put position, the investor can write (sell) an option with the same terms to establish a short call or a short put. In effect, these transactions cancel each other out and the investor has closed the position. A closing transaction can also be done if the investor has a short call or short put position. If the investor buys a long call or long put position with the same terms as the short position, the investor has closed the position. Because of OCC, the investor is guaranteed to be able to close out the position by buying an offsetting option with the same terms for the same stock. Remember, though, that there's no price guarantee (the investor may lose money), but at least the investor can close out the position and eliminate the uncertainty without waiting for expiration.

Limits. There are several kinds of limits that are discussed throughout this textbook. With regard to options, the relevant ones to know are position limits and exercise limits. **Positions limits** are the maximum number of listed options that an individual, or group of individuals working together, can own in the same underlying security. (The numbers are adjusted frequently, and vary by exchange and trading volume of the underlying security.) These limits apply to all expiration dates on the same side of the market. For example, long calls and short puts are on the same side of the market, so they're added together when looking at position limits.

Exercise limits are the maximum number of contracts of any one option class that can be exercised within five business days of each other. (The numbers are adjusted frequently, and can vary by exchange and even the trading volume of an individual security.) Each contract represents 100 shares of stock in the underlying security.

Position limits and exercise limits are put in place by the OCC to ensure that large investors cannot manipulate the market with the incredible leverage that options give. Also of interest to the OCC and investors are the total number of options that are still an open interest. **Open interest** is the total number of options contracts that have not been exercised, closed out, or still have not expired. This is useful information to options traders, and is published daily in some newspapers.

OCC Settlement. Since all exercise notices go through OCC, there is a standard OCC settlement procedure. After the OCC randomly chooses a broker-dealer, then the broker-dealer chooses a client who will be exercised. The broker-dealer can select clients randomly, or use any other fair and consistent method. Buying and selling options are settled the next business day; exercised options are settled within three business days after OCC gets the exercise notice. (The date that OCC gets the exercise notice is considered the trade date.)

Also, upon expiration, OCC automatically exercises options if they are ¼ point (25 cents) in-the-money for broker-dealers, and ¾ point (75 cents) in-the-money for other clients. OCC must be notified if an investor does not want this automatic exercise of options upon expiration.

Breakeven Points. The **breakeven point** for option contracts is the market price the stock must attain so that the investor will not lose money (nor make money). Breakeven points consider the premium in the calculations, so the math is the strike price, plus or minus the premium, depending on the type of option contract. For a call option, the breakeven point is the strike price plus the premium. For a put option, the breakeven point is the strike price minus the premium.

There are more complex breakeven points for trades that involve more than one option contract. We will look at those breakeven points in upcoming sections as we discuss those trades. To calculate the **expiration breakeven points,** simply use the strike price of the option and consider the expiration date as the trade date. Then calculate breakeven amounts at the expiration of aggregate positions relative to movements in the underlying security.

Note that breakeven is different from when an option is at-the-money. At-the-money options occur when the strike price equals the price of the underlying stock, but at-the-money does *not* take into account the premium paid to buy the option.

Covered and Uncovered Options. All of the option contracts that we have discussed thus far can be either covered or uncovered. A **covered option** means that the writer of the option actually owns the stock to back up the contract. An **uncovered option** (also called a **naked option**) means that the writer of the option does not own the stock to back up the contract. Let's look at the implication of this.

Suppose our investor client wants to try to increase portfolio income so he writes a call on some of the stock he owns. He thinks the stock price is stable, or maybe thinks that some recent bad news will send the stock price down. Let's review our terms. The investor has a short call. Since he owns the stock, this is a **covered call.** If the stock price does indeed stay stable or drop, the option stays out-of-the-money, it expires worthless, and the investor gets to keep the premium. If the price of the stock goes up above the strike price, the investor has to surrender his stock when he gets called because the option buyer will likely exercise the option once it gets in-the-money.

But what if the investor sells the stock even though the short call has not expired? Or what if the investor writes a call on a stock he doesn't own? He writes the call for the same reasons: he wants to make the premium, and he thinks the stock price will stay the same or go down. But since he does not own the stock, this is an **uncovered call.** If the stock price stays stable or drops, the situation is the same as before: the option expires worthless and the investor keeps the premium. But if the stock price goes above the strike price, the investor has unlimited potential risk. The investor is obligated to sell the stock at the option strike price, but because he does not own it he must buy it at the current market price—whatever the price is! **Ratio call writing** is when the investor writes multiple calls on the same stock, some covered and some uncovered. This generates more portfolio income, and hedges *some* of the risk, but the investor still has unlimited risk for the naked calls.

There are other ways to limit this risk, even if the investor does not own the stock. This involves multiple option strategies where the investor is buying more than one option position in the same company's stock. We will introduce a few of these next, and then discuss them in greater detail a little later.

Spreads, Straddles and Combinations. These are some of the common multiple option strategies that investors can use to accomplish different objectives. We will define them here, and then go through a progressive explanation of different option strategies in an upcoming section. A **spread** is an option position that has one long contract and one short contract on the same stock. Investors buy this option position when they think the stock price will move in a particular direction. The difference between the long strike price and the short strike price is what produces the spread. The potential gain is limited, but so is the potential loss. A **straddle** is an option position that has an equal number of call contracts and put contracts on the same stock with the same strike price and the same expiration date. Investors buy straddles when they expect major movement in the stock price, but they're not sure which direction the price will move. Investors sell straddles when they expect little movement in the stock price. A **combination** is an option position that has two long contracts or two short contracts on the same stock, but either with different strike prices or different expiration dates. Investors buy this option because they accomplish some of the same objectives as straddles, but are less expensive.

Rotations. Trading rotation is always the business day before expiration. **Opening rotation** orders are orders which must be executed by the Order Book Official (OBO) or specialist at the beginning of the trading day, or not at all. Opening rotation consists of calling for bids and offers from the crowd for each option series. **Closing rotation** orders are executed by the Order Book Official (OBO) or specialist in order to ensure a closing price or quote for each option series. Through the closing rotation process, the bids will be representative of, and in relationship to, the price of the underlying instrument. **Market-on-close** orders can be executed only during the official closing session at the end of the trading day.

Options Disclosure Documents. There are several documents which must be given to the client. First is the options disclosure document from the OCC entitled "Characteristics and Risks of Standardized Options." This document must be given to all clients before their first options trade is executed. Future revisions of the document must also be given to clients along with the confirmation of their most recent trade. The OCC also has an options agreement that clients must sign. The main provisions of this agreement have clients agreeing to be bound by the rules and regulations of the OCC. This document must be signed and returned within 15 days. Finally, many broker-dealers have information, disclosures, and documents for clients to sign, ensuring that they understand the risks and rules of options trading.

3.6.1.2 Characteristics of Specific Options

Thus far, every time we have discussed options, we have talked about them using company stocks as the underlying security. In reality, though, there are other kinds of securities and instruments that can have listed options. In addition to equity options, there are index, debt, and foreign currency options. Each has unique characteristics that we will explore.

EQUITY OPTIONS. Equity is ownership interest in a company, so equity options are options that are bought and sold with company stock as the underlying security.

- ▷ **Underlying Instrument:** NYSE, NASDAQ and other listed company stocks
- ▷ **Contract Size:** 100 shares of stock (round lot)
- ▷ **Premium Increments:** 1/16 of a dollar up to 3, 1/8 of a dollar above 3
- ▷ **Expiration Date:** three, six, or nine months from the date of issue (except LEAPS); actual day is always on Saturday after the third Friday of expiration month
- ▷ **Exercise Settlement:** five business days after exercise; writer of a call will deliver stock if exercised; writer of a put will deliver cash if exercised

There are a few additional characteristics that are unique to equity options. If an investor is holding an option on a stock that declares a dividend, splits, or issues rights (rights offering), the terms of the options contract are adjusted as follows:

1. **cash dividends:** no adjustment to listed option contracts. (OTC option contracts may have strike price reduced to reflect dividend amount.)
2. **stock dividends:** strike price of options contract is adjusted (downwards and number of shares contract can buy is adjusted (upwards).
3. **stock splits:** for round lots (multiples of 100 shares), option contract splits equal to stock split and strike price is adjusted—e.g., a 2-for-1 split has contract double to control 2 times the shares and strike price is cut in half; for non-round lots (less than 100 shares), option contract is adjusted proportionally as is the strike price (but in opposite directions).

4. **rights:** for rights, warrants and other such offerings, the options contract is adjusted to reflect the strike price of the distributed securities (rounded to nearest 1/8 point), and the number of shares in the contract are adjusted by rounding down to the next lowest whole share.

(You'll likely see a few questions about option splits, dividends on Series 7 exam.)

LEAPS, Long-term **E**quity **A**ntici**P**ation **S**ecurities, are special options contracts that expire in 24–39 months, instead of the nine-month limit on regular option contracts. The premiums are higher, though, because investors must pay extra for the time value of holding the option contract open longer. All contracts expire in January. LEAPS are offered on most blue chip companies and other large cap stocks.

(Equity options are not the same as stock options offered by companies to employees or executives. Those usually have longer holding periods, are not tradeable on the open market, and do not go through OCC, but instead are issued by the company itself. They are similar to calls in that they give the holder the right to buy stock at a specific price prior to expiration, but there's no corresponding put option available.)

INDEX OPTIONS. An **index** is a statistical composite that measures up and down price movements of a representative sample from a particular group as a means of tracking the overall health and direction of the markets, an industry, a sector, etc. An example would be the Standard & Poor's 500 (S&P 500) index which tracks the average performance of 500 widely held stocks that trade on the NYSE. So, index options are options that are bought and sold based on an underlying index, allowing an investor to trade in a particular market or industry and benefit from anticipated up and down movements, without having to buy all of the stocks individually.

- ▷ **Underlying Instrument:** various market indices. Broad-based index tracks 20 to 1,700+ securities that track the market as a whole; narrow-based index tracks movement in a particular industry group; some indices include the S&P 500, Russell 2000, Wilshire 5000, and other industry specific indices.
- ▷ **Contract Size:** varies according to contract.
- ▷ **Premium Increments:** varies according to contract.

  Premium Amount × $100 = Option Price

  Strike Price × $100 = Total Dollar Value of Index
- ▷ **Expiration Date:** three, six, or nine months from the date of issue (except LEAPS); actual day is always on Saturday after the third Friday of expiration month.
- ▷ **Exercise Settlement:** next business day after exercise; cash only.

Capped index options are special options contracts that reduce risk because they are set up like a spread. They are sold in pairs, with one index option contract at-the-money and the other contract above or below that strike price (out-of-the-money), depending on whether the investor wants to own a call or put option contract position. For a *call,* buy the cap with the second contract *above* the first strike price; for a *put,* buy the cap with the second contract *below* the first strike price. The cap spread (interval) is set (usually at about 30 points) when the option is first listed. Capped index options are automatically exercised when the cap is hit, or can be exercised by the owner *only* on the last business day before the option expires.

Long-term index options are available as **LEAPS,** with expirations 24–39 months out. Premiums are higher because of longer time value. All contracts expire in January.

DEBT OPTIONS. These are exchange-traded debt options on T-bills, T-notes, and T-bonds. They act as an inflation hedge, so they're also called **interest rate options.**

- ▷ **Underlying Instrument:** 13-week U.S. Treasury bills (T-bills), five and 10 year U.S. Treasury notes (T-notes), and 10+ year U.S. Treasury bonds (T-bonds)
- ▷ **Contract Size:** T-bills: $1,000,000 (100 units at $10,000 per unit face amount); T-note/T-bond: $100,000 (100 units at $1,000 per unit face amount)
- ▷ **Premium Increments:**

  T-bills: 1/100 of 1 percent of underlying principal amount

  But 13 weeks is only 1/4 of a year, so premium quote is multiplied only times 1/4 of $10,000 face amount ($2,500 is used, *not* $10,000); thus, if a T-bill option premium is .8, the premium is $2,000 (.8 × $2,500).

  T-note/T-bond: 32nd of a point of underlying security. These work like the bonds/notes. If premium is quoted as :16 (or .16), that is really 16/32, so premium is 16/32 x $1,000 face = (16 ÷ 32) x $1,000 = $500.

You'll likely see one or both debt option premium calculations on Series 7 exam.

- ▷ **Expiration Date:** varies according to exchange and underlying security.
- ▷ **Exercise Settlement:** T-bills: Thursday of the following week; T-note/T-bond: second business day after exercise; note/bond plus accrued interest or cash

Yield-based options are similar to debt options, except that yield-based options trade based on changes in yield instead of changes in price like debt options. This means that yield-based options have a positive relationship with interest rates, instead of the inverse relationship that debt options have. Everything else is the same, except how strike prices are quoted.

With debt options, strike prices are quoted in the same way as the bonds: percentage of face value. So a debt option on a T-bond, quoted at 105 has a strike price of $105,000 (105% × $100,000 face value of the contract). But with yield-based options, our strike price *is* the yield. So a yield-based option with a strike price of 75 represents a yield of 7.5 percent for that option contract.

If a portfolio manager or investor expected interest rates to go up, he or she would buy debt put options or buy yield-based call options. Both of these option positions would hedge against rising interest rates. As interest rates rise, bond prices fall because of their inverse relationship (remember the balance diagrams). Since bond prices are falling, it would be advantageous for the investor to be able to put (sell) the bonds at a higher predetermined price. The same strategy is at work for the yield-based calls: as the bond prices are falling, it would be advantageous for the investor to be able to call (buy) bonds that are offering a better rate of return.

To take advantage of rising rates, the investor could also sell debt call options or sell yield-based put options. Think through these strategies in light of the last paragraph.

Conversely, if a portfolio manager or investor expected interest rates to go down, he or she would buy debt call options or buy yield-based put options. Both of these option positions would hedge against falling interest rates. As interest rates fall, bond prices rise because of their inverse relationship (remember the balance diagrams). Since bond prices are rising, it would be advantageous for the investor to be able to call (buy) the bonds at a lower predetermined price. The same strategy is at work for the yield-based puts: as bond prices are rising, it would be advantageous for the investor to be able to put (sell) the bonds offering a lower rate of return.

To take advantage of falling rates, the investor could also sell debt put options or sell yield-based call options. Think through these strategies in light of the last paragraph.

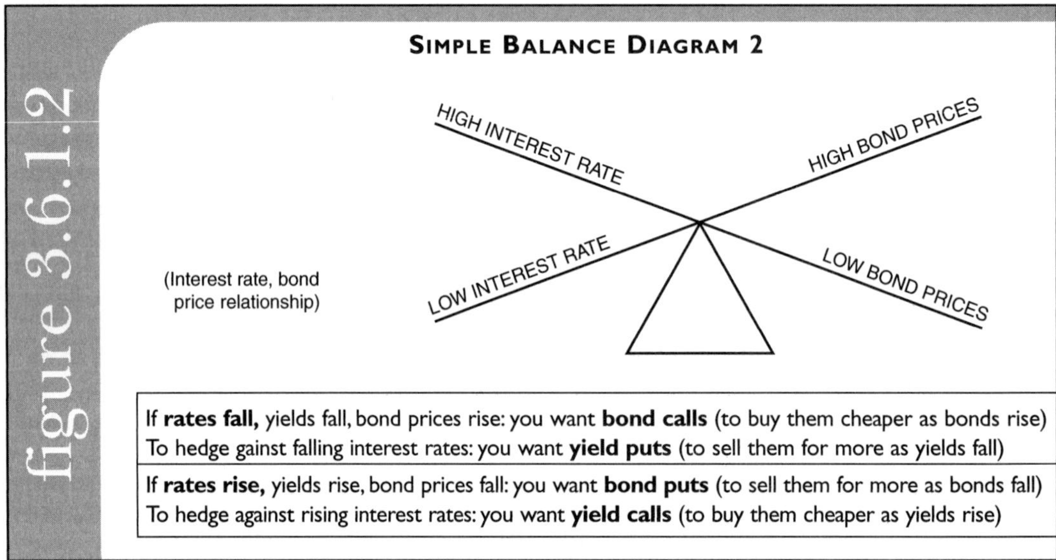

You'll likely see questions on the Series 7 exam that ask you how to hedge a portfolio against expected changes in interest rates, or how to take advantage of rate changes.

FOREIGN CURRENCY OPTIONS. These provide a means to protect the value of revenue or investments paid in foreign currency, or can be used for speculation.

- **Underlying Instrument:** various foreign currencies; many options use the Interbank market spot price or other spot price exchange rates
- **Contract Size:** varies according to currency, but usually very large
- **Premium Increments:** most premiums and strike prices are quoted in U.S. cents, except French francs (1/10th of a cent), Japanese yen (1/100th of a cent). So premium of 2.5 lira is actually 0.025 cents x contract amount = contract cost, thus controlling 50,000 Italian lira costs $1,250. (50,000 units × .025 premium).

- ▷ **Expiration Date:** 11:59 p.m. E.S.T. on the Saturday preceding the third Wednesday of the expiration month of the option
- ▷ **Exercise Settlement:** varies by contract, but must be settled in the foreign currency. Settlement can be either European style or American style: **European style** option contract can be exercised only on expiration date; **American style** option can be exercised at any time before the expiration.

Although they can be used for speculation, foreign currency option contracts are most often used to hedge an existing risk; for example, an international company that pays wages in a foreign currency, or an exporter who doesn't get paid in dollars. Foreign currency options also have an inverse relationship—as the foreign currency goes up, the value of the dollar goes down, and vice versa.

You'll likely see a foreign currency premium calculation on the Series 7 exam.

If you have to pay in foreign currency and you are worried that the foreign currency will go up in value, you could buy a call on that currency. That way, even if the currency goes up, you can use your call option to buy the foreign currency at the lower price that you have locked in with your option contract. If the currency goes down, buy the foreign currency at the lower market price and allow the option contract to expire worthless.

If you will be paid in a foreign currency and you are worried that the foreign currency will drop in value, you could buy a put on that currency. That way, even if the currency goes down, you can use your put option to sell your foreign currency at the higher price that you have locked in with your option contract. If the currency goes up, sell the foreign currency at the higher market price and allow the option contract to expire worthless.

U.S. dollar is benchmark currency for all foreign currency options contracts, so *options on the U.S. dollar are not available!* (Watch this on the Series 7 exam.)

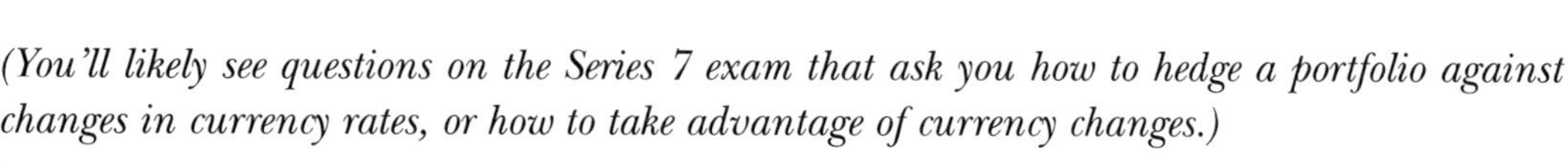
(You'll likely see questions on the Series 7 exam that ask you how to hedge a portfolio against changes in currency rates, or how to take advantage of currency changes.)

3.6.1.3 Characteristics of Option Strategies

There are two basic kinds of options players: hedgers and speculators. Hedgers already have something at risk, and are looking for ways to reduce that risk through the use of option contracts. Speculators have no existing risk, but think the markets will move a certain way and buy option contracts to try to capitalize on this.

Option strategies can either be **bullish** (positive outlook, think markets will rise), **bearish** (negative outlook, think markets will decline), or neutral. They can involve one option contract, or multiple option contracts used together to achieve the desired objective. Let's revisit some of the options that we defined earlier in this section, and show how they fit in with our option strategies.

LONG CALL: A long call is bullish. The person who is "long the call" thinks the stock price will rise, so buying the long call option contract will lock in his or her right to buy the stock at a lower price being agreed to now. If the person is correct, when the stock goes up he or she can exercise the call, buy the stock at that lower price, and resell it in the marketplace for a profit. In fact, the contract holder has a potential maximum gain that is unlimited. (The person could also sell the option contract instead of actually exercising it.) The maximum loss the long call buyer could have is the option premium paid.

EXAMPLE

1 XYZ Jun 75 call at 5

If stock goes to 90, gain is 10 per share = \$1,000. (90 – 75 + 5) × 100

If stock goes to 80, this is the breakeven. (75 + 5)

If stock stays below 75, loss is premium of \$500. (5 × 100)

SHORT CALL: A short call is bearish or neutral. The person who is "short the call" thinks the stock price will drop or stay the same, so writing the short call option contract allows the seller of the option to collect the premium. If the person is correct, the option contract will not go in-the-money, will not be exercised, and will expire worthless. The maximum gain for the call writer is the premium. The maximum potential loss is unlimited (if the call is not covered, meaning the call writer does not actually own the stock).

EXAMPLE

1 XYZ Jun 75 call at 5

If stock stays below 75, gain is premium of \$500. (5 × 100)

If stock goes to 80, this is the breakeven. (75 + 5)

If stock goes to 90, loss is 10 per share = \$1,000. (90 – 75 + 5) × 100

LONG PUT: A long put is bearish. The person who is "long the put" thinks the stock price will drop, so buying the long put option contract will lock in his or her right to sell the stock at a higher price being agreed to now. If the person is correct, when the stock goes down he or she can exercise the put and sell it to the put holder for the higher put price. This is more like insurance for the put holder, because the maximum potential gain is only the strike price minus the premium. The maximum loss is the option premium paid.

EXAMPLE

1 XYZ Jun 75 put at 5

If stock goes to 60, gain is 10 per share = \$1,000. (75 – 60 – 5) × 100

If stock goes to 70, this is the breakeven. (75 – 5)

If stock stays above 75, loss is premium of \$500. (5 × 100)

SHORT PUT: A short put is bullish or neutral. The person who is "short the put" thinks the stock price will rise or stay the same, so writing the short put option contract allows the seller of the option to collect the premium. If the person is right, the option contract will not go in-the-money, won't be exercised, and will expire worthless. The maximum gain for the put writer is the premium. The maximum potential loss is the strike price minus the premium.

EXAMPLE

1 XYZ Jun 75 put at 5

If stock stays below 75, gain is premium of $500. (5 × 100)

If stock goes to 70, this is the breakeven. (75 – 5)

If stock goes to 60, loss is 10 per share = $1,000. (75 – 60 – 5) × 100

chart 3.6.1.3

BASIC OPTIONS POSITIONS

BULLISH	**LONG CALL**	**SHORT PUT**	**(same side of the market)**
BEARISH	**LONG PUT**	**SHORT CALL**	**(same side of the market)**

Let's see how these basic, single option contracts can be combined with stock positions or other option contracts to achieve various investment objectives.

Neutral Option Strategies. There are three neutral strategies that we will look at in greater detail: covered call writing (at market), straddle writing, and combination writing.

COVERED CALL WRITING (at market): Writing a covered call at market is a neutral position. It indicates that the investor does not have an indication of which way the market will go. So the investor's trade would look like this:

Long 100 shares ABC company at 50

1 Short ABC Nov 50 call at 3

The client bought the ABC shares at $50, but then sold a 50 call on the shares. This is a covered call since the investor owns the stock, but what was the point of the trade? If the stock goes down, the investor will lose money. If the stock goes up before November, the investor will likely get exercised and have to surrender the stock so he won't make money there.

The investor made this trade to **increase portfolio income** by collecting the premium. He or she can help offset the cost of the stock by writing the call. If the stock stays where it is, the investor has reduced the cost of the stock. If the stock goes up, the investor surrenders the stock but still keeps the premium collected. And, if the stock drops, the premium helps offset the loss. In fact, the investor's breakeven is only 47 because he or she paid 50 for the stock, but collected 3 in premium, so 50 – 3 = 47. Even if the stock drops to 47, the investor will still not lose money.

STRADDLE WRITING: Writing a straddle is a neutral position. It indicates that the investor does not think there will be much movement in stock prices. Remember, a **straddle** is an option position that has an equal number of call contracts and put contracts on the same stock with the same strike price and the same expiration date. So the investor's trade would look like this:

1 Short ABC Nov 50 call at 3

1 Short ABC Nov 50 put at 6

To see if the client can profit from this trade, the first thing we need to do is figure out how much the trade cost the investor. To do that, you simply add the premiums together, so here we have 3 + 6 = 9, for a total premium of $900. Since 9 is our total premium, we need to add 9 to the call and subtract 9 from the put, so our breakevens are 59 call and 41 put. So as long as the stock does not go above 59, nor below 41, the investor makes money from this trade. To figure out how much money, we need to know where the stock is trading when one of the options gets exercised. The profit is the difference between the market price and the closest breakeven point. The maximum potential profit for the investor with this trade is the total of the premiums collected, if the stock stays at 50 for the entire option period.

If the price of the stock goes above 59 or below 41, the investor loses money on this trade. The loss is the difference between the market price and the closest breakeven point. Because of the short call, there is unlimited risk with this trade and so the maximum potential loss is also unlimited.

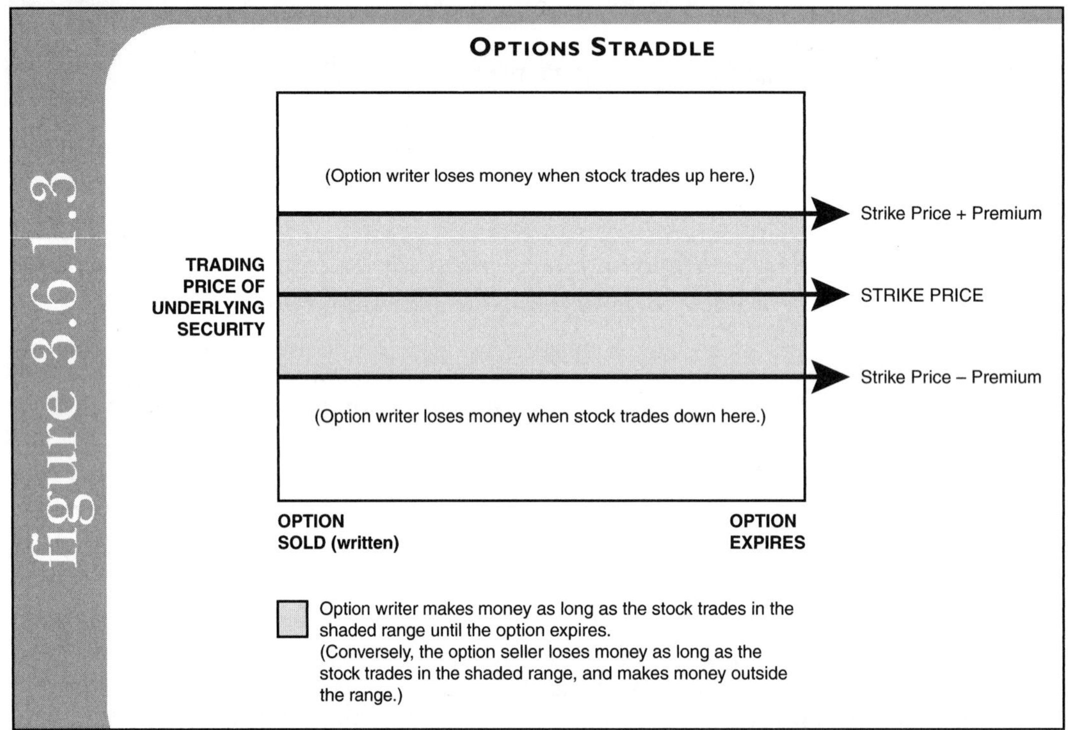

COMBINATION WRITING: Writing a combination is a neutral position. It indicates that the investor does not think there will be much movement in stock prices. Remember, a **combination** is an option position that has two long contracts or two short contracts on the same stock, but with different strike prices and/or different expiration dates. Here's an investor's trade:

1 Short ABC Nov 50 call at 2

1 Short ABC Jan 50 put at 4

The mechanics here are almost the same as the straddle. The first thing we need to do is figure out how much the trade cost, so adding the premiums we get 2 + 4 = 6, for a total premium of $600. Since the total premium is 6, add 6 to the call and subtract 6 from the put, so the breakevens are 56 and 44. As long as the stock trades between 56 and 44 the investor makes money. The profit is the difference between the market price and the closest breakeven point. The maximum potential profit is $600—the total of premiums collected.

If the price of the stock goes outside our range of 56–44, the investor loses money on this trade. The loss is the difference between the market price and the closest breakeven point. Because of the short call, there is unlimited risk with this trade and so the maximum potential loss is also unlimited.

Bearish Option Strategies. There are five bearish strategies that you need to be familiar with. We have already looked at two of them: put purchase (long put) and uncovered call writing (short call). Let's explain the other three: covered call writing (below market), covered put writing, and bear spreads.

COVERED CALL WRITING (below market): Writing a covered call below market is a bearish position. It indicates that the investor is concerned that the stock will drop in value and wants to limit this downside risk, like so:

Long 100 shares ABC company at 50

1 Short ABC Nov 45 call at 2

The client bought the ABC shares at $50, but then sold a 45 call on the shares. This is a covered call since the investor owns the stock. If the stock goes down, the investor will lose money, but the call reduces the downside risk by the premium amount. The investor's breakeven is only 48 because 50 was paid for the stock, but 2 was collected in premium, so 50 – 2 = 48. So if the stock drops as the investor expects, the downside risk is cushioned a bit.

COVERED PUT WRITING: Writing a covered put is a bearish position, used by an investor who is trying to protect a short sale position. Here the put is covering a short sale, not shares the investor actually owns. Example:

Short 100 shares ABC company at 50

1 Short ABC Nov 50 put at 2

The client shorted the ABC shares at $50, but then wrote a 50 put on the shares. This is a covered call since the investor already had the short position, but wants to protect himself. The investor is bearish on the stock, but with this trade the investor will not lose as much money if the stock goes up. The investor's breakeven is 52 because he can collect 50 from the sale of the stock that was shorted and 2 from the premium, so the risk is less with the put.

BEAR SPREAD: A **spread** is an option position that has one long contract and one short contract on the same stock. The difference between the long strike price and the short strike price is what produces the spread. Whatever you do with the more expensive option determines whether you are a bull or a bear. Since we are discussing bear spreads, we are looking for trades where the investor bought the puts or sold the calls. Here's a sample trade:

1 Long ABC Nov 50 put at 8

1 Short ABC Nov 40 put at 6

Since the investor bought the more expensive option, the predominant trade was buying the put. Remember from the first group of four options we discussed, a long put is bearish so we do indeed have a bear spread. With a bear spread, the breakeven point is calculated by taking the net difference between the premiums and subtracting that from the higher strike price.

So here our net premium is 2, and higher strike price is 50, so 50 – 2 = 48. The breakeven is 48. An easy way to remember the formula, is:

BREAKEVEN for Puts = PuSH ——→ Put, Subtract Higher

Now let's figure the client's maximum potential gain and loss. Since the client is a bear, the maximum gain comes at the lower strike price, so the spread of 10 minus net premium of 2 means the max possible gain is 8, or $800. (10 – 2 = 8) And since the client bought one contract at 8 and sold one for 6, the client owes some money: 8 – 6 = 2. The client owes $200 for the net premium amount, which is the maximum loss the client could have from this trade.

Another correlation we need to discuss with spreads is the concept of debit spreads and credit spreads. A **debit spread** is one where the more expensive option was bought, thus the trade results in money being taken out of the investor's brokerage account. A **credit spread** is one where the more expensive option was sold, thus the trade results in money being deposited into the investor's brokerage account. A bear spread can actually be a debit or credit spread, depending on what type of option is in the trade. Here the more expensive option was a long put, so we have a debit bear spread.

On the Series 7 exam, you may get questions about spreads that do not show the premiums. Many times, the question will ask you only the logic of the trade: Is it a bull spread or a bear spread? Is it a debit spread or a credit spread? To answer these types of questions, all you need to know is which option is more valuable, and thus is more expensive. You can derive this from the strike price of the options. For calls, the lower strike price option is more valuable. (Being able to buy stock cheaper is worth more.) For puts, the higher strike price option is more valuable. (Being able to sell stock for more money is worth more.) *Remember, whatever you do with the more expensive option determines whether you are a bull or a bear.* Also, if you spent more money buying an option, you would have a debit spread; and if you spent more money selling an option, you would have a credit spread. Here's a chart to help you.

chart 3.6.1.3

BULL-BEAR SPREAD CHART

Type of Spread	Want Premiums to:	Call or Put	Type of Spread	
BULL	**W** widen	**C** call	**DR** debit	—Initial Debit = Maximum Loss
BEAR	**N** narrow	**C** call	**CR** credit	—Initial Credit = Maximum Gain
BULL	**N** narrow	**P** put	**CR** credit	
BEAR	**W** widen	**P** put	**DR** debit	

READ CHART ACROSS. To help you build the chart, remember doors (DR) and windows (W) go on the outside.

With this chart, you don't need to waste time on the test figuring out the client's strategy. Just ask yourself what was done with the more expensive option. If you bought the more expensive option, you spent more money, so you have a debit spread. If you sold the more expensive option, you made more money, so you have a credit spread. Suppose the more expensive option was a call option. You have a credit call spread, so look on your chart for CR and C: you're on the second line. You know it's a bear trade looking for the premiums to narrow.

Bullish Option Strategies. There are four bullish strategies that you need to be familiar with. We have already looked at two of them: call purchase (long call) and uncovered put writing (short put). Let's examine the other two: covered call writing (above market) and bull spreads.

COVERED CALL WRITING (above market): Writing a covered call above market is a bullish position. It indicates that the investor thinks the stock will rise in value and is willing to lock in a profit at a comfortable level. Take a look:

Long 100 shares ABC company at 50

1 Short ABC Nov 75 call at 4

The client bought the ABC shares at $50, but then sold a 75 call on the shares. This is a covered call since the investor owns the stock. If the stock goes up past 75, the investor will be forced to sell, but at high enough level where he or she will feel comfortable with the profit made, plus the premium amount. The investor's breakeven is only 46 because 50 was paid for the stock, and 4 was collected in premium, so 50 – 4 = 46. The investor has limited the upside potential from unlimited back to 79 (75 + 4), but has collected immediate cash from the premium and lowered the breakeven.

BULL SPREAD: A **spread** is an option position that has one long contract and one short contract on the same stock. The difference between the long strike price and the short strike price is what produces the spread. Whatever you do with the more expensive option determines whether you are a bull or a bear. Since we are discussing bull spreads, we are looking for trades where the investor bought the calls or sold the puts. Here's a sample trade:

1 Long ABC Nov 40 call at 10

1 Short ABC Nov 50 call at 7

Since the investor bought the more expensive option, the predominant trade was buying the call. And remember from the first group of four options we discussed, a long call is bullish so we do indeed have a bull spread. With a bull spread, the breakeven point is calculated by taking the net difference between the premiums and adding it to the lower strike price. So here our net premium is 3, and lower strike price is 40, so 40 + 3 = 43. The breakeven is 43. An easy way to remember the formula, is:

BREAKEVEN for Calls = CALL ⟶ Call, Add Lower

Now let's figure the client's maximum potential gain and loss. Since the client is a bull, the maximum gain comes at the higher strike price, so the spread of 10 minus net premium of 3 means the max possible gain is 7, or $700. (10 – 3 = 7) And since the client bought one contract at 10 and sold one for 7, the client owes some money: 10 – 7 = 3. The client owes $300 for the net premium amount, which is the maximum loss the client could have from this trade. Furthermore, since the net premium amount is a debit, we know this is a debit spread.

Let's do another example using our Bull-Bear Spread Chart.

Example

A client's trades consisted of the following:

B MNO Oct 90 Call

S MNO Oct 105 Call

What is the maximum potential gain and loss for the client?

The first thing we should do is draw our table to help us analyze the problem.

Type of Spread	Want Premiums to:	Call or Put	Type of Spread	
BULL	**W** widen	**C** call	**DR** debit	—Initial Debit = Maximum Loss
BEAR	**N** narrow	**C** call	**CR** credit	—Initial Credit = Maximum Gain
BULL	**N** narrow	**P** put	**CR** credit	
BEAR	**W** widen	**P** put	**DR** debit	

READ CHART ACROSS. To help you build the chart, remember doors (DR) and windows (W) go on the outside.

Next, we need to ask what was done with the more expensive option. The more expensive call is the one with the lower strike price. Since the client bought the more expensive option, we have a debit call spread—first line of the chart. We can see that this trade is bullish, so we know that the maximum gain is at the higher strike price: 105; and the maximum loss is the initial debit: 90.

Let's do another example with a twist.

Example

A client wants you to do the following trades:

B XYZ May 40 Call at 11

S XYZ May 45 Call at 6

What is will be the most the client can make from this trade?

We can look at our table above if we want to help us analyze the problem, but the question has given us the strike prices and is asking us something a little different. In asking us how much the client can make from this trade, watch for a breakeven. Let's first see what was done with the more expensive option. Since the client bought the more expensive option, we have a debit call spread—first chart row. It's a bullish trade, so the maximum gain is 45 (the higher strike price). Let's use the prices we were given. Our breakeven is the difference between the premiums, plus and minus the two strike prices. The difference between the premiums is 5, but the difference between the strike prices is also only 5. *This is really a trick question.* The client can't make money on this trade because the spread between the strike prices equals the spread between premiums. You should not recommend this trade. This is called an **uneconomic trade** and is considered unethical. *Watch for a trick like this on the Series 7 exam.*

Here's another easy way to do a quick analysis to see if a spread is a bull spread or a bear spread: What did you do with the *lower* strike price? If you bought= own=hold=long the lower strike price, you are bullish. If you sold=wrote=short the lower strike price, you are bearish. With this method, it doesn't matter whether you are dealing with call spreads or put spreads.

Finally, here are a few more miscellaneous spread options that you should be aware of in case you are asked to identify them on the Series 7 exam:

PRICE SPREAD (VERTICAL SPREAD): same expiration, different strike prices

Example:
LONG DEF MAY 40 CALL AT 4
SHORT DEF MAY 55 CALL AT 3

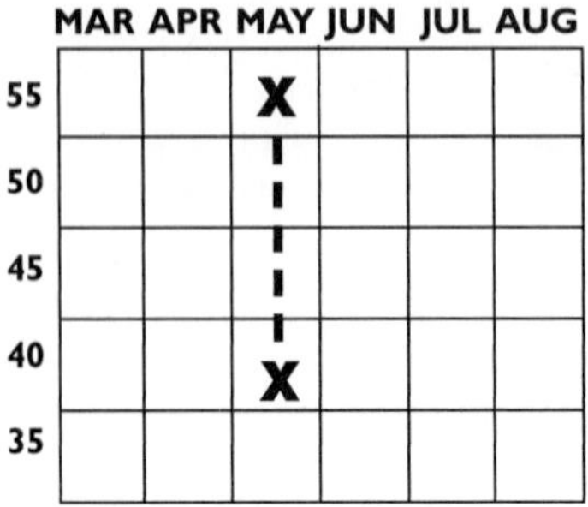

TIME SPREAD (HORIZONTAL SPREAD): same strike prices, different expiration: (also called CALENDAR SPREAD)

Example:
LONG DEF MAR 40 CALL AT 4
SHORT DEF JUL 40 CALL AT 6

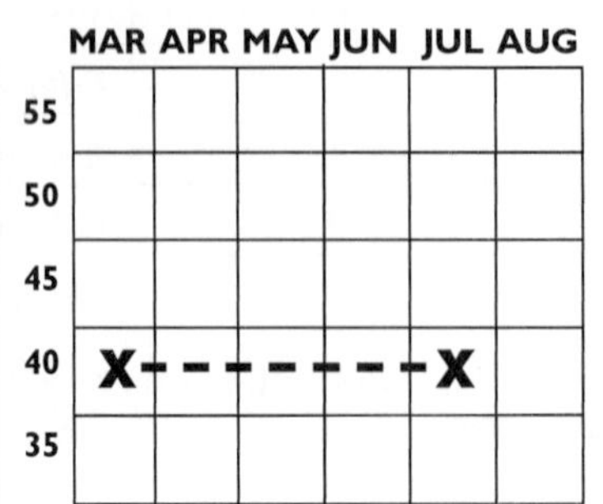

DIAGONAL SPREAD: different expiration and different strike prices:

Example:
LONG DEF APR 50 CALL AT 5
SHORT DEF JUL 40 CALL AT 3

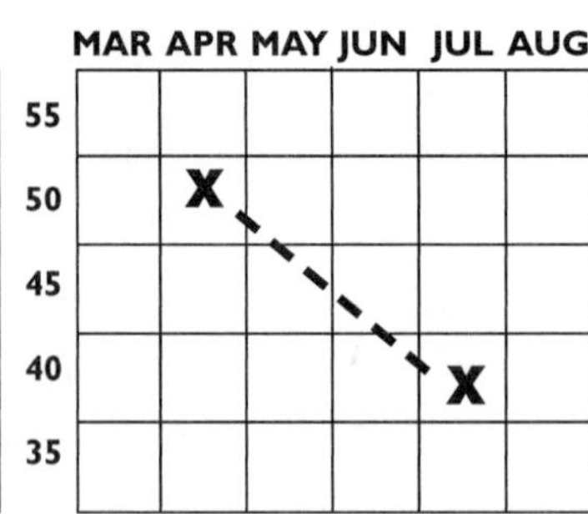

3.6.1.4 Tax Treatment of Options

Options transactions have unique tax rules, but the rules apply the same whether the options traded are equity, index, foreign currency, debt, or yield-based. As with all option contracts, there is a buyer and seller that have different tax rules depending on what they do with the options.

The buyer can exercise the option, sell the option contract, or let it expire. If the buyer exercises the option, the cost basis is equal to the price paid for the stock, plus the option contract premium. Capital gains are determined when the stock is ultimately resold. If the buyer sells the contract, the difference between what the contract was purchased for and what it was sold for is the gain (loss). If the buyer allows the option contract to expire, then the premium paid is a loss. The one exception to this rule is that if stock was purchased the same day as the option contract, the option premium becomes part of the cost basis of the stock.

The seller can be exercised, buy an offsetting contract to close the position, or allow the option to expire. If the seller is exercised, call options have the premium added to the sale price to determine the gain (loss); put options have the premium subtracted from the purchase price to determine the cost basis. If the seller buys an offsetting contract, the difference between the price of the option contracts is the gain (loss). If the option expires, the premium is considered a short term capital gain.

There are a few additional points worth mentioning. LEAPS that expire are considered short-term gains to sellers (even if they are held for over 12 months), but can be long-term losses for buyers. Furthermore, investors may not use options to lock in gains from stocks, then wait and not physically sell the stocks until after the 12 month long-term capital gain period has passed. Finally, trading puts and calls in stocks an investor owns will stop the long-term capital gains clock from ticking, such that the holding period must be 12 months already before an option is acquired, or the 12 months must begin from the date the option is no longer in effect (resold, expired, etc.). The reason for this is that the IRS does not consider the investment to be at risk when the investor can use options to hedge a position.

3.7 Retirement Plans and Estate Tax Considerations

Most investors have two goals: save money for retirement and avoid as much taxation as possible. Many retirement plans help achieve both of these goals. Proper estate planning is essential so that as much as possible of an investor's hard-earned money can be passed on to heirs instead of the government. This section will not turn you into an estate tax expert, but will help you speak intelligently with clients about the subject—and know when to advise clients to seek professional advice.

3.7.1

Individual Plans

Individual retirement plans are a means for investors to build up money that will be available to them when they reach retirement age. Some of the more popular ones are variations of the **Individual Retirement Account (IRA),** which is a personal, tax-deferred retirement account. The main incentive to open an IRA and contribute to it (aside from having income to spend during retirement) is that the money invested is permitted to grow tax-deferred until it is withdrawn from the account. Furthermore, there are provisions for some of the contributions to be tax deductible so this also can reduce an investor's immediate tax burden.

Eligibility for Contributions. Anyone who earns income (from other than investments) is eligible to make tax deferred contributions of up to $2,000 per year to an individual retirement account (IRA). Nonworking spouses may also make a tax deferred contribution of up to $2,000 if they file a joint tax return. Persons with earned income (and nonworking spouses) may contribute to IRAs until age 70½. Contributions are fully deductible if the investor is not eligible to be in another retirement plan (e.g., a company-sponsored plan). In other situations, contributions may be fully, partially, or not deductible based on the individual's adjusted gross income and other factors. Contributions may be made up until April 15 following the tax year of eligibility. Even if the investor is not eligible to make tax deductible contributions, he or she may still make nondeductible contributions with after-tax dollars that can grow tax-deferred until they are withdrawn at retirement age.

Taxation and Distributions. Funds invested in IRAs are permitted to grow tax deferred until distribution at retirement. Dividends and capital gains from IRA investments are also tax deferred as long as the money stays invested in the plan. Distribution options upon retirement (or disability) include receiving regularly scheduled payments (e.g., monthly), or receiving a lump sum payment. Distributions are taxed as ordinary income when received, unless they are rolled over into another qualifying plan within 60 days. Lump sum payments are immediately taxable, and may not be averaged out to lower the tax burden.

Age Requirements. The minimum age to begin receiving IRA distributions without incurring penalties is 59½. If IRA distributions are taken before age 59½, the funds are taxed as ordinary income with an added 10 percent tax penalty. Funds can be withdrawn before age 59½ without incurring penalties if the person becomes disabled, or will use the money to pay medical expenses, to pay educational expenses, or as a down payment for the first-time purchase of an investor's principal residence.

The latest that a person can begin taking distributions without incurring penalties is age 70½. If IRA distributions have not begun by age 70½, the IRS estimates the amount of distribution that should have been made and taxes the funds at the person's ordinary income with an added 50 percent tax penalty.

Permissible Investments. Contributions can be invested in stocks, bonds, government securities, mutual funds, limited partnerships, annuities, CDs, standard bank accounts, U.S. gold, or silver coins. IRA contributions may *not* be invested in antiques, paintings, collectibles, rare coins, gold bullion, or life insurance.

Plan Considerations. Change of employment does not affect the plan, as long as the IRA is transferred directly from one custodian to another. Furthermore, the investor may take possession of the IRA funds once each year, as long as the funds are redeposited into another IRA account within 60 days. This is called a **rollover.** Lump sum distributions from a qualified retirement plan (e.g., when a person changes employers) may be rolled over into a new retirement plan without incurring tax consequences. There is no limit on the amount that an investor can roll over, but any amount not rolled over within that time frame is subject to ordinary income tax (and an added 10 percent penalty if the investor is not yet 59½ years of age).

Remember, though, that there is a limit on the amount of annual contributions that an investor may make: $2,000 for individuals, $4,000 for married couples filing jointly. If these limits are exceeded, there is a 6 percent excess contribution penalty imposed by the IRS. Rollovers are not subject to these limits.

3.7.1.1 IRAs

There are several varieties of IRAs now available to the investor. Two IRA plans of note are the Roth IRA and the SEP-IRA. The **Roth IRA** is a retirement plan with contributions that are *not* tax deductible, but which permits qualified distributions to be taken tax-free upon retirement. Since the Roth IRA funds are taxed before they go into the plan, they are allowed to come out tax free. Like regular IRAs, the Roth IRA permits persons with earned income to invest up to $2,000 individually or $4,000 for married couples filing jointly. Roth IRA contributions must have been invested in the plan at least five years prior to distribution in order to qualify for tax free distribution. And like a regular IRA, a 10 percent penalty is imposed on distributions that start before age 59½, except in the case of disability, medical expenses, education expenses, first-time home purchase, or death. Unlike regular IRAs, there are no mandatory distributions that must occur by age 70½. Regular IRAs may be converted to Roth IRAs without incurring any early withdrawal penalties, but ordinary income tax must be paid on the fund amount.

The **SEP-IRA** (Simplified Employee Pension-IRA) is a tax-deferred retirement plan that is often used by small businesses or sole proprietors who do not offer other retirement plans. Employers can make contributions equal to 15 percent of the employee's total compensation, up to a maximum of $25,500. Contributions and investment earnings grow tax-deferred until distributions begin at retirement (age 59½) or disability. All distributions are taxed as ordinary income. Except for higher contribution limits, all rules for regular IRAs apply, including early withdrawal penalties.

3.7.1.2 Keogh Plans

H.R.-10 (Keogh) plans are available to self-employed people who want to save for retirement. This plan may be contributed to in addition to an IRA plan. Keogh plans are tax deductible to the contributor, and the funds accumulate tax free until distribution at retirement at age 59½. Distributions are taxed as ordinary income. There is a 10 percent penalty for withdrawals before age 59½, and withdrawals must start no later than age 70½.

To be eligible, a person must have self-employed income. This can be in addition to any regular job or regular wages earned. If the self-employed person has full-time (1,000 hours) adult employees (21 years old) who have worked for the employer at least one year, they must be included in the plan as well. Maximum contributions by the employer are 25 percent of net earned income or $30,000, whichever is *less*. The 25 percent of net income earned equals 20 percent of pre-contribution income. The calculation for a person making $80,000 gross is $80,000 gross × 20% = $16,000. Or, take $80,000 – $16,000 = $64,000 × 25% = $16,000. So the math is the same, just watch this on the Series 7 exam: *use* ***20 percent gross, 25 percent net.***

3.7.2

Employer-Sponsored Plans

Employer-sponsored retirement plans come in many varieties as well. The ones we will talk about in this section all allow tax-deferred growth of invested dollars, but the main difference is to the employer. Some retirement plans allow the corporation to deduct contributions from their corporate tax burden (qualified plans), others do not (unqualified plans).

Qualified plans have several characteristics that distinguish them from unqualified plans. In addition to providing companies with a tax deduction for contributions, qualified plans must be approved by the IRS. Qualified plans must also treat all employees equally. The plan is a trust with a document that specifies the rights of the employees. The plan is funded by the employer (except 401k's), with the money being put in on behalf of the employee. The employee pays regular income tax on distributions from the fund upon retirement.

Unqualified plans have several unique characteristics. Because contributions are not tax deductible, they do not need IRS approval. Furthermore, because they are paid with after-tax dollars, the distributions are taxed only on the investment income earned above the cost basis. The plan is not a trust, and the employer is allowed to treat employees differently within the plan—or exclude some altogether. This is the main reason that employers use unqualified retirement plans. They can be "golden handcuffs" that retain a key employee. If more salary were offered, the employee might just shop around with headhunters to get paid more elsewhere, but by offering a larger retirement package, the employee must stay with the firm to collect it. If an employee leaves the company early, the retirement benefits may be cancelled or reduced.

Deferred Compensation Plans. This is an unqualified retirement plan, where the employees agree to receive less money now in exchange for retirement benefits. This is only a contract, though, not a trust or guarantee, so the employees can lose out if the company is not able to pay in the future or the employee leaves the company. When benefits are paid out during retirement, they are taxed as ordinary income to the recipient, and become a tax deduction to the corporation in the future at the time when the benefits are actually paid out.

Profit-Sharing Plans. With this type of plan, the employer agrees to make contributions to the retirement accounts of employees annually when the company makes profits above a certain level. When all employees are treated equally, this is a qualified plan. Benefits paid out during retirement are taxed as ordinary income to the recipient.

Defined Contribution Plan. This is a retirement plan where contribution amounts are fixed at a certain level, but benefit payouts are adjusted based on the return on investment of the retirement account funds. In some plans, employees make voluntary contributions, which may or may not be matched by the company. In other plans, the money is contributed by the employer based on an employee's salary and years of service to the company. The employee usually has options as to where the money will be invested. Benefits that are paid out during retirement are taxed as ordinary income to the recipient.

Defined Benefit Plan. This is a retirement plan where benefit amounts are fixed at a certain level based on the employee's years of service to the company. Contributions may come solely from the employer, or sometimes from employees as well. Such plans pay no taxes on their investments.

Tax-Deferred Annuity Plan [403(b)]. This plan is also referred to as a **tax sheltered annuity** plan or **TSA.** This is a retirement plan that allows employees of nonprofit organizations, tax-exempt organizations, and schools to invest money tax deferred, usually through some type of payroll deduction plan. Employees may contribute up to $10,500, and employers can match up to 25 percent of employee's compensation or $30,000, whichever is less. Distributions may begin at age 59½, and must start by age 70½. Early withdrawal penalty is 10 percent. Benefits paid out during retirement are taxed as ordinary income to the recipient.

Note that even though "annuity" is part of the name, TSA funds can invest in CDs, mutual funds, etc. Also, on Series 7 exam, assume "annuity" means nondeductible, unqualified retirement plan unless you are specifically told in a question that you're dealing with a TSA.

Payroll Deduction Savings Plan. The most common payroll deduction plan used for retirement is the **401(k) plan.** This is a qualified plan, whereby employees can elect to contribute pre-tax dollars to a retirement account where the money will grow tax-deferred. Many employers also match their employees' 401(k) contributions. Employees may contribute up to $10,000, but this number (like most numbers quoted in this section) is subject to constant revisions. Employees can usually choose from a number of investment options. Distributions may begin at age 59½, and must start by age 70½. Early withdrawal penalty is 10 percent. Benefits paid out during retirement are taxed as ordinary income to the recipient.

Ironically, most other payroll deduction plans are unqualified. That is, all contributions must be made with after-tax dollars. Of course, making contributions with after-tax dollars means that the investor has a cost basis, which will make that portion of the retirement distributions tax-free.

Rollovers. When a person changes employers, but has built up some money in a retirement plan which has vested, he or she is usually entitled to move the account as long as it is transferred directly from one custodian to another. Furthermore, the investor may take possession of the funds provided they are redeposited into another account within 60 days. Lump sum distributions from a qualified retirement plan may be rolled over into a new retirement plan without incurring tax consequences. There is no limit on the amount that an investor can roll over, but any amount not rolled over within that time frame is subject to ordinary income tax (plus a 10 percent penalty if the investor is not yet 59½ years of age).

3.7.3

Employees Retirement Income Security Act (ERISA)

Congress felt that employers were abusing company retirement plans, mostly favoring the owners and executives at the expense of the hourly workers. In an effort to protect them and ensure that they were treated fairly, ERISA was enacted in 1974. ERISA applies only to corporate (and other private sector) retirement plans, but excludes government (and other public sector) retirement plans. (Watch this on the Series 7 exam!)

In order to maintain their favorable tax treatment, all qualified plans must follow ERISA guidelines. ERISA defines certain rules and procedures that must be adhered to by employers in order to take tax deductions for contributions made to employees' retirement plans. Some of the key points of the ERISA legislation are noted in this section.

Employee Participation. All full-time, adult employees who have worked for the employer at least one year must be included in the plan. Full-time, adult employees are defined as workers over the age of 21 who have worked at least 1,000 hours in the preceding year.

Funding. Contributions must be invested separately from other corporate funds, and all IRS limits must be observed.

Fiduciary Responsibility. Plan administrators have a fiduciary responsibility to protect the assets of the fund for the beneficiaries. Risk must be a primary consideration when investing. Investments such as short sales, naked options, and buying securities on margin are not allowed.

Vesting. **Vesting** is the right of ownership that an employee gains in retirement plans and other benefits from years of service at a company. Once this right is gained, it cannot be taken away just because a person leaves the company. Instead, benefits accrue in the retirement pension plan, or the employee is given a chance to roll over the funds into another account. This stops companies from firing workers before they reach retirement age just to avoid paying retirement benefits. Under the Tax Reform Act of 1986, employees must be 100 percent vested after their fifth year, or 20 percent vested after their third year with 20 percent more each year until 100 percent in their seventh year.

Nondiscrimination Tests. The formula used to determine the percentage of contributions made by the employer must be the same for all employees in the plan. Treating workers differently is a sure way to have the plan disqualified.

Communications. All employees must receive a written description of the retirement plan, including their rights under the plan, contribution amounts, and distribution information. Qualified plans must also provide employees with a means to name a beneficiary for their contributions upon death. A vesting schedule must be provided as well. Employees must be told what options are available to them, including amounts, if any, they may invest, and matching funds available from the company. They must be given an annual statement that shows the status of their account. Any updates to the plan must also be provided in writing to employees as soon as they are made or scheduled for implementation.

3.7.4

Federal Estate and Gift Tax Considerations

Federal estate and gift taxes are due on securities and other assets that are transferred from a donor to a recipient. The rules that apply, and the exceptions to those rules, can be complicated, but there are a few basic points you need to know.

Unification of Gift and Estate Taxes. Estate taxes and gift taxes are taxed at the same progressive rate. For estates, taxes are due upon death for the value of the estate as of the date the person died, minus exclusions. Taxes must be paid by the estate. For gifts, taxes are due in the year the gift was given for the value of the gift as of the date it was given, minus exclusions. Taxes must be paid by the person who gave the gift (donor).

Lifetime Exclusion, Annual Gift Exclusions. Estates are given an exclusion of $700,000 upon which no tax is due. This amount is current for the 2002 and 2003 tax years, and will gradually rise up to $1,000,000 by 2006. Estates that are transferred to spouses, however, are given a marital deduction that excludes the entire estate from paying tax during the life of the surviving spouse. Upon death of the second spouse, estate taxes are due.

Donors are given an exclusion of $11,000 per year per recipient. Once this annual gift exclusion amount is reached, the donor must then pay tax on any portion over the exclusion amount. This annual amount can't be compounded or annualized.

UGMA/UTMA Accounts. The Uniform Gift to Minors Act (UGMA) provides a simple way for property to be transferred to minors without a formal trust account and without an official guardianship having to be established. Instead, a custodian is appointed, who acts as trustee of the account in charge of affairs for the minor. When a UGMA account is set up, there are several points you need to know.

There can be only one minor and one custodian per account. The account uses the minor's social security number for tax purposes, and pays at the parents' tax rate until age 14, when the minor begins to pay tax on the account. Any amount can go into the account, but amounts over $11,000 may be subject to gift taxes. Once money or securities go in, they may not be taken back. The custodian has a fiduciary responsibility to the minor, and full control over the account's investments. The custodian cannot give discretionary power over the account to another party, cannot invest in options, nor use margin buying for the account. The custodian can loan money to the account, but cannot borrow from the account. Upon the death of the minor, the account goes into the minor's estate. (It does not go to the parents or custodian.)

The Uniform Transfer to Minors Act (UTMA) has been adopted by all 50 states. Most provisions of the UGMA also apply to the UTMA with two notable exceptions. The kind of gifts that may be given to a minor's account has been expanded beyond cash and securities to include real estate, and other assets. Also, the age at which minors can take control of the account was raised to 21 or 25, depending on the state.

Securities as Gifts, Securities as Bequeaths. For securities given as a gift, the recipient receives the donor's cost basis. For securities that are inherited, the heir has the cost basis stepped up to the value of the securities on the date of death. The nature of the gains or losses (whether long-term or short-term) is the same as the donor's for gifts, but inherited securities are always considered long-term holdings.

3.X Summary

3.1 Risk of principal is chance that invested capital will decrease in value. Investment risk is chance that adverse conditions will affect relative value.

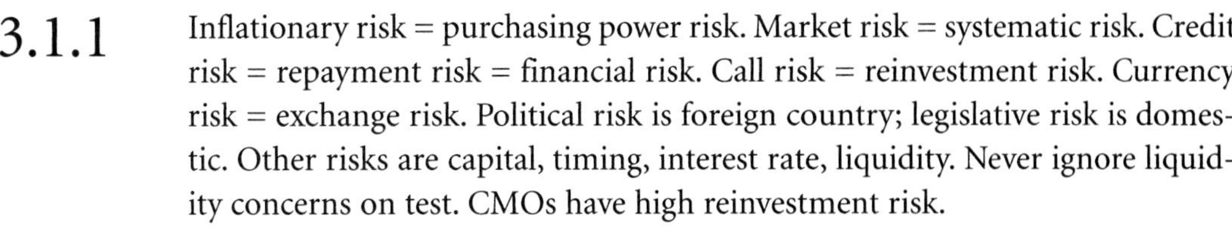

3.1.1 Inflationary risk = purchasing power risk. Market risk = systematic risk. Credit risk = repayment risk = financial risk. Call risk = reinvestment risk. Currency risk = exchange risk. Political risk is foreign country; legislative risk is domestic. Other risks are capital, timing, interest rate, liquidity. Never ignore liquidity concerns on test. CMOs have high reinvestment risk.

3.1.2 Defensive investing: bonds, blue chip, utilities. Aggressive: hi-tech, margin.

3.2

Taxation is important investment portfolio concern: minimize, defer, avoid.

3.2.1 Earned income (a.k.a. active): labor, services, pension, social security, annuity. Investment income (a.k.a. unearned): interest, dividends, capital gains. Passive income: limited partnership, real estate. Losses offset only passive income.

3.2.2 U.S. citizens owe tax on foreign interest, capital gain. If withheld in foreign country, get tax credit (dollar for dollar reduction in amount of tax owed).

3.2.3 Wash sale is when substantially similar securities (or options on them) are bought, sold within 30 days before or after (61-day window). Losses can't be deducted. Bond swap: exception if bonds change two things (e.g., rate, date).

3.3

Equity securities are ownership interest in company: stocks, derivatives.

3.3.1 Stock can be authorized, issued, outstanding, treasury. Treasury can't vote or get dividends. Issued – Treasury = Outstanding. Stock price driven by supply and demand (market value). Shareholders don't vote on dividends, buy back. Stock is transferred by endorsement, transfer agent maintains records and is final arbiter in authenticity disputes. Registrar watches over all stock issues, must be independent entity and can't be same as transfer agent.

3.3.2 Common stock is company ownership, limited liability. Rights: preemptive (antidilution), dividends, access to books, voting, residual claim to assets. Voting: board of directors, dilution issues, change in company direction, splits. Voting can be statutory (1 share = 1 vote), cumulative (total shares voted for one director), proxies (absentee); nonvoting classes of stock exist.

Types of stock: blue chip (stable, well-known), growth (hi-tech), emerging (new tech), income (utilities), cyclical (auto, home), counter-cyclical (food), defensive (blue chip, counter-cyclical), speculative, special situation (news).

Dividends: distribution of company earnings to stockholders by board vote. Paid pro-rata quarterly to stockholders of record on certain date. Taxable. Stock split: adjust stock price downward by increasing outstanding shares. Current stockholders keep same ownership: more shares, less value per share. Reverse split: decrease shares to raise price (so won't get delisted).

3.3.3 Preferred stock is company ownership that pays specified dividend rate. Limited liability, no voting, no preemptive rights, no capital appreciation. Has

priority over common stock for dividends, asset claims in bankruptcy. Kinds of preferred: cumulative (unpaid is future liability), noncumulative, participating (bonuses), nonparticipating, convertible (trade for common stock at fixed price), callable (can redeem early), sinking fund, adjustable rate.

3.3.4 Derivative security has value dependent on underlying security (e.g., option). Rights offering: offer new shares to existing stockholders before public (due to preemptive rights); subscription price is usually lower than price to public; B-D does standby underwriting: guarantees company it will buy all unsold shares. Warrants are future right to buy stock at preset price; given as a sweetener. ADRs are foreign stock for United States; no SEC; banks hold; no voting, less liquid.

3.3.5 Dividends: taxed as ordinary income in year received; corporation exclusion = 70 percent.

Adjusted cost basis is original price, plus commission and allowable expense. Loss is decrease below adjusted cost basis, gain is increase above adjusted cost basis. 12-month hold for long-term capital gain, favorable tax rate. (Puts can restart)

Net gains and losses, long term and short term, offset each other first, then additional loss up to $3,000 can be deducted against ordinary income. Hold period for securities begins on trade date ("when issued" use trade date too).

Stock acquired by conversion: holding period, cost basis same as original. Stock dividends, splits, etc.: holding period same as original, cost basis is same total but divided by increased number of shares so it's less per share. Inherited stock: already one year, cost basis stepped up to FMV on death date. Gift stock: holding period same as donor's, if FMV > donor's basis, gain or loss is donor's basis, if FMV < donor's basis, gain is same, loss is gift's FMV.

Selling part of a position: IRS uses FIFO (early sales usually have lower cost basis so can collect more tax); investor can use LIFO or identify shares.

3.3.6 DPPs are limited partnership; gains, losses flow through so avoid double tax. IRS says DPP can have only four of six corporate features: central management is hardest for DPP to avoid; continuity of existence, freely transferable are easiest to avoid. DPP does not exist until certificate is filed with state; investor is not limited partner until general partner signs subscription agreement accepting limited partner.

Advantages of DPP: limited liability; flow-through of income, losses (passive losses can only offset passive income). Limited partners can't do day-to-day management, can vote on sale, change business/general partner, etc. When dissolved, payout order: secured creditors, unsecured creditors, limited partners, general partner.

Common DPPs: real estate, oil and gas, equipment leasing. Don't sell for tax advantage.

Subscription agreement must be signed by investor, then becomes limited partner when general partner signs. Private offering is done to accredited investors using a private placement memorandum; public offering uses a prospectus.

3.4 Debt instruments are mainly bonds. Can be bearer or registered. Bearer have coupons, so interest rate still called coupon rate. Bonds also called fixed-income securities. Bonds with no collateral are debentures. Bonds are issued by U.S. government, corporations, and municipal governments.

3.4.1 U.S. government bonds are called Treasuries. All kinds use book entry registration. T-Bills: 1 year or less, $10,000 face, quoted at a discount from par (no interest); bid price is higher than ask price because quoted at a discount from par. T-Notes: 1–10 years, $1,000 face, quoted as percent of par, 1/32 increment. T-Bonds: 10+ years, $1,000 face, quoted as percent of par, 1/32 increment. STRIPS are U.S. government backed zero-coupon bonds; T-receipts not government backed.

T-Notes, T-Bonds trade "and interest." Accrued interest calculation is done based on 365-day actual year, settlement is trade + 1 day, don't include settlement day. T-Bills, STRIPS, T-receipts trade flat (no accrued interest because no interest is paid).

Yield has inverse relationship with bond price. Current yield/CY is coupon rate divided by bond price. Yield-to-maturity/YTM is total return investor gets holding bond to maturity. Premium $ = low CY, YTM; Discount $ = high CY, YTM.

3.4.2 U.S. government agencies, entities issue debt to help certain groups lower borrowing costs (e.g., farmers, students). Ginnie Maes are pass-through certificates, securitized by mortgages, backed by the United States government. Reinvestment risk is high.

3.4.3 Asset-backed securities include CMOs (private mortgage-backed securities). Principal, interest payments pass through to investors. CMOs are put into tranches (groups) based on maturity. Can buy standard CMO, interest only, principal only, TAC, PAC. TAC & PAC use companion tranches to help offset risk of prepayment (TAC & PAC) and default (PAC only). CMO has four risks: interest rate (lower rates = refinance), prepayment (if paid off early need replacement investment), extension (late payment), repayment (default). Relatively safe because backed by mortgages, but not backed by the U.S. government.

3.4.4 Corporate bonds, backed by issuer, par = $1000. Need indenture agreement: between corporation and trustee, *not* corporation and bondholder. Corporate bonds have term maturities (all due at once). Ownership: bearer, registered, registered coupon and book entry. Interest paid semiannually, redeemable at par at maturity. If callable, company may pay call premium, holder may get call protection period.

Convertible bonds can be exchanged for common stock at preset price. Parity is price bond value = stock value. Convertible bond and stock usually move in tandem, but stock can drop lower since bond has yield value to support price.

Redeeming bonds: maturity, calling, tender offer, buy on market, refunding, conversion. Bonds paying no interest or in default trade flat. Other trade "and interest." Accrued interest calculation is done based on 360-day year, 30-day months, settlement is trade + 3 days, don't include settlement day.

Yield has inverse relationship with bond price. Corporates use CY, YTM, YTC. YTC (yield-to-call) is total return investor gets holding bond to first call date. Premium price = low CY, YTM, YTC; Discount price = high CY, YTM, YTC.

Corporate bonds rated by Moody's, S&P. Investment grade are four highest ratings for each (a.k.a. bank grade). S&P uses all caps; Moody's uses upper-, lowercase.

3.4.5 Bond interest is taxable when received. Accrued interest is *not* added to cost basis. Zero coupon bonds have imputed interest figured, and tax is due. Corporate bonds bought at premium, investor can amortize premium or add it to cost basis. Corporate bonds bought at discount, discount amount is accreted over life of bond, tax is due each year on that portion. Amortizing and accreting cause adjustments to the cost basis so at maturity there's no capital gain or loss.

3.4.6 Corporations pay tax on 100 percent of interest income, but are given a 70 percent exclusion on dividends received from other U.S. corporations. Corporations are also subject to alternative minimum tax (AMT): tax preference items are added back into adjusted gross income; after exemptions, pays lesser of 20 percent of new total or regular tax.

3.4.7 Money market instruments are short-term debt obligations (1 year or less): REPOs (buy-sell agreements), Federal funds (loans between banks), commercial paper (issued by corporation, *not* banks), CD ($100,000 face, negotiable), Eurodollars (U.S. dollars in foreign banks), banker's acceptances (time drafts, exports).

3.4.8 Municipal securities: debt of state, local governments. Most are tax-exempt. Municipal issuers exempt from SEC, etc. rules (except fraud), but not B-D. Muni interest rates are usually lower because they offer tax advantages.

Many munis have indenture agreement—not required by law, but by market. Price quote is basis price (a percent based on YTM—used for serial, series), or dollar price (percent of par, like corporate—used for term maturities). Ownership is bearer, registered, registered coupon, book entry. Interest paid twice a year. Unqualified legal opinion assures investor bonds are eligible for tax-exempt.

G.O. bonds are paid with tax dollars; backed by full faith and credit of issuer; voter approval may be needed, legal limits on indebtedness must be observed; competitive underwriting; safest because of municipalities' taxing authority.

Revenue bonds paid from project revenues (income), not taxes; feasibility study needed; may have indenture agreement with flow of funds statement; negotiated underwriting; only as sound as underlying project because no tax. Industrial revenue bonds paid by company lease payments, not taxes; feasibility study; negotiated underwriting; most risky muni bond; *not* tax-exempt.

Short term project notes (PNs) are backed by full faith and credit of U.S. government thru HUD because used to finance public housing. Special types of munis are special assessment (fees collected from beneficiaries), moral obligation (state may help pay if default), advance refunded (waiting to retire old debt), double barreled (revenue bonds also backed by taxes), OID (original issue discount), AMT (qualify as tax-exempt, but must be added back as tax preference item).

Marketability factors include: quality rating, maturity, call features, interest rate, block size, liquidity, dollar price, issuer, default, sinking fund, safety.

Early debt retirement can be done through call, put option (holder can choose to sell back), tender offer (issuer can offer to buy), redemption, extraordinary call (e.g., source of revenue is destroyed), refunding. Refunding methods are direct exchange, advanced refunding, refund at call, escrow to maturity.

3.4.8+ Muni pricing is dollar price (percent of par, like corporate—for term maturities); yield with basis price (a percent based on YTM—used for serial, series). Yield has inverse relationship with bond price. Corporates use CY, YTM, YTC. YTC (yield-to-call) is total return investor gets holding bond to first call date. Premium price = low CY, YTM, YTC; Discount price = high CY, YTM, YTC. Munis trade "and interest." Accrued interest calculation is done based on 360 day year, 30-day months, settlement is trade + 3 days, don't include settle day.

Odd-first coupon is when bond is issued more than 6 months prior to first interest payment. Accrued interest is due when buying bond, refunded with first interest payment. Interest figured from dated date (date bond issued).

Muni bonds bought at premium, investor must amortize premium. Muni bonds bought at discount in secondary market must accrete discount over life of bond, but no tax is due. OID: no accretion. Amortizing and accreting cause adjustments to the cost basis so at maturity there's no capital gain, loss.

Taxable equivalent yield is formula that shows investor how much less of a rate is acceptable on tax-exempt muni bonds compared to taxable corporate bonds. Net yield after tax is formula to show how much yield goes to pay capital gain tax.

Yield has inverse relationship with bond price. Corporates use CY, YTM, YTC. YTC (yield-to-call) is total return investor gets holding bond to first call date. Premium price = low CY, YTM, YTC; Discount price = high CY, YTM, YTC.

(THIS IS VERY IMPORTANT FOR THE SERIES 7 EXAM.)

Basis point = 1/100% = .01; Bonds paying no interest or in default trade flat. Tax issues you must know for muni bonds include treatment of discounts and

premiums, OID, margin purchases (interest expense is not deductible), tax on capital gains is still due if bond is sold for a gain, state and local taxes are often exempt if bondholder is a resident, taxable equivalent yield, accrued interest that is paid when buying a muni bond is added to cost basis.

3.5 Packaged securities combine other investments; mutual funds, UIT, REITs.

3.5.1 Three categories of packaged securities:investment companies—separate corporation to collect money, invest, manage portfolio; variable annuity—insurance company manages portfolio to provide income for life; REIT—manages real estate.

3.5.2 Investment companies are non-managed (e.g., UIT) or managed (e.g., mutual fund). Management companies are open-end or closed-end. Closed end: fixed number of shares, buy and sell on exchange, only whole shares, price is supply and demand.

Open end: no limit to number of shares, continuous primary offering—need prospectus, partial shares o.k., buy/sell thru issuer, public offering price = NAV + sale charge.

Mutual funds, three pluses: liquidity (7 days), diversification, pro management. Board of Directors hires Investment Advisor; Underwriters market the fund; Custodian keeps securities safe; Shareholders have right to vote, sell fund. Fund objectives: growth, income, preserve capital, balanced (asset allocate). Fund types: bond, money market, sector, index (match it, not beat it!).

3.5.2+ All clients pay POP. POP = NAV + sales charge. (NASD members get discount.) POP = "ask" price; NAV = "bid" price; NAV = (assets – liabilities) ÷ number of shares. Forward pricing means orders are placed before price is known since NAV is calculated at end of day. Dollar cost averaging is investing same amount each time, but amount buys different number of shares. Result: lower cost/share.

NAV isn't affected by buying, selling shares; mostly by stock value in fund.

Client can save sales charges: 1. reinvesting dividends, capital gains (taxable!) 2. exchanging in same family of funds, 3. breakpoints, 4. letters of intent, 5. rights of accumulation. (Breakpoint selling is violation of NASD rules.)

Sales charge (spread or load): no-load, load (front or back), 12b-1 market fee. Front end, customer buys fewer shares; Back end, all money buys shares and fee is paid when sold (lower if fund held longer); 12b-1 maximum 75 percent—load and .25 percent—no load.

Distribution fee maximum is 8.5 percent if breakpoints offered, auto reinvest, accumulation rights; if not, maximum is 6.25 percent. Only distribution fee paid to underwriter from sales charge.

Fund must redeem within 7 days at NAV price. Payout can be lump sum, fixed percentage or fixed payments (not for life). May have restrictions.

Conduit theory: if 90 percent cap. gains, dividends pass thru, fund is tax exempt.

Unit Investment Trust (UIT): no active management, has fixed portfolio, so low fees.

Taxes on distributions depend on how long fund held the security, not the investor. Reinvest capital gains, dividends and exchanges are taxable events.

3.5.3 Annuities are payments for life. Fixed guarantees amount, variable doesn't. Fixed investments go into general account, variable go into separate account. Separate account can be directly managed (regulated like mutual fund), or indirectly managed (invest. advisor is outside contractor so reg. like UIT).

Variable annuity has accumulation units, annuity units. Conversion done at retirement and Assumed Interest Rate (AIR) is chosen. If separate account rate of return is higher than AIR, payment goes up; if lower than AIR payment falls.

Payouts can be immediate or deferred. Can take lump sum or systematic withdrawal; or if annuitized take life annuity (highest, but no money to heirs), life with period certain, life with amount certain, life with joint survivor.

AIR is constant, number of annuity units is constant, value of units and payment can change.

Qualified annuities (e.g., IRA) paid with pre-tax dollars, so taxed as income when taken out at 59½. Money grows tax deferred, but 10 percent penalty for early withdrawal. If investor surrenders contract, treated as a withdrawal. Death benefits, tax treatment transfers to beneficiary. Annuities have no capital gains.

3.5.4 REITs manage real estate. Favorable tax if 75 percent real estate assets, 75 percent income from real estate, 90–95 percent income pass through. Investors share gains, but not losses.

3.6 Derivatives have value dependent on underlying security, e.g., options.

3.6.1 Options can be OTC or exchange traded (listed). Options give holder the right, but not the obligation to do something (buy or sell). Call buyer has option to buy; put buyer has option to sell. Strike price is price that holder can exercise option. Exercise means make use of a right before it expires. Random assignment of exercise notice given by Options Clearing Corp. (OCC issues, guarantees, clears options. Allows investor to close a position.)

Option price is premium. Premiums increase portfolio income. Option has intrinsic value (in-the-money) and time value. Intrinsic value only = parity.

In-the-money means option is at point where holder could make money (if don't consider commission). Out-of-the-money means option can't make money.

Opening transaction: buyer = owner = holder = long; seller = writer = short. Closing transaction: liquidate position by buying offsetting option. There are position limits and exercise limits (max contracts can own and use). OCC settlement: buy/sell, next business day; exercise, three days after notice.

Breakeven is premium plus strike price for call, minus strike price for put. Breakeven for multiple options is difference of premiums plus and minus strike prices to find range where investor will make or lose money.

Covered option means option writer owns the stock. Naked (uncovered) option means writer doesn't own stock. Ratio call writing is some of each.

Spread is one long, one short option on same stock. Straddle is equal calls or equal puts on same stock, same price, same date. Combination is two or more options on same company, but different price or dates.

Equity options: listed stocks, 100 shares round lot, expire 3–6–9 months except LEAPS (24–39 mos.), stock splits affect option contract terms, prices (p.149). Index options: various market indexes, expire 3–6–9 months except LEAPS. Debt options: Treasuries (T-bills figure premium × 0.25 because 13 weeks). T-note/T-bond quoted 1/32 point, bond options move opposite interest rate. Yield-based options trade based on yield changes, move with interest rate. Foreign currency option: U.S. cents, except 1/10 cent Francs, 1/100 for yen, no U.S. dollar options. European: exercise last day; American: exercise anytime.

Long call, short put = bullish (optimistic). Short call, long put = bearish. Neutral strategies: write covered call to collect premium; write straddle when don't think there will be much price movement; write combination. Bearish strategies: write covered call; write covered put to protect short sale; bear spread. Put breakeven = PUSH (put, subtract higher). Chart page 158. Bull strategies: write covered call (above market); bull spread. Breakeven for Call = CALL (call, add lower). Review other spread charts on page 160.

If buyer exercises option, premium is added to cost basis. If option expires, premium = loss. If seller is exercised, premium is part of gain/loss. If option expires, premium = short term capital gain (including LEAP). Options can't be used to turn short into long cap gains. Options can restart cap gains hold time.

3.7

Retirement and tax avoidance are two goals of many investors.

3.7.1

Individual retirement plans open to anyone who makes earned income (not from investment). IRA $2,000 contribution limit, plus $2,000 for spouse. Amount is tax deductible if person isn't eligible for another plan. Money grows tax deferred. Withdrawals at age 59½ –70½ with no penalties. If not, 10 percent tax penalty early, 50 percent tax penalty if late. Can invest in stocks, bonds, mutual funds, etc., but not antiques, collectibles, coins, etc. Rollover is o.k.

Roth IRA is not tax-deductible, but using after-tax dollars means tax-free later. SEP-IRA has higher limits (15 percent of pay., max is $25,500). Other rules same. Keogh plans for self-employed. All employees must be allowed to do plan. Maximum contribution is the lesser of 25 percent net earnings (20 percent gross) or $30,000.

3.7.2 Employee sponsored plans are qualified or unqualified. Qualified is tax deductible if treat all employees same, have trust account, follow rules. Unqualified is not tax deductible, but can give selectively to employees. Deferred compensation is unqualified, and employee may lose if leaves company. Profit-sharing can be qualified if all participate. 401(k) is payroll deduction where employer may match funds. 403(b) is for non-profits. Defined benefit and defined contribution with fixed amounts. (Details on page 164.)

Rollover: can take it out but must reinvest within 60 days or pay penalty.

3.7.3 Tax favorable plans must follow ERISA guidelines. All full-time (1,000 hrs.) adult (age 21) employees must be included. Funds must be kept separate from company accounts. Fiduciary duty means no risky investments. Vesting must be 100 percent in fifth year, or 20 percent each year beginning in third year. Must treat all employees in plan equally (nondiscrimination). Everyone must get written description of plan, annual report of contributions, means to name beneficiary, vesting schedule, and details of available options.

3.7.4 Federal estate and gift taxes due transfer from donor to recipient. Tax rate is same for both. Estate exclusion is currently $700,000, but entire estate is excluded for spouse. Donor limit is $11,000 per year tax free.

UGMA/UTMA gives simplified asset transfer to minors. Only one minor and one custodian per account. Use minor's social security number. Parents' tax rate until age 14, then minor's tax rate. Once asset goes in, can't take it back. Custodian has fiduciary duty. Upon death of minor, account goes into minor's estate, not to custodian and not to parents.

For gifted securities, cost basis and holding period (short or long) same as donor. For inherited securities, cost basis is stepped up to value on date of death, and inherited securities are always considered long-term capital gains.

Chapter 3 Review Quiz

1. Which of the following means a decline in the value of assets relative to prices?
   a. capital risk
   b. purchasing power risk
   c. interest rate risk
   d. systematic risk

2. Passive income:
   a. is derived from investments.
   b. can be offset by passive losses.
   c. both a and b.
   d. neither a nor b.

3. Which of the following types of stock is not eligible to vote?
   a. authorized and outstanding
   b. issued and outstanding
   c. outstanding
   d. treasury

4. Which of the following would be voted on by shareholders?
   a. decision on stock buy-back
   b. merger and acquisition activity
   c. dividend payments
   d. Board of Directors' salaries

5. Which of the following helps a company fulfill its preemptive rights obligation?
   a. warrants
   b. standby underwriting
   c. preferred stock
   d. banker's acceptance time draft

6. An example of counter-cyclical stock would be:
   a. IPO stocks.
   b. housing stocks.
   c. high-tech stocks.
   d. food stocks.

7. Preferred stock:
   a. pays a dividend.
   b. confers preemptive rights.
   c. gives stockholder voting rights.
   d. all of the above

8. The value of a derivative security is dependent on all of the following *except:*
   a. value of the underlying security.
   b. market conditions.
   c. expiration of the derivative.
   d. interest rate paid on bonds.

9. The dividend exclusion rule says that:
   a. preferred stock payments are made before common stock dividends.
   b. corporations don't need to pay tax on 70 percent of dividends received.
   c. dividends qualify for a tax credit.
   d. investors can deduct foreign dividends received from ADR holdings.

10. An investor's adjusted cost basis:
    a. is found by taking the purchase price and adding allowable deductions.
    b. is subtracted from the sale price of an asset to figure tax liability.
    c. must be accreted to count imputed interest when OID bonds are purchased.
    d. all of the above

11. "When issued" means:
    a. a security has been issued but not yet authorized.
    b. for tax purposes, holding period begins when a stock is issued and paid for.
    c. an official settlement date is not yet known, but stock can be purchased now.
    d. all of the above.

12. What is the reason FIFO is used by the IRS when figuring tax liability?
    a. because the first shares purchased would have the highest cost basis, and thus maximize tax revenues.
    b. because the first shares purchased would have the lowest cost basis, and thus maximize tax revenues.
    c. because the investor is not permitted to choose an alternative method.
    d. the IRS doesn't used FIFO, it uses LIFO.

13. For limited partnerships to be afforded preferable tax treatment, the IRS says that they can have no more than four of the following traits:

    I. business associates, II. profit motive, III. centralized management structure, IV. limited liability, V. continuity of existence, VI. freely transferable shares

    Which of the above are most easily avoided in a limited partnership?
    a. I and III
    b. IV and VI
    c. V and VI
    d. II and V

14. When does an investor become a limited partner?
    a. When the general partner signs the subscription agreement.
    b. When the general partner receives the check and subscription agreement.
    c. When the investor signs the subscription agreement.
    d. When broker-dealer or registered representative accepts the subscription agreement.

15. What's the main advantage you should use to sell clients on limited partnerships?
    a. tax advantages
    b. unlimited growth potential
    c. chance to get in on deals where they've had no previous experience
    d. economic soundness of the deal

16. Which of the following are not backed by the full faith and credit of U.S. government?
    a. T-bills
    b. U.S. Treasury Notes and Treasury Bonds
    c. Treasury Receipts
    d. STRIPS

17. When bonds trade "and interest," it means that:
    a. accrued interest is added to the quoted price of the bond.
    b. interest is being paid on the bond.
    c. the bond is trading flat.
    d. the bond is a zero coupon which pays full face value at maturity.

18. Accrued interest calculations for U.S. treasury bonds:
    a. use a 365-day year.
    b. use 30-day months.
    c. settle trade + 3 business days.
    d. all of the above

19. A U.S. Treasury bill (face value of $10,000) has bid price of 3.00, ask price of 2.75. How much accrued interest is due if an investor buys it on Monday, May 1?
    a. $300
    b. $275
    c. $0
    d. need more information

20. When bonds are purchased at a discount, this means that:
    a. the purchase price is less than the face amount.
    b. the current yield is higher than the coupon rate.
    c. the yield-to-call is higher than the yield-to-maturity.
    d. all of the above

21. Which of the following bonds are backed by the full faith and credit of U.S. government?
    a. Sallie Maes
    b. Ginnie Maes
    c. Freddie Macs
    d. Fannie Maes

22. A collateralized mortgage obligation is:
    a. backed by a pool of mortgages.
    b. divided into tranches.
    c. both a and b.
    d. neither a nor b.

23. An indenture agreement is required for which of the following?
    a. corporate bonds
    b. municipal bonds
    c. both a and b
    d. neither a nor b

24. Term maturities are associated with which type(s) of bonds?
    a. corporate bonds
    b. dollar-priced municipal bonds
    c. both a and b
    d. neither a nor b

25. Calculating conversion parity is important for corporate bonds because:
    a. investors want to know when the call protection period has expired.
    b. investors need to know if they should convert the bond to common stock.
    c. investors need to watch for interest rate fluctuations.
    d. investors know a falling stock price moves in tandem with bond prices.

26. Prerefunding is used by a bond issuer:
    a. when he is tendering shares in the open market.
    b. when a mass conversion of convertible bonds is imminent.
    c. so the issuer can sell bonds now at favorable rates, then call old ones.
    d. to avoid bankruptcy.

27. A trade reads: 5 ABC 8¼% F+A callable 102 after ’06. What does “5” mean?
    a. The premium for the trade is 5.
    b. The trade is for 5 units.
    c. The strike price is 5.
    d. Interest is due on the 5th of the month.

28. Why would a security “trade flat”?
    a. The broker forgot to calculate interest.
    b. No interest is being paid on the bond.
    c. The price has not fluctuated for a period of time.
    d. The security is preferred stock.

29. Whose highest bond rating is "Aaa"?
    a. Moody's
    b. S&P's
    c. Fitch's
    d. Washington, DC

30. When a bond trades "and interest," how is this treated for tax purposes?
    a. The interest is accreted over the life of the bond.
    b. It is a deduction against interest earned for the buyer who pays the interest.
    c. It is added to the cost basis of the bond.
    d. It is amortized over the life of the bond.

31. Which of the following is *not* a money market instrument?
    a. repurchase agreement
    b. commercial paper
    c. banker's acceptance
    d. standard CDs

32. Which of the following is a characteristic of general obligation bonds?
    a. backed by full faith and credit of the issuer
    b. paid from income generated by a specific project
    c. negotiated underwriting
    d. all of the above

33. Which of the following is a characteristic of revenue bonds?
    a. backed by the full faith and credit of the issuer
    b. paid from income generated by a specific project
    c. competitive underwriting
    d. all of the above

34. A moral obligation bond:
    a. is one a county was not going to pay, but then decided it would not default.
    b. is tax-exempt at all levels of government.
    c. is one where the state legislature has passed a resolution that it would pay the debt in the event that the issuer defaults.
    d. is one where repayment is taken on as a binding obligation of the state.

35. An AMT bond:
    a. has the interest exemption added back into one's AMT tax computation as a tax preference item.
    b. is issued by a bank or savings & loan.
    c. is tax-exempt.
    d. pays from the revenue stream of a project and from taxes.

36. Diversification in bond holdings would entail:
    a. buying bonds from different parts of the country.
    b. buying some revenue bonds and some GO bonds.
    c. buying different bond maturity dates.
    d. all of the above.

37. Early retirement of muni bonds can be done in all of the following ways, *except:*
    a. tendering.
    b. extraordinary call.
    c. direct exchange.
    d. forced conversion.

38. When the basis price of a bond is lower than the coupon rate, the bond is:
    a. trading at a premium.
    b. trading at a discount.
    c. trading at par.
    d. trading flat.

39. With an odd first coupon:
    a. the investor will miss one interest payment.
    b. the issuer will miss one interest payment.
    c. the investor must pay accrued interest from the dated date.
    d. the issuer will pay additional interest when the bond matures.

40. Taxable equivalent yield tells an investor:
    a. how much higher of a yield is required on municipal bonds.
    b. how much lower of a yield is required on corporate bonds.
    c. how much tax the investor will pay on municipal bonds.
    d. how much lower of a yield is acceptable with tax-exempt bonds.

41. When tax-exempt municipal bonds are purchased on margin, the investor:
    a. may deduct interest expenses.
    b. may not deduct interest expenses.
    c. must add any deduction back into his or her AMT calculation.
    d. both b and c

42. When do closed-end investment companies need to give out a prospectus?
    a. Always, because the closed end offering is a continuous primary offering.
    b. Exchange traded securities must always give prospectuses.
    c. SEC rules say they must each time old shares are sold.
    d. Closed-end companies need to give out prospectuses only at initial offering.

43. An asset allocation mutual fund would have funds:
    a. invested in open-end and closed-end investment companies.
    b. invested in stocks, bonds, and annuity contracts.
    c. invested in stocks, bonds, and cash.
    d. invested in REITs and UITs.

44. An index fund has the fund manager:
    a. try to beat the index.
    b. try to match the index.
    c. lag behind the index.
    d. ignore the index.

45. The NAV of a mutual fund:
    a. is made up of the fund's net assets divided by the number of shares outstanding.
    b. is an equivalent term to "bid" price used for other securities.
    c. is figured once at the end of each day, so orders use forward pricing.
    d. all of the above

46. Which of the following has the most impact on NAV?
    a. money going into the fund (new buyers)
    b. money going out of the fund (redemptions)
    c. dividend payments from companies the fund is holding
    d. the value of the stocks in the fund

47. When computing the sales charge:
    a. POP is always greater than NAV.
    b. NAV is always greater than POP.
    c. POP and NAV are equal.
    d. the management fee must always be added to POP.

48. All of the following are characteristics of variable annuity contracts, *except:*
    a. funds are deposited into a separate account.
    b. insurance companies bear the entire market risk.
    c. payments are guaranteed for the life of the contract holder.
    d. payments are based on comparison of actual return to assumed interest rate.

49. Given the following information about a variable annuity payout schedule, what will the third month's payment be?

MONTH	PRIOR MO. RETURN	AIR	PAYMENT
1	n/a	6%	$537
2	9%	6%	$565
3	7%	6%	$?

    a. $537
    b. $556
    c. $565
    d. $573

50. Which type of annuity payout would pay a client the highest monthly payment?
    a. life annuity
    b. life annuity with period certain
    c. life annuity with amount certain
    d. life annuity with joint and last survivor

51. What percentage of REIT income must pass through to qualify for favorable taxes?
    a. 25%
    b. 75%
    c. 90–95%
    d. 5–10%

52. Which group is responsible for guaranteeing and clearing options contracts?
    a. SEC
    b. OCC
    c. SRO
    d. NASD

53. When is the following option in-the-money?

    B IBM May 60 call at 5

    a. when IBM reaches 65
    b. when IBM reaches 60
    c. when IBM reaches 55
    d. in the month of May

54. What is the client's maximum risk writing an uncovered call IBM 60 at 5?
    a. Maximum loss is the initial debit amount.
    b. Maximum loss is strike price, minus premium collected,
    c. Maximum loss is 60 if stock goes to zero.
    d. Maximum loss is unlimited.

55. When a cash dividend is declared, what happens to an option's strike price?
    a. Strike price is adjusted downwards and number of shares is adjusted up.
    b. Option contract splits and strike price is adjusted.
    c. No adjustment is made.
    d. Options contract price is adjusted to reflect strike price of other securities.

56. Yield-based options:
    a. trade with an inverse relationship to interest rates.
    b. trade with a positive relationship to interest rates.
    c. trade the same as bond options.
    d. can't be traded in the marketplace.

57. Why would an investor write a covered put?
    a. to protect a short sale position
    b. to protect against losses in a stock the investor owns
    c. because the investor is bullish on the stock
    d. the investor made a mistake and really meant to write a covered call

58. Given the following trade, is the investor bullish, bearish, or neutral?
    1 Long XYZ Oct 50 call at 8
    1 Short XYZ Oct 60 call at 5
    a. bullish
    b. bearish
    c. neutral
    d. need more information

59. If a client does not begin taking distributions from a qualified IRA account by age 59½, are there any consequences?
    a. Yes, there is a 10 percent tax penalty.
    b. Yes, there is a 50 percent tax penalty.
    c. No, the client can withdraw at any time with no penalty.
    d. No, as long as withdrawal begin before age 70½.

60. An employer wants to retain some key employees and so devises a special unqualified retirement package just for them. Which of the following rules apply?
    a. ERISA says all employees must be treated equally.
    b. Employees must have 100 percent vested ownership in the plan by the fifth year.
    c. All employees must receive a written description of the plan and a payout schedule of benefits.
    d. No rules apply because it is an unqualified plan.

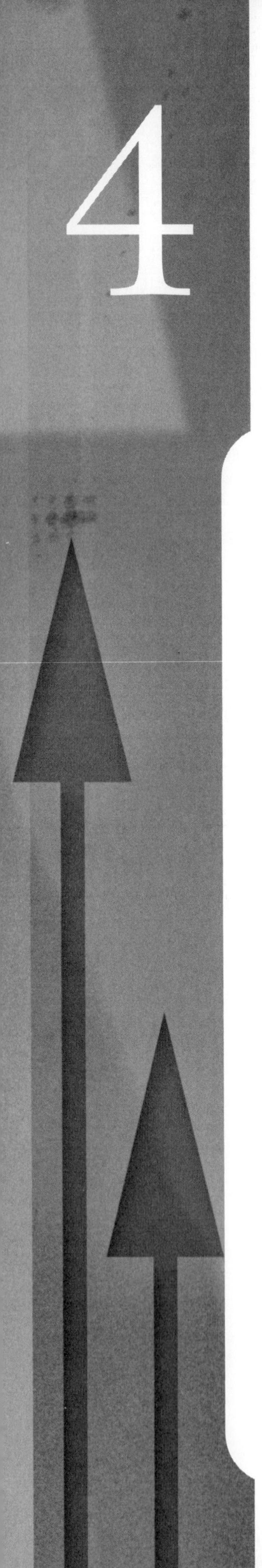

4 Managing Customer Accounts and Records

"Managing Customer Accounts and Records" is the fourth of the seven critical functions that are performed by a Registered Representative. When working with customer accounts, it is important to inform the customer of all basic types of accounts available and discuss the appropriateness of each. Obtaining all required customer documentation is important. This ensures that accounts and transactions that are prohibited for a customer are not initiated.

The RR must be sure to obtain all required approvals to open an account. The customer must also be kept informed about the conditions under which the account will be maintained. This includes both regulatory requirements and broker-dealer firm policies. The RR should retain copies of all correspondence with the customer, as part of this duty to maintain and update customer account records. The RR also has a responsibility to execute appropriate customer requests, such as withdrawal of funds or securities, after obtaining all of the necessary documents, approvals, or power of attorney.

This fourth critical function, covered in Chapter 4 ("Managing Customer Accounts and Records"), represents about 11 percent of the total exam: approximately 25–29 questions of the total 250 questions on the Series 7 Exam. Much of the material covered in this chapter builds on what you have already learned in the first three chapters. This information will help you on the Series 7 exam, and later as you function as an RR in the securities industry.

This chapter will be broken up into three sections:

4.1 **Requirements for Opening Customer Accounts.** This first section will go through lots of definitions of the different kinds of customer accounts that may be opened. This will touch on everything from simple basic accounts, to joint accounts, corporate accounts, minors' accounts, and confidential accounts. The chapter will also discuss discretionary authority, power of attorney, and related topics.

4.2 **Rules Governing the Conduct of Accounts.** The requirements and regulations that must be observed when dealing with customer accounts will be examined in this section. Rules governing discretionary accounts will be looked at in more depth. Other customer requests will be discussed, including circumstances for refusing a request or restricting account activity, procedures to follow upon the death of a client, and other circumstances for closing or transferring accounts. State regulations with regard to fiduciary accounts will be the final area looked at in this section.

4.3 **Margin Accounts.** This section will define key terms dealing with margin accounts, go through the requirements and characteristics of margin accounts, then discuss important calculations regarding equity positions in margin accounts. These calculations will likely appear on the Series 7 exam, as will questions about short sales, which is the last topic covered in this section and in this chapter.

key terms

Excess equity: any value that is in a margin account above the minimum Reg. T requirement.

Exempt securities: securities which do not fall under the rules or jurisdiction of a particular oversight body.

Fiduciary: a person in a position of trust, held by law to high standards of good faith and loyalty.

Hypothecation: using something as collateral. A **hypothecation agreement** allows the broker-dealer to use the securities as collateral.

Loan value: the maximum percentage of current market value that a broker-dealer can lend on nonexempt marginable securities (currently 50 percent of value).

Margin: the amount that a customer must have on deposit with a broker-dealer to buy securities on credit.

Margin call: a demand that a customer deposit additional cash or securities to bring the margin amount up to the minimum requirement.

Marginable securities: securities that are eligible for a client to buy and sell in a margin account.

Nonexempt securities: securities which are under the jurisdiction of a particular oversight body, and thus must comply with their rules, e.g., SEC or Reg. T.

Shorting against the box: a technique where an investor does a short sale with the same security in which the investor also owns a long position. The short sale locks in a gain against drops in price, and the long stock the investor owns can be delivered later to cover the short sale. Tax law changes have curtailed the use of this technique.

Special memorandum account (SMA): a bookkeeping entry used by broker dealers to keep track of excess equity that clients have built up through their trades in their margin accounts.

4.1

Requirements for Opening Customer Accounts

When opening new customer accounts, there are many documents to fill out and procedures to follow. Some of these will vary by broker-dealer; others are more standard because they follow NYSE, NASD, or MSRB guidelines. Much of this falls under the "know your customer" rules that we discussed in Chapter 2.

Just to review, the "know your customer" rule says that it is the responsibility of the broker-dealers and RRs to have a complete and accurate understanding of a client's financial situation so that they are in a position to give appropriate advice and make suitable recommendations to the client. To this end, most brokerage firms have special forms that new clients must fill out as a means of gathering the necessary information to satisfy this requirement.

Much of this information is standard: name, address, phone number, age (not required, but must note for a retirement account—also, minors can't open accounts), occupation, employer information, income, estimated net worth, bank references, previous brokerage experience. Of course, the social security number is also required (for tax reporting purposes), but one that may surprise you is citizenship. Two items of note that are *not* on the new account forms used by broker-dealer are education level and race/ethnicity. It is also interesting to note that the new customer is *not* required to sign the new account form if he or she is opening a cash account. The RR and branch manager or other principal of the firm must sign for the broker-dealer, but the customer needs to sign only if securities will be bought on margin (credit).

Additional requirements by the NYSE, NASD, and MSRB include a statement about how the account was acquired, whether or not the customer is an employee of another member broker-dealer firm, and whether or not the customer is an officer, director, executive, or shareholder (10 percent or higher) of any publicly traded company. This is to help monitor potential conflicts of interest, insider trading, or illegal activity.

4.1.1

Account Specifics

All new accounts require a new account form. There are other items that the broker-dealer may need in order to set up and handle the account properly (for example, MSRB requires a B-D to know the tax status of a client). Some of these items depend on what kind of account will be opened, who will own the account, and who is authorized to trade for the account. These choices may entail additional restrictions or require more documentation, which we will mention as we discuss each topic.

CASH ACCOUNTS. A cash account (sometimes called a **special cash account**) is one of the two basic types of accounts that can be opened. With a cash account, all securities are paid for in cash, either from funds already on deposit with the broker, or by the customer delivering cash or a check within the settlement rules established by the broker-dealer for the type of trade involved. Some accounts, such as IRAs, can be opened only with a cash account.

When doing trades in the account, the customer can choose to have securities handled one of three ways: **transfer and ship** (securities transferred into customer's name and shipped to customer), **transfer and hold** (securities transferred into customer's name, but held by the broker-dealer), or **hold in street name** (securities left in broker-dealer's name and held by broker-dealer to facilitate future sales).

MARGIN ACCOUNTS. A margin account is the other basic type of account that can be opened. Opening a margin account means that the customer is going to buy securities on credit. **Margin** is the amount that a customer must have on deposit with a broker-dealer to buy securities on credit. The customer is permitted to borrow only a portion of the securities price, and must cover the balance with cash or by depositing other securities that the customer owns. Federal Reserve Board Regulation T (**Reg T**) states that a person must have on deposit the higher of $2,000 or 50 percent of the purchase price of the eligible securities bought on margin. Broker-dealers can establish their own margin rules requiring more to be on deposit.

When opening a margin account, there are some additional documents that the customer must sign. These include a **credit agreement** (spelling out the terms of credit from the broker-dealer) and a **hypothecation agreement** (allowing the broker-dealer to use the securities as collateral).

Exam Topic Alert

The broker-dealer may also ask the customer to sign a **loan consent agreement** (allowing the securities to be loaned to other broker-dealers), but *this form is the only one not required.*

OPTIONS TRADING. If a customer wants to trade options, some additional forms are needed. We saw this in the last chapter when we discussed options. The Options Clearing Corporation (OCC) has an **options disclosure document** that must be given to the customer before any trades can be made. An **options agreement** must also be signed by the customer within 15 days, acknowledging receipt of the OCC disclosure document, and agreeing to be bound by the rules and terms of OCC and the broker-dealer with regard to options trading. Furthermore, the new account agreement must be **signed by a registered options principal** (ROP) from the firm, acknowledging that he or she has examined the customer's financial situation and investing history, and the customer is suitable for options trading. Some brokerage firms also have additional documents that clients are required to sign prior to options trading.

INDIVIDUAL ACCOUNTS. An individual account is set up with only one named person on the account. That individual, though, can grant power of attorney to another party, giving that party trading authority over the account. Granting **limited authorization** would permit only buy-sell orders to be executed by that person; **full authorization** would also allow the person to withdraw funds from the account. The individual can also grant discretionary power to the RR or broker-dealer. Documents must be signed by the customer (and kept on file by the broker-dealer) any time trading authorization is granted to others. We will discuss this topic in more detail shortly.

JOINT ACCOUNTS. A joint account is set up with two or more people named on the account. With any type of joint account, all parties own an undivided interest in the account. This means that everyone owns a part of each stock; there is no way to separate out who owns which stocks. Because of this, any one of the joint owners can enter a buy or sell order on behalf of the account. This also means that whenever any security is sold, the check must be written to *all* parties jointly. There are actually three different kinds of joint accounts that can be set up.

Joint Tenants with Right of Survivorship (JTROS) is a type of joint account where upon the death of one party, that party's interest in the account is passed to the other parties of the account. To have this arrangement, all parties must have an equal share in the account. This is a common arrangement between spouses.

Joint Tenants In Common (JTIC) is a type of joint account where upon the death of one party, that party's interest in the account is passed to his or her estate. This means that each of the joint tenants can name a beneficiary. With this arrangement, parties can have unequal shares.

Community property is a type of joint account that is not recognized in all states. States that do recognize it have their own rules regarding ownership rights and transfer upon death. Just be aware that these types of accounts do exist in places.

SOLE PROPRIETORSHIPS. Sole proprietorship accounts are set up and maintained very similarly to the way individual accounts are. Generally, only the person named on the account may make trades unless other persons are authorized. If the sole proprietorship is using a fictitious name, that information must be part of the file. Other relevant information or documents may be requested as needed. Of course, a new account form is also required.

PARTNERSHIPS. Partnerships are a contract between two or more persons to pool money, resources, and talents in a business, project, or venture, in exchange for a share of the profits (or losses) generated by their association. To open a securities account (cash or margin), the broker-dealer needs a copy of the partnership agreement, and any other documentation that details who has the authority to open the account and make trades on behalf of the partnership. A new account form is needed also.

Unincorporated associations may be set up as a partnership, or in some other business arrangement. In order to open an account, the broker-dealer must be provided with appropriate documentation, such as a resolution, stating who has authority to open an account and make trades, and under what conditions.

CORPORATIONS. A corporation is a separate legal entity organized under state law. As such, the broker-dealer requires the company's Articles of Incorporation and/or Corporate Charter stating that the corporation is authorized to buy and sell securities. The broker-dealer also needs a specific corporate resolution stating which person(s) are authorized to make trades on behalf of the corporation. This is in addition to the new account form required any time a new account is opened.

Insiders are any persons who have access to confidential or sensitive information about a company before it is released to the public. Included in this definition are officers, directors, and key employees of a company, as well as any stockholder who owns more than 10 percent of a publicly traded company. Any such person must disclose this to the RR and broker-dealer firm when opening a new account.

TRUST ACCOUNTS. Trust accounts are set up to benefit one party (beneficiary), but are controlled by a third party (fiduciary). A **fiduciary** is a person in a position of trust, held by law to high standards of good faith and loyalty. As such, the fiduciary must be prudent with the trust account, and act solely in the best interests of the beneficiary. Speculative trades, selling short, and many times even margin accounts are not permitted. Some states limit the investments that a fiduciary can make, publishing a list of securities acceptable for investment. A fiduciary cannot delegate authority or responsibility for the account, nor share in the profits of the account.

The fiduciary is authorized by court order or appointed by another official document to manage the account. The broker-dealer will need a copy of either of these along with the new account form.

UGMA/UTMA ACCOUNTS. The Uniform Gift to Minors Act (UGMA) and Uniform Transfer to Minors Act (UTMA) provide a simple way for property to be transferred to minors without a formal trust account. Instead, a custodian is appointed.

The **custodian** has a fiduciary responsibility to the minor, and full control over the account's investments. The custodian cannot give discretionary power over the account to another party, cannot invest in options, nor use margin buying for the account. The custodian can't borrow from the account. There can be only one minor and one custodian per account, but the minor can have many accounts and a custodian can be appointed to many different accounts. An account uses the minor's social security number. Securities cannot be held in a street name, and be transferred to the minor's name when he or she reaches the age of majority in that state. The B-D needs the appropriate information (custodian name, minor name, etc.) to set up the account.

INVESTMENT ADVISERS. Investment advisers are persons registered to give investment advice for a fee. In addition to providing one-on-one advice to clients or issuing newsletters to dispense investing advice, some investment advisors actually invest money on behalf of clients. This can be done in a blind pool (called an omnibus account) where client identities are not disclosed, or in a fully disclosed account where the client identities are known. In the latter instance, the broker-dealer is responsible for obtaining new account forms and any necessary agreements or documents from each client, as well as maintaining current client data.

DISCRETIONARY AUTHORITY. The client may choose to authorize the RR to make buy-and-sell decisions on the client's behalf. We will explore the rules covering discretionary authority in the next section. For now, know that the client must sign a document granting this authorization before any trades by the RR can take place.

POWER OF ATTORNEY. This instrument authorizes one person to act on behalf of another. The document details exactly what authority the person has. A limited power of attorney grants limited authorization (can execute only buy-sell orders); a full power of attorney gives full authorization (can withdraw funds from the account).

EMPLOYER'S AUTHORIZATION. The NYSE requires written permission from a current B-D employer before an RR (or relative of an RR) can open an account with another firm. NASD and MSRB rules provide for notification to the employer, but not permission. Duplicate trade confirmations of the RR's activity are automatically sent by NYSE and MSRB to the RR's employing B-D firm; NASD does so upon request.

RETIREMENT PLANS. Any accounts that are opened as retirement plans must be cash accounts—no margin. The broker-dealer needs the new account form and other appropriate information (custodial records and authority, tax information for IRS). If the retirees will be traveling, the broker-dealer needs appropriate mailing instructions. A broker-dealer (*not* the RR) can hold a client's mail up to 60 days while clients travel in the United States; up to 90 days when they travel overseas.

NUMBERED ACCOUNTS. Accounts that a client requests be identified only by a number (or symbol) must be accompanied by appropriate documentation to show that the client does, in fact, own the account. Numbered accounts may be used to maintain the confidentiality of clients, but the clients must agree to disclose their identities to the proper authorities, if necessary.

4.2 Rules Governing the Conduct of Accounts

Once an account has been opened, there are a number of rules and regulations that must be followed. In addition, broker-dealer firms are likely have their own procedures in place which must be followed. Most of these rules have to do with ensuring that clients' interests are protected, especially with regard to executing orders, using discretionary authority, transferring accounts, and closing accounts.

4.2.1 Designation of Accounts and Account Requests

When dealing with customer accounts, it is very important to follow all rules and procedures put in place by the broker-dealer. These are designed to ensure compliance with the regulations of the various SROs. Customer complaints and violations in dealing with customer accounts are taken very seriously.

DESIGNATION OF ACCOUNTS. When opening new accounts, you must ensure that the new account form is filled in completely and accurately. One of the most important parts is the designation of the account as a cash account, margin account, or option account. As we saw in the last section, each of these has different documents that must be signed and requirements that must be met. Furthermore, proper designation of account ownership is important, because only those persons may make trades in the account and have access to account records. Finally, it is important to note whether or not any discretionary authority has been granted.

ACCOUNTS FOR EMPLOYEES OF OTHER B-Ds. Another area where caution is advised is when opening and carrying accounts for employees of other broker-dealer firms. In fact, the new account form asks if the client, spouse, or relative works for *any* financial institution, not just the B-D. The rules for each are slightly different.

NYSE broker-dealers must give written permission before their employees can open accounts with other broker-dealers. Furthermore, if an account is approved, duplicate trade confirmations for all trading activity must be sent automatically to the NYSE broker-dealer where the client works. Finally, the NYSE does not allow its members (including the RR) to open accounts with fictitious names.

NASD broker-dealers must be given written notice before one of their employees opens an account with another broker-dealer. The NASD firm has the option of requesting duplicate trade confirmations for all trading activity.

MSRB broker-dealers must be given written notice before one of their employees can open an account with another broker-dealer. Furthermore, if the account is approved, then duplicate trade confirmations for all trading activity must be sent automatically to the MSRB broker-dealer where the client works. Prior approval for each trade, though, is not required.

Banks, trust companies, and insurance companies must give written permission before their employees can open *margin* accounts with broker-dealers. Permission is *not* required for cash accounts. Duplicate trade confirmations are not needed.

DISCRETIONARY ACCOUNTS. Discretionary accounts give the RR the authority to make trades on behalf of the client, without the client's prior knowledge. This is an area where the RR must be careful to follow all guidelines precisely. You could see lots of questions on the Series 7 exam about handling discretionary accounts.

An RR can have discretionary authority over an account only if the client gives explicit written permission by signing a power of attorney or other trading authorization document that is provided by the broker-dealer firm. This authorization must be received, and approved by a principal, before any discretionary trades can be made. Authorization can last a maximum of three years before it must be renewed.

All trades must be marked "discretionary," and a principal must sign off on (initial) all discretionary trades (at least the same day). Furthermore, all trades must stay within the investment objectives that the client has laid out for you. If the client wants safe blue chips, it could be a violation to buy her an Internet stock. Finally, all persons monitoring a discretionary account are sensitive towards signs of churning the account to generate commissions. It's not the volume of trades, per se, but rather the change in trade volume since the account became discretionary.

Note that prior written consent is still required if the RR wants to buy a stock or bond from an issuer with which the firm has a control relationship.

For the Series 7 exam, you need to know what constitutes a discretionary trade. Just because you as the RR decide at what price to buy or sell a security for the client does not mean you have made a discretionary trade. It would be a discretionary trade only if you chose the security, and the amount of shares, and whether they would be bought or sold. All three elements are necessary (picked by you, the RR) for a trade to be considered discretionary. So if a client tells you to buy IBM stock when you think it's at a good price, that is not a discretionary trade because you did not pick the stock. But if a client tells you to pick a good bio-tech stock, and you pick one—and decide how many shares—that is a discretionary trade.

If you are choosing only the timing of the trade, or the price at which to buy or sell, that alone does not make it a discretionary trade. *If you are not picking the stock, it's not a discretionary trade.*

SENDING ACCOUNT STATEMENTS. Customer statements are sent at the end of the month if there is activity in the preceding month. Account statements must be sent to clients *at least quarterly*, even if there has been no activity in the account. The account statement must show any security positions the client has open as well as any cash balances. Clients can designate to where and to whom account statements and duplicate order confirmations should be sent. If the client requests that materials be sent to someone who does not hold power of attorney, or even if statements are going anywhere other than the client's residence or business address, it should be done in writing.

RETENTION OF CUSTOMER MAIL. At a client's written request, a broker-dealer (*not* the RR) can hold client mail up to 60 days while clients travel in the United States; up to 90 days when they travel overseas. Also note that customers can choose to have the broker-dealer mail or hold dividend checks.

CHANGES IN ORDER DESIGNATIONS. Changes in order designations must be thoroughly documented, and may need to be approved by a principal. Furthermore, it is the responsibility of the RR to double-check the accuracy of all order information, and be aware of any additional documentation that may be required because of the order change.

ERRONEOUS REPORTS TO CUSTOMERS. Any erroneous reports to customers must be corrected immediately. Order execution reports must be double-checked against the order ticket, and checked again on the client's confirmation. The order execution must be reported to the client, and any errors must be reported to the proper person within the broker-dealer firm. The RR should not attempt to correct the problem by making any additional trades until instructions are received from a principal of the firm. Written confirmations of transactions may be amended to correct details, but are deemed correct by the client unless written notice to the contrary is received within ten (10) days from the date the confirmation is received.

REVIEW/APPROVAL OF CORRESPONDENCE. All members are required to keep a written record of all transactions and correspondence its RRs make in connection with the execution of any securities trade. Written approval must be given by a supervisory-level person for all external communications by the RR, but internal memos are excluded from this requirement.

CUSTOMER COMPLAINTS. Arbitration is available for disputes involving less than $25,000. Clients may also file complaints with the NASD. Such complaints fall under the NASD Code of Procedure, which gives the NASD the right to inspect the records of the broker-dealer, the right to request statements from the parties involved, and the right to require an appearance before the hearing board. While the investigation is still ongoing, the NASD may not ask the member to waive any rights, sign a statement of fact, or offer a settlement. Penalties that may be levied against a member found in violation include fines, censure, suspension, and expulsion.

The MSRB complaint procedure is to log in the complaint, indicate what actions have been taken, and deliver the MSRB's Investor Brochure to the client. Complaints, like all records, must be kept for six years.

ACCEPTANCE OF C.O.D. ORDERS. Cash-on-delivery (C.O.D.) orders may be accepted by the broker-dealer if prior arrangement is made with the client and the recipient of the securities. With this kind of transaction, the broker-dealer delivers securities to a bank (or other third-party guarantor), and cash payment is made promptly. This is also referred to as "delivery against payment" (DAP), or "delivery vs. payment" (DVP), and is popular with institutional investors.

UPDATING CUSTOMER RECORDS. It is the RR's responsibility to verify and update client information every time he or she takes over a new account. In addition to keeping track of personal changes and adjusting investment objectives, the RR must also maintain records about the securities that the client owns and all transactions that have been made with the firm. These detailed records are sometimes referred to as the "customer book." This, along with client statements and confirmations, must be kept for six years (the past two years should be accessible). In fact, all correspondence and records should also be kept for the same period of time.

EXECUTING CUSTOMER REQUESTS. All appropriate requests by the client must be executed in a timely fashion. Furthermore, the RR is required to get the best possible price for the client in the OTC market. If the RR feels that a trade is not appropriate for the client, he or she can still make the trade if the customer insists but should mark the order ticket as "unsolicited" so that the record will show that the RR did not encourage the trade. (A signed statement from the client may also be required by the broker-dealer.) Sometimes, though, there are reasons not to execute a transaction that the client requests.

4.2.1.1 Circumstances for Restricting Activity

There are situations for refusing customer requests: the proposed transaction would exceed the client's margin limits, the client's credit has been cancelled, the account is closed or in dispute, the client has changed jobs (perhaps now works for another B-D), additional documents are needed (e.g., options agreement), the stock endorsement is incorrect or illegible, or the RR can't verify the location of the securities being held long by the customer (and not in the B-D account).

Most account restrictions are money issues. For example, cash accounts may be restricted if any balance owed for a cash transaction is still outstanding after 20 business days (or five business days for DAP transaction). Restrictions may be removed from the account on payment of amount owed, or transferring the account to a margin account. With margin accounts, if a customer becomes undermargined (by B-D standards or Reg T) the account is restricted until the client deposits cash or securities. Once restricted, the only allowable trades are ones which reduce the margin deficiency in the account. If a client doesn't answer a Reg T call by depositing cash or securities within five days, the broker must sell out the position and freeze the account for 90 days. Furthermore, accounts may be closed by a B-D if unpaid balances are outstanding, securities are not delivered as promised, or violations occur.

Prohibited accounts include numbered accounts for NASD members, secret accounts for NASD members, and accounts for persons who have not disclosed a directorship, relationship, or ownership (10 percent+) interest in an exchange listed company. Accounts may be legally restricted or frozen if any of these previously mentioned conditions are found to be true, or if the account is under investigation by the SEC or an SRO, or if the account is the subject of litigation or under a court order.

Death of a Client. Upon receiving notice of the death of a client, there are three procedures that the RR must follow. The RR must cancel all pending orders, ensure that no new orders are placed, and wait for instructions from the executor of the estate as to how to proceed. In the case of a JTROS account, the interest transfers to the surviving party(ies) so this is less complicated.

With the death of the beneficial owner of a trust account, it is important to note that the assets of the account go to the person's estate—*not* to the fiduciary. The same is true with a minor's account: the assets go to the minor's estate, *not* to the custodian and *not* to the minor's parents.

Transferring Accounts. Accounts may be closed or transferred on customer request. In such cases, the client initiates a transfer by completing an authorization form and submitting it to the new broker-dealer, who will hold the client's account. The new B-D sends notice to the original B-D, who then has **three business days** to affirm or disaffirm the transfer authorization. If affirming, the original B-D makes a complete inventory of the client's securities, margin and cash position and forwards that to the new B-D. This validates the transfer. The account is then frozen for **four business days** to allow the transfer to be completed. (Options expiring during this seven-day window only may be executed during this time; other activity is not permitted.)

There are two other possibilities that you need to be aware of. One is that the new firm may decide that it can accept only a partial transfer, perhaps because some of the margined securities do not meet the new firm's minimum margin requirement. In that case, that portion stays with the original firm pending the client's instruction. The other possibility is that the original B-D may not be able to transfer all of the client's account, possibly a mutual fund that only the B-D can trade in. Again, the client would decide whether to leave the fund with the original B-D, or liquidate it.

4.22

State Regulation of Fiduciary Accounts

Fiduciary accounts are often subject to state regulations. These are designed to protect the interests of the beneficiary of the account, who usually has no say in how the account is handled. The rules vary by state, but two mechanisms used by many states are the implementation of a legal list and enforcement of the Prudent Man Rule.

The **legal list** is an official list of securities that are selected by the state as being acceptable for investment by fiduciaries. To protect the interests of the beneficiaries, only high grade debt and equities appear on the list. Investments may be made only in securities that appear on the restricted legal list.

The **Prudent Man Rule** says that fiduciaries must act as any prudent man or woman would when making investment decisions; with care and skill, to preserve capital, seek reasonable income, and avoid unreasonable risk and speculative investments. This rule serves as a guideline for those who have the duty and responsibility of investing money on behalf of beneficiaries.

Here are a few points to remember for the Series 7 exam. A principal must approve every new account, but *doesn't have to approve before the first trade* can be made. The RR and principal must sign all new account forms; the client doesn't have to for cash accounts, but must for margin accounts. A registered options principal (ROP) must approve options accounts. The loan consent form is the only optional form with margin accounts; the credit agreement and hypothecation agreement are not. MSRB rules require that tax information be an important consideration for trades.

A trade is discretionary only if you choose the security and the amount of shares, and whether they will be bought or sold.

One of the keys to look for is whether or not the client told you the *name* of the stock to trade. *If you are not picking the name, it's not a discretionary trade.*

Accounts may be restricted if left unpaid for 20 days. Upon the death of a client, the RR must cancel all pending orders, ensure that no new orders are placed, and wait for instructions from the executor of the estate as to how to proceed. Account transfers occur if the original broker-dealer approves after three days, then the new broker-dealer has four days to transfer the account.

4.3 Margin Accounts

Borrowing money to buy securities allows clients to use leverage, controlling more securities with less cash. Since margin accounts use credit, there is more risk involved so there are additional rules and regulations that must be followed. This is to protect the broker-dealer as well as the client. As we examine margin accounts in greater detail, note that this is also an area that receives particular attention on the Series 7 exam. There aren't many questions (maybe 5 percent of the test), but you *will* see some. You will need to know definitions, margin requirements, margin calculations, and short sale rules. Let's define the terms, then look at how margin accounts work.

4.3.1 Key Margin Terms

There are several important words that are unique to margin accounts. These words deal with the accounts themselves, the agreements required, the way securities are handled, and eligibility requirements.

MARGIN. This is the name applied to the type of account where clients can borrow money to pay for a portion of the securities they buy, but watch its real definition. **Margin** is the amount that the customer must have on deposit with the broker-dealer to buy securities. Margin is *not* the amount of money being borrowed. Remember that the customer is permitted to borrow only a portion of the securities price, and must cover the balance with cash or by depositing other securities she owns.

HYPOTHECATION. This is one of the agreements that must be signed by a client before opening a margin account. **Hypothecation** is using something as collateral for a loan.

The **hypothecation agreement** (also called **margin agreement**) allows the broker-dealer to use the securities as collateral. The broker-dealer gets this authorization because the B-D will sell the securities if the client does not pay on the margin account. Title to the securities is not transferred unless there's a default.

REHYPOTHECATION. **Rehypothecation** is when a broker-dealer pledges a client's securities as collateral for a loan. The broker-dealer needs this authorization because the B-D is going to borrow the money to buy the securities that the client is buying on margin. If the broker-dealer could not hypothecate the client's securities, then the B-D would have to pay cash for the securities or get a loan with its own collateral. Here too, title to the securities is not transferred unless there's a default.

MARGINABLE SECURITIES. Not every stock or security can be purchased on margin. **Marginable securities** are securities that are eligible for a client to buy and sell in a margin account. These include listed stocks, listed bonds, and some over-the-counter (OTC) securities identified by the Federal Reserve Board. Some items of note that are *not* marginable are OTC securities that are not designated by the Federal Reserve Board, new stock issues, mutual funds, and option contracts.

EXEMPT, NONEXEMPT. **Exempt securities** are ones that do not fall under the rules or jurisdiction of a particular oversight body. In this case, it is the Federal Reserve Board that oversees rules with regard to margin accounts, specifically with Regulation T (Reg. T). For example, U.S. government and municipal bonds do not have to comply with Reg. T, so they are considered exempt securities. **Nonexempt securities** are ones that are under the jurisdiction of a particular oversight body, and thus must comply with their rules, such as the SEC or Reg. T.

Individual broker-dealers are permitted to establish their own rules with regard to exempt securities in margin accounts; they must follow existing rules and guidelines for nonexempt securities.

LOAN VALUE. This has to do with the Federal Reserve Board Reg. T requirements for margin accounts. **Loan value** is the maximum percentage of current market value that a broker-dealer can lend on nonexempt marginable securities.

MARGIN CALLS. There are two things at work that we must consider with margin accounts. First are the Reg. T requirements and broker-dealer rules regarding how much can be borrowed in a margin account. Second is the fact that the value of securities constantly fluctuates up and down. Where these two intersect we get margin calls. A **margin call** is a demand that a customer deposit additional cash or securities to bring the margin amount up to the minimum required.

We will discuss when and how margin calls happen in an upcoming section. For now, just know that it is a common occurrence with margin accounts. And if the client does not respond and bring the account into compliance, securities can be sold and even the entire account may be liquidated and closed.

SMA. A **special memorandum account (SMA)** is almost the opposite of a margin call. It occurs when there is excess equity in the customer's margin account (above Reg. T requirements). This may be because some securities were sold, extra cash or securities were deposited by the client, or because the securities in the account have appreciated in value. The client may not withdraw funds based on the SMA without approval, as the broker-dealer (not Reg. T) may require that some be kept in the account in case of future margin calls. Remember, this SMA is not cash, but rather it is more like a line of credit that can be tapped based on the excess equity in the account. It does not really become cash, but can be used to buy additional securities on credit without depositing more funds. Sometimes clients can borrow against the SMA funds to get cash. (We'll discuss SMA calculations in an upcoming section.)

4.3.2

Requirements and Characteristics

Now that we have discussed what some of these terms mean, let's examine how the actual rules and regulations operate. There are specific requirements that Reg. T places on broker-dealers with respect to margin accounts, and these requirements are augmented by the various SROs.

APPROVALS, INELIGIBLE ACCOUNTS. In addition to the other requirements we discussed for opening a new brokerage account, margin accounts have some additional requirements before they can receive approval for margin trades. The credit agreement and hypothecation agreement are essential parts of the margin account approval process. In addition, it is important for the RR and principal to inquire about the client's previous margin trading experience (listed on the margin account approval form) before signing off to approve the new margin account.

Before giving final approval, it is also important for the RR and principal to be sure that the kind of account being opened is eligible for margin trades. Most fiduciary and trust accounts (including UGMA/UTMA) are ineligible to be margin accounts. The broker-dealer may also choose to declare corporate and partnership accounts ineligible for margin trades, unless clients can produce written approval that the partnership agreement or corporate bylaws expressly permit margin trades.

Finally, the NASD has established new approval guidelines for day traders who are eligible to do margin trades. When a day traded account has less than US $25,000 balance, it will not be able to open more than three positions (stock margin trades) in any five-day period. This is to ensure that day traders meet margin requirements.

ELIGIBLE, INELIGIBLE SECURITIES. Eligible securities for margin account trading include listed stocks, listed bonds, corporate convertible bonds, and other OTC securities as declared eligible from time to time by the Federal Reserve Board. This eligibility is granted to stocks on the OTC margin list when the Fed determines that there is enough investor interest and marketability in a particular security. Convertible bonds and some warrants are also eligible, depending on the issuing company, conditions of the security, etc.

Ineligible securities include new stock issues, mutual funds, insurance contracts, option contracts, rights offerings, and other OTC securities that are not on the Fed's eligible list. Option contracts and rights offerings are not permitted because they expire. Mutual funds are not eligible because they are always considered new issues, although they can be deposited in the margin account as collateral to help meet margin requirements. Likewise, other new stock issues may be used as collateral 30 days after they are acquired and paid for.

Remember, too, that government bonds and municipal securities are exempt. This means that their eligibility and requirements are left up to the discretion of the individual broker-dealers.

REG. T, SRO REQUIREMENTS. There are two important areas where Reg. T and SRO requirements come into play—initial deposits and minimum margin requirements. When the rules between Reg. T and SROs differ, the more stringent standard is applied.

Initial Deposits. Reg. T requires that all clients deposit 50 percent of the purchase price of all eligible, nonexempt securities that are purchased on margin. SROs (NASD, NYSE, etc.) go one step further and require a minimum initial deposit of $2,000, unless the price of the securities is under $2,000 (except short sales). What this means is that if a client is buying stock worth $8,000, the client must deposit at least $4,000 into the margin account. Reg. T rules are stricter so they apply. If the client is buying stock worth $3,000, Reg. T would say the initial deposit is only $1,500, but the SROs require a minimum of $2,000, so here the client must deposit $2,000 because the stricter SRO rules win. Our third example is a client who's buying $1,000 worth of stock on margin. Reg. T rules would say that only $500 needs to be deposited, but the SRO rule saying the deposit is the price of the securities for sales under $2,000 means the client needs to deposit the entire $1,000. (The exception to this is that the minimum amount for short sales must be at least $2,000, regardless of price.)

Minimum Margin Requirements. In addition to these rules governing initial deposits, there are other margin rules you need to be aware of. After the initial deposit, Reg. T still applies to account activity. If the account falls below 50 percent, there is no margin call, but the account becomes restricted and a **retention requirement** kicks in. This means that the client is required to leave in the account 50 percent of the cash received from any sales to help get the account back closer to its initial margin level.

In addition to these Reg. T requirements, SROs have a minimum maintenance requirement of 25 percent. This means that if the value of a client's equity in his margin account drops below 25 percent, then the client is given a margin call and must deposit additional cash or securities he owns outright. *Notice the difference:* Reg. T's minimum margin requirements do not immediately trigger a margin call. Instead they just restrict the account and implement the retention requirement. SRO minimum maintenance requirements trigger a margin call. Also note that an account can trade in between—say 33 percent, and thus is restricted by Reg. T, but is not low enough to trigger a margin call. We will look at these calculations in the next section.

Keep this in mind to help you remember the distinction clearly: The Reg. T requirements instituted by the Federal Reserve Board are in place because they are concerned with how investors get into margin accounts. The SROs, on the other hand, are more interested in how investors stay in the account.

Calculations of Equity in Margin Accounts

As we begin to look at the calculations for margin accounts, keep in mind that securities can actually be purchased long or short in margin accounts. With a **long margin account,** the investor desires to own the securities and so he or she *borrows money* from the broker-dealer firm to buy them. "Long" here is used like it is with stocks or options in that the customer wants to buy and hold securities, he or she just doesn't want to have to pay for them all in cash. With a **short margin account,** the investor desires to sell the securities and so she *borrows the securities* from the broker-dealer firm to sell them. "Short" here is used a little differently than we have seen before, but the customer is still looking to sell; she just doesn't own the securities, so she borrows them now and hopes to repay them later by buying them at a reduced price and making money. (If the price goes up, though, the investor loses money.) Let's look at some of the concepts and calculations with margin accounts.

4.3.3.1 Basic Margin Accounting

When working with margin accounts, there are several concepts and values that must be understood. Keep in mind that some of these differ, depending on whether we are dealing with a long margin account or a short margin account. We will point out any important differences as we go.

Long Market Value. Long market value (LMV) is the present worth of a client's portfolio at the end of the valuation period. With a long margin account, this number is calculated at the end of each trading day. In figuring the LMV, the closing price is used for all listed securities; the latest bid price is used for OTC securities. (Another word for long market value is **current market value,** but you will likely see long market value and LMV used more on the Series 7 exam.)

Short Market Value. Short market value (SMV) is the present worth of the client's short stock position at the end of the valuation period. With a short margin account, this number is calculated at the end of each trading day. In figuring the SMV, the closing price is used for all listed securities; the latest bid price is used for OTC securities. (Short market value and SMV will be used on the Series 7 exam.)

Debit Balance. Debit balance (DR) is the money that a client owes to the broker-dealer for loans used to purchase securities. A debit balance is like any other debt: even if the value of the item fluctuates, DR does not change unless more money is borrowed or more money is paid into the account. Think of a new car loan. Even though a car depreciates the minute you drive it off the lot, you still owe the original debt amount you agreed to when you bought the car. The only way to lower the debt is to pay part of it off. Better yet, look at a home. A home's value can go up or down, but the amount owed on it goes up only if you borrow more, or down if you pay off more of the debt. Likewise, DR does *not* go up and down with the value of the securities.

The "R" in "DR" stand for "registry" or "register" as in a bookkeeping entry. Debit balance and DR are used with long margin accounts and LMV on the Series 7 exam.

Credit Balance. Credit balance (CR) is the money deposited by a client into an account, plus the proceeds from any short sales and the value of any securities deposited. As with the DR, even if the value of the item fluctuates, the CR does not change. CR changes only if cash is taken out, or more money or securities (must be owned 100 percent by client) are deposited into the account to meet margin requirements.

The "R" in "CR" stand for "registry" or "register" as in a bookkeeping entry. Credit balance and CR are used with short margin accounts and SMV on the Series 7 exam.

Initial Reg. T Requirements. For initial margin purchases in a long margin account, Reg. T requires that clients deposit 50 percent of the purchase price of all eligible, nonexempt securities. For **long margin** positions, this means that the client has a **debit balance,** and must make the deposit within five business days to meet the 50 percent rule. (Most SROs, though, require the deposit within three business days.) If the price of the security fluctuates before the deposit is made, the requirement is still for 50 percent of the purchase price from when the trade was made (remember our car example).

The deposit can be in cash or securities that the client owns, but if using securities, the client must deposit double the value. This is because only the loan value (or 50 percent of the securities) can be counted towards the Reg. T cash requirement.

EXAMPLE

Chris is buying $10,000 worth of stock on margin. To meet the Reg. T initial margin requirement, $5,000 in cash must be deposited, or $10,000 of fully paid securities.

Let's do a simple balance sheet diagram to help visualize this example.

LMV (long mkt. value)	**DR (debit balance)**
10,000 (initial stock value)	**5,000 (amount client owes)**
	5,000 EQ (equity client put in)

In a short margin account, Reg. T also requires that clients meet the 50 percent initial margin requirement. For **short margin** positions, the client immediately receives a **credit balance** for the short sale of the security, but must still make the 50 percent deposit within five business days. (Most SROs, though, require the deposit within three business days.) Remember, the client has borrowed the securities and already sold them, so he doesn't own anything—except an obligation to replace the securities by a certain date.

The deposit can be in cash or securities that the client owns, but if using securities, the client must deposit double the value. This is because only the loan value of 50 percent of the securities can be counted towards the Reg. T cash requirement. Also note that when selling short, the client gets an immediate credit for the amount of the short sale.

Example

Chris is selling $10,000 worth of stock short. To meet the Reg. T initial margin requirement, $5,000 must be deposited in the account. Chris also got $10,000 for the short sale of stock, so Chris's credit balance is $15,000.

CR (credit balance)	**SMV (short mkt. value)**
15,000 (value in account)	**10,000 (amount client got from short sale)**
	5,000 EQ (equity client put in)

Ongoing Reg. T Requirements. Even though Reg. T requirements are primarily concerned with the initial position of a client getting into a margin account, Reg. T does come into play for established accounts as well. All margin accounts have their valuations adjusted at the end of the trading day to reflect current market values. This is called **mark to the market,** and broker-dealers do this to ensure that margin accounts still meet minimum margin and maintenance requirements. If the equity in an account drops below the 50 percent required by Reg. T, the account becomes a **restricted account.** If the equity in the account drops below 25 percent for long accounts or 30 percent for short accounts, then clients receive a **margin call** or a **maintenance call.**

Restricted accounts are allowed to make additional purchases only if they improve the margin deficiency, and any sale is subject to a **retention requirement,** meaning the client is required to leave in the account 50 percent of the cash received from any sales to help raise the equity in the account and get it back to the 50 percent margin level. Receiving a maintenance call or margin call means that the client must deposit additional cash or securities to bring the margin back to the 25 percent or 30 percent required by the SRO.

Remember for established accounts: Reg. T minimums restrict accounts; SRO minimums trigger a margin call.

Loan Value. Loan value is the maximum percentage of current market value that a broker-dealer can lend on nonexempt marginable securities. This is established by the Federal Reserve Board Reg. T requirements for margin accounts. The loan value is actually applied in two different situations. The first we have already talked about: the broker-dealer is permitted to loan only 50 percent of the value of marginable securities when a client buys in a long margin account. But loan value also applies to equity positions that a client maintains in long margin accounts and short margin accounts. This is the second situation.

Since a broker-dealer can loan only 50 percent of the value on marginable securities, if a client deposits securities to cover margin requirements, then only 50 percent of the cash value of those securities can be considered when computing minimum margin requirements. The effect of this is that a client must deposit twice as much in security value as would be needed in cash to meet minimum margin requirements.

Excess Equity. **Excess equity** is any value that is in a margin account above the minimum Reg. T requirement. To calculate equity use the following formulas:

Long Margin Account	**EQ = LMV – DR**
Short Margin Account	**EQ = CR – SMV**

When these equity calculations produce a number greater than the minimum Reg. T maintenance requirements, the account has **excess equity.** Excess equity may occur because some securities in the account were sold, extra cash or securities were deposited by the client, dividends or option premiums were received, or because the securities in the account have appreciated in value. This excess equity gets applied towards a **special memorandum account (SMA).**

Buying Power of Deposited Securities. Before, we said that when depositing securities in a margin account to meet margin requirements, only 50 percent of their value counts. Once Reg. T minimum margin requirements are exceeded, deposited securities raise excess equity in the account. This in turn raises SMA by 50 percent of their value. When buying securities, buying power is double the SMA amount, so the net effect of depositing securities to create excess equity translates into a 1-for-1 ability to buy more stock on credit. We will discuss SMA calculations in an upcoming section.

4.3.3.2 Recalculating after Transactions

As we go through examples to help you better understand margin accounting, there is one important point you should always remember. When we are dealing with long margin accounts, no matter what transactions take place, the debit balance (DR) can be affected only by cash coming into or going out of the account. Likewise, when we are dealing with short margin accounts, no matter what transactions take place, the credit balance (CR) can be affected only by cash coming into or going out of the account. DR and CR do not change with the market value of the stocks. (Remember our car loan analogy.)

Additional Purchases. After the initial purchase, additional purchases may or may not require a 50 percent deposit of the purchase price depending on the market value of the account, the equity, and the SMA. Remember, if the equity falls below

50 percent of the LMV, the account is restricted and can make only purchases which improve the margin deficiency. In essence, with a restricted account, the client must deposit 50 percent of the purchase amount just like a new purchase. On the other hand, activity in the account may have altered the equity balance such that the client does not have to deposit as much money. (SMA can also play a role here, but we will ignore it for now to simplify our explanation, and talk about SMA calculations in the next section.)

Let's go back to our example and look at what happens when the stocks go up.

Example

Before, Chris bought $10,000 worth of stock on margin (100 @ $100).

LMV (long mkt. value)	**DR (debit balance)**
10,000 (initial stock value)	**5,000 (amount client owes)**
	5,000 EQ (equity client put in)

Now the stock has gone up to $130 per share. (Remember, DR stays same.)

LMV (long mkt. value)	**DR (debit balance)**
~~10,000~~ **13,000 (stock value)**	**5,000 (amount client owes)**
	~~5,000~~ **8,000 EQ (equity)**

So Chris could buy up to $3,000 more stock before having to deposit more money. Chris's LMV is $13,000, so 50 percent of that is $6,500 to meet Reg. T requirement. Chris has EQ of $8,000, but needs only $6,500 so ($8,000 – $6,500 = $1,500), Chris can buy $3,000 worth of stock (all on credit), and still fit under Reg. T.

LMV (long mkt. value)	**DR (debit balance)**
13,000 (value) **+3,000 (new stock)** **16,000 (total stock value)**	**5,000 (amount client owes)** **+3,000 (client owes for new stock)** **8,000 (total debit balance)**
	8,000 EQ (equity)

Our balance sheet is still correct. We have $16,000 on the left, and $16,000 total on the right ($8,000 DR + $8,000 EQ). (We'll show how SMA fits in soon.)

Now let's see what happens when the stocks go down.

EXAMPLE

Before, Chris bought $10,000 worth of stock on margin (100 @ $100).

LMV (long mkt. value)	DR (debit balance)
10,000 (initial stock value)	5,000 (amount client owes)
	5,000 EQ (equity client put in)

Now the stock has gone down to $80 per share. (Remember, DR stays same.)

LMV (long mkt. value)	DR (debit balance)
~~10,000~~ 8,000 (stock value)	5,000 (amount client owes)
	~~5,000~~ EQ 3,000 EQ (equity) – 38% of LMV

Chris would not get a margin call, though, because the $3,000 EQ is 38 percent of LMV, which is still more than 25 percent, but this is a restricted account. So because this is a restricted account, Chris can make a purchase only if it improves the margin deficiency. Chris would need to make a 50 percent deposit with any additional purchases, and this will improve his margin. Let's look at this.

Additional Sales. Additional securities sales in a long margin account are restricted only if the equity falls below 50 percent of the LMV. With a restricted account, any sale is subject to a **retention requirement,** meaning the client is required to leave in the account 50 percent of the cash received from any sales to help raise the equity in the account. Additional sales in a short margin account are permitted if the account has sufficient equity or SMA that can be tapped. (SMA is like a line of credit. We will talk about it in the next section.)

Cash Withdrawals. Cash withdrawals from a long margin account are restricted only if the equity falls below 50 percent of the LMV. With a restricted account, the client must deposit securities (100 percent owned) with a value equal to double the withdrawal amount. (This is because the loan value of securities is only 50 percent.)

Stock Withdrawals. Stock withdrawals from a long margin account are restricted only if the equity falls below 50 percent of the LMV. With a restricted account, the client must deposit cash equal to half the value of the securities to be withdrawn, or other securities with a value equal to the ones to be withdrawn.

Liquidation of Securities. A client may liquidate securities to withdraw cash, meet a Reg. T margin call, or meet a maintenance call. If the account is restricted (which it is if client is liquidating to meet a margin call), the client needs to sell twice as much stock as the cash she needs or wants to receive. This is because half of the amount sold must pay down the debit balance. Remember, with a restricted account, the client can only do things which do not make the deficiency worse.

Simultaneous Purchases. When trades are made the same day, they can be considered simultaneous. The mark-to-the-market is performed at the end of the day as usual, but only the net amount is used for figuring LMV and equity in the account. If the purchases and sales are for the same amount, there is no net effect to the margin requirement because the sales cancel each other out.

Sales of Unequal Value. When trades are made the same day, they can be considered simultaneous. The mark-to-the-market is performed at the end of the day as usual, but only the net amount is used for figuring LMV and equity in the account. If the trades are unequal, the normal rules go into effect. For example, if there is a sale for $5,000 and a purchase for $2,000, there is a net sale of $3,000. This amount can be withdrawn from the margin account, unless it is restricted, in which case only $1,500 may be withdrawn. If there is a sale for $7,000 and a purchase for $9,000, there is a net purchase of $2,000, so if there is no excess equity or SMA (or if the account is restricted) there would be a margin requirement of $1,000 for the transaction.

Current Dollar Value If Liquidating. If the client decides to liquidate some of a long margin position to meet a maintenance call, there is a simple formula that will tell how much stock the client needs to sell to get the account back above the minimum level. Take the dollar amount of the call, times 4/3, and that equals the amount of stock that must be liquidated to bring the equity back above 25 percent of LMV.

Current Dollar Value If Depositing. If the client decides to deposit securities to meet a maintenance call, the amount needed is simply double the amount of the call needed to bring the equity back above 25 percent of LMV. Remember, double the securities are needed because the loan value is only 50 percent.

4.3.3.3 SMA

A **special memorandum account (SMA)** is a bookkeeping entry used by broker-dealers to keep track of the excess equity that clients have built up through their trades in their margin accounts. We saw before that **excess equity** is any value that is in a margin account above the minimum Reg. T requirement. This excess equity translates into SMA. The difference, though, is that once the SMA goes up, it stays at that level until it is used, whereas the excess equity rises and falls with the market value of the securities in the account. In fact, even a restricted account can still have SMA if it had excess equity at one time, but the value of the account has since dropped.

Thus, you can see that the purpose of the SMA is to preserve the client's buying power. Without SMA, the client would feel compelled to withdraw cash or securities every time the excess equity rose. With SMA, the client can take advantage of the appreciation of the account at any time, without having to worry about when the account might drop in value. Keep in mind, though, that SMA is not cash or any other asset in an account somewhere. Rather, it is like a line of credit that the client can tap as needed (except to meet maintenance calls).

SMA Balance. The SMA balance is like a line of credit that a client can use to buy additional stocks, apply towards Reg. T requirements, or borrow against to withdraw cash. Remember, SMA is equal to an account's equity in excess of Reg. T requirements, and once increased it drops only when it is used.

The SMA balance can increase from excess cash being deposited into the account, excess cash left in the account (sale of securities, dividends, etc.), or an increase in the LMV of securities in the account above the 50 percent Reg. T requirements.

Let's go back to our example and look at what happens when SMA go up.

Example

Before, Chris bought $10,000 worth of stock on margin (100 at $100). Adding excess equity and SMA to our chart, you can see that both equal zero.

LMV (long mkt. value)	DR (debit balance)
10,000 (initial stock value)	**5,000 (amount client owes)** **SMA = 0**
	5,000 EQ (equity client put in) **Excess Equity = 0**

The stock has gone up to $130 per share. (Remember, DR stays same.)

LMV (long mkt. value)	DR (debit balance)
~~**10,000**~~ **13,000 (stock value)**	**5,000 (amount client owes)** **SMA = 1,500**
	~~**5,000**~~ **EQ** **8,000 EQ (equity)** **Excess Equity = 1,500**

Chris's LMV is $13,000, so 50 percent of that is $6,500 to meet Reg. T requirement. Chris' has EQ of $8,000, but needs only $6,500 so ($8,000 – $6,500 = $1,500), gives Chris a total of $1,500 of excess equity, which gets applied to Chris's SMA.

Now the stock has gone down to $80 per share. (Remember, DR stays same.)

LMV (long mkt. value)	DR (debit balance)
~~**10,000**~~ **8,000 (stock value)**	**5,000 (amount client owes)** **SMA = 1,500**
	~~**5,000**~~ **EQ** **3,000 EQ (equity) – 38% of LMV** **Excess Equity = 0**

Notice how when the stock value (LMV) dropped, so did the equity and excess equity numbers. But the SMA did not drop! This will stay where it is until used by the client (we'll look at that next). In fact, this is now a restricted account because the equity is only at 38 percent of LMV. When an account becomes restricted, the broker-dealer may or may not also place restrictions on what the SMA can be used for.

The SMA balance can decrease when more securities are purchased against the SMA balance, securities are withdrawn from the account, or excess equity is withdrawn from the account (whether borrowed against the SMA or not).

Let's go back to our example and look at how SMA can go down.

Example

Before, Chris bouth $10,000 worth of stock on margin (100@$100). The stock rose to $130 per share, giving Chris SMA of $1,500. Let's begin here.

LMV (long mkt. value)	**DR (debit balance)**
~~10,000~~ **13,000 (stock value)**	**5,000 (amount client owes)** **SMA = 1,500**
	~~5,000~~ EQ **8,000 EQ (equity)** **Excess Equity = 1,500**

Chris wants to withdraw cash, but does not want to liquidate any securities to do so. Chris may borrow up to the SMA value, but must also debit the SMA by the amount to be withdrawn. Furthermore, because this is a loan, the DR balance must be increased because Chris owes the broker-dealer more money.

LMV (long mkt. value)	**DR (debit balance)**
13,000 (stock value)	**~~5,000~~ (original DR)** **6,500 (new amount client owes)** **SMA = ~~1,500~~ SMA = 0**
	~~8,000~~ EQ (equity) **Excess Equity = ~~1,500~~** **6,500 EQ (equity)** **Excess Equity = 0**

Essentially, Chris took out the excess equity. Notice, though, that the equity in the account dropped because Chris took it out. The DR actually increased here, because Chris borrowed the $1,500 against the SMA balance and Chris must repay this money to the broker-dealer in the future.

Note that with all of our calculations, the DR amount changed only when Chris actually owed more money. The change in value of the stocks did not affect DR. From this second example, perhaps you can see why the SMA was instituted. If there was no SMA, Chris would always have to withdraw money when the stock price increased, or lose it forever when the value of the stocks dropped again. With the SMA, Chris could choose to leave the money in the account, knowing that the stock appreciation raised the SMA. Then later, even if the stocks dropped in value, Chris could use the SMA to buy more stocks or tap it like a line of credit and borrow money. Using the SMA this way raises the amount of money that Chris owes.

Exam Topic Alert

Another important note: SMA may be used to meet initial Reg. T margin requirements when buying stock, but SMA may *not* be used to meet a maintenance call when equity drops below 25 percent. In fact, SMA cannot be used at all once there's a maintenance call.

Buying Power of SMA Balance. SMA allows a customer to buy double the amount of stock. A $1,000 SMA balance allows a client to buy $2,000 worth of stock. This is because when a client buys $2,000 worth of stock, $1,000 is borrowed from the broker-dealer and $1,000 is the initial margin requirement a client must contribute. But if the client has an SMA balance of $1,000, the SMA credit can be used to pay for the initial Reg. T margin requirement that the client normally pays in cash. Thus, the client was able to buy stocks equal to two times the SMA balance, all on credit, without having to put in any cash. Of course, since the client is using all credit, that means the DR balance must be increased by the full amount of the stock purchase.

SMA Balance To Meet a Reg. T Call. An SMA balance can be used only to pay for an initial Reg. T margin requirement. An SMA balance cannot be used to pay a regular margin call or maintenance call. That would be like borrowing money to pay off another loan, or moving credit card balances from one card to another. But since all of these "loans" are with the same broker-dealer, this is not permitted.

SMA Balance, Excess Equity. Excess equity is value in a margin account above Reg. T requirements, and this excess equity translates into SMA. But be aware that excess equity and SMA are not always equal. That's because excess equity can rise and fall with market value, but SMA does not. And once the SMA goes up, it stays at that level until it is used, even if the excess equity disappears for one reason or another. SMA is always the greater of the new excess equity amount or the previous SMA balance. Remember, even a restricted account can still have SMA if it had excess equity at one time, but the value of the account has since dropped.

Additional Deposit of Securities. Deposited securities above the 50 percent Reg. T minimum margin requirements create excess equity in the account, which in turn raises SMA by 50 percent of their value. This is because of the loan value of the securities being only 50 percent. So an additional deposit of securities in the amount of $20,000 would raise the SMA to $10,000. (Remember, though, this is only if SMA is below that level. For example, if the account is above 50 percent equity, but already has $30,000 of SMA, the SMA would remain at $30,000.)

Receipt of Cash Dividends, Interest. The value of any cash dividends received on stocks held in the margin account, or interest earned on securities in the margin account, are applied against the DR debit to reduce it, and thus increase SMA.

Liquidation of Securities. When securities in the margin account are sold, the SMA is increased by 50 percent of the proceeds from the sale. For example, if a client sells $10,000 worth of stock, the SMA balance would increase by $5,000.

Cash or Securities Withdrawals. Withdrawing cash or securities from a margin account reduces the SMA balance. For cash withdrawals, the SMA is debited by the amount of the withdrawal. A client could also choose to borrow money against the SMA, and have the SMA debited by that amount. For securities withdrawals, the SMA must be reduced by 50 percent of the value of the securities. If the client does not have enough SMA to allow the withdrawal, then additional cash (or other securities) must be deposited to raise SMA to a high enough level to allow the 50 percent deduction before making the withdrawal.

New Margin Securities Purchased or Sold Short. When new margin securities are purchased or sold short, the SMA decreases by 50 percent of the Reg. T initial requirement. Of course, this is assuming that the client put in no cash and chose to use the SMA balance to cover the Reg. T requirement. If the client paid for the Reg. T requirement in cash, there would be no excess equity generated and so the SMA balance would stay the same.

Here are a few points for you to be careful of for the Series 7 exam. If a client is buying securities and also sells an option (covered call), how much of the option premium can count towards Reg. T requirements? The answer is zero! Option premiums can stay in the account and be credited as cash, but for initial Reg. T requirements, the investor must deposit cash. Also watch new account minimums: minimum deposit is *$2,000 for short accounts,* even if trade cost is below that level. Another tip is if you see "when issued" securities in a question, that tells you they are new issues and must be paid for 100 percent in cash—no margin. Remember that broker-dealers are *not permitted* to hypothecate customers' securities in *cash accounts.*

Here are some tips with calculations. If given numbers, draw a chart right away. This is especially helpful with short accounts. Use SMV + EQ = CR, then don't change the credit amount! Use end of day (mark to the market) to figure new Reg. T and SRO requirements based on *new* LMV figure. Calculate the change to LMV based on information in the question, then figure new 50 percent Reg. T and 25 percent SRO maintenance requirements to see if account is restricted or will get a margin call.

One question you could see on the Series 7 exam might ask how low or high stocks could move before triggering a margin call. Here are two formulas you can use:

How low can the LMV go before the client would get a margin call? To figure this, LMV must be greater than or equal to 4/3 of the debit amount. So, **DR × 4/3** will tell you the LMV threshold that will trigger a margin call.

How high can the SMV go before a client would get a margin call? To figure this, SMV must be less than or equal to 10/13 of the credit amount. So, **CR** × **10/13** will tell you the SMV threshold that will trigger a margin call.

4.3.4

Short Sales

Short sales occur when an investor sells a security which he or she doesn't own. The investor *borrows the security* from a broker-dealer firm to sell it now, and hopes to repay the security later by buying it at a reduced price at some point in the future. When the investor makes the short sale now, she is credited with the amount received from the short sale. If the price of the security does, in fact, go down, the investor purchases the security at that reduced price and gives the security back to the broker-dealer before the agreed upon date. The difference between the original amount the investor received from the sale, and the price the investor later bought the replacement security for is the investor's profit. If the price of the security goes up, though, the investor loses money on the transaction because she is forced to spend the current higher price to replace the security she borrowed before.

4.3.4.1 Characteristics and Purposes

Although short sales are not done as much anymore because of their potential for unlimited risk (the price of the security has no limit to how high it could go), there are still some valid reasons for doing it.

Speculation. One of the basic reasons that investors do short sales is speculation that the price of a stock or other security will decline. Investors can make a nice profit from guessing correctly. If the investor is wrong, however, the potential loss is unlimited, unless the short sale is covered by a stock position the investor owns.

Hedging. Hedging is trying to offset an investment risk. If you own a long position in a stock, but are afraid that a near-term problem could cause the price to plummet, you might consider shorting the stock you own. You could also do this with put options because they have less risk, but selling short is generally cheaper—and if you own the stock your cash risk is minimal (although your opportunity to sell your long shares at a profit could evaporate).

Selling some stock short to cover part or all of your long position would hedge your long position. If the price falls, you make money on the short sale. If the price rises, you can use the shares you already own to replace the ones you borrowed, so you don't have to go out and buy the replacement shares at market price.

Tax Purposes. With short sales, tax liability is not incurred until the shares are replaced because only then can the investor calculate the gain or loss. Doing a **short sale against the box** is a technique where the investor does a short sale with the same security in which he also owns a long position. The short sale locks in a gain against drops in price, and the long stock the investor owns can be delivered later to cover the short sale. Tax laws, though, do not allow the use of this technique to turn a short-term gain into a long-term gain, and tax law changes have severely restricted the ability of this technique to delay a gain until a later tax year. (We will detail these rules in the last section of this chapter.)

Covering the Short Position. The short position is best covered when the investor is long the stock that is being shorted. In other words, if the price drops the investor wins. If the price rises, the investor is covered by using shares already owned to replace the borrowed ones. Other strategies can be used to cover option positions and convertible securities.

Market Arbitrage. Short sales are involved in different types of arbitrage strategies. Short sales can be used to take advantage of differences in pricing between stocks that are expected to move a certain way in the marketplace. For example, the announcement of a merger or acquisition might send one of the company's stock in a certain direction. When the market doesn't react favorably, the price can drop, and short selling can profit from this.

Arbitrage Between Equivalent Securities. Short sales can be used to take advantage of differences in pricing between stocks and futures contracts, stocks and convertible bonds, and any other pair of equivalent securities. Theoretically, the price of two equivalent securities should be equal, but this is not always the case. Short selling can take advantage of the price drop of one of those securities as they seek the balance and equilibrium that the market always strives to achieve.

Margin Treatment for Arbitrage. Federal Reserve System rules state that a broker-dealer who reasonably anticipates a short sale may borrow securities up to one standard settlement cycle in advance of the trade date. The standard settlement cycle is currently considered to be three business days.

Risk Arbitrage. Short sales are involved in numerous different arbitrage strategies trying to hedge investment risks. Some strategies do not use individual stocks, but rather use a market basket of securities from different industries to hedge against various risks. Short positions can cover exposure in a portfolio when signals are mixed, interest rates are uncertain, and overvaluation is a concern.

4.3.4.2 "Plus Tick" Rule

The "Plus Tick" rule governs when short sales can occur. The idea is that when the market is already going down, investors selling short could continue to place more short orders in an effort to drive the market even lower, because that would be in their own self-interest. To keep this from happening, the **"Plus Tick" rule** says that short sales can occur only on a plus tick or a zero-plus tick. To understand these, let's look at each of the four possible trade points.

Plus Tick. This term is used when the previous trade occurred at a higher price than the one before it. In essence, the price of the security is heading up. This is also referred to as an **uptick.** So if the previous trade was at 12, and the trade before that was at 11⅞, this is considered a "plus tick" and short sales may be entered. Note that at the beginning of the trading day, the last trades of the previous day are used.

Zero-Plus Tick. This term is used when the previous trade occurred at the same price as the one before it, and higher than the last different price. The price of the security is stable, but still in an upward trend. This is also referred to as a **zero uptick.** So if the previous trade was at 12, and the trade before that was at 12, and the trade before that was 11⅞, then this is considered a " zero-plus tick" and short sales may be entered. Trades going back to the previous day are used if needed.

Minus Tick. This term is used when the previous trade occurred at a lower price than the one before it. In essence, the price of the security is heading down. This is also referred to as a **downtick.** So if the previous trade was at 12 and the trade before that was at 12⅛, this is considered a "minus tick" and short sales are not permitted. At the start of the trading day, the last trades of the previous day are used.

Zero-Minus Tick. This term is used when the previous trade occurred at the same price as the one before it, but at a price lower than the last different price. The price of the security is stable, but still in a downward trend. This is also referred to as a **zero downtick.** So if the previous trade was at 12, and the trade before that was at 12, and the trade before that was 12⅛, this is considered a " zero-minus tick" and short sales may not occur. Trades from the previous day are used if needed.

Exceptions. Orders that are marked "long," meaning the investor intends to buy and hold the stock, are exempt from the plus tick rule. Other exceptions to the short sale rules are made if a long position is being liquidated (less than a round lot), and an offset odd lot order is received from a customer. Certain international and special arbitrage accounts are also often exempt from the plus tick rules.

4.3.4.3 Tax Treatment

With short sales, the tax consequences of a trade cannot be calculated until the shares are replaced and the position is closed out. Before then, it would be hard to know whether or not the investor would have a gain or a loss and for how much. But since the short seller never actually holds the securities, they never have a holding period, so all gains or losses are short term.

Shorting Against the Box. Shorting against the box is when a client does a short sale on a security in which he or she also owns a long position. The short sale locks in a gain against price drops now, and the investor can deliver the long stock later to cover the short sale. Tax law changes, though, have severely restricted the ability of this technique to delay a gain until a later tax year. In fact, taxes can be deferred only if the short position is closed within 30 days of the end of the tax year (or fiscal year), and the customer must own the stock for at least 60 more days.

Finally, let's review some of the special risks associated with margin accounts that you and your clients need to be aware of. These include:

- ▷ client can lose more funds than deposited in the account (if value declines)
- ▷ broker-dealer firm has the right to sell securities in the account

- ▷ broker-dealer can sell securities to meet a margin call even without contacting the client, and client has no say over which securities should be sold
- ▷ broker-dealer firm can raise maintenance/margin requirements at any time
- ▷ broker-dealer firm does not have to give client more time to meet a margin call

All or some of these may appear on the Series 7 exam in one form or another. If there isn't a direct question asking you to identify or list margin account risks, then there will certainly be a question where you are given a client's situation and asked if the risk is acceptable, or asking you to suggest a means to hedge an overt or implied risk.

4.X Summary

4.1 Accounts opened with NYSE, NASD, MSRB rules; "Know your customer." New account form: include citizenship; *not* education, race. Principal signs. Also need to know if customer works for other B-D, owns 10 percent + of public company.

4.1.1 Cash account: transfer and ship, transfer and hold, street name. IRA is cash only. Margin account: need credit and hypothecation agreement, loan consent optional. Option account: OCC option disclosure document, option agreement; ROP signs.

Individual account: one person; can give limited authorization (trade only); full (take money). Joint account: 2+ people; JTROS (equal share), JTIC (unequal), community property. Partnership account: need partner agreement; Corp account: need charter, resolution. Trust account: fiduciary duty, can't delegate; UGMA/UTMA: 1 minor, 1 custodian.

4.2 Rules protect clients' interest: execute order, discretionary, transfer, close.

4.2.1 For RR account: NYSE requires written employer authorization and duplicate orders; NASD gets notice, duplicate on request; MSRB gets notice, duplicate authorization.

Discretion authority: client's written permission, principal signs (after o.k.). RR picks stock, amount, buy or sell. If don't pick stock, not discretionary.

Accounting statement sent monthly (if active), quarterly (at least). RR can't hold mail. Note order changes; report error right away, correct only if principal says. Keep trade/statement/communication records 6 years. Arbitrate complaint if <$25K.

Restrict account: need documents, margin high, bad endorsements, no payment, account problem. Client death: cancel order, no new order, wait on

executor. Assets to estate. Transfer account: affirm 3 days, transfer 4 days. Partial if margin, mutual fund.

4.2.2 State rule for fiduciaries: legal list (of approved invest.), Prudent Man Rule.

4.3

Margin is buying securities using credit to leverage (control more, less money).

4.3.1 Margin is deposit amount, *not* amount borrowed. Hypothecation is using stock as collateral; rehypothecation is B-D pledging client stock for loan. Marginable securities are exchange-traded, Federal list. Exempt securities are not under SRO, SEC rules (e.g. Treasuries). Loan value is 50 percent of value. Margin call is demand to deposit more money, stock. SMA is like line of credit.

4.3.2 Some accounts (e.g., fiduciary) can't do margin. Some stock not marginable. Reg. T initial deposit: 50 percent. SRO initial deposit: 50 percent or $2,000 or trade cost, whichever is less. SRO takes precedence. Short margin account minimum is $2,000. If account LMV or SMV goes below Reg. T. minimum of 50 percent, then account is restricted. Retention requirement says 50 percent of transaction must stay in account, only can do trades to improve margin deficiency. If account LMV or SMV goes below SRO minimum of 25 percent, get maintenance call for more money.

4.3.3 Long margin acct: borrow money, own stock. Short margin: borrow stock, owe money.

LMV = current market value at end of day. SMV = position value at end of day.

DR = debit (money owed); CR = credit (money in account). DR, CR don't change.

LMV, SMV calculated daily to see if need Reg. T margin, SRO maintenance call.

If account value above CR or DR then have excess equity (EQ). EQ raises SMA. SMA rises when dollars go in. Deposited securities raise SMA by 50 percent; can buy more securities up to 100 percent of value, though. More sales or buys change LMV and SMA. If restricted, 50 percent of withdrawals must stay in acct; must deposit double stock value of cash want to take out, or equal value to take stock out. Margin call if LMV > or = 4/3 debit, or SMV < or = 10/13 credit. SMA pages 209–214.

4.3.4 Short sale is selling securities you don't own. Do it for speculation, hedge, arbitrage, taxes. Short against box: sell stock you own short to lock in gain. Can't use to make short gain into long, and tax use is restricted. Can short only on plus tick or zero-plus tick. Margin risks: lose more, firm can sell.

Chapter 4 Review Quiz

1. Which of the following documents is *not* required to open a margin account?
   a. credit agreement
   b. hypothecation agreement
   c. loan consent agreement
   d. new account form

2. Which type of joint account allows an automatic transfer to a spouse at death?
   a. JTROS
   b. JTIC
   c. community property
   d. probated estate

3. UGMA/UTMA accounts have which of the following?
   a. one custodian
   b. one minor
   c. both a and b
   d. neither a nor b

4. Under what conditions may discretionary authority be given?
   a. if client gives written consent
   b. if principal signs off on all trades before they are made
   c. if registered representative signed a power of attorney
   d. all of the above

5. Which of the following applies to accounts opened by registered reps?
   a. NYSE requires written permission and duplicate trades.
   b. NASD requires notice and can request duplicate trades.
   c. MSRB requires notice and duplicate trades.
   d. all of the above

6. A client tells you to buy stock in that big software giant when it hits 50:
   a. This is a discretionary trade because a company name was not mentioned.
   b. This is not discretionary because client told you to buy and the price.
   c. This is a discretionary trade because the client didn't say what day to buy.
   d. This is not discretionary because you are not selling stock for the client.

7. If an erroneous report is sent to a customer, you should immediately:
   a. make a trade to correct the problem.
   b. notify the exchange to reverse the trade.
   c. notify the client and wait for your supervisor's instructions.
   d. don't do anything because if 10 days pass, then customer can't complain.

8. Which of the following is a valid reason to restrict a customer's account?
   a. The proposed transaction would exceed the customer's margin limits.
   b. You're not sure if the customer can pay for the trade after buying a new car.
   c. The client forgot to make his appointment with you.
   d. all of the above

9. Upon learning of the death of a client, you should:
   a. cancel all pending orders.
   b. ensure no new orders are placed.
   c. wait for instructions from the executor of the estate.
   d. all of the above

10. A client opens an account. The first trade is shorting QRS for $800. The deposit:
    a. must be $400.
    b. must be $800.
    c. must be $1,600.
    d. must be $2,000.

11. A nonrestricted account has $1,000 SMA. What is the most stock that a client can buy without having to put in any additional money?
    a. $500
    b. $1,000
    c. $2,000
    d. Client can't use SMA to buy stock.

12. Client's DR is $9,000. How low can LMV go before client gets a margin call?
    a. $12,000
    b. $9,000
    c. $6,923
    d. need more information

13. When can a client execute a short sale?
    a. on a plus tick or zero-plus tick
    b. on a minus tick or zero-minus tick
    c. anytime, as long as the RR submits the order ticket marked "short"
    d. only if shorting against the box

Explaining Various Securities Markets

"Explaining Various Securities Markets" is the fifth of the seven critical functions performed by a Registered Representative. Customers need to understand how the various markets work, and how they affect the issuance and trading of their securities investments. The effects of other economic factors, both at home and abroad, are also important to understanding the securities markets.

This chapter gives you an understanding of the purpose and workings of the primary marketplace, and how new issues of securities are sold, as well as a thorough examination of the secondary marketplace. This chapter will also explain the relevance of economic events around the country and around the globe, showing you how to assess and explain those events as they affect the markets. That way, you as an RR can impart this knowledge to your clients as needed. Finally, you will learn where to obtain economic news and data, and how to assess its effect on the markets.

This fifth critical function covered in Chapter 5 ("Explaining Various Securities Markets") represents about 21 percent of the total exam: approximately 50–55 questions of the total 250 questions on the Series 7 Exam. As usual, much of the material covered in this chapter builds on what you have learned, and will provide a foundation for learning future concepts. Many questions on the Series 7 exam come from here also.

This chapter will be broken up into four sections:

5.1 Self-Regulatory Organizations (SROs). This first section will examine the structure and authority of each SRO, as well as the scope and nature of SRO rules and regulations. The first section will also discuss prohibited practices, and look at arbitration, complaint procedures, and disciplinary proceedings.

5.2 Primary Marketplace. This section will look at how new issues are brought to market, including the role of investment banking. Regulations concerning new issue offerings will also be examined in great detail.

5.3 Secondary Marketplace. This section does an analysis of the regulations and participants in the secondary market, with a brief overview of penny stock rules and the role and function of the SIPC. Explanations of the secondary markets for equity securities, options, municipal securities, and U.S. government securities follow. Other secondary market securities will be discussed, including corporate bonds, commercial paper, Eurodollar bonds, and CMOs. Finally, the currency markets will be discussed, followed by brief mention of the third and fourth markets.

5.4 Principal Factors Affecting Securities Markets, Prices. This section begins with a discussion of the business cycle and principal economic theories. Next, it will discuss the role of the Federal Reserve Board in the economy in detail, followed by a section on the effects of international economic factors on securities markets. Finally, the section ends with an overview of business data sources.

key terms

Blue Sky laws: name given to various state laws requiring issuers to register their new issues and provide financial information for securities sold in their state. Comply by filing notice, coordinating registration, and qualifying independently.

Competitive sale: where the issuer considers offers from several underwriters or underwriting syndicates before selecting a firm to work with. Also called **competitive bid** or **competitive underwriting.** Compare: **negotiated sale.**

CPI: **C**onsumer **P**rice **I**ndex: measures the fixed cost of a market basket of goods and services. CPI includes food, transportation, energy, housing, clothing, etc.

GDP: **G**ross **D**omestic **P**roduct: measures the value of all goods and services produced in the United States. Includes consumer spending, government spending, net value of exports.

IPO: **I**nitial **P**ublic **O**ffering: when a company that is going public for the first time sells new shares in a new issue stock offering.

Market maker: brokerage firm that has taken a position (built up an inventory) in a certain stock, and stands ready to honor quoted bid and ask prices for round lots. Market makers help maintain stability in OTC market, allowing OTC to function.

Negotiated sale: where the issuer selects an underwriter, then underwriter and issuer agree on the price and terms of the issue, and the spread. Also called **negotiated bid** or **negotiated underwriting.** Compare: **competitive sale.**

Primary market: sale of new securities issues directly by the issuer to investors.

Primary offering: sale of stock in the primary market, with the proceeds from the sale of stock going into the company treasury.

Secondary market: place where securities are bought and sold after original issue, with proceeds going to the investor selling the security.

Secondary offering: sale of stock in the primary market, with the proceeds from sale of stock going to present shareholders.

Securities Act of 1933: requires all securities to be registered before they can be sold to the public, requires use of a prospectus with full disclosure of all pertinent information, and prohibits false and misleading information with several anti-fraud provisions. (Focus is on the primary market.) Also called the **Paper Act.**

Securities Exchange Act of 1934: regulates secondary market activity, outlaws fraud and market manipulation, regulates sales and activity by company insiders, requires broker-dealer firms and sales reps to be registered, and created the Securities & Exchange Commission (SEC). Also referred to as the **People Act.**

Specialist: member of stock exchange given authority to act as broker and dealer (agent and principal) for other brokers, and given responsibility of maintaining a fair and orderly market. Specialist must be ready to buy and sell from firm's own account to stabilize the market when there are supply and demand imbalances.

Takedown: balance of spread paid out in commissions to members of the syndicate.

5.1 Self-Regulatory Organizations (SROs)

As we saw in Chapter 1, **Self-Regulatory Organizations (SROs)** were created by federal securities laws to help maintain a fair and orderly trading environment, to help oversee various aspects of the securities industries, and to aid in the enforcement of securities rules and regulations. SROs fall under the jurisdiction of the SEC and are responsible for the conduct of their own members. As such, each has adopted and enforces its own set of "industry rules," which members agree to abide by as a condition of participation in the market or exchange.

Fortunately, most of these rules have been adopted uniformly by the various SROs. Thus, when we examine the rules later in this section, we will have one large discussion of the rules and regulations as a group, pointing out differences between them as they exist because they may be addressed on the Series 7 exam. First, though, we will briefly explain the structure and authority of each SRO separately.

Structure and Authority of Each SRO

As pointed out before, each major exchange has its own SRO charged with oversight of activity within that marketplace. The three largest SROs are the New York Stock Exchange (NYSE), the National Association of Securities Dealers (NASD), and the Municipal Securities Rulemaking Board (MSRB). Let's look at each of these.

NYSE. The **New York Stock Exchange (NYSE)** is an SRO that is responsible for all activities related to securities listed and traded on the New York Stock Exchange. To become a member firm, one of the 1366 individual "seats" must be purchased. Member firms and salesperson employees of member firms must register with the NYSE and agree to abide by its rules and regulations. NYSE also has responsibility for some regional stock exchanges in the United States (e.g., Philadelphia Stock Exchange).

The NYSE is governed by a 21-member Board of Directors: one Board chairperson, ten NYSE members, and ten Board members representing the public. The Board supervises all NYSE activities, including listing and de-listing of stocks, membership activities and approvals, and setting NYSE rules and policies. One important role for the Board is determining who can be a specialist. We will discuss this function when we discuss the workings of the secondary market later in this chapter.

- ▷ NYSE member firms **must be open every day trading occurs** on the NYSE.
- ▷ All trades must be **charged commission** by member firms (but no minimum).
- ▷ Registered Principals of member firms are responsible for all office activities, supervising RRs, and must approve all new accounts and client trades.
- ▷ Principals who own 5 percent + of firms' voting stock are **allied members** of NYSE, but are **not permitted to trade** on the NYSE floor.
- ▷ RRs must be registered with the NYSE through their employing member firms; **120-day apprenticeship period** to pass Series 7 exam, then RR can collect commissions for trades and interact with the public.
- ▷ NYSE member RR must have **written permission to take any outside jobs.**
- ▷ RR **must resign and reapply** (not transfer) to join another member firm.
- ▷ RR may voluntarily leave a member firm; NYSE has jurisdiction for one year.
- ▷ All compensation must be paid through the broker-dealer firm.
- ▷ Disputes must go through arbitration.
- ▷ Disciplinary matters heard by NYSE panel; appealed to Board of Directors.
- ▷ Penalties can include fine, censure, suspension or expulsion.

NASD. The **National Association of Securities Dealers (NASD)** is an SRO that is responsible for all activities related to securities sold in the over-the-counter market. Any broker-dealer registered and in good-standing with the SEC may apply to become an NASD member. Salesperson employees of member firms must also be registered with NASD and agree to abide by its rules and regulations. The NASD also has regulatory authority over investment banking, investment companies, and limited partnerships.

NASD has a national Board of Governors and 13 District Offices run by district committees. The Board supervises all national NASD activities, including membership activities and approvals, handling complaint appeals, and setting NASD rules and policies. One important rule adopted by the Board is the 5 percent markup policy (discussed later). District Offices handle complaints via District Business Conduct Committees (DBCC), and also take care of nonpayment and nondelivery issues.

- ▷ Registered Principals of member firms are ultimately responsible for all office activities and supervision of Registered Representatives, and must approve all new accounts, client trades, sales literature, and ads.
- ▷ Registered Principals must have Principal License (Series 24) and register with NASD; Registered Options Principal needs ROP License (Series 4).
- ▷ RR must be registered with the NASD through employing member firm after passing the Series 7 exam; can collect commissions, interact with public and trade most securities, but **can't sell commodities futures.**
- ▷ NASD member RR can take **outside job with knowledge plus consent of firm.**
- ▷ RR **must resign and reapply** (not transfer) to join another member firm.
- ▷ RR may voluntarily leave a member firm; no retest if rejoining within two years.
- ▷ Continuing education: Firm Element (annual training given by firms); and Regulatory Element (within 120 days of second year, then every three years; NASD varies content of this computer-based regulatory training).
- ▷ **NASD name or logo can't be bigger** or more prominent than member name.
- ▷ All compensation must be paid through the broker-dealer firm.
- ▷ Disputes must go through arbitration; follow Code of Procedure.
- ▷ Disciplinary matters heard by DBCC; appealed to Board of Governors.
- ▷ Summary complaint procedure for undisputed minor violations: $2,500 fine.
- ▷ Penalties can include fine, censure, suspension or expulsion.

MSRB. Municipal Securities Rulemaking Board (MSRB) is an SRO responsible for all activities related to municipal bonds and other intrastate government securities that are issued, sold or traded. Firms and employees associated with those firms must be qualified in accordance with MSRB rules, become members, and agree to abide by its regulations. MSRB reexamines all broker-dealers every 24 months.

- ▷ Principals of member firms are ultimately responsible for all office activities and must approve all new accounts, client trades, sales literature, and ads.
- ▷ RR must be registered with the MSRB through employing member firm; **90-day apprenticeship;** 180-day window to pass Series 7 (or 52) exam, then RR can collect commissions for trades and interact with public.
- ▷ MSRB member RR can take **outside job with the knowledge and consent of firm.**

- ▷ RR **must resign and reapply** (not transfer) to join another member firm.
- ▷ RR may voluntarily leave a member firm; no retest if rejoining within two years.
- ▷ All compensation must be paid through the broker-dealer firm.
- ▷ MSRB does *not* have power to enforce its own rules; relies on SEC, other SRO; disputes must go through arbitration.

Remember: 1) NYSE and NASD have the power to enforce their regulations on registered member firms and registered representatives who work for those firms. 2) NYSE and NASD do not have power to enforce each other's rules and regulations; they may discipline only their own members. 3) MSRB does *not* have power to enforce its rules, but instead relies on NASD, other SROs, and SEC for enforcement.

Exam Topic Alert

5.1.2

Scope and Nature of SRO Rules

In addition to some of the main points of the SROs we discussed in the prior section, there are additional rules and regulations you must be familiar with. These are interspersed throughout this textbook where applicable, but there are a few rules and regulations that we will highlight here because they are popular test question material for the Series 7 exam. Many of these rules and regulations originated with NASD, and have been adopted by the other SROs. Where differences occur between the SROs over how a rule is implemented, this will be mentioned.

UNIFORM PRACTICE. **Uniform Practice Code** is a set of rules set up by NASD to establish standard methods and procedures for transactions between members. These rules have to do with how trades are executed and settled. For example, it is the Uniform Practice Code which has the regular-way transactions for corporate and municipal securities settled in three business days (T + 3). It is important for all member broker-dealers to follow these rules to ensure that trades are completed in a smooth and timely fashion. There are a number of aspects of interdealer trading that are facilitated by Uniform Practice Code rules, such as good delivery rules, confirmation procedures, and the assignment of ex-dates, among other things.

PRICES AND COMMISSIONS. SROs have rules that concern the way issues are priced and the commissions that broker-dealers may charge the public. For example, **firm quotes** mean that the broker-dealer must be willing to sell or buy at least one round lot (100 shares of stock or 5 bonds) at that price. But a firm quote is good for only the number of shares quoted; if more are needed, a new firm quote is needed. Backing away from a firm quote is a violation of NASD rules. Instead, the rules allow **subject quotes** (still negotiable or subject to final confirmation, not firm) or **workout quotes** (approximate depending on size of order or market activity).

Markups. NASD has a special 5 percent markup rule that applies to all nonexempt OTC securities transactions. (Exempt from this rule are U.S. government bonds, municipal bonds, listed securities, mutual funds, and new issues. This rule does not apply to NYSE transactions.) A **markup** is money added to the price of securities when a customer buys securities from a broker-dealer. A **markdown** is money subtracted from the price of securities when a broker-dealer buys securities for customers. The rule says that 5 percent is a reasonable guideline for markups, markdowns, or commissions, but this is subject to interpretation and exceptions.

Many factors are considered when determining a "fair" markup, and exceptions are made all the time. For example, one of the guidelines says that if a customer sells securities, then uses the proceeds to buy other securities, the *total* markup/markdown/commission should be no more than 5 percent. But, if too much time elapses between the transactions, it might be perfectly reasonable for the broker-dealer to make 5 percent each time.

Another exception to consider is a **riskless transaction** where the broker-dealer is simply filling a buy order of a widely traded security for a customer. In this case a 5 percent commission would likely be considered excessive since the broker-dealer has nothing at risk. And even if the broker-dealer actually purchased the security before reselling it to the client, this is considered a **simultaneous transaction** where the broker-dealer has no risk, so a 5 percent markup would likely be considered excessive also. On the other hand, if the security in question is an obscure, thinly-traded issue, and the broker-dealer has to expend considerable effort to find a buyer or seller, charging more than 5 percent may not be considered excessive even if the broker-dealer is strictly filling an order.

As you can see, there are few hard and fast rules. Remember, 5 percent is a guideline, so read test questions carefully, looking for unusual circumstances. Another thing to keep in mind is that when the broker-dealer is figuring a markup, it is *not* the dealer's cost basis that is used for figuring the 5 percent. Instead, the broker-dealer must look at *all* market makers in the security, find the best price for the client, and use this best "ask" price of the "inside market" when adding the markup to be charged.

Only if there is **no** *market activity in the stock can the dealer's cost basis be considered.*

Other factors may be considered when determining a "fair" charge by the broker-dealer. These include the type of security (bonds are less risky than stocks), availability of security (thinly-traded issues are more risky), price of security (small trades justify higher percentages than larger volume trades). Profit considerations of the broker-dealer firm ("We need to make X amount.") is *not* a valid consideration. Remember, the 5 percent markup rule applies to *all* nonexempt OTC transactions.

Markups and markdowns are charged when broker-dealers **act as dealers** and sell or buy securities with **their own inventory,** whereas **commissions** are charged when broker-dealers **act as brokers** and **arrange transactions** for clients.

Free Riding, Withholding. **Free riding** is when a broker-dealer holds back part of a new issue of stock so that it can be resold later at a better profit than the original public offering price. **Withholding** is when a broker-dealer holds back part of a new issue so that it can be kept in the broker-dealer's own account, or sold to family members, employees, or other insiders. **Both of these practices are prohibited by NASD rules.** Broker-dealers who are selling a new issue are required to make a bona fide offering at the public offering price, and are required to sell hot issues to the public on a first-come, first-served basis.

Exceptions to the withholding rules allow for immediate family members, employees, and others to buy hot issues if they can demonstrate that it is part of their normal investment practice, they are buying an insubstantial amount of the hot issue, and that the broker-dealer has sold 10 percent or less of its total stock to restricted people or restricted accounts.

OTHER REGULATIONS. Some other NASD or SRO regulations you may be asked about on the Series 7 exam have to do with gift rules and confidential information.

Gifts, Gratuities. SRO rules state that gifts or gratuities to employees of other firms must be approved by the firm, and can't be conditioned on sales or performance. The annual gift limit established by NASD and MRSB is $100, with a $50 limit for mutual fund distributors. Although occasional gifts may exceed this limit (e.g., meal, tickets to a game), lavish gifts are always unacceptable (e.g., vacation, season tickets).

Use of Information. Information obtained in a fiduciary capacity may not be used beyond its original intended purpose, and may be used only to benefit the client. For example, it is not acceptable to feed information to telemarketers about a client's investment portfolio.

Confidential information may be used or revealed only by specific written authorization of the client, or pursuant to a court order. Firms must have a written privacy policy and confidentiality policy in place.

5.13

Prohibited Activities

There are a number of activities and practices that are specifically prohibited by NASD and other SROs. Some of them we have discussed before, others will be more relevant when talking about a future topic. Some of the important prohibited activities that may be asked on the Series 7 exam are listed here, with brief explanations.

- **selling away**—doing a trade or collecting a commission that does not go through the broker-dealer firm
- **making unsuitable trade recommendations**—too speculative for client's investment objectives, beyond customer's purchasing capabilities, or not right for client's tax situation—MSRB only

- ▷ **making unauthorized trades**—without discretionary authority or properly executed power of attorney
- ▷ **churning**—excessive trading to generate commissions, usually determined by significant increase in trades after account became discretionary
- ▷ **short-term mutual fund trades**—because of excessive sales charges
- ▷ **breakpoint selling**—keeping client trades just below breakpoints where they would save on mutual fund sales charges
- ▷ **selling dividends**—telling clients to buy stocks right before ex-date just to capture a dividend is considered unethical since stock prices will drop the dividend amount after ex-date, but the client has an immediate tax event

Exam Topic Alert

Note: On the Series 7 exam, if a question suggests buying stocks to capture dividends is a good idea, *it's probably a trick.*

- ▷ **unauthorized use of client's money**—this includes hypothecating customer securities that are fully paid for and in a cash account
- ▷ **sharing client profits**—except in proportion to money RR actually invested
- ▷ **borrowing money**—from clients or **lending money** to clients
- ▷ **guaranteeing profits**—or promising future buybacks at set prices

5.14

Arbitration

Arbitration is an alternative means of dispute resolution whereby an impartial third party or panel of people listen to evidence presented by both sides and render a decision, thus avoiding the court system. Arbitration is often final and binding, although appeals to the court system may be allowed in limited circumstances. Member firms and RRs agree to submit disputes to arbitration as a condition of becoming registered members. Often customers sign arbitration agreements when opening accounts with broker-dealers.

PURPOSES. Arbitration is chosen to settle disputes because it is faster and cheaper than settling disputes through the court system. In fact, the Supreme Court has stated that arbitration is a fair, equitable, and efficient method for settling disputes in the securities industry. Any dispute is eligible for arbitration. Members who have disputes with other members are required to submit the matter to arbitration. Disputes involving members and customers may also be submitted to arbitration, if the customer has signed an arbitration agreement when opening the account.

PROCEDURES. All matters that are in dispute can be submitted for a hearing of impartial arbitration. The proper documentation is filled out and submitted to the Board of Arbitration for NYSE disputes, or the Director of Arbitration for NASD disputes. NASD disputes involving rules violations or misconduct go through the Code

of Procedure (COP—detailed in the next section). NASD disputes involving money go to arbitration following the NASD Code of Arbitration Procedure (CAP).

Note that the COP (for misconduct) *is **not** the same as CAP (for money disputes)!*

Exam Topic Alert

Self-Regulatory Organizations (SROs)

Arbitration is mandatory for NASD members. Customers can also choose arbitration in disputes with members, but members can compel customers to use it only if the customer has signed an arbitration consent form. Once the claimant files the arbitration paperwork and pays the required fee, the respondent has 45 days to answer the complaint, with an additional 10 days for the claimant to reply. After this initial written discovery phase, hearings are held. During this time, the matter may be resolved prior to the final ruling. The arbitration ruling is final and binding.

SRO RULES. Arbitration claims involving NYSE stockbroker activities must be filed within six years of the disputed incident. A securities customer has the right to require a stockbroker who works for a NYSE member firm to submit to arbitration. When a customer chooses arbitration to resolve the dispute, he or she waives the right to pursue the matter in court. Arbitration is final and binding.

NASD disputes involving money also go to arbitration, following the NASD Code of Arbitration Procedure. This is mandatory for NASD members. The size of the arbitration panel is determined by the amount involved in the dispute. Arbitration claims must also be filed within six years of the disputed incident involving NASD members. Members are required to settle disputes through arbitration. Clients who choose arbitration to resolve disputes waive their right to pursue the matter in court also. Arbitration is final and binding.

For NYSE claims involving $10,000 or less, or NASD claims involving $25,000 or less, simplified arbitration is an option. The advantage to simplified arbitration is that the parties do not have to appear in person at a hearing, which could make it a less costly choice. With simplified arbitration, the arbitrator renders a decision by reviewing documents and written accounts of the facts from the parties involved.

5.15

Trade Practice Complaints and Disciplinary Proceedings

For complaints and disciplinary proceedings, the NYSE holds a disciplinary hearing before a panel selected by the NYSE Board of Directors. The member has 25 days to respond to the complaint. The decision of the panel can be appealed to the Board of Directors, but they have the final say in the matter. Penalties that may be imposed for rules violations include censure, fines, suspension, termination of membership, prohibition against association with other members or member firms, and other sanctions as deemed appropriate by the NYSE.

For complaints and disciplinary proceedings, the NASD has a Department of Enforcement that arranges a hearing following the detailed procedures laid out in the NASD Code of Procedure. The Hearing Officer appointed to the case gives the respondent 45 days to respond to the charges. If the respondent files an Offer of Settlement, he or she waives the right to a hearing and the matter goes to the National Adjudicatory Council (NAC) for approval. If the Offer is rejected, hearings begin (but the Offer is null and void, and can't be held against the member). If the hearing goes against a respondent, sanctions begin 30 days after a final written report. Appeals may be made within 25 days to the SEC and then to federal court.

The NASD Code of Procedure deals with NASD rules violations, as well as MSRB rules violations and federal securities laws infractions. Penalties that may be imposed for rules violations include censure, fines, suspension, termination of membership, prohibition against association with other members or member firms, and other sanctions as deemed appropriate by NASD.

In lieu of a hearing, the Department of Enforcement (DOE) may also make an Acceptance, Waiver and Consent (AWC) offer, whereby the respondent signs a letter acknowledging the violation and accepting the penalties imposed by the DOE. If accepted by the NAC, the matter is closed. Another option for a minor rule violation (MRV), such as an advertising-related infraction or the untimely filing of a report, is that the DOE may also make an MRV offer, whereby the respondent signs the MRV letter acknowledging the violation. In this case, the maximum NAC penalty is a $2,500 fine.

Also, be aware that often a complaint names the principal supervisor in any complaint proceedings. Remember that any penalties or sanctions for rules violations may be cumulative. For example, an RR who is a member of the NYSE and NASD who commits fraud could be investigated and punished by the NYSE, NASD, SEC and state securities authorities.

5.2 The Primary Marketplace

The primary marketplace is where new securities issues are sold. Some examples are Initial Public Offerings (IPOs) where companies sell new stock, or a new bond issue sold by a municipality. What distinguishes a primary offering transaction is that the sale proceeds from the securities go to the issuer. This is much different from the secondary marketplace, where stocks change hands between investors. With the primary marketplace, there are many additional rules and regulations which must be followed. For example, a prospectus must be given out to investors when primary issues are sold. Furthermore, there are different players and procedures that are involved with selling a new issue. Investment bankers and underwriting are two of the terms you will need to become familiar with to understand how the primary marketplace functions.

5.2.1

Bringing New Issues to Market, Investment Banking

When companies or municipalities want to raise money, one way they can do that is to contact an investment banker and try to sell stock or bonds to the public. The investment banker is not a typical banker, but rather a broker-dealer that specializes in underwriting new securities issues. The underwriter works on behalf of the company or municipality to sell securities to the investing public. The investment banker makes a spread between the price charged to the public (public offering price) and the money given to the issuer selling the securities. Let's first focus on the investment banking process used when companies sell securities, then later we'll look at how the process differs when selling municipal issues.

5.2.1.1 Functions of the Investment Banker

The broker-dealer firm that takes on the role of investment banker has two functions. The investment banker's first function is an advisory role, helping the issuer to determine the best means of raising capital, helping the issuer price the securities and advising the issuer on the regulatory procedures for doing so according to securities laws. For example, with a corporation, the investment banker will help determine if a stock or bond issue is more suitable for the corporation. Considerations include what interest rates may have to be paid to attract capital, the bottom line cost of each source of capital (including tax implications), and which may be easier to sell to the public. The investment banker may also suggest issuing stock with warrants or bonds that are convertible to ensure the acceptance of the new issue by the investing public.

The investment banker's second function is distribution, finding the best way for getting the securities into the hands of investors. The investment banker will study the new issue and the market, and then come up with a distribution plan. Some of the decisions will be whether the investment banker will work alone or put together a team, and whether or not the investment banker will guarantee a sell out of the issue. You will see how each of these decisions impacts the underwriting process.

Nature of Underwriting Procedure. Once the company and the investment banker have decided to sell stock, there are still some additional decisions that they must make. There are actually two types of stock issues and two types of offerings. A company going public for the first time sells new shares as a **new issue** stock offering. This is what is commonly referred to as an **initial public offering,** or **IPO.** A company that is already public but looking to sell more stock can do an **additional issue** stock offering.

With either of these types of issues, there can be a primary offering or a secondary offering. In a **primary offering,** the proceeds from the sale of stock go into the company treasury. In a **secondary offering,** the proceeds from the sale of stock go to present shareholders. This is one way that founders and employees can take money out of the company. The offering can also be a **combined offering,** where some of the proceeds go to the company and some go to current shareholders.

Exam Topic Alert

Do not confuse secondary *offering* with secondary *market.* The only similarity is that present stockholders receive money from the sale of stock. But a secondary offering for company insiders must be done through an investment banker following the SEC rules for stock issues, whereas stock sold in the secondary market is an investor-to-investor transaction that takes place on an exchange.

5.2.1.2 Formation of the Underwriting Syndicate

In the last section, we said that one of the decisions the investment banking firm will make is whether to work alone or put together a team. Much of this decision will depend on the size of the offering. The investment bank can work together with other investment banking firms and arrive at a **competitive bid** to do the offering, or it can do a **negotiated underwriting** by working out the details of the issue with the issuer first and then put together a syndicate. A **syndicate** is a group of investment banking firms that agree to work together to purchase all of the securities from an issuer, and resell them to the public. A syndicate is also called a **purchase group,** to distinguish it from a **selling group** which may be formed to help distribute and sell the issue to the public. (Selling group members do not invest money to buy part of an offering.)

Underwriting Commitments. The other decision the investment banking firm will make is whether or not to guarantee a sell out of the issue. This decision will be influenced by many factors: market conditions, quality of the company (or municipality), etc. The two broad categories that an underwriting commitment can fall into are firm commitment and best efforts. **Firm commitment** is a guarantee by the investment banking firm that the entire issue will be sold. The issuer is guaranteed the money because the investment banker agrees to buy up all unsold shares or bonds. One type of firm commitment which we saw before was a **standby underwriting,** meaning that the investment banking firm guarantees to buy all shares that are not bought as part of a rights offering.

Best efforts is an agreement with the investment banking firm acting as agent and broker in selling the securities, buying only what it needs to fills orders, and without any obligation to purchase unsold securities from the issuer. There are two common types of best efforts offerings: all or none and mini-max. With **all or none,** the firm sells as much of the issue as possible, but if the entire issue is not sold then the offering is cancelled and the investors' checks (which are escrowed until the offering is complete) are returned. With **mini-max,** the offer will be cancelled only if a certain minimum amount of the issue is not sold (e.g., half of the issue), but even after that minimum is reached, the investment banking firm will continue to sell on a best-efforts basis up to the maximum authorized offering amount.

Note that the *purchase group assumes 100 percent of the risk with a firm commitment,* and is acting as a principal in the offering when underwriting the deal with a guarantee. On the other hand, the purchase group assumes *no risk when making a best efforts commitment* to doing the underwriting, since they are acting only as an agent for the corporation in trying to sell the issue. And of course, the *selling group also has no risk* since they, too, are merely acting as agents. With any of these underwriting commitments, though, the investment banking firm will usually have a **market-out clause** that permits the firm to postpone or cancel the offering if market conditions change (or for other stated reasons) before the offering has begun.

5.2.1.3 The Registration Process

All corporate securities must be registered with the SEC before they can be sold to the general public on a national scale. The company and investment banking firm prepare and file a **registration statement** (also called a **registration letter**). After filing, there is a **20-day cooling off period** during which time the SEC reviews a company's registration statement. The SEC often requests revisions, so the process may actually take longer than 20 days. During this time, the investment banking firm can distribute a preliminary prospectus to potential investors to gauge interest, but no securities may be sold yet.

Due Diligence. Due diligence is actually an ongoing process of researching information, gathering data, and verifying what is learned about the company. After the cooling off period, a formal **due diligence meeting** is called, during which a final analysis and verification takes place, particularly with regard to the company's financial information and use of proceeds. Once all questions are answered to everyone's satisfaction, the details of the registration statement, final prospectus, and underwriting agreement are finalized. The price of the issue is also set.

Preliminary Prospectus. A preliminary prospectus is prepared and distributed during the cooling off period. The preliminary prospectus gives some details about the offering to gauge investor interest, but must clearly state that it is "not an offer to sell securities nor solicit orders." (Because this warning is printed in red, a preliminary prospectus is sometimes referred to as a **red herring.**) The final public offering price does not appear in the preliminary prospectus, because it would not have been decided at the point when the preliminary prospectus was prepared. The preliminary prospectus, though, does give financial details about the issue and about the company, including a detailed use of proceeds statement. Other details include history of the company, management team, and risks to investors in the issue. All information, however, is subject to change before the final prospectus is issued.

Final Prospectus. The final prospectus is distributed on the effective date of the offering period, which begins once the SEC has cleared the prospectus for distribution. The final prospectus is basically the same as the preliminary prospectus, but with changes requested by the SEC, as well as additions of the final offering price and sales spread that the investment banking firm will make for selling the issue. At this point, the SEC has reviewed the prospectus, but the SEC does *not* approve the stock issue, nor guarantee the accuracy of the information. The SEC in no way states or implies that an issue is a good investment, and it is a violation of SEC laws for an investment banking firm or company to give the impression that the SEC has approved the stock being sold. In fact, a statement to the effect that the SEC has not approved the securities must be printed on the front of every prospectus. A copy of the final prospectus may be sent to all those who expressed interest during the cooling off period, and sales may be solicited. A copy of the final prospectus must also be sent to investors no later than with the sales confirmation.

Underwriting Agreement. The underwriting agreement is entered into between the company issuing securities and the managing underwriter, who is the lead investment banker and the agent representing the entire underwriting group. In the agreement, the underwriters agree to purchase the securities, and give the proceeds to the issuer by a stated settlement date. The issuer agrees to make all required SEC filings, comply with all laws, and use the proceeds as stated in the prospectus. The underwriting agreement also states the final public offering price and the spread the underwriters will make from the sale of securities to the public.

This underwriting agreement is different from the **agreement among underwriters,** where all investment banking broker-dealer firms who are part of the underwriting syndicate agree to appoint the originating investment banking firm as managing underwriter. The agreement also sets out how long the syndicate will last, details the proportionate share of the issue that each underwriter is committed to buying and reselling to the public, and gives the managing underwriter the authority to enlist a sales group.

Selling Group Agreement. The selling group agreement details the relationship between the purchase group and the sales group. Important terms of this agreement set forth the amount of commission that will be paid (called the **seller's concession**) and the length of time the contract will be in force (often only 30 days). Usually the selling group is *not* responsible for buying any unsold shares and bears no liability if shares are unsold. The *selling group is merely an agent,* and is not bound by any agreements the underwriting manager or other syndicate members may have entered into. The underwriter, on the other hand, is acting as a principal, and is completely at risk and responsible for buying any unsold shares if they have entered into a firm commitment underwriting.

Blue Sky Rules. The Blue Sky Laws in various states require issuers to register their new issues and provide financial information for securities that will be sold in that state. The investment banking firm decides in which states it has potential clients that it might like to sell the issue. Then the company and the issuer work together to assemble the required information and file the necessary registration statements in those states so that the securities can be sold there.

Although the laws vary by state, most contain provisions that prohibit fraud, regulate broker-dealers doing business in the state, and require registration of securities. In many states, some of these requirements are integrated with federal securities laws, so no separate action is needed. Municipal securities are generally exempt from state securities laws, but broker-dealers selling them must still comply.

There are three ways that an issue can comply with Blue Sky Laws. **Filing a notice** is the simplest of the three. For states that allow this, a notice is filed putting the state on notice that a federal SEC registration statement has been filed. Additional financial information may be required, but not a complete repeat filing of all registration materials. **Coordinated registration** is the second method, and has the same registration information filed simultaneously with the SEC and each state so that they both run on the same timetable. **Qualifying independently** is the final method, where a registration is filed with individual states for an intrastate offering only (which is exempt from SEC registration requirements).

5.2.1.4 Pricing Practices

Pricing a new security issue must take many factors into account. For a primary offering, the main factors have to do with the strength of the issuing company. A strong company with a good history of sales and a solid management team can command a higher price than a start-up company with no sales and unproven talent. Another important factor in setting the price is the level of interest that was generated from the preliminary prospectus (red herring) and any tombstone ads that may have been run. Market conditions also play a role, especially when the new issue is compared with other similar stocks. And, if it is an additional issue offering, then the existing stock price is a factor. Finally, the price has to be at a level that can raise enough money to make it worthwhile for the issuing company, and pay enough of a concession to make the deal acceptable to the underwriters.

Determination of Underwriter's Compensation. The underwriter's compensation is determined primarily by the type of commitment that is made. Since a firm commitment entails more risk, that allows the underwriters to command a larger spread for taking on that risk. The underwriter's **spread** is the difference between what the underwriters pay the company to buy the issue, and what public offering price they are able to sell the securities for. Other factors that can influence the spread are the type of issue (bonds are often easier to sell than stock), the strength of the company (a strong company makes the issue easier to sell), and even the size of the issue (selling more shares allows a smaller profit margin on each).

Components of the Underwriter's Spread. The underwriter's spread is made up of three main components, representing each group that must be paid. **Managing underwriter's fee** is paid to the syndicate manager for coordinating and overseeing the deal. This fee is the smallest part of the compensation at **10–20 percent.** There is an **underwriting fee** paid to the syndicate members to compensate them for the risk they undertook by buying the issue. This is typically **20–30 percent** of the spread *regardless of who sells the securities.* Finally, the **takedown** is paid to the selling group or other parties as a commission for actually selling the security to an investor. When outside selling groups are used, the **seller's concession** is part of the takedown. The takedown is by far the largest part of the spread at **50–60 percent** of the total spread. Note that these percentages are used by NASD as guidelines for determining the fairness of underwriter's spread and the various components of the spread.

Selling Group Concession and Reallowance. The selling group concession is a negotiated amount that a selling group member receives for each security sold. The concession can be a set dollar amount or a fixed percentage per unit sold. The concession here is also given at a discount, just like it is when the underwriting syndicate buys the issue from the issuer. Remember, though, the selling group members usually do not have to commit to sales so they can either buy only enough securities to fill orders, or simply return unsold securities to the underwriter since they are not their responsibility. **Reallowance** is a small part of the concession that is paid to any firms who sell the issue, but are not part of the syndicate or selling group. In all cases, the syndicate retains at least a portion of the total underwriter's concession to compensate them for the risk and expense of buying the issue.

5.2.1.5 Selling Practices

The selling of a new securities issue has two possible situations that the managing underwriting must be prepared for: the issue is too hot or the issue is too cold. A **hot issue** is one in which the market price moves above the public offering price almost immediately after the stock begins trading in the open market (aftermarket). We have already discussed the prohibited practices of **free riding** (part of a new issue is held back so that it can be resold later at a profit) and **withholding** (part of a new issue is held back and sold to family, other insiders). The NASD also watches to ensure that there is a bona fide public distribution, with no one person or small group being able to buy too much of an issue. Beyond these prohibited practices, though, the managing underwriter can get hit with a situation where the issue is too hot, and too much of it is sold. We will discuss this shortly.

The other problem is when an issue is too cold and there is not much demand. If the commitment is best efforts, this may not be a problem. But for a firm commitment, this is always a problem. What can make the problem even worse is if the market price starts to drop below the public offering price. This can result in the need for the underwriter to make a stabilizing bid.

Stabilizing Bid. A **stabilizing bid** is a buy order placed by the managing underwriter to ensure that the new issue price does not fall below the public offering price during the initial offering period while the issue is still being sold. Another term for this is **pegging.** Normally, this type of action would be considered manipulation of the market, and would be illegal. But the NASD allows the use of a stabilizing bid for new issues, as long as the bid is 1) disclosed in the prospectus as a possibility, 2) done only by the managing underwriter, and 3) done at or below the public offering price.

A stabilizing bid can never be above the public offering price.

Another way that the managing underwriter can try to keep prices somewhat in control is to set up penalty system for syndicate members. The managing underwriter offers a monetary concession to syndicate members and to sales group participants if they distribute the issue to customers who have an interest in the company and want to buy and hold the stock. The concession is offered because the managing underwriter wants to try to keep from having to place a stabilization bid to ensure that an orderly market exists in the stock during the initial trading period. If customers "flip" their stock and sell it during the initial trading period (also called the penalty period), the syndicate or sales group member may have to pay back the concession earned to the managing underwriter as a **penalty bid** or **penalty fee.** The problem with penalty fees, though, is they're perceived to be disproportionately applied against retail investors, but not institutional investors.

Note, too, that directors, officers and other company insiders are usually restricted by the managing underwriter from selling their shares of stock right away in an IPO situation. This is referred to as a **lock-up period,** and usually lasts for at least 180 days after the IPO shares begin trading.

Overallotments. Sometimes an issue is too hot and too much of it is sold. This situation is referred to as **overallotment, overselling,** or **oversubscribed.** When this happens, one of two things can be done to resolve the situation. If the syndicate (or selling group) sell more stock than is available, the managing underwriter has his firm in a short position. The underwriting syndicate members must get together and buy some additional shares in the open market to cover that position. The cost (loss) for that is divided up among all of the underwriters, based on their percentage of participation in the syndicate.

The other option is that the company might agree to issue more stock. If the issuer increases the number of shares available, the short position of the managing underwriter is covered. The issuance of additional shares is required if the underwriting agreement has a green shoe clause. A **green shoe clause** says that if there is an extraordinary demand for the stock, the issuer will agree to authorize additional shares and allow them to be sold by the underwriters.

Tombstone Ads. One of the ways the managing underwriter can know ahead of time if there might be a problem with the issue being too hot or too cold is the response that is received during the cooling off period. Remember, we said that during the cooling off period, no stock can be sold and no orders can be taken, but the underwriter can gauge interest in the offering through the distribution of a preliminary prospectus (red herring) and through the use of tombstone ads.

Tombstone ads are ads that an underwriter can run during the cooling off period as long as they clearly state that the ad is not an offering for sale or a solicitation for orders. Instead, the tombstone ad serves to announce the upcoming offering to the public. Tombstone ads are never required, but they can be a useful gauge of investor interest for the underwriter. In addition to the disclaimer, the ad states the size of the offering, the public offering price, and the names of the members in the underwriting group syndicate which can be contacted to obtain a prospectus. (Note that no other information can be distributed, except for the preliminary prospectus, and selling group members can't distribute the preliminary prospectus.)

5.2.1.6 Shelf Distributions

This is a special situation where a person affiliated with a company can sell off portions of his or her stock holdings at any time in the future after the holding period has ended. This is called a shelf distribution because the request is written into a registration statement that is filed early, then allowed to "sit on a shelf" until the person is ready to use this privilege. By selling later and over a long period of time, though, the person helps the market absorb the additional shares of stock without adversely affecting the price too much.

5.2.2

Regulation of New Issue Offerings

New issue offerings are one of the more heavily regulated aspects of the securities industry. The SEC was established by the Securities Exchange Act of 1934 specifically to enforce the regulations of new issue offerings that were detailed in the Securities Act of 1933.

5.2.2.1 Securities Act of 1933

This Act requires that all securities must first be registered before they can be sold to the public. The Act also requires the use of a prospectus to provide full disclosure of all pertinent information relative to a company's business and finances so that investors can make informed investment decisions. Finally, the Act prohibits false and misleading information from being disseminated with several antifraud provisions.

The Securities Act of 1933 is sometimes referred to as the **Paper Act** because of all the paperwork and filings that it requires. The focus of the Act is on the primary market for new issues. Much of the language of the law focuses on the duties and responsibilities of the investment banking firm as well as the issuer. Keep in mind that the Act does *not* approve securities, nor does it ascertain the value of an issue or the worth of a company. The Act only clears a registration, allowing a public offering to take place. The purpose of the Act is to ensure that investors are provided with full and fair disclosure about the issue and the issuer.

5.2.2.2 Registration Statement

There is certain specific information required to be in a registration statement. The **registration statement,** sometimes called a **registration letter,** must disclose the purpose of the offering, how much money the company is going to raise, how the money will be spent, information on the company and its business, information on the company's principals (especially any prior securities trouble), any legal proceedings the company is involved in, and any other pertinent facts that investors would need to know to make an informed decision about buying the company's stocks or bonds.

5.2.2.3 Filing Period

When a registration statement is received by the SEC it is time-stamped, and that **filing date** begins the cooling-off period. The **cooling-off period** is the time after the registration statement is filed, but before the securities can be offered for sale to the public. During this period, the SEC reviews the registration statement and preliminary prospectus. The investment banking firm continues its due diligence, and may place tombstone ads or distribute a preliminary prospectus to potential investors to gauge interest. No securities may be sold during this time.

The cooling off period is supposed to last 20 days, although it can be extended if the SEC requests additional documentation or wants changes made to the prospectus. When final clearance has been received from the SEC, this is considered to be the **effective date of registration.** From that point on, the underwriters may solicit orders to sell securities as long as the final prospectus is also sent to investors.

5.2.2.4 Offering Material

With new issues, different types of offering materials may be given out at different times before, during, and after the registration process. In the **pre-filing period** before any registration statement has been filed, no materials of any kind may be used by the company or underwriter. No prospectus, no advertising, and no information may be sent out, and no solicitations for orders. During the **cooling-off period** (after the registration statement is filed with the SEC but before receiving SEC clearance), only indications of interest can be solicited. A preliminary prospectus (red herring) can be delivered to those who request one, tombstone ads may be run, but no other info (e.g., research reports) may be sent out, no solicitations for orders can be made, and no securities can be sold during this time. The **post-registration period** (the offering period) begins with the effective date of registration after receiving final clearance for the offering from the SEC. At this time, securities may be sold to the general public provided that a copy of the final prospectus is sent no later than the order confirmation, and advertising may be done for the issue as long as it is truthful and complies with all SEC rules and regulations.

5.2.2.5 Prospectus Requirements

The final prospectus that is produced by the underwriter and issuing company is really an amalgamation of all the other documents that have come before it.

First is the **registration statement.** It must disclose

- ▷ the purpose of the offering,
- ▷ how much money the company is going to raise,
- ▷ how the money will be spent ("use of proceeds" statement),
- ▷ information on company (history, strategy, financials, market, competitors),
- ▷ information on company's principals (salary, resume, past five years experience),
- ▷ any legal proceedings the company is involved in, and
- ▷ any other pertinent facts.

Although timeliness of the information is not guaranteed, companies are required to notify the SEC with updated filings if any material facts included in the registration statement change during review.

The **preliminary prospectus** builds on this information. It includes

▷ the purpose of the offering,
▷ how much money the company is going to raise,
▷ how the money will be spent ("use of proceeds" statement),
▷ information on company (history, strategy, financials, market, competitors),
▷ information on company's principals (salary, resume, past five years experience),
▷ any legal proceedings the company is involved in,

PLUS:

▷ legal opinion on the validity of the corporation,
▷ description of the underwriting,
▷ risks to purchasers,
▷ disclaimer that this is "not an offer to sell securities nor solicit orders," and
▷ any other pertinent facts.

The **final prospectus** includes the same information as the preliminary prospectus, but may contain updates, corrections or changes from the SEC. The final prospectus also includes the offering price, selling discounts and a different disclaimer. The final prospectus includes:

▷ the purpose of the offering,
▷ how much money the company is going to raise,
▷ how the money will be spent ("use of proceeds" statement),
▷ information on company (history, strategy, financials, market, competitors),
▷ information on company's principals (salary, resume, past five years experience),
▷ any legal proceedings the company is involved in,
▷ legal opinion on the validity of the corporation,
▷ description of the underwriting,
▷ risks to purchasers,
▷ any other pertinent facts;

PLUS:

▷ offering price,
▷ selling concessions,
▷ statement that stabilizing bids may be used, and
▷ disclaimer that "These securities have not been approved by the SEC."

The final prospectus must be delivered to each investor no later than with the sales confirmation. This requirement lasts for different periods of time, depending on what type of offering is being done.

For **new issues (IPOs) listed on NASDAQ,** a final prospectus must be delivered for **25 days** past the effective date (beginning) of the offering period.

For **new issues OTC and others not listed,** the requirement is **90 days.**

For **additional issue offerings listed on NASDAQ,** a final prospectus must be delivered only **until the issue has sold out.**

For **additional issues OTC and others not listed,** a final prospectus must be delivered for **40 days** past the effective date.

After these times, it is assumed the stock is trading in the secondary market and no longer available only from the underwriter, so the prospectus is no longer needed.

5.2.2.6 Restrictions on Solicitations

There are certain restrictions placed on prospecting and soliciting that may be done while a security is in registration. The underwriter may not solicit orders nor sell stock during the registration process. After the registration statement has been filed, then a preliminary prospectus can be used in a limited way to get an indication of interest from potential investors. Remember, the preliminary prospectus must clearly state that it is "not an offer to sell securities nor solicit orders." Investors can indicate their interest in buying the issue, but they cannot place an order.

Once the registration statement and preliminary prospectus have been filed, the SEC imposes a **quiet period.** During this time, the company is prevented from sending any materials other than the preliminary prospectus. This quiet period lasts concurrently with the cooling off period, then continues for an additional 25 days after a stock starts trading. This means that a company is prevented from promoting the issue, and must let the prospectus be the vehicle to explain and sell the issue.

5.2.2.7 Reg. A Offerings

Certain provisions of the Securities Act of 1933 allow for streamlined securities registration. One such exception is called **Reg. A,** named after Regulation A of the '33 Act. Reg. A provides for a simplified securities registration process for companies doing stock offerings of less than $5 million within a 12-month period. With a Reg. A offering, the company does not need to file a lengthy registration statement and prepare a full prospectus. Instead, a shorter document called an **offering circular** is used. Much of the information that is required in an offering circular is the same as a prospectus, but there may be less detail. Also, the company's financial statements do not need to be audited, which can save time and money. With a Reg. A exemption, the company must still notify the SEC and keep them apprised of any developments with the offering, including how much money has been raised.

5.2.2.8 Exempt from Registration

Some provisions of Securities Act of 1933 provide for certain securities and/or transactions to be exempt from registration. U.S. government and municipal securities are two exempt securities that we have already discussed. Others are bank issues, savings & loan issues, trust company issues, farm cooperative issues, nonprofit issues, insurance products, and any commercial paper or other money market instruments that will mature in 270 days (nine months) or less.

In addition to these exempt issuers, some exempt transactions include any transaction between private individuals, brokers executing unsolicited requests from customers, and Reg. D private placements.

Private Placements. Regulation D of the Securities Act of 1933 provides an exemption for investment transactions where the securities are purchased with the intent of being held for investment purposes, rather than for resale. This is because securities acquired through a private placement are generally restricted securities which can be repurchased only by the issuer. In fact, when stock is acquired by means other than a typical SEC registered offering, it is likely to be **restricted stock** that must be held for a certain period of time before it can be resold.

There are three investor categories of people who are eligible for investing in a Reg. D private placement: accredited investors, officers or those affiliated with the issuer, and an investment group consisting of no more than 35 nonaccredited investors. **Accredited investors** are individuals with a net worth of at least $1 million or annual income of at least $200,000. There is no limit to how many accredited investors can join a deal, but each person's investment cannot exceed 20 percent of their net worth. The thinking behind this exemption in the law is that accredited investors who have amassed a certain amount of wealth can look out for themselves. (Financial institutions and other institutional investors also fall under the accredited investor exception.) These accredited investors also do not count against the group limit of 35 nonaccredited investors.

Note, though, that all investors must still receive (or have access to) detailed information about the company (its history, its finances, its market position, etc.), and all the other information that would have been in a prospectus if the issue were registered. Also, a broker-dealer can only invite accredited investors to a private placement meeting, but cannot contribute or participate in any other way. (And a broker-dealer may have prohibitions against even this, so an RR must check with the policies of his or her employing broker-dealer firm.)

Rule 144. This Rule is part of the Reg. D private placement regulations. Rule 144 involves the use of an investment letter which investors sign stating, among other things, that the private placement stock they are buying is being purchased for investment purposes, and furthermore that they agree not to sell the stock for a certain period of time and/or under certain conditions.

Rule 144 distinguishes between control securities held by control persons, and restricted securities. **Control persons** are people who own 10 percent or more of a company, and their stock is referred to as **control stock.** People related to or affiliated with control persons are also classified as control persons, and their stock is also classified as control stock. Rule 144 limits the amount of control stock that may be sold in a 90-day period. The total control stock sold may be not more than 1 percent of the outstanding stock (of the same class) or not more than the average weekly trading volume reported over the past month, whichever is greater.

Restricted stock is stock that is acquired by means other than a typical SEC registered offering (e.g., through a private placement). Rule 144 dictates that restricted stock must be held for at least one year before it can be sold. If restricted stock is held by an insider or someone affiliated with an insider, then the restricted stock is also subject to the control stock sale limits after the one-year holding period. If the restricted stock is held by someone who is not defined as an insider, after the one-year holding period there are volume limits for the second year, and no volume limits beginning in the third year.

Any time that restricted stock or control stock is sold in excess of 500 shares or $10,000, a Rule 144 Form 144 must be filed. Form 144 is valid for only 90 days. If these restricted or control shares are sold following a valid Form 144 filing, the shares are then considered registered, and the new owner receives the stock *without* the restrictions (unless they are also an insider). Just to clarify, understand that control persons always have control stock. Control persons' control stock may or may not also be restricted stock, depending on whether or not the stock they own was part of an SEC registered issue. Remember, too, that control stock does not necessarily have holding periods; only volume limits. Other terms for **restricted stock** are **unregistered stock, legended stock** (because it contains a legend on the face detailing the restrictions), or **lettered stock** (because investors must sign a letter stating that they agree to the terms of the restricted stock offering).

Note that on the Series 7 exam, *any time you see these words for* ***restricted stock*** *or* ***control stock,*** *the question or answer is likely referring to a Reg. D private placement or Rule 144.*

Rule 144a. This Rule provides for an exception to the holding period requirements. The exception applies if the securities are nonregistered foreign securities sold to institutional investors in the United States. The institutional investor must qualify under securities rules as a QIB (qualified institutional buyer) with at least $100 million in assets, and meet certain other qualifications.

Rule 145. This Rule applies to stock acquired through a merger, consolidation or transfer. In essence, persons who acquire stock through one of these means are permitted to resell their shares without registration. This is done to protect investors by allowing them to dispose of shares in the new entity without registration so that management cannot do a merger, consolidation, or transfer with the sole intent of keeping investors in a perpetual holding period with their stock. There are stipulations that must be followed when selling the stock, but those are beyond the scope of this textbook.

5.2.2.9 Blue Sky Laws

This is the generic name given to the various state laws that require issuers to register their new issues and provide financial information for securities that will be sold in a particular state. There are three ways that an issue can comply with Blue Sky Laws.

Filing a notice is the simplest of the three. For states that allow this, a notice is filed putting the state on notice that a federal SEC registration statement has been filed.

Additional financial information may be required, but not a complete repeat filing of all registration materials.

Coordinated registration is the second method, and has the same registration information filed simultaneously with the SEC and the individual states so that they both run on the same timetable.

Qualifying independently is the final method, where a registration is filed with individual states for an intrastate offering only (which is usually exempt from SEC registration requirements).

Remember that Blue Sky Laws cover state registrations. The investment banking firm decides in which states it has potential clients that it might like to sell the issue. Then the company and the issuer work together to assemble the required information and file the necessary registration statements in those states so that the securities can be sold there.

5.2.2.10 Trust Indenture Act of 1939

This Act was passed by Congress to give corporate bond investors the same kinds of protection that corporate stock investors have under the law. If a company is selling bonds within a 12-month period that are valued at more than $5 million and with maturities of longer than 270 days (nine months), the Act requires corporate bonds to have a **bond indenture agreement.**

The **indenture agreement** provides for the appointment of a qualified, independent trustee to watch over the interests of the bondholders. The trustee is responsible for holding the corporation accountable in keeping the protective clauses and list of promises to bondholders. The corporation is also responsible for giving semiannual financial reports to bondholders, and for making periodic SEC filings to show compliance.

Exam Topic Alert

*Note that although the indenture agreement is for the benefit of bondholders, and designed to protect them, the bond indenture is a contract between the corporation and trustee—*not *between the company and bondholder.* Watch this on the Series 7 exam.

5.2.2.11 Primary Market for Municipal Securities

The primary market for municipal securities consists of new bond issues sold by municipalities at various levels of state and local government. Because municipal bonds are exempt from the Securities Act of 1933, there is no centralized registration process like there is for corporate bonds. (Remember, though, that the broker-dealer firms who underwrite and sell municipal bond issues are still subject to securities laws.) Although municipal securities have their own methods and documents, the underwriting procedures share some similarities with corporate bonds. Let's take a look at these.

Methods. Underwriting a primary offering can be accomplished a number of ways. The two primary methods used for bonds sales are competitive sale and negotiated sale. A **negotiated sale** (or **negotiated bid, negotiated underwriting**) is where the issuer selects an underwriter, and then the underwriter and the issuer agree on the price and terms of the issue. They also agree on the spread that the underwriters will make, thus the amount that the issuer will receive from the sale of the securities is the difference between the issue price and the spread. Negotiated sales is the way that most corporate issues are done, and some municipal bonds. Municipal revenue bonds that are paid from user fees of the project are often done with negotiated bids. But with general obligation (GO) bonds where tax money is involved, the fiduciary responsibility that the municipality has to the public usually dictates that GO bond issues are done with a competitive bid.

A **competitive sale** (or **competitive bid, competitive underwriting**) is where the issuer will consider offers from several underwriters or underwriting syndicates before choosing a firm to work with. This ensures that the municipality receives the most money possible from the sale of the securities, thus protecting the public's best interests.

A **public offering** of municipal securities is accomplished with either a negotiated bid or a competitive bid. Both of these, however, are usually done on a firm commitment basis. (Another option would be to do a public offering that was done on a best efforts basis.)

A **private placement** offering can also be done with municipal securities. This is not so much to get accredited investors (since there is no registration requirement to make this an advantage), rather it is to sell the issue to institutional investors. The advantage to the private placement (both with municipals and corporates) is that a much larger chunk of the investment can be sold off at one time to one investor. A private placement with a large amount sold to a few select, large investors (institutional or otherwise) can save a tremendous amount of effort when compared to selling the issue $1,000 or $5,000 at a time to small investors.

Advance refundings are a method of primary financing that lowers the interest rate of a municipality's debt obligation by selling more bonds when rates are lower, to replace bonds that are at a higher rate. This method can be coordinated with an underwriting firm using any of the previous four methods to actually sell the issue.

Documents. There are several documents provided by the issuer which play an important role in the selling of a municipal bond issue. Unlike the underwriting agreement that is used with corporate deals, there is no single document that covers everything. Instead, the municipality and the underwriter enter into a bond contract which actually involves multiple documents. There are three documents that stand out in importance, and thus will be discussed here.

The **authorizing resolution** is the issuer's authority to sell the bond issue. It may be voted on at the government level (legislature, committee, etc.), or it might be the result of voters saying "yes" to a ballot issue. In any case, the resolution must authorize the action, describe the size of the issue, the interest rate on the bonds, and cover other legal issues. As part of the authorizing resolution, or as a separate action, the municipality will also have an award resolution, awarding the securities underwriting contract to the chosen underwriter.

The **bond indenture agreement** is very similar to the corporate one. Although municipalities are exempt from the Trust Indenture Act of 1939, and hence do not legally need to provide an indenture, this has become a prerequisite in the marketplace for the municipal issue to sell. One important item that a municipal bond indenture has that a corporate one doesn't is a **flow of funds** statement. With revenue bonds, this is important to investors because they want to know the priority that their debt obligation is to the municipality.

The **official statement** is the final important document that we will discuss. It is very similar in scope and function to the prospectus used in corporate offerings. There is even a preliminary official statement and a final official statement. Let's look at this in greater detail.

Official Statements. The **official statement** serves as the means of communication between the issuer and investor, giving very detailed and pertinent information about the municipality, the purpose of the bond issue, and the terms of repayment. The official statement is all about disclosure. The preliminary official statement is also used to solicit interest, so that the size and price of the issue can better be determined. The final official statement must be delivered no later than the order confirmation. It contains the final offering price, the size of the issue, and other information that is as up-to-date as possible when it is distributed.

The official statement contains much of the same information as the corporate prospectus. It discloses the purpose of the offering, how much money will be raised, how the money will be spent, information on the municipality, any legal proceedings the municipality is involved in, and any other pertinent facts that investors would need to know to make an informed decision about buying the bonds. The official statement will also provide a feasibility study (for revenue bonds), a legal opinion regarding the legitimacy of the municipality to levy the tax to repay the bonds (for GO bonds), and tax information to show whether or not the issue is tax exempt, including on what basis that determination was made.

Function of Bond Attorney. A bond attorney plays an important role in municipal bond issues. The issuer hires a bond attorney to render a legal opinion as to whether or not the issue qualifies for tax exempt status. The independent attorney examines all state and local laws, relevant legislation, and court opinions with regard to the bond issue. The attorney then issues an unqualified or qualified legal opinion.

An **unqualified legal opinion** states that the attorney has thoroughly researched the contemplated bond issue, and that the municipality has the legal authority to issue the bonds. If the bonds are eligible for tax exempt status, this will also be stated in the legal opinion. An unqualified legal opinion is the most desirable for the issuer, and the most attractive for investors. This also allows the issuer to charge more for the bonds.

A **qualified legal opinion** is issued if the attorney finds some problem with the issue. The legal opinion will state that the attorney has found that the bond issue is valid only with certain qualifications (such as pending litigation, or the inability to confirm some essential fact). This is not as attractive as an unqualified legal opinion, but it is better than no legal opinion. Thus, the price falls between the two extremes.

The legal opinion is made part of the official statement for the bond issue. The legal opinion is also distributed with the bonds, and may actually be printed right on the face of the bond. Smaller issuers may choose not to have a legal opinion done to save the expense, and thus they stamp **ex-legal** on all of their bond documents. This is acceptable if agreed to by the buyer prior to making any purchase of bonds, but it is the least attractive of the options and causes the price to be lower than if a legal opinion was attached to the bonds.

Underwriting Procedures. The sale of municipal securities is similar to that for corporates. The underwriting procedures share some similarities, but also have some differences that we need to explore. If the municipality is getting ready to issue revenue bonds, they will contact investment banking firms and choose one to handle the issue through a negotiated bid. Even though there is no official registration statement that must be filed, the issuing municipality and underwriters still meet and go through much of the same due diligence, information gathering and document preparation to get ready to bring the new issue to market.

If the municipality is going to issue GO bonds, then the competitive bid process is a little different. The municipality will advertise an "official notice" or "intent to sell" in a financial publication, such as the Bond Buyer, and solicit bid offers from investment banking firms. The municipality will give proposed details of the bond offering it wants to do, including size, date, purpose, maturity, etc. Investment banking firms and underwriters will choose to form different groups on their own to determine the best way to submit a winning bid to sell the issue.

1. Account formation is a process that takes place independent of the issuer. Instead, investment banking firms get together with others they know or have worked with before in an effort to come up with a bid they think will be successful. Members are chosen based on their experience and ability to sell new issues. The group would likely sign a **syndicate letter** that outlines the framework for their joint bid effort. The next step would be to determine the scale necessary to fulfill the goals of the municipality. (**Scale** is the number of bonds, maturity date, coupon rate, and offering price.) Members who want to participate in the bond offering would then commit to selling a certain percentage of the issue, and this would form the basis for the bid to be submitted by this particular syndicate group. The same process goes on other places, as many different independent underwriting groups get together to contemplate bidding on the municipal bond issue.

2. Underwriting account agreements consist of one or more contracts which detail the responsibilities and relationships of the different parties. In addition to the syndicate letter mentioned above (which is not binding), the group will also likely sign an **agreement among underwriters** (which is binding). This is different from the underwriting agreement signed between the managing underwriter and company with corporate issues. The **agreement among underwriters** appoints the originating investment banking firm as managing underwriter, gives the managing underwriter the authority to enlist a sales group, and sets out how long the syndicate will last. The agreement also details the proportionate share of the issue that each underwriter is committed to buying and reselling to the public, and the type of account arrangement that will exist between the syndicate members.

3. Types of accounts can be either undivided or divided. The difference between these two types of syndicated accounts has to do with how the issue of unsold bonds will be resolved after the initial order period is over. With the **undivided account** (or **Eastern account**), each member has an undivided interest in all bonds and an undivided interest in, and liability for, all issues that remain unsold after the initial sale period. For example, if underwriter #3 commits to selling 20 percent of the issue, after the initial sales period is over, all remaining unsold issues are gathered up and redistributed a second time based on each underwriter's initial sales commitment. Thus, underwriter #3 will still be responsible for selling 20 percent of the unsold issues that get redistributed—even if underwriter #3 sold 50 percent of the issue during the initial sales period, or sold only 10 percent of its original allotment.

With the **divided account** (or **Western account**), each member has no interest nor liability nor responsibility for any bonds that remain unsold after the initial sale period. The Western account member is responsible only for her own allotment. Thus, if an underwriter commits to selling 20 percent of the issue, and is unable to sell the 20 percent, it simply sends in a check to buy the balance of what it didn't sell. Although this method seems to be simpler (and more fair), it is actually used less often.

4. Role of the underwriter is different for the managing underwriter and the members. The managing underwriter (or lead underwriter) is the one who has responsibility for arranging the deal, handling the paperwork, and making sure that everything gets done. Being the lead underwriter, though, does not necessarily mean that that firm has the biggest allotment of the issue to sell. The responsibility of the other syndicate members is often as simple as selling their portion of the issue, and following the guidelines established for the group.

5. Determination of the syndicate bid is also a responsibility borne mostly by the managing underwriter, although the other syndicate members participate as well. In fact, there are usually several meetings where the bid is discussed before it is finalized. To aid with the bidding process, the managing underwriter will often order a new issue worksheet from the Bond Buyer, which gives details about the municipality's bid solicitation. Some of the factors taken into consideration are the placement ratio of other new issues during prior weeks, the 11-year bond index and 20-year bond index, which both measure current market interest rates, and the visible supply numbers which list new offerings announced for the next 30 days. All of these factors help determine the final bid price. The syndicate wants to price the issue high enough to make money, but low enough so that investors will buy up the entire issue. Remember, the syndicate's bid will be a firm commitment.

6. Computation of the bid involves the managing underwriter writing the scale. **Writing the scale** is the process the underwriter goes through to figure out how much the bonds can be sold for in the marketplace. The computation will consider the other issues in the marketplace (as discussed above), but will also consider when the bonds will mature, the interest rate, and what the firm can charge for the bonds (the spread). *The par value of the bonds at maturity is* not *considered.* (Watch for this on the Series 7 exam.) Also, when the bid form is submitted, it simply states the coupon rate and the dollar amount bid. The underwriter does not show the municipality any of the re-offering yield schedules that the underwriter computed when it figured the writing the scale calculations.

7. Factors relevant for the basis of award can vary depending on how the municipality examines the bids. The municipality wants the lowest interest cost, but some consider the present value of money; others only look at the net interest cost. With **net interest cost (NIC),** any money received by the municipality over par value is subtracted from the interest cost. It does not matter when the money is received or paid. Only the total interest amount the municipality will pay is used in the comparison of bids. With **true interest cost (TIC),** all moneys received are also considered, but money paid or received earlier is weighted more heavily than money that will be paid or received at some point in the future. In other words, TIC uses standard time value of money calculations as part of its overall comparison of bids. Usually, the underwriting syndicate that offers the lowest total interest payout is awarded the bid contract, and signs with the municipality to begin selling the issue.

8. Syndicate operation procedures then dictate how the rest of the offering will go after the bid has been accepted. Most of these procedures have already been decided in the syndicate letter and/or the agreement among underwriters. The two most important considerations are priority provisions during the order period, and the concessions and takedown allocations.

Priority provisions during the order period determine who can buy bonds and how the commissions for those sales will be shared among the syndicate members. The **order period** is a time during which orders are taken and bonds are allocated based on the type of order rather than the exact time that the order was received. MSRB rules allow this to take place for a short window after the syndicate's successful bid. Remember, when orders are placed during this order period, how the order is placed is more important than when the order is placed for determining priority. These priority provisions often come into play when an issue is oversold.

Priority provisions are the sequence in which bond orders are filled.

1. **p**resale orders: orders taken before pricing and terms of the issue were finalized. Commission is shared with all syndicate members.
2. **g**roup net orders: orders taken after terms and price were finalized. Commission is shared proportionately with all members.
3. **d**esignated orders: orders received during order period but don't get high priority. Commission goes only to selling firm and managing firm.
4. **m**ember at takedown orders: orders for firm's own account, thus get lower priority. Commission all goes to firm, but issue may be sold out.

There may be questions on the Series 7 exam about order priority with municipal bonds, so to remember the order think: PGDM: **P**retty **G**ood **D**ance **M**usic.

Exam Topic Alert

Concession and takedown allocations are the final area of syndicate operations that need to be discussed. Concession and takedown are actually components of the spread. **Spread** is the difference between what the underwriters pay for the bonds to buy the issue, and what price they are able to sell the bonds for. In other words, the spread is the entire amount of money that can be made from selling a bond to the public at the offering price. The spread is made up of two basic components: the manager's fee and the total takedown. The **manager's fee** is a fixed amount that comes off the top of every sale and is paid to the managing underwriter firm no matter who sells the bond. There is also an **underwriting fee** that goes to all members to help defray costs and compensate them for the risk of taking on the bond issue. The **takedown** is the balance of the spread that is paid out in commissions to members of the syndicate group. Sometimes the entire takedown amount is divided up proportionately among the syndicate members (such as with presale orders and net group orders). Other times, the takedown is further subdivided into two parts. One subpart of the takedown is called the **additional takedown.** This amount is paid to the syndicate member who is responsible for selling the bond; that member retains this part of the takedown even if a sales group helped sell the issue. The other subpart of the takedown is called the **seller's concession,** which is the commission paid to the firm that actually sells the bond to an investor.

5.3 The Secondary Marketplace

The secondary marketplace is the place where securities are bought and sold after their original issue. What distinguishes a secondary market transaction is that the sale proceeds from the securities go to the investor or broker-dealer who holds the stock, not the company who originally issued it. This is much different from the primary marketplace, where the money from securities goes to the issuers (or company insiders). With the secondary marketplace, there are different rules, regulations and procedures that must be followed. For example, if the securities are listed on an exchange, prices can change frequently under the "double auction" method of pricing. Specialists and market makers are two of the terms you will need to become familiar with to understand how the secondary marketplace functions.

Regulation and Participants

When stocks are traded on the exchanges or over-the-counter (OTC) there are specific rules that must be followed. The activities of broker-dealers and others are regulated so that stock prices cannot be manipulated, and so that average investors cannot be taken advantage of by professionals who know how to use the system better. Much of these regulations are part of the Securities Exchange Act of 1934.

5.3.1.1 Securities Exchange Act of 1934

This Act regulates secondary market activity by outlawing fraud and market manipulation, regulating sales and activities by company insiders, and requiring broker-dealer firms and securities sales representatives to be registered. This Act also created the Securities and Exchange Commission (SEC) to oversee the securities markets and enforce the regulations of this Act and the Securities Act of 1933.

The Securities Exchange Act of 1934 is sometimes referred to as the **People Act** because of all the various people required to be registered under the Act, or whose activities the Act regulates. The focus of the Act is on the secondary markets where outstanding stock issues are traded on exchanges or OTC. The purpose of the Act is to protect investors and investments from fraud and manipulation. In fact, even if securities or transactions are exempt from registration under the Act of 1933 or for some other reason, there is *never* an exemption for any security or any person from the antifraud provisions of the Securities Exchange Act of 1934.

You may be asked lots of questions about the Securities Exchange Act of 1934 (also called the **Exchange Act** or People Act). Before we cover some important topics in detail, here's a synopsis of what the Act of '34 covers. Remember **SIMMERS PAN** or **SIMMER + PAN.**

- ▷ **S**EC was created,
- ▷ **I**nsider activities regulated,
- ▷ **M**argin rules were created,
- ▷ **M**anipulation of the markets was prohibited,
- ▷ **E**xchanges and all people who trade on them are required to be registered with the SEC,
- ▷ **R**egistration and filings are required to be done regularly by listed companies,
- ▷ **+S**hort sales were regulated with the "plus tick" rule,
- ▷ **P**roxies were required to include specific information so voters are informed,
- ▷ **A**nnual statements from broker-dealers were required to be given to clients,
- ▷ **N**et capitalization rules applied to broker-dealers to limit their indebtedness.

5.3.1.2 Regulation of Insider Activities

The Exchange Act of 1934 did much to curb the activities of insiders. **Insiders** are defined by the 1934 Act as any officers or directors of a company, or any person who owns 10 percent or more of a company's stock. Prior to the Act, insiders would buy stock before making a major announcement that would send the stock up, or, more commonly, sell stock before releasing bad news that would send the stock down. The 1934 Act prohibits those insiders who have access to privileged information from using that information to trade in their companies' securities before the information is made public. (The distinction of the Act as being the 1934 Act is important, because the Insider Trading Act of 1984 greatly expanded the definition of "insider" to include almost anyone who has non-public information.)

Furthermore, the 1934 Act also prohibits short selling by insiders (except shorting against the box), and requires insiders to file reports with the SEC any time there is a change in their company holdings or a transaction is executed on their behalf.

5.3.1.3 Regulation of Proxies

The Exchange Act has specific proxy solicitation rules. Remember, a **proxy** is a kind of absentee ballot, whereby the stockholder can vote on matters without having to attend the annual stockholders' meeting. Proxy solicitations must be sent to the SEC for approval before the company can send them to stockholders. Proxy fights, which attempt to alter control of a company, must have all parties register with the SEC or risk criminal penalties.

Any type of proxy solicitation where someone is trying to persuade a shareholder to vote a certain way must be first filed with the SEC, and comply with SEC rules. Proxy solicitations must contain a proxy statement disclosing exactly what is being voted upon, names of proposed members of the Board of Directors, their compensation, any conflicts of interest, and details of any major change or resolution that will be voted upon. Furthermore, proxy rules require that an annual report be sent to all shareholders. Finally, any false or misleading statements or omissions in a proxy statement are prohibited by the Exchange Act and the SEC.

Rules governing the proxy itself state that the card on which a shareholder can vote must clearly show who is being voted on by name, and what is being voted on by description. There cannot be an option to vote blindly, for unnamed candidates, or give the management discretion on how to vote on behalf of the shareholder. The proxy must be voted when received, and votes on the proxy cannot be changed except by a new proxy from the shareholder, or attendance at the annual meeting in person.

5.3.1.4 Regulation of Broker-Dealer Activities

The Exchange Act of 1934 requires that all broker-dealers register with the SEC, even if they are dealing with exempt securities. The Act goes even further to regulate the activities of broker-dealers, specifically prohibiting or placing restrictions on a number of practices.

Trading for Own Accounts. When trading for their own accounts, broker-dealers must place customer orders ahead of their own. Furthermore, broker-dealers are required to disclose to their clients if they are acting as a broker or a dealer in a transaction. This means that if a firm is selling stock to a client from the broker-dealer's own account, that fact must be disclosed to the client. For transactions involving OTC securities, the broker-dealer must also disclose the amount of the markup that the firm is charging the client on the transaction.

Specialist Activities. Specialists are members of a stock exchange given authority to act as brokers and dealers (agents and principals) for other brokers, and charged with the responsibility of maintaining a fair and orderly market. The specialist must be ready to buy and sell from the firm's own account in an effort to stabilize the market when there are supply and demand imbalances. We will discuss the role of the specialist in greater detail in an upcoming section.

The activities of the specialist are subject to special rules laid out by the '34 Act. The specialist may not trade for his or her own account while other unexecuted orders are open at the same price for the same security, and the specialist may make trades for his or her own account only between (not at) the current bid and ask price. Also, the specialist is prohibited from taking any action which would destabilize the balance of supply and demand in a stock (such as making opening trades in a stock).

Broker, Dealer in Same Transaction. It is prohibited for broker-dealers to act as both a broker and a dealer in the same transaction. In other words, a firm can't collect a commission from a client (acting as a broker) while buying the firm's own stock (acting as a dealer) and also charge a markup on the same transaction.

Manipulative and Deceptive Practices. A number of practices are illegal under the Exchange Act of 1934 because they either move a stock in a direction that it is not actually going on its own, or make it look as if there is more trading activity in a stock than there actually is. Some examples of prohibited practices include

> **Pegging:** intervention in the markets by a broker-dealer, when a broker-dealer places a nonexistent buy order, or places its own buy order, to move a stock up to that price or keep it from falling any lower than the price that the broker-dealer bid. (This is allowed for new issue sales, though.)
>
> **Painting the tape:** when one or more broker-dealer firms act in a coordinated effort, or within a group or ring, to buy and sell the same stock several times in succession to show trading activity, or make a stock appear hot. (This is also referred to as **matched order** or **sales pools** or **sales rings.**)
>
> **Wash sales:** buying and selling the same stock to show trading activity. (Although the name is the same, and both involve selling and buying the same stock, do not confuse this with the wash sale rules preventing tax avoidance.)

Short Tendering of Stock. This is a prohibited act, whereby broker-dealers borrow stock (take short positions) to take advantage of a purchase request (tender offer) by a company. In other words, if a company offers to buy back some of its stock, a broker-dealer cannot immediately go out and borrow shares to sell to the company.

Trading by Participants. When broker-dealers are involved in the distribution of a security, they are prohibited from trading in it. This is to avoid situations where the broker-dealer might issue overly-optimistic sales forecasts for the company and then recommend purchase or sale of the security without a reasonable basis for such recommendations, all as a means of manipulating the price to its own benefit. Broker-dealers are permitted only to trade with other members of the syndicate for legitimate purposes necessary to carry out the stock offering. The law is also aimed at making sure that broker-dealers do not have any type of buyback arrangement with clients if the stock price falls or does not rise to meet expectations.

Stabilizing Bids. Stabilizing bids are illegal, except during the original sales offering of a new issue. They may be called pegging, or some other term, but in effect they have the broker-dealer set a buy price to keep the stock from falling any lower than the broker-dealer's bid price. When the stock hits that price, the broker-dealer buys it to artificially support the price above where the market dictates.

Extension of Credit for New Issues. It is illegal for a broker-dealer to allow a client to buy a new issue on margin, or extend credit in any other way to the client for the purchase of new issues. New issues may be used as collateral on other margin loans after the securities are held, fully paid, for 30 days.

Segregating, Pledging Customer Securities. All customers' securities that are fully paid must be kept separate from the broker-dealer's securities. Excess margin securities must be segregated as well. Commingling of the customers' securities and the firm's securities is strictly prohibited. Broker-dealers must have express written consent before they can pledge a customer's securities or loan them out for any purpose. The broker-dealer is also prohibited from pledging more of the customer's securities than are needed to obtain financing for the client's debit account balance amount. Rehypothecation of securities is also permitted only with express written consent, and only to the extent necessary to cover customers' credit requirements for their own account. (Cash account securities may not be loaned out.)

Net Capital Requirements. The net capital requirements provided for in the '34 Act ensure that broker-dealers remain solvent. The current ratio is 15:1 of required liquidity to indebtedness. Other provisions are that the broker-dealer must give an annual statement from the firm to all clients, and balance sheets for the firm must be available upon request, but the firm is *not* obligated to disclose its investments nor show a detailed profit and loss statement.

5.3.2

Penny Stock Regulations

There are additional regulations that cover "penny stocks." **Penny stocks** are over-the-counter (OTC, i.e. non-listed) equity securities that trade for less than $1 per share (although they may trade as high as $5–10 per share), but are highly volatile because the companies who issue the stock usually have short and erratic operating histories.

In fact, if penny stocks are issued by a company that has not yet begun operations, the funds raised must be put into an escrow account until the offering is complete and the company has started its business.

Because of their highly speculative nature, the SEC has also adopted the Penny Stock Cold Calling Rules to protect unsophisticated investors. The RR must first attempt to ascertain the prospect's suitability for the investment, and a suitability statement must be signed by the prospect before any penny stock trades can be executed. Certain disclosures are also required under SEC rules for penny stocks:

- the name of the stock,
- the number of shares being sold,
- the current price of the shares, and
- the amount of commission to be paid to the RR and to the firm.

Furthermore, a monthly statement must be provided showing the number of penny stock shares a client holds and the current market value.

5.3.3

Securities Investor Protection Corporation (SIPC)

The **Securities Investor Protection Corporation (SIPC)** was established as a nonprofit corporation by an act of Congress in 1970 to protect investors from broker-dealer insolvency. The SIPC provides a fund that insures the cash and securities in an investor's account up to $500,000 total, with a limit of $100,000 paid in cash. These limits are for each separate customer account, so a husband and wife with separate accounts would count as two customer accounts, and if the husband and wife had a third joint account, that would count as a third separate customer account.

If a brokerage firm fails, the SIPC first tries to merge it with another firm. If that is not possible, then the SIPC liquidates the firm's assets and pays off customer accounts up to the stated limits. All debit balances owed by the customer are subtracted from the market value of the securities when determining the payout amounts due. If the amount due a customer exceeds the maximum SIPC payout limit, the investor becomes a general creditor of the bankrupt broker-dealer firm.

Note for the Series 7 exam that *the SIPC does not protect investors against market risks or bad investments, and SIPC is* not *an agency of the U.S. government.*

5.3.4

Secondary Market for Equities

Secondary markets are the exchanges and over-the-counter (OTC) markets where investors buy and sell securities after their initial offering. All proceeds from sales in the secondary markets go to the investors and others who actually hold the securities, not to the issuing companies. The secondary market for equities is made up of several exchanges, with the main one being the NYSE. Equities are also traded on the NASDAQ and in the OTC markets. Let's look at some of the characteristics of each, and point out some of the unique ways that they function.

5.3.4.1 Exchange Auction Market

Exchanges act as a centralized trading floor where listed securities can be bought and sold using a **double auction** pricing mechanism. What this means is that the markets are constantly getting pricing information from buyers and sellers. The instant reporting of trades provides for a true free market, where supply and demand dictate the price of a particular stock issue. All of this is made possible by floor brokers who try to get the best possible prices for clients, and the specialist who ensures that orders are matched up in a fair and orderly process.

Role of the Specialist. The **specialist** is a member of a stock exchange given authority to act as broker and dealer (agent and principal) for other brokers, and charged with the responsibility of maintaining a fair and orderly market. The specialist must be ready to buy and sell from the firm's own account in an effort to stabilize the market when there are supply and demand imbalances. The specialist is appointed by the NYSE to supervise order execution in his or her designated trading post area. The specialist conducts auctions between buyers and sellers, acting in the capacity of an agent when there is sufficient market activity. When there is little or no trading volume, the specialist acts in the capacity of principal and trades from his or her own account. In this respect, the specialist is a market maker.

The specialist also fills orders from the Specialist's Book. The **Specialist's Book** is a record of limit orders, stop orders, short sales and the specialist's own inventory of securities. (A **limit order** is an order that a particular security should be bought or sold, but only at a certain price. A **stop order** is an order that a particular security should be bought or sold at the market price, once a certain threshold has been met or exceeded. These will be explained in detail in Chapter 6.) Only SEC or NYSE officials may look at the Specialist's Book. If other traders want an idea of the market, they can ask the specialist for the current range or the size of the market. The specialist will reveal only the inside quote and the number of shares at each price point.

Example

The inside quote is 37–37¼. This means that the range is 37 bid and 37¼ ask. If there are total orders for 300 shares waiting to buy when the price drops to 37, and 500 shares waiting to sell when the price rises to 37¼, then the specialist says the quote is "37–37¼, 3 × 5." This is not a firm quote, but gives the trader an indication of the market. The specialist may have 800 more shares available for sale if the price reaches 37½, or an order to buy 1,000 more shares if the price drops to 36½, but a specialist is *not* allowed to disclose this information because it is beyond the inside quote.

The specialist does not reveal more information, because this could distort the market. Traders might wait longer or flood the market with more shares if they knew which way the market was heading because of the total volume of the limit orders waiting to be executed. (Stop orders do not count when the specialist reveals range or size of the market.)

Two other things the specialist does are arrange the opening orders and stopping the stock. Before the start of trading each day, the specialist takes all **opening orders** that have come in since trading closed the previous day and tries to match them up. If there is an imbalance, then the start of trading may be delayed. **Stopping the stock** involves the specialist holding open a quote for a floor trader for a certain period of time. This allows the floor trader to shop around to try to get a better price for the client without missing the market. Even if the market has moved beyond the price quoted by the specialist when the stock was stopped, the trade can still be executed at the quoted price. This can be done only for public orders, not broker-dealer account trades. Also note that the trading activity in the stock does *not* stop when the specialist stops the stock. Stopping the stock only means that the price quote is held open.

There are a number of things that the specialist is prohibited from doing. We just saw that the specialist may not stop the stock for broker-dealer trades. The specialist also may not trade for his or her own account while other unexecuted orders are open at the same price for the same security. And the specialist may make trades for his or her own account only between (not at) the current bid and ask price. Also, the specialist is prohibited from taking any action which would destabilize the balance of supply and demand in a stock (this may include making opening trades in a stock). Finally, the specialist is not permitted to act as a broker and a dealer in the same transaction, and is also prohibited from performing the duties of an underwriter in a primary offering.

Purpose of Exchange Listing. There are reasons why companies want to be listed on a major exchange, such as the NYSE. One of the big advantages is that exchanges provide a centralized trading floor that offers immediate access to buyers and sellers. In fact, you may see a question on the Series 7 exam asking what is the primary role of the NYSE. It is *not* buying and selling stocks from the American public. The NYSE only provides the trading floor and a centralized location that provides a forum for the buying and selling.

The NYSE approves companies and traders, and monitors trading activities for fraud, but that is the extent of its involvement. Watch this on the exam.

Another big advantage is the double auction mechanism for pricing of securities. This, coupled with the instant reporting of trades, leads to a true up-to-the-minute gauge of market value based on supply and demand. Other reasons companies list on exchanges include lower cost of capital, ready access to capital, availability of institutional investors, greater liquidity, and higher visibility and prestige.

Limits on Trading During Market Declines. There are several ways that exchanges attempt to prevent the markets from going into a free-fall once significant declines occur. These measures are often referred to collectively as **circuit breakers,** and are an attempt to allow the market time to rebalance supply and demand. For example, the NYSE halts or curtails trading when the Dow Jones Industrial Average falls 10 percent, 20 percent, or 30 percent. The numbers are revised quarterly, and the rules are subject to change from time to time. There are also provisions to curb automated trading (**program trading**) and limit price movements on index futures (to reduce **index arbitrage**). The rules are actually rather complicated, and take into account many variables (including the time of day and market activity). For the Series 7 exam, though, you just need to know that these exist, and understand the key terms that are associated with the halt of trading during volatile market conditions.

5.3.4.2 Over-the-Counter (OTC) Market

The over-the-counter (OTC) market is a decentralized trading environment that relies on negotiated bid and ask (buy and sell) prices between investors and market makers. A **market maker** is a brokerage firm that has taken a position (built up an inventory) in a certain stock, and stands ready to honor quoted bid and ask prices for round lots. Market makers help maintain stability in the OTC market, and are the reason OTC markets can function.

Role of the Market Maker. The market maker acts as a principal dealer for the stocks in which the firm has taken a position. The position of market maker means that the firm is willing to honor the publicly quoted bid and ask price, and trade in a round lot at any time. This gives the OTC market much needed liquidity so that investors know they will always have a means to sell their shares.

Every stock must have at least two market makers. Market makers must meet NASDAQ minimum net capital requirements, and must demonstrate that they are willing to execute trades for minimum lots of 100 shares at the firm bid and ask quotes that they provide. The market maker's role is chiefly that of principal, buying and selling for the firm's account, but may in some circumstances coordinate a trade where the firm is merely the intermediary acting in an agency capacity. In the first instance where the firm is the principal, it charges a markup or markdown. In the second instance where the firm is an agent, it collects a commission. And here too, rules prohibit the firm from acting as both broker and dealer in the same transaction.

Quotations. The market maker is the one who gives quotes on OTC stocks. Sometimes they are based on the most recent transaction; other times the quotes represent the firm's bid and ask prices. There are actually several different types of quotes that a market maker can give for a particular stock. Two of the more common ones you'll hear are firm quote and subject quote.

Firm quotes mean that the broker-dealer is willing to sell or buy at least one round lot (100 shares of stock or 5 bonds) at that price. But a firm quote is good only for the number of shares quoted; if more are needed, the B-D must ask for a new firm quote. Backing away from a firm quote is a violation of NASD rules. Instead, the rules allow **subject quotes,** meaning that the quote must still be verified or confirmed, and the market maker is not ready to trade right away at that price. Subject quotes are not firm, but if the market maker says only the price (e.g., "It's 35–35¼." or "It's quoted at 35–35¼.") and doesn't qualify the statement (e.g., "It's 35–35¼, subject." or "It's about 35–35¼."), it is considered a firm quote.

Other terms you should at least be aware of are **nominal quotes** (pricing quote for informational purposes only, and must be qualified similar to subject quote), **workout quotes** (approximate quote that must still be negotiated, because it depends on size of the order or market activity), **bid wanted** (there is no activity in the stock, but the dealer is looking to sell some and wants traders to submit a bid), and **offer wanted** (there is no activity in the stock, but the dealer is looking to buy some and wants traders to submit an ask price).

One final point about quotes. We mentioned this before, but it bears repeating. **Size obligations** are important. A firm quote is good for 100 shares only, unless a number of shares is also quoted. If a number of shares is quoted, the bid is good for only that many shares, or fewer (in round lot numbers). If more shares than the quote was for are needed, the trader needs to ask for a new firm quote. The market maker is not obligated to sell more shares than the price was quoted for.

Transaction Reporting. All transactions in the OTC market are required to be reported within 90 seconds of execution. When two market makers make a reported trade, the stated price allows other computerized and NASDAQ trades to be executed automatically at the same price. Up to 1,000 shares of National Market System stocks and up to 500 shares of NASDAQ stocks may trade at that price electronically, without the intervention of another broker-dealer. If reporting a trade within 90 seconds is not possible, a trade must be designated as "late." (Late reporting does not allow short sales to take place.) Market makers must also make daily trade volume reports for each stock for which they are a market maker. Finally, reports are optional for trades that were not round lots (odd lots), computer assisted trades, option-related transactions, and trades in new issues.

Purpose of NASDAQ Listing. There are several reasons why companies want to be listed on NASDAQ. NASDAQ provides increased secondary market liquidity for smaller companies. While the disclosure and accounting norms required for getting listed on the NASDAQ are very stringent, the company size and capitalization requirements are not as high as the NYSE. NASDAQ also offers an exchange with high efficiency, good settlement processes, and low cost of operation. All of this is enhanced by the large capital commitment from market makers, and increased competition, which provides very competitive bid and ask prices for securities. Finally, there is the reputation, prestige, and visibility of being on an exchange recognized for its high growth companies.

Exchange Options Markets

As we saw in Chapter 3, there are two types of options: over-the-counter options and exchange-traded options. **Over-the-counter (OTC) options** do not trade on an exchange because their contract terms are negotiated on an individual basis. **Exchange-traded options,** also called **listed options,** are options that are freely tradeable on a given market exchange because they have standardized contract terms, such as expiration dates. There are listed options for stocks, commodities, indexes, foreign currency, and some kinds of debt. The largest exchange (and only exclusive one) where options are traded is the Chicago Board Options Exchange (CBOE). The exchange sets the terms for acceptable options, and the Options Clearing Corporation (OCC) issues the options and is their guarantor.

The options markets function as a risk management tool, providing leverage and a means of gauging future price directions. Options markets redistribute risk as hedgers try to reduce the risk of an underlying asset, protecting themselves from a price decrease (if they own the asset) or from a price increase (if they need to buy the asset in the future). Speculators try to profit by taking on the risk the hedgers are trying to get rid of, thus providing needed liquidity to the options markets.

The big advantage with options is leverage. They allow an investor to control a large block of securities for a relatively small investment. The options markets can also be used as a gauge of market expectations for future price directions. Massive short selling can signal a bear market with lower expected future prices. Other options contracts can be measured to determine price direction as well. Let's review.

Function. The **Options Clearing Corporation (OCC)** issues, guarantees and clears options contracts for securities and instruments that are traded on the exchanges. OCC guarantees that an investor can exercise an option, or close out an options contract by buying an offsetting option position, but does not guarantee price.

The person who **buys a call** has the *option* to buy the security; the person who **sells a call** has the *obligation* to sell the security at that price if the buyer exercises the option. The person who **buys a put** has the *option* to sell the security; the person who **sells a put** has the *obligation* to buy the security at that price if the buyer exercises the option. The option can be exercised at the strike price before the expiration date, which is three, six, or nine months from the date of issue (except LEAPS). The actual expiration is always on Saturday after the third Friday of the expiration month, so the last possible trade or exercise day is that third Friday (if no holiday).

Exercise means that the contract holder will make use of his or her rights to buy or sell securities under the contract. To exercise an option, the broker gives an **exercise notice** to OCC. OCC does a **random assignment of exercise notice,** choosing a broker who sold that series of option to make the trade, according to the terms of the options contract. Settlement for exercise is three business days after OCC gets the exercise notice (next day settlement when buying or selling options).

Floor Participants. There are three main trading floor participants in the options exchange markets you should know. **Market makers** (or Registered Options Traders) act as intermediaries, buying and selling option contracts for their own accounts and to help keep the market in balance. A **board broker** is an employee of CBOE who handles away from the market orders, which are recorded in an **order book** until they can be executed. (Thus, a board broker is also known as an **order book official.**) **Floor brokers** work for firms and execute client orders on the exchange floor.

5.3.6

Secondary Market for Municipal Securities

Secondary markets are the markets where investors can also buy and sell municipal securities after their initial offering. Remember that in the secondary market, all proceeds from sales go to the investors and others who actually hold the securities, not to the issuing municipalities. All municipal bonds trade in the OTC market. To gauge the status of municipal securities offered in the secondary market, traders can consult the Blue List. The **Blue List Total** is the total par values of all municipal securities offered for sale, and as such is one measure of the supply of municipal securities available for purchase.

5.3.6.1 Types of Orders, Offerings

There are several ways that municipal bond orders or offerings are carried out in the secondary market. Bonds are typically sold **at advertised yield.** This means that bonds are sold at their stated yield as required by regulations, but that they are sold less a discount given to the buying dealer. This is done for trades between municipal bond dealers, where this is referred to as trading on a **concession basis.**

Bonds lots can be offered as all-or-non (AON), or multiples. **All-or-none (AON)** is a type of offering where a buyer is required to bid for all of the securities being offered if the party wishes to buy any. **Multiples** allow the buyer to bid for round lots of bonds (usually in multiples of $1,000 or $5,000).

Another point to note about municipal bonds is that NASD rules prohibit short sales if the bonds are in a **down bid.** This means that the current bid price quoted is below the previous bid. This is similar to the short sale rule for stocks, which also prohibits a short sale if there is a down-tick, instead requiring an up-tick. Likewise, bonds can be shorted only if there is an up bid. Note, though, that it is a little more difficult for investors to short bonds because they are not as actively traded, so it may be difficult to replace the bonds an investor borrowed to do the short sale.

5.3.6.2 Types of Business Activity

There are several places where municipal bond are traded with various customers. Although all **retail** activity takes places through the exchange, some **institutional** bond buyers are offered entire bond issues or large parts of bond issues directly. Another type of activity occurs through the **interdealer systems.** These are computer based systems that allow dealers to execute transactions electronically with other dealers. Finally, there is the **broker's broker** service, whereby brokers transact business with other brokers, but as a fully anonymous service. They do not deal with the retail public, and do not reveal any information about the clients or customers they are working for.

5.3.6.3 Role of the Municipal Bond Trader

Municipal bond traders work for broker-dealer firms as a bond trading specialist. They attempt to get the best bid and ask prices for the bonds they trade, whether working for a client or trading for their own account. If the bond trader gives a quote for a municipal bond, then the quote must be bona fide. **Bona fide** means that the trader is actually ready, willing and able to trade the bond at that quoted price. If the trader does not have the bond in the firm's own inventory, he or she must know where the bond can be readily obtained. The quote must represent the trader's best assessment as to the reasonable market value of the bond, and may also reflect the expected market direction.

5.3.7

Secondary Market for U.S. Treasury Securities, Agencies, Pass-Throughs

Secondary market activity also exists for U.S. Treasury securities, government agency securities, and government-backed pass-through certificates. Again, when traded in the secondary market, the proceeds from the sale of these securities go to the investors, not the government. Let's look at the characteristics of these securities, and then briefly discuss some of the primary dealers and marketing methods.

5.3.7.1 General Characteristics

U.S. Treasury securities are debt obligations of the U.S. government, backed by the full faith and credit of the U.S. government. They are considered the most risk-free investment money can buy, so they have lower yields than corporate bonds. The four types of U.S. Treasury securities are

- **T-Bills** (mature 1 year or less, $10,000 face, quoted at discount from par—no interest);
- **T-Notes** (mature 1–10 years, $1,000 face, quoted as percent of par, 1/32 increment);

- ▷ **T-Bonds** (mature 10+ years, $1,000 face, quoted as percent of par, 1/32 increment);
- ▷ **STRIPS** (U.S. government backed zero-coupon bonds—no interest).

Government agency securities, known as **government sponsored entities (GSEs),** are privately owned, but publicly chartered entities which were created by the government to help out farmers, students, homeowners, and others by lowering borrowing costs. The GSEs sell securities to investors, then take the money from the investors and provide low interest loans to people in those targeted groups who meet certain criteria, or use the funds to buy mortgages in the secondary market. Most GSE securities are backed by the agency issuing them, and are *not* backed by the full faith and credit of the U.S. government.

Federally related institutions are arms of the U.S. government that have the authority to issue securities for the needs of their agencies. Most federally-related securities are backed by the full faith and credit of U.S. government. An example is the **Ginnie Mae pass-through certificates,** which are backed by a pool of insured mortgages (FHA, VA). The certificates have a face value of $25,000 and are quoted based on a 12-year planned repayment, but may be paid off early. Government insures them against repayment risk, and interest is fully taxable at all government levels.

5.3.7.2 Primary Dealers, Marketing Methods

There are several banks and investment companies authorized to buy and sell government securities directly with the Federal Reserve Bank of New York. These entities must meet certain qualifications of size, capacity, reputation, etc. This is part of the government's open market operations. Government securities sales and auctions are part of the means through which the federal government implements fiscal and monetary policy.

5.3.8

General Characteristics, Secondary Market Participants

Secondary markets deal not only in stocks and municipal bonds, but also in a number of other security instruments. These include corporate bonds, repurchase agreements, commercial paper, negotiable CDs, Eurodollar bonds, bankers' acceptances, and collateralized mortgage obligations. Let's review their characteristics.

5.3.8.1 Corporate Bonds

Corporate bonds are debt obligations of a private corporation. They pay interest semiannually, and return the principal face amount ($1,000 par value) upon maturity. Corporate bonds are issued for 1–20 years, and have **term maturities,** meaning that the bonds all come due at once. Corporate bonds are required to have an **indenture agreement,** appointing a qualified, independent trustee, with protective clauses for bondholders, requiring a semiannual financial report to bondholders and periodic SEC filings to show compliance. Corporate bonds are backed by the issuer, and may or may not have collateral associated with them. The bond is a promise by the issuer to repay a fixed sum of money with interest, but does not confer any right of ownership in the corporation. Bondholders are creditors of the corporation. Bonds are actively traded in the secondary market. **High-yield** corporate bonds are bonds with a credit rating of "BB" or lower. They are sometimes referred to as **junk bonds** because the company issuing them may have a poor credit rating or short operating history with little sales or earnings to base the bond price.

Secondary market participants for corporate bonds include institutional investors, private investors, and other corporations. Broker-dealer firms also trade in bonds for their own accounts.

Exam Topic Alert

One other rule you need to be aware of is the **nine bond rule.** This NYSE rule says that any order for nine bonds or less must go to the floor first for one hour to seek a market before being filled OTC. Since most NYSE bond activity is with large institutional investors and smaller bond orders trade OTC anyway, this rule is rarely used. Still, it is designed to help small investors—*and may be on the Series 7 exam.*

5.3.8.2 Repurchase Agreements (REPOs)

Repurchase agreements are an arrangement between buyer and seller to sell an asset now, and then buy it back for a fixed price, and usually within a stated time-frame. It is very similar to a loan, but it is actually the sale of an asset with a locked-in agreement to buy it back. The assets involved in these types of transactions are often U.S. government securities, but they can be anything of value that is agreed upon by the parties. This arrangement is more attractive than other options because the parties have more flexibility to negotiate terms that fit their particular situation. Repos are a way to park funds and make interest, or can be used by corporations, banks, and governments to cover shortfalls in inventory positions, reserve requirements, or balance sheet items. The Federal Reserve also uses repo agreements to buy and sell securities when implementing monetary policy.

Secondary market participants for repos include banks, institutional investors, corporations, and the Federal Reserve.

5.3.8.3 Commercial Paper

Commercial paper is short-term debt that is issued by corporations to finance inventories, accounts receivable, and other obligations. Maturities range from 2–270 days to avoid registration requirements. Commercial paper issued by corporations is typically unsecured, although it is often backed by bank lines of credit. Corporations prefer commercial paper because they can get better rates than using their bank lines, plus the repayment terms can be negotiated to be more flexible. Such debt is rated by the rating agencies discussed before, but some money market managers will not buy commercial paper since it is unsecured.

For the Series 7 exam, *if you see an answer to a question stating that commercial banks issue commercial paper, it is most likely a trick and probably the wrong answer.*

Secondary market participants for commercial paper include institutional investors and corporations.

5.3.8.4 Certificates of Deposit (CDs)

Certificates of Deposit (CDs) are debt securities, usually issued by a financial institution. Negotiable CDs have a minimum face value of $100,000 and are offered by commercial banks to investors as a time deposit. Since these so-called "jumbo" CDs are negotiable, they are considered a money market instrument. (These negotiable CDs should not be confused with the "standard" CDs that are offered by neighborhood banks to depositors. Standard CDs are available in much smaller face amounts, and are not negotiable so they are not considered money market instruments.)

Secondary market participants for CDs include institutional investors, banks, and corporations. Broker-dealer firms also trade in these for their own accounts.

5.3.8.5 Eurodollars

Eurodollars are U.S. dollars that are held in foreign banks. The banks can be anywhere outside of the United States—although many are in Europe, they do not have to be there. These funds are available for settling transactions between companies on an international scale. **Eurodollar bonds** are debt securities that pay interest and principal in Eurodollars. These are usually traded at lower interest rates than U.S. bonds and have fewer regulatory concerns, so they are a popular money market security especially for dealing with international transactions. (Eurodollars and Eurodollar bonds should not be confused with the new Euro currency that is being implemented as a pan-European currency. There is no connection between the two.)

Secondary market participants for Eurodollar bonds include banks, institutional investors, corporations, and other entities that deal in international goods.

5.3.8.6 Bankers' Acceptances (BAs)

Bankers' acceptances (BAs) are a time draft drawn on a particular bank, whereby the bank accepts responsibility for payment. The time draft designates the date on which payment will be made. BAs are a tool for handling the extension of credit. Essentially

BAs work like a letter of credit, and are often used for import and export financing, and the purchase of goods and services when doing international business. Because of the bank's backing, BAs are often used as money market instruments.

Exam Topic Alert

For the Series 7 exam remember that *when you see "time draft" in a question, look for "banker's acceptances" in the answer (and vice versa).*

Secondary market participants for BAs include institutional investors, banks, corporations, and other entities that deal in international goods.

5.3.8.7 Pass-Throughs and CMOs

A **Collateralized Mortgage Obligation (CMO)** is a vehicle for issuing mortgage-backed securities, separated into different groups based on maturity dates. CMOs are pass-through certificates, backed by a pool of mortgages. Payments are made monthly, and interest payments are taxable at all government levels (federal, state, local). CMOs are not backed by the U.S. government. CMOs are separated into different maturity groups called **tranches.** Each CMO has various tranches with staggered maturities from a few months up to 20 years, and pay varying rates of interest depending on when the tranche matures. Tranches with the shortest term receive the lowest interest rate of return; the longest term tranches receive the highest rate of return. As mortgage payments are made by homeowners, money is collected and redistributed to investors.

Exam Topic Alert

Remember, *if you see "tranches" in a question, look for "CMOs" in the answer (and vice versa).*

Secondary market participants for CMOs include institutional investors, private investors, and others looking for an income stream.

5.3.9

The Currency Market

The **currency markets** are the unregulated international trading of foreign currencies between banks. This is also referred to as the **interbank market.** Trading in this market is what establishes the foreign exchange rates. The currency market is decentralized, but banks are linked via computers and other electronic means. Trades can be either spot trades or forward trades. **Spot trades** are settled in cash and completed within one or two business days. This spot market trading is also sometimes called the

cash market. Forward trades are more like futures contracts, where settlement can be anywhere from two days to 18 months. This forward market trading is much more speculative.

Aside from the usual systematic (market) risks, currency markets are risky because prices are highly volatile. And since currency positions are usually highly leveraged (often only 3 percent to 20 percent of the value of the contract is paid), a relatively small price movement in a contract may result in immediate and substantial losses to the investor—even in excess of the amount invested. This coupled with an unregulated environment poses unique risks for traders in the currency markets. For example, there is no limit on daily price movements in most currency markets. In addition, principals who deal in interbank markets are not required to continue to make markets. This can make it difficult, if not impossible, to liquidate a position. Deregulation of fixed trading in a currency can also make liquidation difficult. Furthermore, at times it may be impossible to execute stop-loss or stop-limit orders, inhibiting efforts to limit losses. Finally, in an unregulated environment there is a tremendous potential for conflicts of interest and recommendations of excessive trading, plus a risk of loss of deposited funds if a trading center goes bankrupt.

TERMINOLOGY. Let's look at a few more terms that are unique to the currency markets. They are important for you to know, and may appear on the Series 7 exam.

Exchange rate: the price at which one country's currency can be converted into another country's currency.

Floating exchange rate: when the exchange rate is permitted to respond to the market forces of supply and demand.

Fixed exchange rate: when the exchange rate between two currencies is held at a set amount, and not allowed to move in response to market forces.

Exchange rate controls: these can be achieved using a fixed exchange rate, or by limiting the amount of currency that may be converted, or by controlling the amount of foreign investment that can go into or out of a country.

Central bank interventions: when a government attempts to manipulate the price of its currency through **pegging** or **stabilization,** which involves buying the currency in the open market when it dips below a certain level.

Devaluation: when the value of a country's currency falls relative to other currencies (or other currencies rise). This can be from market forces or government action.

Revaluation: when the value of a country's currency rises relative to other currencies (or other currencies fall). This is usually from government action.

For the Series 7 exam, remember the *key words to associate with the currency markets* are interbank market, unregulated, decentralized, spot trades, and forward trades. Also, pegging and stabilization can be associated with foreign governments here (and also with broker-dealers doing primary issues).

FACTORS AFFECTING EXCHANGE RATES. There are several factors that can affect the exchange rate of a specific currency and cause price movements up and down relative to other currencies. These numerous influences are beyond a person's control, and most can't be foreseen or planned for. They include changes in supply and demand; government policies (trade, fiscal, monetary); U.S. and foreign political and economic events; foreign or domestic interest rate changes; foreign or domestic inflation; foreign country credit rating; currency devaluation; and market sentiment.

5.3.10

The Third Market

The **third market** is the buying and selling of exchange-listed stocks in the over-the-counter market by non-exchange member brokers and institutional investors. The third market has resulted in large orders being made off the exchange floor in an effort to save commissions on large volume orders by large institution investors. Institutional investors include pension funds, insurance companies, mutual funds, banks, universities or other institutions.

Transaction rules dictate that before a member can sell securities to a nonmember in an off-the-floor transaction, the member must first fill any limit orders (in the specialist's book) at the same price or better. The rules also require that off-the-floor orders be executed before any on-the-floor orders. Reporting requirements are that all transactions of listed securities which are traded in the third market must appear on the consolidated tape no later than 90 seconds after the transaction. (Consolidated tape is explained in detail in Chapter 7.)

5.3.11

The Fourth Market

The **fourth market** is the direct trading of large blocks of securities between institutional investors to avoid brokerage commissions. Quotes can be obtained through an electronic communications network service called **Instinet,** an acronym for Institutional Networks Corporation, which is owned by Reuters. The purpose of the system is to allow direct trading between institutional investors (such as mutual funds), while avoiding the brokerage commissions of trading on the exchange floor or going through a brokerage firm.

Instinet is registered with the SEC as a stock exchange. All members are linked directly by computer, which allows for after-hours trading as well. Since these transactions are done directly between large institutional investors and other members, there is no need for broker-dealer assistance. The system allows all subscribers to post requests, indicate interest in a certain volume of security, and show quotes (bid or ask) to others on the system.

5.4 Principal Factors Affecting Securities Markets and Prices

Aside from all of the market factors that we have been pointing to in an effort to explain how securities rise and fall in value, we also need to consider business cycles, the economy, and other principal business factors that affect the securities markets and securities prices. The simple fact is that all of these securities are issued by companies or municipalities or the U.S. government. And since the values of the securities are based on the strength of the issuing entities, we in turn need to look at how the strength of these entities is affected by business cycles and the economy.

5.4.1 Business Cycle

The **business cycle** is general swings in business activity, going through periods of **e**xpansion, **p**eak, **c**ontraction and **t**rough during different phases of the cycle, then repeating. (EPCoT can help you remember the four phases of the business cycle.) Cycles last for varying lengths of time. Business cycles affect corporate cash flow and profits, making it an important consideration for dividend payouts and bond payments. Business cycles also affect tax revenue and project revenues, making it an important consideration for municipal bonds. Business cycles can also be a factor in the inflation rate, making it an important consideration for U.S. Treasuries. The rate of inflation also affects the relative rate of return on all investments.

Economic theory says that supply and demand always seek to balance each other, and thus the market responds. When demand for a product exceeds supply, the price for that product will rise, thereby stimulating more production (expansion). As production increases, more of the demand is satisfied until eventually the supply outstrips demand. At that point, prices will fall and production will slow until demand catches up with supply (contraction), then the cycle starts over.

5.4.1.1 Definition and Characteristics

There are several key terms for you to know if you are to understand the business cycle. It is also a plus if you can explain various measures of the level of business activity and inflation indicators.

Expansions in the economy are generally accompanied by increases in industrial production, consumers who are eager to buy more goods and services, increased demand for housing (especially more new home permits), and a rising stock market.

Contractions in the economy are generally accompanied by decreases in industrial production, falling consumer demand, heavy debt loads for consumer and businesses, increases in bankruptcies (personal and corporate), rising unemployment, and a falling stock market.

Key terms: terminology used to describe the business cycle and its phases, measurements, and indicators.

Depression is a severe economic downturn caused by excess supply and rising unemployment that leads to falling demand, reduced purchasing power, and deflation of prices. Depressions are characterized by dramatic rises in unemployment and acute public caution and fear.

Recession is a less severe economic downturn, characterized by two consecutive quarters of decline in the country's level of business activity as defined by the gross domestic product (GDP).

Inflation is an increase in the cost of goods or services. This is also called **cost inflation** because it's the result of manufacturers and others passing along to the consumer increases in their costs. **Inflation** is also defined as too much money chasing too few goods. This is also called **demand inflation** because it's driven by demand, where too many people want to buy the same thing.

Peak is the top of a business cycle, where expansion begins to level off as demand catches up with supply. From this point, production and prices will begin to fall.

Trough is the bottom of a business cycle, where contraction begins to stop its descent and turn upward. Supply no longer exceeds demand, so from this point production and prices begin to rise.

Contraction is a period of business activity marked by falling production, which is slowing down until demand catches up with the supply.

Recovery is a period of business activity marked by increasing production as supply is trying to catch back up to increasing demand. This is the precursor to an expansion phase of the business cycle and growth for the economy.

Cycle is a recurring pattern of activity. For example, the **business cycle** is general swings in business activity, going through periods of expansion, peak, contraction and trough during different phases of the cycle, then repeating.

Measure of the level of business activity is a measurement that analyzes current business output, as a means of comparison with past statistics (e.g., GDP), to determine if business activity is generally rising or falling.

Gross domestic product (GDP) measures the value of all goods and services produced within the United States. This includes consumer spending, government spending, and the net value of exports. (On the test you may also see the gross national product [GNP], but this measure is not used as frequently since it also includes net foreign investments in the total.)

Note that GDP figures are adjusted for inflation. That is, the comparisons between the current number and previous numbers use constant dollars, so that comparisons represent the true core value of output without inflation.

Inflation indicators are the measurements that analyze past and current inflation, as a means of forecasting the future direction and rate of inflation (e.g., CPI), to determine if price levels in the economy are generally rising or falling.

Consumer price index (CPI) measures the fixed cost of a market basket of goods and services. CPI includes components from the food, transportation, energy, housing, and clothing sectors, as well as other items. The figure is published monthly, and used as an inflation adjuster for such things as Social Security benefits, union wage contracts, and other cost of living adjustments.

Note that CPI figures are often quoted two ways: one with the complete theoretical market basket of goods, and one that excludes the volatile food and energy sectors. Also note that taxes are not part of the CPI.

5.4.1.2 Business Cycle Indicators

Like the indicators for inflation, there are several indicators that can be used to analyze and measure business activity and the business cycle. These measurements, though, are able to use past and present data to indicate future business activity much more efficiently. That's because the indicators used to determine if the business cycle and the economy are generally expanding or contracting are based on several types of data. Each of these can be analyzed independently, but when they are all analyzed together they give a much clearer picture of where the business cycle has been, and where it is headed.

Leading Economic Indicators. These measure changes *before* the economy has changed, and thus are good for predicting future economic activity. For example, building permits are a good leading indicator because when they rise, that means that there will also likely be a rise in other industries and businesses that supply the building market: lumber, carpet, etc. There are eleven component figures used to compile an index of leading economic indicators that can accurately forecast ups and downs in the business cycle. Those eleven components are:

- building permits
- production workweek
- unemployment insurance claims
- money supply (M2)
- stock prices
- vendor performance (deliveries)
- changes in materials pricing
- orders for plant and equipment
- orders for durable goods
- orders for consumer goods
- consumer confidence index (more debt)

Coincident Economic Indicators. These measures change *while* the economy is changing, and thus are good for confirming the state of current economic activity. There are five coincident indicators used to compile this index:

- industrial production
- manufacturing
- trade sales
- nonfarm payrolls
- net personal income

Lagging Economic Indicators. These measures change *after* the economy has changed, and thus are good for verifying past economic activity (and predictions). For example, some of the items that make good lagging indicators can be found on companies' financial statements. These are accurate because they reflect back on what happened at a company in the previous quarter or over the previous year. There are six lagging indicators used to compile this index:

- ▷ unemployment rate
- ▷ labor costs
- ▷ business spending
- ▷ interest rates (prime rate)
- ▷ outstanding debt
- ▷ inventory book value

Exam Topic Alert

Note that for the Series 7 exam, you may be given some of these indicators, and asked to categorize them as leading, coincident, or lagging, and you may be asked to identify which measure past, present, and future business cycle activity.

5.4.1.3 Effects of Business Cycle on Securities Markets

The business cycle has many direct effects on the securities markets. As business cycles go through different phases, this causes investors to constantly shift money back and forth between the bond market and the stock market as they seek the best rate of return given current and future economic conditions.

BOND MARKETS. Inflation and the perception of inflation have a direct impact on bond yields. As we look at this impact, we'll also explain how to analyze a yield curve.

Effects of Inflation/Deflation. During expansion periods in the business cycle, inflation tends to creep upward. As inflation rises, interest rates tend to rise as well. When interest rates go up, bond prices fall, making bonds a less attractive investment vis-à-vis stocks.

During contraction periods in the business cycle, there is more of a deflationary tendency as prices drop to attract more spending. As inflation falls, interest rates tend to fall as well. When interest rates go down, bond prices rise, making bonds a more attractive investment compared with stocks.

Impact on Yield Spreads. Yield spreads are the differences in return on investment between various issues of securities. More specifically, yield spread usually reflects the markets' expectations of future monetary policy and credit demand. Business cycles can directly affect yield curves through expectations.

If business is doing well and the business cycle is in an upswing, it is expected that increased demand will lead to increases in spending and credit, which will lead to increased interest rates. When this happens, investors expect future interest rates to rise, so the yield spread widens. The spread also widens when there is economic uncertainty because investors expect to be compensated more for risks.

Conversely, when business is not doing well and the business cycle is in a downswing, there is falling demand, less spending, and less borrowing. When this happens, investors expect future interest rates to be lower as well, so the yield spread narrows. **Disintermediation** is when funds flow out of banks and institutions, and into other short term investments seeking higher yields.

Yield Curve Analysis. A **yield curve** is a line on a graph that shows the relationship between yields and maturity dates for a set of similar bonds, by plotting the yields of all bonds from the shortest maturity to the longest maturity. This yield curve graph shows if short-term rates are higher or lower than long-term rates. Bond prices generally fall in line with the yield curve based on their maturity dates.

When looking at yield curves, there are three possible relationships.

- ▷ **Normal yield curve** is a situation where long-term bonds have higher yields than short-term bonds. This is also called a **positive yield curve.** This is in line with market expectations that an investor should be compensated more for taking on the extra risk and uncertainty of receiving future payments.
- ▷ **Inverted yield curve** is an unusual situation where long-term bonds have lower yields than short-term bonds. This is also called **negative yield curve.** This can happen if investors expect future interest rates to be much lower, so they try to lock in a rate now before the anticipated steep drop in rates.
- ▷ **Flat yield curve** is when short-term bonds and long-term bonds have the same yield. This is also called an **even yield curve** or a **humped yield curve.**

EQUITIES MARKETS. Business cycles also affect the equities markets. Here we must not only consider inflation and the perception of inflation, but also cyclical stocks and expectations of future profits.

Effects of Inflation/Deflation. During expansion periods in the business cycle, inflation tends to creep upward. As inflation rises, interest rates tend to rise as well. As business expands and profits rise, buying stocks is more attractive because of their high potential returns. But this can also be a double-edged sword, because as inflation rises, new issues of fixed-income securities (bonds) are also offering higher yields, making them an attractive alternative with less risk than stocks.

During contraction periods in the business cycle, there is more of a deflationary tendency as prices drop to attract more spending. As inflation falls, interest rates tend to fall as well. As businesses struggle and profits decline, buying stocks is less attractive because of their lower potential returns than the fixed-income securities (bonds), which are seeing their prices rise.

Some investors believe that deflation is beneficial because it helps maintain moderate economic growth, with falling real wages and raw material costs, which theoretically should lead to higher corporate profits. In reality, though, deflation can keep businesses from raising prices or passing on cost increases, and falling wages tend to decrease consumption, all of which make it hard to maintain or grow profits.

Interest-Rate-Sensitive Stocks. These are stocks that are affected mainly by changes in interest rates. Some examples of these are bank stocks, which feel the effects of any move by the Federal Reserve to adjust interest rates, and utility stocks, which are highly leveraged and must pay out more in debt service.

Cyclical, Defensive Stocks. **Cyclical stocks** are common stocks that generally rise and fall quickly in response to economic conditions. Some examples of cyclical stocks are automobile stocks and housing related stocks. **Counter cyclical stocks** are common stocks that generally rise when economic conditions worsen. The best example of a counter cyclical stock is the food sector (because demand is constant regardless of economic conditions).

Defensive stocks are common stocks with prices that are more stable over time than the broad market. Some examples of defensive stocks would be utility stocks, counter cyclical stocks, and certain blue chip stocks. These stocks are more conservative than average, and thus may experience slower growth during economic expansions, but should fare better during contractions or recessions because the underlying products are necessities of everyday life.

Expectations of Future Profits. In theory, stock prices are the present discounted value of expected future earnings and profits. Although stock prices can fluctuate for reasons other than changes in profitability, in general this principle is sound. Expectations of future profits reflect the level and growth of profits in the recent past, so current stock prices are trying to anticipate the level and growth of profits in the future. This leads to the use of a company's PE ratio as a way to compare companies across an industry. This also explains why at times a company's stock price will drop even if it is profitable—and sometimes even when it beats analysts' expectations. In these situations, investors have determined that even though the company is doing well now, the current profit numbers do not warrant such a high valuation for expected future earnings of the company. In other words, the expectations of future company business profits are not as high as once thought, or the stock price was already high because better growth expectations were already figured into the price, so the current stock price has changed based on these new expectations.

5.4.2

Principal Economic Theories

An economic theory is a set of statements or principles that show cause and effect when market forces (such as supply and demand) or external forces (such as government) allocate scarce products and resources between competing objectives.

When studying economic theories, the main ones that need to be discussed are Keynesian (demand side), supply side, and monetarist theories.

5.4.2.1 Keynesian Theory

Keynesian economics is an economic theory that says government intervention should be used to achieve full employment and stable prices. This theory is named for economist John Maynard Keynes, who said that insufficient demand caused unemployment and too much demand caused inflation, so it was up to the government to manipulate demand via expenditures and thus achieve balance through demand-side management of the economy. This is also referred to as **demand-side economics.**

The ultimate goal of demand-side economics is full employment. Demand-siders believe that the role of government in economic policy is to put people to work. Government should spend money initiating programs that put people to work so that the people can earn money, spend money, and create demand through consumption.

By contrast, **supply-side economics** says the economy is better served by government reducing tax rates, especially for businesses and those able to create jobs, as a means of creating employment opportunities and stimulating savings and investment for the benefit of everyone. The ultimate goal of supply-side economics is *laissez-faire* (nonintervention) policies by government that allow capital to be invested in the economy to create job opportunities, so that people can earn more money and pay less taxes, giving them more to spend, save and invest.

Key terms: terminology used in various economic theories.

Consumption is buying a product or service and using it until it has no remaining value.

Investment is when capital is used to create money via income-producing instruments, or to create capital appreciation from a risk-oriented venture.

Savings is when a portion of income or other money is not spent immediately.

Multiplier effect is the effect that investment has in creating additional income and other benefits to all those who participate in a project, through ownership, providing labor, or being a supplier to that business. (In monetary theory, this also refers to the expansion of the money supply resulting from a bank's ability to lend money in excess of its reserves.)

Marginal propensity to consume is the amount that consumption changes due to incremental changes in disposable income.

(change in consumption ÷ change in disposable income)

Liquidity preference is the supply of credit available because people are willing to forgo liquidity and save money. In other words, if people will accept only cash, and want to spend the cash immediately and refuse to save, then there is no money left for borrowing or investing.

5.4.2.2 Monetarist Theory

Monetarist theory says that the size of the money supply is the most important economic determinant. Proponents of monetarist theory say that too much money in circulation causes inflation, and that too little money causes deflation and recessions. Monetarists believe that the money supply should be increased by a fixed rate annually, thus allowing for businesses, consumers, investors, and other money managers to plan accordingly. The theory holds that this would allow resources to be used as efficiently as possible, since there would not need to be any contingencies planned to manage risk and uncertainty (as least as far as inflation is concerned).

Key terms: terminology used in relation to the money supply.

Money supply is the total amount of money in circulation in a country's economy at a given time, including not only cash, but also deposits in savings and checking accounts. Too much money in circulation can lead to inflation.

M1 is the most stringent measure of money supply because it represents only money that can be spent immediately or easily converted to cash. M1 includes all coins and currency in circulation, traveler's checks, checking account balances, NOW account balances, credit union accounts, and draft accounts.

M2 is a key measure of money supply, and an indicator for forecasting economic growth and inflation. M2 counts all of the items in M1, plus savings accounts, time deposits (e.g., CDs), noncommercial money market accounts, and overnight repurchase agreements.

M3 is the broadest measure of money supply, which includes all items from M1 and M2, plus large time deposits (jumbo CDs), repossessions held by commercial banks (maturing in over one day), and institutional money market accounts.

5.4.3

Role of the Federal Reserve

The Federal Reserve Board plays a large role in controlling the level of business activity through interest rates, and other means. The **Federal Reserve Board** (also referred to as **the Fed**) is responsible for U.S. monetary policy, maintaining economic stability, regulating commercial banks, and setting margin requirements. **Monetary policy** is the government's mechanism through which it can exert control over the supply and cost of money. Monetary policy also has the goals of economic growth, full employment and international balance of payments, plus monetary policy tries to maintain stability in prices, interest rates and financial markets.

The Fed uses monetary policy to make more or less money available for banks to lend, in effect raising or lowering interest rates for business. Higher interest rates mean tougher credit and lower interest rates mean easier credit. By making credit easier or tougher, the Fed also controls the level of business activity. We will discuss four tools used by the Fed to implement monetary policy and affect interest rates:

- open market operations,
- discount rates,
- reserve requirements, and
- margin requirements.

OPEN MARKET OPERATIONS. Open market operations are when the Fed sells or buys government securities (bonds) as a means of controlling the supply of, and demand for, money. Interest rates are affected because when the Fed buys and sells securities, it makes more or less money available for banks to lend.

To accomplish the Fed's goals, the Federal Open Market Committee (FOMC) meets regularly to discuss the present and future state of the economy, including where interest rates should ideally be to accomplish the Fed's long-term objectives of economic growth and stability with minimal inflation. One of the things the Fed does at its FOMC meeting is to try and exert indirect influence over long-term interest rates by establishing a target Fed funds rate. The **Fed funds rate** affects the short-term interest rate that banks charge when they borrow money in the Fed funds market (usually very short term loans for a day or two to help banks cover reserve requirements caused by the normal daily fluctuations in their deposits).

To hit its target Fed funds rate, the Fed will sell or buy securities. When the Fed *sells* Fed fund securities, it is increasing its stockpile of cash and taking money out of circulation. Since the banks have less money available to lend out, this raises interest rates. Conversely, when the Fed *buys* securities, it is decreasing its stockpile of cash and putting more money into circulation. Since the banks that sold the security (or the banks of the customers that sold the security) have more money available, the banks want to quickly re-lend the money somewhere else so that they can earn interest on the money instead of just letting it sit in their banks. Since the banks have more money to lend out, they will lower interest rates.

Keep in mind, though, that other factors, such as inflation, may be applying upward pressure on interest rates at the same time that an increase in money supply is exerting downward pressure. And, the Fed can exert influence only on short-term Fed funds interest rates.

The Fed does not set the prime rate, and the Fed's actions have no direct effect on the prime rate, but long-term rates do usually follow the lead established by the Fed funds rate movement. There are times, though, when long-term interest rates don't follow the lead of short-term interest rates. This may occur if there are other perceived long-term risks, such as fear of future inflation.

Exam Topic Alert

(The Fed can also buy and sell U.S. dollars as part of its open market operations if there's an imbalance in international supply and demand for U.S. dollars. Although this can also affect inflation and interest rates, it is beyond the scope of this text.)

DISCOUNT RATES. Discount rates or **federal discount rates** are the interest rates charged by Federal Reserve Banks on loans to member commercial banks. This is another way the Fed can change interest rates—and it's easier to remember. If Federal Reserve Banks charge higher discount rates when they lend money to commercial banks, then the banks will pass along those higher costs to their customers in the form of higher interest rates. A cut in the discount rate also filters down to the loans that banks make to their customers (but usually not as fast). So, an increase in the discount rate equals an increase in interest rates to customers; a decrease in the discount rate equals a decrease in interest rates to customers.

Now, though, the discount rate is less of a policy tool. The Fed discourages banks from borrowing funds directly from the Fed, unless they are in financial trouble and not able to borrow from other banks on the open Fed funds market. The discount rate is still important, however, because money managers watch the discount rate.

Adjusting the discount rate in line with the Fed funds rate is seen as confirmation of the Fed's true long-term outlook and bias for future monetary policy decisions.

RESERVE REQUIREMENTS. Reserve requirements are the percentage of deposits that commercial banks are required to keep on deposit, either on hand at the bank or in the bank's own accounts—in other words, money the bank can't lend to customers. The original purpose of reserve requirements was to help avert financial panic by giving depositors some confidence that their deposits were safe and accessible. Reserve requirements, however, have also become a policy tool.

By raising or lowering reserve requirements the Fed controls the supply and cost of money, and the quality of credit. If you wanted to raise interest rates, make credit tougher to get and/or improve the quality of credit, then you'd raise the reserve requirements because raising reserve requirements decreases the money supply available for banks to loan. When there's a smaller supply of money, you can be more selective about who borrows it and thus improve the quality of loans (and hopefully have less bad debt losses). When there's a smaller supply of something, you want to decrease demand—and higher interest rates should decrease demand! (See chart 5.4.3, Part A below.)

Conversely, if you wanted to lower interest rates or make credit easier to get, then you'd lower the reserve requirements. Lowering the reserve requirements increases the money supply available for banks to loan out. When there's a larger supply of money, you can be less selective about who borrows it. You also want to increase demand—and lower interest rates should increase demand! (See chart 5.4.3, Part B below.)

Using reserve requirements to adjust interest rates and control inflation has become a less important near-term Fed tool, and instead reserve requirement changes are used in the face of a severe recession or severe inflation. This is because changing reserve requirements has a large effect on the money supply since it affects *all* of the deposit assets of banks. Instead, the Fed is able to have a similar outcome but on a smaller, more manageable, scale with FOMC open market operations.

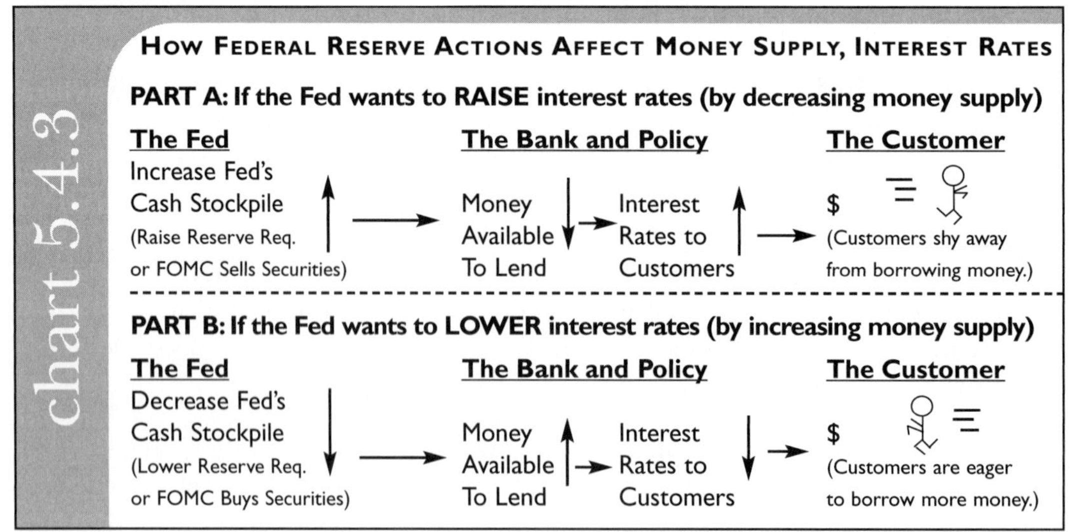

MARGIN REQUIREMENTS. **Margin requirements** are the amount of money that an investor must deposit in a margin account before buying stock on credit or selling short, as required by Reg. T. This is another way the Fed can control the money supply since margin is a form of credit. Raising margin requirements takes money out of circulation, which should push interest rates higher. Lowering margin requirements leaves more money in circulation, which should push interest rates lower. Changes in margin requirements, though, are not seen as effective a policy tool as the others we've discussed, because margin affects less people and money.

INTEREST RATES, ECONOMIC ACTIVITY AND MONEY SUPPLY. The Fed actively tries to manage the economy through the use of monetary policy. Interest rates have a direct effect on economic activity, and the Fed tries to control this with changes in the money supply. Since higher interest rates mean tougher credit and lower interest rates mean easier credit, the Fed is able to discourage or encourage economic activity. During expansion periods in the business cycle, the Fed is generally worried about inflation, so by using monetary policy to lower the money supply and increase interest rates, the Fed can curtail business and consumer spending to try and keep inflation in check.

Conversely, during contraction periods in the business cycle, the Fed is generally trying to stimulate the economy to avoid recession, so by using monetary policy to increase the money supply and lower interest rates, the Fed can encourage borrowing to spur business and consumer spending. The balancing efforts of the Fed are directed towards managing the growth of the money supply to allow adequate growth of the economy at reasonable interest rates, without fueling inflation or fears of inflation which could lead to higher interest rates.

Part of the Fed's role in managing interest rates is to deal not only with actual inflation, but also with anticipated inflation. In recent years, the Fed has adopted a policy of trying to anticipate future economic conditions rather than simply reacting to them as it had in the past. This has also involved trying to further reduce the size and impact of swings in the business cycle. Most economists and businesses watch the Fed's actions when the FOMC meets to see if they will raise interest rates to reduce growth and head off inflation, or lower rates in an effort to spur economic growth and head off recession. Although many believe that inflation is less of a threat in our current global economy, the Fed still plays an important role in managing economic growth and business activity, as well as money supply and interest rates.

Here are a few things to remember for the Series 7 exam. First, the Fed does *not* set the prime rate nor the fed funds rate. Instead, the Fed influences these with its open market operations of buying and selling securities. The Fed sets the discount rate, margin and reserve requirements. Reserve requirements cause the largest change (because of the multiplier effect), margin requirements cause the smallest change (because fewer people affected). Monetary policy is the Fed influencing interest rates by various means; fiscal policy is government taxes and spending.

5.4.4

International Economic Factors

International economic factors can play an important role in our domestic securities markets and our business cycles. This is true not only because many U.S. companies are international in scope and depend on foreign manufacturing subsidiaries and export sales, but also because of competition in the marketplace. We are not only talking about competition between companies offering similar goods and services, but also competition for the limited dollars that consumers have to spend, and the competition that exists for investment dollars staying in the U.S. securities markets or flowing to other countries to obtain better returns.

These same international factors also affect money coming into the United States from other countries. The United States balance of payments measures money flowing into or out of the U.S. economy, exchange rates affect the purchasing power people have to buy goods and make investments, and foreign interest rates relative to those in the United States can also determine which direction money will flow. Let's examine each of these.

U.S. BALANCE OF PAYMENTS. The **balance of payments** measures the difference between all goods and services purchased between two countries. This includes all transactions made over a certain time period, comparing the amount of foreign currency taken in with the amount of domestic currency paid out. For example, the United States has a negative balance of payments with Japan. This means that the United States has sent more money to Japan than Japan has sent to the United States.

The balance of payments figure is made up of several components. One element is the **balance of trade,** which counts only goods and ignores the services and investment components. This is also referred to as the **current account.** Another component is the **capital account,** which shows the net capital expenditures (investments) each country made in the other country. Other components include services expenditures, investments, and all other spending.

These balance of payments figures serve to indicate the trade situation between two countries. By looking deeper, though, they can also indicate future trends. When there is a deficit in the balance of payments, that usually indicates that that country's currency is weaker. A weaker currency can help business activity by encouraging more exports. A stronger currency encourages imports. The currency can also have an impact on investments, as we will see in the next section.

EXCHANGE RATES. The **exchange rates** are the prices at which one country's currency can be converted into another country's currency. Talking about the strength or weakness of a currency is all relative, depending on whether the country is talking about its own currency or that of another country. Let's use the dollar as an example. A **weak dollar** is when the dollar can be exchanged for less of a foreign currency. This makes foreign imports expensive, but encourages other countries to buy more U.S. goods. A **strong dollar** is when the dollar can be exchanged for more of a foreign currency. This makes foreign imports cheaper, but makes it more expensive for other countries to buy U.S. goods. Also, a strong dollar attracts deposits and foreign investment money into the United States. Foreign investment dollars don't buy as much initially, but foreign investors want their investment to enjoy capital appreciation (income or interest) in the stronger U.S. dollar so they can get more of their own currency later when the investment matures or is liquidated.

INTEREST RATES. Foreign and domestic interest rate differentials also affect our domestic securities markets because U.S. dollars and foreign investment money will always flow to where it can get the best rate of return. We saw this in the last section. Exchange rates and interest rates must both be considered. Higher interest rates abroad do not necessarily translate into immediate capital flight out of the United States and into that country (and vice versa). Here's why.

As the interest rates or rates of return offered by foreign investments rise, they become more attractive to both U.S. and foreign investors. Worldwide, the demand for these foreign investments rises as well. Suppose some investors sell some assets in the United States to try to shift the proceeds into those foreign investments offering better interest rates. The proceeds from the sale must be converted from U.S. dollars into the foreign currency to buy the foreign investment. Thus, demand for the foreign currency rises and the U.S. dollar depreciates, which lowers the overall profitability of the transaction. This helps the market achieve interest rate parity between the two countries. Here, too, expectation of future exchange rate movements between the two currencies can also be a factor.

For the Series 7 exam, though, just know that a rise in foreign interest rates leads to a depreciation of the U.S. dollar relative to the foreign currency. This reinforces the fact that a weak dollar makes U.S. investments less attractive to foreigners anyway. And know that a strong dollar attracts deposits and foreign investment money into the U.S. markets.

5.45

Sources of Business Data

There are many sources of data on business conditions and corporate profits that you can consult for information on securities and the securities markets. You can get anything from general market trend data to specific financial information on a company you and your client are interested in. One of the best places to get data on corporate profits of a specific company is from the company itself. Publicly traded companies have annual statements and other investor relations material that they send out upon request. And, of course, the Internet has a myriad of sources where research can be done, and the company itself may even have its own website with information posted for reading or that can be downloaded for a client presentation.

Information regarding the level of business activity can also be gleaned from a variety of sources. Some require interpretation; others provide straightforward commentary. Major financial publications come in all media these days. Typically, though, when people talk about major financial publications, the main one they are referring

figure 5.4.5

Sample Financial Information

NEW YORK STOCK EXCHANGE COMPOSITE TRANSACTIONS
Quotations as of 4 p.m. 04/01/02

YTD % CHG	52 WEEKS HI	52 WEEKS LO	STOCK (SYM)	DIV	YLD %	PE	VOL 100S	LAST	NET CHG
+ 22.1	17.45	6.96	AAR **AIR**	.10	.9	dd	1439	11	+ 0.23
+ 17.2	38.20	24.96	ABM Ind **ABM**	.72	2.0	29	719	36.75	+ 0.05
+ 17.7	20.43	14.20	ABN Am ADS **ABN**	.80e	4.2	...	1680	19.16	+ 0.20
+ 4.1	44.76	18.10	ACE Ltd **ACE**	.60	1.4	dd	10062	41.79	+ 0.09
− 44.6	52.25	3.40	AES Cp **AES**		...	18	23396	9.06	+ 0.06
− 35.3	79.74	11.20	AES Tr	3.38	15.1	...	829	22.40	− 0.10
+ 19.6	35.24	23	AFLAC **AFL**	.24f	.8	23	8564	29.37	− 0.13
+ 39.2	23	7.90	AGCO Cp **AG**	.04	.2	71	9010	21.96	− 0.86
+ 1.7	24.50	18.95	AGL Res **ATG**	1.08	4.6	...	1108	23.42	− 0.08
+ 27.3	16.15	9.52	AgSvcAm **ASV**		...	13	24	14	...
+ 6.7	48.15	30.30	AIPC **PLB**		...	24	421	44.86	− 0.54
+ 24.1	15	7.50	AK Steel **AKS**	j	...	dd	4752	14.12	− 0.18
+ 5.9	27.65	22.75	AMB Prop **AMB**	1.64f	6.0	19	622	27.54	+ 0.04
− 14.6	7.50	3.82	AMCOL **ACO**	.06	1.0	14	280	6.15	+ 0.10
+ 0.3	26	21.75	AMLI Resdntl **AML**	1.92	7.6	12	135	25.30	+ 0.08
+ 14.6	39.50	15.10	AMR **AMR**	stk	...	dd	10780	25.56	− 0.85
− 27.5	58.51	22.10	AOL Time **AOL**		...	dd	166515	23.27	− 0.38
− 6.3	4.35	2.15	APT Satelt **ATS**	.15e	4.8	...	44	3.10	− 0.05
− 87.4	11.30	0.13	APW **APW**		...	dd	11131	0.21	+ 0.03
− 37.7	21.10	7.67	AT&T Wrls **AWE**		...	...	70799	8.95	...
− 12.7	21.46	14.18	AT&T T s	.15	.9	7	90051	15.84	+ 0.14
− 11.0	25.40	14.51	AVX Cp **AVX**	.15	.7	31	1807	20.99	+ 0.05
+ 7.3	31.48	15.40	AXA ADS **AXA** s	.50e	2.2	...	1402	22.55	+ 0.10
− 15.4	25.79	14.20	AZZ **AZZ**	.16	.9	11	10	17.81	− 0.09
+ 39.3	23.15	14.45	AaronRent **RNT**	.04	.2	37	375	22.70	− 0.15
+ 61.1	22.25	10.50	AaronRent A **RNTA**	.04	.2	35	41	21.75	− 0.30
− 16.7	18.95	6.10	ABB ADS **ABB** n		...	...	149	7.84	+ 0.04

NASDAQ SMALL-CAP ISSUES
April 01, 2002

ISSUES	SYM	VOL 100s	LAST	CHG
FrntlrComm wt	FCCNW	220	0.13	+ 0.03
FuelTech	FTEK	407	5.75	...
GLB Bcp	GLBK	1	9.89	− 0.01
GWilliFod	WILCF	3	3.25	+ 0.04
GtwyBk&Tr wts	GBTSW	222	1.17	− 0.01
GtwyFncl	GBTS	6	9	− 0.40
GeeringWade	GEER	16	1.19	+ 0.08
GeoRes	GEOI	5	1.51	...
GETGO	GTGO	654	0.10	− 0.03
GishBioMed	GISH	150	0.52	+ 0.01
GlenBurnie	GLBZ	28	20.65	− 1.75
GlycoGensys	GLGS	616	1.56	− 0.83
Go2Phrmcy	GORX	14	0.80	...
GdTimeRestr	GTIM	45	4.50	− 0.10
GrandCntlFnl	GCFC	4	11.05	+ 0.05
GrandToys	GRIN	43	2.68	+ 0.01
GranitBdcst	GBTVK	96	2.04	− 0.06
GtLakAviatn	GLUX	103	0.69	+ 0.05
GtDelValSvg	ALLB	15	25.95	− 1.05
GreenDan	DAGR	48	9.65	− 0.09
GreeneCnty	GCBC	1	17.99	...
GrillCncpts	GRIL	477	1.57	+ 0.17
GuardnTch	GRDN	660	0.25	− 0.01
Gyrodyn	GYRO	1	17.80	− 0.01
HCB Bcshs	HCBB	170	14.43	+ 0.08
HansnNtrl	HANS	173	4.25	+ 0.03
HarveyElec	HRVE	109	1.28	− 0.03
Hathaway	HATH	12	2.68	− 0.11
Hlthwatch	HEAL	46	0.19	− 0.06
Hemagen	HMGN	21	0.97	...
HemagenDiag wt	HMGNW	200	0.10	+ 0.04
HemlkFedFnl	HMLK	25	24.17	...

MONEY RATES
April 01, 2002
Note: These rates are a guide and may not be based on actual transactions.

PRIME RATE: 4.75% (effective 12/12/01). The base rate on corporate loans posted by at least 75% of the nation's 30 largest banks.
DISCOUNT RATE: 1.25% (effective 12/11/01). The charge on loans to depository institutions by the Federal Reserve Banks.
FEDERAL FUNDS: 2 1/16% high, 1 5/8 % low, 1 11/16% near closing bid, 1 3/4 % offered. Reserves traded among commercial banks for overnight use in amounts of $1 million or more. Source: Prebon Yamane(U.S.A) Inc. FOMC fed funds target rate 1.75% effective 12/11/01.
CALL MONEY: 3.50% (effective 12/12/01). The charge on loans to brokers on stock exchange collateral. Source: Reuters.
COMMERCIAL PAPER: Placed directly by General Electric Capital Corp.: 1.80% 30 to 62 days; 1.84% 63 to 89 days; 1.93% 90 to 121 days; 2.03% 122 to 182 days; 2.22% 183 to 213 days; 2.31% 214 to 244 days; 2.41% 245 to 270 days.
EURO COMMERCIAL PAPER (March 28 trading): Placed directly by General Electric Capital Corp. : 3.33% 30 days; 3.37% two months; 3.41% three months; 3.46% four months; 3.50% five months; 3:55% six months.
DEALER COMMERCIAL PAPER: High-grade unsecured notes sold through dealers by major corporations: 1.78% 30 days; 1.82% 60 days; 1.80% 90 days.
CERTIFICATES OF DEPOSIT: Typical rates in the secondary market. 1.85% one month; 1.95% three months; 2.28% six months.
BANKERS ACCEPTANCES: 1.88% 30 days; 1.93% 60 days; 1.99% 90 days; 2.11% 120 days; 2.23% 150 days; 2.33% 180 days. Offered rates of negotiable, bank-backed business credit instruments typically financing an import order. Source: Reuters
EURODOLLARS (March 28 trading): 1.88% - 1.75% one month; 1.94% - 1.81% two months; 2.06% - 1.94% three months; 2.13% - 2.00% four months; 2.25% - 2.13% five months; 2.38% - 2.25% six months.
LONDON INTERBANK OFFERED RATES (LIBOR) (March 28): 1.87875% one month; 2.0300% three months; 2.3300% six months; 3.0025% one year. British Banker's Association average of interbank offered rates for dollar deposits in the London market based on quotations at 16 major banks. Effective rate for contracts entered into two days from date appearing at top of this column.
EURO LIBOR (March 28 trading): 3.36000% one month; 3.45000% three months; 3.59300% six months; 3.95163% one year. British Banker's Association average of interbank offered rates for euro deposits in the London market based on quotations at 16 major banks. Effective rate for contracts entered into two days from date appearing at top of this column.
EURO INTERBANK OFFERED RATES (EURIBOR) (March 28 trading): 3.362% one month; 3.448% three months; 3.594% six months; 3.953% one year. European Banking Federation-sponsored rate among 57 Euro zone banks.
FOREIGN PRIME RATES: Canada 3.75%; Germany 3.25%; Japan 1.375%; Switzerland 3.50%; Britain 4.00%. These rate indications aren't directly comparable; lending practices vary widely by location.
TREASURY BILLS: Results of the Monday, April 1, 2002, auction of short-term U.S. government bills, sold at a discount from face value in units of $1,000 to $1 million: 1.790% 13 weeks; 2.110% 26 weeks. Tuesday, March 26, 2002 auction: 1.770% 4 weeks.
OVERNIGHT REPURCHASE RATE: 1.89%. Dealer financing rate for overnight sale and repurchase of Treasury securities. Source: Reuters.
FREDDIE MAC: Posted yields on 30-year mortgage commitments. Delivery within 30 days 6.93%, 60 days 7.02%, standard conventional fixed-rate mortgages: 3.375%,2% rate capped one-year adjustable rate mortgages. Source: Reuters.
FANNIE MAE: Posted yields on 30 year mortgage commitments (priced at par) for delivery within 30 days 7.03%, 60 days 7.13%, standard conventional fixed-rate mortgages; 4.80%, 6/2 rate capped one-year adjustable rate mortgages. Source: Reuters.
MERRILL LYNCH READY ASSETS TRUST: 1.56%. Annualized average rate of return after expenses for the past 30 days; not a forecast of future returns.
CONSUMER PRICE INDEX: February, 177.8, up 1.1% from a year ago. Bureau of Labor Statistics.

DIVIDENDS REPORTED APRIL 1

COMPANY	PERIOD	AMT.	PAYABLE DATE	RECORD DATE
	REGULAR			
Cardinal Fin'l pfA	Q	.0906	4-26-02	4-05
Clarcor Inc	Q	.12	4-26-02	4-12
Conectiv	Q	.22	4-30-02	4-11
GreatSthrnCap Tr I	Q	.225	4-01-02	3-28
GreatSthrnCap Tr I	Q	.225	7-01-02	6-28
GreatSthrnCap Tr I	Q	.225	9-30-02	9-27
GreatSthrnCap Tr I	Q	.225	12-31-02	12-30
Inter-Tel Inc	Q	.02	4-15-02	3-31
MetroCorp Bancshs	Q	.06	4-15-02	r3-31
NPB Capital Tr Pfd	Q	.5625	3-31-02	3-15
National City Corp	Q	.295	5-01-02	4-11
Noland Co	Q	.08	4-25-02	4-15
NStar	Q	.53	5-01-02	4-10
PIMCO Corp Inco	M	.10625	5-01-02	4-12
Pro-Fac Co-op pfA	Q	.43	4-29-02	4-12
ProLogis Trust pfE	Q	.5469	4-30-02	4-15
Sandy Sprg CapTr	Q	.585938	4-01-02	3-29
Sandy Sprg CapTr	Q	.585938	7-01-02	6-28
Sandy Sprg CapTr	Q	.585938	9-30-02	9-27
Sandy Sprg CapTr	Q	.585938	12-31-02	12-30
Westbank Corp	Q	.11	4-19-02	4-12
Wireless Telecom	Q	.02	4-30-02	4-12
X-Rite Inc	Q	.025	5-10-02	4-12
YadkinVlyBk&Tr NC	Q	.10	4-26-02	4-05

EX-DIVIDEND STOCKS ON APRIL 3

COMPANY	AMOUNT
ACM Govt Opportun	.06
ACM Inco Fd	.0825
ACM MngdDollarInco	.0675
ACM MngdInco	.0425
ACM MuniSecsInco	.0725
AlexandriaRlEst	.50
AlexandriaRlEstpfA	.59375
AlexandriaRlEstpfB	.52451
AllianceWldDolGvII	.09
AllianceWldDolGv	.0925
AmerExpress	.08
Amvescap PLC ADS	t.2054
Annaly Mtg Mgt	.63
BristolMyersSq Inc	.28
ColonialNYInsdMuni	.085
Commerce Bncp NJ	.15
CommrclMetals	.13
Credicorp Ltd	t.20
CrSuisseMgmtInco	.06
Genl Gwth Props pf	.4531
Glatfelter	.175
MerLynPharmHOLDRs	t.0504
Mkt2000+ HOLDRs	.0046
Mkt2000+ HOLDRs	.0084
Mrgn(JP)Chs	.34
Jefferson Smurfit	t.4055
LL&E Royalty Tr	.00781
Masco Corp	.135

LISTED CORP. BONDS
Quotations as of 4 p.m. 04/01/02

BONDS	CUR YLD.	VOL.	CLOSE	NET CHG.
AES Cp 4½05	cv	200	65½	+ ¼
AES Cp 8s8	10.5	150	76	− ¾
AMR 9s16	9.3	42	96¾	+ ⅛
ATT 6½02	6.4	30	101¼	...
ATT 6¾04	6.6	12	102	− 1⅛
ATT 5⅝04	5.6	440	100	− ⅛
ATT 7s05	6.9	100	102	− ⅛
ATT 7½06	7.3	45	102⅝	...
ATT 7¾07	7.5	10	103⅝	+ ¼
ATT 6s09	6.4	161	93⅝	+ ⅝
ATT 8⅛22	8.1	56	99⅞	− ⅛
ATT 8⅛24	8.2	46	99⅛	− ¼
ATT 6½29	7.9	142	82¾	− ⅛
ATT 8⅝31	8.4	22	102½	− ⅛
ARetire 5¾02	cv	95	76	+ 8
BauschL 6¾04	6.7	164	101¼	+ 1

KEY INTEREST RATES

	Week Ended: Mar. 29, 2002	Mar. 22, 2002
Treasury bills (90 day)-a	1.79	1.82
Commrcl paper (Finl., 90 day)-a	1.90	1.89
Commrcl paper (Non-Finl., 90 day)-a	1.91	1.88
Certfs of Deposit (Resale, 3 month)	1.97	1.94
Certfs of Deposit (Resale, 6 month)	2.29	2.22
Federal funds (Overnight)-b	1.70	1.76
Eurodollars (90 day)-b	1.96	1.93
Treasury bills (one year)-a	2.70	2.66
Treasury notes (two year)-c	3.71	3.70
Treasury notes (three year)-c	4.31	4.32
Treasury notes (five year)-c	4.88	4.84
Treasury notes (ten year)-c	5.38	5.37
Treasury bonds (25+ years)-c	5.95	5.95

a-Discounted rates. b-Week ended Wednesday, March 27, 2002 and Wednesday, March 20, 2002 c-Yields, adjusted for constant maturity.

to is *The Wall Street Journal.* Other major financial publications of note include the *Financial Times, Investor's Business Daily, Barron's, Forbes,* and *Fortune.* Then there are news bureaus, such as Bloomberg and Reuters, plus numerous websites, including sites put up by many of these same entities, as well as online only offerings from the likes of The Motley Fool (Fool.com) and Yahoo! Finance.

Business indexes and statistics are also compiled by a number of investment research firms. Some offer reports and advice for a fee; others are selling their own packaged securities or offering brokerage services. Some of these players include Standard & Poor's, Moody's, Wilshire, Morningstar (with their Mutual Fund Data), and many more. Everything from broad market indexes to the narrowest of sector analysis can be found. These offer more in-depth analysis and trends than is offered in the typical newspapers and periodicals mentioned before. Many of those investment newspapers and periodicals mentioned previously, however, offer additional depth of reporting available on their websites, through subscription to news services or purchase of in-depth reports or analyses.

Finally, one source of a wealth of information that often gets overlooked is the U.S. government. This is where some of the most authoritative data can be found on present business conditions, current business activity, and future trends. The government compiles data on prices, spending, inventories, consumer confidence, and numerous other business and economic indicators. Almost all are free for the asking.

5.X Summary

5.1 SROs oversee securities industry with "industry rules," but many rules are same.

5.1.1 NYSE: must be open every trading day, must charge commission, allied members can't trade on floor, 120-day apprenticeship, written o.k. for other job, must resign and re-apply, NYSE has jurisdiction for one year after leaving, all compensation through firm, disputes to arbitration, discipline is NYSE panel, appeal to Board of Directors, penalties: fine, censure, suspension, expulsion.

NASD: principal needs Series 24, ROP needs Series 4, RR can't sell commodity futures, present firm must have knowledge and give consent for the RR to take another job, must resign and reapply, no re-testing needed if rejoining within two years, continuing education: firm part and NASD part (within 120 days of second year, then every three years), NASD name/logo can't be bigger, all compensation through firm, disputes to arbitration, discipline is DBCC, appeal to Board of Governors, minor rule violation fine is $2,500, penalties: fine, censure, suspension, expulsion.

MSRB: 90-day apprenticeship, knowledge and consent of present firm to take another job, must resign and reapply, no retest if rejoin in two years, all money through firm, no power to enforce.

5.1.2 Uniform Practice Code is standard trade execution, settlement rules. (T+3) Firm quote means B-D ready, willing, able to trade one round lot (100 shares, 5 bonds); backing away is NASD violation, instead subject or workout quote.

Markup rule: 5 percent guideline (less for riskless, more for more difficult trade). Prohibited: broker and dealer in 1 trade, free riding, withholding, gift $100+.

5.1.3 More prohibited practices: selling away (trade, commission not through firm), unsuitable recommendation, unauthorized trades, churning (excessive trades to make commission), short-term mutual fund trades, breakpoint selling (keep customer below commission breaks), selling dividends (push stock trades to get dividend), use client money, share profit, borrow/lend client money, guarantee profit.

5.1.4 Arbitration can solve disputes faster, cheaper than courts. NASD Code of Procedure (COP) for discipline, Code of Arbitration Procedure (CAP) for money. Simple arbitration (no personal appearance) for NYSE <$10K, NASD <$25K.

5.1.5 NYSE: discipline panel hears case, can appeal to Board of Directors (final say). NASD: Dept. of Enforcement appoints discipline hearing officer, can make Offer of Settlement, can appeal to SEC or federal court, can sign Acceptance Waiver and Consent, or Minor Rule Violation letter (for ads, etc.) fine $2,500.

5.2

Primary market: new issues sold. Uses investment bankers, underwriters.

5.2.1 Investment banker is special B-D who underwrites new issues. New stock issue is IPO. Primary offering: money to company; secondary offering: money to shareholders (company founders, insiders). Underwriting can be competitive or negotiated. Syndicate is purchase group of underwriters; sell group helps sell. Commitments can be firm (guarantee) or best efforts (all-or-none, mini-max).

5.2.1+ Registration process: registration statement, 20-day cooling off period, due diligence, preliminary prospectus (red herring), clearance, final prospectus.

Underwriting agreement between issuer and managing underwriter: agree on price, spread, settlement date, company use of funds, SEC filings compliance. Agreement among underwriters: appoint managing underwriter, how long syndicate will last, each member responsible sales amount, use sell group. Selling group agreement: relationship, time, amount of seller's concession.

Blue Sky is required by state registration rules to sell in a particular state.

Issue price based on market conditions, strength of issuer. Underwriter makes the spread (difference between offering price and money to issuer). Spread: management fee + underwriter fee + takedown (additional takedown + seller concession)

Hot issue when market price moves above offering price. B-D can't free ride or withhold. Oversold, company may issue more (green shoe clause) or syndicate may buy more and split cost. To keep market price from dropping below offering price, underwriter may do stabilizing bid (pegging). Normally not allowed, but o.k. for new issue if stated in prospectus and bid is at or below public offering price. Firm may have penalty bid for sellers whose investors flip stock too quickly, may have lock-up period so insiders can't sell too soon. Shelf distribution lets insiders join registration now, then sell some later.

5.2.2 Securities Act of '33 (Paper Act): regulates new issues, primary markets, investment banking, promotes full and fair disclosure. Registration procedures in place; prospectus requirements. Need complete company info, history, financials, market, management, use of proceeds. Prospectus also needs risk assessment, legal opinion, legal action. Preliminary prospectus must state "This is not an offer to sell securities nor solicit orders." (often in red ink so called red herring); Final prospectus includes offering price, spread, and state "These securities have not been approved by SEC."

Need prospectus with new issues for a time (p. 216); quiet period is 25 days.

Reg. A: offering circular, non-audited books for less than $5 million in 12 months.

Reg. D: private placement, securities for investment (restricted), insiders accredited investors ($1 million worth, $200,000 income), 35 non-accredited. Rule 144: restricted stock (non-registered): must be held for one year; control stock: insiders with 10 percent+; selling over 500 shares or $10,000 require Form 144. Rule 144a: foreign, qualified institutional buyers (QIB) don't have restrictions. Rule 145: stock acquired thru merger, acquisition, sale doesn't have restriction.

Blue Sky: various state registration rules. Three ways: file notice, coordinate with SEC registration, independent filing in each state.

Trust Indenture Act of '39 requires indenture agreement (between trustee and corporation) to protect bondholders. Company must keep promises, make semiannual reports to bondholders, and do periodic SEC filings.

5.2.2+ Municipal securities are exempt from '33 Act so no centralized registration. Still do paperwork, due diligence, etc. with underwriter. Can be negotiated sale (usually for revenue bonds) or competitive sale (usually for GO bonds).

Issuer does resolution by appointing underwriter. Indenture agreement is not required by law, but done for market acceptance. Municipal official statement is like corporate prospectus. Bond attorney does legal opinion: unqualified (no problems, tax exempt) or qualified (found some questions). Also do ex-legal.

Underwrite procedure: 1) account formation (syndicate letter), 2) underwriting account agreement (details relationships among members), 3) type of account (undivided/Eastern—shared responsibility; divided/Western—only take care of own), 4) underwriter roles (manager does paperwork, but not always most sales), 5) bid determination (manager looks at index for current rate, visible supply), 6) compute bid (writing the scale—figure maturities, rates, spread, but not par value), 7) award based on net interest cost (NIC) or true interest cost (TIC) to issuer, 8) order priority (presale, group net, designated, member); spread is shared.

5.3

Equity securities are ownership interest in company. Stock, derivatives.

5.3.1

Securities Exchange Act of '34 (People Act): regulates outstanding issues, secondary market, fair and orderly markets, antifraud provisions (NO ONE is exempt), proxies required, registration of firms and people, created SEC.

The '34 Act defined insiders as officers, directors, people own 10 percent + stock. Made it illegal to trade on information before it became public.

Proxies required to give stockholders a vote without attendance at annual meeting. Annual report must be sent to shareholders. Proxies must clearly state what is being voted on, and can't leave vote to discretion of management.

Broker-dealers must disclose if trading from own account, markup charged. Can't be broker and dealer in same transaction. Specialist can't trade for own account while orders at same price are outstanding. Manipulative practices prohibited (pegging nonnew issues, painting the tape, sales ring, wash sale). Can't short tender (borrow when company offers to buy stock); can't make buyback guarantees; can't give credit on new issues; must keep clients' securities separate, only pledge if agreement; must meet net capital requirements, 15:1 liquidity.

5.3.2

Penny stock rules include monthly statement of shares, value to clients. If calling, must identify stock name, number of shares, current price, firm commission.

5.3.3

SIPC protects investors from B-D insolvency (not bad investments). Each account is insured to $500,000 total, $100,000 cash. If firm fails, SIPC tries to merge, then liquidates and pays. Debit balances subtracted. If not enough, investor become general creditor of firm. SIPC is *not* agency of U.S. government.

5.3.4

Secondary market for equities is OTC, exchange. Exchange is double auction. Specialist at NYSE keeps orderly market; buys/sells from own account; keeps Book of limit, stop orders; can arrange opening orders or stop the stock.

5.3.4+

Stopping the stock keeps price quote open for trader to try for better price, but it does *not* stop trading in the stock. (Can't stop stock for B-D trades.)

NYSE is centralized trading floor, approves members, watches for fraud.

When market is falling, circuit breakers can halt trading, limit program trading, and limit price movements in index futures to reduce index arbitrage.

OTC market is decentralized, linked by electronic means, relies on negotiated bid ask between investors and market makers. Market maker must be ready to give firm quote to buy or sell round lots. Can also do subject quotes, workout. Transactions must be reported within 90 seconds (allows other computerized trades).

5.3.5 Listed options trade on exchanges, depend on OCC as issuer and guarantor of options. If exercised, OCC does random assignment. Settlement is three days for exercise, one day if buy/sell options. Market maker (keeps trade balance), board broker (board employee, fills book orders), floor broker (client orders).

5.3.6 Municipal securities trade OTC in secondary market. Blue List shows total par value for all munis and thus is good measure of supply. Bond offerings can be all-or-none (where buyer takes whole lot) or multiples (round lots). Bonds can't be sold short on down bid. Some institutional buyers use interdealer systems (computer based, direct). Broker's broker helps sell bonds anonymously. Bond specialists must give bona fide quotes (ready to trade).

5.3.7 Treasuries secondary markets exist. Some banks, investment companies can sell direct.

5.3.8 Many securities trade in secondary market: corporate bonds (9 bond rule says order must go to NYSE floor for one hour before go to OTC market), repo agreements (flexible term buybacks, also used by Fed), commercial paper (*not* issued by commercial banks), CDs (only jumbo $100K+ are negotiable), Eurodollars (U.S. dollars in foreign banks), Banker's Acceptance ("time draft" used like a letter of credit), pass-thrus and CMOs (tranches to spread risk).

5.3.9 Currency markets are unregulated, decentralized, risky. Interbank market trades are spot trades (1–2 days) or forward trades (2 days–18 months). Market makers don't have to allow a trade, difficult to liquidate position, may be impossible to do stop limit/stop loss orders, risk of bankruptcy. Central bank intervention is government trying to buy currency to support price, stop devaluation. Risks: government policy, political events, interest rates, inflation, devaluation.

5.3.10 Third market is OTC by non-members. Usually large institutional investors trying to save commissions. Transactions must be reported in 90 seconds.

5.3.11 Fourth market is Instinet. Direct computerized trades between institutional investors. Instinet is registered with the SEC as an exchange.

5.4

Beyond market and exchange factors, business and economic conditions have a great impact on markets and securities prices.

5.4.1 Business cycle: swings in the economy: expansion, peak, contraction, trough. (Remember: EPCoT). Supply and demand seek balance. Expansion is rise in production, demand, prices, stocks. Contraction is fall in demand, production. Recession is 2 consecutive quarters of declining GDP. Inflation can be cost (passing along price increases) or demand (too much money, too few goods).

Gross Domestic Product (GDP) is value of all goods and services produced in the United States (may also see GNP on test, which counts net foreign investment). Consumer Price Index (CPI) measures fixed cost of market basket of goods; includes food, transportation, energy, housing, clothing. Used as inflation adjuster.

Leading economic indicators measure changes before economy (e.g., housing). Coincident economic indicators measure current economy (e.g., production, income). Lagging economic indicators measure changes after economy (e.g., company financials).

Bond prices affected by business cycle because inflation, interest rates, yields. Expansion = rates rise, bond prices fall. Contraction = rates fall, bonds rise. Yield spread is difference between long and short rates. During upswings, investors expect rates to rise so spread widens. In downswings, investors expect rates to fall so spread narrows. Normal yield curve has long bond yields higher than short-term yields. Inverted has short higher than long.

Equities prices affected by business cycle because expansion equals rising profits, which equals rising stock prices. Contraction equals falling profits which equals falling stock prices. Some stocks are very sensitive to cycles (e.g., autos), others are counter cyclical because demand is constant (e.g., food). Interest rate sensitive stocks include banks, utilities. Stock price = present discounted value of expected future profits.

5.4.2 Economic theories are Keynesian or demand-side (government should spend money and intervene to keep full employment and stable prices), supply-side (government should cut taxes and regulation to allow job creation and investment), and monetarist (money supply growth should be constant to allow efficient plans).

5.4.3 Federal Reserve (Fed) affects interest rates by adjusting money supply through open market operations (buy and sell securities to hit target fed funds rate), discount rates (rate charged from member bank loans), reserve requirements (money banks must keep in their accounts), margin requirements (Reg. T). If more money is available, rates should fall; less money, rates should rise. Fed does *not* set prime rate; reserve requirements = largest effect, margin = smallest.

5.4.4 International economic factors include balance of payments (difference between all goods and services sold); exchange rates (weak dollar helps foreign countries buy exports, strong dollar makes imports cheaper and attracts foreign investment); interest rates can draw investment money, but offset by exchange rates.

5.4.5 Many sources of business data including newspapers (*The Wall Street Journal*), magazines, new bureaus, websites. Great sources of information also include individual companies and the U.S. government, which publishes many statistics.

Chapter 5 Review Quiz

1. Which of these SROs require written permission for an RR to take another job?
   a. NYSE
   b. NASD
   c. MSRB
   d. all of the above

2. The Uniform Practice Code is a set of rules:
   a. that established the three-business-day settlement rule.
   b. that determine what constitutes good delivery.
   c. set up by NASD.
   d. all of the above

3. The NASD markup rule says that:
   a. 5 percent is a guideline for the markup charged by broker-dealers in OTC trades.
   b. sometimes 5 percent is too much of a markup on a trade.
   c. sometimes a markup can exceed 5 percent on a trade.
   d. all of the above

4. All of the following are prohibited activities, *except:*
   a. selling away.
   b. extending margin credit.
   c. churning.
   d. selling dividends.

5. Simplified arbitration:
   a. allows for more discovery than regular arbitration.
   b. is a good first step in seeking redress through the court system.
   c. does not require the parties to make a personal appearance.
   d. all of the above

6. The primary marketplace:
   a. allows only primary offerings to be done.
   b. is the place where investors come first when they want to sell securities.
   c. is where issuers can sell new issues.
   d. all of the above

7. Which of the following statements is true?
   a. A primary offering has proceeds paid into the company treasury.
   b. A secondary offering has proceeds paid to shareholders.
   c. The secondary market has proceeds paid to investors.
   d. all of the above

8. A firm commitment means:
   a. the investment banking firm has agreed to do a standby underwriting.
   b. the underwriter will buy any unsold shares.
   c. the underwriter will do the offering on an all-or-none basis.
   d. a syndicate has agreed to terms on working together.

9. During the 20-day cooling off period:
   a. additional due diligence is performed.
   b. the SEC may request additional changes to the prospectus.
   c. the underwriter may send out a red herring.
   d. all of the above

10. Which of the following is a component of the underwriter's spread?
    a. issuer's concession
    b. underwriting fee
    c. 12b-1 management fee
    d. all of the above

11. When are tombstone ads used?
    a. before the registration statement is filed
    b. during the cooling off period
    c. when soliciting orders for a new issue
    d. Tombstone ads are not permitted.

12. All of the following are associated with the Securities Act of 1933 *except:*
    a. registration of new issues.
    b. probibition of the dissemination of false, misleading, or fraudulent materials.
    c. registration of broker-dealer firms.
    d. the Paper Act.

13. All of the following are associated with the Securities Exchange Act of 1934, *except:*
    a. the registration statement must be filed.
    b. it prohibits fraud and market manipulation.
    c. registration of sales representatives.
    d. the People Act.

14. For how long must the final prospectus be delivered with a new issue?
    a. 25 days past the effective date of the offering period for new OTC issues
    b. 25 days past the effective date of the offering for new NASDAQ issues
    c. until the issue is sold out for a new initial public offering
    d. indefinitely

15. Rule 144 says that restricted stock:
    a. may only be sold by control persons.
    b. must be part of a Reg. D private placement before it can be sold.
    c. must be held for at least one year before it can be sold.
    d. is also considered control stock by SEC rules.

16. Blue Sky laws:
    a. are irrelevant for national stock issues registered with the SEC.
    b. are individual state registration procedures which must be followed.
    c. always take precedence over SEC regulations.
    d. are important only for intrastate stock offerings.

17. All of the following are true about trust indentures *except:*
    a. the Trust Indenture Act of 1939 requires a company to issue a bond indenture.
    b. the bond indenture is an agreement between a company and bondholders.
    c. a bond indenture agreement is required by the marketplace for municipal bonds.
    d. the indenture agreement requires the company to make SEC filings.

18. When a bond attorney issues a qualified legal opinion, it means that:
    a. the bond attorney is stating that he or she is qualified to render an opinion.
    b. the issue has been examined and is qualified for tax exempt status.
    c. the attorney has some unresolved questions about the legality of the issue.
    d. the issue is qualified as an AMT bond under the IRS code.

19. When bond underwriters enter into a Western style account agreement:
    a. all underwriters are agreeing to share equally in selling the issue.
    b. all underwriters are agreeing to share proportionately in selling the issue.
    c. each underwriter is responsible for selling its committed amount.
    d. each underwriter is jointly liable for selling everyone's amount.

20. When writing the scale, the managing underwriter looks at all of these *except:*
    a. when the bonds will mature.
    b. the interest rate at which the bonds will be issued.
    c. the spread the firm can charge on the issue.
    d. the par value of the bonds at maturity.

21. Put the following bond orders in priority, from first to get filled to last:
    a. member, designated, group net, pre-sale
    b. pre-sale, group net, designated, member
    c. pre-sale, member, designated, group net
    d. pre-sale, designated, member, group net

22. Which of the following Acts created the SEC?
    a. Paper Act
    b. People Act
    c. Trust Indenture Act
    d. Insider Trading Act

23. According to the Exchange Act of '34, who is defined as an insider?
    a. officers and directors of a company
    b. anyone who has confidential information
    c. investors who own at least 5 percent of the company stock
    d. all of the above

24. Which of the following is true about the SIPC?
    a. It is a government agency.
    b. It guarantees investors' accounts against market risk.
    c. It insures investors' money against broker-dealer insolvency.
    d. all of the above

25. Which of these is an advantage for stocks listed on the NYSE?
    a. double auction pricing
    b. decentralized trading environment
    c. lower capitalization requirements
    d. all of the above

26. When the specialist stops the stock:
    a. all trading activity ceases until the specialist releases the hold.
    b. open orders are filled before any more trades occur.
    c. trades can be executed only for the stock in the OTC market.
    d. the quoted price is held open for a period of time.

27. Exchange circuit breakers:
    a. are designed to limit downside volatility.
    b. can halt or curtail trading due to large drops in a given index or average.
    c. can curb program trading and limit price movements of index futures.
    d. all of the above

28. The role of the Options Clearing Corporation is to:
    a. issue and guarantee options contracts.
    b. exercise calls and puts whenever the market dictates.
    c. stabilize the options markets by making offsetting contracts hard to get.
    d. guarantee minimum exercise amounts for options contracts.

29. A bond offering that is all-or-none means:
    a. the underwriter is doing it on a best efforts basis.
    b. the underwriter is doing it on a firm commitment basis.
    c. a buyer is required to take all of the bonds being offered, or buy none of them.
    d. a buyer can buy any number of round lots desired at the quoted price.

30. Ginnie Maes are:
    a. the same thing as CMOs.
    b. mortgage pass-through certificates.
    c. backed by the full faith and credit of FHA.
    d. all of the above.

31. All of the following are true about commercial paper *except:*
    a. they are usually a money market instrument.
    b. their maturities are from 2–270 days.
    c. they are always issued by commercial banks.
    d. the debt is usually unsecured.

32. Eurodollars are:
    a. U.S. dollars held in foreign banks.
    b. foreign currency held in U.S. banks.
    c. debt securities that pay interest and principal in Euros.
    d. a new unit of currency being issued and used throughout Europe.

33. A recession is defined as:
    a. two consecutive years of decline in GDP.
    b. increase in business activity following a recovery period.
    c. the part of the business cycle that immediately follows expansion.
    d. two consecutive quarters of decline in GDP.

34. The Consumer Price Index:
    a. measures housing starts.
    b. measures the fixed cost of a market basket of goods.
    c. is a good indicator of future gasoline prices.
    d. is a direct function of the GDP.

35. Which of the following are leading economic indicators?
    a. building permits
    b. non-farm payrolls
    c. interest rates
    d. all of the above

36. When analyzing a yield curve, if long-term rates are higher than short-term:
    a. it is a normal yield curve.
    b. it is a negative yield curve.
    c. it is a humped yield curve.
    d. need more information

37. Stock prices are:
    a. present inflation adjusted value of earnings from the previous quarter.
    b. present discounted value of expected future earnings and profits.
    c. current asset value of the company if it were liquidated.
    d. a speculative measure of future market averages, adjusted for inflation.

38. Which economic theory says that control of money supply should be paramount?
    a. Keynesian economic theory
    b. demand-side economic theory
    c. supply-side economic theory
    d. monetarist theory

39. The method most used by the Fed to adjust interest rates is:
    a. open market operations.
    b. adjustment of discount rates.
    c. reserve requirements.
    d. margin requirements.

40. Which of the following is best for U.S. exports?
    a. negative balance of trade
    b. capital account surplus
    c. strong dollar
    d. weak dollar

6 Processing a Customer's Instructions

"Processing a Customer's Instructions" is the sixth of the seven critical functions performed by a Registered Representative. A customer needs to be informed about how the order process works, the basic types of orders available, and how these choices relate to his or her investment objectives. After completing the order ticket according to the customer's instructions, the RR needs to verify the order with the customer prior to entry.

After verifying the order, the RR checks the open order notices. It is the responsibility of the RR to ensure that the customer understands the settlement procedures for each type of security. After entering all orders appropriately, the RR must promptly report trade confirmations to the customer and ensure that the transaction is recorded in the customer's account.

This sixth critical function covered in Chapter 6 ("Processing a Customer's Instructions") represents about 5 percent of the total exam: approximately 10–15 questions of the total 250 questions on the Series 7 Exam. This is again somewhat deceptive, though, because the concepts in this chapter are helpful in understanding some of the other things we have discussed. This chapter should help fill in some of the gaps that may have been left up to this point. Furthermore, this chapter has a few key concepts for the Series 7 exam, and later for your career as an RR in the securities industry.

This chapter will be broken up into three sections:

6.1 **Securities Orders and Confirmations.** This first section will detail the different types of securities orders that you will encounter, then go through some of the order execution qualifiers that you are likely to encounter. Filling out the order ticket is also an important skill that will be discussed here. The purposes of and restrictions on automated execution systems will be touched upon before this section closes with a discussion of the RR recordkeeping responsibilities and customer confirmations.

6.2 **Delivery and Settlement of Transactions.** This section deals with the important subject of good delivery and explains what exactly constitutes good delivery of securities. Automated clearance of book entry securities will be touched on before going into the heart of this section: settlements. Settlement of securities transactions will examine the primary market and secondary market before going on to negotiated settlements, options settlements, U.S. Treasury settlements, and municipal settlements. "DK" procedures will also be explained briefly.

6.3 **Recordkeeping.** This section will define recordkeeping responsibilities of the RR with regard to customer account information and customer holdings, then cover industry regulations with regard to the firm's recordkeeping responsibilities.

key terms

All or none: an order qualifier that says the entire order must be filled, but that it does not necessarily have to be filled right away. All or none says a partial order will not be accepted, but the order should not automatically be canceled either.

CUSIP number: Committee on Uniform Securities Identification Procedures number used to identify all listed stocks and registered bonds. The CUSIP number can be used for easy tracking of securities, and aids in settlement of trades.

Customer book: detailed records kept by RRs about the securities a client owns and all transactions that have been made with the firm.

Date of record: cutoff date for an investor to be considered the owner of record and eligible to receive rights, dividends, etc.

Day order: an order that is valid only for the trading day that it is entered.

DK: "don't know" (DK); a trade comparison response where one party challenges the validity of a trade. If there is no response to a DK within four days, the disputing party can disaffirm the questioned trade.

Ex-date: the last date that a person can buy a stock and still have time to settle the transaction and be the owner of record to receive rights or dividends.

Execution: to fulfill or perform an order as directed. (Also: the act of signing.)

6.1

Securities Orders and Confirmations

This is the chapter where we begin talking about actually trading securities. Orders and confirmations are the beginning of the trading process. Most of what we see is the electronic price quotes that come across the computers or show up on the financial programs. But buying and selling securities is still an old-fashioned auction, where everyone is trying to get the best price as the market moves towards an equilibrium price between supply and demand.

When a typical order comes in, the one with the highest bid to buy and the lowest offer to sell is filled first. Beyond that, the orders are filled based on priority, precedence and parity. (*To help you remember, think **reverse** alphabetical order.*) **Priority** simply says that if prices are equal, the order that is placed first (with the best price) is filled first. When done electronically, it is the order that arrives first; when done on the trading floor, it is the order that the specialist hears first. **Precedence** says that, all things being equal, the larger order gets filled first. **Parity** says that if everything is the same (same time, same size), orders are filled randomly.

Customers should be informed about how the order process works so that they can have a clear understanding of how their trades are handled. (If they get shut out, they will want to understand why.) To be an effective RR, you also need to ensure that your customers are fully informed about the basic types of orders available.

Fill or kill: an order qualifier that says the entire order must be filled, and that it must be done right away. Fill or kill says that partial orders will not be accepted, and the order should automatically be canceled if it can't be filled.

Good-till-canceled: an open order until it gets filled or canceled. (Good-till-canceled orders are cleared off the Specialist's book twice a year [April, Oct.], so they must be reentered.)

Immediate or cancel: an order qualifier that says the entire order does not have to be filled, but it must be done right away. Immediate or cancel says that partial orders are okay, but if the balance can't be filled right away, it should be canceled.

Limit order: an order that a particular security should be bought or sold, but only at a certain price (or better).

Market order: an order that a particular security should be bought or sold immediately at the best available price.

Stop limit order: an order that becomes a stop order once a certain trigger has been met or exceeded; that stop order then becomes a market order after a second trigger has been met or exceeded.

Stop order: an order that a particular security should be bought or sold at market price, once a certain trigger price has been met or exceeded. Once the trigger is hit, the stop order becomes a market order.

Trigger: price at which an order is executed or an order status is changed.

Types of Securities Orders

Different types of orders help fulfill different investment objectives. As we go through the various possibilities, be aware that the orders accepted vary by SRO as well as the market exchange where the securities are traded. We will point out a few.

MARKET ORDER. A **market order** is an order that a particular security should be bought or sold immediately at the best available price. With market orders, the price of the stock is the market price, determined by supply and demand at the exchange where the security is traded. This is a "typical" order on most exchanges.

LIMIT ORDER. A **limit order** is an order that a particular security should be bought or sold, but only at a certain price (or better). Here the customer limits what price is acceptable for the trade. A limit order is not filled unless or until the price matches the customer's restriction (limit).

STOP ORDER. A **stop order** is an order that a particular security should be bought or sold at the market price once a certain **trigger** price has been met or exceeded. Once the price of the security meets or exceeds the trigger set by the customer, the stop order becomes a market order. There is no guarantee, though, that the market order can be executed at all because the security may never hit the trigger price. Trigger does not equal execution! The trigger changes only the status of the order, so that it becomes a market order. Only then does it have a chance of being executed.

If the security does hit the trigger price, this is not a guarantee that the order can be executed at the trigger price. The next trade could already be beyond the trigger, or the orders in line ahead of this new market order might use up all of the inventory at that price, pushing the next available market trade beyond the trigger.

Stop orders can be buy stop orders (with a trigger above current market price) or sell stop orders (with a trigger below current market value). You should also note that stop orders are *not* permitted in the OTC market.

STOP LIMIT ORDER. A **stop limit order** is an order that becomes a stop order once a certain trigger has been met or exceeded, then that stop order becomes a market order after a second trigger has been met or exceeded. Here, there is no guarantee that the stop limit order will become a stop order or a market order. The security may never hit either trigger price. If the security does hit the trigger price, there is no guarantee that the order can be filled at the trigger price. Since stop orders are not permitted in the OTC market, obviously stop limit orders would not be allowed either. The American Stock Exchange allows stop limit orders only where the two trigger prices are equal.

chart 6.1.1

PLACEMENT OF STOP AND LIMIT ORDERS

(This may be on Series 7 exam.)

Orders Placed **Above** Current Stock Price: **Sell Limit, Buy Stop** (SLoBS)

Current Stock Trading Range

Orders Placed **Below** Current Stock Price: **Buy Limit, Sell Stop** (BLeSS)

DAY ORDER. A **day order** is an order that is valid only for the trading day that it is entered. Orders are assumed to be day orders unless the trade specifies another expiration qualifier. Note, too, that you can combine a day order qualifier with other trades. For example, you could have a limit order that is also a day order.

GOOD-TILL-CANCELED (GTC). A **good-till-canceled order (GTC)** is an open order until it gets filled or canceled. These orders, though, still get cleared off of the Specialist's book twice a year (end of April, end of October), so they must be reentered. The customer does not lose priority if the order is reinstated. As an RR, it is important for you to be aware of this so that you can reinstate any orders your client wants to have left open.

Exam Topic Alert

This may also be a good source for a tricky test question on the Series 7 exam. If the customer specified that a GTC be valid for eight months (customers may specify time limits for GTC), and you placed the order in April, you would have to enter the order a total of three times: once in April when first received from the customer, once again on the first trading day in May, and again on the first trading day of November. Again, too, you should note that the GTC order qualifier can be combined with other trades (e.g., you could have a GTC stop limit order).

6.12

Order Execution Qualifiers

In addition to the types of orders we saw in the last section which were concerned with the price at which an order got filled or when an order got filled, there are also qualifiers which are concerned with execution instructions. This means that the order must be filled a certain way, or not at all. These qualifiers can all be used with the order types we discussed in the last section. Let's look at some of these.

ALL OR NONE. **All or none** is an order qualifier that says the entire order must be filled, but that it does not necessarily have to be filled right away. All or none says that partial orders will not be accepted, but the order should not automatically be canceled either.

FILL OR KILL. **Fill or kill** is an order qualifier that says the entire order must be filled, and that it must be done right away. Fill or kill says that partial orders will not be accepted, and the order should automatically be canceled if it can't be filled.

IMMEDIATE OR CANCEL. **Immediate or cancel** is an order qualifier that says the entire order does not have to be filled, but it must be done right away. Immediate or cancel says that partial orders are okay, but the balance of whatever can't be filled right away should be canceled.

NOT HELD. **Not held** is an order qualifier for an order which is not given to the specialist, but rather is given to a floor broker. The floor broker is given some latitude on price and timing of the trade (usually because it is a rather large order). The floor broker is supposed to shop around and get the best price, but the floor broker is "not held" responsible for variations in price when filling the order.

Note that even though the floor broker is given some discretion over the time and price of the trade, this is *not* considered a discretionary trade. (*Watch this for the Series 7 exam.*)

Exam Topic Alert

6.13

Filling Out the Order Ticket

This is an area where RRs need to pay special attention, because this is one area where mistakes are easiest to make. Transpose a number or mis-enter some data and a trade can have a serious mistake. The order ticket is what the RR fills out as he or she is accepting the order from the client.

INFORMATION REQUIRED. The order ticket must have certain details about the trade. If the trade is a limit order or a stop limit order, the order ticket would also include the limit price. If not, the RR enters the price on the order ticket and circles it after receiving confirmation. Information that must be on an order ticket includes

- where traded (NYSE, OTC, bond, etc.)
- order execution (buy, sell, sell short)
- number of units to trade
- designation of security (name or symbol)
- kind of order (market, limit, stop, etc.)
- customer name (or code number)
- date and time of order
- initiator of trade (solicited or unsolicited)
- identification of RR, broker (name or number)

Exam Topic Alert

Two important items to note that *may appear on the Series 7 exam.* First, if an order execution is marked sell (sell long), the *RR must know the location of the securities.* Often they are held by the broker in street name for ease of transfer, but this is not always the case. If the securities are being held by a client, the RR must be reasonably sure that they can be delivered on time. And second, an order ticket must be approved by a principal by the end of the trading day, but *the order ticket does not have to be approved by the principal before the trade is made.*

USE OF AUTOMATED QUOTATIONS. An RR is allowed Level 1 access to the NASD Automated Quotations Service (NASDAQ). This shows the highest bid price and lowest ask price (the "inside quotes") for any NASDAQ stock that has at least two active market makers. These quotes, though, are not firm until confirmed by another broker-dealer. (Level 2 and Level 3 access to NASDAQ are for institutional investors and market makers, respectively, and will be discussed in more detail in Chapter 7.)

IDENTIFICATION OF SELL ORDERS. It is an SEC requirement that orders to sell be marked as long or short. Sales that are marked long indicate that the securities are in the customer's account, or that they can be delivered by the settlement date. That's why we said earlier that the RR must know the location of the securities. Sales that are marked short are subject to the Plus Tick rule.

6.14

Automated Execution Systems

Automated execution systems are used by the NYSE and NASDAQ to handle small market orders more quickly and efficiently. NYSE uses the Designated Order Turnaround (DOT) system, which routes small market orders directly to the specialist from the member firm, thereby bypassing the need for the floor broker. NASDAQ uses the Small Order Execution System (SOES), which aggregates small market orders of less than 1,000 shares and executes them using firm quotes from market makers in the stock that put quotes on the NASDAQ system.

6.15

RR Recordkeeping Responsibilities

The RR is responsible for retaining all records of correspondence with customers regarding trades. This is especially important in case a dispute arises in the future. Records of transactions, including confirmations and account statements, must be kept for six years, with easy access to the past two years. Furthermore, it is the RR's responsibility to check the accuracy of all data entered and all trades made. After making a successful trade, the RR must compare the report of the trade execution against the order ticket, and then report the trade execution to the customer.

ERRONEOUS REPORTS. Order execution reports must be double-checked against the order ticket, and checked again against the client's confirmation. The order execution must be reported to the client, and any errors must be reported to the proper person within the broker-dealer firm. Even if there is an error in the trade, once the order execution is received, the trade is considered confirmed and is binding on the client. The only exception is for trades made outside the customer's limits. The RR should not attempt to correct any problem by making additional trades until receiving instructions from a principal of the firm.

CHANGES IN ORDER DESIGNATIONS. Customers may change order designations at any time up until the trade is actually executed. The RR, though, needs to be careful so as not to jeopardize the client's priority position. For example, if a client gives you a day limit order to buy a stock at a certain price, then the client later calls back and wants to change the order designation to GTC (good-till-canceled), the RR should *not* cancel the first order because then the client would lose his or her place in line to buy the stock at that price. Instead, you should wait until the end of the day, and if the order has not been filled, enter a new GTC order. Watch for a trick question like this on the Series 7 exam.

You should cancel orders only if the customer's new order, or order change, contradicts the previous one. If there is no contradiction, then you should not cancel the first order so that you can preserve the customer's priority status.

6.16

Customer Confirmations

Customer confirmations are the formal record of a transaction given by the broker-dealer to the client. The confirmation includes all details about the transaction, including whether the firm acted as a broker or as a dealer in the transaction. If the firm acted as a broker (arranging the trade with another broker-dealer firm), details about the other party involved in the transaction, as well as the source and amount of commission charged by the firm, must be disclosed. If the firm acted as a dealer (trading with its own inventory), that fact must be disclosed along with the markup or markdown amount charged.

COMPONENTS. The confirmation contains basically the same information as the order ticket, with a few additional items. We have already discussed the fact that the confirmation will indicate the firm's role in the transaction and the commission or markup (down) charged. The confirmation will also indicate the price and net price for the trade, any "and interest" amount due for bond trades, and a CUSIP number. The **CUSIP** (Committee on Uniform Securities Identification Procedures) **number** is a number identifying all listed stocks and registered bonds. The CUSIP number can be used for easy tracking of securities, and aids in the settlement of trades.

For bonds, MSRB Rule G-15 requires that the customer's written confirmation contain the identity of the parties to the transaction, a description of the securities, the trade date, the settlement date, yield to maturity or dollar price, the capacity in which the firm or bank is acting, and other specified information (e.g., the time of trade execution and CUSIP number).

WHEN SENT. Customer confirmations must be sent to the client in writing on or before the settlement date. Remember, settlement varies: for corporate securities (T + 3), municipal securities (T + 3), for U.S. government securities (T + 1). Buy/sell option contracts settle the next business day (but three days if delivering securities). Mutual fund trade confirmations may be sent as late as the day after the settlement date.

Note that *all broker-to-broker confirmations use the settlement as the next business day (T + 1). Watch this point for the Series 7 exam.*

WHERE SENT. Customer confirmations are usually sent to the same place where customer statements are sent. Clients, though, can designate to where and to whom duplicate order confirmations should be sent. If the client requests that materials be sent to someone who does not hold power of attorney on the account, or if confirmations are being sent to a place other than client's residence or business address, it might be good idea to have the request done in writing. Check with your employing broker-dealer for their policies in this area.

6.2 Delivery and Settlement of Transactions

After the order and confirmation, the next step is delivery and settlement. This is where the securities actually change ownership and are paid for. It is imperative that customers understand the delivery and settlement procedures for the type of trade executed on their behalf. This includes everything from good delivery of the securities to payment within the rules of the securities industry.

6.2.1

Regulations and Practices Relating to "Good Delivery"

When detailing what constitutes "good delivery" there are several items that must be discussed. These include physical condition of the securities, proper endorsement of the securities, and physical delivery by the settlement date. This is why it is important for the RR to know the physical location of the securities. If the securities are being held by the brokerage firm in street name, then none of these factors are an issue. If the firm is holding the securities for a customer, but they are in the customer's name, then the firm must have a valid, executed stock power. There should be minimal problems for good delivery.

Problems can arise, though, when the customer is physically holding the securities. If they are damaged, missing coupons, or soiled enough to obscure the writing on the face, the transfer agent will need to be notified to rectify the situation. The transfer agent may issue new certificates, or require a surety bond if the authenticity of the certificate is in question.

Two points of "good delivery" that are unique to bonds are also important for you to know. First, if the bond is a bearer bond, then a signature endorsement is not necessary. And second, municipal bond issues must have the legal opinion attached or be stamped ex-legal in order for them to be considered as a "good delivery."

PROPER ENDORSEMENT. When looking at what constitutes "good delivery," proper endorsement is one of the most important considerations. Without proper endorsement, the securities cannot legally be transferred. Proper endorsement includes such things as complete and legible signature, signature of all parties, and additional documentation if needed. Signatures must be guaranteed by the member broker-dealer firm, a bank, other party approved by the transfer agent. If certificates are in the possession of the seller and are going to be endorsed by the seller,

- ▷ every certificate must bear a complete and accurate signature.
- ▷ the signature must match the name printed on the face exactly (only two exceptions: "and" can be "&", and "company" can be "co.").
- ▷ certificates with two or more named persons must bear signatures of all persons (or submit a power of attorney).
- ▷ deceased persons can have only certificates endorsed by their estates, or signed and dated before death (firm liable if forged).
- ▷ stock/bond power may be used in lieu of a customer's signature.
- ▷ additional documents may be required for good delivery (e.g., corporate resolution authorizing the sale).

DENOMINATIONS. Different delivery amounts are considered acceptable for equity securities and bonds. To be considered good delivery, stock certificates must be in round lots of 100-shares, or separate certificates that can be combined to create 100-share round lots. For example, if a customer has five certificates for 80 shares each, this is not considered good delivery because the certificates cannot be combined to make 100-share sets. In this situation, the broker-dealer must send the stock certificates to the transfer agent, and have new certificates reissued as 4 × 100 share certificates. On the other hand, if the customer had eight certificates for 50 shares each, this is good delivery, because two of the 50-share certificates can be combined into a lot. This is why clients are discouraged from buying odd lots of certificates. Buying odd lots can also lead to a client paying higher commissions, which is referred to as the **odd lot differential.**

For bonds, good delivery is bearer bonds in face value denominations of $1,000 or $5,000. Registered bonds are acceptable only for good delivery if they are cleared beforehand and deemed acceptable by the receiving party.

AUTOMATED CLEARANCE. Automated clearance for book-entry securities is often used. There are various automated confirmation/comparison and book-entry settlement systems that are used in connection with the clearance of certain inter-dealer and customer transactions for municipal securities. Ownership of book-entry securities is transferred by notifying the appropriate clearinghouse and requesting a transfer from one owner to another. For example, the Government Securities Clearing Corporation (GSCC) provides automated clearance and guaranteed settlement for eligible U.S. Treasury securities.

6.2.2

Settlement of Securities Transactions

Settlement practices for securities transactions have been standardized somewhat by the Uniform Practice Code of the NASD, but still vary by the type of security and the market where the security is traded. Federal Reserve Board Regulation T requirements call for settlement to occur within five business days, but the various markets and SROs have established their own, more stringent standards. This gives broker-dealers and other market players some extra time to ensure that they are in compliance with Reg. T. For example, the NYSE settlement rule for stock transactions is three business days. So if the client or broker-dealer is not able to comply with the three-day settlement rule, the parties still have two more days to try to rectify the situation before they run afoul of Reg. T rules. We have discussed settlement procedures in various contexts in previous chapters, but we will summarize some of the important points here as a review. (Remember: **Reg. T = T + 5; SRO = T + 3**)

6.2.2.1 Primary Market

In the primary market, when new issues of securities are being sold, one settlement problem that can occur is that the certificates are not always ready for good delivery at the time the securities are initially being sold. When this occurs, the securities are sold on a when issued (WI) basis. This is short for "when, as, and if issued," meaning that the securities are offered conditionally upon the final issuance, but trade now as if they've already been issued and will be delivered when ready. **When issued (WI)** settlement is date of **issue + three business days (i + 3).**

6.2.2.2 Secondary Market

In the secondary market, several factors must be considered when discussing settlement dates of securities. Of course, cash settlement is always same day. **Regular way** settlement is **trade + three business days (T + 3)** for most stock issues. But for stocks that are paying dividends or doing a rights offering, there are some other factors to consider with the settlement.

For rights offerings and dividend payments, the buyer is not considered the owner until the settlement date. Since rights and dividends go only to owners of record as of a certain date (called the **date of record**), the actual trade must occur early enough to make sure that the settlement date will be *before* the date of record. The last date that a person can buy a stock and still have time to settle the transaction and be the owner of record to receive rights or dividends is called the **ex-date.** After the ex-date, the stock trades ex-rights or ex-dividend (without those things).

When stocks trade **ex-rights** that means the stock no longer gives the holder the right to buy shares from the new rights offering at a discounted rate. **Ex-dividend** means the stock no longer gives the holder the right to collect the upcoming dividend that was announced.

Trades must occur three business days before the date of record so that the new owner will settle in time to be the owner of record and qualify for the rights or dividend. (Of course, cash settlement is the same day, so a cash trade could occur the day before the ex-date and still entitle the new owner to the rights or dividend.) If the trade occurs three days before the ex-date, but settlement gets delayed until after the ex-date, or if there was a cash settlement after the ex-date that was missed in the owner of record list, the new owner will not collect a dividend check. In this situation, the new owner will send a statement of money owed (called a **due bill**) to the original owner (or broker) asking that a that a **due bill check** be sent for the dividend amount.

6.2.2.3 Negotiated Settlements

There are a few settlement variations that can occur between parties, as long as they are agreed to beforehand by the parties involved. Cash settlement for **cash-on-delivery (C.O.D.)** orders (where the broker-dealer delivers securities to a bank) when used by institutional investors can be negotiated to settle as much as 35 calendar days beyond the settlement date.

Delayed delivery is another option where delivery of securities is later than the usual settlement date. This is also known as **seller's option** or **buyer's option,** depending on who chooses delivery date. Delivery date can be anywhere from the fourth business day to the date written in the contract. This is acceptable only with a contract in place between all parties. In fact, almost any alternate arrangement can be made **as mutually agreed upon,** as long as all parties agree and there's a contract in place.

6.2.2.4 Options Settlement

Options transactions have some unique characteristics that you need to be aware of. First, whether opening or closing a position, when options are bought or sold, settlement is the next business day. When options are exercised, however, settlement is the third business day after OCC receives the option holder's exercise notice. Exercised option contracts are assigned by OCC on a random basis to any of the member firms, who in turn assign the contract to a client.

Second, exchange traded index options settlement is always the next business day with cash payments, whereas exchange traded debt options settle two business days after submission of the exercise notice. Finally, some types of options (e.g., foreign currency options) can have settlement that is either European style or American style: **European style** options can be exercised only on expiration date; **American style** options can be exercised at any time before the expiration date.

6.2.2.5 U.S. Government, Government Agency Settlements

There is an important difference between government securities and government agency issues. U.S. government securities have a settlement of **trade + one business day (T + 1).** U.S. government agency issues have a settlement of **trade + three business days (T + 3).**

6.2.2.6 Municipal Securities Settlements

In the municipal securities market, MSRB rules also follow Uniform Practice. **Cash settlement** is always the **same day. Regular way settlement** is **trade + three business days (T + 3).** When new issues are being sold and the certificates are not ready for good delivery, the securities are sold on a when issued (WI) basis. This is short for "when, as, and if issued," meaning that the securities are offered conditionally upon the final issuance, but trade now as if they've already been issued and will be delivered when ready. **When issued (WI)** settlement is date of **issue + three business days (i + 3).**

Delayed delivery is delivery of securities later than the usual settlement date. This is also known as **seller's option** or **buyer's option,** depending on who chooses the delivery date. The delivery date can be anywhere from fourth business day to the date written in the contract. This is acceptable only with a contract in place between all parties. In fact, almost any alternate arrangement can be made **as mutually agreed upon,** as long as all parties agree and there is a contract in place.

6.2.2.7 "DK" Procedures

Part of the Uniform Practice deals with how to handle discrepancies in trade data between two broker-dealers. The day after a trade, each broker-dealer sends the other a comparison (*not* confirmations that go to customers) that details the trade that took place between them. The parties have up to four business days to dispute any element of the transaction. If one party challenges, the other has four business days to respond. Response can be either "confirm" or "don't know" (DK). If there is no response, the disputing party can disaffirm the questioned trade.

6.3 Recordkeeping

Keeping good records is a critical task for RRs and all members of the securities industry. This is one area where the SEC and the various SROs place great emphasis. We have discussed some of these issues in other sections of the book, but will summarize two important areas here, just to review.

6.3.1 RR's Recordkeeping Responsibilities

The RR has an important responsibility to verify and update client information every time he or she takes over a new account, and to keep the account information current and updated on a regular basis. In addition to keeping track of personal changes and adjusting investment objectives, the RR must also maintain records about the securities that the client owns and all transactions that have been made with the firm. These detailed records are sometimes referred to as the **customer book.** The RR should also keep all order tickets, execution reports, and trade confirmations. These, along with client statements, must be kept for six years (the past two years should be accessible). It is probably advisable to keep all correspondence and records for the same period of time. You should check with your broker-dealer to find out the firm's policies in this area.

6.3.2

Industry Regulations of Firm's Recordkeeping Responsibilities

SEC Rules in Section 17 (a) on recordkeeping require the creation, retention, and preservation (for a period of six years) of numerous records, including the following:

- itemization of all purchases and sales of securities, all receipts and deliveries of securities (including certificate numbers), all cash receipts and disbursements, and all other debits and credits;
- a general ledger reflecting all assets and liabilities, income and expenses, and capital accounts;
- ledgers separately itemizing all securities transactions and all debits and credits in each account;
- position books reflecting all long and short positions in each security as of each clearance date;
- memoranda of each brokerage order or instruction, indicating the account, the time of entry, the terms of the order, and the details of the execution;
- copies of all confirmations of securities transactions and all debit and credit advices;
- records containing the name, address, and signatures of all persons for whom accounts are carried;
- detailed information concerning the identity, background, and qualifications of all employees; and
- monthly trial balances and other information in connection with "net capital" computations.

This summarizes some of the basic record creation, retention, and maintenance requirements. In addition, the firm must keep copies of all records and books (including customer books), keep copies of all account information transmitted to customers, maintain a file of customer complaints and their disposition, and keep copies of all advertising and sales literature. There are also rules about other recordkeeping items, but these are not likely to appear on the Series 7 exam.

6.X Summary

6.1 Market orders filled based on priority (first one for best price), precedence (same time, then larger order first), parity (if all equal, then random).

6.1.1 Order types: market (trade immediately at best price); limit (wait for stated price before trade); stop order (wait for trigger, then becomes limit order); stop limit order (double trigger: stop limit becomes stop, then becomes limit); day order (valid only day entered); good-till-canceled (wait until filled, but cleared in April and October, so need to reenter). No stop orders for OTC.

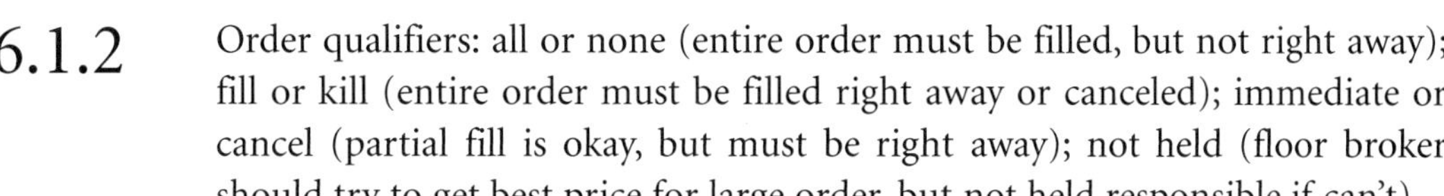

6.1.2 Order qualifiers: all or none (entire order must be filled, but not right away); fill or kill (entire order must be filled right away or canceled); immediate or cancel (partial fill is okay, but must be right away); not held (floor broker should try to get best price for large order, but not held responsible if can't).

6.1.3 Order ticket needs client and trade information, type of order, marked long or short. RR must know location of securities. Principal must approve order ticket at end of day. RR has NASDAQ Level 1 access to inside quote (best bid, ask).

6.1.4 Automated execution for small trades. NYSE = DOT; NASDAQ = SOES.

6.1.5 RR must check accuracy of trades, keep records for six years. If errors, tell principal but don't do trades to fix unless told. Trade is binding on client. Be careful when changing order designation so as to not cancel client's priority.

6.1.6 Confirmation must disclose firm's role in trade, markup, or commission. CUSIP number identifies all trades for easy tracking. Confirmations must be sent to client on or before settlement date. (All broker-to-broker trades are T+1.)

6.2

Delivery and settlement are when securities change ownership and are paid.

6.2.1 Good delivery: good physical condition, proper endorsement, timely delivery. Proper endorsement includes all signatures, power of attorney, other documents. Stocks must also be round lots of 100 shares, bonds in $1,000 or $5,000 face.

6.2.2 Settlement rules: Reg. T is T+5, so SROs are T+3 to give two-day cushion to catch and fix problems. When issued, trade issue date + 3 days (i+3); cash is same day; regular way is T+3 (except government—T+1). Delivery can be delayed, seller's option, buyer's option, as mutually agreed, with written contract.

Ex-date is last date can buy stock and still have time to settle transaction and be owner of record to receive rights or dividends.

6.3

Recordkeeping is important task for RR. Great emphasis by SEC, SROs.

6.3.1 Customer book is detailed record kept by RR about securities client owns and all transactions, etc. Must keep this, all statements, letters, etc. for six years.

6.3.2 Firm must keep detailed records about client, accounts, transactions, for six years.

Chapter 6 Review Quiz

1. The price at which a stop order becomes a market order is called the:
   a. trigger.
   b. execution price.
   c. market price.
   d. stop limit order price.

2. Which of the following would *not* be placed below the current stock price?
   a. buy limit order
   b. sell stop order
   c. buy stop order
   d. sell stop limit order

3. Which order of the following orders would *not* have to be filled immediately?
   a. immediate or cancel order
   b. market order
   c. fill or kill order
   d. all or none order

4. When filling out an order ticket, the registered rep must:
   a. get immediate approval of a principal.
   b. get immediate confirmation from the floor trader.
   c. get the order approved by a principal before the end of the day.
   d. get the order approved by a principal before sending confirmation to client.

5. What is CUSIP?
   a. a special order qualifier
   b. a tracking number
   c. a type of order
   d. a kind of security

6. Which of the following variations would still be considered proper endorsement of a stock certificate?
   a. The stock face said "company" but the person signed "co."
   b. One of three parties named on a certificate could not be located so the other two signed her name.
   c. Both of the above would be considered acceptable.
   d. No variations of any kind are acceptable for proper endorsement.

7. When is delayed delivery acceptable?
   a. If the buyer cannot come up with the cash on time.
   b. If the seller cannot come up with securities on time.
   c. Only if all parties agree in writing.
   d. It is never acceptable.

8. How long must the registered representative keep the customer book?
   a. until all trades have been executed
   b. two years
   c. six years
   d. until the client closes the account

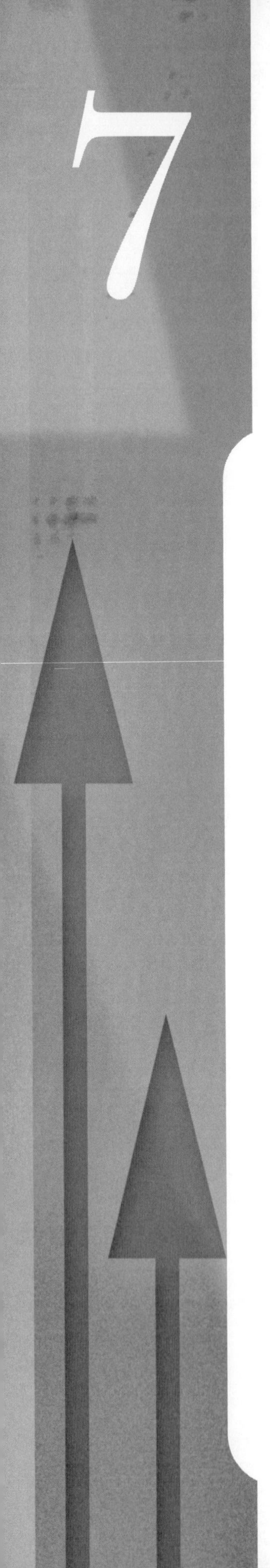

Monitoring a Customer's Portfolio

"Monitoring a Customer's Portfolio" is the last of the seven critical functions that are performed by a Registered Representative. Now that you have worked with the customer to identify investment objectives, then made investments to work towards those objectives, you must routinely review the customer's account to ensure that investments continue to be suitable. Clients' needs change; the markets change.

The RR must be vigilant to suggest to the customer which securities to acquire, liquidate, hold, or hedge. The RR needs to explain how news about an issuer's financial outlook may affect the performance of the securities, and determine which sources of information would best answer a customer's investment questions. The RR must use information from appropriate sources to provide the customer with relevant information, and keep the customer informed about his or her investments.

This seventh and final critical function covered in Chapter 7 ("Monitoring a Customer's Portfolio") represents about 8 percent of the total exam: approximately 20–24 questions of the total 250 questions on the Series 7 Exam. The material in this chapter is part of an ongoing pursuit for knowledge and insight for the Series 7 exam and your career as a successful RR.

This chapter will be broken up into four sections:

7.1 **Portfolio Analysis.** This first section will discuss the changing factors that affect customers' investment objectives. Portfolio management policies and portfolio theory will also be discussed as they apply to securities selection for customers.

7.2 **Securities Analysis.** This section will examine the equities markets, talk about the role of indices and averages, and explain the principal theories of market behavior using technical analysis and fundamental analysis. Factors used in comparisons of mutual funds will also be looked at, as will ways to analyze municipal bonds, specifically general obligation and revenue bonds.

7.3 **Sources of Price and Securities Information.** This section will explore ways to get more analysis and information from and about each of the major exchanges and securities, including muni bond report sources and options reports.

7.4 **Sources of Investment Research Information.** This section will discuss the publications that are important to the market, as well as explain some of the key indexes used by investors and professionals to track the markets.

key terms

Bottom line: company's operating income (EBIT), minus debt service, minus taxes. Also referred to as **net income** or **net income after tax (NIAT).**

Breakout: movement of a stock price past a resistance level or support level. Theory: Once the stock has a breakout past one of these levels, that is seen as an indication that the stock is going to continue to move in that direction.

Correction: a price decline in the overall market resulting from an overbought situation. Theory: Because there are few buyers left, a price drop is imminent.

Debt-to-equity ratio: a measure of the company's ability to effectively use leverage to enhance the rate of return on shareholder's equity.

Debt-to-Equity Ratio = Long Term Debt ÷ Stockholder's Equity

EBIT: Earnings Before Interest & Taxes: a company's gross sales, minus returns, minus cost of goods sold, minus selling expenses, minus depreciation. EBIT is also referred to as **operating income.**

EPS: Earnings per Share: straight division of profit by the number of common, outstanding shares. Also called **Earnings per Common Share.**

Earnings per Share = Common Earnings ÷ Outstanding Common Shares

Fundamental analysis: examines the financial statements and management of a company. (Analysis focuses on the earnings history and sales prospects for the company in relation to competitors in an effort to predict future share price.)

Price-Earnings (PE) ratio: an indication of how much an investor is paying for a company's earning power. A company with high growth potential can command a higher PE multiple. PEs can measure company's intrinsic value and value relative to other companies.

Price-Earnings (PE) Ratio = Market Price per Share ÷ Earnings per Share

Profit margin: equal to a company's operating income divided by its net sales.

Resistance level: technical term for highest price at which a stock has peaked on several occasions in previous trades. Theory: A stock has difficulty rising above a resistance level because there's more supply than demand at that price.

Support level: technical term for lowest price at which a stock has bottomed out on several occasions in previous trades. Theory: A stock has difficulty falling below the support level because there is more demand than supply at that price point.

Technical analysis: examines the supply and demand for a security based on its historical trading volumes and prices. (Analyst focuses on movement of the stock price in relation to other market trends in an effort to predict future share price.)

Visible supply: an index that shows all bonds which are scheduled to be offered within a 30-day period. This is published in *The Bond Buyer.*

7.1 Portfolio Analysis

Early on, we discussed the importance of examining the investment profile of a customer so that you as the RR could give the best advice possible to your client. Now that you have helped your client build a portfolio of investments, it is not time to stop the evaluation process. In fact, a client's financial needs and investment objectives change over time. As clients gain investment experience and build up some capital appreciation in their portfolios, it may be time to take a second look at the management of their portfolios, and see if perhaps a different portfolio theory is in order. "Know your customer" isn't an event; it's an ongoing process.

7.1.1 Changing Factors and Investment Objectives

There are many factors that affect a customer's investment objectives. These include age, marital status, family responsibilities, education, and investment experience. Notice how these are nonfinancial considerations. Presumably, you are up-to-date on your client's financial situation, as seen through the investment portfolio you have helped your client build. But as clients go through life, they are also going through changes—some of which you may not be aware of, so you need to ask. Certainly age is important for retirement planning, and you should already have this in your client's profile. As a client gets closer to retirement age, a more conservative, income-oriented portfolio strategy may be in order.

What about family responsibilities? These can and do change. Not only do the kids grow up, but sometimes clients want to provide for an elderly parent or a niece who needs help with education expenses. A portion of the client's portfolio may need to go in a safer direction to care for the elderly parent, and a portion may need to go in a more aggressive direction to pay for the education expenses. These factors should all be part of an ongoing dialogue with clients.

When reassessing these factors, it is important to discuss with a client if a change in investment objectives warrants a change in investment strategy. As a client gains more investment experience and knowledge, it may be time to introduce some new portfolio techniques that may be more appropriate to reach the client's revised financial goals.

7.12

Portfolio Management Policies

Portfolio management is a means of bringing a portfolio in line with customer investment objectives. While it is not as sophisticated as the portfolio theory we will discuss in the next section, portfolio management has its place nonetheless. Portfolio management policies at their basic level have the customer's overall objectives in mind, but with a more subjective component to the portfolio composition. Part of the problem here is that portfolio management does not use the objective measurement criteria that portfolio theory does. Portfolio management moves the overall investment strategy in one direction or another, tilting the balance from extremely aggressive to very conservative. But what is an aggressive investment to one investor, may not be to another. Still, portfolio management is useful in helping the average investor achieve his or her goals.

AGGRESSIVE. Aggressive investments are stocks of rapidly growing companies that have prospects for above-average growth, but with prices that are highly volatile over time when compared with the broader market. Some stocks that would be in a typical "aggressive" portfolio would be high-tech companies and other start-ups. These stocks are generally relied upon solely for capital appreciation since they usually offer no dividend income. An aggressive portfolio would have very little in the way of bonds or other investments with fixed returns. An aggressive portfolio would also have a portion of securities bought on margin to gain maximum leverage with its funds. The more aggressive the portfolio is, the greater the risks. But investors who want to maximize their return on investment understand that the greater the risks, the greater the potential rewards.

DEFENSIVE. Defensive investments are stocks with prices that are more stable over time than the broad market, and high grade bonds. Some stocks that would be in a typical "defensive" portfolio would be utilities, certain blue chip stocks, and some high grade preferred stock. The blue chips would allow for some moderate growth, and may even pay a dividend, while maintaining the safety component that the investor requires. A defensive portfolio would also hold debt securities as a larger portion of the overall portfolio. These bonds would be government issued, or high grade corporate bonds from companies that have an excellent debt rating. Safety and preservation of capital are goals here. The investor may also desire to generate some income. Safety and moderate growth are best achieved through the use of defensive investments.

BALANCED PORTFOLIO. In reality, most investment portfolios fall somewhere in the middle. This is at the heart of diversification: deciding exactly how much of a portfolio should be in what types of investments. Portfolio management techniques suggest two possible ways to diversify: constant dollar and constant ratio.

Constant dollar says that a fixed dollar amount should be kept in stocks, and the balance in bonds. If the equity rises above the fixed amount chosen, then the additional equity amount is liquidated to buy bonds. If the equity amount falls below a fixed chosen amount, then some bonds are liquidated to raise the equities portion.

Constant ratio says that a fixed percentage of all assets should be kept in equity stocks and a fixed percentage in bonds. If the value of one portion rises, it should be sold off to bring the ratios back in line.

As we discuss different ways to analyze securities, remember that no two portfolios will look the same because investors have different factors affecting their lives and investment objectives. Only careful planning can help clients achieve the right balance of aggressive and defensive strategies to accomplish their goals.

7.1.3

Portfolio Theory

Portfolio theory is a much more sophisticated investment approach. This approach gives investors objective benchmarks that measure risk against return in a portfolio. Unlike traditional securities analysis, though, portfolio theory doesn't worry about the specific securities that are in the portfolio. Instead, the idea is to have a diversified mix of asset classes to achieve the investor's goals. In other words, it doesn't matter that much which particular stocks are owned, as long as there are some from that representative group or industry.

Modern portfolio theory says that it is the relationship between the different types of investments, and their proportion of the entire investment portfolio that will determine the success of the portfolio. If investors have sufficiently diversified out as much risk as possible, while retaining enough reward in the overall portfolio, it's possible to meet the financial investment objectives they hope to achieve.

With modern portfolio theory, it is important to go through each of the four basic steps in order to make an appropriate allocation of assets. These steps must be applied to all securities selected for inclusion in the portfolio.

7.1.3.1 Portfolio Diversification

This first step of modern portfolio theory takes each type of asset and describes it in terms of expected return and expected risk. Looking at all types of assets ensures that the investor considers all investment opportunities, which in the end will provide a more well-rounded, diverse portfolio. This step is also called **security valuation.**

7.1.3.2 Capital Asset Pricing Theory (CAPT)

This step involves a sophisticated analysis of the relationship between expected risk and expected return. This relationship is quantified by considering the asset's rate of return as if it had no risk, then assigning a risk premium to add to that price. Doing this puts all assets on a level playing field, and allows the choice of securities to be based on which portfolio combination would offer the best rate of return for a given level of risk. This step is also called **portfolio optimization.**

7.1.3.3 Asset Allocation Principles

This step determines the final allocation of stocks and bonds, based on the distribution of the securities into different classes of investments. This distribution is based on risk analysis done in the prior steps, and will form the basis for how the final portfolio will look: how much of it will be in stocks or bonds or other assets, and what the expected return (and risk) of the portfolio is given its final composition. This step is also called **asset allocation decision.**

7.1.3.4 Alpha and Beta Considerations

This final step measures the performance of the portfolio, to see if its rate of return is in line with expectations. Each security's performance is divided into market-related and industry-related risk and return categories, and evaluated against different benchmarks. Two such benchmarks are *alpha* and *beta.* This step is also called **performance measurement.**

The **alpha** measurement is used to gauge performance apart from risk factors of the market. Any number of items related to a portfolio can be gauged: a specific stock, the portfolio as a whole, the portfolio manager, etc. A positive alpha means that the performance being analyzed was better than expected, relative to other investments. A negative alpha means performance was relatively worse.

The **beta** measurement is used to gauge the portfolio's performance versus some chosen index. The beta number is an indicator of how volatile the portfolio is (how much wider its price fluctuations are) when compared to overall market. A well-diversified portfolio is one that moves even with the index, and would have a beta of 1. The higher the beta number, the more susceptible the portfolio is to the risk-reward ratios. That means that in good times the portfolio will perform better than the market (giving more reward), but in bad times the portfolio will perform worse than the market (indicating more risk). A beta that is below 1 would indicate a more conservative investment portfolio that does not enjoy the big gains when the market is doing well, but does not take the big hits when the market is doing poorly.

7.2 Securities Analysis

Securities analysis involves investment research into the securities markets. The investor, analyst, or RR is looking for anything that might indicate the future direction of a particular security, a certain industry, or the market in general. These include behavior patterns of the market, financial condition of corporations, comparisons of mutual funds, and strength of municipal issues and issuers.

7.2.1 Analysis of Equities Markets

There are many market theories that one can look at when analyzing the equities markets. Each one has advantages and disadvantages, but all have people who follow them closely. Some of these indicators must be analyzed in conjunction with other market indicators; others are more useful when compared with previous readings.

MARKET SENTIMENT. This simply refers to whether the market overall is in a bullish (upward) mood or a bearish (downward) mood. Some indicators of market sentiment might be the reaction to economic news, advance-decline ratio, and trading volumes of stock.

ADVANCE-DECLINE INDEX. This is a measurement of the number of stocks that rise in price, compared with the number of stocks that decline in price. When advancers lead decliners, that is a bullish market sentiment. When decliners lead advancers, that is a bearish market sentiment. As this index is tracked over time, the steeper the line, the stronger the market sentiment is said to be in that direction.

PUT-CALL RATIO. This is a measurement of the number of put options traded, compared with the number of call options traded. A higher volume of puts indicates a bearish sentiment. A higher volume of calls indicates a bullish sentiment.

MARKET MOMENTUM. The speed, volume, and change of stock prices is said to be an indicator of the market's direction at a given point in time. The momentum swings up and down like an oscillator feeding on itself until the momentum carries it back in the other direction.

AVAILABLE FUNDS. This is an indicator that tracks the amount of money that is not currently invested in the market. When available funds are high, that is a bearish sentiment because it means investors are not fully invested in the stock market. On the other hand, the available funds sitting on the sidelines could indicate an imminent bullish trend when that pent-up money is finally invested in the market.

TRADING VOLUME. Large volumes indicate that the current market trend is strong. For example, if an index dropped during a period of heavy trading volume that would indicate a bearish sentiment. Conversely, a rally that is supported by heavy trading volume indicates confidence in the bullish sentiment. Trading volumes in options and futures can also be an indication of future market trends, as can the volume of short selling that occurs.

7.2.2

Use of Market Indexes and Averages

Indexes and averages are a popular means of market analysis. The most familiar index or average is the **Dow Jones Industrial Average (DJIA).** It is a price-based average of 30 industrial stocks that trade on the NYSE. Dow Jones also has a number of other averages that track the transportation sector, utility concerns, and others. In fact, **Dow Theory** says that the averages in these other sectors must confirm the movement of the DJIA to signal a true change in market direction.

There are better indicators of overall market performance. Take for example, the S&P 500 index. The S&P 500 addresses many of the flaws inherent in the DJIA. First, the S&P 500 tracks 500 companies—a far better sample than the 30 tracked by the DJIA. Second, this wider sampling of companies with the S&P 500 allows it to have components from all sectors of the economy. And finally, the S&P 500 is a market cap weighted index. This means that larger companies with a large market capitalization will move the index more than small cap companies.

The indexes and averages do have their limitations, however. For example, the DJIA is not a weighted index and does not consider the market capitalization of the companies that comprise the average. The S&P 500 considers only U.S. companies. Furthermore, just because an index rises, does not mean that all companies did well.

In fact, theoretically, all companies that are not part of the average could drop, but the average would still rise. To a casual observer, it would look like the market did well, but the gains may have been shared by only a handful of companies. Still, though, indexes and averages are a good indication of the overall trend of the market.

7.2.3

Principal Theories of Market Behavior

There are two types of Wall Street analyses: technical analysis and fundamental analysis. Both use very different methodologies to try to predict future stock price movements. **Technical analysis** examines the supply and demand for a security based on its historical trading volumes and prices. The technical analyst focuses on the movement of the stock price in relation to other market trends in an effort to predict future share price and stock direction. **Fundamental analysis** examines the financial statements and management of a company. The fundamental analyst focuses on the earnings history and sales prospects for the company in relation to competitors in an effort to predict future share price and stock direction.

7.2.3.1 Technical Analysis

Technical analysis uses basic chart patterns to track stock price movements. (For that reason, technical analysts are called **chartists.**) When technical analysts look at a company, they don't care too much about what the company makes, or the management of the company, or the company's market position, or any market advantage. Instead they focus on stock price movements over a period of time, checking trading volume, index comparisons, short stock positions, and other stock movement patterns. Technical analysts think that past price information (and other factors) will be useful in predicting future prices.

Trend Lines. **Trend lines** are technical chart patterns that track stock price by connecting the peaks or valleys over a period of time to see which general direction (up or down) the stock is moving. A trend line that tracks upwards over time is called an **uptrend.** A trend line that tracks downwards over time is called a **downtrend.**

Saucer. A **saucer** is a technical chart pattern that shows a stock price has declined over a period of time, but has bottomed out and is now in an upward trend. An **inverted saucer** is a technical chart pattern that shows a stock price has risen over a period of time, but has peaked and is now in a downward trend.

Head-and-Shoulders. The **head-and-shoulders** is a technical chart pattern that resembles the outline of the head and shoulders of a person. The chart shows a stock that was in an upward trend, reached a few peaks, but was not able to sustain them and is headed in a downward trend. This is a bearish reversal of fortune. An **inverted head-and-shoulders** is a technical chart pattern that shows a stock that was in a downward trend, reached a few valleys, but was able to rally and is headed in an upwards trend in a bullish reversal of fortune.

Breakout, Resistance, Support. **Resistance level** is a technical term for the highest price at which a stock has peaked on several occasions in previous trades. The theory is that the stock has difficulty rising above the resistance level because there is more supply than demand at that price point. **Support level** is a technical term for the lowest price at which a stock has bottomed out on several occasions in previous trades. The theory is that the stock has difficulty falling below the support level because there is more demand than supply at that price point.

Technical analysts see support levels and resistance levels as important psychological barriers for the stock price. Once the stock has a **breakout** past one of these levels, that is seen as an indication that the stock is going to continue to move in that direction.

Accumulation, Distribution. An **accumulation area** is a technical chart pattern that shows trading in a narrow range for an extended period of time, followed by an expected upward trend as more buying interest is generated following the accumulation period. A **distribution area** is a technical chart pattern that shows trading in a narrow range for an extended period of time, with investors careful not to sell below the range to avoid pushing the price downward.

Moving Averages. **Moving averages** is a means of technical analysis which shows the trend of a stock price by computing the average price of the security over a set interval, and repeating that over time. For example, a six-week moving average would compute the average stock price over the past six weeks; each week a new average would be computed by adding a new week and dropping the earliest week. The trend line would thus show a more smooth average stock price over the period of time, flattening out any wild fluctuations, and giving a better indication of the true price trend.

Trading Channels. **Trading channels** is a technical chart that shows the long-term direction of a security price, by drawing a line connecting the peaks the security has reached and another line connecting the valleys where the security has traded over the same time frame. This is also referred to as a **trading pattern.**

Consolidation, Stabilization. **Consolidation** is a technical chart pattern that shows trading in a narrow range for an extended period of time, with a trend line that

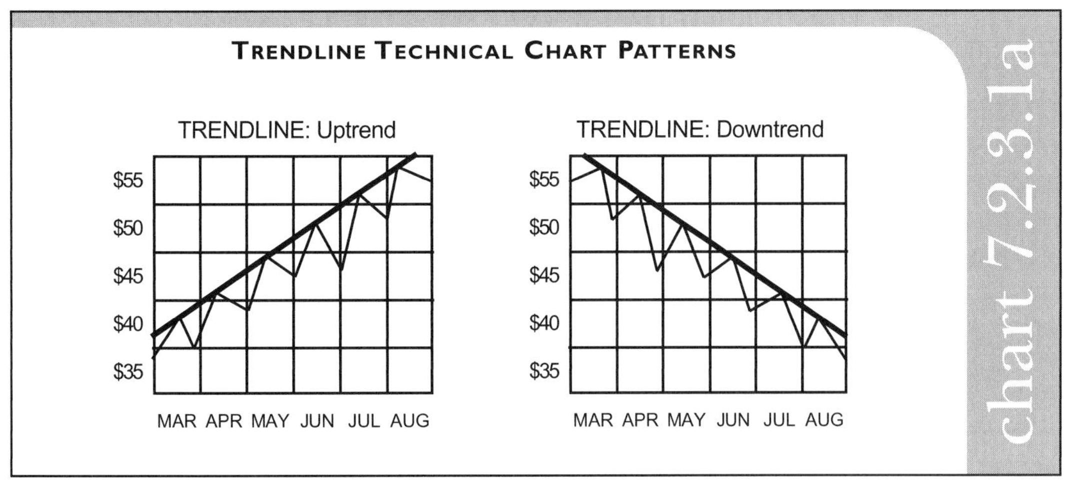

chart 7.2.3.1a

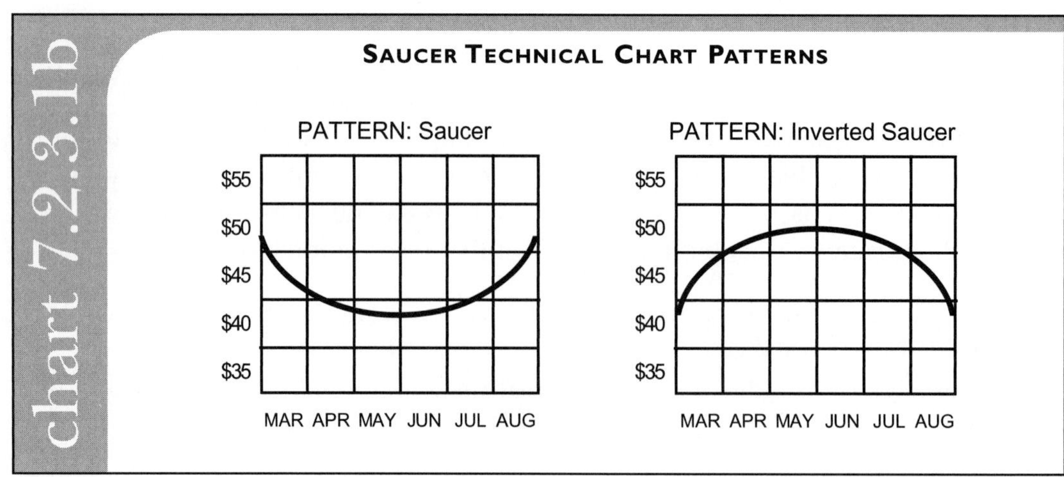
chart 7.2.3.1b
SAUCER TECHNICAL CHART PATTERNS
PATTERN: Saucer
$55
$50
$45
$40
$35
MAR APR MAY JUN JUL AUG
PATTERN: Inverted Saucer
$55
$50
$45
$40
$35
MAR APR MAY JUN JUL AUG

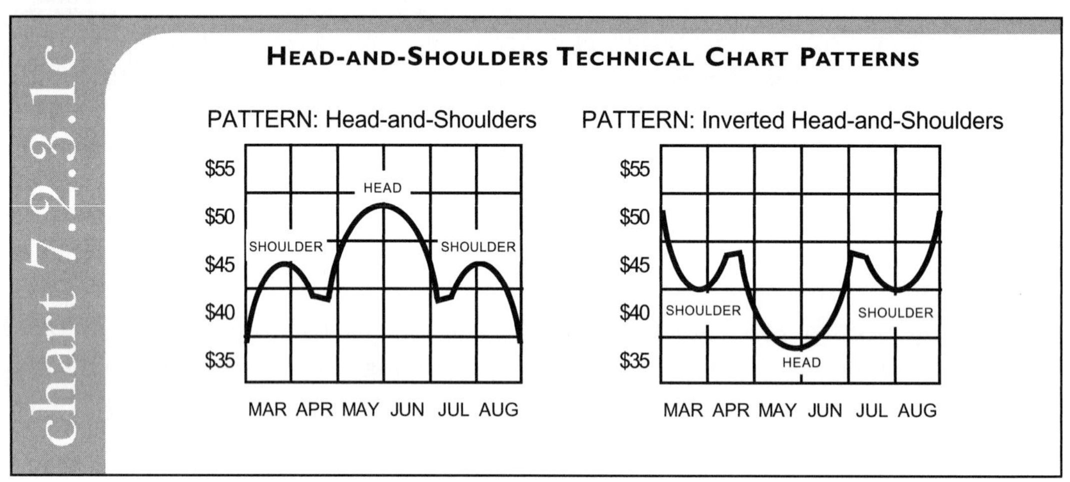
chart 7.2.3.1c
HEAD-AND-SHOULDERS TECHNICAL CHART PATTERNS
PATTERN: Head-and-Shoulders
$55
$50
$45
$40
$35
HEAD
SHOULDER
SHOULDER
MAR APR MAY JUN JUL AUG
PATTERN: Inverted Head-and-Shoulders
$55
$50
$45
$40
$35
SHOULDER
SHOULDER
HEAD
MAR APR MAY JUN JUL AUG

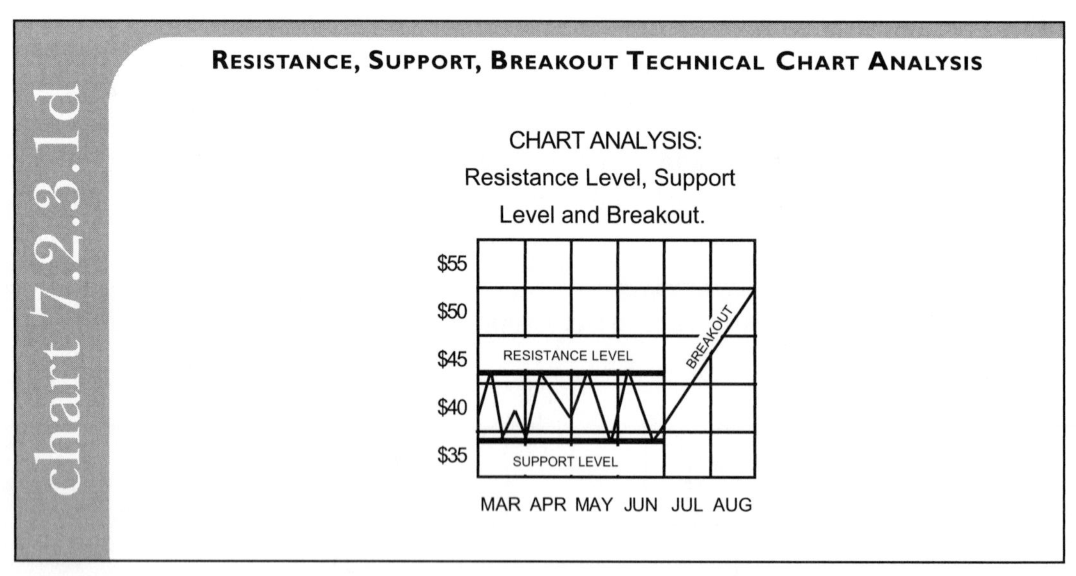
chart 7.2.3.1d
RESISTANCE, SUPPORT, BREAKOUT TECHNICAL CHART ANALYSIS
CHART ANALYSIS:
Resistance Level, Support
Level and Breakout.
$55
$50
$45
$40
$35
RESISTANCE LEVEL
BREAKOUT
SUPPORT LEVEL
MAR APR MAY JUN JUL AUG

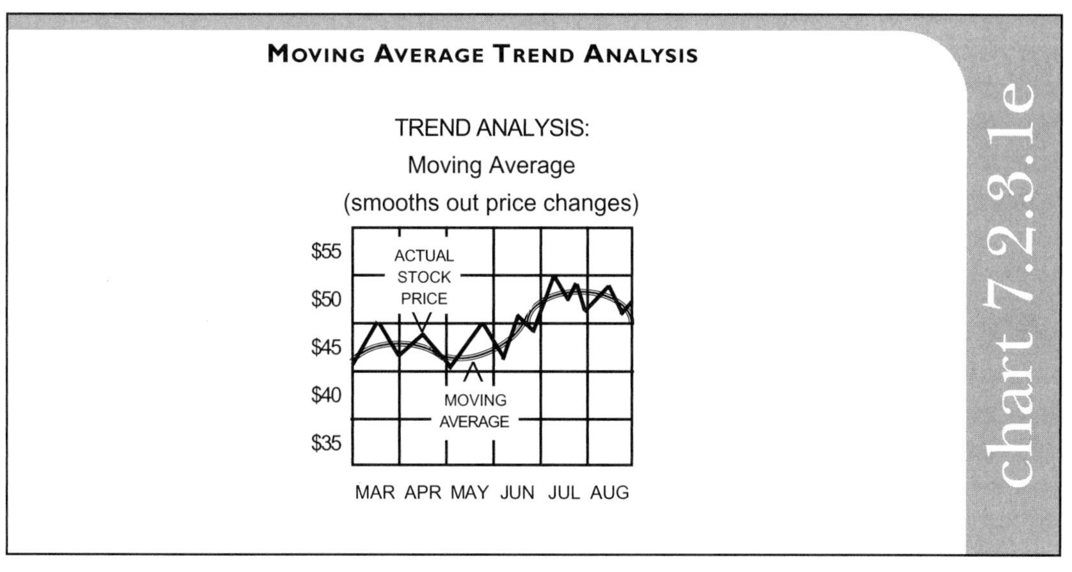

is relatively flat (horizontal), neither showing an uptrend nor a downtrend. Stabilization is a technical chart pattern that shows little price fluctuation.

Overbought, Oversold. **Overbought** is a market condition whereby prices have risen so sharply that some are predicting a price decline **(correction)** in the overall market: because there are few buyers left, a price drop is imminent. **Oversold** is a market condition whereby prices have fallen so sharply that some are predicting a price rise in the overall market: because there are few sellers left, a price rise is imminent.

7.2.3.2 Fundamental Analysis

Fundamental analysis uses various financial statements from the company and other indicators of a company's health as a way of anticipating stock price movements. When technical analysts look at a company, they are very concerned about what the company makes, whether it is in a growing or declining industry, management of the company, the company's market position relative to other companies in the same industry, and any other market advantage the company might have. Fundamental analysts think a company's past, present, and future strengths and weaknesses are useful in predicting future stock prices.

Financial Statements. A company's financial statements include key financial information about the health of the company. Assets, debts, income and profitability can all be ascertained by looking at the various financial documents prepared by the company. The two most common financial statements are the balance sheet and income statement. A **balance sheet** is a financial report that shows the financial status of an entity with regard to **assets, liabilities** and **net worth** as of a particular date. An **income statement** is a financial report that summarizes an entity's income and expenses over a given period of time, and thus is also called a **profit and loss statement.**

Both a balance sheet and income statement are included in a company's annual report, along with any footnotes which tell if certain items were excluded from the figures, or what assumptions or accounting methods were used to arrive at the numbers. These are important for interpreting the numbers presented in a financial statement. There are other key terms and concepts that you need to understand in order to have a clear understanding of a company's financial statements.

- **Assets** are anything of value that are owned or in one's possession. Assets would include such things as cash, stocks, or real estate.
- **Liabilities** are any debt, financial obligation, or claim that another has on the ownership of an asset.
- **Shareholders' equity** is the total value that is left over after adding up all assets and subtracting all liabilities from that total. Also called **net worth.**
- **Depreciation** is amortization of a *man-made* asset so as to allocate its loss in value over its expected useful life (e.g., buildings, vehicles, equipment).
- **Depletion** is amortization of a *natural* asset so as to allocate its loss in value over its expected useful life (e.g., oil, minerals, timber).

Remember, a *balance sheet* covers only a *specific point in time* (usually the last day of the fiscal year), whereas an *income statement* covers a *certain period of time* (usually the preceding 12 months).

Components of a Balance Sheet. The balance sheet can give the fundamental analyst a good indication of the company's financial strength, including its capital structure. A company's capital structure is equal to shareholders' equity plus all long-term debt. Shareholders' equity is money that has come into the company, derived from adding up all stock sold by the company (common stock, preferred stock), paid-in capital, and retained earnings. Liabilities are money owed out by the company, including all long-term debt and current liabilities (accounts payable, notes due, wages outstanding).

Note that current liabilities are *not* considered part of the company's capital. *Watch for this on the Series 7 exam.*

The other important component of a company's balance sheet is the assets. Assets can be current assets (fairly liquid), fixed assets (buildings, equipment), and intangible assets (patents, trademarks, goodwill). Current assets can include such things as cash on deposit, marketable securities, accounts receivable and inventory. When examining how a company values its inventory or calculates depreciation, there are certain terms you need to be aware of.

- **LIFO (last in, first out)** inventory method considers the last goods produced or acquired to be the first items sold. This can make gross sales appear higher, and profit margins lower, because the most recent goods made would have higher raw material costs compared to raw materials bought awhile ago.

- ▷ **FIFO (first in, first out)** inventory method considers the first goods produced or acquired to be the first items sold. This can make gross sales appear lower, but profit margins higher, because older goods would have been made less expensively before inflation raised the cost of raw materials.
- ▷ **Fixed asset depreciation** is the present net depreciated value of assets as stated on the balance sheet. When this depreciation method is used, assets have a depreciation amount deducted from their cost for valuation purposes.
- ▷ **Straight line depreciation** is a depreciation method where the total cost is divided by the estimated useful life of an asset, minus a figure for salvage value. That amount is then deducted from stated income each year.
- ▷ **Modified accelerated cost recovery system (MACRS)** is a modified depreciation model which allows for faster depreciation of some assets, with greater tax benefits early on (e.g., computers, but *not* buildings).

Here are a few other balance sheet-related formulas that could help you answer questions that may appear on the Series 7 exam:

1. **Total Capital = Net Worth + Long Term Debt**
2. **Working Capital = Current Assets – Current Liabilities**
3. **Debt Ratio = Total Debt ÷ Total Capital**
4. **Preferred Ratio = Preferred Stock ÷ Total Capital**
5. $$\textbf{Common Ratio} = \frac{\textbf{common stock + capital excess of par + retained earnings}}{\textbf{Total Capital}}$$

Components of an Income Statement. The income statement can give the fundamental analyst a good picture of the company's ongoing financial health, including its income and expenses. An income statement shows the company's gross sales, cost of goods sold, and other detailed expenses. The last number after all costs, expenses, interest, taxes, and dividends have been paid is **retained earnings** (also called **earned surplus**). If all remaining money were to be paid out in dividends, there would be no retained earnings, but typically companies pay out only a portion of this money as a dividend and keep some retained earnings to reinvest in the company for research and development or other purposes. This figure gets transferred to the balance sheet. (Losses from previous years reduce retained earnings.)

Sometimes the income statement is accompanied by a **cash flow statement,** which breaks down sales and expenses by showing the month in which they were incurred. This can be a useful tool in determining the stability of a company, as well as its future earnings potential. A number that increases over the months can signal growth prospects; a number that fluctuates from month to month can signal a volatile company that is more vulnerable to economic conditions or seasonality.

One of the most important things that can be learned from a company's income statement is its profitability. A company's **profit margin** is equal to its operating income divided by its net sales. It is also important, though, to look at a company's earnings numbers before and after tax and interest figures to get an accurate picture of the company's real earnings. In fact, when people refer to a company's **bottom line,** they are referring to net income after tax. When examining the numbers on the income statement, there are certain terms and calculations you need to be aware of.

chart 7.2.3.2a

Sample Company Balance Sheet

CCC Company
Consolidated Balance Sheet—December 31, 2002

ASSETS	
Current Assets	**Dec. 31, 2002**
Cash and Cash Equivalents	$1,611,000
Short Term Investments	$201,000
Receivables	$1,798,000
Inventories	$1,076,000
Prepaid expenses and other	$1,794,000
Total Current Assets	$6,480,000
Long Term Assets	
Long Term Investments	$8,916,000
Property, Plant, and Equipment	$4,267,000
Goodwill/Intangible Assets	$1,960,000
Total Assets	$21,623,000
LIABILITIES	
Current Liabilities	
Accounts Payable	$4,483,000
Short Term Debt	$5,373,000
Total Current Liabilities	$9,856,000
Long-Term Liabilities	
Long Term Debt	$854,000
Other Liabilities	$902,000
Deferred Long Term Liability Charges	$498,000
Total Liabilities	$12,110,000
Shareholder's Equity	
Common Stock	$867,000
Capital Surplus	$2,584,000
Retained Earnings	$20,773,000
Other Stockholder Equity	($1,551,000)
Treasury Stock	($13,160,000)
Total Equity	$9,513,000
TOTAL ASSETS AND LIABILITIES	$21,623,000

chart 7.2.3.2b

Sample Company Income Statement

CCC Company
Income Statement—January 1 thru December 31, 2002

Total Revenue from Sales	$19,805,000
Cost of Goods Sold	$6,009,000
Gross Profit	$13,796,000
Other Expenses	$9,814,000
Net Operating Profit (Operating Income or EBIT)	$3,982,000
Bond and Interest Expense	$77,000
Equity Income	$184,000
Pre-tax Income (EBT)	$3,819,000
Income Taxes	$1,388,000
Net Income (NIAT or EAT or Bottom Line)	$2,431,000

▷ **EBIT (earnings before interest & taxes)** is a figure that shows the gross sales of the company, minus returns, minus cost of goods sold, minus selling expenses, minus depreciation. EBIT is also referred to as operating income.

▷ **EBT (earnings before taxes)** is the operating income (EBIT), minus the interest paid by the company to service its bonds and other debt. This is an important figure to compare to EBIT to see the debt load of the company.

▷ **EAT (earnings after taxes)** is figured by subtracting the taxes that are owed by the company. EAT is also referred to as **net income** or **net income after tax (NIAT),** and is the figure people commonly call **the bottom line.** It is a true indication of the money that was actually made by the company.

Here are a few other income statement-related formulas that could help you answer questions which may appear on the Series 7 exam:

1. **Operating Income = Gross Sales – Returns – Cost of Goods – Selling Expense – Depreciation**

2. **Net Income = Total Income – Interest – Taxes**

3. **NIACS = Net Income – Preferred Dividend Payout**
   Net Income Available to Common Shareholders—paid as dividend or kept as retained earnings

4. **Cash Flow = Operating Income ÷ Net Sales**
   Net Sales = Gross Sales – Returns

Measurement Tools. There are several tools that can be used to analyze a company's financial statements. Many of these involve the application of formulas to interpret and compare data presented in the balance sheet and/or income statement. Some of these tools are useful for comparing companies against others within their industry; others are good for comparing the rate of return that can be earned from investments in companies across different sectors. All of these can give you an indication of the financial strength of the companies in the past, their health at the present moment, and their prospects for continued growth and stability in the future. (Unfortunately, this does not always guarantee a positive correlation with a company's stock price.)

LIQUIDITY: the ability to convert assets to cash, or have cash readily available as needed. This is an important indication of a company's financial stability. A company's liquidity is its ability to meet ongoing payroll and other obligations. This is what keeps a company solvent and able to weather the inevitable economic downturns on its way to profitability. Some important concepts:

1. Working Capital is amount of cash a company has readily accessible, such as in its bank accounts. Working capital is the money a company lives off of while it is waiting to manufacture more goods, waiting for more sales, or waiting to collect accounts receivable payments from its customers. Companies with low overhead need less working capital than capital intensive ones.

Working Capital = Current Assets – Current Liabilities

2. Current Ratio is an indication of a company's ability to pay its current debts from its current assets. Companies that have steady cash flow or good paying customers or low inventory requirements can safely have a lower ratio.

Current Ratio = Current Assets ÷ Current Liabilities

3. Quick Assets are a measure of a company's liquid assets, excluding inventory. This is a better indication of a company's ability to quickly meet expenses should sales be interrupted or inventory become outdated, because inventory isn't that liquid at full price. This is also called **Acid Test Ratio.**

Current Ratio = (Current Assets – Inventory) ÷ Current Liabilities

RISK OF BANKRUPTCY: the danger that a company will not be able to meet its debt service obligations. This is an important indication of a company's financial strength and credit risk. A company that is leveraged too much may not be able to pay off its debts if rates rise or the economy declines.

1. Bond Ratio is the percentage of a company's debt that is represented by bonds. A ratio above 1:3 (33 percent) is considered high, except for utility companies.

Utility companies are always highly leveraged. (Watch this on Series 7 exam.)

Bond Ratio = Bonds ÷ Capitalization

2. Debt-to-Equity Ratio is a measure of the company's ability to effectively use leverage to enhance the rate of return on shareholder's equity. In a good year, highly leveraged companies have positive earnings to distribute to fewer shareholders (because there is more debt than equity). In a bad year, earnings may not be enough to cover the company's debt service.

Debt-to-Equity Ratio = Long Term Debt ÷ Stockholder's Equity

EFFICIENT USE OF ASSETS: the ability to sell inventory quickly so that the same money can be put to work again building more units. This is an important indication of company productivity and sales force prowess. These numbers can be compared both against the company's prior years and other companies in the same industry to indicate the relative strength of sales.

1. Inventory Turnover Ratio is a number that shows how many times a company's inventory is sold and replaced during the fiscal year. Inventory is a non-producing asset, and makes money for the company only when it is sold. This number must compare favorably with other companies in the same industry, or the company will likely experience a loss of market share.

Inventory Turnover Ratio = Annual Sales ÷ Inventory

2. Cash Flow is an indication of a company's ability to generate revenue to meet its financial obligations. Companies need steady cash flow so that they do not have to dip into reserves to pay debts. Cash flow can be more important than assets, because assets are not always liquid enough to meet expenses.

Note that depreciation is added back to net income. (Watch this on the Series 7 exam.)

Depreciation is added back in, because it is really an accounting entry that does help with taxes, but does not help meet current expenses.

Cash Flow = Net Income + Depreciation

PROFITABILITY: the ability to generate money above costs, expenses, and overhead. This is the most important indicator of all. A company must be able to generate a profit if it is to provide a rate of return on invested capital. There are actually a few ways to measure profit. We will look at pre- and post-tax.

1. Margin-of-Profit Ratio is the relationship of operating income to net sales. This is a measure of the operating efficiency of a company, and is a good means of comparison. The number can be compared with prior years, to see if the number is improving, or against other companies to see if the company is productive and price competitive. (Note this is pre-tax.)

Margin-of-Profit Ratio = Operating Income ÷ Net Sales

2. Net Profit Ratio is an indication of a company's relative profitability. This is another measure of a company's efficiency, productivity, and price strategy. (Note this is after tax.)

Net Profit Ratio = Net Income ÷ Net Sales

ASSET COVERAGE, SAFETY OF INCOME: the extent that a company's (net) assets can cover its debt obligations. These are different measures that can help an investor determine the adequacy of a company's assets and cash flow to cover its debt, and how much protection can be expected in a worst case scenario with the company being liquidated in bankruptcy proceedings.

1. Net Asset Value per Bond is the relationship of net assets in a company and all claims that must be paid prior to bonds, to the bonds themselves. This is a measure of the safety level of the bonds if the company is liquidated.

$$\textbf{Net Asset Value Per Bond} = \frac{\textbf{net asset value} - \textbf{intangible assets} - \textbf{all liabilities with prior claim}}{\textbf{Total Bonds}}$$

2. Bond Interest Coverage is the number of times a company's interest payments could be paid with cash flow. This is used to gauge the safety of the income stream paid to a bondholder (or preferred stockholder).

Bond Interest Coverage = Total Income ÷ Interest Expense

3. Book Value per Share is the ultimate value of a company's securities in the event that a company is liquidated. This figure is used by some analysts to pick undervalued stocks.

$$\textbf{Book Value Per Share} = \frac{\textbf{net tangible assets} - \textbf{all liabilities} + \textbf{par value of preferred stock}}{\textbf{Number of Shares of Outstanding Common Stock}}$$

EARNINGS PER SHARE: the value of a company's profit, figured as if it were distributed to all stockholders. This is actually a common benchmark used when evaluating a company and its profitability. There are several calculations that can be done with earnings to produce meaningful results.

1. Earnings per Share (EPS) is the straight division of profit by the number of common, outstanding shares. Also called **Earnings per Common Share.**

Earnings per Share = Common Earnings ÷ Outstanding Common Shares

2. Fully Diluted Earnings per Share is the EPS recalculated so that it considers what effect it would have if all types of convertible securities were converted and all warrants were exercised. This is a second method of EPS that must be calculated and reported per accounting rule changes in 1998.

Fully Diluted EPS = Common Earnings ÷ All Total Possible Common Shares

3. Price-Earnings Ratio (PE) is an indication of how much an investor is paying for a company's earning power. Companies with high growth potential can generally command higher PE multiples. PEs are a commonly used indicator of company's intrinsic value, and value relative to other companies.

Price-Earnings (PE) Ratio = Market Price per Share ÷ Earnings per Share

4. Dividend Payout Ratio is the actual percentage of earnings paid out in dividends to common stockholders. Generally, mature companies (e.g., blue chips, utilities) have higher payout ratios than high growth companies (which tend to retain earnings to reinvest them in research and development).

Dividend Payout Ratio = Common Dividends ÷ Common Earnings

5. Current Yield is the actual rate of return a stock pays in dividends based on its current market price. This gives investors a gauge of the actual rate of return on their stock investment, just like CY calculations do for bond yields.

Current Yield = Dividends per Share ÷ Market Value per Share

COMPETITIVENESS: a measure of comparative performance. This is one method investors use to measure return on investment. It also provides for a mechanism to compare the performance of a company with previous years, with other companies in same industry, and with companies across sectors.

1. Return on Common Equity is the amount earned on a company's stock over a given period of time (usually for the previous year). This tells investors how efficiently money is being used by a company, and gives a means of comparison against prior years' performance and against competitors.

$$\text{Return on Common Equity} = \frac{\text{Common Stock Earnings}}{\text{retained earnings + paid in surplus + common stock par value}}$$

Now that you have a plethora of formulas to contemplate and remember for the Series 7 exam, let's look at a few examples as to how the test might expect you to apply them. It is unlikely that you will have to do complex calculations (and even if you do, it may be one or two questions at most), but you may run into a simple math problem like example #1, or a theory-based question like example #2.

Example #1

A company had $50 million of net IACS, and paid $20 million out in common dividends. What is the company's dividend payout ratio?

Answer #1

Ratio is 2:5. This is just a matter of recognizing what the question is asking and knowing the NIACS to dividend relationship, rather than math.

Example #2

Suppose a company's interest expense is all from convertible debt. If all holders converted to common stock, what would the effects be?

Answer #2

Of course on the Series 7 exam, you would receive multiple answers to choose from. Instead, here we will mention five possible things that could happen. You won't see explanations on the test, but you need to have this thought process to figure out what the question is trying to ask you. 1) Interest costs would drop to nothing. 2) Pre-tax income would rise because there would be no interest expenses. 3) Taxes would rise because there's no interest being deducted. 4) Net IACS would rise since pre-tax income rose. 5) EPS would drop since earnings are now divided by more common shares.

7.2.4

Factors in Comparison of Mutual Funds

Mutual funds have a number of factors that need to be compared when deciding which one best fits a particular client's financial objectives. The fund's characteristics and philosophy are important, but so are the fees and returns. Let's look at some of the different criteria that can be used when making mutual fund comparisons.

7.2.4.1 Nonstatistical Comparisons

There are a number of nonstatistical means that can be used to compare the advantages and disadvantages of various mutual funds. Even though numbers are not involved, it is important that the comparisons be made as objectively as possible.

Investment Objectives and Policies. When you look at mutual funds, one of the first decisions must be what type of mutual fund is right for the client. There are mutual funds that invest solely in stocks, some that invest only in bonds, and others use a balanced approach to investing. Even within these broad categories, there are different choices. Stock funds can be growth funds, income funds, hybrid funds, or specialized funds. Bond funds can be U.S. government bonds, municipal bonds, corporate bonds, or preferred stock. Within each of those groups, the funds can emphasize growth, income, safety, or any of these in varying combinations. Investors should read the fund's prospectus carefully to determine the fund's objectives, then look at the fund's portfolio to see if the objectives are being met.

Minimum Purchase Amounts. This is an important consideration for many investors. Some mutual funds have a minimum amount that must be invested with each purchase; others allow investors to contribute any amount they want after making the initial purchase.

Conversion Privileges and Reinvestment Costs. Some investment companies allow customers to combine mutual fund purchases across the same family of funds to reach breakpoints and receive sales charge discounts; others do not. Some allow exchanges without sales charges as long as the investor is converting the mutual fund to another in the same family of funds; others do not. And some allow dividends and other payments to be reinvested without sales charges; others do not. All of these possibilities must be investigated before a mutual fund is purchased.

Various Sales Charge Methods. Mutual fund sales charges are called **loads.** Sales charges can be collected as a **front-end load,** where a commission is paid when the mutual fund is purchased; or as a **back-end load,** where a commission is paid when the fund is sold. Back-end loads are sometimes referred to as **contingent deferred**

sales loads (CDSL) when the percentage of load decreases the longer the fund is held, and usually reaches 0 percent after about the fifth year. A third fee option is a small **level load** charged yearly for the life of the fund, similar to the 12b-1 fee of up to 1 percent charged by **no-load** funds for marketing expenses.

Withdrawal Options. Of course, mutual fund shares can be redeemed for cash in a lump sum withdrawal, but some funds also offer several systematic withdrawal plans for investors whose shares are worth a certain minimum amount of money. Withdrawal plans may be fixed dollar amount (paid monthly or quarterly), fixed percentage (where a fixed number or certain percentage of shares are redeemed on a regular schedule), or fixed time (where the fund's value is divided by a chosen period of time, then redeemed on that schedule in even payments). Investors need to check if the choice they desire is offered by a fund.

Letter of Intent (LOI). Certainly another consideration in comparing mutual funds is whether or not the fund will allow use of a LOI. Some will, some won't. Remember, a letter of intent is a commitment by an investor to invest a certain amount of money within 13 months, in exchange for being entitled to receive breakpoint sales charge rates now. The letter may be back-dated up to 90 days to encompass previous investments by that person. Funds are not required to offer this to clients, but many do because it encourages more investment.

Right of Accumulation (ROA). Another optional mutual fund feature, which investors may find beneficial, is ROA. Remember, rights of accumulation are breakpoint sales offered at a future time once the total amount of money invested has reached the breakpoint. From then on, all newly invested money qualifies for the reduced sales charges. Rights of accumulation do not count the initial investment, and aren't retroactive, but they do accumulate indefinitely until the goal is reached. Again, funds aren't required to do this, so investors should seek this if it's important.

Diversified Portfolio. A diversified fund portfolio can emphasize growth, income, safety, or any of these in combination. The investor or RR needs to look at the actual investments that the fund is holding to see if the fund's portfolio objectives are being met. For an equity fund, that involves looking to see in which industry sectors the fund has invested, as well as ensuring that the fund has invested in a variety of companies and industries. For a bond fund, that involves looking at the maturity years of its holdings and seeing if it holds any tax-exempt bonds, as well as ensuring that the fund holds different types of bonds from different geographic areas.

Eligibility for "Conduit Theory." Conduit Theory allows for income to be passed through to fund holders so that the investment company does not also get taxed on the investment income. If a mutual fund does not distribute at least 90 percent of net investment income to fund holders, the mutual fund must pay taxes on 100 percent of the net investment. This extra level of taxation can take its toll on the assets of the fund, so investors and RRs should be sure to investigate the eligibility of any fund.

No-Load Features. As stated before, some mutual funds do not have a sales charge when investors put money in. Other funds have a sales charge for the initial investment, but do not charge for reinvestment of dividends or payouts. And some funds have a sales charge any time additional money is used to buy more shares, regardless of the source. This is an important point of comparison with mutual funds, as sales charges can quickly eat into any returns that the fund may achieve.

Early Termination Charges. Early termination charges is an area that must be thoroughly investigated. Early termination charges can add up, especially with back-end load funds, where the fee is inversely proportional to how long the investor has owned the fund. Even some no load funds charge a redemption fee, early or otherwise. Other funds, though, do allow exchanges within the same family of funds at any time with no sales charges or penalty fees.

7.2.4.2 Statistical Comparisons

The bottom line with any investment is making money, so a comparison of mutual funds must also include a comparison of fees, sales charges, and expense ratios in order to make an informed choice. Other objective numbers can be used to get a better picture of which mutual fund is right for a client.

Sales Charges. Mutual fund sales charges are called **loads.** These loads are the cost of buying a fund (as opposed to the expense ratio which is the fees and other total costs of owning a fund). Sales charges can be computed one of several ways.

Front-end loads are commissions paid when the mutual fund is purchased. These can range up to an average of 5 percent, and come off the top of the investor's investment dollars. Spending $10,000 on a mutual fund with a 5 percent front-end load, means that the investor is really buying only $9,500 worth of mutual fund shares. (Mutual funds with front-end loads are often referred to as **Class A shares.**)

Back-end loads are commissions paid when the fund is sold. The lure of a back-end load is that the entire investment amount goes to buy mutual fund shares. Of course this means that the load percentage is taken off of a larger amount if the mutual fund grows while the investor owns it. One feature of back-end loads, though, is that the percentage of load often decreases the longer the fund is held, and usually reaches 0 percent after about the fifth year. We will compare load charges over time shortly. (Back-end loads are sometimes called **contingent deferred sales loads (CDSL),** and mutual funds with back-end loads are often referred to as **Class B shares.**)

Level loads are small fees charged yearly for the life of the fund, similar to the 12b-1 fee of up to 1 percent charged by funds (including **no-load** funds) for marketing expenses. If a fund is held for a long period of time, a level load can be a significant cost concern. (Mutual funds with level loads are often referred to as **Class C shares.**)

Distribution Fees. The **12b-1 distribution fee** is a marketing fee that can be charged by load funds and no-load funds. This fee can range from 0.25 percent – 1.0 percent of a fund's assets. The fee really does little to enhance the fund, other than advertising to attract new investors, so this is one area that investors and RRs need to compare. It is one of the components of a fund's expense ratio, which we will discuss shortly.

Performance Over Time. A mutual fund's return is the total return of the fund minus any fees paid. From an investment standpoint, total return should be one of the first considerations. Growth and income are also important points of comparison among mutual funds, but the total return that the fund allows the investor to keep is the ultimate measure of success. If fees are high, then the performance of the fund (growth and/or income) needs to be that much better to compensate.

Expense Ratio. The **expense ratio** is the amount of expenses that a fund charges its fund holders each year for running the fund. The expense ratio is the cost of owning a fund (as opposed to the sales charge which is the cost of buying a fund). The expense ratio is charged as a percentage of the fund's assets.

The expense ratio includes all the various costs and expenses (investment advisory fee, administrative costs, 12b-1 distribution fees, and other operating expenses) into one number. A typical expense ratio is about 1.5 percent for an actively managed mutual fund. This amount is paid regardless of the fund's performance. With indexed funds and other funds that are not actively managed, the expense ratio is typically around 0.25 percent. Expense ratios of mutual funds can be found on the Internet and in financial sections of many newspapers.

Comparison of Loads Over Time. The way mutual fund loads are computed and collected can have a serious impact on the total return that the investor gets to keep from a mutual fund investment. One factor that must be considered is how long the client anticipates keeping the fund. Let's look at a sales charge comparison.

As you can see in the comparison chart, our sample 1.5 percent front-end sales charge seems much lower than the 5 percent back-end charge. But when total cumulative charges are compared, it is a better deal only if the fund is held for fewer than 5 years.

Portfolio Turnover. Mutual funds buy and sell their holdings at varying paces. Turnover is expressed as a percentage of a fund's portfolio that's sold during the year.

Turnover Rate = Gross Proceeds From Sales ÷ Total Assets

Average turnover rate for managed mutual funds is about 85 percent per year. Indexed and non-actively managed funds are significantly less. There are two reasons why turnover is important from an investor's standpoint. First, more turnover of

chart 7.2.4.2a

FRONT-END SALES CHARGES

Year	Annual 12b-1	Cumulative Charge 12b-1	Entrance Fee	Cumulative Sales Charge
1	1%	1%	1.5%	2.5%
2	1	2	1.5	3.5
3	1	3	1.5	4.5
4	1	4	1.5	5.5
5	1	5	1.5	6.5
6	1	6	1.5	7.5
7	1	7	1.5	8.5
8	1	8	1.5	9.5
9	1	9	1.5	10.5
10	1	10	1.5	11.5

Year	Annual 12b-1	Cumulative Charge 12b-1	Exit Fee	Cumulative Sales Charge
1	1%	1%	5%	6%
2	1	2	4	6
3	1	3	3	6
4	1	4	2	6
5	1	5	1	6
6	1	6	0	6
7	1	7	0	7
8	1	8	0	8
9	1	9	0	9
10	1	10	0	10

Back-End Sales Charges — chart 7.2.4.2b

funds means the fund is paying more in sales commissions that can eat into a fund's assets. And second, the sale of a fund's holdings generates a taxable event—and it's a short term capital gain if the stock was held for fewer than 12 months. Investors should investigate the historical turnover of a fund as a gauge of its likely future turnover.

7.2.5

Analysis of Municipal Securities

Although there are many types of municipal bonds, the two that you will likely see the most questions about on the Series 7 exam are general obligation bonds (GO) and revenue bonds. Let's look at some of the different characteristics of these two types of municipal bonds, and some different ways to analyze them.

7.2.5.1 Analysis of General Obligation Bonds

General obligation bonds are bonds paid for out of the general revenue of the municipality, which may also use additional tax revenues or borrow funds to cover any shortfall. GO bonds are backed by the full faith and credit of the issuer, and GO bonds offer a high level of safety to investors because they are backed by the taxing authority of the issuer. When analyzing GO bonds, there are several things that need to be considered.

Characteristics of the Issuer. This has to do with the economic and social aspects of the issuer in helping to determine ability to repay in a timely manner.

- **tax base:** Does issuer have authority to receive taxes from multiple sources?—income tax, property *(ad valorem)* tax, sales tax, user fees—
- **diverse economy:** Is issuer's economy diverse enough to sustain downturn?
- **budgetary practices:** Is issuer fiscally responsible or does it run deficits?
- **current financial condition:** Does issuer have lots of outstanding debt?

- ▷ **unfunded liabilities:** Does issuer have hidden expenses that must be paid?
- ▷ **population trends:** Is issuer experiencing growth or decline in tax base?
- ▷ **tax collection record:** Does issuer have high delinquency or can it collect?
- ▷ **history of debt repayment:** Has issuer paid debts on time in the past?

Nature of Issuer's Debt. In assessing a bond offering, it is important to examine issuer's debt plans for repaying the current debt along with its other obligations.

- ▷ **debt trends:** Does issuer have habit of taking on too much debt? Is debt rising?
- ▷ **debt service schedule:** Is new debt schedule realistic, given its other debts?
- ▷ **contemplated financing:** Is issuer considering other concurrent financing or will issuer need to issue more debt in the near future, which could negatively impact municipality's credit rating on this present issue?
- ▷ **relation of debt to life of improvement:** Although this is more a consideration with revenue bonds, will issuer need to issue new debt to repair or replace the current item before this present issue is paid in full?

Factors Affecting Issuer's Ability to Pay. The tax limitations of the issuer and tax burden of citizens are important considerations in deciding if issuer can pay on time.

- ▷ **tax limitations:** Is voter approval required? Are there legal limits on taxes?
- ▷ **priority of claim:** Is issuer obligated to pay other debts ahead of this one?
- ▷ **non-tax revenues:** Are other revenue sources able to contribute to pay debt?
- ▷ **tax rates, trends, comparisons:** Are tax rates already high in the municipality compared with other areas, and could this cause people to move?
- ▷ **tax collection record:** Does issuer have good history of tax collection?
- ▷ **trends in assessed value:** Is it experiencing growth or decline?
- ▷ **overlapping debt:** Does coterminous debt exist? Will it overburden citizens?

Municipal Debt Ratios. When analyzing a municipal bond issue, it is important to consider it in light of the municipality's total outstanding debt load.

- ▷ **net debt to assessed valuation:** This calculation has to do with the total debt of a municipality compared to the assessed property values within its boundaries. This is useful when evaluating an issue backed with *ad valorem* (property) taxes. But when comparing debt from two different municipalities, this is not very useful because the basis for valuation each uses is likely different.
- ▷ **net debt to estimated valuation:** This calculation is also useful for issues backed by property taxes, but uses estimated values instead of assessed values.
- ▷ **net debt per capita:** This is useful when comparing bonds issued by different municipalities. This formula helps investors measure tax burden, see if it has improved from prior years, and gauge issuer's fiscal responsibility based on whether number is rising or falling. Also, larger cities can afford more debt.

Debt per Capita = Net Total Debt ÷ Population

Note: When calculating municipality debt, there's Total Debt and Net Total Debt. The key is that Net Total Debt does not include any revenue bond debt because it is self-supporting, nor does it include debts that will be paid by a sinking fund.

7.2.5.2 Analysis of Revenue Bonds

Revenue bonds are bonds paid for from the the income (revenue) generated by a specific project. These are usually used for public works projects, such as roads or water treatment plants. The revenue bonds are backed by fees from the project, not taxes, so they are less secure than GO bonds. Because revenue bonds are supposed to be self-supporting, they require more analysis, but not about taxes or per capita debt. Instead, sources of revenue, security of issue, flow of funds, and earnings coverage are all analyzed in the feasibility study.

Feasibility Study. This is conducted to demonstrate to investors the economic soundness of the proposed bond project. It is not any kind of guarantee with regard to principal or interest payments, but rather gives investors information to make an informed decision. It will generally include engineering reports with the financials.

▷ **financially:** Can the debt service on the project be supported from the projected revenue stream estimates? Are estimates realistic?

▷ **physically:** Can the project be built with the amount of funds the bond issue is projected to generate? What's the chance of cost overruns?

Sources of Revenue. This considers the source, strength, and stability of the source of revenue, and considers how discretionary the project usage is (toll road vs. stadium).

▷ **user charges:** Are they mandatory? Are there ready substitutes for users?

▷ **concessions, fees:** How elastic is demand for these items?

▷ **special taxes:** Are special taxes and assessments going to be enacted?

▷ **rental, lease payments:** Is there a stable base of potential tenants or users?

▷ **legislative appropriation:** Any chance it can become a moral obligation bond?

Security. This looks at any additional assurance offered by the issuing municipality. Often, an indenture agreement is a market condition for acceptance of the bonds, so one is offered with several covenants, documents, repayment provisions, etc.

▷ **protective covenants of bond indenture:**

1. rate covenant—user fees will be adjusted to cover costs plus debt service
2. insurance covenant—facility will remain insured until debt is paid
3. maintenance—facility will be maintained during debt period

▷ **financial report, audit:** economic justification for facility, funding adequate

▷ **restriction on issuing additional bonds:** new bonds only after a percentage of the debt is paid down

1. open-end indenture—new bonds can at most be equal to this issue
2. closed-end indenture—no new bonds unless this issue takes priority

Flow of Funds. This is a statement that details the order in which revenues will be used. This analysis also considers the source, strength, and stability of the source of revenue, and considers how discretionary the project usage is.

▷ **application of revenue:**

1. net revenue pledge—after operating expenses and maintenance costs are paid, a sinking fund will be established

2. gross revenue pledge—debt service on bonds is paid as first priority

▷ **debt service coverage:** sinking fund or reserve fund may be established

Earnings Coverage. Ratio that shows how many times the project's revenues can meet annual debt service costs (2:1 is adequate for munis, but not for corporates).

chart 7.2.5

COMPARISON OF GO BONDS AND REVENUE BONDS
(These may be on Series 7 exam.)

Comparison Points	GO Bonds	Revenue Bonds
Backed By:	full faith & credit of issuer	trust indenture (convenants)
Underwriting Bid:	competitive bid	negotiated bid
How Debt is Repaid:	issuer's taxing authority	revenue from project
Source of Authority:	often needs voter approval	feasibility study
Overcoming Obstacles:	legal debt limits	flow of funds, sinking fund
Ratios Analyzed:	all ratios but debt service	only debt service-to-earnings
Extra Protection:	double barreled	moral obligation of state

7.2.5.3 Sources of Credit Information

There are multiple sources of information that investors and RRs can turn to when researching credit of bond issuers.

Issuer. Most municipal bond issuers put out a debt statement with GO bonds. The debt statement will include information on the various tax ratios we discussed, and include property valuations, population figures, and total debt calculations.

Advisory Councils. There are for-profit and nonprofit advisory councils that produce information on municipal bond issues.

State Services. Some states provide public information with regard to the credit rating, payment history, and tax records and projections of municipalities.

Commercial Research Services. Several commercial research services track municipal bonds, including Moody's, S&P and other bond credit rating services. They provide fee-based research reports. (We will discuss these in the next few sections.)

Industry, General Publications. Financial magazines and newspapers provide bond credit information, as do several special industry publications, such as *The Blue List, The Bond Buyer* and computer-based Munifacts. (Details in next section.)

7.2.5.4 Rating Services

Municipal bond credit rating can be obtained from several different ratings services. The two you should be familiar with from our corporate discussion are Moody's and Standard & Poor's. Moody's top four bond ratings are "Aaa," "Aa," "A," and "Baa." S&P's top four bond ratings are "AAA," "AA," "A," and "BBB." Moody's may also assign a "1," "2," or "3" to modify a rating, such as "Baa3" to indicate the lowest of that group. S&P uses "+" or "–" to modify some ratings. Moody's also rates short-term municipal notes, with ratings of MIG-1 thru MIG-4 being investment grade. Municipal bond ratings signify the likelihood an issuer will default on the debt. The higher the bond rating, the more marketable the bond is. Some bonds are not rated because the size of the issue is too small.

7.2.5.5 Credit Enhancements

Several private companies offer insurance to investors that guarantees the principal and interest payments on municipal bonds. The insurance can be purchased by the investor, or purchased by a municipality that wants to offer a lower coupon rate. Two of the largest municipal bond insurers are Municipal Bond Investors Assurance (MBIA) and AMBAC Indemnity. When either of these insure an issue against default, the bonds become "AAA" rated.

7.3 Sources of Price and Securities Information

There are a number of sources available to investors, RRs, and others that can provide price and securities information. Some of the sources are able to provide up to the minute information; others present quotes at the end of the day. In addition to traditional sources, such as newspapers, each type of security has its own sources that provide specialized information. Let's look at a few that you should be familiar with for the Series 7 exam, and for your career as an RR.

7.3.1 Exchange-Traded Equities

The primary exchange market consists of NYSE and other regional exchanges. Final prices of exchange-traded equities are listed daily in various newspapers. But, for the up-to-the-minute quotes needed to do trades, other sources must be used. When these stocks trade in the OTC market, broker-dealers and RRs rely on a system called consolidated trading that relies on the use of **Consolidated Tapes.**

CONSOLIDATED TAPES. This is an electronic service providing quotes on NYSE, Amex and some regional stock exchange issues. This service allows these stocks to be traded in the OTC market as long as trades are reported within 90 seconds of execution. Reading the ticker tape-like readout or terminal display is not difficult, and may appear in a question or two on the Series 7 exam. Here's a sample tape:

IBM	Dsny	GE	IBM	WX
61¾	4s27½	49.50	2s62¼.½	$7^{S}_{S}52$

Reading the Tape. There are a few conventions used on the tape:

1. Prices reported are for round lots of 100 shares when no notation is made; # tells you to multiply the number times 100 shares, so **Dsny 4s27½** is 400 shares; $\#^{S}_{S}$ is fewer than 100 shares, so multiply times 10, thus **WX $7^{S}_{S}52$** is 70 shares; if more than 10,000 shares are traded, then the actual number is shown.
2. Consecutive trades for the same security are separated by a "."—this is *not* a decimal point. (Even though real trades are now in decimals, some questions on the Series 7 exam still use fractions. Your course instructor will update you as the Series 7 exam moves more of its questions to reflect decimal trades.)

   Consecutive trades are read as follows: **GE 49.50** is 100 shares of GE traded at 49, followed by a consecutive trade of 100 shares of GE traded at 50; **IBM 2s62¼.½** is 200 shares of IBM traded for 62¼, then 100 shares for 62½.
3. There are several abbreviations used on the tape. Some of these represent the exchange where a stock trade took place; others indicate omitted information or messages to traders. On the Series 7 exam, the only one you need to concern yourself with is SLD. **SLD** means "Sale Delay." This means that the trade did not appear within the 90-second requirement or was reported out of sequence.

If SLD appears after a price, it cannot count as a "plus tick" or "zero-plus tick," so **SLD does not allow a short sale to occur,** regardless of the trading price.

7.3.2

OTC-Traded Equities

The Over-the-Counter (OTC) market consists of broker-dealers trading in unlisted securities. Final prices for OTC-traded equities are also listed daily in various newspapers. For trading information, though, the OTC market relies on a number of different systems, depending on the trading volumes of the securities.

NASDAQ NATIONAL MARKET ISSUES. Stock issues that are actively traded OTC issues on NASDAQ are listed on this electronic system that quotes up-to-the-minute prices as trades occur. These are generally large, easily identifiable stocks.

OTC BULLETIN BOARD. This is an electronic listing of bid and ask quotes for OTC stocks not meeting the minimum net worth (or other) requirements of NASDAQ. This is a step up from the pink sheets, where pricing info is updated only once daily.

NASDAQ SYSTEM. NASD Automated Quotations Service (NASDAQ) links broker-dealers by telephone and computer to facilitate trades. The service has three levels:

> **Level 1:** This shows *only* the highest bid price and lowest ask price (the **inside quote**) for any NASDAQ stock that has at least two active market makers. These quotes, though, aren't firm until confirmed by another broker-dealer. RRs have access to this level, but cannot use it to guarantee any prices.
>
> **Level 2:** This provides quotes from *multiple market makers,* showing the current firm quote (good for a minimum of 100 shares) and the quote size available. This level of access is primarily for institutional investors.
>
> **Level 3:** This has the same info as levels 1 & 2, but also lets market makers *update or change their stock quotes*. This level is for market makers only.

Note: NASDAQ system provides a stock's trading volume only at the end of the day.

PINK SHEETS. This is the name of the daily publication of the National Quotation Bureau showing wholesale interdealer listing bid and ask prices of OTC **stocks** not listed on the NASDAQ. The pink sheets get their name from the color of paper they are printed on. There are three things you should know about the pink sheets:

1. They are interdealer quotes only, and not for public consumption.
2. Stocks are usually at the low end of price scale (under $5 = **penny stocks**).
3. Pink sheets are never firm quotes, because they may not be two-sided.

Of course, dealers must be ready to quote a firm price when called upon to do so, but if the Series 7 exam asks about calculating a bid or ask, the correct answer probably is that you can't because they're not a firm quote.

7.3.3

Corporate Bonds

Many corporate bonds are traded in the OTC market. For the public, final prices for OTC-traded bonds are listed daily in various newspapers. Broker-dealers and RRs rely on the various computers linking dealers, and also on the **yellow sheets.**

YELLOW SHEETS. This is the name of the daily publication of the National Quotation Bureau showing wholesale interdealer listing bid and ask prices of OTC **bonds** not listed on NASDAQ. Yellow sheets are also named for their color of paper.

7.3.4

Municipal Securities

Although the secondary market for municipal bonds is not a formal market like the NYSE, munis are still traded on a regular basis both in auction markets and in the

OTC market. OTC is by far the more common of the two markets for muni trades. For the public, bond prices for major issues can be found in some newspapers, but specialized sources are best (see below). Broker-dealers and RRs rely on a number of industry publications and services for the trading and pricing info they need.

THE BLUE LIST. This is a daily publication (put out by an S&P subsidiary) that lists comprehensive price, yield, volume, and other information about bonds offered for sale, including many municipal bond issues. Information is also available online at bluelist.com. The **Blue List Ticker** is the computerized subscription service that provides up-to-the-minute additions and deletions of bond offerings.

THE BOND BUYER. This daily publication has important indexes, statistics, and other information used by broker-dealers and others who trade in the bond market. *The Bond Buyer* publication includes the visible supply, computes many indexes (all described in the next section), and provides Bond Buyer new issue worksheets to aid in comparisons and bond calculations. **Munifacts** is the computerized subscription service offered by *The Bond Buyer* that provides municipal bond information.

MOODY'S BOND SURVEY. This is the weekly newsletter that updates the bond ratings and other information listed in *Moody's Bond Record.* The publication also offers more detailed information on certain select municipal bond issues.

DEALER OFFERING SHEET, BROKER'S BROKER SYSTEM. Dealer **offering sheets** are weekly inventories of municipal bonds that are held by individual dealers and offered for sale. (Contain investor names, type of bond, bond yield, price.) Computer systems allow for direct communication among muni bond brokers.

PUBLIC NEWSPAPERS, PUBLICATIONS. Generally, newspapers do not carry complete information on municipal bonds, current prices, and trading data. Instead, investors must turn to bond publications. *Moody's Municipal & Government Manual* is an annual publication with complete information on bond issuance, pricing, and trading, organized by state, city, town, etc. The book includes all bond issues, and offers additional information, such as state tax revenues and census figures. A bimonthly update newsletter is available, listing new or changed issues and call notices.

7.3.5

Listed Options

Listed options are traded in the OTC market. For the public, prices for OTC-traded options are listed daily in certain newspapers. Broker-dealers and RRs rely on the various computers linking dealers, subscription services, and publications.

OPRA. **O**ptions **P**rice **R**eporting **A**uthority is a computer-based subscription service that gives inside quotes (highest bid, lowest ask price) and last sale data for options.

FINANCIAL NEWSPAPERS. *The Wall Street Journal* and *New York Times* are just two of the newspapers that publish prices for options in their financial sections for a wide range of underlying options. If more information is needed, implied volatility can be calculated using the option market price, terms, underlying price and interest rate.

7.4 Sources of Investment Research Information

Investment research is plentiful, but it is the source that makes it valuable. In addition to discussing research from securities firms and investment publications, we'll also briefly mention research information sources for stocks or municipal bonds.

7.4.1 Research Departments of Securities Firms

When we talk about "broker-dealers," one of the implications of that term is that a securities firm has investment advisors and research departments. While it can be helpful for investors to receive information that is already assembled, investors should still seek information on their own to corroborate what they are being told. Furthermore, investors should inquire how research results and conclusions were reached, and find out what is done (if anything) at the firm to maintain the research department's independence from undue influence. Investors should also inquire how the broker-dealer is trading their accounts given the research results.

7.4.2 Market Indexes

Market indexes are useful as a standard for comparing the performance of individual stocks, or the market as a whole. When compiling investment research and basing any conclusions on the various market indexes, it is helpful to know a little about the index and how it is calculated.

DJIA. Dow Jones Industrial Average is a price-based average of 30 industrial stocks that trade on the NYSE. Dow Jones also has a number of other averages that track the transportation sector, utility concerns, and others. The Dow Jones Composite Index combines the DJIA, Dow Jones Transportation Average (DJTA), and Dow Jones Utility Average (DJUA) into a single number. **Dow Theory** says that the averages in these other sectors must confirm the movement of the DJIA to signal a true change in market direction.

NYSE COMPOSITE. The NYSE Composite measures all common stocks listed on the New York Stock Exchange, including four subindexes (Industrials, Transportation, Utilities, Finance). The index tracks the change in market value of NYSE stocks, adjusted to reduce the effects of market capitalization changes, new listings and de-listings. Market value for each stock is figured by multiplying its per share price times the number of shares listed.

WILSHIRE 5000. This index measures the performance of all U.S.-based exchange-traded stock companies. Bulletin board traded companies are excluded because there is no readily available price data. The index is adjusted on a regular basis, with over 6,500 capitalization-weighted stock returns.

S&P 500. Stocks are chosen to achieve a distribution by broad industry groupings, roughly relative to the composition of the total NYSE market. Each stock is thought to be representative of its industry group, with price movements that are fairly responsive to changes in that sector. Total market capitalization of the stock and its trading volume are important considerations, as stocks in the index are weighted.

7.4.3

Investment Advisory Services

Various investment advisory services also stand ready to provide investment research information for a fee. Some specialize in certain investment areas, while others offer broad research capabilities. Some also offer additional services, such as targeted research information, custom analysis, publications, and credit ratings.

MOODY'S. Moody's Investors Service is a rating service providing information on bond issues, commercial paper, preferred stock, and municipal short-term notes. It publishes several bond and stock books that provide thorough analyses of the issuers.

STANDARD & POOR'S. S&P provides numerous investment-related services including credit ratings, debt ratings, indexes, and research information.

VALUE LINE. Value Line Investment Survey (VL) is a weekly subscription advisory service that ranks hundreds of investment debt securities for safety of principal and timeliness of repayment. It estimates which will have the best or worst price performance in the coming year, and assigns each corporate debt issuer a risk rating based on stock price movements compared to market averages. Other information on the companies is also available through various research reports and analyses.

OTHERS. There are many other sources of investment research information. The goal is to find a reliable, objective source that documents its research findings.

Municipal Market Indicators

Municipal bond market indicators are important in helping dealers spot market trends, gauge future supply and demand, and measure bond risk at a given yield. There are a number of municipal bond research information providers. Some of the best known indexes are computed and published by *The Bond Buyer.*

Note that on the Series 7 exam, you may be asked the source of some of these indexes. With the exception of *The Blue List* Total, the rest of these indexes come from *The Bond Buyer.*

THE BLUE LIST TOTAL. This represents the total par value of all municipal securities offered for sale in *The Blue List.* This measures the supply of municipal bonds available for purchase (indicates status of secondary market for muni bonds).

PLACEMENT RATIO INDEXES. This shows the proportion of all bonds over $1 million (competitive and negotiated) that were distributed during the past week. This is published in *The Bond Buyer.*

TWENTY BOND GO INDEX. This shows the yield on a GO bond with a 20-year maturity, and is calculated using bonds from 20 actual issuers that have bond ratings in the middle of Moody's top four credit ratings. This is published in *The Bond Buyer.*

ELEVEN BOND GO INDEX. This uses 11 of the 20 issuers from the 20-Bond Index with an average rating of Aa from Moody's. This is published in *The Bond Buyer.*

THIRTY-YEAR REVENUE INDEX. This shows the yield of a 30-year revenue bond based on a variety of bonds from 25 issuers. This is published in *The Bond Buyer.*

THE VISIBLE SUPPLY. This shows all bonds which are scheduled to be offered within a 30-day period. This is published in *The Bond Buyer.*

7.X Summary

7.1 Client's investment profile must constantly be examined and updated. "Know your customer" is an ongoing process, not an event.

7.1.1 Client's family situation is most likely to change, necessitating a change in investment strategy. As client gains investing experience, can try new things.

7.1.2 Portfolio management is more subjective. Aggressive investments: growth companies with more volatile stock prices, few bonds, use some leverage. Defensive investments: utilities, blue chip, high grade debt. Constant dollar has fixed dollar amount in stocks, bonds. Constant ratio uses percentages.

7.1.3 Portfolio theory uses relationship between asset classes rather than worry about specific stocks held. Portfolio diversification (assets have return part and risk part), capital asset pricing (put all assets on same level without risk part), asset allocation (determine allocation of stocks and bonds). Alpha gauges performance apart from risk; beta measures against market.

7.2 Securities analysis uses research to indicate future value, market direction.

7.2.1 Equities market analysis looks at market sentiment (overall market trend: bullish or bearish); advance-decline ratio (more advancers = bullish); put-call ratio (more calls = bullish, more puts = bearish); momentum (activity swings); available funds (money on sidelines is bearish, but bull market may start when money gets invested); trading volume (high volume confirms trend).

7.2.2 Indexes can track stocks. Dow Jones Industrial Average (DJIA): 30 price averaged stocks. Dow Theory says sector indexes must confirm changes in DJIA direction. S&P 500: 500 capitalization weighted stocks.

7.2.3 Technical analysis: uses chart patterns to track stock price movements and predict future direction. Not interested in particulars about company, but instead look at trendline, moving average, resistance level, support level.

Fundamental analysis: uses company financials, other data to determine company health, market position to predict future stock prices. Three important documents: balance sheet (assets, liabilities, net worth as of a certain time), income statement (income, expenses over time), and cash flow.

Earnings Before Interest & Taxes (EBIT) is operating income: sales minus costs minus returns minus depreciation. Bottom line is earnings after tax: EBIT minus interest minus taxes. Profit margin is income divided by sales.

Debt-to-equity ratio shows how company uses leverage to maximize return. Earnings per share is value of company's profit if it were distributed to all shareholders. Earnings per diluted share assumes all conversions happen. Price-earnings (PE) ratio says how much investor is paying for company's future earning power. High growth companies have high PEs. PE is common means of comparison between companies.

7.2.4 Mutual fund comparisons can be nonstatistical, statistical. Should check fund objectives vs. actual portfolio investments, check withdrawal options, other rights and charges. Statistical comparisons include load charges (front end vs. back end vs. level over time), expense ratios (cost of owning a fund including management fees), asset turnover (how often it sells stocks).

7.2.5 Municipal bonds include GO, revenue. GO bonds: full faith & credit of issuer, competitive bid, issuer's taxing authority, often needs voter approval, legal debt limits considered, analyzes all ratios (but debt service), double barreled. Revenue bonds: need trust indenture (covenants), negotiated bid, revenue from project, need feasibility study with flow of funds (sinking fund?), only debt service-to-earnings ratio analyzed, extra help if moral obligation of state.

Credit information can come from non-profits, state service, industry publications, rating companies. "AAA" (S&P) and "Aaa" (Moody's) are best. Moody's also uses MIG-1 to –4. Municipal bond insurance against default from MBIA, AMBAC make bonds "AAA."

7.3

Price info in daily publications (for clients), or up-to-minute (for B-D, RR).

7.3.1 Exchange-traded equities use consolidated tapes so NYSE can trade OTC. Review how to read these on p. 341. Remember SLD (sale delay) prohibits short sale.

7.3.2 NASDAQ: Level 1: RR can see inside quote. Level 2: institutional investors see quotes from multiple market makers. Level 3: market makers can update. Pink sheets are daily non-firm quotes on OTC stocks too small for NASDAQ.

7.3.3 Yellow sheets are daily non-firm quotes on OTC bonds too small for NASDAQ.

7.3.4 Municipal securities have information listed daily in The Blue List. The Bond Buyer is main publication that has many indexes, including visible supply. (Munifacts is computerized version.) Moody's Bond Survey is weekly newsletter. Offering sheets are dealer reports.

7.3.5 OPRA (Options Price Reporting Authority): computerized quotes for options.

7.4

Investment research is plentiful, but must consider if source is reliable.

7.4.1 Broker-dealers have research departments, but need to make sure research and information is unbiased and independent from sales department.

7.4.2 DJIA (Dow Jones Industrial Average) is 30 stock price average. Dow Theory says sector averages must agree with DJIA to signal market change. NYSE composite measures all NYSE stocks. Wilshire 5000 measures all exchange stocks (capitalization weighted). S&P 500 is capitalized weighted index of 500 stocks.

7.4.3 Investment advisory services include Moody's, Standard & Poor's, Value Line.

7.4.4 Municipal market indicators include *The Blue List* Total (total par value of all municipals offered for sale: measures municipal bond supply). *The Bond Buyer* published indexes: placement ratio index, 20 bond GO index, 11 bond GO index, 30 year revenue, visible supply (shows all bonds scheduled to be offered within 30-day period).

Chapter 7 Review Quiz

1. Changing customer objectives always entail:
   a. changing a customer's portfolio strategy.
   b. updating the "know your customer" information.
   c. putting clients in more risky investments as they gain experience.
   d. all of the above.

2. A defensive portfolio would most likely *not* have which of the following?
   a. utility stocks
   b. preferred stocks
   c. blue chip stocks
   d. margin stocks

3. A portfolio that has a beta coefficient of 0.85 is:
   a. more likely to underperform the market.
   b. more likely to outperform the market.
   c. likely to have more volatility than the chosen index.
   d. not possible.

4. If advancers lead decliners, which is the best statement about the market?
   a. There are more people buying stocks on margin.
   b. Short selling of stocks has been near a record level.
   c. Trading volume must have been exceptionally light.
   d. Market sentiment is bullish, but more information is needed to know how strong.

5. Dow Theory says:
   a. Dow Jones Industrial Average is the best indicator of market performance.
   b. Dow Jones Industrial Average is a poor indicator of market performance.
   c. market movements must be confirmed by sector averages to signal a trend.
   d. other indexes, such as S&P 500, must be considered with the Dow.

6. A stock has been trading within a range for several weeks, but rose dramatically today beyond the range. What would a technical analyst say about the movement?
   a. The stock has lost its support level.
   b. The stock has had a breakout.
   c. The stock has hit a resistance level.
   d. The stock is in an accumulation area.

7. Which of the following would be equal to the company's "bottom line?"
   a. NIAT
   b. EAT
   c. net income
   d. all of the above

8. Diluted earnings per share measures:
   a. the profit a company would have made under different conditions.
   b. the value of a company's profit figured as if distributed to current shareholders.
   c. EPS calculated as if all conversions took place, warrants exercised, etc.
   d. earnings before taxes.

9. With a mutual fund, what does the expense ratio measure?
   a. the ratio of expenses to total portfolio investments
   b. the cost of owning the fund
   c. the cost of acquiring the fund
   d. the cost of management fees divided by the sales charge load

10. Portfolio turnover is:
    a. the percentage of a mutual fund's portfolio sold during the past year.
    b. the number of stocks your client has sold since opening the account.
    c. the number of people who have invested money in a mutual fund.
    d. the percentage of people buying a fund compared to the number selling.

11. All of the following are true about a GO bond, *except:*
    a. debt per capita is an important consideration.
    b. negotiated bid underwriting is used.
    c. it is backed by the full faith and credit of the issuer.
    d. debt limits need to be considered.

12. All of the following are true about a revenue bond, *except:*
    a. a feasibility study must be done.
    b. a trust indenture is used.
    c. a flow of funds statement is important.
    d. the net debt to assessed valuation ratio is important.

13. On the consolidated tapes, SLD means:
    a. the name of the stock traded.
    b. the stock was sold long rather than sold short.
    c. a delayed trade report follows.
    d. short sales are allowed if the price that follows is an uptick.

14. The pink sheets:
    a. are firm quotes given by the market maker.
    b. are OTC corporate stocks not big enough to be listed on NASDAQ.
    c. are OTC corporate bonds not big enough to be listed on NASDAQ.
    d. are published weekly.

15. Listed options use which of the following computerized trading systems?
    a. Instinet
    b. Munifacts
    c. DOT
    d. OPRA

16. Which of the following indexes indicates all bonds scheduled for the next 30 days?
    a. Visible Supply
    b. *Blue List* Total
    c. 30-Year Revenue Index
    d. Placement Ratio Index

Exam Manual Extras

Series 7 Securities Practice Exam #1

1. The term *NAV* means:
   I. Not Available Values
   II. Net Asset Value
   III. Share value of a mutual fund
   IV. Current yield
   A. I, II
   B. II, III
   C. I, IV
   D. IV

2. A person who wants an "ownership position" in a company should buy:
   A. Bonds
   B. Common stock
   C. Both common stock and bonds
   D. Neither common stock or bonds

3. Authorized Stock is:
   A. Open end amount
   B. Specific number of shares
   C. Insider purchases
   D. Control purchases

4. LIFO refers to:
   I. Zero tax liability for an annuity
   II. Last in–First out
   III. Normal taxation for an annuity
   IV. None of the above
   A. II
   B. II, III
   C. IV
   D. I

5. Zero coupon bonds have the following characteristics:
   A. Interest paid every 6 months
   B. Very stable resale price
   C. No reinvestment risk
   D. Should never be purchased

6. The term *Inverted Yield* means:
   A. Long term bonds have a higher yield
   B. Long term bonds have a lower yield
   C. This situation never occurs
   D. Rating of bonds may be improving

7. According to S&P a bond may be of investment quality, or bank grade, if it has a rating of at least:
   A. BBB
   B. C
   C. NR
   D. BB

8. A speculative bond issue, sometimes called a *junk bond,* will have a S&P rating of ____, or lower.
   A. BBB
   B. C
   C. NR
   D. BB

9. An account designated JTWROS is a joint account with the following characteristics:
   I. Right of survivorship
   II. 50 / 50 ownership
   III. May be passed without probate
   IV. May have unequal ownership
   A. I
   B. II
   C. I, II, IV
   D. I, II, III

10. The abbreviation SLD means:
    A. Sale not reported on time
    B. Opening sale on AMEX
    C. Long stock position
    D. Closing price

11. An option with a strike price of $55 means:
    A. The option contract protects a price of $55 until expiration
    B. Does not relate to options
    C. Applies only to puts
    D. Applies only to calls

12. The term or terms that describe successive security transactions is (are):
    I. Uptick
    II. Downtick
    III. Zero plus tick
    IV. None of the above
    A. II
    B. III
    C. IV
    D. I, II, III

13. An Underwriter could be any of the following:
    A. Issuer
    B. Corporation receiving issue proceeds
    C. Investment banker
    D. Bond counsel

14. Regulation T settlement refers to:
    A. T + 3
    B. T + 5
    C. T + 7
    D. None of the above

15. Stock represents ownership in a company. Bonds represent a loan to a company.
    A. Both statements are true
    B. Both statements are false
    C. Stock represents ownership
    D. Bonds represent a loan

16. Bonds are sometimes described as the "junior" security.
    A. Bonds are junior because they are at the bottom of the liquidation priority
    B. Bonds are never secured
    C. Common stock is the "junior" security
    D. Bonds are "junior" in their claim to assets, as compared to stock

17. To calculate current yield for a bond, divide:
    A. Semiannual interest by current market price
    B. Semiannual interest by par value
    C. Annual interest by current market value
    D. Annual interest by the OID

18. CUSIP numbers are used:
    I. Only for bonds
    II. Only for stocks
    III. For both stocks and bonds
    IV. Only for commission purposes
    A. I
    B. I, II
    C. III
    D. IV

19. Which of these preferred stocks will provide the highest dividend?
    A. Convertible Preferred
    B. Callable Preferred
    C. Straight Preferred
    D. Cumulative Preferred

20. Limited liability is often discussed as a reason to own common stock. This means:
    A. Stock value is guaranteed
    B. Loss is limited to the amount of the stock purchase price
    C. Common stock has less risk than a bond held to maturity
    D. Common stock always pays a dividend

21. Participating preferred stock:
    A. Allows owners to participate in company profits
    B. Guarantees a dividend payment
    C. Never allows payment of a fixed dividend
    D. May be called by the company

22. Preferred stock:
    A. Usually will have voting rights
    B. Never will have voting rights
    C. Except for rare instances, does not have voting rights
    D. None of the above

23. If an investor buys a bond at a premium:
    I. The purchase price is above par
    II. Yield to maturity will be higher than the coupon rate
    III. Yield to maturity will be lower than the coupon rate
    IV. The investor may want the bond at a premium, since the interest rate will be higher
    A. I
    B. I, II
    C. III, IV
    D. I, III, IV

24. All of the following bonds are Zero Coupon Bonds except:
    A. STRIPS
    B. Treasury Receipts
    C. Zero Corporates
    D. MBIA

25. A dollar bond may sell at par, discount, or at a premium. Under which of these situations would the bond usually sell at a price other than par?
    I. At issue
    II. In the resale market
    III. In the secondary market
    IV. Never; the price is set at issue
    A. I
    B. I, II
    C. I, IV
    D. II, III

26. A buyer of a call wants the market to:
    A. Go up
    B. Go down
    C. Stay the same
    D. None of the above

27. An investor has the following option position: Long DEF Jun 45 call at 4. The current market value (CMV) is 49.
    I. This contract is in the money by 4.
    II. Intrinsic Value is 4.
    III. If exercised, the investor will make a profit.
    IV. The contract is out of the money.
    A. I
    B. IV
    C. I, II
    D. III

28. General Obligation (GO) bonds are:
    A. Backed by revenues
    B. Corporate AAA bonds
    C. Municipal Bonds backed by the taxing authority of the municipality
    D. Double-barreled bonds

29. Time value of an option contract means:
    A. The amount the contract is in the money
    B. The amount the contract is out of the money
    C. The perceived worth of the contract, based upon time
    D. No such value exists

30. An example of a non-equity option is:
    A. Stock option
    B. Put option
    C. Call option
    D. Index option

31. The risk of the market overall is called:
    I. Market risk
    II. Systematic risk
    III. Interest-rate risk
    IV. Timing risk
    A. I, IV
    B. III, IV
    C. I, II
    D. I, III

32. SMA is:
    A. Insufficient funds in an investor's account
    B. Excess equity in an investor'saccount
    C. Initial margin position
    D. Used only in a short sale

33. State security (blue sky) laws require registration of:
    I. Broker-dealers
    II. Securities sold within the state
    III. Registered Representatives
    IV. Securities not sold in the state
    A. I, III, IV
    B. I, IV, II
    C. I, II, III
    D. I, III

34. A standby underwriting:
    A. Could occur if current stockholders purchased all the additional stock offered by the company
    B. Could occur if current stockholders did not purchase all the additional stock offered by the company
    C. Could occur if the company is in need of "immediate cash"
    D. Would never contain a "firm commitment"

35. The consolidated tape system is designed to deliver real-time reports on securities transactions. Real-time reporting is:
    A. 60 seconds
    B. 90 seconds
    C. 120 seconds
    D. 45 seconds

36. Major factors regarding DPP programs include:
    I. Lack of liquidity
    II. Limited secondary market
    III. Ability to shelter ordinary income
    IV. Liability for recourse loans
    A. I, II
    B. III, IV
    C. III
    D. I, II, IV

37. The purpose of an investment company is to:
    A. Pool investors' money
    B. Offer only well-diversified open-end mutual funds
    C. Manage money toward a specific objective
    D. Both A and C

38. Policies broker-dealers establish to restrict passing nonpublic information between departments is known as:
A. Internal barrier
B. Chinese wall, or firewall
C. Firm element
D. Regulatory element

39. Accrued interest calculations are made for corporate bonds and municipal bonds on the basis of:
I. 365-day year
II. 360-day year
III. 360-day year based upon 11 months
IV. 365-day year with 30 days for February
A. I
B. I, IV
C. II
D. III

40. All of these companies are considered to be investment companies. Which type investment company has no provision for redemption of outstanding shares?
A. Mutual fund
B. Unit investment trust (UIT)
C. Closed-end company
D. Open-end company

41. An investor with no other holdings purchases a call. The maximum loss the investor may encounter is:
A. Unlimited
B. Premium paid
C. Strike price minus premium paid
D. Strike price plus premium paid

42. The maximum sales charge for a mutual fund in the first year is:
A. 5%
B. 8%
C. 8½%
D. None of the above

43. Back End Load mutual funds:
I. Contain charges called Contingent Deferred Sales Charges
II. May be referred to as "no-load funds"
III. Usually contain a "holding period" that will reduce the load to zero over time
IV. Limit sales charges to 5% in the first year
A. I, II, III
B. I, II
C. I, IV
D. I, III

44. Money-market funds are considered to be good choices for:
I. Liquidity
II. Safety of principal
III. Long-term investment
IV. Growth
A. I, IV
B. II, IV
C. II, III
D. I, II

45. ERISA would consider employees eligible if they:
A. Have worked 1,000 hours or more in the past year
B. Have completed one year or more in employment
C. Are 21 years or older
D. All of the above

46. A defined benefit retirement plan may favor one of the following groups of employees:
A. Younger
B. Older
C. Both younger and older
D. Neither younger or older

47. Limited Partnership programs have the following characteristics:
    I. Intended for lower income investors
    II. Usually of more value to higher income investors
    III. Almost always used to shelter ordinary income
    IV. Should be purchased because they are "economically viable"
    A. I, IV
    B. III
    C. IV
    D. II, IV

48. M2 money supply, building permits (housing starts), new orders for consumer goods, and stock prices are considered to be:
    A. Lagging indicators
    B. Coincident indicators
    C. Leading indicators
    D. Measures of the CPI

49. Throughout history, business cycles go through four stages. In order of occurrence, they are:
    A. Expansion, peak, contraction, trough
    B. Peak, trough, expansion, contraction
    C. Contraction, trough, peak, expansion
    D. Trough, peak, expansion, contraction

50. A person who gives investment advice for a flat fee or percentage of assets must register under the:
    A. Investment Company Act of 1940
    B. Investment Advisors act of 1940
    C. Maloney Act of 1938
    D. NASD "people act"

51. SIPC is an independent, government sponsored corporation that collects annual assessments from broker-dealers. The maximum limits for this protection are:
    A. $500,000 in securities plus $100,000 in cash
    B. $500,000 in securities, including $100,000 in cash
    C. $1,000,000 in total "asset" coverage
    D. SIPC is not government sponsored

52. An investor believes an announcement will have a strong effect upon the value of HTM stock. The problem is the investor does not know which direction the market will move. Which one of these strategies would be best?
    A. Write a call
    B. Write a put
    C. Buy a straddle
    D. Sell a straddle

53. A client owns 100 HTM with CMV presently at 40. The client hedges the risk of owning this stock by writing a 45 call and going long with a 35 put.
    I. This strategy is not desirable, due to the uncovered position and unlimited risk of the short call.
    II. This strategy is acceptable and will protect the downside risk of the long-stock position.
    III. This strategy is known as a collar.
    IV. This strategy is known as a diagonal spread.
    A. I
    B. I, III
    C. II, IV
    D. II, III

54. Before trading may take place in an options account, the account must be approved by a:
   A. Registered Representative
   B. Registered Principal
   C. Registered Options Principal
   D. Registered Dealer

55. Options contracts are adjusted for several conditions. A few examples would be:
   A. Forward stock splits
   B. Reverse stock splits
   C. Stock Dividends
   D. All of the above

56. Tax rates are a primary concern in determining suitability for:
   A. Corporate Bonds
   B. Common Stock
   C. Preferred Stock
   D. Municipal Bonds

57. Serial maturity bonds have these characteristics:
   I. Maturity is on one single date.
   II. Maturity is on different dates.
   III. They may be sold on yield-to-maturity.
   IV. None of these apply.
   A. I
   B. II, III
   C. IV
   D. I, IV

58. An IPO is released and, after a period of time, the selling group is beginning to believe it will not be entirely sold. These actions could be taken by the broker-dealers involved in the IPO:
   A. Enter into matching transactions
   B. Participate in a ring
   C. Create a favorable review for the IPO
   D. None of the above

59. A very famous client of yours becomes concerned about having her name on your broker-dealer's records. You may:
   A. Suggest she put the account in your name with a limited POA
   B. Designate the account by number
   C. Change her name for your records
   D. None of the above, all are illegal

60. During one year, the gifts a broker-dealer may give employees of another broker-dealer may not exceed:
   A. $25
   B. $50
   C. $100
   D. $500

61. Within a brokerage firm, an order is placed by the client and written by the Registered Representative. This order then goes to:
   A. Margin, or credit department
   B. Order, wire room
   C. Purchase, or sales department
   D. None of the above; as a listed security, the order goes directly to the specialist

62. A client has a variable annuity with you and wants to know about the "separate account" he has heard about. You tell the client:
   I. This type of account is illegal and does not exist.
   II. The separate account is where the investments are located within the annuity.
   III. The separate account contains only fixed rate investments.
   IV. The separate account contains systematic risk.
   A. I
   B. II, IV
   C. III
   D. III, IV

63. A customer trade confirmation must:
    A. Be sent before the completion of the transaction
    B. Be sent to the client no later than T+7
    C. Contain an approximate "amount due"
    D. None of the above

64. SMA is commonly referred to as:
    A. Regulation T requirement
    B. Initial margin requirement
    C. Excess equity
    D. Special managed account

65. Your client has the following position. Short XYZ 45 call at 4. The position is "uncovered."
    A. Maximum gain is $400
    B. Maximum loss is $400
    C. Maximum gain is unlimited
    D. Both A and B

66. When considering a municipal bond, which of these areas are of prime concern to the client?
    I. Client's tax rate
    II. Client's credit rating
    III. Issuer's credit rating
    IV. Issuer's tax rate
    A. I, III
    B. II, IV
    C. IV
    D. I, IV

67. Municipal bonds are tax exempt. Therefore, when a muni bond is purchased at a discount:
    A. No tax will be due
    B. Tax must be paid on the gain
    C. There is no gain
    D. None of the above

68. DPPs may be structured as:
    A. Subchapter S corporations
    B. Limited partnerships
    C. Both A and B are true
    D. Neither A or B is true

69. The "prospectus" was created by the:
    A. Securities Act of 1933
    B. Securities Exchange Act of 1934
    C. Maloney Act
    D. MSRB

70. Retirement plans may be either "qualified" or "nonqualified."
    I. Only qualified plans may be used in corporations.
    II. Only nonqualified plans may be used in corporations.
    III. Qualified plans may discriminate.
    IV. Nonqualified plans may discriminate.
    A. I
    B. I, III
    C. IV
    D. II, IV

71. Identify the following options positions:
    I. Long call, short put is bearish
    II. Long call, short put is bullish
    III. Long put, short call is bearish
    IV. Long put, short call is bullish
    A. I, IV
    B. II, III
    C. IV, II
    D. I, III

72. In municipal bond offerings, a presale order:
    A. Is never allowed
    B. Is allowed
    C. Is illegal
    D. May not be a part of a public offering

73. The term *DK procedures:*
    A. Has no meaning
    B. Stands for Don't Know procedures
    C. Would be a violation against a registered representative
    D. None of the above

74. An SRO is part of the SEC oversight functions. The following would be classified as SROs:
   A. NYSE
   B. NASD
   C. CBOE
   D. All of the above

75. *Ad Valorem* taxes are:
   I. Property taxes
   II. Paid on a property's assessed value
   III. Paid on a property's market value
   IV. Value-added taxes
   A. I, III
   B. IV, III
   C. I, II
   D. None of the above

76. A variable annuity is considered to be:
   A. An open-end management investment company
   B. A closed-end management investment company
   C. Neither A or B is true
   D. Both A and B are true

77. Retained earnings for a corporation represent the total of earnings held since the corporation was formed, less any dividends paid out to stockholders.
   A. These earnings are also called *earned surplus*
   B. Operating losses in any year reduce retained earnings from previous years
   C. Both of these statements are true
   D. Neither of these statements is true

78. A new customer account form must contain these items:
   I. Client's signature
   II. Registered Representative's signature
   III. Registered Principal's signature
   IV. Client's date of birth
   A. I, IV
   B. II, III
   C. I, II, IV
   D. I, II, III, IV

79. A client is in the 37% tax bracket and is considering a 4% municipal (muni) bond. The tax equivalent yield for this bond is:
   A. 6.8%
   B. 4.25%
   C. 10.8%
   D. 6.35%

80. A class of option refers to:
   A. All calls of an issuer
   B. All puts of an issuer
   C. Both A and B are true
   D. None of the above

81. Municipal bonds are considered to be a method of investing in tax-free income. Some advantages may be:
   A. Income received will be free of federal taxes
   B. Income received may also be free of state and local taxes for certain issues
   C. Both A and B are true
   D. Only A is true

82. Many of our clients consider donations to charity. Some of the tax benefits donors could receive for donations to charity are:
    I. Donor receives tax deduction equal to market value on the date of the donation
    II. Donor receives tax deduction equal to the cost basis of the donation
    III. Recipient receives cost basis of donation equal to the donor's basis
    IV. Recipient receives cost basis of donation equal to higher market value
    A. I, III
    B. II, IV
    C. I, IV
    D. II, III

83. A DPP has two types of partners:
    A. General Partner, Limited Partner
    B. Senior Partner, Limited Partner
    C. Limited Partner, Fiduciary Partner
    D. None of the above

84. A client has a long position in a call option. How would you describe "break-even" for this position?
    A. Strike price plus premium paid
    B. Exercise price plus premium paid
    C. Strike price minus premium paid
    B. Both A and B

85. A client has a long position in a put option. How would you describe "break-even" for this position?
    A. Strike price plus premium paid
    B. Exercise price plus premium paid
    C. Strike price minus premium paid
    D. Both A and B

86. You have a client who wants to sell short. You explain to the client:
    I. Short selling is done in a margin account
    II. A loan agreement will be required
    III. Short selling has unlimited risk
    IV. Exchange short sale rules apply
    A. I, II
    B. I, II, IV
    C. I, II, III
    D. I, II, III, IV

87. Arbitration is the method normally used to solve customer complaints, and most new account forms contain a predispute arbitration clause.
    A. This statement is true
    B. Arbitration is used but new account forms do not contain an arbitration clause
    C. Arbitration is never used. Class Action Suits are the normal method for solving customer complaints
    D. Arbitration may be used, but is normally more expensive than court action

88. A trust indenture for corporate bonds contains at least this provision:
    A. Regulation for bonds, which are considered corporate junior securities
    B. Regulation for bonds, which are considered corporate senior securities
    C. A trust indenture applies only to debentures
    D. A trust indenture applies only to income bonds

89. While reviewing current underwriting your firm is involved with, you see a secondary offering which may be coming in the near future. This type offering could involve the following:
   A. CEO retiring
   B. Private placement
   C. Proceeds going to stockholders, rather than to the issuer
   D. Both A and C

90. A new issue of a municipal (muni) bond is often sold on a "when issued" basis because:
   I. The bonds have been issued
   II. The bonds have not been issued, only authorized
   III. Two trade confirmations will be received by a purchaser of a W/I bond
   IV. The investor starts receiving interest on the settlement date
   A. I
   B. II
   C. II, III
   D. II, III, IV

91. Regulation T set the loan value for most securities at:
   A. 25%
   B. 50%
   C. 75%
   D. 100%

92. The price at which an individual investor may purchase a security in the OTC market is called:
   A. Best asking price
   B. Best bid price
   C. Highest asking price
   D. Highest bid price

93. A municipal bond issue may be issued with the following:
   A. Ex-legal
   B. A qualified legal opinion
   C. A nonqualified legal opinion
   D. All of the above

94. A CUSIP number is important to know, because:
   A. It is used on all correspondence regarding specific securities
   B. It is used on all trade confirmations
   C. It is used as an ID number by the transfer agent
   D. All of the above

95. Many DPP programs offer depreciation allowances. These allowances are used to:
   A. Recover the cost of buildings wearing out over time
   B. Recover the cost of equipment wearing out over time
   C. Recover the cost of land
   D. Both A and B

96. NYSE member firms must register all sales persons with the exchange.
   A. Not a true statement; only NASD requires registration
   B. True; sales personnel may also be denied registration by NYSE
   C. Not a true statement; only the CBOE requires registration
   D. None of the above

97. Dollar-cost averaging:
   I. Involves always buying the same number of shares
   II. Involves always buying the same dollar amount
   III. Involves guaranteeing a profit
   IV. Is more desirable when used with individual stocks, as compared to mutual funds
   A. I
   B. II
   C. III
   D. I, III, IV

98. A Territorial bond is:
   A. Free from federal, state, and local taxes in all 50 states
   B. Free of federal tax in all 50 states
   C. Taxable and considered to be a corporate issue
   D. Taxable and considered to be a private activity bond

99. A stock split, such as 2 for 1, means:
   A. An investor will have twice as many shares
   B. The value of each share is reduced by one-half
   C. Total par value of stock is not affected
   D. All of the above

100. A syndicate has been formed to underwrite a municipal bond issue. Which of the following are true?
   A. A Western account will designate a certain percentage of bonds to be sold by each member.
   B. A Western account will not designate a certain percentage of bonds to be sold by each member.
   C. An Eastern account will designate a certain percentage of bonds to be sold by each member.
   D. Both B and C

101. Roth IRA allows:
   I. After-tax contributions
   II. Before-tax contributions
   III. Upon distribution, funds will be taxed as ordinary income
   IV. Upon distribution, funds will be not be taxed
   A. I, IV
   B. II, III
   C. II
   D. III

102. In a DPP, all investors must disclose:
   A. Net worth
   B. Annual income
   C. Statement of understanding regarding risk of the limited partnership
   D. All of the above

103. Current liabilities are liabilities due within the next:
   A. 10 months
   B. 12 months
   C. 18 months
   D. 24 months

104. Examples of depreciating assets are:
   A. Buildings
   B. Equipment
   C. Land
   D. Both A and B

105. Money Market Funds may generally be described as:
   I. No-load funds
   II. Open-end mutual funds
   III. Parking place for money
   IV. Cash equivalent
   A. I, II
   B. I, II, IV
   C. II, IV
   D. I, II, III, IV

106. A bond fund would have as its major objective:
   A. Short-term growth
   B. Long-term growth
   C. Short-term income
   D. Long-term income

107. A client has as major objectives growth and small capital gains. You should recommend the following:
   A. Small-cap fund
   B. Large-cap fund
   C. Index fund
   D. Government-bond fund

108. Under the guidelines for safeguard of nonpublic information:
   I. The person who gives the tip is not liable
   II. The person who receives the tip is not liable
   III. Both the tipper and the person receiving the tip are liable
   IV. No trade needs to be made to have liability under the guidelines
   A. I
   B. II
   C. II, III
   D. III, IV

109. If a member firm uses a person to provide a testimonial, the firm should:
   A. Not disclose that a fee has been paid to the spokesperson
   B. Disclose that a fee has been paid to the spokesperson
   C. Disclose the qualifications of the spokesperson
   D. Both B and C

110. A straddle is written on JKL corporation at 4 on both sides. The risk for the writer of the straddle is as follows:
   I. Maximum gain is both premiums paid
   II. Maximum gain is both premiums received
   III. Maximum loss is unlimited
   IV. Maximum loss is premiums received
   A. I, III
   B. II, III
   C. IV
   D. II

111. A penny stock:
   A. Could be found OTC in the "pink" sheets
   B. Is a stock under $5 per share
   C. Is considered to be of high risk
   D. All of the above

112. Your client has indicated the need for immediate execution of a purchase, if at all possible. You should:
   A. Tell the client this is not possible
   B. Enter a market order
   C. Enter a stop order
   D. Enter a limit order

113. When a stock goes ex-dividend, as a financial advisor, you should recommend:
   A. Immediate purchase before the dividend
   B. Purchase after the ex-dividend date
   C. No purchase for 6 months
   D. None of the above apply to the situation

114. An investor establishes the following option position. Buys 1 ABC Jun 40 put for 5. Sells 1 ABC Jun 35 put for 3.
   I. The investor is bearish.
   II. The investor is bullish.
   III. The overall position is called a debit-put spread.
   IV. The overall position is called a credit-put spread.
   A. I, IV
   B. II, III
   C. I, III
   D. I

115. A traditional IRA could be used by a client for several reasons, which may include:
A. Possible tax deduction
B. Amount placed into an IRA account will be tax deferred
C. Both A and B
D. Neither A or B

116. Two advantages of purchasing IPOs on margin are:
A. More securities may be purchased with less cash outlay
B. Our customer can leverage his account, which can provide a better return
C. Both A and B
D. Neither A or B

117. A muni bond is offered at 104.
I. This price indicates a dollar bond.
II. This price indicates a serial bond.
III. The bond is offered at a discount.
IV. The bond is offered at a premium.
A. I, III
B. I
C. II, IV
D. I, IV

118. For a variable-rate municipal bond:
A. Interest rates are tied to the movement of some other interest rate
B. Interest rates are always stable
C. Secondary pricing is more stable
D. A and C

119. A zero-coupon municipal bond:
A. Does not exist
B. Could provide tax-free growth
C. Is always purchased at a deep discount
D. Both B and C

120. A client wants to buy stock you cannot recommend. You should:
A. Refuse to do the transaction
B. Mark the trade "unsolicited"
C. Discuss the trade with Compliance
D. Mark the trade "solicited"

121. Listed options are traded most heavily on the:
A. CBOE
B. NYSE
C. AMEX
D. OTC

122. Preferred stock:
A. Usually is nonvoting
B. Is considered the "junior" security
C. May have a par value of $100
D. Both A and C

123. You are considering a municipal bond priced at a premium, callable at par in three years.
I. YTC will be lower than CY.
II. YTM will be lower than CY.
III. YTM will be higher than CY.
IV. YTC will be higher than CY.
A. I, II
B. II, III
C. I
D. II

124. You enter a buy limit order and do not mark any time designation for execution. The order will be assumed to be a:
A. Day order
B. GTC order
C. All or none
D. Immediate or cancel

125. The only type of advertising that may be done prior to a new issue coming to market is known as:
   A. Tombstones
   B. Generic
   C. Targeted
   D. Nontargeted

END OF FIRST HALF OF THE FINAL EXAM. IF YOU WERE TAKING THE TEST AT THE TESTING CENTER, YOU WOULD BE REQUIRED TO TAKE A BREAK BEFORE STARTING THE LAST HALF OF THE EXAM.

YOU WOULD NOT BE PERMITTED TO GO BACK AND CHANGE ANSWERS ON THE FIRST HALF ONCE YOU STARTED THE SECOND HALF.

2nd HALF—PRACTICE EXAM #1

126. A company going public by selling shares of stock for the first time may do any of the following:
   I. Conduct an IPO
   II. Conduct a primary offering
   III. Conduct a secondary offering
   IV. Offer additional issues
   A. I, II
   B. II, III
   C. II, III, IV
   D. IV

127. A client sells 1 XYZ 60 call for 5, and immediately closes the position for 5. After further review, he decides to buy a round lot of XYZ. The stock is purchased for $45. The client holds XYZ for a period of time and sells 100 shares for $52. The client has realized:
   A. $7,000 loss
   B. $7,000 gain
   C. $700 loss
   D. $700 gain

128. In a long-margin account, the minimum NASD/NYSE maintenance requirement is:
   A. 30%
   B. 25%
   C. 40%
   D. 50%

129. The document which serves as full disclosure or municipal bonds is called:
   A. Prospectus
   B. Preliminary prospectus
   C. Preliminary Official Statement
   D. Official statement

130. Open-end mutual funds:
   A. Are authorized with a specific number of shares for issue
   B. May issue an unlimited number of shares
   C. Do not issue shares
   D. Participate in an active secondary market

131. Equity options expire:
   I. The Saturday following the third Friday of the expiration month
   II. The Friday following the end of the third week of the month
   III. If new options, at end of 9 months
   IV. If new options, at end of 6 months
   A. I, IV
   B. II, III
   C. III
   D. I, III

132. An aggressive-growth mutual fund will usually be defined as:
   A. Newer, smaller companies, paying cash dividends
   B. Well-established companies with a record of small stock dividends
   C. Newer, smaller companies, reinvesting cash in the business
   D. Well-established companies with a new management team

133. Selling away refers to:
   A. Private securities transaction not approved by your broker-dealer
   B. Private placement of securities
   C. Selling away from your client's needs
   D. Selling a security your competition does not offer

134. Regular way settlement refers to:
   A. T + 3
   B. T + 5
   C. T + 7
   D. T + 10

135. The name of the publication in which the "30-day visible supply" is published is:
   A. *Bond Buyer*
   B. *Munifacts*
   C. *The Blue List*
   D. *Pink Sheets*

136. A variable annuity may be purchased as:
   I. Single-premium deferred annuity
   II. Periodic-payment deferred annuity
   III. Immediate deferred annuity
   IV. None of the above
   A. I, II, III
   B. III
   C. I, II
   D. IV

137. Disintermediation may occur under these circumstances:
   A. Low-yielding bank savings accounts are transferred to higher-yielding investments in the marketplace
   B. Higher-yielding mutual funds are transferred to higher-risk growth stocks
   C. Low-yielding bank savings accounts are transferred to higher-yielding bank CDs
   D. None of the above

138. Advertising is considered to be:
   A. Targeted as to who reads it
   B. Untargeted as to who reads it
   C. Both A and B
   D. None of the above

139. Revenue bonds are municipal bonds which depend upon which of the following for repayment?
   A. Township taxes
   B. Revenues from a toll road
   C. Full faith and credit of taxing authority
   D. Revenue bonds do not exist

140. An investment-grade corporate bond is priced at 91 on the secondary market. It has 5 years until maturity with a call in two years at 104. The coupon is listed as 6%. What is this bond's current yield?
   A. 6%
   B. 6.6%
   C. 3.3%
   D. 5.5%

141. A client wants to buy an option. What are the main advantages of a long-option purchase?
   A. Speculation
   B. Deferring a decision on buying or selling a stock
   C. Limited loss
   D. All of the above

142. A client owns a foreign stock. What additional risk does the client have?
   A. Interest-rate risk
   B. Timing risk
   C. Credit risk
   D. Currency risk

143. BANs, TANs, RANs are:
   A. Muni anticipation notes
   B. Corporate anticipation notes
   C. Low-grade corporate bonds
   D. Low-grade municipal notes

144. Forward pricing refers to:
   I. Mutual funds
   II. Corporate bonds
   III. Municipal bonds
   IV. Private activity bonds
   A. I, II, III
   B. III, IV
   C. II, III
   D. I

145. One of your clients has completed the following position: Sold 1 ABC Oct 35 call at 4½. CMV is 42 and the client is exercised. What is the client's profit or loss?
   A. $500 profit
   B. $500 loss
   C. $250 profit
   D. $250 loss

146. If an individual has "full power of attorney" over an account, this means the individual may:
   A. Make decisions to buy and sell
   B. Make deposits or withdrawals
   C. Neither A or B
   D. Both A and B

147. Rights, sometimes called *subscription rights,* are used to allow current stockholders to:
   A. Maintain their present percent of ownership
   B. Buy additional stock at a price lower than current market price
   C. "Subscribe" to future issues of new stock
   D. Both A and B

148. Trade confirmations using municipal dollar bonds must disclose:
   A. The price of the bond
   B. The lowest potential yield
   C. Both A and B
   D. None of the above

149. By definition, a broker:
   A. Arranges trades for customers
   B. Arranges trades for brokers
   C. Charges commissions
   D. Both A and C

150. A new issue has been registered with the SEC by the issuer. There is a period of time after the issuer files for registration, before it may become effective, known as:
   I. Filing period
   II. Cooling off period
   III. Preliminary period
   IV. Syndicate period
   A. II
   B. II, IV
   C. III
   D. IV

151. Special situation funds are mutual funds with these characteristics:
   A. An objective allowing "short selling"
   B. May invest in turnaround situations
   C. Invested in international securities
   D. Known as "sector funds"

152. Selling a stock "short" may not be done by:
   A. Investors owning 5% or more of the company's stock
   B. Directors of the company
   C. Both A and B
   D. Investors holding "long" positions

153. The price for XYZ stock has remained in a narrow range for the past 11 months, and recent trades have been near the support level. This means the stock is trading:
   I. Near the top of the trading range
   II. Near the bottom of the trading range
   III. Near the resistance level
   IV. At breakout
   A. I, III
   B. III
   C. II
   D. IV

154. DPP (limited partnerships) may pass the following to an investor:
   I. Income
   II. Losses
   III. Gains
   IV. Tax credits
   A. I, II
   B. II, III
   C. I, II, IV
   D. I, II, III, IV

155. IRA accounts may not contain:
   A. Individual stocks
   B. Individual bonds
   C. Life insurance
   D. Both A and B

156. The tax equivalent yield for a 4% muni bond for a client in the 15% tax bracket is:
   A. 4.7%
   B. 6.5%
   C. 7.1%
   D. 26.66%

157. You are reviewing possible investments for your client and a 4% municipal bond, is a possible choice. Using the 15% tax rate, as discussed in the previous question, this bond would:
   A. Be acceptable, because of its high tax equivalent yield
   B. Not be acceptable, because of its low tax equivalent yield
   C. Be acceptable, since tax equivalent yield does not apply to this bond
   D. Be an AMT consideration for the client

158. Your client holds 5 DEF Oct 60 calls. For the client to make money on this option, the market must:
   A. Widen
   B. Narrow
   C. Maintain its present levels
   D. None of the above

159. You are reviewing a number of front-end load mutual funds. One fund you are analyzing has a POP of $10 and NAV of $9.40, and over the past 12 months has distributed $.60 in dividends and long-term capital gains of $.40. What is the current yield for this fund?
   A. 10%
   B. 6%
   C. 6.4%
   D. 4.3%

160. Zero coupon bonds are purchased at a discount. This discount is called:
   A. Markdown
   B. Accreted discount
   C. Best bid
   D. OID

161. Taxation on a bond purchased at a discount, such as 91, will have a gain to report. This gain is:
A. Long-term capital gain
B. Ordinary income
C. Not reportable
D. 50 percent reported as ordinary income

162. You are opening a new account with a client. During the process of completing the new account forms, you discover the new client is a "control" person. The importance of this information is:
A. Not important
B. Very important, since unusual trades will be monitored by the NYSE
C. Only unsolicited trades may be made in this account
D. Unimportant, because client is a control person with only one company

163. An example of a listed stock would be a stock listed on:
I. NYSE
II. AMEX
III. Regional Exchange
IV. OTC
A. I, II, III, IV
B. I, II, IV
C. I, II, III
D. III, IV

164. You have entered an order at the client's instruction to Sell 1,000 shares of T. Instead of marking the ticket *Sell,* you marked it *Buy.* Clearly your mistake!
A. The trade is binding on the customer.
B. The trade is not binding on the customer.
C. Cancel the customer's account immediately.
D. Tell the client you overrode her decision.

165. A client is long 2 ZR Sep Put at 4. What is the maximum possible loss in this position?
A. $800
B. $8,000
C. $400
D. $4,000

166. Buying puts is considered to be:
A. Bullish
B. Bearish
C. Neutral
D. Risky, because of possible unlimited loss

167. The corporation that handles options transactions is known as:
A. MSRB
B. FNMA
C. GNMA
D. OCC

168. Your client owns a number of debentures as a part of an account transferred to your firm. You are reviewing the client's holdings with him and find the client believes debentures are secured debt. You advise the client that:
I. Debentures are debt obligations
II. Debentures are lower value equities
III. An owner of a company's debentures is considered to have a general creditor position
IV. Debentures are secured debt obligations
A. I, IV
B. II
C. I, III
D. II, III

169. The Nine Bond Rule:
    A. Refers to fewer than 10 bonds
    B. Must be presented ahead of larger orders
    C. Exempts bonds with a maturity of less than 12 months
    D. All are correct

170. LMN has a CMV of 63. Our client is long a LMN Jul 65 put at 4.50. What is the time value of this position?
    A. 1
    B. 2
    C. 2.5
    D. 3

171. Our client is considering the income choices available for her variable annuity. For this particular annuity, annuitization is considered to be desirable. In discussing these options, she asks you to rank these monthly payment options from highest to lowest. You respond:
    A. Life annuity, life with period certain, joint life
    B. Life with period certain, joint life, life only
    C. Joint life, life only, life with period certain
    D. Life annuity, joint life, life with period certain

172. The minimum margin maintenance requirement for a short position is:
    A. 25%
    B. 50%
    C. 45%
    D. 30%

173. Since revenue bonds are issues designed to be self-supporting, which of the following are true?
    I. These bonds are part of the constitutional debt limit.
    II. These bond are not part of the constitutional debt limit.
    III. If the revenue is insufficient to support the project financed by revenue bonds, the bondholders bear the risk of loss.
    IV. Bondholders do not have risk of default since revenue bonds are based on the taxing authority of a community.
    A. I, IV
    B. II, III
    C. II, IV
    D. IV

174. When a discount muni bond is purchased, callable at par, the highest yield will be:
    A. Coupon
    B. Nominal rate
    C. Yield to maturity
    D. Yield to call

175. When a broker-dealer is operating as a principal for municipal securities, it could be:
    I. Buying securities for its own account
    II. Selling securities from its own account
    III. Charging mark-ups
    IV. Charging mark-downs
    A. I, II, III, IV
    B. I, II
    C. III, IV
    D. I

176. You receive notice one of your clients is now deceased. You should:
   A. Do nothing at the present time
   B. Cancel all open orders
   C. First, freeze the account, cancel open orders, await instructions
   D. Cancel the account

177. UGMA accounts:
   A. May have only one custodian
   B. May have only one beneficial owner
   C. Neither of the above
   D. Both A and B

178. An investor has these positions:
   - Owns 100 FAB at a basis of 43.
   - Writes a FAB Aug 45 call at 3.

   What is the maximum gain for this overall position?
   A. $1,000
   B. $500
   C. $250
   D. $0

179. You have completed suitability forms for a client. His profile suggests that a mutual fund with moderate growth potential may be appropriate for money he wants to invest now. You recommend:
   A. Government bond fund
   B. Blue-chip stock fund
   C. Gold fund
   D. Technology, or sector, fund

180. A buy stop order is unique in that it is always entered above the current market price. This statement is:
   A. Not true
   B. True—always used for a long position
   C. True—always used for a short position
   D. True—if the investor's overall position contains a short call

181. A client of yours has an options account and is comfortable with most option strategies. He believes the market outlook for TX is going to very stable for an extended period of time. A possible strategy could be:
   A. Buy a call
   B. Buy a put
   C. Buy a straddle
   D. Write a straddle

182. The Securities Exchange Act of 1934 addresses these areas:
   I. Creation of the SEC
   II. Regulation of the exchanges
   III. Regulation of insider transactions
   IV. Creation of the prospectus

   A. I, II
   B. I, II, III
   C. III, IV
   D. II, III

183. Shareholder's equity is also known as:
   A. Net worth of the company
   B. Owner's equity
   C. Creditor's equity
   D. Both A and B

184. In a long-call options position, the exercise of the option:
   A. Does not create an immediate capital gain
   B. Creates an immediate gain
   C. Creates a gain if the underlying stock obtained by the exercise is sold
   D. Both A and C

185. NHA bonds may be described as:
   I. New housing authority bonds
   II. The most secure of all municipal bonds
   III. Public housing authority bonds
   IV. Revenue bonds
   A. I, II, III
   B. I, II
   C. III
   D. III, IV

186. Recruitment advertising may be placed by broker-dealers as blind advertising.
   A. This is a false statement.
   B. This is a true statement.
   C. Blind ads cannot be placed.
   D. Both A and C

187. If prices have risen so sharply that some experts are predicting a price decline, this is a market condition referred to as:
   A. Overbought
   B. Oversold
   C. Correction
   D. None of the above

188. In many instances, DPP programs offer attractive returns. As always, suitability of the investment for the investor is of prime concern. As you discuss the features of a DPP program, which of the following is likely to make the investment unsuitable?
   A. Lack of liquidity
   B. Complex nature of DPPs
   C. Lack of GP's experience
   D. All of the above

189. An open-end mutual fund is always redeemed at:
   A. POP
   B. Asking price
   C. NAV
   D. Market price

190. Which of the following stock certificates would be considered "good delivery" if properly endorsed?
   A. 5 certificates for 80 shares each
   B. 8 certificates for 50 shares each
   C. Both A and B
   D. None of the above

191. One of the factors having an effect upon the value of an options contract is the relationship of the strike price to the CMV. For a call:
   A. The lower the strike price, the higher the option's premium
   B. The higher the strike price, the higher the option's premium
   C. Strike price is not a factor
   D. Strike price is of concern if the contract is "in the money"

192. A 4½% municipal bond is offered on a yield to maturity basis and is being offered for sale at par if the YTM is:
   A. 4%
   B. 4½%
   C. 4¾%
   D. 4¼%

193. Will the coupon rate of a muni bond vary under any of these circumstances?
   I. Premium bond
   II. Discount bond
   III. New issue
   IV. Resale issue
   A. I, III
   B. II, IV
   C. III
   D. None of the above

194. Since options are traded without a certificate, what is proof for the client that she owns the option?
   A. Book entry or BE
   B. Trade confirmation
   C. Broker-dealer statement
   D. OCC statement

195. Which of these options is considered to be non-equity options?
A. Both B and C
B. Index options
C. Currency options
D. Stock options

196. The exchange markets operate as:
I. Auction market
II. Double auction market
III. Negotiated market
IV. Market maker
A. I, IV
B. I, III
C. I, II
D. III, IV

197. Your client has purchased a muni bond that settles as a cash trade. This means the money for payment of the bond will be due:
A. Regular way settlement
B. Regulation T settlement
C. On the trade date
D. When issued

198. You have sold a municipal bond for an existing client and find out, after the fact, that the certificate may be severely damaged. Who will determine if the damaged certificate is negotiable?
A. Registered Principal
B. Broker-dealer managing partner
C. MSRB
D. Transfer agent

199. What is the maximum gain for an investor who sells 3 KA Oct 65 calls at 4?
A. $400
B. $800
C. $1,200
D. $1,600

200. Simplified arbitration is available by agreement between both parties for an amount in dispute of _________, or less.
A. $10,000
B. $25,000
C. $50,000
D. Is not available to clients

201. Our client has purchased 2 LMN Jun 70 calls at 6, and is short 2 LMN Aug 70 calls at 5. A period of time elapses, and our client closes out the position and buys 2 LMN Aug 70 calls at 3 and sells 2 LMN Jun 70 calls at 4. What is the pre-tax loss or gain?
A. $600
B. $800
C. $1,200
D. $0

202. You have attempted to get all of the information requested on the new account forms. The client will not answer several of the questions asked on the new account form. Describe the situation.
I. The account will not be opened.
II. The account may be opened.
III. The situation requires the review, and approval, of the Registered Principal to open the account.
IV. The situation requires the review, and approval, of the firm's General Manager.
A. I
B. II, IV
C. IV
D. II, III

203. It is now several years since you have become a Registered Representative, and you want to transfer to another broker-dealer.
   A. You may not "transfer" to another broker-dealer. You must resign and reapply with the new broker-dealer
   B. You may transfer between two broker-dealers
   C. You resign from your present broker-dealer by submitting a U4
   D. None of the above

204. Corporations, if they will invest in securities from other companies, receive favorable tax treatment on dividends. This statement is:
   A. False: only individuals receive an exclusion for dividends
   B. True: the exclusion on dividends is 35%
   C. True: the exclusion for dividends is 70%
   D. None of the above

205. Index options could be used by an investor to:
   A. Profit by movements of the market, or a market segment
   B. Hedge a market swing up or down
   C. Both A and B
   D. Neither A or B

206. For a publicly traded company, a "control person" is a person identified as:
   I. An investor owning 15% or more of a company's common stock
   II. A director of a company
   III. An investor owning 10% or more of a company's common stock
   IV. An investor owning 25% or more of a company's common stock
   A. II, III
   B. I, II
   C. II, IV
   D. I

207. The safety of a municipal GO bond is determined by several factors, which would include:
   I. Revenues
   II. Property values
   III. Local bank deposits
   IV. Population growth, or decline
   A. I, II, III, IV
   B. II, III, IV
   C. I, II, IV
   D. II, IV

208. NASD has the authority to impose almost any disciplinary action other than:
   A. Fines
   B. Sanctions
   C. Jail
   D. Broker-dealer sanctions

209. Through what option strategy could an investor improve return for a long stock position?
   A. Buy a call
   B. Sell a call
   C. Write a call
   D. Both B and C

210. Commercial paper and banker's acceptances are generally found in which one of these securities?
A. Money market
B. DPP
C. MSRB
D. Growth mutual funds

211. Your firm is a part of an underwriting syndicate for a new stock issue, and the issue is now in its "cooling-off period." What actions may you take during the cooling-off period?
I. Take orders in anticipation of the new issue coming to market
II. Take indications of interest
III. Send "red herrings"
IV. Do nothing at this time, await instructions
A. I, III
B. II
C. II, III
D. IV

212. For the exchange markets, there are three critical people for each transaction. These people are:
A. Broker, buyer, seller
B. Buyer, seller, specialist
C. Buyer, seller, broker
D. Buyer, seller, broker-dealer

213. A limit order for the purchase or sale of stock is an effort to limit the acceptable buying and/or selling price. This order:
A. May not execute at the price designated because of "stock ahead"
B. Always executes at the exact price listed
C. Is always second in priority to a market order
D. Both A and C

214. The holding period for stock is important because of the difference between tax rates for short- and long-term gains. Options may or may not be of benefit in helping this situation because:
A. Options may not be used to postpone the sale of a stock to generate long-term vs. short-term gains
B. Options may be used to postpone the sale of a stock to generate long-term vs. short-term gains
C. Options transactions are classified as long-term gains
D. None of the above

215. Your discussions with a client, age 71, suggest a concern for safety and income, without the need for immediate liquidity or an absolute guarantee of principal. Your recommendations could include:
I. Government bond fund
II. High-grade corporate bond fund
III. Gold stock fund
IV. Corporate bond UIT
A. I, II, III, IV
B. I, II, IV
C. I, II
D. II, IV

216. A bond issued at par with a 6.5% coupon is now selling on the resale market at 103. The bond is callable at 101 in three years. What is the current yield for this bond?
A. 6.37%
B. 6.5%
C. 6.4%
D. 6.31%

217. The risk for an uncovered put is:
   I. Unlimited
   II. Going to occur if the stock were to drop to zero
   III. Defined as the put's strike price minus the premium received
   IV. Defined as the put's strike price plus the premium received
   A. I
   B. II, III
   C. IV
   D. II, IV

218. An "issuer" of a security is known as:
   A. An underwriter
   B. The company
   C. The syndicate
   D. The broker-dealer

219. The owner of either a put or a call has three basic decisions available to her. These are:
   A. B, C, and D below
   B. Sell the option before expiration date
   C. Let the option expire
   D. Exercise the option

220. Traders who take advantage of differences in pricing of a security listed on two exchanges would enter into one, or more, of the following:
   A. Market arbitrage
   B. DPP arbitrage
   C. An illegal activity
   D. Both A and B

221. A Registered Principal must:
   A. Approve all new accounts
   B. Approve all trades
   C. Approve all new accounts and trades on a daily basis
   D. All of the above

222. Oil and gas limited partnerships may, if income is being generated, use:
   A. Land depreciation
   B. Depletion allowance
   C. Accelerated land depreciation
   D. None of the above

223. Open-end mutual funds always redeem shares from investors at:
   A. Market price
   B. POP
   C. NAV
   D. Asking price

224. A municipal bond that is issued as a revenue bond, but also backed by a larger entity, such as the community's tax base, is known as:
   A. An advanced-refunded bond
   B. A special-tax bond
   C. A double-barreled bond
   D. A moral-obligation bond

225. An investor has established the following position: Long 1 ZOR Aug 50 put at 5; short 1 ZOR Aug 45 put at 3. What's this position called?
   A. Debit put spread and is bullish
   B. Debit put spread and is bearish
   C. Credit put spread and is bullish
   D. Credit put spread and is bearish

226. When entering into a transaction with a customer, a broker-dealer may:
   A. Act only as a broker
   B. Act only as a dealer
   C. Act both as broker and dealer
   D. Not be on both sides of the trade and must disclose its position on the trade confirmation

227. Our client holds 1 ZOR Dec 50 put at 5. The CMV is now at 46. This position is said to have:
   A. Intrinsic value of 4
   B. A break-even of 55
   C. Time value of 3
   D. Time value of 5

228. The market for a specific stock, as viewed by the specialist for the retail client, will be:
   A. Highest bid, lowest asking price
   B. Lowest bid, highest asking price
   C. The specialist does not determine these prices
   D. The exchange determines the bid and asking prices for each stock

229. Our client, with no other position, is short 3 KAT Sep 60 calls at 4.
   I. Potential loss is $1,200
   II. Potential loss is $400
   III. Potential loss is unlimited
   IV. Maximum gain is $1,200
   A. I
   B. II, IV
   C. III, IV
   D. I, IV

230. Corporate profits, labor cost per unit, ratio of inventories to sales are examples of:
   A. Leading indicators
   B. Lagging indicators
   C. Coincident indicators
   D. Inflation

231. Suitability of an investment for our client is a prime concern in our industry. As the result:
   A. NYSE (Rule 405) requires brokers to know their customer's financial status
   B. MSRB requires the registered representative to inquire about tax status
   C. CBOE requires the registered representative to inquire about previous investment experience
   D. All of the above

232. Charts, graphs, and other support materials used in a sales presentation:
   A. Must be approved prior to use
   B. Do not need prior approval
   C. Does not include computer software
   D. May be altered by the registered rep

233. A stock's beta is a measure of volatility. If the beta coefficient is:
   A. Less than 1—the stock will move less than the overall market
   B. More than 1—the stock will move more than the overall market
   C. Neither statement is true
   D. Both statements are true

234. In options positions, full versus partial protection is often discussed.
   I. Full protection means being long in the option contract.
   II. Full protection means being short in the options contract.
   III. Partial protection means being long in the options contract.
   IV. Partial protection means being short in the options contract.
   A. II, III
   B. I, IV
   C. I
   D. I, IV

235. MSRB rules mandate an examination of all broker-dealers every:
   A. 12 months
   B. 24 months
   C. 36 months
   D. 48 months

236. A premium bond callable at par will have as its lowest yield (sometimes referred to as "yield to worst") the:
   A. Nominal rate
   B. Yield to call
   C. Yield to maturity
   D. Current yield

237. The term *issued stock* means:
   A. Authorized and distributed to investors
   B. Authorized only
   C. Outstanding stock in hands of investors
   D. Treasury stock

238. A *hot stock issue:*
   A. Will be designated "hot" before the issue comes to market
   B. May be purchased by associated persons
   C. May be purchased only by a client with a "restricted account"
   D. Can become a "hot issue" only by selling above the IPO on the secondary market

239. You have a client who has sold 1 KA 85 Aug put at 4. Soon after the company announces dismal earnings for the previous quarter, the CMV drops to 70.50 and the put is exercised. The client immediately sells the stock acquired from the exercise of the put and gets a market price of $70.50 for KA. What is your client's gain or loss.
   A. $1,050 gain
   B. $400 loss
   C. $1,050 loss
   D. $400 loss

240. Rule 144 is often referred to by number, and the rule relates to:
   A. Regulation of control securities
   B. Odd lot (small investor) sales
   C. Restricted securities
   D. Both A and C

241. When buying stock for a client, we often discuss the desirability for the client to buy a "round lot" versus an "odd lot." The reason for our discussion is that an odd lot costs the client more in commission. This is called:
   A. A mark-up
   B. Odd-lot trade price
   C. Odd-lot differential
   D. Odd-lot margin

242. Limited partnerships that could pass through tax credits to the investor would be:
   A. Raw land
   B. Government assisted housing
   C. Historic rehabilitation
   D. Both B and C

243. A client has the following options position. Short 1 KAT Nov 55 call at 6 and short 1 KAT Nov 55 put at 5. What is the name for this position?
   A. Long straddle
   B. Short straddle
   C. Diagonal spread
   D. Vertical spread

244. All broker-dealers must have, and maintain, a do-not-call-list. If a prospect does not want to be called, the prospect's name will be placed on the list for a period of:
   A. 10 years
   B. 5 years
   C. Indefinitely
   D. 2 years

245. In periods of time when interest rates are trending down, a company may want to buy back its bonds to refinance at a lower rate. If the outstanding bonds are not callable, how would the company proceed to buy back its bonds?
   A. Establish a "call" for the amount of bonds desired to call back
   B. Make a "tender offer"
   C. Pre-refund the issue
   D. Release the "sinking fund"

246. Trading discretion for an account is described as having the ability to choose the:
   I. Activity
   II. Asset
   III. Amount
   IV. Amount of withdrawal of funds from the account
   A. III, IV
   B. II, III
   C. I, II, III
   D. IV

247. Regulation D refers to private placement of a company's stock. Private placement stock is:
   A. Restricted stock
   B. Control stock
   C. Issued in only one state
   D. None of the above

248. A limited partnership (DPP) is known for its:
   A. Lack of liquidity
   B. Ease of selling on the secondary market
   C. Short-term investment objective
   D. Suitability for a low-income investor

249. The Trust Indenture Act of 1939 applies to:
   A. Municipal bonds
   B. IPOs
   C. Treasury bonds
   D. Corporate bonds

250. Customer statements must be provided at least:
   A. Quarterly
   B. Monthly
   C. As activity occurs, but not more often than monthly
   D. Both A and B

End of Practice Exam #1

Series 7 Securities Practice Exam #2

1. A client has an options position holding 1 KAT Jan 40 call at 6 and is short 1 KAT Jan 50 call. What is this options position called?
   A. Straddle
   B. Calendar spread
   C. Diagonal spread
   D. Price, or vertical spread

2. A broker's broker is used to place unsold portions of new municipal bond issues. This type of broker would be helpful to:
   A. Retail customers
   B. Institutional customers
   C. Options exchanges
   D. None of the above

3. Common stock "book value" is often described as:
   I. Assets – Liabilities = Net Worth
   II. Liquidation value of a common stock
   III. Perception of the stock's price
   IV. A value used for accounting purposes
   A. I, II
   B. III, IV
   C. I, III
   D. IV

4. A margin account is said to be restricted if:
   A. Equity is 100% or less
   B. Equity is 75% or less
   C. Equity is 50% or less
   D. Equity is 25% or less

5. You are now in production with your broker-dealer, and want to prospect for new clients by cold calling. You may call potential prospects between the hours of:
   A. 10:00 a.m. – 10:00 p.m.
   B. 9:00 a.m. – 9:00 p.m.
   C. 8:00 a.m. – 8:00 p.m.
   D. 8:00 a.m. – 9:00 p.m.

6. The separate account in a variable annuity is intended to offer a number of choices for our clients. These choices may be of benefit in:
   A. Keeping the annuity diversified
   B. Keeping pace with inflation
   C. Both A and B
   D. Neither A or B

7. All mutual funds have expense ratios, and these general statements apply:
   I. Bond funds generally have higher expenses, as compared to stock funds
   II. Bond funds generally have lower expenses, as compared to stock funds
   III. Stock funds have lower expenses, as compared to bond funds
   IV. Stock funds have higher expenses, as compared to bond funds
   A. I, III
   B. II,
   C. II, IV
   D. IV

8. In an auction market, the specialist maintains an order book. What may be found in this book?
   A. Limit orders
   B. Stop orders
   C. Market orders
   D. All of the above

9. You have a client who has done extensive review about a company and is convinced the stock will remain very steady for the next year. The client has an options account and is experienced in a number of option strategies. There are a number of options contracts available for this company. What is a likely strategy for the client to use?
   A. Sell a straddle
   B. Buy a straddle
   C. Sell a put
   D. Buy a call

10. A broker-dealer acting as a principal will charge a customer:
    A. Mark-down
    B. Mark-up
    C. Both A and B
    D. Agency fee

11. The death of one party in a JTIC account provides for the proceeds of the deceased person to:
    A. Automatically pass to the remaining tenant's estate
    B. Be retained by the remaining tenant's estate
    C. Be tax exempt
    D. Remain in the deceased tenant's estate

12. You live in an area where the school system is shared by two communities. The debt for the school system is known as:
    A. Municipal debt
    B. Coterminous debt
    C. Revenue debt
    D. Current debt

13. Economists compare one period with another by using:
    A. Constant dollars
    B. Inflated dollars
    C. Deflated dollars
    D. Actual dollars

14. Excessive trading in both frequency and size is called:
    A. Twisting
    B. Churning
    C. Specialized trading
    D. Matching

15. A client has sold an LMN Sep 50 put at 5.
    I. This position has unlimited risk.
    II. Possible loss will be the strike price minus the premium received.
    III. Risk will be the premium paid.
    IV. The premium will be received by the client.
    A. I, II, IV
    B. II, III
    C. III
    D. II, IV

16. When calculating accrued interest for a municipal bond, you will use:
    A. 360-day year
    B. 365-day year
    C. A settlement date 10 days after trade confirmation and 360-day year
    D. None of the above

17. Restricted stock:
    A. Has a 12-month holding period
    B. Does not have a holding period
    C. Is known as legend stock
    D. Both A and C

18. There are two basic types of stock—common and preferred. Which type normally pays a quarterly dividend?
   A. Common
   B. Preferred
   C. Both A and B
   D. Neither A or B—only cumulative stock will pay a consistent dividend

19. A client wants you to do a trade you do not believe is in his best interest. You should:
   A. Refuse to do the trade
   B. Do the trade and notify Compliance
   C. Cancel his account
   D. Do the trade—mark the ticket "unsolicited"

20. Full power of attorney is someone other than the account owner who has the right to:
   A. Make investment decisions
   B. Deposit or withdraw cash from the account
   C. Make investment decisions, but not have authority to make deposits or withdraw cash from the account
   D. Both A and B

21. A client has the following options position: Owns 1 ZOR Oct 40 call at 3 and is short 1 Feb ZOR 40 call at 6. Describe this options position:
   A. Diagonal spread
   B. Calendar spread
   C. Time spread
   D. Both B and C

22. Calculate the number of days of accrued interest for a corporate M & S bond purchased May 8 settled regular way:
   A. 70 days
   B. 71 days
   C. 60 days
   D. 72 days

23. DPP programs have an agreement which is unique to this security. Of the following choices it is the:
   A. Authorized agreement
   B. Subscription agreement
   C. Corporate agreement
   D. Convertible agreement

24. A KEOGH (HR-10) plan would be used for:
   I. Self-employed persons
   II. Owners of business with a corporate structure
   III. A qualified retirement plan
   IV. A nonqualified retirement plan
   A. I, II
   B. II, III
   C. I, IV
   D. I, III

25. The firm-element portion of continuing education for Registered Representatives refers to:
   A. Annual compliance meeting—not mandatory
   B. Annual compliance meeting which is mandatory
   C. Completion of the computer-based training requirement to be taken within 120 days of your second anniversary
   D. None of the above

26. The publication that provides the most information about the municipal bond secondary market is:
    A. *The Bond Buyer*
    B. *Munifacts*
    C. *The Blue List*
    D. Both A and B

27. In the absence of a price for a call, the lower the strike price, the:
    A. Higher the option premium
    B. Lower the option premium
    C. Neither A or B
    D. The closer the option will be to "out of the money"

28. In a short margin account, the minimum maintenance percentage allowable is:
    A. 25% of LMV
    B. 30% of SMV
    C. 50% of LMV
    D. 50% of SMV

29. A reduction of the sales charge due to more money being invested in a mutual fund is called:
    A. Back-end load
    B. Front-end load
    C. Breakpoint
    D. Breakpoint selling

30. In some oil and gas DPPs, the write-off for drilling may be 100% in the first year. If available, this deduction is called:
    A. Depletion allowance
    B. Intangible drilling cost
    C. Tangible drilling cost
    D. No such deduction exists

31. NYSE Rule 405 generally discusses suitable recommendations for clients. Under these guidelines, who has the responsibility to determine the validity of customer's financial status information?
    I. Manager of the broker-dealer
    II. Broker-dealer compliance officer
    III. Registered Representative
    IV. Sales assistant
    A. I, II
    B. II, III
    C. III
    D. IV

32. If an insured municipal bond defaults, the insurance will pay:
    A. Principal
    B. Principal and interest
    C. Interest
    D. Neither principal nor interest

33. An insured municipal bond will generally have a rating of:
    A. BBB
    B. A
    C. AA
    D. AAA

34. The highest degree in safety for a security is:
    I. Direct obligations of the U.S. government
    II. Government agency issues, such as FNMA
    III. Municipal securities
    IV. GNMA
    A. I, II
    B. II, IV
    C. III
    D. I, IV

35. The definition for *settlement date* means:
   A. Ownership changes between buyer and seller
   B. Trade date
   C. DTD
   D. T + 7 working days

36. Unit Investment Trusts are investment companies, but they differ from open-end mutual funds because:
   A. They do not have a board of directors
   B. They do not actively manage the trust
   C. They do not have an investment advisor to manage or trade the account
   D. All of the above are correct

37. The term *legislative risk* is used in various discussions. What does this term mean?
   A. Laws could change and the new laws could have a negative effect upon an investment.
   B. If laws change, there will no change to any investment a client already owns.
   C. Any discussion on suitability must include a discussion of any changes in laws known to be pending.
   D. Both A and C

38. Reinvestment risk is an important consideration for the following reason(s):
   A. If interest rates go down, money coming from the investment probably cannot be reinvested at the same rate as the original investment
   B. Normally this is not a consideration
   C. Both A and B
   D. None of the above

39. There are two types of voting rights available to common stockholders—cumulative and statutory:
   I. Statutory voting means one share, one vote.
   II. Cumulative voting means votes may be allocated to favor certain issues.
   III. Statutory voting favors the small stockholder.
   IV. Cumulative voting favors the small stockholder.
   A. I, II
   B. I, II, III
   C. I, II, IV
   D. II, IV

40. A client has an options position as follows: Long 1 XYZ Oct 35 call for 4 and short 1 XYZ Feb 50 call for 2. This options position is called:
   A. Calendar spread
   B. Price spread
   C. Diagonal spread
   D. Vertical spread

41. A client owns a "variable rate municipal bond" and wants you to review its features. You could say:
   I. The coupon rate does not vary
   II. The coupon rate varies, because the rate for this type of bond is indexed to some other interest rate
   III. The resale price for this type of bond is reasonably stable
   IV. The resale price for this type of bond follows the resale market for all other bonds and would not be considered to be stable
   A. I, III
   B. II, III
   C. I, IV
   D. III

42. When a company is considering whether or not additional bonds or additional stock should be issued for capital needed, taxation could be a prime concern because:
    - I. Interest on bonds is tax deductible
    - II. Interest on bonds is not tax deductible
    - III. Cash dividends are paid out to stockholders on an after-tax basis
    - IV. Cash dividends are paid out to stockholders on a before-tax basis

    A. I, III
    B. II, IV
    C. II, III
    D. I, IV

43. Your client asks why so many choices are available in the "family of funds" her mutual fund offers. You reply:
    A. Every fund has an objective
    B. Funds may be allocated to meet investment objectives
    C. Funds offer diversification of a portfolio
    D. All of the above

44. If desired, all annuities offer choices in receiving a lifetime income. Consider the following annuity choices: life income, life with period certain, and joint life. Which option offers the least amount of income per month?
    A. Life with 10 years certain
    B. Life with 15 years certain
    C. Life only
    D. Joint life

45. An allied member of a member firm is:
    A. An executive officer of a member firm who has more than 5 percent of the outstanding voting stock
    B. An executive officer of a member company who has more than 10% of the outstanding voting stock
    C. Common stockholders of a member firm
    D. Preferred stockholders of a member firm

46. A maintenance call could occur if:
    A. Market value for securities in the margin have declined
    B. Market value will not be a factor
    C. Insufficient equity is in the account
    D. Both A and C

47. Calculate the daily interest for a corporate bond selling at 92 with a coupon of 6.25%:
    A. .171233 cents per day
    B. .1736 cents per day
    C. .205 cents per day
    D. .3472 cents per day

48. Any client requesting approval for trading options must complete the options agreement and return it within:
    A. 30 days
    B. 45 days
    C. 15 days
    D. 90 days

49. The mandatory distribution for a traditional IRA must begin:
    I. By April 1 of the year in which the individual holding the IRA turns 70½
    II. By April 1 of the year in which the individual holding the IRA turns 59½
    III. Mandatory distribution does not apply to a traditional IRA
    IV. Mandatory distribution applies only to the Roth IRA
    A. I
    B. III, IV
    C. III
    D. IV

50. A municipal bond may carry an NR rating because the issue is not large enough to be rated.
    A. This statement is true.
    B. This statement is false.
    C. All bond issues are rated, regardless of size.
    D. NR is a superior rating.

51. In general, the minimum amount of equity which must be in a long-margin account before the first purchase may be made is:
    A. $1,000
    B. $5,000
    C. $2,000
    D. 100% of the purchase price above $5,000

52. The primary market refers to:
    A. Resale of IPOs
    B. Proceeds of sale going to Issuer
    C. Proceeds of sale going to Underwriter
    D. None of the above

53. When a "trading halt" occurs:
    I. All trading stops in the market where the halt was declared
    II. Open orders may be canceled
    III. The security may still trade in other markets
    IV. Options may be exercised
    A. I, II, III, IV
    B. I, II
    C. I, IV
    D. II, III, IV

54. The "record date" for dividends is described as:
    A. The date used to identify the holders of the security who are eligible to receive the dividend
    B. The date declared by the BOD
    C. Both A and B
    D. Neither A or B

55. A client orders you to buy 1,000 shares of ZORG on Monday morning. He further states the check for the purchase of ZORG will be brought to your office on Thursday. Tuesday afternoon the client orders you to sell 1,000 shares of ZORG, which are not in his account. You warn the client this action will:
    A. Freeze the account
    B. Be known as insider trading
    C. Be satisfactory, and you sell the stock
    D. Require the approval of your ROP

56. A new issue of a municipal bond will normally contain a dated date (DTD) and a settlement date. These dates:
    I. May differ
    II. Refer to when interests starts to accrue
    III. Refer to when the buyer will begin receiving the bond's interest
    IV. Always include the settlement dates for the interest calculation
    A. I, II, III, IV
    B. I, II,
    C. II, III, IV
    D. II, III

57. Options traded on exchanges are known as:
    A. Listed options
    B. OTC options
    C. Standardized options
    D. Both A and C

58. A fiduciary account may:
    I. Have a legal list of securities approved for use within the account
    II. Not permit the use of uncovered options
    III. Require the use of the prudent-person rule
    IV. Require a court order or certificate to open
    A. I, II
    B. II, III, IV
    C. III, IV
    D. I, II, III, IV

59. A recourse loan may sometimes be used in a limited partnership. The use of this type loan:
    A. Will increase an investor's liability
    B. Is illegal
    C. Will limit the liability of the investor
    D. Is used to guarantee DPP results

60. A corporation successfully sold its IPO last year and now has additional stock to sell to the public. It is on record to provide a preemptive right to its existing stockholders, which means:
    I. Existing stockholders will not have special consideration for the additional stock
    II. Existing stockholders will receive rights to purchase additional stock below the current market price
    III. Existing stockholders will receive warrants to purchase additional stock below current market price
    IV. Control persons will be eliminated from this offering
    A. I
    B. II, IV
    C. III
    D. II

61. The entity responsible for cancellation of stock or bond certificates sold and the reissue of new certificates in the name of the new owner is known as:
    A. Custodian
    B. Transfer Agent
    C. Trustee
    D. MSRB

62. The *trough* is known as the period at the:
    A. End of a declining period of business activity
    B. End of an increasing period of business activity
    C. Beginning of a downward trend in business activity
    D. Beginning of an upward trend in business activity

63. A client wants to purchase an NHA municipal bond. You tell the client:
    I. An NHA bond is not secure
    II. An NHA bond is a direct obligation of the government
    III. Since he is in the 15% tax bracket, the purchase is not suitable
    IV. Since he is in the 15% tax bracket, a taxable purchase will be suitable

    A. I, II
    B. II, III
    C. I
    D. I, IV

64. A foreign currency option will:
    A. Not be suitable for many investors
    B. Be suitable for most investors
    C. Allow for the speculation on foreign currency interest rates
    D. Not allow for fluctuation in currency exchange rates

65. Upon the completion of new account opening documents for a client, you mention some of the investments you could recommend contain the risk of "capital loss."
    A. Capital loss is of no concern
    B. Capital loss means the possibility for real loss of the original investment
    C. You have ways of preventing capital loss and will take immediate action, without her approval, if the client cannot be located
    D. This loss is always unrealized and should be of no concern to the client

66. A significant increase in trading activity after an account becomes discretionary could be an indication of:
    A. Front-running
    B. Matching transactions
    C. Capping
    D. Churning

67. What is the client's break-even for Long 3 ZOR Nov 65 calls at 5?
    A. 65
    B. 62
    C. 60
    D. 70

68. One of your larger clients has a total tax rate of 46%, when the combination of federal, state, and local taxes are considered. You have found within her state of residence a municipal bond with an interest rate of 4% selling at 95. What is the tax equivalent yield?
    A. 7.4%
    B. 7.8%
    C. 8.5%
    D. 4%

69. You are evaluating an options position as follows: Long 1 LMN Feb 55 call at 4 and long 1 LMN Feb 55 put at 5. What are the break-even points?
    A. 64, 55
    B. 5, 46
    C. 5, 55
    D. 64, 46

70. Most new account forms contain some type of predispute arbitration agreement. Does this type of agreement also include class-action suits?
    A. The statement is in error, since most new account forms do not include an arbitration agreement
    B. Class action suits are a part of arbitration agreements
    C. Class action suits are not subject to arbitration
    D. None of the above apply

71. GNMA issues are subjected to what type(s) risk?
    A. Risk of principal if held to maturity
    B. Reinvestment risk
    C. Major concern for loss of principal, since GNMA issues are not of investment grade
    D. Capital risk due to the underlying securities being common stocks

72. A client wants you to explain why his growth mutual fund has a distribution of capital gains and a 1099 was issued, since he did not withdraw any money from the fund in the past year. You comment:
    I. The client owns a portion of the overall fund
    II. The fund manager for the mutual fund traded stocks within the fund and realized gains, which are taxable
    III. The fund manager has been removed from the fund, since a number of errors were made and all gains should have been unrealized
    IV. Since the client did not take a distribution from the fund, he should disregard any funds distribution
    A. I, II
    B. II
    C. III
    D. IV

73. A *convertible security* is convertible to:
    A. DPPs
    B. Preferred stock
    C. Common stock
    D. Straight preferred stock

74. Common stock may be either voting (class A) or nonvoting (class B). What are the advantages of non-voting stock from the company's viewpoint?
    A. No dilution of present ownership
    B. Dilution of present ownership
    C. Does not require shareholder approval
    D. Removes limited liability provision of common stock

75. When a new account is opened for a client, we must:
    I. Obtain the approval of a Registered Principal
    II. Obtain risk tolerance information
    III. Always include the loan agreement
    IV. Always have a specific mailing account
    A. I, II, III
    B. I, II, IV
    C. I, IV
    D. II, IV

76. A few examples of regional exchanges are:
    A. AMEX, Boston, Pacific, Philadelphia
    B. NYSE, Cincinnati, Pacific, Philadelphia
    C. OTC, Cincinnati, Pacific, Philadelphia
    D. Boston, Cincinnati, Pacific, Chicago

77. In a margin account, the "DR" refers to:
    A. Long-market value
    B. Short-market value
    C. Debt due the broker-dealer
    D. Draft register in a short account

78. A closed-end fund is:
    I. Publicly traded
    II. Also called ETF (exchange traded funds)
    III. Sold by prospectus in its IPO
    IV. Redeemed by selling shares on the secondary market
    A. I, II, IV
    B. I, II, III, IV
    C. II, III
    D. I, IV

79. Your client has heard about defensive stocks and would like you to explain a few basics. You reply:
    A. Defensive stocks have higher risks and are more affected by business cycles
    B. Defensive stocks have higher returns
    C. Defensive stocks have lower risks and are less affected by business cycles
    D. An example of a defensive industry would be raw materials, such as steel

80. A variable annuity is taxed as:
    I. FIFO
    II. LIFO
    III. Ordinary income on gains
    IV. Long-term capital-gains rate on appreciated value
    A. I, IV
    B. II, IV
    C. I, III
    D. II, III

81. You have recommended a municipal bond to a client that trades "cash settlement." This means this bond:
    A. Will always be AAA
    B. Settles the regular way
    C. Settles T + 3
    D. Settles on the trade date

82. An investor sells short 100 shares of RSK at 62 and is long 1 RSK Sep 65 call at 5. What is the investor's maximum gain?
    A. $6,500
    B. $5,700
    C. $6,200
    D. Unlimited

83. Using question number 82 as the overall position, what is the investor's maximum loss?
A. $500
B. $300
C. $800
D. Unlimited

84. On both of the major exchanges, buyers and sellers are brought together in what type market?
A. Auction market
B. Negotiated market
C. Seller's market
D. Buyer's market

85. You know of a company which offers its key employees the option of a deferred compensation plan. The S&P rating for this company is B. What would be your major point(s) of discussion for anyone electing a deferred compensation plan with this company?
A. A key employee is a secured debtor of the corporation.
B. A key employee is a general creditor of the corporation.
C. The benefit is payable upon the employee's retirement as ordinary income.
D. Both B and C

86. A customer's margin account contains stock owned with a market value of $110,000 and has a debt balance of $45,000. What is the equity in the account?
A. $65,000
B. $45,000
C. $55,000
D. $50,000

87. The difference between the asking price and the bid price for a security is called:
A. Markup
B. Markdown
C. Spread
D. Takedown

88. The OTC market is:
A. An interdealer market
B. An exchange market
C. The options market
D. The MSRB

89. A general partner in a DPP may:
A. Share in a small portion of revenues but usually has a major portion of the expenses
B. Share in a small portion of the expenses but usually has a major portion of the revenues
C. Not have any form of POA
D. None of the above

90. An option is often referred to as a contract and is traded without a certificate. What is the proof of ownership for the client?
A. Trade confirmation
B. W/I
C. BE
D. A copy of the contract

91. The syndicate management fee is a part of the spread in a municipal bond issue. Which of the following is true?
I. It is calculated as a fee per bond.
II. This fee comes out before any other fees.
III. This fee comes out after all other fees.
IV. It is not calculated on a per-bond basis.
A. I, III
B. II, IV
C. I, II
D. III, IV

92. An investor buys 100 shares of BAT at 60 and immediately buys 1 BAT Oct 55 put at 4. What is this position called?
A. Married put
B. American put
C. Both A and B
D. Neither A nor B

93. You have recommended a new issue municipal bond which has been released for sale. The client must receive:
   A. Prospectus
   B. Preliminary prospectus
   C. Preliminary Official Statement
   D. Official Statement

94. Your client wants you to buy a "penny stock," and you have advised against the purchase. The client insists upon the purchase.
   A. Do not buy the stock for the client, since it is not in the client's best interest
   B. Buy the stock and mark the order "unsolicited"
   C. Buy the stock and mark the order "solicited"
   D. Don't buy the stock, since your firm does not have an analyst devoted to this issue

95. In the exchanges, the specialist may have "stock ahead," which means:
   A. The new limit order you have placed for the client may not execute at this time
   B. The specialist may have other orders in the book at the same price
   C. The specialist may have orders ahead which will take precedence over your order
   D. A, B, and C

96. One of the most widely used terms is *price to earnings ratio* (PE). How is this ratio calculated?
   A. Annual dividend divided by market price
   B. Market price divided by annual dividend
   C. Earnings divided by current market price
   D. Market price divided by earnings

97. For Registered Representatives, the continuing-education requirement is known as the regulatory Element and Firm Element.
   A. The firm element refers to an annual meeting which all representatives *must* attend
   B. The firm element refers to an annual training meeting which representatives should attend
   C. The regulatory element refers to an annual meeting which all representatives *must* attend
   D. The regulatory element refers to an annual meeting which all representatives should attend

98. Yield to maturity for a premium bond will be:
   A. Higher than the coupon
   B. Lower than the coupon
   C. Higher than the nominal yield
   D. Higher than the interest rate

99. The CBOE is the SRO for:
   A. Municipal issues
   B. OTC issues
   C. Options transactions
   D. AMEX

100. A client has a margin account with an equity position of over 70%.
   A. An IPO may be purchased on margin under these circumstances
   B. An IPO may never be purchased on margin
   C. An IPO must always be purchased "fully paid"
   D. Both B and C

101. One reason to buy an option on an equity issue is to:
   A. Defer a decision about the issue
   B. Increase income for a position held
   C. Keep the premium for the option
   D. None of the above

102. In the course of opening a new account, you find the client is an employee of another broker-dealer. Under these circumstances you should:
   I. Not open the account
   II. Advise your new client the employing broker-dealer must be notified of the new account
   III. Advise the client that duplicate statements may be sent to her employer if requested
   IV. In this instance, make an exception and not notify her broker-dealer

   A. I
   B. I, III
   C. IV
   D. II

103. There are two styles of options: American and European. Describe each style.
   I. An American-style option may be exercised at any time during the option period
   II. A European-style option may be exercised at any time during the option period
   III. An American-style option may be exercised only on the day preceding expiration
   IV. A European-style option may be exercised only on the day preceding expiration

   A. I, IV
   B. II, III
   C. I, II
   D. III, IV

104. One of the main features of individual stocks and bonds is a term called *transfer of ownership.*
   A. The statement is not correct, since neither stocks nor bonds may be transferred
   B. The statement is true for either individual stocks or bonds, since both may trade in the secondary market
   C. Bonds offer ease of transfer; stocks do not
   D. Stocks offer ease of transfer; bonds do not

105. There are many type orders you may enter on behalf of a client. From the information listed, determine which of the following are true?
   I. A "market order" is executed at a preset price
   II. A "market order" is executed immediately at the current market price
   III. A "day order" expires at the end of the day, if not filled
   IV. A "day order" expires at the end of the current week, if not filled

   A. I, IV
   B. II
   C. IV
   D. II, III

106. When a public offering is made by your firm, there are guidelines which must be followed. These guidelines would include:
   A. The IPO must be sold at the POP
   B. Unless an IPO is a "hot issue," no broker-dealer employee may buy at the POP
   C. An IPO may be sold to family members, since they are not employees of the broker-dealer
   D. An IPO may always be sold to a person with a "restricted account"

107. A mutual fund will normally offer a number of funds within a "family of funds." Which statements apply to this situation?
   I. Usually an investment may be allocated between funds without additional sales charges.
   II. After an initial fund allocation is made, the investor can usually revise the allocation without additional sales charges.
   III. An exchange between members of the fund family may be a taxable event.
   IV. An exchange between members of the fund family is never a taxable event.
   A. I, II, IV
   B. I, II, III
   C. I, III
   D. IV

108. The Trust Indenture Act of 1939 is concerned with:
   A. Corporate bond offerings over 5 million dollars in value
   B. Municipal notes
   C. Authorized stock limits
   D. Municipal bond offerings under 5 million dollars

109. You are preparing for a meeting with a client regarding the details of a recommendation. You notice that the market research report you have chosen to use does not indicate the source of the information contained within the report.
   A. You may not use this report
   B. You may use the report if you place your name on it as the source
   C. You may go to the Internet and use a similar report produced by the competition
   D. None of the above

110. The Insider Trading and Securities Fraud Enforcement Act of 1988 specifies certain guidelines and penalties. A few of these are:
   I. Nonpublic information is covered by this act
   II. Anyone acting upon nonpublic information is liable
   III. This law pertains only to insiders and not the general public
   IV. A trade need not be made for a violation to occur
   A. I, III
   B. I, III, IV
   C. II
   D. I, II, IV

111. Certain limited partnership programs offer tax credits. What is the importance of tax credits for an investor?
   A. Tax credits are dollar-for-dollar reductions in taxes due.
   B. Tax credits are important, but cannot be the overriding reason to purchase a DPP.
   C. Any tax credits a DPP may offer are not of value to an investor
   D. Both A and B

112. If an issuer of a municipal bond states that the bond will operate under a "gross revenue pledge," we know the following:
   A. The bond is a revenue bond
   B. The bond is a GO bond
   C. Debt service is paid first
   D. Both A and C

113. An issue of a GO bond has published a debt statement rather than a revenue pledge.
   A. This procedure is in accordance with a GO bond.
   B. The issue is probably not in compliance and will make a revenue pledge at a later date.
   C. Since this is a GO bond, the debt statement is of no concern.
   D. When the revenue pledge is made, the bond will increase in rating.

114. If you have discretion over an account, you have the following authority:
   I. May choose the security
   II. May decide to either buy or sell
   III. May choose the size of the trade in units, shares, etc.
   IV. May deposit, or withdraw, funds
   A. I, II, III, IV
   B. I, II, III
   C. I, II, IV
   D. IV

115. You now are in production and are notified of the death of a client. What should you do?
   A. Freeze the account
   B. Cancel open orders
   C. Await instructions
   D. All of the above

116. The SEC may conduct an investigation of any person suspected of insider trading. What are the maximum penalties which may be imposed?
   I. 300% of profits made
   II. 300% of losses prevented
   III. Up to 10 years in jail
   IV. 100% of profits made
   A. I, II, III
   B. II, III, IV
   C. III
   D. IV

117. A person in the 15% tax bracket is considering the purchase of a 3.5% municipal bond. You reply:
   A. With a tax equivalent yield of 3.5%, the investment is not suitable
   B. With a tax equivalent yield of 4.1%, the investment is not suitable
   C. Municipal bonds are always suitable investments, due to their quality
   D. Municipal are always suitable investments, due to their tax-exempt status

118. A client has purchasd 1 APE Nov 45 Call for 4 and the current market price for APE is $48 per share.
   A. The intrinsic value of the option is 1 and the time value is 3
   B. The time value for the option is 4
   C. The time value of the option is 0 and the intrinsic value is 4
   D. The time value of the option is 1 and the intrinsic value is 3

119. An order ticket you write to buy or sell stock for a client must be approved:
   A. By the Registered Principal no later than the end of the trading day
   B. By the Registered ROP no later than the end of the trading day
   C. By the Compliance Officer no later than noon the next trading day
   D. By the Manager no later than noon the next trading day

120. In setting up a basic margin account to pledge securities as collateral, what form is needed?
   A. Loan agreement
   B. Reg U form
   C. Reg T form
   D. Hypothecation agreement

121. Consider these indicators: number of hours worked, employment levels, personal income, and industrial production. They are known as:
   A. Leading indicators
   B. Lagging indicators
   C. Coincident indicators
   D. GDP

122. How do options settle?
   A. Next business day
   B. Stock delivered is settled regular way
   C. Regular way
   D. Both A and B

123. A "sell-stop" order is placed:
   A. Above the CMV
   B. Below the CMV
   C. Always as a "day" order
   D. Always as an IOC order

124. The order of priority for liquidating a DPP is:
   I. General partner(s)
   II. Limited partners
   III. Secured creditors
   IV. General creditors
   A. III, IV, I, II
   B. I, III, II, IV
   C. III, IV, II, I
   D. I, II, III, IV

125. In takeover situations, there are some investors who buy the stock of a company being acquired and short the stock of the acquiring company. These investors would be doing:
   A. Market arbitrage
   B. Risk arbitrage
   C. Insider trading
   D. Restricted trading

END OF FIRST HALF OF THE FINAL EXAM. IF YOU WERE TAKING THE TEST AT THE TESTING CENTER, YOU WOULD BE REQUIRED TO TAKE A BREAK BEFORE STARTING THE LAST HALF OF THE EXAM.

YOU WOULD NOT BE PERMITTED TO GO BACK AND CHANGE ANSWERS ON THE FIRST HALF ONCE YOU STARTED THE SECOND HALF.

2nd HALF—PRACTICE EXAM #2

126. An investor has researched the stock for ZR corporation and believes the stock will remain stable over the next 9 months. What action may be appropriate?
    A. Write a call
    B. Sell a call
    C. Buy a call
    D. Both A and B

127. The underwriting spread consists of several components. Which one is the largest?
    A. Managing underwriters fee
    B. Reallowance
    C. Selling concession
    D. Underwriting fee

128. An account listed as JTIC:
    I. Always has equal ownership for all parties to the account
    II. May have unequal ownership within the account
    III. Would feature "right of survivorship"
    IV. Upon death of an owner, the portion of securities owned in the account go directly to deceased person's estate
    A. I, IV
    B. II, III
    C. IV
    D. II, IV

129. A client is long 1 KA Sep 35 put at 4. What is the break-even point for this position?
    A. 31
    B. 35
    C. 39
    D. 40

130. You are about to advise a client to place a life insurance contract in her traditional IRA.
    A. The recommendation will be in error, since life insurance may not be placed into an IRA
    B. The recommendation will be suitable
    C. The recommendation will be suitable, if it is no more than 5% of the account
    D. The recommendation will not be suitable, since an IRA is a nonqualified retirement plan

131. In a short margin account, the short market value:
    A. Must go up for the client to make a profit
    B. Must go down for the client to make a profit
    C. Must remain constant
    D. Will not have an effect upon the equity in the account

132. All customer signatures must be "guaranteed." A customer signature guarantee may be performed by a:
    A. Commercial bank
    B. Broker-dealer
    C. Both A and B
    D. Neither A nor B

133. In general, records must be kept for a period of:
    A. 3 years
    B. 6 years
    C. 2 years
    D. 10 years

134. A client is concerned about safety of principal within his account. Which of the following strategies will be suitable for this client?
   I. Purchase aggressive growth stock
   II. Purchase a GNMA mutual fund
   III. Purchase a growth stock
   IV. Purchase a high-yield bond fund
   A. I, IV
   B. II, IV
   C. II
   D. IV

135. Stock dividends are frequently paid by companies who are:
   A. Well established
   B. Considered to be growth companies
   C. In a "turnaround situation"
   D. "Cash rich"

136. Cash dividends are paid out to stockholders from:
   A. After-tax dollars
   B. Before-tax dollars
   C. Are not taxable to stockholders
   D. Both B and C

137. Does the specialist for a stock participate in every transaction?
   A. Yes
   B. No, but all transactions must take place in front of the specialist assigned to the stock
   C. Yes, including transactions for the specialist's own account
   D. None of the above

138. The "inside" OTC market refers to:
   A. Highest bid – lowest asking price
   B. Lowest bid – highest asking price
   C. Insider trading
   D. Restricted stock

139. A client has the following spread: Long 1 APE May 50 put at 4 and Short 1 APE May 40 put at 3. What is maximum gain and maximum loss?
   I. Maximum gain $1,000
   II. Maximum gain $900
   III. Maximum loss unlimited
   IV. Maximum loss $100
   A. I, III
   B. II, IV
   C. II, III
   D. I, IV

140. When viewing trading patterns, a stock which has been trading within a narrow range for several months moves upward to the top of the trading range. This is known as:
   A. The resistance level
   B. The support level
   C. Bullish breakout
   D. Bearish breakout

141. The Securities Exchange Act of 1934:
   I. Created the SEC
   II. Created oversight for exchanges
   III. Regulates extension of credit
   IV. Regulates insider transactions
   A. I, II, IV
   B. II, III, IV
   C. III, IV
   D. I, II, III, IV

142. A UGMA account:
   A. Is a custodial account considered to be a revocable trust
   B. Is a custodial account considered to be an irrevocable trust
   C. May be for the benefit of more than one child
   D. May contain more than one custodian

143. A "special situation" mutual fund may contain:
   A. A high level of risk
   B. Companies undergoing a major management change
   C. Companies that are takeover candidates
   D. All of the above

144. In the NASDAQ market, sales transactions must be reported by market makers within:
   A. 60 minutes
   B. 60 seconds
   C. 90 minutes
   D. 90 seconds

145. Within a variable annuity, switching from one fund to another fund within the same family of funds would be considered:
   A. Inappropriate
   B. A taxable event
   C. Not a taxable concern within an annuity
   D. A taxable unrealized gain

146. Options are called *derivative securities.* What does this term mean?
   A. Options derive value from other securities
   B. Derivative securities are just another name for a product
   C. Derivatives are usually considered to be speculative in nature
   D. None of the above

147. Eurodollars are U.S. dollars:
   A. Deposited outside the United States and denominated in foreign currency
   B. Deposited outside the United States and remain denominated in U.S. dollars
   C. On deposit in the United States designated for foreign trade
   D. On deposit in Europe for currency speculation

148. A client has $650,000 in Treasury Notes on deposit in her account and is concerned she is not "insured." You reply:
   A. Treasury notes are a direct obligation of the government and are fully backed by the government's taxing authority
   B. Only $500,000 is backed up by FDIC
   C. SIPC will cover the entire amount
   D. None of the above

149. An *accredited investor* is one who:
   A. Has at least $1,000,000 in net worth
   B. Has an annual income of $200,000, or more over at least the past two years
   C. Reasonably expects income will remain at $200,000 or more in the current year
   D. All of the above

150. A zero-coupon bond increases in value each year, and this process is called:
   A. Accumulation
   B. Accretion
   C. Accrual
   D. Recovery

151. A basis point is, among other uses, a measure of a bond's yield. Therefore, an increase in a bond's yield from 4.5% to 5.0% would be:
   A. 500 basis points
   B. 100 basis points
   C. 50 basis points
   D. .5 basis points

152. When analyzing a balance sheet, *current liabilities* refer to:
   A. Debts due within 12 months
   B. Debts due within the next 90 days
   C. Debts due within the next 30 days
   D. Accounts receivable

153. Calculate the sales charge for Zip funds. Public offering price $12.60. NAV $12.15.
A. 3.0%
B. 3.6%
C. 3.7%
D. 4.0%

154. In options trading, the same side of the market refers to:
I. Long calls – short puts
II. Long puts – short calls
III. Long calls – short calls
IV. Long puts – short puts
A. I, II
B. III, IV
C. III, II
D. IV, II

155. You have a client who needs to sell 5,000 BAT shares of stock. There is no doubt the client owns the shares, but due to unusual circumstances the stock certificates cannot be delivered the regular way. Your broker-dealer:
A. States there is no way a delay in the delivery of the certificates may be accomplished
B. Allows the client to use a Regulation U settlement
C. Uses the W/I procedure
D. Sets up a seller's option contract

156. Your client has stock which has increased in value to $80 per share, and would like to sell at that price. Since the client has owned the stock for 10 months, she elects to buy a $80 put and defer the sale price.
I. The put will delay the sale of the stock
II. For tax purposes, the sale will be a short-term gain
III. For tax purposes, the sale will be a long-term gain
IV. The put will not delay the date of sale for tax purposes
A. I, II
B. I, II, IV
C. III
D. II

157. The members of an underwriting syndicate make an agreement to commit to a certain portion of the issue through:
A. Syndicate letter
B. Selling group agreement
C. Manager's letter
D. Lead manager's letter

158. You see a resale muni bond with a high interest rate, and a premium. Your client is in need of income.
A. This bond is unsuitable
B. In view of the premium, the bond may be suitable if there is a reasonable time remaining to maturity
C. In view of the premium, the bond may be suitable if there is a reasonable time remaining to call
D. Both B and C

159. Members of the syndicate may buy municipal bonds at what price?
A. POP minus total takedown
B. POP minus total spread
C. POP
D. POP minus concession

160. Under what circumstances may a corporate offering be made on a private placement basis?
I. Must be private and not offered to the public
II. An institution could buy the entire issue
III. A small group of wealthy investors could buy the entire issue
IV. Must be for investment purposes, not speculation
A. I, IV
B. I, II, IV
C. IV
D. I, II, III, IV

161. In analyzing and rating a GO municipal bond, an analyst must consider:
A. Total outstanding debt
B. Per capita debt
C. Community's "attitude"
D. All of the above

162. Anyone who supervises people or manages a member firm's investment activities must be a:
A. Registered Representative
B. Registered Principal
C. Registered Associated Person
D. None of the above

163. SIPC is a government-sponsored corporation that collects assessments on an annual basis from broker-dealers. Its purpose is:
A. Consumer protection
B. Broker-dealer protection
C. Issuer protection
D. Market-maker protection

164. An investor buys 1 KAT Feb 60 call and sells one KAT Feb 70 call. What is the investor's market attitude?
A. Bullish
B. Bearish
C. Neutral
D. Uncertain

165. Your client owns a closed-end fund and comments that he would like to redeem shares from the fund. You mention:
A. This will not be possible since shares must be sold in the resale market to liquidate
B. The 800 number which should be called for fund redemption
C. Liquidation for the closed-end fund may be made in fractional shares
D. Redemption may be made, but getting the cash from the fund will take 10 days

166. You have entered into a business relationship with three other partners and have not notified your broker-dealer of this additional business interest.
A. You must get approval from the NASD for this business activity
B. You must get the approval of your broker-dealer for this business activity
C. No other business activity is allowed
D. Approval of your broker-dealer is not required

167. ERISA regulations cover:
A. Roth IRAs
B. Public retirement plans
C. Federal-employee retirement plans
D. Private retirement plans

168. A fund may charge up to 8½% sales charge if it offers:
   A. Reinvestment of dividends and gains at the NAV
   B. Breakpoints
   C. Rights of accumulation
   D. All of the above

169. When you are preparing a sell order for a client, you must indicate the following:
   A. If the client is "long," the security
   B. If the client is "short," the security
   C. Both A and B
   D. Neither A nor B

170. A client wants a recommendation from you for an investment-grade bond. Your recommendation could include any of the following:
   I. Corporate bond
   II. Income, or adjustment, bond
   III. Municipal bond
   IV. Government bond
   A. I, II, III
   B. I, IV
   C. III
   D. I, III, IV

171. You have discovered a triple tax exempt 4.5% municipal bond available on the resale market. You have this bond in mind for a client who is in the 46% tax bracket. What is the tax equivalent yield?
   A. 8.33%
   B. 6.74%
   C. 5.0%
   D. 4.5%

172. Where do you find municipal bonds for sale?
   A. NYSE
   B. AMEX
   C. PHLX
   D. OTC

173. An investor is short 100 shares of APE at 33 and long 1 APE Jul 35 call at 4. What is the maximum loss for this position?
   A. $200
   B. $600
   C. $500
   D. $1,200

174. A stop limit order when it reaches the stop price:
   A. Becomes a market order
   B. Becomes a limit order
   C. Will execute on the next uptick
   D. Will execute on the next downtick

175. If annuitization is chosen for a variable annuity:
   I. The assumption is called the AIR
   II. Annuity units are calculated
   III. Income may vary month to month
   IV. Income will not vary from month to month
   A. I, II, IV
   B. I, II III
   C. II, III
   D. I, IV

176. When funds are withdrawn from a mutual-fund account, there are three accepted accounting methods used for determining the cost basis. These are:
   I. FIFO
   II. LIFO
   III. Average basis
   IV. Share identification
   A. I, II, III
   B. II, III, IV
   C. I, II, IV
   D. I, III, IV

177. An investor sells 7 ZOR May 60 calls at 4. What is the maximum gain?
A. $2,800
B. $700
C. $5,400
D. $400

178. What is the maximum loss for the position described in question 177?
A. Unlimited
B. $2,800
C. $400
D. $700

179. The consolidated tape shows the message SLD for ZORK. What does this message mean?
A. ZORK is being removed from the tape.
B. The latest transaction for ZORK was delayed.
C. Trades for ZORK will be delayed for the entire trading day.
D. ZORK has new option contracts available.

180. The number of issues closing up or down in a particular day is known as:
A. Market depth
B. Market breadth
C. Market volume
D. Both A and C

181. Under NASD rules for freeriding and withholding, the "immediate family" is described as:
I. Parents and in-laws
II. Brothers or sisters
III. Brothers- or sisters-in-law
IV. Any relative receiving support from the Registered Representative
A. I, II, IV
B. II, IV
C. I, IV
D. I, II, III, IV

182. For the buyer of either a put or a call to make money, the market must:
A. Widen
B. Narrow
C. Both A and B
D. Neither A nor B

183. For the seller of either a put or a call to make money, the market must:
A. Widen
B. Narrow
C. Both A and B
D. Neither A nor B

184. All of the major exchanges have specialists who are assigned a particular group of stocks. What are a few of the job functions for a "specialist"?
I. Maintain a fair and orderly market
II. Perform as an agent
III. Perform as a principal
IV. Buy and sell for his own account
A. I, II
B. I, III
C. I, II, III
D. I, II, III, IV

185. A "book entry" bond is purchased by the client.
A. You are concerned because there is no certificate and the client will not be in a position to have proof of ownership
B. Book entry bonds furnish certificates upon request
C. The trade confirmation is proof of ownership for a book entry bond
D. There is nothing unusual about the book entry bond, and a certificate will be provided

186. In Direct Participation Programs, the GP cannot:
   I. Borrow from the partnership
   II. Compete with the partnership
   III. Commingle funds
   IV. Transfer fiduciary responsibility
   A. I, II, III
   B. II, III
   C. IV
   D. I, II, III, IV

187. If a client believes her broker-dealer used any form of deceptive practices in the course of doing business, she:
   A. May sue within a period of 5 years
   B. May sue within a period of 3 years
   C. May not sue, due to an arbitration agreement in force
   D. None of the above

188. If you are using the telephone to solicit business, what time period may be used?
   A. 5:00p.m. – 8:00p.m.; perfect for dinner hour!
   B. 10:00a.m. – 10:00p.m.
   C. 10:00a.m. – 9:00p.m.
   D. 8:00a.m. – 9:00p.m.

189. There are a number of theories about buying and selling stocks. The "capital asset pricing" theory:
   A. Involves a sophisticated analysis of the relationship between expected risk and expected return
   B. Says that all investments should be "defensive"
   C. Says that all investments should be "aggressive"
   D. No such theory exists

190. You may receive a gift from another broker-dealer of no more than:
   A. $200 per year
   B. $100 per year
   C. $500 per year
   D. You may not accept a gift

191. What publication would you use to find details about the secondary market for municipal bonds?
   A. *The Blue List*
   B. *The Bond Buyer*
   C. *Munifacts*
   D. None of the above

192. The type of bond you would use to speculate on the bond market would be:
   A. Corporate coupon bond
   B. Municipal coupon bond
   C. Intermediate government T bond
   D. Zero coupon bond

193. The liquidation priority for a corporation if it is going out of business is:
   I. Unpaid wages, taxes, secured debt
   II. Unsecured debt—general creditors
   III. Subordinated debt, preferred stock
   IV. Common stock
   A. I, III, IV
   B. I, II, IV
   C. I, II
   D. I, II, III, IV

194. A cumulative preferred stock will pay dividends in the following manner:
   A. Quarterly
   B. If a dividend is missed it is paid in arrears
   C. If a dividend is missed, it need not be paid in the future
   D. Both A and B

195. An investor has purchased the following options position: Long 1 RSK Jun 45 call at 5 and Short 1 RSK Jun 35 call for 7. What type position does the investor hold?
   A. Debit spread—bearish
   B. Credit spread—bearish
   C. Debit spread—bullish
   D. Credit spread—bullish

196. The term *trade date* is used throughout our industry. What does it mean?
   A. The date the transaction was executed
   B. The date the securities were paid
   C. The quote date
   D. For bonds, 3 business days after execution

197. Mutual funds held in a regular investment account (not tax deferred) pay out, from time to time, both dividends and capital gains. How are they taxed?
   A. If reinvested, tax is deferred
   B. If reinvested, tax is due
   C. If not reinvested, tax is due
   D. Both dividends and capital gains are taxable if reinvested or if taken in cash

198. A limited partner in a DPP may:
   A. Lose no more than the initial investment, unless recourse loans are a part of the partnership
   B. Have management responsibility
   C. Sue the general partner
   D. Both A and C

199. A *territorial bond* is:
   I. A municipal bond from Puerto Rico
   II. A corporate bond from a corporation within Puerto Rico
   III. A municipal bond from Guam
   IV. A municipal bond from the U.S. Virgin Islands
   A. II
   B. I, III
   C. I, III, IV
   D. IV

200. The two basic types of equity securities are:
   A. Common and preferred
   B. Common and closed end
   C. Common and corporate bond
   D. Common and participating preferred

201. Limit orders may not be used for OTC trades.
   A. There is no specialist for OTC.
   B. OTC is an auction market and there is a specialist.
   C. A specialist adds too much cost for OTC transactions.
   D. None of the above statements is true.

202. A specialized fund:
   A. Is also known as a "sector" fund
   B. May contain more risk for the client
   C. Is not considered to be diversified
   D. All of the above

203. A client has the following options position: Short 1 RSK Nov 35 call at 6 and owns 1 RSK Nov 45 call at 4. What is this position called?
   A. Diagonal spread
   B. Neutral spread
   C. Vertical spread
   D. Calendar spread

204. Examples of OTC securities are:
   I. ADR's
   II. Municipal bonds
   III. Bank stocks
   IV. U.S. government securities
   A. II, III
   B. I, IV
   C. I, II, III
   D. I, II, III, IV

205. A client is considering a DPP involving raw land. What type of risk is associated with this type of partnership?
   A. Speculation
   B. Income producing, conservative
   C. Well established, low risk
   D. Medium risk, with limited tax credits

206. The term *option income* is associated with this particular type of option activity:
   A. Uncovered calls
   B. Covered call writing
   C. Ratio call writing
   D. Uncovered put writing

207. Complaints regarding municipal bonds received from clients must be kept on file for:
   A. 5 years
   B. 3 years
   C. 6 years
   D. 10 years

208. If your firm receives a complaint from a municipal bond client, what procedure must be followed?
   I. Log the complaint into a complaint file
   II. Indicate what actions have been taken
   III. Deliver an Official Statement (OS) to the client
   IV. Deliver the MSRB's investor brochure to the client
   A. I, II, III
   B. I, II, IV
   C. IV
   D. II, IV

209. A firm that is providing research and/or advisory services for municipal bond investors is known as a(n):
   A. Municipal bond dealer
   B. Municipal bond principal
   C. Broker-dealer
   D. Advisor

210. For municipal activities, all records must be kept in an easily accessible place for at least:
   A. 1 year
   B. 2 years
   C. 3 years
   D. 6 years

211. A "mutilated certificate" comes to you from a client who wants to sell what appears to be 20 bonds. Where does your firm go to find out if this certificate will be considered "good delivery"?
   A. Compliance officer
   B. Registered principal
   C. Transfer agent
   D. Home office

212. There are basic option activities a client may enter into. These are:
    I. Buy an option
    II. Sell an option
    III. Trade an option
    IV. Hold an option
    A. I, II, III, IV
    B. I, II
    C. I, II, IV
    D. I, II, III

213. On the secondary market for option contracts, what is the result when an underlying stock goes down in value?
    A. The value of calls will go down.
    B. The value for puts will rise.
    C. Values will stay the same.
    D. Both A and B

214. The owner of either a put or a call has several choices that may be made as expiration of the contract nears. These choices include:
    I. Sell the option in the open market
    II. Rewrite the option at a different contract value
    III. Let the option expire
    IV. Exercise the option
    A. I, III, IV
    B. II
    C. I, II, III
    D. I, II, III, IV

215. A *broker* is described as:
    A. An individual, or a firm, who charges mark-ups
    B. An individual, or a firm, who charges commissions and arranges trades
    C. An individual, or a firm, who acts as "principal"
    D. An individual, or a firm, who charges mark-downs

216. When reviewing overall options contracts the term *same side of the market* is often mentioned in regard to position limits. What does this term mean?
    A. All options contracts are considered to be bullish
    B. All options contracts are considered to be bearish
    C. Both A and B
    D. Neither A nor B

217. The resale price for a variable-rate municipal bond:
    A. Is very volatile
    B. Is very stable
    C. Cannot vary from issue
    D. None of the above

218. What effect does a "reverse split" have upon an issue of stock a client is holding?
    A. The client has fewer shares than before the split.
    B. The client has more shares than before the split.
    C. In either instance, there would be no concern on your part if you are writing an order to sell the stock.
    D. None of the above

219. Every firm associated with municipal securities must establish a registered principal to supervise Registered Representatives. In addition, the principal must:
    A. Approve all new accounts
    B. Approve every muni transaction
    C. Approve all correspondence regarding municipal trades
    D. All of the above

220. In municipal bonds, if more than _____% of the proceeds are going to private parties, the bond is not automatically granted tax-exempt status.
A. 5
B. 10
C. 15
D. 20

221. During the 20-day cooling-off period for corporate securities, the broker may:
I. Take orders
II. Take indications of interest
III. Deliver the "Red Herring" to those indicating interest
IV. Not distribute sales literature
A. I, III
B. II, III, IV
C. III
D. III, IV

222. The NASD may impose almost any disciplinary action, except:
A. Jail sentence
B. Fines
C. Fines and a jail sentence
D. Cancellation of license

223. An investor has established a short straddle. Which of the following best describes the strategy?
A. The maximum gain is the premium collected
B. The maximum loss is unlimited
C. The investor hopes the market will narrow
D. All of the above

224. A client setting a short margin account must deposit:
A. At least $2,000
B. At least $2,000, or fully pay for the first trade if under $2,000
C. At least $4,000—full Reg T requirement
D. $1,000

225. You need to know where the market may be for an inactively traded OTC stock. You talk with a broker-dealer and request:
A. A workout quote
B. A nominal quote
C. A firm quote
D. A negotiated quote

226. Listings for penny stocks are found:
A. In the yellow sheets
B. In the pink sheets
C. On the regional exchanges
D. On CBOE

227. The NASD 5% markup policy is in place to:
A. Ensure investors receive fair treatment
B. Allow for a higher-than 5% policy
C. Both A and B
D. None of the above

228. An odd lot of equity securities is known as:
A. 99 shares, or less
B. 100 shares, or more
C. 50 shares, or more
D. 50 shares, or less

229. The trade confirmation will list:
A. The trade date
B. The settlement date
C. The quantity purchased
D. All of the above

230. Unit Investment Trusts (UITs) are groupings of securities and come in under The Investment Company Act of 1940. What are the unique features of the UIT?
A. They are not actively managed.
B. They do not have a board of directors.
C. Both A and B
D. None of the above

231. The basic requirements to establish a mutual fund are:
   A. Private capitalization of $100,000
   B. Clearly defined investment objectives
   C. At least 100 investors
   D. All of the above

232. An open-end investment company is said to be in a continuous public offering. This means:
   I. A prospectus must be provided for the client either at the time of the sales presentation, or prior
   II. A preliminary prospectus must be provided
   III. A secondary market for the shares does not exist
   IV. A secondary market for the shares does exist
   A. I, III
   B. II, IV
   C. I, IV
   D. II, III

233. Current liabilities for a company include:
   A. Accounts payable
   B. Accounts receivable
   C. Accrued wages payable
   D. Both A and C

234. Commodities are not backed up by SIPC. Why?
   A. Commodities are not considered to be securities
   B. Commodities are securities and are an exclusion from SIPC
   C. As a Registered Representative, you are licensed to sell commodities
   D. Commodities are backed by the FDIC

235. Your client has indicated the need for balanced, or moderate, growth. You recommendations could include:
   A. Aggressive-growth stocks
   B. Blue-chip stocks
   C. Balanced mutual fund
   D. Both B and C

236. At the request of the client, you have purchased a municipal bond at a discount for the client's account.
   I. The discount will be treated as ordinary income
   II. The discount will be treated as a long-term gain
   III. The discounted price is not taxed for a municipal bond
   IV. The discount may be offset by the interest rate
   A. I, IV
   B. I
   C. II
   D. IV

237. Insider trading is known by someone who divulges this information to the authorities. The informer may:
   A. Not receive any compensation
   B. Receive a merit consideration
   C. Receive up to 10% of the amounts recovered
   D. Receive up to 20% of the amounts recovered

238. The term *inside market* is used many times, particularly OTC. What is the inside market?
   A. Highest bid (retail selling price)
   B. Highest ask (retail buy price)
   C. Both A and B
   D. None of the above

239. What are the advantages of a margin account for the client?
   A. Can purchase more securities with less actual cash outlay
   B. Can use the loan value of securities with the margin account
   C. Can leverage the account by borrowing a portion of the purchase price
   D. All of the above

240. At expiration of an options contract, an options
   I. Buyer loses the premium
   II. Buyer keeps the premium
   III. Seller loses the premium
   IV. Seller keeps the premium
   A. I, IV
   B. II, III
   C. I, III
   D. II, IV

241. An investor owns an OEX Jun 450 call at 5. OEX is at 470 and the option is exercised. What is the investor's profit?
   A. $2,000
   B. $1,500
   C. $1,000
   D. $500

242. A proxy is used for:
   A. Absentee balloting
   B. Voting, in person, at the annual stockholder's meeting
   C. Neither of the above
   D. Cumulative voting

243. How would you describe a "moral obligation" municipal bond to a client?
   I. May be a "state issued" bond
   II. Usually backed by revenues
   III. If revenues are insufficient to pay the debt service for the bond issue, the state legislature may appropriate the funds needed.
   IV. Usually backed by taxing authority
   A. I, III, IV
   B. I, IV
   C. I, II, III
   D. III

244. Your firm may decide to become a syndicate member for a new municipal bond issue. What are a few of the key factors it will consider in making its decision?
   I. The extent of its liability
   II. The anticipated demand for the bond
   III. The scale and spread of the issue
   IV. Existence of any pre-sale orders
   A. I, II, III, IV
   B. I, II, III
   C. II, III
   D. II

245. A Registered Representative is responsible for keeping records for each customer's account. These records must include at least:
   I. Customer's name, address, and phone number(s)
   II. Account number(s) and type of account
   III. Investment objective
   IV. List of all securities on deposit with the firm
   A. I, II, IV
   B. I, II, III
   C. IV
   D. I, II, III, IV

246. Blue sky laws cover the registration of:
A. Registered Representatives
B. Broker-dealers
C. Securities
D. All of the above

247. An investor writes 1 BAT Jul 65 put at 6. It is now several weeks later, and the put is exercised when the CMV is 42. The investor immediately sells the newly acquired stock and gets 42 for BAT. What is the profit or loss for this position?
A. $600 profit
B. $1,700 profit
C. $1,700 loss
D. $2,300 loss

248. An aggressive growth mutual fund may have a turnover of 100%. What does this mean?
A. The average holding period for this fund is short term—one year or less
B. The investment manager may be churning the account
C. The average holding period is over one year
D. The fund is of lower risk

249. A defined contribution retirement plan favors:
A. Neither younger nor older employees
B. Younger employees
C. Older employees
D. None of the above

250. What type bond would be useful for accumulation of money for college, since it contains no reinvestment risk?
A. Coupon corporate bond
B. Coupon municipal bond
C. Zero coupon bond
D. Treasury bond

End of Practice Exam #2

Glossary

The definitions given here explain how the listed terms are used in the securities markets. Some of the terms have additional meanings, which can be found in a standard dictionary.

Accredited Investors—defined as people who have at least $1 million of net worth or an annual income of at least $200,000, and meet certain other criteria.

Accrete—the act of accretion. SEE: **Accretion.**

Accretion—amortizing the beneficial amount over the remaining life of a bond, and adjusting the cost basis accordingly.

Accrued Interest—interest that has accumulated because it has not yet been collected.

Accumulation, Rights of—SEE: **Rights of Accumulation.**

Accumulation Area—a technical chart pattern that shows trading in a narrow range for an extended period of time, followed by an expected upward trend as more buying interest is generated following the accumulation period. COMPARE: **Distribution Area.**

Accumulation Stage—the time when the investor is making regular payments into the separate account as an investment, and determines the amount of accumulation units. ALSO SEE: **Accumulation Units.** COMPARE: **Annuity Stage.**

Accumulation Units—the measure of how much of an interest the investor owns in the separate account, based on the amount of payments the investor makes into the separate account during the accumulation stage. ALSO SEE: **Accumulation Stage.** COMPARE: **Annuity Units.**

Acid Test Ratio—SEE: **Quick Assets.**

Active Income—SEE: **Earned Income.**

Additional Issue—when a company that is already public is looking to sell more stock. ALSO SEE: **Initial Public Offering.**

Additional Takedown—part of the takedown paid to the entire syndicate group (proportionately) to help defray costs and compensate them for the risk of taking on the bond issue. (The other part of the takedown is the seller's concession.) ALSO SEE: **Seller's Concession, Takedown.**

Adjusted Cost Basis—the original price, plus any commissions, adjustments or allowable expenses. (Used for computing tax liability.) Also referred to simply as **Basis** or **Cost Basis** although these latter two terms should technically refer to the original price only.

ADR—SEE: **American Depository Receipts.**

Advance-Decline Index—a measurement of the number of stocks that rise in price, compared with the number of stocks that decline in price. When advancers lead decliners, that is a bullish market sentiment. When decliners lead advancers, that is a bearish market sentiment. As this index is tracked over time, the steeper the line, the stronger the market sentiment is said to be in that direction.

Advance Refunded Bonds—new bonds sold in anticipation of replacing ones that are coming to maturity, or replacing bonds that are callable. (Usually this is done when interest rates are more favorable to the issuer, and may be done well in advance of the original bonds actually becoming due.)

Advance Refunding—a method of primary financing that lowers the interest rate of a municipality's debt obligation by selling more bonds when rates are lower, to replace bonds that are at a higher rate. ALSO SEE: **Advance Refunded Bonds.**

Advantages, Tax—SEE: **Tax Advantages.**

Advertising—any kind of public communication that comes from the brokerage firm, but is not specifically distributed by the firm, and as such the brokerage firm has no control over who receives the material. (e.g., TV, magazine, website). COMPARE: **Sales Literature.**

Aggressive Investments—stocks of rapidly growing companies that have prospects for above-average growth, but with prices that are highly volatile over time when compared with the broader market. (Some stocks that would be in a typical "aggressive" portfolio would be high-tech companies and other start-ups, and an aggressive portfolio would use margin.) COMPARE: **Defensive Investments.**

Agreement, Indenture—SEE: **Indenture Agreement.**

Agreement, Repurchase—SEE: **Repurchase Agreement.**

Agreement Among Underwriters—agreement where all investment banking broker-dealer firms who are part of the underwriting syndicate agree to appoint the originating investment banking firm as managing underwriter. The agreement also sets out how long the syndicate will last, details the proportionate share of the issue that each underwriter is committed to buying and reselling to the public, and gives the managing underwriter the authority to enlist a sales group. ALSO SEE: **Selling Group Agreement.** COMPARE: **Underwriting Agreement.**

AIR—SEE: **Assumed Interest Rate.**

All or None—1. a best efforts underwriting commitment whereby the firm sells as much of the issue as possible, but if the entire issue is not sold then the offering is cancelled and the investors' checks (which are escrowed until the offering is complete) are returned. (COMPARE: **Mini-Max.**) 2. all-or-none (AON) is a type of offering of municipal securities where a buyer is required to bid for all of the securities being offered if the party wishes to buy any. (COMPARE: **Multiples.**) 3. an order qualifier that says the entire order must be filled, but that it does not necessarily have to be filled right away. All or none says a partial order will not be accepted, but the order should not automatically be canceled either.

Alpha—measurement is used to gauge performance apart from risk factors of the market. Any number of items related to a portfolio can be gauged: a specific stock, the portfolio as a whole, the portfolio manager, etc. A positive alpha means that the performance being analyzed was better than expected, relative to other investments. A negative alpha means performance was relatively worse. COMPARE: **Beta.**

Alternative Minimum Tax (AMT)—a tax calculation designed to ensure that all wealthy individuals and corporations pay at least some tax, by also figuring the tax obligation without the inclusion of excessive deductions to which the entity may legally be entitled. By computing tax liability with and without those items, and making certain allowances, there is a minimum tax amount that must be paid.

Alternative Minimum Tax Bonds—SEE: **AMT Bonds.**

AMBAC Indemnity—municipal bond credit insurance company. SEE: **Credit Enhancement.**

American Depository Receipts (ADR)—a U.S. substitute for foreign common stock. Investors can hold ADRs rather than having to deal with trying to obtain stock in a foreign country. With ADRs, foreign companies can sell shares to U.S. investors without having to go through the lengthy and expensive SEC registration process. ADRs allow investors in the U.S. to collect dividends and enjoy the capital gains of the foreign stock, but do not usually come with voting rights or preemptive rights.

American Style—options that can be exercised at any time before the expiration date. COMPARE: **European Style.**

Amortization—the process of reducing an amount, by dividing it into smaller equal payments over a period of time.

Amortize—the act of amortization. SEE: **Amortization.**

AMT—SEE: **Alternative Minimum Tax.**

AMT Bonds—Alternative Minimum Tax (AMT) bonds are municipal bonds that provide tax-free interest income to the holder for regular income tax purposes, but which are considered tax preference items and must be added back in when figuring out an investor's AMT calculation for federal income tax purposes.

And Interest—when the buyer of a security must pay the quoted price of the bond or note, plus accrued interest since last interest payment was made. COMPARE: **Traded Flat.**

Annuities—a series of equal payments, often set up as insurance contracts because they are for the life of the holder. ALSO SEE: **Variable Annuities, Fixed Annuities.**

Annuitize—to convert an annuity contract from the accumulation stage to the annuity stage, so that the investor can begin to collect payments from the value that has built up in the annuity.

Annuity, Deferred—SEE: **Deferred Annuity.**

Annuity, Immediate—SEE: **Immediate Annuity.**

Annuity Stage—the time when the investor is receiving payments from the separate account. At the time that the variable annuity contract is converted from the accumulation stage to the annuity stage, a calculation is done to determine the basis for future payments. ALSO SEE: **Annuity Units.** COMPARE: **Accumulation Stage.**

Arbitrage—profiting from the price differential between two like securities, commodities, etc., that are trading simultaneously in two different markets.

Arbitration—an alternative means of dispute resolution whereby an impartial third party or panel of people listen to evidence presented by both sides and render a decision, thus avoiding the court system. (Often final and binding.)

As Mutually Agreed Upon—SEE: **Delayed Delivery.**

Ask—offer to sell at a quoted price. COMPARE: **Bid.**

Asset Allocation Fund—a balanced mutual fund that has multiple asset classes, and which tilts its asset balance between stocks, bonds, and cash depending on market conditions.

Asset Coverage—the extent that a company's (net) assets can cover its debt obligations. These can help determine the adequacy of a company's assets and cash flow to cover its debt, and how much protection can be expected in a worst case scenario with the company being liquidated in bankruptcy proceedings. SEE: **Net Asset Value per Bond, Bond Interest Coverage, Book Value per Share.**

Assets—things of value that are owned or in one's possession. (e.g., cash, stock, land). ALSO SEE: **Liabilities, Net Worth.**

Assumed Interest Rate (AIR)—an estimated interest rate that the insurance company uses when calculating the projected payout on a variable annuity contract. (This is not a guaranteed rate of return, but rather a means to calculate the conversion from accumulation units to annuity units. The AIR is a set figure, used as the benchmark for measuring performance of the separate account, and thus determining payout amounts.)

At Advertised Yield—bonds are sold at their stated yield as required by regulations, but are sold less a discount given to the buying dealer. (This is done for trades between municipal bond dealers, where this is referred to as trading on a **concession basis.**)

At-the-Money—when the strike price equals the price of the underlying stock, but at-the-money does *not* take into account the premium paid to buy the option. (This is not the same as **breakeven.**) COMPARE: **Breakeven, In-the-Money, Out-of-the-Money.**

Authorization, Full—SEE: **Full Authorization.**

Authorization, Limited—SEE: **Limited Authorization.**

Authorized Stock—the stock originally approved by a corporation in its Articles of Incorporation. (This is the maximum number of shares that the company may create.)

Authorizing Resolution—the issuer's authority to sell the bond issue, authorizing the action, describing the size of the issue, the interest rate on the bonds, and covering other legal issues. (As part of the authorizing resolution, or as a separate action, the municipality will also have an award resolution, awarding the securities underwriting contract to the chosen underwriter.)

Available Funds—an indicator that tracks the amount of money that is not currently invested in the market. When available funds are high, that is a bearish sentiment because it means investors are not fully invested in the stock market. On the other hand, the available funds sitting on the sidelines could indicate an imminent bullish trend when that pent-up money is finally invested in the market.

Averaging, Dollar Cost—SEE: **Dollar Cost Averaging.**

BA—SEE: **Banker's Acceptance.**

Back End Load—when a sales charge is added to an investment when it is sold (e.g., with a mutual fund, the length of time the investment is held often determines the sales charge that is added at time of sale—and often can drop to 0% by about the fifth year). If the load declines over time, it is often referred to as a **contingent deferred sales load (CDSL).** Back end load funds are often referred to as **Class B shares.** COMPARE: **No Load, Front End Load.**

Balance of Payments—measures the difference between all goods and services purchased between two countries. This includes all transactions made over a certain time period, comparing the amount of foreign currency taken in with the amount of domestic currency paid out. COMPARE: **Balance of Trade.**

Balance of Trade—one component of the balance of payments counts only goods and ignores the services and investment components. This is also referred to as the **current account.** COMPARE: **Balance of Payments.**

Balance Sheet—a financial report that shows the financial status of an entity with regard to assets, liabilities and net worth as of a particular date. COMPARE: **Income Statement.**

Balloon Maturity—when a bond issue has some bonds with staggered redemption dates, but a larger number of bonds coming due on the last maturity date.

Bank Grade Bonds—SEE: **Investment Grade Bonds.**

Banker's Acceptance (BA)—a time draft drawn on a particular bank, whereby the bank accepts responsibility for payment. Essentially BAs work like a letter of credit, and are money market instruments.

Basis—the original price. ALSO SEE: **Adjusted Cost Basis.**

Basis Point—1/100%, or .01 of yield. A basis point is the smallest unit of measure used to quote yields. It takes 100 basis points to equal 1%. (For example, if we say that the yield on a bond is 1/4 point higher, we are saying that it rose 0.25%, or 25 basis points.)

Basis Price—an investor's yield-to-maturity at a particular bond price.

Bear—one who has a negative view of the market, and thinks that the market will fall. COMPARE: **Bull.**

Bear Spread—a spread trade where the more expensive option was selling (short) call or buying (long) put. COMPARE: **Bull Spread.**

Bearer Bonds—bonds where the person who holds the bond is the owner. The bonds have coupons that are detached and submitted to collect interest payments. COMPARE: **Registered Bonds.**

Bearish—negative outlook, thinking that the markets will fall. COMPARE: **Bullish.**

Best Efforts—an agreement with the investment banking firm acting as agent and broker in selling the securities, buying only what it needs to fill orders, and without any obligation to purchase unsold securities from the issuer. ALSO SEE: **All or None, Mini-Max.** COMPARE: **Firm Commitment.**

Beta—measurement used to gauge a portfolio's performance vs. some chosen index. The beta number is an indicator of how volatile the portfolio is (how much wider its price fluctuations are) when compared to overall market. A well-diversified portfolio is one that moves even with the index, and would have a beta of 1. The higher the beta number, the more susceptible the portfolio is to the risk-reward ratios. Thus, in good times the portfolio will perform better than the market (giving more reward), but in bad times the portfolio will perform worse than the market (indicating more risk). A beta below 1 would indicate a more conservative investment portfolio that does not enjoy big gains when the market is doing well, but does not take big hits when the market is doing poorly. COMPARE: **Alpha.**

Bid—offer to buy at a quoted price. COMPARE: **Ask.**

Bid Wanted—bid request by a broker-dealer when there is no activity in the stock, but the dealer is looking to sell some and wants traders to submit a bid. COMPARE: **Offer Wanted.**

Blue Chip—common stocks from well-known companies who have a long history of growth and a reputation for good management. Dividends are usually paid out on a fairly consistent basis. Blue chips are usually nationally known corporations, and their products or services are familiar to many people. The common stock of these companies is considered relatively safe and stable, and thus it commands a higher price in the marketplace even with low yields.

Blue List, The—daily publication (put out by an S&P subsidiary) that lists comprehensive price, yield, volume, and other info about bonds offered for sale, including many municipal bond issues. Info is also available online at bluelist.com. The **Blue List Ticker** is the computerized subscription service that provides up-to-the-minute additions and deletions of bond offerings.

Blue List Ticker—the computerized subscription service that provides up-to-the-minute additions and deletions of bond offerings.

Blue List Total—the total par values of all municipal securities offered for sale, and as such is one measure of the supply of municipal securities available for purchase.

Blue Sky Laws—name given to various state laws requiring issuers to register their new issues and provide financial information for securities sold in their state. Compliance can be achieved by filing notice, coordinated registration, or qualifying independently. ALSO SEE: **Filing a Notice, Coordinated Registration, Qualifying Independently.**

Bona Fide—means that the trader is actually ready, willing and able to trade the bond at the quoted price. (If the trader does not have the bond in the firm's own inventory, he or she must know where the bond can be readily obtained.)

Bond—security that pays interest, and returns the principal investment amount upon maturity. Also called a **fixed-income security.**

Bond Buyer, The—daily publication has important indexes, statistics, and other information used by broker-dealers and others who trade in the bond market. *The Bond Buyer* publication includes the visible supply, computes many indexes and provides Bond Buyer new issue worksheets to aid in comparisons and bond calculations. **Munifacts** is a computerized subscription service offered by *The Bond Buyer* providing municipal bond information.

Bond Indenture Agreement—SEE: **Indenture Agreement.**

Bond Interest Coverage—the number of times a company's interest payments could be paid with cash flow. This is used to gauge the safety of the income stream paid to a bondholder (or preferred stockholder). Bond interest coverage is figured by taking total income divided by interest expense.

Bond Ratings—SEE: **Ratings.**

Bond Ratio—the percentage of a company's debt that is represented by bonds. A ratio above 1:3 (33%) is considered high, except for utility companies (which are highly leveraged.) Bond ratio is figured by taking the amount of bonds outstanding, and dividing it by capitalization.

Bonds, Advance Refunded —SEE: **Advance Refunded Bonds.**

Bonds, AMT —SEE: **AMT Bonds.**

Bonds, Bank Grade —SEE: **Investment Grade Bonds.**

Bonds, Bearer —SEE: **Bearer Bonds.**

Bonds, Double Barreled —SEE: **Double Barreled Bonds.**

Bonds, Eurodollar —SEE: **Eurodollar Bonds.**

Bonds, General Obligation (GO) —SEE: **General Obligation Bonds.**

Bonds, Investment Grade—SEE: **Investment Grade Bonds.**

Bonds, Moral Obligation—SEE: **Moral Obligation Bonds.**

Bonds, Put—SEE: **Put Bonds.**

Bonds, Registered —SEE: **Registered Bonds.**

Bonds, Revenue —SEE: **Revenue Bonds.**

Bonds, Special Assessment —SEE: **Special Assessment Bonds.**

Bonds, Special Tax —SEE: **Special Tax Bonds.**

Bonds, Taxable —SEE: **Taxable Bonds.**

Bonds, Zero Coupon —SEE: **Zero Coupon Bonds.**

Book Entry Bonds—registered bonds that do not have a certificate given with them.

Book Value—net worth figure for a company divided by the number of shares outstanding.

Book Value per Share—the ultimate value of a company's securities in the event that a company is liquidated. This figure is used by some analysts to pick undervalued stocks. Book value per share is figured by taking net tangible assets minus liabilities and adding par value of preferred stock, then dividing that by the number of outstanding common shares.

Bottom Line—a company's operating income (EBIT), minus debt service, minus taxes. Also referred to as **net income** or **net income after tax (NIAT).**

Bracket, Tax—SEE: **Tax Bracket.**

Breakeven Point—for option contracts, the market price the stock must attain so that the investor will not lose money (nor make money). (Breakeven points consider the premium in the calculations. For call options, the breakeven point is strike price plus premium [call=CAL= Call, Add Lower]. For put options, the breakeven point is strike price minus premium [puts=PuSH: Put, Subtract Higher].)

Breakout—movement of a stock price past a resistance level or support level. Theory: once the stock has a breakout past one of these levels, that is seen as an indication that the stock is going to continue to move in that direction. ALSO SEE: **Resistance Level, Support Level.**

Breakpoint—the investment dollar level at which investors are eligible for a reduced sales charge. COMPARE: **Letters of Intent, Rights of Accumulation.**

Breakpoint Selling—keeping a client's trades just below breakpoints where the investor would save on sales charges. (This is a violation of NASD rules.)

Broker—one who arranges trades for a commission as an agent.

Broker-Dealer—securities brokerage house and/or investment banking firm.

Broker-Dealer's Concession—part of the sales charge paid to compensate the broker-dealer.

Broker's Broker—service whereby brokers transact business with other brokers, but as a fully anonymous service. (They do not deal with the retail public.)

Bull—one who has positive view of the market, and thinks the market will rise. COMPARE: **Bear.**

Bull Spread—a spread trade where the more expensive option was buying (long) call or selling (short) put. COMPARE: **Bear Spread.**

Bullish—positive outlook, thinking that the markets will rise. COMPARE: **Bearish.**

Business Cycles—general swings in business activity, resulting in expanding activity and contracting activity during different phases of the cycle. The phases in the cycle are expansion, peak, contraction, trough. (See each entry separately.)

Buyer—one who buys something. Also called **long.** SEE: **Long.**

Buyer's Option—SEE: **Delayed Delivery.**

Call—1. redeeming a bond or preferred stock before maturity by paying principal and interest owed, and often a call premium, as per terms stated in the security; 2. option that gives an investor the right to buy a certain number of shares of a security, at a pre-determined price, before a certain date. COMPARE: **Put.**

Call, Extraordinary—SEE: **Extraordinary Call.**

Call, Ratio—SEE: **Ratio Call Writing.**

Call Features—part of the Indenture Agreement put forth by a bond issuer, which spells out the schedule and price for redemptions prior to maturity.

Call Premium—additional money paid to a bond holder when the bond is called and paid off early.

Call Protection—Period of time during which a bond may not be called early.

Call Risk—the chance that a bond issuer or company that has issued preferred stock may call (redeem) the security before the actual maturity date. ALSO SEE: **Reinvestment Risk.**

Capital, Paid-In—SEE: **Paid-In Capital.**

Capital, Preservation of—SEE: **Preservation of Capital.**

Capital Account—one component of the balance of payments which shows the net capital expenditures (investments) each country made in the other country. SEE: **Balance of Trade, Balance of Payments.**

Capital Gain—the increase in value above the adjusted cost basis that is realized by an investor when an asset is sold. COMPARE: **Capital Loss.**

Capital Growth—an investment objective that tries to make the original amount of invested money appreciate over the long term.

Capital Loss—the decrease in value below the adjusted cost basis that is realized by an investor when an asset is sold. COMPARE: **Capital Gain.**

Capital Risk—the chance that an investment will go down in value or lose money without something bad having happened to the underlying company.

Capped Index Options—special options contracts that reduce risk because they are set up like a spread. They are sold in pairs, with one index option contract at-the-money and the other contract above or below that strike price (out-of-the-money).

Cash Flow—an indication of a company's ability to generate revenue to meet its financial obligations. Companies need steady cash flow so that they do not have to dip into reserves to pay debts. Cash flow can be more important than assets, because assets are not always liquid enough to meet expenses. Cash flow is figured by taking net income plus depreciation (because, although it makes a good tax write-off, you can't spend depreciation).

Cash Flow Statement—income statement which breaks down sales and expenses by showing the month in which they were incurred. SEE: **Income Statement.**

Cash Market—SEE: **Spot Trades.**

Cash Settlement—settlement occurs the same day when paying cash. (COMPARE: regular way settlements, which settle T + 3 or T + 1.)

CD—SEE: **Certificate of Deposit.**

CDSL—Contingent Deferred Sales Load. SEE: **Back End Load.**

Central Bank Intervention—when a government attempts to manipulate the price of its currency through **pegging** or **stabilization,** which involves buying the currency in the open market when it dips below a certain level.

Certificate—SEE: **Stock Certificate.**

Certificates of Deposit (CD)—debt securities, usually issued by a financial institution. (There are actually two kinds of CDs: "standard" CDs offered by neighborhood banks to depositors, and "jumbo" CDs that have a minimum face value of $100,000 and are offered by commercial banks to investors as a time deposit. Standard CDs are non-negotiable, but jumbo CDs *are* negotiable and as such are considered money market instruments.)

Chartists—another name for technical analysts.

Churning—excessive trading to generate commissions, usually determined by significant increase in trades after account became discretionary. (Prohibited by NASD rules.)

Circuit Breakers—ways that exchanges attempt to prevent the markets from going into a free-fall once significant declines occur, allowing the market time to rebalance supply and demand. (For example, the NYSE halts or curtails trading when the Dow Jones Industrial Average falls 10%, 20% or 30%, and also places limits on automated trading and price movements of index futures.)

Class—options of the same type (e.g., all calls) with the same underlying security. COMPARE: **Series.**

Class A Shares—mutual fund with a front end load. SEE: **Front End Load.**

Class B Shares—mutual fund with a back end load. SEE: **Back End Load.**

Class C Shares—mutual fund with a level load. SEE: **Level Load.**

Closed End Management Company—investment company that offers a fixed number of shares to investors, and uses the funds raised to operate a packaged security. The company is "closed end" because, after the initial offering of shares to the public, the fund is closed out and no further investments are accepted. Shares of the closed end fund trade on an exchange, and this serves as the vehicle for investors to buy and sell their positions after the initial offering. COMPARE: **Open End Management Company.**

Closing Rotation—orders executed by the Order Book Official (OBO) or specialist in order to ensure a closing price or quote for each option series. (Through the closing rotation process, the bids will be representative of, and in relation to, the price of the underlying instrument.) COMPARE: **Opening Rotation, Market-on-Close.**

Closing Transaction—liquidating a position in an option by buying an offsetting option with opposite terms (or by exercising the option). COMPARE: **Opening Transaction.**

CMO—SEE: **Collateralized Mortgage Obligation.**

CMV—Current Market Value. SEE: **Long Market Value.**

Coincident Economic Indicators—measure changes *while* the economy is changing, and thus are good for confirming the state of current economic activity. There are 5 coincident indicators used to compile this index: industrial production, non-farm payrolls, manufacturing, net personal income, trade sales. COMPARE: **Leading Economic Indicators, Lagging Economic Indicators.**

Cold Calling—any telephone solicitation made when the caller does not have a prior relationship with the party being called. (As defined by the Telephone Consumer Protection Act of 1991.)

Collateralized Mortgage Obligations (CMOs)—a vehicle for issuing mortgage-backed securities, separated into different groups based on maturity dates, which pass-through principal and interest payments to investors. CMOs are private sector issues backed by a pool of Fannie Mae, Freddie Mac and other mortgages.

Combination—an option position that has two long contracts or two short contracts on the same stock, but either with different strike prices or different expiration dates. (Investors buy this option because they accomplish some of the same objectives as straddles, but are less expensive.) ALSO SEE: **Spread; Straddle.**

Combined Offering—sale of stock in the primary market, with some of the sale proceeds going to the company treasury, and some going to present shareholders. ALSO SEE: **Primary Offering, Secondary Offering.**

Commercial Paper—short-term debt issued by corporations to finance inventories, accounts receivable, and other obligations. (*not* issued by commercial banks.)

Commission—small percentage of transaction price collected by a broker-dealer when it acts in a brokerage capacity to arrange a trade. NASD 5% Markup Rule says that 5% is a reasonable guideline for markups, markdowns, or commissions—but this is subject to interpretation and exceptions. COMPARE: **Markup, Markdown.**

Common Equity—SEE: **Return on Common Equity.**

Common Ratio—common stock plus capital in excess of par plus retained earnings, divided by total capital. COMPARE: **Debt Ratio, Preferred Ratio.**

Common Stock—an ownership interest in a corporation that conveys to the holder certain rights, including the right to vote for the board of directors and certain other issues, and the right to receive a proportionate share of any declared dividend. COMPARE: **Preferred Stock.**

Community Property—a type of joint account that is not recognized in all states.

Companies, Investment—SEE: **Investment Companies.**

Companies, Management—SEE: **Management Companies.**

Companies, Nonmanagement—SEE: **Nonmanagement Companies.**

Company—a business entity. SEE: **Corporation.** COMPARE: **Partnership.**

Competitive Bid—SEE: **Competitive Sale.**

Competitive Sale—when the issuer considers offers from several underwriters or underwriting syndicates before selecting a firm to do an offering of securities. This is also referred to as **competitive bid** or **competitive underwriting.** COMPARE: **Negotiated Sale.**

Competitive Underwriting—SEE: **Competitive Sale.**

Competitiveness—a measure of comparative performance. This is one method investors use to measure return on investment. It also provides for a mechanism to compare the performance of a company with previous years, with other companies in same industry, and with companies across sectors. SEE: **Return on Common Equity.**

Concession—SEE: **Underwriter's Concession, Seller's Concession, Broker-Dealer's Concession.**

Concession Basis—when bonds are sold between municipal bond dealers at advertised yield as required by regulations, but are sold less a discount given to the buying dealer.

Conduit Theory—theory that says if the investment company passes through at least 90% of its dividends and net income from capital gains, and meets other IRS guidelines, then the fund is merely a conduit for passing through capital gains, thus allowing those monies to be taxed only once at the personal level. Also referred to as **Subchapter M theory** or **pipeline theory.**

Consent Agreement—SEE: **Loan Consent Agreement.**

Consolidated Tapes—an electronic service providing quotes on NYSE, Amex and some regional stock exchange issues. This service allows these stocks to be traded in the OTC market as long as trades are reported within 90 seconds of execution.

Consolidation—a technical chart pattern that shows trading in a narrow range for an extended period of time, with a trend line that is relatively flat (horizontal), neither showing an uptrend nor a downtrend.

Constant Dollar—says that a fixed dollar amount should be kept in stocks, and the balance in bonds. If equity rises above the fixed amount chosen, then the additional equity amount is liquidated to buy bonds. If equity amount falls below a fixed chosen amount, then some bonds are liquidated to raise the equities portion. COMPARE: **Constant Ratio.**

Constant Ratio—says that a fixed percentage of all assets should be kept in equity stocks and a fixed percentage in bonds. If the value of one portion rises, then it should be sold off to bring the ratios back in line. COMPARE: **Constant Dollar.**

Consumer Price Index (CPI)—measures the fixed cost of a market basket of goods and services. CPI includes components from food, transportation, energy, housing, clothing, etc. (Often used as an inflation adjuster for cost of living increases.)

Consumption—buying a product or service and using it until it has no remaining value.

Contingent Deferred Sales Load (CDSL)— SEE: **Back End Load.**

Contraction—falling demand and business activity, generally accompanied by decreases in industrial production, falling consumer demand, heavy debt loads for consumer and businesses, increases in bankruptcies (personal and corporate), rising unemployment, and a falling stock market. COMPARE: **Expansion.** ALSO SEE: **Business Cycles.**

Control Persons—people who own 10% or more of a company. (The stock they own is considered control stock.)

Control Stock—stock owned by control persons, which falls under Rule 144 limiting the amount of control stock that may be sold in a 90-day period to not more than 1% of the outstanding stock (of the same class) or not more than the average weekly trading volume reported over the past month, whichever is greater.

Conversion—exchanging one security for another (usually convertible bonds or convertible preferred stock are exchanged for a fixed number of shares of common stock).

Conversion, Forced—SEE: **Forced Conversion.**

Conversion Price—the price at which a stock should trade before a bondholder considers conversion.

Conversion Privilege—1. the right of a bondholder to exchange (convertible) bonds for a fixed number of shares of common stock. 2. the redemption of shares from one family and using the proceeds to buy another mutual fund within the same families of funds. (Often there is a time limit within which the conversion must be completed to qualify for reduced or waived sales charges.)

Conversion Ratio—number of shares of stock an investor would receive for converting bonds.

Convertible Preferred Stock—preferred stock that can be traded in for common stock in the company at a preset price. (Because of this feature, the price of convertible preferred stock may fluctuate in line with the common stock, and the dividend paid on convertible preferred stock is usually lower.

Cooling Off Period—the time after the registration statement is filed, but before the securities can be offered for sale to the public. During this period, the SEC reviews the registration statement and preliminary prospectus. The investment banking firm continues its due diligence, and may place tombstone ads or distribute a preliminary prospectus to potential investors to gauge interest. No securities may be sold during this time. (The time period is supposed to last 20 days, but is often longer, especially if SEC requests changes.)

Coordinated Registration—a means of compliance with Blue Sky Laws whereby the same registration information is filed simultaneously with the SEC and each state so that they both run on the same timetable. ALSO SEE: **Blue Sky Laws, Filing a Notice, Qualifying Independently.**

Corporates—another term for "corporate bonds."

Corporation—a separate legal entity organized under state law. COMPARE: **Partnership, Sole Proprietorship.**

Correction—a price decline in the overall market resulting from an overbought situation. Theory: since there are few buyers left, a price drop is imminent. SEE: **Overbought.**

Cost Basis—SEE: **Adjusted Cost Basis.**

Cost Inflation—an increase in the cost of goods or services. COMPARE: **Demand Inflation.**

Coterminous—debt situation where multiple taxing authorities have jurisdiction over the same group of people, and both issue debt that taps the same taxpayer. (An example is a county and city that share boundaries, and both issue bonds.) Also called **overlapping debt.**

Counter Cyclical Stocks—common stocks that generally rise when economic conditions worsen. The best example of a counter cyclical stock is the food sector (because demand is constant regardless of economic conditions). COMPARE: **Cyclical Stocks.**

Coupon—nominal interest rate the issuer will pay on a security, expressed as a percentage. (Term comes from old bearer bonds which had physical coupons that were detached and submitted to collect interest payments.)

Covered Option—when the writer of the option actually owns the stock to back up the contract. COMPARE: **Uncovered Option.**

CPI—SEE: **Consumer Price Index.**

CR—Credit Registry; an accounting entry that shows a credit, or money is surplus. ALSO SEE: **Credit Balance.** COMPARE: **DR.**

Credit, Tax—SEE: **Tax Credit.**

Credit Agreement—agreement spelling out the terms of credit between the broker-dealer and the customer with a margin account.

Credit Balance—the money deposited by a client into an account, plus proceeds from any short sales and value of any securities deposited. (Even if the value of securities in the account fluctuates, CR does not change. CR changes only if cash is taken out, or more money or securities are deposited into the account.) Also called **CR.** COMPARE: **Debit Balance.**

Credit Enhancements — insurance offered by private companies that guarantees principal and interest payments on municipal bonds. The insurance can be purchased by the investor, or purchased by a municipality that wants to offer a lower coupon rate. Two of the largest municipal bond insurers are **Municipal Bond Investors Assurance (MBIA)** and **AMBAC Indemnity.** If either of these insure an issue against default, bonds become "AAA" rated.

Credit Risk—risk that an investment will lose money because it is not repaid. This is also called **repayment risk** or **financial risk.**

Credit Spread—a spread trade where the more expensive option was sold, thus the trade results in money being deposited into the investor's brokerage account. COMPARE: **Debit Spread.**

CROP—Compliance Registered Options Principal. SEE: **ROP**

Cumulative (Voting)—a type of voting whereby stockholders receive a total number of votes equal to their total number of shares of stock, then the stockholder may place all of those votes for a single board member, or divide the vote anyway he or she wants. (This gives minority shareholders more influence when voting.) COMPARE: **Statutory (Voting).**

Cumulative Preferred Stock—preferred stock allows dividends to accrue so that in the event that dividends cannot be paid, the unpaid dividends become a liability that must be paid in full before any regular dividends can be paid to common stockholders.

Currency Market—the unregulated international trading of foreign currencies between banks. Trading in this market is what establishes the foreign exchange rates. (The currency market is decentralized, but banks are linked via computers and other electronic means.) Trades are either spot trades or forward trades. Also called the **interbank market.** ALSO SEE: **Spot Trades, Forward Trades.**

Currency Risk—the chance of foreign exchange loss because of fluctuations in the value of foreign money vis-a-vis the dollar. Also referred to as **exchange risk.**

Current Account—SEE: **Balance of Trade.**

Current Income—an investment objective that tries to generate an immediate cash flow from a portfolio of investments.

Current Market Value (CMV)—SEE: **Long Market Value.**

Current Ratio—an indication of a company's ability to pay its current debts from its current assets. Companies that have steady cash flow or good paying customers or low inventory requirements can safely have a lower ratio. Current ratio is figured as current assets divided by current liabilities.

Current Yield—1. the coupon rate of the bond divided by the purchase price paid. 2. the actual rate of return a stock pays in dividends based on its current market price. This gives investors a gauge of the actual rate of return on their stock investment, just like CY calculations do for bond yields. Current yield for stocks is figured as dividends per share divided by market value per share.

CUSIP Number—Committee on Uniform Securities Identification Procedures (CUSIP) number used to identify all listed stocks and registered bonds. The CUSIP number can be used for easy tracking of securities, and aids in settlement of trades.

Custodian—person who watches over something, and has a fiduciary responsibility. With a UGMA/UTMA account, the custodian is a fiduciary to the minor, since the custodian has full control over the account's investments.

Customer Book—detailed records kept by RRs about the securities a client owns and all transactions that have been made with the firm. (Should be kept for 6 years, with past 2 years readily accessible.)

Cyclical Stocks—common stocks that generally rise and fall quickly in response to economic conditions. Some examples of cyclical stocks are automobile stocks and housing related stocks. COMPARE: **Counter Cyclical Stocks.**

Date, Expiration—SEE: **Expiration Date.**

Date of Record—cut-off date for an investor to be considered the owner of record, and eligible to receive rights, dividends, etc. ALSO SEE: **Ex-Date.**

Dated Date—the date a bond was issued, and from which date accrued interest is calculated.

Day Order—an order that is valid only for the trading day that it is entered. COMPARE: **Good-Till-Canceled.**

DCA—SEE: **Dollar Cost Averaging.**

Dealer—one who buys and sells from his own inventory for a markup or markdown as a principal.

Debenture—an unsecured bond.

Debit Balance—the money that a client owes to the broker-dealer for loans used to purchase securities. (Even if the value of the securities in the account fluctuates, the DR does not change. DR changes only if money is paid on the account.) Also referred to as **DR.** COMPARE: **Credit Balance.**

Debit Spread—a spread trade where the more expensive option was bought, thus the trade results in money being taken out of the investor's brokerage account. COMPARE: **Credit Spread.**

Debt Options—a measure of a municipality's indebtedness and burden to its citizens, figured by taking net total debt and dividing it by the population of the area. (This is not used for revenue bonds since their income comes from project revenue and not taxes.)

Debt Per Capita—total debt divided by total capital. COMPARE: **Preferred Ratio, Common Ratio.**

Debt Ratio—total debt divided by total capital. COMPARE: **Preferred Ratio, Common Ratio.**

Debt-to-Equity Ratio—measure of a company's ability to effectively use leverage to enhance the rate of return on shareholder's equity. In a good year, highly leveraged companies have positive earnings to distribute to fewer shareholders (because there is more debt than equity). In a bad year, earnings may not be enough to cover the company's debt service. Debt-to-equity ratio is figured as long-term debt, divided by stockholder's equity.

Deduction—reduction in the amount of income taxes are figured on. COMPARE: **Tax Credit.**

Defensive Investments—stocks with prices that are more stable over time than the broad market, and high grade bonds. (Some stocks that would be in a typical "defensive" portfolio would be utilities, certain blue chip stocks, and some high grade preferred stock.) COMPARE: **Aggressive Investments.**

Defensive Stocks—common stocks with prices that are more stable over time than the broad market. Some examples of defensive stocks are utility stocks, counter cyclical stocks and certain blue chip stocks. These stocks are more conservative than average, and thus may experience slower growth during economic expansions, but should fare better during recessions because the underlying products are necessities of everyday life.

Deferred Annuity—an annuity contract that has an accumulation period for a certain amount of time, followed by an annuity stage scheduled to begin at a future date chosen by the contract holder. COMPARE: **Immediate Annuity.**

Deferred Compensation Plan—an unqualified retirement plan, where employees agree to receive less money now in exchange for retirement benefits. (This is only a contract, not a guarantee, so employees can lose out if company is not able to pay in the future or the employee leaves the company. When benefits are paid out during retirement, they are taxed as ordinary income to the recipient, and become a tax deduction to the corporation in the future at the time when the benefits are actually paid out.)

Delayed Delivery—an option where delivery of securities is later than usual settlement date. Also known as **seller's option** or **buyer's option,** depending on who chooses delivery date. Delivery date can be anywhere from fourth business day to date written in the contract. This is only acceptable with a contract in place between all parties. In fact, almost any alternate arrangement can be made **as mutually agreed upon,** as long as all parties agree and there's a contract in place.

Demand Inflation—too much money chasing too few goods. COMPARE: **Cost Inflation.**

Demand-Side Economics—economic theory that says government intervention should be used to achieve full employment and stable prices, by manipulating demand via expenditures, and thus achieve balance through demand-side management of the economy. Also called **Keynesian economics.** COMPARE: **Supply-Side Economics.**

Depletion—amortization of a *natural* asset so as to allocate the loss in value of the asset over its expected useful life. Examples of a depletable asset are oil, minerals and timber. COMPARE: **Depreciation.**

Depreciate—to decline in value.

Depreciation—amortization of a *man-made* asset so as to allocate the loss in value of the asset over its expected useful life. Examples of a depreciable asset are buildings, vehicles and equipment. COMPARE: **Depletion.**

Depreciation, Fixed Asset—present net depreciated value of assets as stated on the balance sheet. When this depreciation method is used, assets have a depreciation amount deducted from their cost for valuation purposes.

Depreciation, Straight Line—a depreciation method where the total cost is divided by the estimated useful life of an asset, minus a figure for salvage value. That amount is then deducted from stated income each year.

Depression—a severe economic downturn caused by excess supply and rising unemployment that leads to falling demand, reduced purchasing power and deflation of prices. Depressions are characterized by dramatic rises in unemployment and acute public caution and fear.

Derivative Security—an instrument whose value is dependent on the value of another underlying security. For example, SEE: **Option.**

Detachable—when warrants (or other paired security) may be sold separately to anyone. COMPARE: **Non-Detachable.**

Devaluation—when the value of a country's currency falls relative to other currencies (or other currencies rise). This can be from market forces or government action. COMPARE: **Revaluation.**

Direct Exchange—when a municipality issues new bonds, and, rather than selling them and paying off the old bonds with the proceeds, exchanges the new bonds directly with current bondholders. (This may be done when the source of revenue is in peril and a direct exchange is preferable to default.)

Direct Participation Program (DPP)—a type of limited partnership investment that allows investors to receive the cash flow, capital gains, losses and tax benefits of the underlying partnership business activity, without the liability that would be incurred with a general partnership.

Discount—the amount below par that is paid for a bond, preferred stock, or other security. ALSO SEE: **OID.**

Discount Rate—the interest rate charged by Federal Reserves banks on loans to member commercial banks. Also referred to as the **federal discount rate.**

Discount Yield—a way to figure yield on T-bills, whereby you divide the discount by the face amount of the bond, and multiply that by 360 divided by the days to maturity.

Disintermediation—when funds flow out of banks and institutions, and into other short term investments seeking higher yields.

Distribution Area—a technical chart pattern that shows trading in a narrow range for an extended period of time, with investors careful not to sell below the range to avoid pushing the price downward. COMPARE: **Accumulation Area.**

Distribution Fees—the compensation paid to the distributor (wholesaler, sponsor, underwriter) from the sales charges. Also referred to as the **underwriter's concession.** ALSO SEE: **12b-1 Fees.**

Diversification, Portfolio—SEE: **Portfolio Diversification.**

Divided Account—type of syndicated account where each member has no interest nor liability nor responsibility for any bonds that remain unsold after the initial sale period. The Western account member is responsible only for his own allotment. Also called an **Western account.** COMPARE: **Undivided Account.**

Dividend Exclusion—rule whereby U.S. corporations do not have to pay corporate income tax on 70% of the dividend income they receive from other U.S. corporations.

Dividend Payout Ratio—the actual percentage of earnings paid out in dividends to common stockholders. Generally mature companies (e.g., blue chips, utilities) have higher payout ratios than high growth companies (which tend to retain earnings to reinvest them in research and development). Dividend payout ratio is figured by taking common dividends divided by common earnings.

Dividends—a distribution of company earnings to stockholders as voted on by the board of directors. Dividends are paid out to shareholders on a *pro rata* basis, based on the percentage of stock ownership in the company. The dividends are usually paid in cash, but they can also be paid out in stock or even sometimes with company products (this is rare, but actually anything of value can be distributed as a dividend).

DJIA—SEE: **Dow Jones Industrial Average.**

DK—"don't know" (DK); a trade comparison response where one party challenges the validity of a trade. If there is no response to a DK within four days, the disputing party can disaffirm the questioned trade.

Dollar Cost Averaging (DCA)—an investment method whereby a set dollar amount is invested at regular intervals. (Investor buys fewer shares when the price is high, but more when the price is low, so the average price per share and total investment cost are both lower because the average price per share is lower than the average share price.)

Dollar Price—bond price expressed as a percentage of face value of the bond.

Don't Know—SEE: **DK.**

Double Auction—pricing mechanism which constantly gets pricing information from buyers and sellers. The instant reporting of trades provides for a true free market, where supply and demand dictate the price of a particular stock issue. COMPARE: **Firm Quote.**

Double Barreled Bond—revenue bonds which are guaranteed by an additional (usually larger) entity than just the issuer, giving the investor two sources (revenue and taxes) from which to collect the interest and principal.

Dow Jones Composite Index—combines the DJIA, Dow Jones Transportation Average (DJTA), and Dow Jones Utility Average (DJUA) into a single number. ALSO SEE: **DJIA, Dow Theory.**

Dow Jones Industrial Average (DJIA)—a price-based average of 30 industrial stocks that trade on the NYSE. (Dow Jones also has a number of other averages that track the transportation sector, utility concerns, and others.)

Dow Theory—says that the averages in these other sectors must confirm the movement of the DJIA to signal a true change in market direction.

Down Bid—when the current bid price quoted is below the previous bid for municipal bonds, preventing short sales as per NASD rules.

Downtick—SEE: **Minus Tick.**

Downtrend—SEE: **Trend Lines.**

DPP—SEE: **Direct Participation Program.**

DR—Debit Registry; an accounting entry that shows a debit, or money being owed. ALSO SEE: **Debit Balance.** COMPARE: **CR.**

Due Bill—a statement of money owed, sent when the issuing company missed a transfer in the owner of record list so the new owner did not collect a dividend check. ALSO SEE: **Due Bill Check.**

Due Bill Check—asked-for check to cover a due bill sent over a miss-sent dividend check. ALSO SEE: **Due Bill.**

Due Diligence—process of researching information, gathering data, and verifying what is learned about the company.

Due Diligence Meeting—meeting that serves as the final analysis and verification of the company's financial information and use of proceeds. (Once all questions are answered to everyone's satisfaction, the details of the registration statement, final prospectus, and underwriting agreement are finalized. The price of the issue is also set.)

Earned Income—money generated from providing labor, goods or services. Also called **Active Income.** (e.g., salary, wages, tips, bonuses, other employee compensation, pensions, social security payments, annuity income payments) COMPARE: **Investment Income, Unearned Income.** ALSO SEE: **Passive Income.**

Earnings After Taxes (EAT)—this is figured by subtracting out the taxes that are owed by the company. EAT is also referred to as **net income** or **net income after tax (NIAT),** and is the figure people commonly call **"the bottom line."** It is a true indication of the money that was actually made by the company.

Earnings Before Interest & Taxes (EBIT)—a company's gross sales, minus returns, minus cost of goods sold, minus selling expenses, minus depreciation. EBIT is also referred to as **operating income.**

Earnings Before Taxes (EBT)—a company's operating income (EBIT), minus the interest paid by the company to service its bonds and other debt. This is an important figure to compare to EBIT to see the debt load of the company.

Earnings Coverage—ratio that shows how many times the project's revenues can meet annual debt service costs. (2:1 is adequate for municipal bonds, but not for corporate bonds)

Earnings Per Share (EPS)—straight division of profit by the number of common, outstanding shares. Also called **Earnings per Common Share.** Earnings per share is the value of a company's profit, figured as if it were distributed to all stockholders. The calculation is common earnings divided by outstanding common shares. ALSO SEE: **Fully Diluted Earnings Per Share, Price-Earnings Ratio, Dividend Payout Ratio, Current Yield.**

Eastern Account—SEE: **Undivided Account.**

EAT—SEE: **Earnings After Taxes.**

EBIT—SEE: **Earnings Before Interest & Taxes.**

EBT—SEE: **Earnings Before Taxes.**

Effective Date of Registration—the date when final clearance of the prospectus is received from the SEC. (From this point, the underwriters may solicit orders to sell securities.)

Efficient Use of Assets—the ability to sell inventory quickly so that the same money can be put to work again building more units. This is an important indication of company productivity and sales force prowess. These numbers can be compared both against the company's prior years and other companies in the same industry, to indicate relative strength of sales. SEE: **Inventory Turnover Ratio, Cash Flow.**

Eleven Bond GO Index—uses 11 of the 20 issuers from the 20-Bond Index with an average rating of Aa from Moody's. (Published in *The Bond Buyer.*)

Employees Retirement Income Security Act (ERISA)—a 1974 law designed to protect workers and ensure that they were treated fairly in their retirement plans. ERISA applies only to corporate (and other private sector) retirement plans, but excludes government (and other public sector) retirement plans. In order to maintain their favorable tax treatment, all qualified plans must follow ERISA guidelines, including participation by all eligible full-time employees, funding segregated from other corporate accounts, vesting of 100% in fifth year or 20% in third year plus 20% more each year to 100%, equal treatment of all employees in the plan and a written description of the plan and the options available distributed to all employees.

EPS—SEE: **Earnings Per Share.**

Equity—1. an ownership interest in a company. 2. the difference between what has been paid on an obligation, and the value of the asset. 3. any value that is in a margin account above the minimum Reg. T requirement.

Equity, Excess—SEE: **Excess Equity.**

Equity, Shareholder's—SEE: **Net Worth.**

Equity Options—options that are bought and sold with company stock as the underlying security.

Equity Securities—instruments that signify an ownership interest in a company. (i.e., stocks)

ERISA—SEE: **Employees Retirement Income Security Act.**

Eurodollar—U.S. dollars that are held in foreign banks. The banks can be anywhere outside of the U.S. Although many of these banks are in Europe (hence the name), they do not have to be there. ALSO SEE: **Eurodollar bonds.**

Eurodollar Bonds—debt securities that pay interest and principal in Eurodollars.

European Style—options that can be exercised only on expiration date. COMPARE: **American Style.**

Even Yield Curve—SEE: **Flat Yield Curve.**

Excess Equity—value in a margin account above the minimum Reg. T requirement. ALSO SEE: **Special Memorandum Account.**

Exchange, Direct—SEE: **Direct Exchange.**

Exchange Privileges—a privilege offered by some mutual funds whereby an investor can change funds within the same families of funds without sales charges. (Even if exchanging within a family of funds does not incur sales charges, it's still a taxable event for the investor.)

Exchange Rate—the price at which one country's currency can be converted into another country's currency.

Exchange Rate, Fixed—SEE: **Fixed Exchange Rate.**

Exchange Rate, Floating—SEE: **Floating Exchange Rate.**

Exchange Rate Controls—these can be achieved using a fixed exchange rate, or by limiting the amount of currency that may be converted, or by controlling the amount of foreign investment that can go into or out of a country.

Exchange Risk—SEE: **Currency Risk.**

Exchanges—place where securities are bought and sold.

Exclusion, Dividend—SEE: **Dividend Exclusion.**

Exchange-Traded Options—option contracts that are freely tradeable on a given market exchange. (There are listed options for stocks, commodities, and many other securities and instruments.) Also called **listed options.** COMPARE: **Over-the-Counter Options.**

Ex-Date—the last date that a person can buy a stock and still have time to settle the transaction and be the owner of record to receive rights or dividends. ALSO SEE: **Date of Record, Ex-Dividend, Ex-Rights.**

Ex-Dividend—stock that no longer gives the holder the right to collect the upcoming dividend that was announced. ALSO SEE: **Date of Record, Ex-Date.**

Execution—to fulfill or perform an order as directed. (Also: the act of signing.)

Exempt Securities—securities that do not fall under the rules or jurisdiction of a particular oversight body. (e.g., U.S. government Treasuries) COMPARE: **Non-Exempt Securities.**

Exercise—the contract holder will make use of his or her rights to buy or sell securities under the contract. ALSO SEE: **Exercise Notice.**

Exercise Limits—the maximum number of contracts of any one option class that can be exercised within 5 business days of each other. (The numbers are adjusted frequently, and can vary by exchange and even the trading volume of an individual security.) ALSO SEE: **Position Limits.**

Exercise Notice—when a broker notifies OCC of option holder's desire to exercise the option.

Exercise Price—the price at which the contract holder can exercise the option. Also called **strike price.**

Ex-Legal—"without a legal opinion;" stamped onto bond documents when a bond issuer does not want to go to the trouble or expense of obtaining a legal opinion on the bond issue.

Expansion—growing demand and business activity, generally accompanied by increases in industrial production, consumers who are eager to buy more goods and services, increased demand for housing (especially more new home permits), and a rising stock market. COMPARE: **Contraction.** ALSO SEE: **Business Cycles.**

Expiration Date—the date before which the option must be exercised, which is 3, 6 or 9 months from the date of issue (except LEAPS). The actual expiration is always on Saturday after the third Friday of the expiration month, so the last possible trade or exercise day is that third Friday (assuming no holiday).

Ex-Rights—stock that no longer gives the holder the right to buy shares from the new rights offering at a discounted rate. ALSO SEE: **Date of Record, Ex-Date.**

Extension Risk—the chance that homeowners will be late making payments on their mortgage, which could in turn affect payouts to investors.

Extraordinary Call—repaying debt early if the source of revenue to repay the bonds no longer exists. (e.g., burned down)

Feasibility Study—an evaluation or study done to demonstrate to investors the economic soundness of a proposed project and revenue bond issue. (Term used with **revenue bonds.**)

Fed Funds Rate—target rate established by the Fed as a means of influencing other interest rates.

Federal Discount Rate—interest rate charged by Federal Reserves banks on loans to member commercial banks. Also called **discount rate.**

Federal Funds—the monies used by commercial banks to cover reserve requirements with the Federal Reserve Banks. Most loans are overnight, and are made at the Fed Funds rate.

Federal Home Loan Mortgage Corporation (FHLMC)—nonprofit, federally chartered institution that functions as a buyer and seller of savings and loan residential mortgages.

Federal Housing Administration (FHA)—government agency that insures mortgage loans.

Federal National Mortgage Association (FNMA)—the nation's largest, privately owned investor in residential mortgages.

Federal Open Market Committee (FOMC)—a body that controls the Fed's sale and purchase of government securities. The body is made up of the seven members of the Federal Reserve Board, plus the President of the Federal Reserve Bank of New York, and four other Federal Reserve Bank Presidents.

Federal Reserve Banks—banks that provide services to financial institutions, e.g. check clearing. (One main office in each Federal Reserve district.) All nationally chartered commercial banks must join Federal Reserve and buy stock in its district reserve bank.

Federal Reserve Board (the Fed)—body responsible for U.S. monetary policy, maintaining economic stability and regulating commercial banks.

Federally Related Institutions—arms of the U.S. government that have the authority to issue securities for the needs of their agency. Most federally related securities are backed by the full faith and credit of the U.S. government. These include the Government National Mortgage Association (GNMA or Ginnie Mae), Small Business Administration, General Services Administration, and many others.

Fees—SEE: **12b-1 Fees, Distribution Fees, Management Fees.**

Fiduciary—a person in a position of trust, held by law to high standards of good faith and loyalty.

Filing a Notice—a means of compliance with Blue Sky Laws, whereby a notice is filed putting the state on notice that a federal SEC registration statement has been filed. Additional financial information may be required, but not a complete repeat filing of all registration materials. ALSO SEE: **Blue Sky Laws, Coordinated Registration, Qualifying Independently.**

Filing Date—when the registration statement is received by the SEC. (This begins the cooling off period.) ALSO SEE: **Cooling Off Period.**

Fill or Kill—an order qualifier that says the entire order must be filled, and that it must be done right away. Fill or kill says that partial orders will not be accepted, and the order should automatically be canceled if it can't be filled.

Final Prospectus—basically the same as the preliminary prospectus, but with changes requested by the SEC, as well as additions of the final offering price, the sales spread that the investment banking firm will make for selling the issue, and a disclaimer that "the securities have not been approved by the SEC" must be printed on the front of every prospectus. (The final prospectus is distributed on the effective date of the offering period which begins once the SEC has cleared the prospectus for distribution. A copy of the final prospectus must be sent to investors no later than with the sales confirmation.) COMPARE: **Preliminary Prospectus.**

Financial Risk—SEE: **Credit Risk.**

Firm Commitment—a guarantee by the investment banking firm that the entire issue will be sold. Issuer is guaranteed the money since the investment banker will buy all unsold shares or bonds. COMPARE: **Best Efforts.**

Firm Quotes—the price at which the broker-dealer must be willing to sell or buy at least one round lot (100 shares of stock or 5 bonds). (Firm quote is good for only the number of shares quoted.) Backing away from a firm quote is a violation of NASD rules. COMPARE: **Subject Quotes, Workout Quotes.**

First In, First Out (FIFO)—inventory method considers the first goods produced or acquired to be the first items sold. (This can make gross sales appear lower, but profit margins higher, because older goods would have been made less expensively before inflation raised the cost of raw materials.) COMPARE: **Last In, First Out.**

Fiscal Policy—the federal government's plan for spending, taxation and debt management. COMPARE: **Monetary Policy.**

Fixed Annuity Contract—an annuity where the payments are a fixed monthly amount. COMPARE: **Variable Annuity Contract.**

Fixed Asset Depreciation—SEE: **Depreciation, Fixed Asset.**

Fixed Exchange Rate—when the exchange rate between two currencies is held at a set amount, and not allowed to move in response to market forces. COMPARE: **Floating Exchange Rate.**

Fixed-Income Security—SEE: **Bonds.**

Flat, Traded—SEE: **Traded Flat.**

Flat Yield Curve—when short-term bonds and long-term bonds have the same yield. Also called a **even yield curve** or **humped yield curve.** COMPARE: **Normal Yield Curve, Inverted Yield Curve.**

Flipping—when buyers of a new issue resell their stock quickly. ALSO SEE: **Penalty Bid.**

Floating Exchange Rate—when the exchange rate is permitted to respond to the market forces of supply and demand. COMPARE: **Fixed Exchange Rate.**

Flow of Funds—statement (often as part of the Indenture Agreement) which details the order in which revenues will be used. (Term used with **revenue bond.**) ALSO SEE: **Net Revenue Pledge, Gross Revenue Pledge.**

Forced Conversion—when a company calls its bonds, and makes it more advantageous for the bondholder to convert to common stock than surrender the bond.

Foreign Currency Options—option contracts that provide a means to protect the value of revenue or investments paid in foreign currency (or can be used for speculation).

Forward Pricing—when buy and sell orders for something (such as mutual fund shares) are placed before the final price is known, but the purchase or sale price is based on the next value (NAV) calculation.

Forward Trades—currency trades more like futures contracts, where settlement can be anywhere from 2 days to 18 months. (This forward market trading is much more speculative.) COMPARE: **Spot Trades.**

Front End Load—when a sales charge is added to the sales price of an investment when it is purchased (e.g., with a mutual fund, invested amount buys a reduced number of shares because of the load). Front end load funds are often referred to as **Class A shares.** COMPARE: **No Load, Back End Load.**

401(k) Plan—a qualified payroll deduction plan used for retirement, whereby employees can elect to contribute pre-tax dollars to a retirement account where money grows tax-deferred. Many employers also match employees' 401(k) contributions. Employees may contribute up to $10,000 (subject to constant revisions). Distributions may begin at age 59½, and must start by age 70½. Early withdrawal penalty is 10%. Benefits paid out during retirement are taxed as ordinary income to the recipient.

403(b) Plan—SEE: **Tax Deferred Annuity Plan.**

Fourth Market—the direct trading of large blocks of securities between institutional investors to avoid brokerage commissions. Quotes can be obtained through an electronic communications network service called **Instinet.**

Free Riding—when a broker-dealer holds back part of a new issue of stock so that it can be resold later at a better profit than the original public offering price. (This practice is prohibited by NASD rule.) ALSO SEE: **Withholding.**

Full Authorization—authority granted to another person, permitting buy-sell orders to be executed by that person and allowing the person to withdraw funds from the account. COMPARE: **Limited Authorization.**

Fully Diluted Earnings Per Share—EPS recalculated so that it considers the effect if all types of convertible securities were converted, and all warrants were exercised. This is a second method of EPS that must be calculated and reported per accounting rule changes in 1998. The calculation is common earnings divided by all possible common shares.

Functional Allocation—a way of describing how income and expenses are allocated in oil and gas partnerships, whereby limited partners pay most expenses but income is shared; limited partners get IDC deductions, general partner gets depreciation deductions. COMPARE: **Reversionary Work Interest.**

Fundamental Analysis—examines the financial statements and management of a company. (Analysis focuses on the earnings history and sales prospects for the company in relation to competitors in an effort to predict future share price.) COMPARE: **Technical Analysis.**

Gain—SEE: **Capital Gain.**

GDP—SEE: **Gross Domestic Product.**

General Obligation (GO) Bonds—bonds paid for out of the general revenue of the municipality, which may also use additional tax revenues or borrow funds to cover any shortfall. GO bonds are backed by the full faith and credit of the issuer, however, most require voter approval (especially if the bond issue will raise taxes). COMPARE: **Revenue Bonds.**

Ginnie Mae—mortgage-backed pass-through certificate, backed by the full faith and credit of the U.S. government. (Named for the GNMA government agency. SEE: **Government National Mortgage Association.**)

GNMA—SEE: **Government National Mortgage Association.**

GNP—SEE: **Gross National Product.**

GO Bonds—SEE: **General Obligation Bonds.**

Good-Till-Canceled (GTC)—an open order until it gets filled or canceled. (But still cleared off the Specialist's book twice a year [end of April, end of Oct.], so they must be re-entered.) COMPARE: **Day Order.**

Government National Mortgage Association (GNMA)—government-owned corporation that guarantees payment of principal and interest to investors that buy its mortgage backed securities on the secondary markets.

Government Sponsored Entities (GSE)—privately owned, but publicly chartered entities which were created by the government to help out farmers, students, homeowners and others by lowering borrowing costs. Most GSE securities are backed by the agency issuing them, and are *not* backed by the full faith and credit of the U.S. government. Some GSEs include Federal Farm Credit Consolidated Bank, Federal Home Loan Bank, Student Loan Marketing Association (Sallie Mae), Federal National Mortgage Association (FNMA or Fannie Mae), and Federal Home Loan Mortgage Corporation (FHLMC, Freddie Mac).

Green Shoe Clause—clause in the underwriting agreement that says that if there is an extraordinary demand for the stock, the issuer will agree to authorize additional shares and allow them to be sold by the underwriters. ALSO SEE: **Overallotment.**

Gross Domestic Product (GDP)—measures the value of all goods and services produced in U.S. Includes consumer spending, government spending, and net value of exports. (Does *not* include net foreign investment.) COMPARE: **Gross National Product.**

Gross National Product (GNP)—measures the value of all goods and services produced in U.S., as well as all net foreign investment. GNP includes consumer spending, government spending, and net value of exports. COMPARE: **Gross Domestic Product.**

Gross Revenue Pledge—promise that debt service on the bonds is paid as a first priority—even before operational expenses. COMPARE: **Net Revenue Pledge.**

Growth, Capital—SEE: **Capital Growth.**

Growth Stocks—common stocks from companies that have shown faster than average increases in earnings over past several years, but are likely not paying dividends. (Usually have higher price-earnings ratios.)

GSE—SEE: **Government Sponsored Entities.**

GTC—SEE: **Good-Till-Canceled.**

Head-and-Shoulders—technical chart pattern that resembles the outline of the head and shoulders of a person. The chart shows a stock that was in an upward trend, reached a few peaks, but was not able to sustain them and is headed in a downward trend. This is a bearish reversal of fortune. An **inverted head-and-shoulders** is a technical chart pattern that shows a stock that was in a downward trend, reached a few valleys, but was able to rally and is headed in an upwards trend in a bullish reversal of fortune.

High-Yield Bonds—corporate bonds with a credit rating of BB or lower. Also referred to as **junk bonds** because the companies issuing them may have a poor credit rating or short operating history with little sales or earnings on which to base the price of the bond.

Hold in Street Name—securities left in broker-dealer's name and held by the broker-dealer to facilitate future sales. COMPARE: **Transfer and Ship, Hold in Street Name.**

Hot Issue—issue where the market price moves above the public offering price almost immediately after the stock begins trading in the open market (after-market). ALSO SEE: **Free Riding, Withholding.**

Humped Yield Curve—SEE: **Flat Yield Curve.**

Hypothecation—using something as collateral. ALSO SEE: **Hypothecation Agreement, Rehypothecation.**

Hypothecation Agreement—allows the broker-dealer to use the securities as collateral. Also referred to as a **margin agreement.**

IA—SEE: **Investment Advisor.**

IDB—SEE: **Industrial Development Bond.**

Immediate Annuity—an annuity contract that is purchased with a lump sum payments, with the annuity stage scheduled to begin immediately (usually no longer than 2 months out). COMPARE: **Deferred Annuity.**

Immediate or Cancel—an order qualifier that says the entire order does not have to be filled, but it must be done right away. Immediate or cancel says that partial orders are okay, but if the balance can't be filled right away should be canceled.

Imputed Interest—equivalent to interest earned on a zero coupon bond due to its appreciation over time. (Used by the IRS in tax and cost basis calculations.)

In-the-Money—when the market price of a stock is *above the strike price of a call option,* or *below the strike price of a put option,* the option contract is said to be in-the-money. In-the-money is the theoretical point at which the option holder could make money, but considers only the strike price and the price of the underlying security, and does not consider price of the option, sales commissions, or any other carrying costs. (Options are always looked at from option holder's position.) COMPARE: **At-the-Money, Out-of-the-Money.**

Income—money generated from any source. ALSO SEE: **Earned Income, Investment Income, Passive Income, Unearned Income.**

Income, Active—SEE: **Earned Income.**

Income, Current—SEE: **Current Income.**

Income, Earned—SEE: **Earned Income.**

Income, Investment—SEE: **Investment Income.**

Income, Passive—SEE: **Passive Income.**

Income, Unearned—SEE: **Investment Income.**

Income Statement—a financial report that summarizes an entity's income and expenses over a given period of time. Also called a **profit and loss statement.** COMPARE: **Balance Sheet.**

Income Stocks—common stocks that regularly pay good dividends to stockholders, and are in industries where companies are expected to continue doing so. Utilities, banks and insurance company stocks are good examples of income stocks.

Indenture Agreement—an agreement that must be part of a corporate bond issue as required by the Trust Indenture Act of 1939. Also called a **trust indenture** or **bond indenture agreement,** the agreement is between the issuer and a qualified, independent trustee who oversees the protective clauses and list of promises to bondholders. (Municipal bonds often use an Indenture Agreement also because the market requires it.)

Index—a statistical composite that measures up and down price movements of a representative sample from a particular group, as a means of tracking the overall health and direction of the markets, an industry, a sector, etc. (e.g., S&P 500)

Index Fund—a type of mutual fund designed to track a particular recognized index and match its portfolio composition and movements.

Individual Retirement Account (IRA)—a personal, tax-deferred retirement account. There are several varieties of IRAs, but most allow contributions of up to $2,000 per person per year, with a spouse also able to put in $2,000 if married and filing jointly. (Some IRA plans have contributions that are immediately tax deductible. All contributions and investment earnings grow tax-deferred until distributions begin at retirement.) ALSO SEE: **Roth IRA, SEP-IRA.**

Industrial Development Bond (IDB)—bonds used to finance fixed assets, which are then leased to private corporations. These are a type of revenue bond, but are usually NOT tax exempt because they are designed to help private parties. Repayment of the debt relies on lease payments from corporate tenants.

Industrial Revenue Bond—SEE: **Industrial Development Bond.**

Inflation—an increase in the cost of goods or services; or, too much money chasing too few goods.

Inflation, Cost—an increase in the cost of goods or services.

Inflation, Demand—too much money chasing too few goods.

Inflationary Risk—chance that the value of assets or income will decline relative to the prices of other goods and services. Also called **purchasing power risk.**

Initial Public Offering (IPO)—when a company that is going public for the first time sells new shares in a new issue stock offering. ALSO SEE: **Additional Issue.**

Inside Quote—highest bid price and lowest ask price.

Insiders—any persons who have access to confidential or sensitive information about a company before it is released to the public. This definition includes officers, directors, and key employees of a company, and stockholders owning over 10% of a publicly traded company.

Instinet—acronym for Institutional Networks Corporation (owned by Reuters). The purpose of the system is to allow direct trading between institutional investors, since all members are linked directly by computer. Instinet is registered with the SEC as a stock exchange.

Instruments, Money Market—SEE: **Money Market Instruments.**

Intent, Letters of—SEE: **Letters of Intent.**

Interbank Market—SEE: **Currency Market.**

Interdealer Systems—computer based systems that allow dealers to execute transactions electronically with other dealers.

Interest—1. a right or share in something (such as a joint account). 2. A charge a borrower pays to a lender for the use of lender's money.

Interest, Accrued—SEE: **Accrued Interest.**

Interest, And—SEE: **And Interest.**

Interest, Imputed—SEE: **Imputed Interest.**

Interest Rate Options—SEE: **Debt Options.**

Interest Rate Risk—risk that changes in interest rates will adversely affect investment value.

Intrinsic Value—the difference between the strike price of the option and the market value of the underlying security. (Intrinsic value is equal to the in-the-money option amount. An out-of-the-money option does not have any intrinsic value; it merely has a speculative value. When an option contract trades at its intrinsic value, with no time value component added to the price, it is said that the option contract is trading at **parity.**) ALSO SEE: **Time Value.**

Inventory Turnover Ratio—a number that shows how many times a company's inventory is sold and replaced during the fiscal year. Inventory is a non-producing asset, and makes money for the company only when it is sold. This number must compare favorably with other companies in the same industry, or the company will likely experience a loss of market share. Inventory turnover ratio is figured as annual sales divided by inventory.

Inverted Yield Curve—unusual situation where long-term bonds have lower yields than short-term bonds. Also called a **negative yield curve.** COMPARE: **Normal Yield Curve, Flat Yield Curve.**

Investment—when capital is used to create money via income-producing instruments, or to create capital appreciation from a risk-oriented venture.

Investment Advisor (IA)—anyone who gives investment advice for a fee. The compensation can be a flat fee or it can be a percentage of the assets managed.

Investment Companies—separate corporations set up for the sole purpose of packaging securities, collecting funds, investing funds, and managing the portfolio.

Investment Grade Bonds—bonds that have one of the top four ratings from Moody's (Aaa, Aa, A, Baa) or S&P (AAA, AA, A, BBB). Also called **bank grade bonds.**

Investment Income—money generated from securities or other assets. This could mean interest from bonds, dividends from stocks, or capital gains from the sale of securities. Also referred to as **unearned income.**

Investment Risk—the chance that adverse conditions will cause the value of an investment to drop.

Investment, Trust—SEE: **Unit Investment Trust.**

Investments, Aggressive—SEE: **Aggressive Investments.**

Investments, Defensive—SEE: **Defensive Investments.**

Investors, Accredited—SEE: **Accredited Investors.**

IPO—SEE: **Initial Public Offering.**

IRA—SEE: **Individual Retirement Account.**

Issue, Additional—SEE: **Additional Issue.**

Issued, When—SEE: **When Issued.**

Issued Stock—stock that has been distributed by the corporation (held by founders, sold to investors, given to employees, etc.).

Joint Tenants In Common (JTIC)—a type of joint account where upon the death of one party, that party's interest in the account is passed to his or her estate. This means that each of the joint tenants can name a beneficiary. With this arrangement, parties can have unequal shares. COMPARE: **Joint Tenants with Right of Survivorship.**

Joint Tenants with Right of Survivorship (JTROS)—a type of joint account where upon the death of one party, that party's interest in the account is passed to the other parties of the account. To have this arrangement, all parties must have an equal share in the account. This is a common arrangement between spouses. COMPARE: **Joint Tenants In Common.**

JTIC—SEE: **Joint Tenants In Common.**

JTROS—SEE: **Joint Tenants with Right of Survivorship.**

Junk Bonds—SEE: **High-Yield Bonds.**

Keogh Plan—H.R.-10 (Keogh) plans are retirement account plans for people who have self-employed income. Keogh plans are tax deductible to the contributor, and the funds accumulate tax free until distribution at retirement at age 59½. Distributions are taxed as ordinary income. There is a 10% penalty for withdrawals before age 59½, and withdrawals must start no later than age 70½. Maximum contributions by the employer are 25% of net (20% of gross) earned income or $30,000, whichever is *less.* (This plan may be contributed to in addition to an IRA plan.)

Keynesian Economics—SEE: **Demand-Side Economics.**

Know Your Customer—concept that says it is the responsibility of the broker-dealer and RR to have a complete and accurate understanding of a client's financial situation so as to give appropriate advice and make suitable recommendations.

Lagging Economic Indicators—measure changes *after* the economy has changed, and thus are good for verifying past economic activity (and predictions). There are 6 lagging indicators used to compile this index: unemployment rate, interest rates (prime rate), labor costs, outstanding debt, business spending, inventory book value. COMPARE: **Leading Economic Indicators, Coincident Economic Indicators.**

Last In, First Out (LIFO)—inventory method considers the last goods produced or acquired to be the first items sold. (This can make gross sales appear higher, and profit margins lower, because the most recent goods made would have higher raw material costs compared to raw materials bought awhile ago.) COMPARE: **First In, First Out.**

Leading Economic Indicators—measure changes *before* the economy has changed, and thus are good for predicting future economic activity. There are 11 leading indicators used to compile this index: building permits, changes in materials pricing, production workweek, orders for plant and equipment, unemployment insurance claims, orders for durable goods, money supply (M2), orders for consumer goods, stock prices, consumer confidence index (more debt), vendor performance (deliveries). COMPARE: **Coincident Economic Indicators, Lagging Economic Indicators.**

LEAPS—Long-term Equity Anticipation Securities: special options contracts that expire in 24–39 months.

Legal List—an official list of securities that are selected by the state as being acceptable for investment by fiduciaries.

Legal Opinion—when a bond attorney examines a bond issue to determine its legality, and whether or not it qualifies for tax exempt status. ALSO SEE: **Unqualified Legal Opinion, Qualified Legal Opinion, Ex-Legal.**

Legislative Risk—the risk of a change in the law that adversely affects an investment. This usually refers to domestic policies, such as new clean air requirements or tax law changes. COMPARE: **Political Risk.**

Letters of Intent (LOI)—a commitment by an investor to invest a certain amount of money within 13 months in exchange for being entitled to receive breakpoint sales charge rates now. (Letter may be back-dated up to 90 days to encompass previous investments.) ALSO SEE: **Breakpoint Sales.** COMPARE: **Rights of Accumulation.**

Level 1—access level on NASDAQ system. SEE: **NASDAQ.**

Level 2—access level on NASDAQ system. SEE: **NASDAQ.**

Level 3—access level on NASDAQ system. SEE: **NASDAQ.**

Level Load—a small sales charge paid annually for the life of a mutual fund. (The amount does not change, hence the word "level.") Level load funds are often referred to as **Class C shares.**

Liabilities—any debt, financial obligation or claim that another has on the ownership of an asset. (e.g., credit card bill, car installment loan, home mortgage). SEE: **Assets, Net Worth.**

LIFO—SEE: **Last In, First Out.**

Limit Order—order that a particular security should be bought or sold, but only at a certain price. ALSO SEE: **Stop Order, Stop Limit Order.**

Limited Authorization—authority granted to another person, permitting only buy-sell orders to be executed by that person, and *not* allowing the person to withdraw funds from the account. COMPARE: **Full Authorization.**

Limited Partnership—an investment structure that allows investors to receive the cash flow, capital gains, losses and tax benefits of the underlying partnership business activity, without incurring the liability of a general partner.

Limits, Exercise—SEE: **Exercise Limits.**

Limits, Position—SEE: **Position Limits.**

Liquid Net Worth—SEE: **Net Spendable Income.**

Liquidation— the selling off of securities or other assets to raise cash for withdrawal, to pay an amount owed, or as the result of a bankruptcy.

Liquidity—ease with which assets can be converted into cash. For a company, the ability to convert assets to cash, or have cash readily available as needed is an important indication of a company's financial stability. Company liquidity is the ability to meet ongoing payroll and other obligations. SEE:

Working Capital, Current Ratio, Quick Assets.

Liquidity Preference—the supply of credit available because people are willing to forgo liquidity and save money. In other words, if people will accept only cash, and want to spend the cash immediately, refusing to save, there is no money left for borrowing or investing.

Liquidity Risk—the chance that an investor may not be able to convert an investment, security or asset into cash when needed.

Listed Options—SEE: **Exchange-Traded Options.**

LMV—SEE: **Long Market Value.**

Load—sales charge added to the price of an investment (e.g., a spread is added to NAV for a mutual fund to get the POP). COMPARE: **No Load, Front End Load, Back End Load.**

Loan Consent Agreement—agreement allowing the broker-dealer to use the customer's securities as collateral.

Loan Value—the maximum percentage of current market value that a broker-dealer can lend on non-exempt marginable securities. (currently 50% of value)

Lock-Up Period—time period during which directors, officers and other company insiders are restricted by the managing underwriter from selling their shares of stock, usually for at least 180 days after IPO shares begin trading.

LOI—SEE: **Letters of Intent.**

Long—a position in a stock, option, etc. when an investor **buys** it. You can also say that the investor is the **owner** or **holder** of the option, or is **long** the option. (These terms are synonymous: **buyer = owner = holder = long.**) COMPARE: **Short.**

Long Call—buy a call option (a bullish strategy). COMPARE: **Short Call, Long Put.** ALSO SEE: **Short Put.**

Long Margin Account—account in which the investor desires to own the securities and so he or she *borrows money* from the broker-dealer firm to buy them. ("Long" here is used like it is with stocks or options in that the customer wants to buy and hold securities, he or she just doesn't want to have to pay for them all in cash.) COMPARE: **Short Margin Account.**

Long Market Value (LMV)—the present worth of a client's portfolio at the end of the valuation period. Also referred to as **current market value.** COMPARE: **Short Market Value.**

Long Put—buy a put option (a bearish strategy). COMPARE: **Short Put, Long Call.** ALSO SEE: **Short Call.**

Long-term Equity Anticipation Securities—SEE: **LEAPS.**

Loss—SEE: **Capital Loss.**

M1—the most stringent measure of money supply because it represents only money that can be spent immediately or easily converted to cash. M1 includes all coins and currency in circulation, traveler's checks, checking account balances, NOW account balances, credit union accounts, and draft accounts.

M2—a key measure of money supply, and an indicator for forecasting economic growth and inflation. M2 counts all of the items in M1, plus savings accounts, time deposits (e.g., CDs), non-commercial money market accounts, and overnight repurchase agreements.

M3—the broadest measure of money supply, which includes all items from M1 and M2, plus large time deposits (jumbo CDs), repos held by commercial banks (maturing in over one day), and institutional money market accounts.

MACRS—SEE: **Modified Accelerated Cost Recovery System.**

Maintenance Call—a demand that a customer deposit additional cash or securities to bring the margin amount up to minimum requirement. (The minimum for a maintenance call is usually considered to be the broker-dealer or SRO-required minimums of 25% (long) or 30% (short). Reg. T requires a minimum of 50% before necessitating a **margin call.**)

Management Companies—companies that are in the business of managing money for other people, and as such have a manager responsible for actively managing the company's investment portfolio. (e.g., **mutual fund;** Management companies can be either open end or closed end.) ALSO SEE: **Open End Management Company, Closed End Management Company.** COMPARE: **Nonmanagement Companies.**

Management Fees—compensation paid to the Financial Advisor, and others responsible for managing the mutual fund portfolio, paid as a percentage of the fund's net asset value.

Manager's Fee—SEE: **Managing Underwriter's Fee.**

Managing Underwriter's Fee—part of the underwriter's spread paid to the syndicate manager for coordinating and overseeing the deal. This fee is the smallest part of the compensation at **10-20%** (and is paid off the top of every sale). Also referred to as the **manager's fee.** ALSO SEE: **Underwriting Fee, Takedown.**

Margin—amount customer must have on deposit with broker-dealer to buy securities on credit.

Margin, Profit—SEE: **Profit Margin.**

Margin Account—one of the two basic types of accounts that can be opened with a broker-dealer (the other being a cash account). ALSO SEE: **Long Margin Account, Short Margin Account.**

Margin Agreement—SEE: **Hypothecation Agreement.**

Margin Call—a demand that a customer deposit additional cash or securities to bring the margin amount up to minimum requirement. (The minimum for a margin call is usually considered to be the Reg. T minimum of 50%. A broker-dealer or SRO requires minimums of 25% (long) or 30% (short) before they demand a **maintenance call.**)

Margin-of-Profit Ratio—the relationship of operating income to net sales. This is a measure of the operating efficiency of a company, and is a good means of comparison. The number can be compared with prior years, to see if the number is improving, or against other companies to see if the company is productive and price competitive. (Note this is pre-tax.) Margin-of-profit ratio is calculated by taking operating income divided by net sales.

Margin Requirements—the amount of money that an investor must deposit in a margin account before buying stock on credit or selling short, as required by Reg. T. This is another way the Fed can control the money supply since margin is a form of credit.

Marginable Securities—securities that are eligible for a client to buy and sell in a margin account.

Marginal—meaning that only the portion of income that falls above each bracket is taxed at that higher level. ALSO SEE: **Tax Bracket, Progressive Tax.**

Marginal Propensity to Consume—the amount that consumption changes due to incremental changes in disposable income.

Mark to the Market—when broker-dealers check the valuations of all margin accounts and adjust them at the end of the trading day to reflect current market values, checking to ensure that margin accounts still meet minimum margin and maintenance requirements.

Markdown—money subtracted from the price of securities when a broker-dealer buys securities for customers. (A **markup** is money added to the price of securities when a customer buys securities from a broker-dealer.) NASD 5% Markup Rule says that 5% is a reasonable guideline for markups, markdowns, or commissions—but this is subject to interpretation and exceptions. COMPARE: **Commission.**

Market Maker—brokerage firm that has taken a position (built up an inventory) in a certain stock, and stands ready to honor quoted bid and ask prices for round lots. (Market makers help maintain OTC market stability, allowing OTC to function.) COMPARE: **Specialist.**

Market Momentum—the speed, volume and change of stock prices is said to be an indicator of the market's direction at a given point in time. The momentum swings up and down, like an oscillator feeding on itself until momentum carries it back the other direction.

Market-on-Close—orders that can be executed only during the official closing session at the end of the trading day. COMPARE: **Opening Rotation, Closing Rotation.**

Market Order—an order that a particular security should be bought or sold immediately at the best available price.

Market-Out Clause — underwriting agreement clause that permits the firm to postpone or cancel the offering if market conditions change (or for other stated reasons) before the offering has begun.

Market Risk—risk that is common to all investments of the same type or classification, owing more to broad market conditions or investor sentiment towards a particular sector of stocks or bonds. This is also called **systematic risk**.

Market Sentiment—refers to whether the market overall is in a bullish (upward) mood or a bearish (downward) mood. Some indicators of market sentiment might be the reaction to economic news, advance-decline ratio, and trading volumes of stock.

Market Value—stock price that investors will pay in the marketplace, driven by supply and demand.

Markup—money added to the price of securities when customer buys securities from a broker-dealer. (A **markdown**

is money subtracted from the price of securities when a broker-dealer buys securities for customers.) NASD 5% Markup Rule says that 5% is a reasonable guideline for markups, markdowns, or commissions—but this is subject to interpretation and exceptions. COMPARE: **Commission.**

Matched Order—SEE: **Painting the Tape.**

Maturity—the date when a bond becomes due and payable. ALSO SEE: **Term Maturity, Series Maturity, Serial Maturity.**

Maturity, Serial—SEE: **Serial Maturity.**

Maturity, Series—SEE: **Series Maturity.**

Maturity, Term—SEE: **Term Maturity.**

MBIA—Municipal Bond Investors Assurance, a credit insurance company. SEE: **Credit Enhancement.**

Mini-Max—a best efforts underwriting commitment whereby the offer will be cancelled only if a certain minimum amount of the issue is not sold (e.g., half of the issue), but even after that minimum is reached, the investment banking firm will continue to sell on a best efforts basis up to the maximum authorized offering amount. COMPARE: **All or None.**

Minus Tick—term for when the previous trade occurred at a lower price than the one before it. In essence, the price of the security is heading down. This is also referred to as a **downtick.** ALSO SEE: **Zero-Minus Tick, Short Sale.** COMPARE: **Plus Tick.**

Modified Accelerated Cost Recovery System (MACRS)—a modified depreciation model which allows for faster depreciation of some assets, with greater tax benefits early on. (e.g., computers, but *not* buildings)

Monetarist Theory—economic theory that says that the size of the money supply is the most important economic determinant, and thus it should be increased by a fixed rate annually, allowing businesses, consumers, investors and other money managers to plan accordingly. COMPARE: **Demand-Side Economics, Supply-Side Economics.**

Monetary Policy—the government's mechanism through which it can exert control over the supply and cost of money. Monetary policy also has the goals of economic growth, full employment and international balance of payments, plus monetary policy tries to maintain stability in prices, interest rates and financial markets. COMPARE: **Fiscal Policy.**

Money, At-, In-, Out- —SEE: **At-the-Money, In-the-Money, Out-of-the-Money.**

Money Market Instruments—short-term debt obligations that are due and payable in 12 months or less. Examples of money market instruments are **repurchase agreements, commercial paper,** and **negotiable CDs.**

Money Supply—the total amount of money in circulation in a country's economy at a given time, including not only cash, but also deposits in savings and checking accounts. Too much money in circulation can lead to inflation. ALSO SEE: **M1, M2, M3.**

Moody's—Moody's Investors Service is a rating service, providing information on bond issues, commercial paper, preferred stock, and municipal short-term notes. It publishes several bond and stock books providing analysis of issuers. (For bond rating service, SEE:

Investment Grade Bonds) Moody's also publishes facts, information and research on bond issues, such as *Moody's Municipal & Government Manual. Moody's Bond Survey.*

Moody's Bond Survey—weekly newsletter that updates the bond ratings and other information listed in *Moody's Bond Record.* The publication also offers more detailed information on certain select municipal bond issues.

Moral Obligation Bond—revenue bonds issued by a municipality, but also backed by moral obligation of the state. This occurs where the state legislature indicates it intends to pay on the debt if issuer defaults, but it is not binding on future legislatures so the debt is a moral obligation only, not a legal one.

Moving Averages—means of technical analysis showing the trend of a stock price by computing the average price of the security over a set interval, and repeating that over time.

MSRB—SEE: **Municipal Securities Rulemaking Board.**

Multiples—a type of offering of municipal securities which allows the buyer to bid for round lots of bonds (usually in multiples of $1,000 or $5,000). COMPARE: **All or None.**

Multiplier Effect—1. the effect that investment has in creating additional income and other benefits to all those who participate in a project, through ownership, providing labor, or being a supplier to that business. 2. In monetary theory, this refers to the expansion of money supply resulting from banks' ability to lend money in excess of its reserves.

Municipal Bond—debt obligations of state and local governments. ALSO SEE: **General Obligation Bonds, Revenue Bonds.**

Municipal Bond Investors Assurance (MBIA)—a credit insurance company. SEE: **Credit Enhancement.**

Municipal Securities—SEE: **Municipal Bonds.**

Municipal Securities Rulemaking Board (MSRB)—self-regulatory organization responsible for all activities related to municipal bonds and other intrastate government securities that are issued, sold or traded.

Municipals—another term for "municipal bonds."

Munifacts—a computerized subscription service offered by *The Bond Buyer* that provides municipal bond information.

Munis—another term for "municipal bonds."

Mutual Fund—a pooled investment, managed by an investment company, offering an undivided interest in the portfolio to holders of shares in the fund. The three main advantages to mutual funds are liquidity, diversification and professional management.

Naked Option— SEE: **Uncovered Option.**

NASD—SEE: **National Association of Securities Dealers.**

NASDAQ—National Association of Securities Dealers Automated Quotation (NASDAQ) system that links broker-dealers by telephone and computer to facilitate trades. The service has three levels:

Level 1: This shows *only* the highest bid price and lowest ask price (the

inside quote) for any NASDAQ stock which has at least two active market makers. These quotes, though, aren't firm until confirmed by another broker-dealer. RRs have access to this level, but cannot use it to guarantee any prices.

Level 2: This provides quotes from *multiple market makers,* showing the current firm quote (good for a minimum of 100 shares) and the quote size available. This level of access is primarily for institutional investors.

Level 3: This has the same info as levels 1 & 2, but also lets market makers *update or change their stock quotes.* This level is for market makers only.

National Association of Securities Dealers (NASD)—self-regulatory organization responsible for all activities related to securities sold in the over-the-counter market, also has regulatory authority over investment banking, investment companies and limited partnerships.

NAV—SEE: **Net Asset Value.**

Negative Yield Curve—SEE: **Inverted Yield Curve.**

Negotiated Bid—SEE: **Negotiated Sale.**

Negotiated Sale—when the issuer selects an underwriter, underwriter and issuer agree on the price and terms of the issue, and the spread. This is also referred to as **negotiated bid** or **negotiated underwriting.** COMPARE: **Competitive Sale.**

Negotiated Underwriting—SEE: **Negotiated Sale.**

Net Asset Value (NAV)—the value of a mutual fund and its shares, derived by taking the funds assets minus liabilities, then dividing that result by the number of outstanding shares. NAV is the "bid" price at which fund shares are redeemed. COMPARE: **Public Offering Price.**

Net Asset Value per Bond—the relationship of net assets in a company and all claims that must be paid prior to bonds, to the bonds themselves. This is a measure of the safety level of the bonds if the company is liquidated. Net asset value per bond is figured as net assets minus intangible assets minus liabilities, divided by total bonds outstanding.

Net Income—SEE: **Earnings After Taxes.**

Net Income After Tax (NIAT)—SEE: **Earnings After Taxes.**

Net Income Available to Common Shareholders (NIACS)—net income minus the preferred dividend payout, which is then paid out as a dividend to common shareholders or kept as retained earnings.

Net Interest Cost (NIC)—any money received by the municipality over par value is subtracted from the interest cost. It does not matter when the money is received or paid. Only the total interest amount the municipality will pay is used in the comparison of bids. COMPARE: **True Interest Cost.**

Net Profit Ratio—an indication of a company's relative profitability. This is another measure of a company's efficiency, productivity, and price strategy. (Note this is after tax.) Net profit ratio is calculated as operating income divided by net sales.

Net Revenue Pledge—promise that after operating expenses and maintenance costs have been paid, a sinking fund will be established to ensure timely payments now, and act as a holding place for excess revenues for future payments, before any money is spent on expanding the facility. COMPARE: **Gross Revenue Pledge.**

Net Spendable Income—figure arrived at by subtracting expenses from income (usually calculated for individuals, not companies).

Net Worth—the value that is left over after adding up all assets and subtracting all liabilities from that total. (Also referred to as **shareholder's equity** when talking about a company's net worth.) ALSO SEE: **Assets, Liabilities.**

New York Stock Exchange (NYSE)—self-regulatory organization responsible for all activities related to securities listed and traded on New York Stock Exchange and some regional stock exchanges (e.g., Philadelphia Stock Exchange).

NIACS—SEE: **Net Income Available to Common Shareholders.**

NIAT—Net Income After Tax. SEE: **Earnings After Taxes.**

NIC—SEE: **Net Interest Cost.**

Nine Bond Rule—NYSE rule says that any order for nine bonds or less must go to the floor first for one hour to seek a market before being filled OTC.

No Load—when no sales charge is added to the price of an investment (e.g., no spread is added to a mutual fund so NAV equals POP). COMPARE: **Load, Front End Load, Back End Load.**

Nominal Quotes—pricing quote for informational purposes only, if given with a qualified statement. COMPARE: **Firm Quotes.**

Non-Detachable—when warrants (or other paired security) can be transferred only with the bond, preferred stock or security they were sold with. COMPARE: **Detachable.**

Non-Exempt Securities—securities that are under the jurisdiction of a particular oversight body, and thus must comply with their rules. (e.g., SEC, Reg. T) COMPARE: **Exempt Securities.**

Non-Management Companies—investment companies with a fixed portfolio of investments that investors put their money into, so there is no need for a portfolio manager. (e.g., **unit investment trust**) COMPARE: **Management Companies.**

Non-Qualified Annuity—variable annuity that had the investment amount paid for with after-tax dollars. This allows it to have a cost basis so that only a portion of the withdrawal amount (interest portion) is subject to taxation. COMPARE: **Qualified Annuity.**

Non-Qualified Retirement Plan—SEE: **Unqualified Retirement Plan.**

Nonvoting Stock—sub-classes of common stock (e.g., Class A, Class B) that do not carry voting rights.

Normal Yield Curve—situation where long-term bonds have higher yields than short-term bonds. Also called a **positive yield curve.** COMPARE: **Inverted Yield Curve, Flat Yield Curve.**

Not Held—an order qualifier for an order which is not given to the specialist, but rather is given to a floor broker. The floor broker is given some latitude on price and timing of the trade (usually because it is a rather large order). The floor broker is supposed to shop around and get the best price, but the floor broker is "not held" responsible for variations in price when filling the order.

NYSE—SEE: **New York Stock Exchange.**

NYSE Composite—measures all common stocks listed on the New York Stock Exchange, including four subindexes (Industrials, Transportation, Utilities, Finance). The index tracks the change in market value of NYSE stocks, adjusted to reduce the effects of market capitalization changes, new listings and de-listings. Market value for each stock is figured by multiplying its per share price times the number of shares listed.

Obligation Bond—SEE: **Moral Obligation Bond.**

OCC—SEE: **Options Clearing Corporation.**

ODD—SEE: **Options Disclosure Document.**

Odd First Coupon—a first bond interest payment that is for more than the standard six months worth of interest.

Offer, Tender—SEE: **Tender Offer.**

Offer Wanted—ask request by a broker-dealer when there is no activity in the stock, but the dealer is looking to buy some and wants traders to submit a bid. COMPARE: **Bid Wanted.**

Offering, Rights—SEE: **Rights Offering.**

Offering Circular—document used for disclosure with Reg. A offerings, containing much of the same kind of information contained in a prospectus, but with less detail and un-audited financial information.

Offering Sheets—weekly published inventories of municipal bonds that are held by broker-dealers and offered for sale.

Official Statement—serves as means of communication between issuer and investor, giving pertinent details about the municipality, purpose of the bond issue, and terms of repayment. (Official statement also provides a feasibility study (for revenue bonds), a legal opinion regarding municipality authority to levy taxes (for GO bonds), and tax information to show if the issue is tax exempt.)

OID—SEE: **Original Issue Discount.**

Open End Management Company—investment company that continually offers shares to investors, and uses the funds raised to operate a packaged security, such as a mutual fund. The company is "open end" because it does a continuous offering, with the fund continuing to grow over time. Shares of the open end fund can be sold and redeemed only by the fund that issued them. COMPARE: **Closed End Management Company.**

Open Interest—the total number of options contracts that have not been exercised, closed out, or still have not expired.

Open Market Operations—when the Fed sells or buys government securities as a means of controlling supply of, and demand for, money. Interest rates are affected because as the Fed buys and sells securities, it makes more or less money available for banks to lend.

Opening Orders—orders that have come in since trading closed the previous day.

Opening Rotation—orders which must be executed by the Order Book Official (OBO) or specialist at the beginning of the trading day, or not at all. (Opening rotation consists of calling for bids and offers from the crowd for each option series.) COMPARE: **Closing Rotation, Market-on-Close.**

Opening Transaction—establishing a position in an option (by buying or selling). COMPARE: **Closing Transaction.**

Operating Income—SEE: **Earnings Before Interest & Taxes (EBIT).**

Opinion—SEE: **Legal Opinion.**

OPRA—SEE: **Options Price Reporting Authority.**

Option—the right, but not obligation, to buy or sell something at a predetermined price and under predetermined conditions (time limit and/or other conditions).

Option, Covered—SEE: **Covered Option.**

Option, Naked—SEE: **Uncovered Option.**

Option, Uncovered—SEE: **Uncovered Option.**

Options, Debt—SEE: **Debt Options.**

Options, Equity—SEE: **Equity Options.**

Options, Exchange-Traded— SEE: **Exchange-Traded Options.**

Options, Foreign Currency—SEE: **Foreign Currency Options.**

Options, Listed—SEE: **Exchange-Traded Options.**

Options, Over-the-Counter—SEE: **Over-The-Counter Options.**

Options, Yield-Based—SEE: **Yield-Based Options.**

Options Clearing Corporation—the largest clearing organization for derivative securities, which issues, guarantees and clears options contracts for stocks, Treasuries, and other securities that are traded on the various exchanges.

Options Disclosure Document (ODD)—a document that explains in detail how options work, various option strategies, and the risk-reward potential of trading in options. (The ODD was developed by the OCC to ensure fair and full disclosure of the risks involved to all potential options traders before they actually begin trading options.)

Options Price Reporting Authority (OPRA)—a computer-based subscription service that gives inside quotes (highest bid, lowest ask price) and last sale data for options.

Order Period—a time during which orders are taken and bonds are allocated based on the type of order rather than the exact time that the order was received. (MSRB rules allow this to take place for a short window after the syndicate's successful bid.) ALSO SEE: **Priority Provisions.**

Original Issue Discount—bonds that are sold at a discount from par value when they are first issued.

Out-of-the-Money—when the option holder would not make money by exercising the option contract. COMPARE: **At-the-Money, In-the-Money.**

Outstanding Stock—stock presently held by shareholders. (i.e., investors, founders, employees, etc.)

Over-the-Counter Options—option contracts distinguished by the fact that they do not trade on an exchange, and thus are non-negotiable. COMPARE: **Exchange-Traded Options.**

Overalottment—when too much of a hot issue is sold. Also called **overselling** or

oversubscribed. SEE: **Green Shoe Clause.**

Overbought—a market condition whereby prices have risen so sharply that some are predicting a price decline (**correction**) in the overall market: because there are few buyers left, a price drop is imminent. COMPARE: **Oversold.** ALSO SEE: **Correction.**

Overlapping Debt—SEE: **Coterminous.**

Overselling—SEE: **Overalottment.**

Oversold—a market condition whereby prices have fallen so sharply that some are predicting a price rise in the overall market: because there are few sellers left, a price rise is imminent. COMPARE: **Overbought.**

Oversubscribed—SEE: **Overalottment.**

Owner—one who possesses (or has the right to possess) something. Also called **long.** SEE: **Long.**

PACs—Planned amortization class CMOs (PACs) utilize a sinking fund to ensure that investors receive their principal and interest payments. PAC obligations are repaid first, using companion tranches to shift prepayments, and to maintain payments if the underlying mortgages do not pay on time. COMPARE: **TACs.** ALSO SEE: **CMOs.**

Packaged Securities—investments which are created by combining several other investments. (e.g., **Mutual Funds, REITs**)

Paid-In Capital—difference between the initial par value of stock and the actual money the corporation receives for selling the stock. (Paid-in capital is money received from investors, as opposed to money actually earned by a company, and is an asset of the company.)

Painting the Tape—when one or more broker-dealer firms act in a coordinated effort, or within a group or ring, to buy and sell the same stock several times in succession to show trading activity, or make a stock appear hot. This is also referred to as **matched order** or **sales pools** or **sales rings.** (NASD rules prohibit this.)

Paper, Commercial—SEE: **Commercial Paper.**

Paper Act—SEE: **Securities Act of 1933.**

Par Value—1. the face value of a security (e.g., $1,000 is typical for a bond). 2. arbitrary value assigned by a company to its authorized stock.

Parity—1. when the value of convertible bonds and the common stock price intersect, such that the conversion would be an even exchange. 2. when an option contract trades at its intrinsic value, with no time value component added to the price. 3. when filling market orders, if everything else is the same (same time, same size), then orders are filled randomly. (ALSO SEE: **Precedence, Priority.**)

Partnership—a contract between two or more persons to pool money, resources, and talents in a business, project or venture, in exchange for a share of the profits (or losses) generated by their association. COMPARE: **Corporation, Sole Proprietorship.**

Passive Income—income derived from any business activity in which the person is not an active participant. (e.g., limited partnerships or real estate). Tax law changes in 1986: passive losses are deductible only against passive income. COMPARE: **Earned Income.**

Payroll Deduction Savings Plan—SEE: **401(k) Plan.**

PE Ratio—SEE: **Price-Earnings Ratio.**

Peak—the top of a business cycle, where expansion begins to level off as demand catches up with supply. From this point, production and prices will begin to fall. COMPARE: **Trough.** ALSO SEE: **Business Cycles.**

Pegging—1. intervention in the markets by a broker-dealer, when a broker-dealer places a non-existent buy order, or places its own buy order to move a stock up to that price or keep it from falling any lower than the price that the broker-dealer bid. (NASD rules prohibit this.) 2. permitted bids for new issues (SEE: **Stabilizing Bid**). 3. intervention by governments to try to control the exchange rate of their currency by buying it in the open market when it dips below a certain level.

Penalty Bid—when the syndicate or sales group member has to pay back all or part of the concession earned to the managing underwriter because buyers of a new issue resold their stock too soon. Also called **penalty fee.**

Penalty Fee—SEE: **Penalty Bid.**

Penny Stock—over-the-counter (OTC, i.e., non-listed) equity securities that trade for less than $1 per share (although they may trade as high as $5-$10 per share), but are highly volatile because the companies who issue the stock usually have short and erratic operating histories.

Penny Stock Cold Calling Rules—SEC rules designed to protect unsophisticated investors by requiring certain disclosures and procedures when making telephone solicitations.

People Act—SEE: **Securities Exchange Act of 1934.**

Performance Measurement— SEE: **Alpha, Beta.**

Pink Sheets—the name of the daily publication of the National Quotation Bureau showing wholesale interdealer listing bid and ask prices of OTC **stocks** not listed on the NASDAQ. (The pink sheets get their name from the color of paper they are printed on.) COMPARE: **Yellow Sheets.**

Pipeline Theory—SEE: **Conduit Theory.**

Placement Ratio Indexes—shows the proportion of all bonds over $1 million (competitive and negotiated) that were distributed during the past week. (Published in *The Bond Buyer.*)

Plus Tick—term for when the previous trade occurred at a higher price than the one before it. In essence, the price of the security is heading up. This is also referred to as an **uptick.** ALSO SEE: **Zero-Plus Tick, Short Sale.** COMPARE: **Minus Tick.**

Plus Tick Rule—rule that says a short sale can only occur on a "plus tick" or "zero-plus tick." ALSO SEE: **Zero Tick, Zero Plus Tick, Short Sale.**

Point—equal to one percent change in the value of a bond. (Fractions of a point are called **Basis Points**).

Point, Basis—SEE: **Basis Point.**

Political Risk—the risk of a change in government policy that adversely affects an investment. This usually refers to a foreign country, such as when an industry is nationalized or protectionist measures are adopted that affect specific import or export products. COMPARE: **Legislative risk.**

POP—SEE: **Public Offering Price.**

Portfolio Diversification—spreading out risk by holding investments in varying types, amounts and asset classes.

Portfolio Management—a means of bringing a portfolio in line with customer investment objectives. Portfolio management moves the overall investment strategy in one direction or another, tilting the balance from extremely aggressive to very conservative. COMPARE: **Portfolio Theory.**

Portfolio Theory—a means of using objective benchmarks that measure risk against return in a portfolio. Unlike traditional securities analysis, though, portfolio theory doesn't worry about the specific securities that are in the portfolio. Instead, the idea is to have a diversified mix of asset classes to achieve the investor's goals. COMPARE: **Portfolio Management.**

Portfolio Turnover—the percentage of a fund's portfolio that's sold during the year, expressed as a percentage to show how often mutual funds buy and sell their holdings. Portfolio turnover is calculated as gross proceeds from sales divided by total assets.

Position Limits—the maximum number of listed options that an individual, or group of individuals working together, can own in the same underlying security. (The numbers are adjusted frequently, and vary by exchange and trading volume of the underlying security.) These limits apply to all expiration dates on the same side of the market. ALSO SEE: **Exercise Limits.**

Positive Yield Curve—SEE: **Normal Yield Curve.**

Power, Stock—SEE: **Stock Power.**

Precedence—when filling market orders, all things being equal, the larger order gets filled first. ALSO SEE: **Priority, Parity.**

Preemptive Rights—the right of existing stockholders to buy, in proportion to their current holdings, additional shares of a new issue by the company before the stock is offered to the public. Also called an **antidilution provision.**

Preferred Ratio—total preferred stock divided by total capital. COMPARE: **Debt Ratio, Common Ratio.**

Preferred Stock—an ownership interest in a corporation that pays a specified dividend rate. Owners of preferred stock have limited liability, get paid dividends before common stockholders, and can recoup assets in a liquidation before common stockholders. Preferred stockholders usually do not receive voting rights or preemptive rights, and do not get to share in the capital appreciation of the company. COMPARE: **Common Stock.**

Preliminary Prospectus—gives some details about the offering to gauge investor interest, but must clearly state that it is "not an offer to sell securities nor solicit orders." (Because this warning is printed in red, a preliminary prospectus is sometimes referred to as a **red herring.**) The preliminary prospectus gives financial details about the issue and about the company, including a detailed use of proceeds statement, history of the company, management team, and risks to investors in the issue. (The preliminary prospectus is distributed during the cooling off period. It does not contain the final public offering price, and all information is subject to change before the final prospectus is issued.) COMPARE: **Final Prospectus.**

Premium—1. the amount above par that is paid for a bond, preferred stock, or other security; 2. the price an investor pays to buy an option contract.

Premium, Call—SEE: **Call Premium.**

Premium, Waiver of—SEE: **Waiver of Premium.**

Preservation of Capital—an investment objective that ensures that the original amount of money invested is as safe as possible.

Price, Exercise—SEE: **Exercise Price.**

Price, Strike—SEE: **Strike Price.**

Price-Earnings Ratio—an indication of how much an investor is paying for a company's earning power. A company with high growth potential can command higher PE multiple. PEs can measure a company's intrinsic value and value relative to other companies. PE is derived by taking the market price per share of stock, and dividing that by the earnings per share.

Pricing, Forward—SEE: **Forward Pricing.**

Primary Market—sale of new securities issues directly by the issuer to investors. COMPARE: **Secondary Market.**

Primary Marketplace—where new securities issues are sold. COMPARE: **Secondary Marketplace.**

Primary Offering—sale of stock in the primary market, with the proceeds from the sale of stock going into the company treasury. COMPARE: **Secondary Offering.** ALSO SEE: **Combined Offering.**

Principal—1. With regard to a loan, the amount originally borrowed. COMPARE: **Interest.** 2. With regard to an investment, the face amount. 3. With regard to a transaction, a person who grants another person (an agent) authority to represent him or her in dealings with third parties. 4. In general, one of the parties to a transaction (such as a dealer), as opposed to those who are involved as agents or employees (such as a broker).

Principal, Risk of—SEE: **Risk of Principal.**

Priority—when filling market orders, if prices are equal, the order that is placed first (with the best price) is filled first. When done electronically, it is the order that arrives first; when done on the trading floor, it is the order that the specialist hears first. ALSO SEE: **Precedence, Parity.**

Priority Provisions—the sequence in which bond orders are filled: pre-sale orders, group net orders, designated orders, member at takedown orders. ALSO SEE: **Order Period.**

Private Placement—SEE: **Reg. D.**

Private Placement Memorandum—document that discloses details of a limited partnership investment, business plan, financial information, and information on the general partners.

Private Placement Offering—selling a municipal bond issue to institutional investors.

Privilege, Conversion—SEE: **Conversion Privilege.**

Pro Rata—a method of proportionate allocation, meaning that each gets a percentage share based on the percentage of stock owned.

Profit and Loss Statement—SEE: **Income Statement.**

Profit Margin—equal to a company's operating income divided by its net sales. ALSO SEE: **Margin-of-Profit Ratio.**

Profit Sharing Plan—plan where the employer agrees to make contributions to the retirement accounts of employees annually when the company makes profits above a certain level. Benefits paid out during retirement are taxed as ordinary income to the recipient. (When all employees are treated equally, this is a qualified, tax deductible plan.)

Profitability—the ability to generate money above costs, expenses and overhead. This is the most important indicator of all. A company must be able to generate a profit if it is to provide a rate of return on invested capital. SEE: **Margin-of-Profit Ratio, Net Profit Ratio.**

Profits, Trading—SEE: **Trading Profits.**

Program Trading—automated, computerized trading. ALSO SEE: **Circuit Breakers.**

Progressive Tax—a system of taxation whereby people with higher incomes pay a higher percentage of their income in taxes. This is accomplished by the use of **tax brackets.** COMPARE: **Regressive Tax.**

Prospectus—a formal written document detailing the financial information, business plan and operating history of a company that is selling securities. ALSO SEE: **Preliminary Prospectus, Final Prospectus.**

Prospectus, Final—SEE: **Final Prospectus.**

Prospectus, Preliminary—SEE: **Preliminary Prospectus.**

Prospectus, Public Offering—SEE: **Public Offering Prospectus.**

Protection, Call—SEE: **Call Protection.**

Proxy—a kind of absentee ballot, whereby the stockholder can vote on matters without having to attend an annual stockholders' meeting.

Proxy Fight—battle over a major issue, change of management, or control of a company, which is done through shareholder voting. (Proxy fights, that attempt to alter control of a company must have all parties register with the SEC or risk criminal penalties.)

Proxy Solicitation—ballot or other document trying to elicit a vote from a shareholder. (Proxy solicitations must be sent to the SEC for approval before the company can send them to stockholders.)

Prudent Man Rule—rule that says that fiduciaries must act as any prudent man or woman would do when making investment decisions: with care and skill, to preserve capital, seek reasonable income, and avoid unreasonable risk and speculative investments. This rule serves as a guideline for those who have the duty and responsibility of investing money on behalf of beneficiaries. COMPARE: **Legal List.**

Public Offering Price (POP)—the price of buying a mutual fund share, derived by taking the NAV and adding the sales charges. POP is the "ask" price at which fund shares are purchased. COMPARE: **Net Asset Value.**

Public Offering Prospectus—document that explains the limited partnership investment, business plan, financial information, and information on the general partners. The prospectus must be filed with the SEC.

Purchasing Power Risk—SEE: **Inflationary Risk.**

Put—option that gives an investor the right to sell a certain number of shares of a security, at a predetermined price, before a certain date. COMPARE: **Call.**

Put Bonds—a bond that gives a bondholder the right to turn in a bond for payment before its maturity date, and redeem the bond at full face value. (Sometimes the put option must be exercised on a specific date, or is offered at a specific interval of time, or can be done at any one time during the life of the bond.)

Put-Call Ratio—a measurement of the number of put options traded, compared with the number of call options traded. A higher volume of puts indicates a bearish sentiment. A higher volume of calls indicates a bullish sentiment.

Put Option—bondholder's right to turn in a bond for payment before its maturity date.

Qualified Annuity—variable annuity that has the invested amount paid for with pre-tax dollars. (e.g., an annuity in an IRA account, or a retirement account paid for by an employer) This means that although the money is allowed to grow tax deferred, all money taken out is fully taxable as ordinary income. COMPARE: **Non-Qualified Annuity.**

Qualified Legal Opinion—a legal opinion issued by a bond attorney that says that the bond issue is valid only with certain qualifications (perhaps because of the inability to confirm some essential fact, or because of pending litigation). COMPARE: **Unqualified Legal Opinion, Ex-Legal.**

Qualified Retirement Plan—an employer-sponsored retirement account paid for with pre-tax dollars. This means that although the money is allowed to grow tax deferred, all money taken out is fully taxable as ordinary income. (Plan must treat all employees equally, must be IRS approved to qualify for tax deductible contributions, and must comply with ERISA.) COMPARE: **Unqualified Retirement Plan.**

Qualifying Independently—a means of compliance with Blue Sky Laws whereby a registration is filed with individual states for an intra-state offering only (which is exempt from SEC registration). ALSO SEE: **Blue Sky Laws, Filing a Notice, Coordinated Registration.**

Quick Assets—a measure of a company's liquid assets, excluding inventory. This is a better indication of a company's ability to quickly meet expenses should sales be interrupted or inventory become outdated, because inventory isn't that liquid at full price. This is also called **Acid Test Ratio.**

Quotes, Firm—SEE: **Firm Quotes.**

Quotes, Nominal—SEE: **Nominal Quotes.**

Quotes, Subject—SEE: **Subject Quotes.**

Quotes, Workout—SEE: **Workout Quotes.**

Rating Agencies—entities that research corporate and municipal bond issues and assign them a rating. Two notable agencies are Moody's and Standard & Poor's (S&P). Also referred to as **rating services.**

Ratings—values on a point scale that represent the likelihood that the issuer will default on a debt obligation. ALSO SEE: **Rating Agencies, Investment Grade Bonds.**

Ratio Call Writing—when the investor writes multiple calls on the same stock, some covered and some uncovered. (This generates more portfolio income, and hedges *some* of the risk, but the investor still has unlimited risk for the naked calls.)

Real Estate Investment Trust (REIT)—separate trusts which specialize in real estate investment, collect funds to control real estate, and manage the portfolio.

Real Estate Mortgage Investment Conduit (REMIC)—a vehicle for issuing mortgage-backed securities, with the flexibility to issue the securities into different groups based on the maturity and the risk level of the pool of mortgages which back the securities.

Reallowance—a small part of the concession that is paid to any firms who sell the issue, but are not part of the syndicate or selling group.

Recession—a less severe economic downturn, characterized by two consecutive quarters of decline in the country's level of business activity as defined by the gross domestic product (GDP).

Record, Date of—SEE: **Date of Record.**

Recovery—a period of business activity marked by increasing production as supply is trying to catch back up to increasing demand. This is the precursor to an expansion phase of the business cycle and growth for the economy. ALSO SEE: **Business Cycles.**

Red Herring—term used to describe the preliminary prospectus because the disclaimer ("This is not an offer to sell securities nor solicit orders.") is often printed on the cover in red ink. SEE: **Preliminary Prospectus.**

Redemption—repayment of a debt obligation at maturity, or earlier.

Redemption, Sinking Fund—SEE: **Sinking Fund Redemption.**

Redemption Price—NAV price for mutual funds.

Refund at Call Dates—redeeming a bond issue by calling the bonds as soon possible, per the terms of the call feature.

Refunding—replacing a debt obligation with another debt security that has different terms, such as a lower interest rate. ALSO SEE: **Advance Refunding.**

Reg. A—exception to the registration requirements of the Securities Act of 1933, providing for a simplified securities registration process for companies doing stock offerings of less than $5 million within a 12-month period. With a Reg. A offering, instead of the registration statement and full prospectus, a shorter document called an offering circular is used, requiring less detail and unaudited financial statements. (Named for Regulation A of '33 Act.)

Reg. D—exception to the registration requirements of the Securities Act of 1933, providing for investment transactions where the securities are purchased as part of a private placement with the intent of being held for investment purposes, rather than for resale. The stock is restricted stock that must be held for a certain period of time before it can be re-sold. Three investor categories are eligible for investing in a Reg. D private placement: accredited investors (with a net worth of at least $1 million or annual income of at least $200,000), officers or those affiliated with the issuer, and an investment group consisting of no more than 35 nonaccredited investors. (Named for Regulation D of '33 Act.)

Reg. T—Federal Reserve Board Regulation T states that a person must have on deposit the higher of $2,000 or 50% of the purchase price of the eligible securities bought on margin. (Reg. T also says that settlement must occur within 5 business days.)

Registered Bonds—bonds where the owner's name is recorded with the registrar, and interest payments are sent automatically or paid electronically. COMPARE: **Bearer Bonds.**

Registered Representative (RR)—an employee of a stock exchange member firm who acts as an account executive for clients, giving advice on which securities to buy and sell, and collecting a commission through the firm for services rendered. RRs must be licensed by the Securities and Exchange Commission (SEC), by one or more of the various self-regulatory organizations (SRO) and by the state or states in which they engage in securities activities.

Registrar—appointed by the corporation to oversee the issuance of stock certificates, to make sure that no more than the total number of authorized shares of stock are in circulation, and to certify the authenticity of corporate bonds. (By law, the registrar must be an entity separate from the company, and the same entity cannot act as both registrar and transfer agent for the same corporation.) COMPARE: **Transfer Agent.**

Registration, Coordinated—SEE: **Coordinated Registration.**

Registration, Effective Date of—SEE: **Effective Date of Registration.**

Registration Letter—SEE: **Registration Statement.**

Registration Statement—statement filed with the SEC that must disclose the purpose of the offering, how much money the company is going to raise, how the money will be spent, information on the company and its business, information on the company's principals (especially any prior securities trouble), any legal proceedings the company is involved in, and any other pertinent facts that investors would need to know to make an informed decision about buying the company's stocks or bonds. Also called a **registration letter.**

Regressive Tax—a system of taxation whereby all people pay the same tax rate, regardless of income (e.g., a sales tax). COMPARE: **Progressive Tax.**

Regular Way—settlement designation of T + 3 for corporate and municipal securities, and T + 1 for U.S. government securities. (COMPARE: cash settlements, which settle same day.)

Regulation A—SEE: **Reg. A.**

Regulation D—SEE: **Reg. D.**

Regulation T—SEE: **Reg. T.**

Rehypothecation—when broker-dealers pledge a client's securities as collateral for a loan. (The broker-dealer needs this authorization because the B-D is going to borrow the money to buy the securities that the client is buying on margin.) SEE: **Hypothecation.**

Reinvestment Risk—risk that the investor cannot replace a paid off investment with one of a similar yield. ALSO SEE: **Call Risk.**

REIT—SEE: **Real Estate Investment Trust.**

REMIC—SEE: **Real Estate Mortgage Investment Conduit.**

Repayment Risk—the chance that homeowners will default on the mortgage loan. ALSO SEE: **Credit Risk.**

REPOs—SEE: **Repurchase Agreement.**

Repurchase Agreement—an arrangement between buyer and seller to sell an asset now, and then buy it back for a fixed price, and usually within a stated timeframe.

Reserve Requirements—the percentage of deposits that commercial banks are required to keep on deposit, either on hand at the bank or in the bank's own accounts—in other words, money the bank can't lend to customers. By raising or lowering reserve requirements the Fed controls the supply and cost of money, and the quality of credit. (The original purpose of reserve requirements was to help avert financial panic by giving depositors some confidence that their deposits were safe and accessible. Reserve requirements, however, have also become a policy tool.)

Reserve Split—an attempt to adjust the price of a stock upward by decreasing the number of outstanding shares without changing the percentage of company ownership held by each stockholder, and without changing the total market value of all outstanding shares. ALSO SEE: **Stock Split.**

Residual Claim (on Assets)—In a bankruptcy, the common stockholders are the last in line to recoup any money. After all creditors and lien holders have been satisfied, though, the common stockholders do have a claim on whatever assets, if any, are left.

Resistance Level—technical term for highest price at which a stock has peaked on several occasions in previous trades. Theory: a stock has difficulty rising above a resistance level because there's more supply than demand at that price. COMPARE: **Support Level.**

Restricted Account—account situation when the equity in an account drops below the 50% required by Reg. T, resulting in the account not being able to make any additional purchases unless the margin deficiency is improved, and making all sales subject to 50% retention requirements. ALSO SEE: **Retention Requirement.**

Restricted Stock—stock that is acquired by means other than a typical SEC registered offering, and thus must be held for a certain period of time before it can be re-sold. Also called **unregistered stock, legended stock,** or **lettered stock.** ALSO SEE: **Rule 144.** COMPARE: **Control Stock.**

Retention Requirement—rule that the client is required to leave in the account 50% of the cash received from any sales to help raise the equity in the account, and get it back closer to its initial margin level. (This occurs when the account becomes a restricted account and keeps it from falling below the 50% Reg. T requirement.) ALSO SEE: **Restricted Account.**

Return, Total—SEE: **Total Return.**

Return on Common Equity—the amount earned on a company's stock over a given period of time (usually for the previous year). This tells investors how efficiently money is being used by a company, and gives a means of comparison against prior years' performance and against competitors. Return on common equity is derived by taking common stock earnings, and dividing that by the total of retained earnings plus paid in surplus plus common stock par value.

Revaluation—when the value of a country's currency rises relative to other currencies (or other currencies fall). This is usually from government action. COMPARE: **Devaluation.**

Revenue Bonds—bonds paid for from the income (revenue) generated by a specific project. These are usually used for public works projects, such as roads or water treatment plants. The revenue bonds are backed by the tolls or user fees from the project. Unless specifically stated, revenue bondholders do not have a claim to other revenue sources or general tax collections to pay the debt. COMPARE: **General Obligation Bonds.**

Revenue Pledge—SEE: **Net Revenue Pledge** or **Gross Revenue Pledge.**

Reversionary Work Interest—a way of describing how income and expenses are allocated in oil and gas partnerships, whereby limited partners pay all expenses and recoup their investment before the general partner receives any money. COMPARE: **Functional Allocation.**

Rights, Preemptive—SEE: **Preemptive Rights.**

Rights of Accumulation (ROA)—breakpoint sales at a future time once the total amount of money invested has reached the breakpoint. (From that point forward, all newly invested money qualifies for the reduced sales charges.) ALSO SEE: **Breakpoint Sales.**

Rights Offering—an offer to existing common stockholders that allows them to buy additional shares of newly issued stock before it is offered for sale to the public. This is done to honor the preemptive rights of existing common stockholders. (Term used with **standby underwriting.**)

Risk, Call—SEE: **Call Risk.**

Risk, Capital—SEE: **Capital Risk.**

Risk, Credit—SEE: **Credit Risk.**

Risk, Currency—SEE: **Currency Risk.**

Risk, Exchange—SEE: **Exchange Risk.**

Risk, Extension—SEE: **Extension Risk.**

Risk, Financial—SEE: **Financial Risk.**

Risk, Inflationary—SEE: **Inflationary Risk.**

Risk, Interest Rate—SEE: **Interest Rate Risk.**

Risk, Investment—SEE: **Investment Risk.**

Risk, Legislative—SEE: **Legislative Risk.**

Risk, Liquidity—SEE: **Liquidity Risk.**

Risk, Market—SEE: **Market Risk.**

Risk, Political—SEE: **Political Risk.**

Risk, Purchasing Power—SEE: **Inflationary Risk.**

Risk, Reinvestment—SEE: **Reinvestment Risk.**

Risk, Repayment—SEE: **Repayment Risk.**

Risk, Systematic—SEE: **Market Risk.**

Risk, Timing—SEE: **Timing Risk.**

Risk of Bankruptcy—the danger that a company will not be able to meet its debt service obligations. This is an important indication of a company's financial strength and credit risk. A company that is leveraged too much may not be able to pay off its debts if rates rise or the economy declines. SEE: **Bond Ratio, Debt-to-Equity Ratio.**

Risk of Principal—the chance that invested capital will decrease in value. Here one thinks of the investor who buys a stock that becomes worthless.

ROA—SEE: **Rights of Accumulation.**

Rollover—when an IRA account balance is transferred directly from one custodian to another, or when the investor takes possession of the IRA funds (permitted once each year) and redeposits the funds into another IRA account within 60 days. (Lump sum distributions from a qualified retirement plan, such as when a person changes employers, may be rolled over into a new retirement plan without incurring tax consequences. There is no limit on the amount that an investor can rollover, but any amount not rolled over within that time frame is subject to ordinary income tax and an added 10% penalty if the investor is not yet 59½ years of age.)

ROP—Registered Options Principal. A person within the broker-dealer firm who approves options-related advertisements, sales literature, and educational materials.

Rotation—SEE: **Opening Rotation** or **Closing Rotation.**

Roth IRA—an Individual Retirement Account (IRA) with contributions that are *not* tax deductible, but which permit qualified distributions to be taken tax-free upon retirement. Since the Roth IRA funds are taxed before they go into the plan, they are allowed to come out tax free. Like regular IRAs, the Roth IRA permits persons with earned income to invest up to $2,000 individually or $4,000 for married couples filing jointly. A 10% penalty is imposed on distributions that start before age 59½, except in the case of disability, medical expenses, education expenses, first-time home purchase, or death.

RR—SEE: **Registered Representative.**

Rule 144—part of the Reg. D private placement regulations, involving use of an investment letter that investors sign stating, among other things, that the private placement stock they are buying is being purchased for investment purposes, and furthermore that they agree not to sell the stock for a certain period of time and/or under certain conditions. ALSO SEE: **Restricted Stock, Control Stock.**

Rule 144a—provides for an exception to the holding period requirements if the securities are nonregistered foreign securities sold to qualified institutional investors in the U.S. who have at least $100 million in assets and meet certain other qualifications.

Rule 145—applies to stock acquired through a merger, consolidation or transfer, permitting the shares to be resold without registration, provided that certain stipulations are followed.

S&P 500—index of stocks chosen to achieve distribution by broad industry groups, roughly relative to composition of the NYSE market. Each stock is representative of its industry group, so price movements are responsive to changes in that sector. Total market capitalization of a stock and its trading volume are important considerations, as stocks in the index are weighted. COMPARE: **DJIA.**

Safety of Income—SEE: **Asset Coverage.**

Sale, Wash—SEE: **Wash Sale.**

Sales Literature—any written, electronic or oral material distributed by a brokerage firm upon the request of a client, sent by the firm to a selected group of people, or disseminated in any other way such that the brokerage firm has control over who receives the material. (e.g., brochure, research report, e-mail newsletter). COMPARE: **Advertising.**

Sales Pools—SEE: **Painting the Tape.**

Sales Rings—SEE: **Painting the Tape.**

Saucer—technical chart pattern that shows a stock price has declined over a period of time, but has bottomed out and is now in an upward trend. An **inverted saucer** is a technical chart pattern that shows a stock price has risen over a period of time, but has peaked and is now in a downward trend.

Savings—when a portion of income or other money is not spent immediately.

Scale—the number of bonds, maturity date, coupon rate, and offering price. ALSO SEE: **Writing the Scale.**

SEC—SEE: **Securities and Exchange Commission.**

Secondary Market—place where securities are bought and sold after original issue, with proceeds going to the investor selling the security. COMPARE: **Primary Market.**

Secondary Marketplace—where securities are bought and sold after their original issue. COMPARE: **Primary Marketplace.**

Secondary Offering—sale of stock in the primary market, with the proceeds from sale of stock going to present shareholders. COMPARE: **Primary Offering.** ALSO SEE: **Combined Offering.**

Securities—any investment relationship with a company (and the instrument that represents that investment). This can be equity in a company (stock), debt with a company (bond), a pooling of investment instruments (mutual fund), or any instrument transferring a future right (option).

Securities Act of 1933—requires all securities to be registered before they can be sold to the public, requires use of a prospectus with full disclosure of all pertinent information, and prohibits false and misleading information with several anti-fraud provisions. (Focus is on primary market.) Also called **Paper Act.**

Securities and Exchange Commission (SEC)—a federal government agency created by the Securities Exchange Act of 1934 to oversee the securities industry, establish regulations governing the issuance and sale of securities, and enforce the securities laws enacted by Congress.

Securities Exchange Act of 1934—regulates secondary market activity, outlaws fraud and market manipulation, regulates sales and activity by company insiders, requires broker-dealer firms and sales reps to be registered, and created the Securities & Exchange

Commission (SEC). (There is never an exemption from the anti-fraud provisions of this Act.) Also called the **People Act.**

Securities Investor Protection Corporation (SIPC)—established as a non-profit corporation by an act of Congress in 1970 to protect investors from broker-dealer insolvency. SIPC provides a fund that insures the cash and securities in an investor's account up to $500,000 total, with a limit of $100,000 paid in cash for each separate customer account.

Security, Derivative—SEE: **Derivative Security.**

Security, Fixed-Income—SEE: **Bonds.**

Self-Regulatory Organization (SRO)—created by federal securities laws to help maintain a fair and orderly trading environment, to help oversee various aspects of the securities industries, and to aid in enforcement of securities rules and regulations. Each SRO also adopts and enforces its own "industry rules."

Seller—one who sells something. Also called **short.** SEE: **Short.**

Seller's Concession—the amount of commission that will be paid to the selling group for issues that they actually sell. ALSO SEE: **Takedown, Additional Takedown.**

Seller's Option—SEE: **Delayed Delivery.**

Selling, Breakpoint—SEE: **Breakpoint Selling.**

Selling Away—doing a trade or collecting a commission that does not go through the broker-dealer firm. (Prohibited by NASD rules.)

Selling Dividends—telling clients to buy stocks right before ex-date just to capture a dividend is considered unethical since stock price will drop equal to the dividend amount right after the ex-date, but client has an immediate taxable event. (Prohibited by NASD rules.)

Selling Group—a group formed to help distribute and sell an issue to the public. (Selling group members do not invest money to buy part of an offering like a syndicate [purchase group] does.) COMPARE: **Syndicate.**

Selling Group Agreement—agreement details the relationship between the purchase group and the sales group, including the amount of commission that will be paid (called the **seller's concession**) and the length of time the contract will be in force (often only 30 days). (Note that the selling group is *not* responsible for buying any unsold shares and bears no liability if shares are unsold. The selling group is an agent, and not bound by any agreements of the other underwriters.) COMPARE: **Agreement Among Underwriters.**

SEP-IRA—a Simplified Employee Pension-Individual Retirement Account with contributions that are tax-deferred, often used by small businesses or sole proprietors without other retirement plans. Employers can make contributions equal to 15% of employees' total compensation, up to a maximum $25,500. Contributions and investment earnings grow tax-deferred until distributions begin at retirement (age 59½) or disability. All distributions are taxed as ordinary income. Except for higher contribution limits, all rules for regular IRAs apply, including early withdrawal penalties. (10% penalty imposed if distributions start before age 59½, except in cases of disability, medical costs, education expenses, first-time home purchase, death. 50% penalty imposed if distributions don't start by age 70½.)

Separate Account—segregated account maintained by an insurance company into which variable annuity contract payments are placed.

Serial Maturity—when bonds are all issued at the same time, but come due on different staggered redemption dates.

Series—a class of options with all the same price and date. COMPARE: **Class.**

Series Maturity—when bonds come due on different dates staggered apart because they were issued at different times.

Shareholder's Equity—SEE: **Net Worth.**

Sharing Agreement—a way of describing how income and expenses are allocated in oil and gas partnerships. There are two main ways these are structured: 1. **Reversionary Work Interest:** limited partners pay all expenses and recoup their investment before the general partner receives any money. 2. **Functional Allocation:** limited partners pay most expenses, but income is shared; limited partners get IDC deductions, general partner gets depreciation deductions.

Sharing Arrangement—SEE: **Sharing Agreement.**

Shelf Distribution—request to sell shares by a company insider written into a registration statement, filed early, then allowed to "sit on a shelf" until the person is ready to use this privilege to sell shares at a later time. Also called a **shelf registration.**

Shelf Registration— SEE: **Shelf Distribution.**

Short—a position in a stock, option, etc. when an investor **sells** it. You can also say that the investor is the **writer** of the option, or is **short** the option. (These terms are synonymous: **seller = writer = short.**) COMPARE: **Long.**

Short Against the Box—SEE: **Shorting Against the Box.**

Short Call—sell a call option (a bearish or neutral strategy). COMPARE: **Long Call, Short Put.** ALSO SEE: **Long Put.**

Short Margin Account—account investor uses to sell securities by *borrowing the securities* from the broker-dealer. ("Short" here is used differently. Customer is selling, he just doesn't own the securities so he borrows them now and hopes to repay them later by buying them at a reduced price and making money.) COMPARE: **Long Margin Account.**

Short Market Value (SMV)—the present worth of the client's short stock position at the end of the valuation period. COMPARE: **Long Market Value.**

Short Put—sell a put option (a bullish or neutral strategy). COMPARE: **Long Put, Short Call.** ALSO SEE: **Long Call.**

Short Sales—when an investor sells a security that he or she doesn't own. (The investor *borrows the security* from a broker-dealer firm to sell it now, and hopes to repay the security later by buying it at a reduced price at some point in the future.)

Short Tendering—broker-dealers borrowing stock (taking short positions) to take advantage of a purchase request (tender offer) by a company. (NASD rules prohibit this.)

Shorting Against the Box—a technique where an investor does a short sale with the same security in which the investor also owns a long position. The short sale locks in a gain against drops in price, and the long stock the investor owns can be delivered later to cover the short sale. Tax law changes have curtailed the use of this technique.

Sinking Fund Redemption—when a municipality calls bonds as soon as it has accumulated enough in a sinking fund to pay off the issue.

SIPC—SEE: **Securities Investor Protection Corp.**

SLD—sale delayed; a notation on the consolidated tapes that a trade did not appear within the 90 second requirement or was reported out of sequence, and thus cannot count as a "plus tick" for short sales. ALSO SEE: **Consolidated Tapes.**

SMA—SEE: **Special Memorandum Account.**

SMV—SEE: **Short Market Value.**

Sole Proprietorship—business enterprise set up by a single individual. COMPARE: **Corporation, Partnership.**

Special Assessment Bonds—revenue bonds that are paid from special assessment collections only. Only those specific individuals benefitting from the project must pay the assessment. For example, the municipality may impose a special assessment and issue special assessment bonds when it needs to put in a new sewer for everyone on the block.

Special Cash Account—alternate name for a cash account; one of the two basic types of accounts that can be opened with a broker-dealer (the other being a margin account).

Special Memorandum Account (SMA)—bookkeeping entry used by broker-dealers to keep track of excess equity clients have built up through their trades in their margin accounts.

Special Situation Stocks—common stocks that are undervalued for a short period of time, but are about to rise significantly because of an upcoming event. This could be a pending merger or acquisition, a new management team or new product introduction.

Special Tax Bonds—revenue bonds that are paid from special tax collections only. Some special taxes include excise taxes on liquor, hotel bed taxes, and other use taxes. Note that special taxes don't have to be related to the project that special tax bonds will finance.

Specialist—member of stock exchange given authority to act as broker and dealer (agent and principal) for other brokers, and given responsibility of maintaining a fair and orderly market. (Specialist must be ready to buy and sell from firm's own account to stabilize the market when there are supply and demand imbalances.) COMPARE: **Market Maker.**

Specialist's Book—a record of limit orders, stop orders, short sales and the specialist's own inventory of securities. ALSO SEE: **Specialist, Limit Orders, Stop Orders, Short Sales.**

Speculation—assuming higher risk in anticipation of higher returns.

Speculative Stocks—common stocks of rapidly growing companies that have prospects for above-average growth, but with prices that are highly volatile. Some examples of speculative stocks would be high-tech companies and other start-ups. These stocks are more aggressive, and are generally relied upon solely for capital appreciation since they usually offer no dividends.

Spendable Income—SEE: **Net Spendable Income.**

Split—SEE: **Stock Split; Reverse Split.**

Spot Trades—currency trades settled in cash and completed within one or two business days. This spot market trading is also sometimes called the **cash market.** COMPARE: **Forward Trades.**

Spread—1. The difference between what the underwriters pay to buy an issue, and the public offering price they are able to sell the securities for. 2. An option position that has one long contract and one short contract on the same stock. (Investors buy this option position when they think the stock price will move in a particular direction. The difference between the long strike price and the short strike price is what produces the spread. The potential gain is limited, but so is the potential loss.) ALSO SEE: **Straddle; Combination, Debit Spread, Credit Spread.**

Spread, Credit—SEE: **Credit Spread.**

Spread, Debit—SEE: **Debit Spread.**

SRO—SEE: **Self-Regulatory Organization.**

Stabilization—1. Intervention by governments to try to control the exchange rate of their currency by buying it in the open market when it dips below a certain level. Also called **pegging.** 2. A technical chart pattern that shows little price fluctuation.

Stabilizing Bid—a buy order placed by the managing underwriter to ensure that the new issue price does not fall below the public offering price during the initial offering period while the issue is still being sold. (This is illegal, except for a new issue when it is disclosed in the prospectus, done only by the managing underwriter, and the bid is at or below the public offering price.) Also called **pegging.**

Standard & Poor's (S&P)—provides numerous investment-related services including credit ratings, debt ratings, indexes, and research information. (For the bond rating service, SEE: **Investment Grade Bonds**) ALSO SEE: **S&P 500.**

Standby Underwriting—when an investment banking firm guarantees the issuing company that the firm will buy all shares that are not bought as part of the new issue offering. (Term used with **rights offering.**)

Statutory (Voting)—a type of voting that follows the one share, one vote rule, whereby stockholders get a single vote on each issue or each board member. COMPARE: **Cumulative (Voting).**

Stock, Authorized—SEE: **Authorized Stock.**

Stock, Common—SEE: **Common Stock.**

Stock, Control—SEE: **Control Stock.**

Stock, Issued—SEE: **Issued Stock.**

Stock, Legended—SEE: **Restricted Stock.**

Stock, Lettered—SEE: **Restricted Stock.**

Stock, Nonvoting—SEE: **Nonvoting Stock.**

Stock, Outstanding—SEE: **Outstanding Stock.**

Stock, Penny—SEE: **Penny Stock.**

Stock, Preferred—SEE: **Preferred Stock.**

Stock, Restricted—SEE: **Restricted Stock.**

Stock, Treasury—SEE: **Treasury Stock.**

Stock, Unregistered—SEE: **Restricted Stock.**

Stock Certificates—instruments that represent equity ownership in the company.

Stock Dividends—SEE: **Dividends.**

Stock Power—a document, separate from the stock certificate, granting another party power of attorney to transfer the stock.

Stock Split—an attempt to adjust the price of a stock downward by increasing the number of outstanding shares without changing the percentage of company ownership held by each stockholder, and without changing the total market value of all outstanding shares. In other words, as of the date of the stock split the stockholders all own the same proportionate share of the company as they did before, and the total value of their stock holdings is also the same. ALSO SEE: **Reverse Split.**

Stop Limit Order—an order that becomes a stop order once a certain trigger has been met or exceeded, and then that stop order becomes a market order after a second trigger has been met or exceeded. ALSO SEE: **Stop Order, Limit Order.**

Stop Order—an order that a particular security should be bought or sold at the market price, once a certain threshold (trigger) has been met or exceeded. ALSO SEE: **Limit Order, Stop Limit Order.**

Stopping the Stock—when the specialist holds open a quote for a floor trader for a certain period of time, allowing the floor trader to shop around to try to get a better price for the client without missing the market. (Even if the market has moved beyond the price quoted by the specialist when the stock was stopped, the trade can still be executed at the quoted price. This can be done only for public orders, not broker-dealer account trades. Also note that the trading activity in the stock does *not* stop when the specialist stops the stock.)

Straddle—option position that has an equal number of call contracts and put contracts on the same stock with the same strike price and the same expiration date. (Investors buy straddles when they expect major movement in the stock price, but they're not sure which direction the price will move. Investors sell straddles when they expect little movement in the stock price.) ALSO SEE: **Spread; Combination.**

Straight Line Depreciation—SEE: **Depreciation, Straight Line.**

Strike Price—the price at which the contract holder can exercise the option. Also called **exercise price.**

STRIPS—zero-coupon bonds backed by the U.S. government.

Strong Dollar—when the dollar can be exchanged for more of a foreign currency. This makes foreign imports cheaper, but makes it more expensive for other countries to buy U.S. goods. Also, a strong dollar attracts deposits and foreign investment money into the U.S. COMPARE: **Weak Dollar.**

Subchapter M Theory—SEE: **Conduit Theory.**

Subject Quotes—price is still negotiable or subject to final confirmation; not firm. ALSO SEE: **Workout Quotes.** COMPARE: **Firm Quotes.**

Subscription Agreement—document that binds the investor to the group as a limited partner, and gives authority to the general partner to act on behalf of the limited partner.

Subscription Price—price at which a new offering is purchased, specifically the price of a rights offering. (Usually must be lower than the market price to absorb the new shares into the marketplace.)

Supply-Side Economics—economic theory that says the economy is better served by government reducing tax rates, especially for businesses and those able to create jobs, as a means of creating employment opportunities and stimulating savings and investment for the benefit of everyone, so that people can earn more money and pay fewer taxes, giving them more to spend, save and invest. COMPARE: **Demand-Side Economics.**

Support Level—technical term for lowest price at which a stock has bottomed out on several occasions in prior trades. Theory: a stock has difficulty falling below the support level because there is more demand than supply at that price point. COMPARE: **Resistance Level.**

Sweetener—SEE: **Warrants.**

Syndicate—group of investment banking firms working together to purchase all of the securities from an issuer, and resell them to the public. A syndicate is also called a **purchase group.** COMPARE: **Selling Group.**

Syndicate Letter—outlines the framework for the joint bid effort among a group of investment banking firms. (The syndicate letter is not binding, whereas the agreement among underwriters is binding.) COMPARE: **Agreement Among Underwriters.**

Systematic Risk—SEE: **Market Risk.**

T + 1—trade plus one business day. Settlement time for U.S. government securities.

T + 3—trade plus three business days. Settlement time for corporate, municipal securities.

T + 5—trade plus five business days. Settlement time as required by Regulation T.

T-Bills—SEE: **Treasury Bills.**

T-Bonds—SEE: **Treasury Bonds.**

T-Notes—SEE: **Treasury Notes.**

T-Receipts—SEE: **Treasury Receipts.**

TACs—targeted amortization class CMOs (TACs) utilize a sinking fund to ensure that investors receive principal and interest payments. TAC obligations are paid first, and prepayments are shifted to other companion tranches. COMPARE: **PACs.** ALSO SEE: **CMOs.**

Takedown—part of the underwriter's spread paid to the selling group or other party as commission for actually selling the security to an investor. (When outside selling groups are used, seller's concession is part of the takedown.) The takedown is by far the largest part of the spread at **50–60%** of total spread. ALSO SEE: **Managing Underwriter's Fee, Underwriting Fee, Additional Takedown.**

Takedown, Additional—SEE: **Additional Takedown.**

Tax, Progressive—SEE: **Progressive Tax.**

Tax, Regressive—SEE: **Regressive Tax.**

Tax Advantages—investment objective whereby money is invested in structured ways or in particular kinds of investments to minimize taxes, defer taxes, or avoid taxes altogether.

Tax Bracket—section on the tax schedule that shows what percentage of income is owed in taxes based on the income being reported. (Tax brackets, though, are **marginal,** meaning that only the portion of income that falls above each bracket is taxed at that higher level.)

Tax Credit—an actual dollar for dollar reduction in the amount of taxes owed. COMPARE: **Deduction.**

Tax-Deferred Annuity Plan—retirement plan that allows employees of nonprofit organizations, tax-exempt organizations and schools to invest money tax-deferred, usually through a payroll deduction plan. Employees may contribute up to $10,500, and employers can match up to 25% of employee's compensation or $30,000, whichever is less. Distributions may begin at age 59½, and must start by age 70½. Early withdrawal penalty is 10%. Benefits paid out during retirement are taxed as ordinary income. Also called a **Tax Sheltered Annuity (TSA)** or **403(b) Plan.**

Tax Sheltered Annuity (TSA)—SEE: **Tax Deferred Annuity Plan.**

Taxable Bonds—long-term bonds issued by a municipality for private purpose projects (e.g., bond issued to build a sports team stadium). Because of the private purpose rules, the interest income on this type of bond is not exempt from federal taxation.

Taxable Equivalent Yield—the yield that would have to be paid out on a taxable bond in order for it to equal the yield paid out on a tax-free bond. (In other words, what yield on a corporate bond would give an investor the same yield as a tax-free municipal bond.)

Taxation—the process of a government levying a charge upon people or things.

Technical Analysis—examines the supply and demand for a security based on its historical trading volumes and prices. (Analyst focuses on movement of the stock price in relation to other market trends in an effort to predict future share price.) COMPARE: **Fundamental Analysis.**

Telephone Solicitation—any telephone call initiated to encourage a person to buy a good or service, or make an investment. (As defined by the Telephone Consumer Protection Act of 1991.)

Tender Offer—an offer to buy bonds (or other securities), often at a premium over current trading levels.

Tendering—when an issuer goes into the secondary market to buy back its own securities.

Term Maturity—when all bonds issued come due at the same time.

The Blue List—SEE: ***Blue List, The.***

The Bond Buyer—SEE: ***Bond Buyer, The.***

Third Market—the buying and selling of exchange listed stocks in the over-the-counter market by nonexchange member brokers and institutional investors.

Thirty-Year Revenue Index—shows the yield of a 30-year revenue bond based on a variety of bonds from 25 issuers. (Published in *The Bond Buyer.*)

TIC—SEE: **True Interest Cost.**

Time Draft—a document which designates the date on which payment will be made. (Term used with **Banker's Acceptances.**)

Time Value—that part of the option that reflects the amount of time remaining until expiration of the option. (The closer the option is to the expiration date, the less value it has.) ALSO SEE: **Intrinsic Value.**

Timing Risk—the danger that an investor will not pick the best time to buy or sell an investment, and thus not maximize his or her gain. (Timing risk actually involves four risks rolled into one: getting in, getting out, transaction costs and tax consequences.)

Tombstone Ads—special ads placed by investment companies, underwriters, or broker-dealer firms to draw attention to a prospectus (or other major business event) without the ad being a specific offer to sell or buy securities. (These can run during the cooling off period.)

Total Capital—net worth plus long term debt. COMPARE: **Working Capital.**

Total Return—an investment objective that seeks capital growth with asset appreciation and interest or dividends.

Traded Flat—when bonds trade at the quoted price without accrued interest. (e.g., zero coupon bonds or when issuer is in default.) COMPARE: **And Interest.**

Trades, Forward—SEE: **Forward Trades.**

Trades, Spot—SEE: **Spot Trades.**

Trading Channels—technical chart that shows the long-term direction of a security price, by drawing a line connecting the peaks a security has reached and another line connecting the valleys where a security has traded over the same time. Also called a **trading pattern.**

Trading Patterns—SEE: **Trading Channels.**

Trading Profits—profits earned from short term trades.

Trading Volume—large volumes indicate that the current market trend is strong. For example, if an index dropped during a period of heavy trading volume that would indicate a bearish sentiment. Conversely, a rally that is supported by heavy trading volume indicates confidence in the bullish sentiment. Trading volumes in options and futures can also be an indication of future market trends, as can the volume of short selling that occurs.

Tranches—separate maturity groups. (Term used with **CMOs.**)

Transfer Agent—appointed by the corporation to maintain ownership records, to issue and cancel certificates, and to resolve problems of lost, stolen or destroyed stock certificates. (The transfer agent is the final arbiter in disputes of stock certificate authenticity.) COMPARE: **Registrar.**

Transfer and Hold—securities transferred into customer's name, but held by the broker-dealer. COMPARE: **Transfer and Ship, Hold in Street Name.**

Transfer and Ship—securities transferred into customer's name and shipped to customer. COMPARE: **Transfer and Hold, Hold in Street Name.**

Treasuries—securities that are debt obligations of the U.S. government, backed by the full faith and credit of the U.S. government. (Considered the most risk-free investment money can buy.) U.S. Treasury securities can be U.S. Treasury bills (T-bills), U.S. Treasury notes (T-notes), U.S. Treasury bonds (T-bonds).

Treasury Bills—U.S. government bonds that mature in one year or less. (Face value is $10,000, price is quoted at discount from par.)

Treasury Bonds—U.S. government bonds that mature in ten years or more. (Face value is $1,000, prices are quoted as a percentage of par in 1/32th increments.)

Treasury Notes—U.S. government bonds that mature in 1–10 years. (Face value is $1,000, prices are quoted as percentage of par in 1/32th increments.)

Treasury Receipts—zero-coupon bonds based on Treasuries, but not backed by U.S. government.

Treasury Stock—stock reacquired by the corporation. (It's issued, but not outstanding. Treasury stock may be held to resell at a future date, or reissued for incentives, bonuses, retirement plans, etc.)

Trend Lines—technical chart pattern that tracks stock price by connecting the peaks or valleys over a period of time to see which general direction (up or down) the stock is moving. A trend line that tracks upwards over time is called an **uptrend.** A trend line that tracks downwards over time is called a **downtrend.**

Trigger—price at which an order is executed or an order status is changed.

Trough—the bottom of a business cycle, where contraction begins to stop its descent and turn upward. Supply no longer exceeds demand, so from this point production and prices begin to rise. COMPARE: **Peak.** ALSO SEE: **Business Cycles.**

True Interest Cost (TIC)—all moneys received are also considered, but money paid or received earlier is weighted more heavily than money that will be paid or received at some point in the future. (TIC uses standard time value of money calculations as part of its overall comparison of bids.) COMPARE: **Net Interest Cost.**

Trust, Real Estate Investment—SEE: **Real Estate Investment Trust.**

Trust Account—an account set up to benefit one party (beneficiary), but is controlled by a third party (fiduciary).

Trust Indenture—SEE: **Indenture Agreement.**

Trust Indenture Act of 1939—Act passed by Congress to give corporate bond investors the same kinds of protection that corporate stock investors have under the law. If a company is selling bonds within a 12-month period that are valued at more than $5 million and with maturities of longer than 270 days (9 months), the Act requires corporate bonds to have a bond indenture agreement. SEE: **Indenture Agreement.**

TSA—Tax Sheltered Annuity. SEE: **Tax Deferred Annuity Plan.**

Turnover—SEE: **Inventory Turnover Ratio** or **Portfolio Turnover.**

12b-1 Fees—special assessments that allow mutual funds to collect money to reimburse marketing and distribution expenses. Also referred to as **distribution fees.**

Twenty Bond GO Index—shows the yield on a GO bond with 20-year maturity, and is calculated using bonds from 20 actual issuers with bond ratings in the middle of Moody's top four credit ratings. (Published in *The Bond Buyer.*)

UGMA—SEE: **Uniform Gift to Minors Act.**

UIT—SEE: **Unit Investment Trust.**

UTMA—SEE: **Uniform Transfer to Minors Act.**

Uncovered Call—when the writer of the call option does not own the stock to back up the contract. (This is a position of unlimited risk.)

Uncovered Option—when the writer of the option does not own the stock to back up the contract. COMPARE: **Covered Option.**

Underwriter's Concession—SEE: **Distribution Fees.**

Underwriter's Spread—compensation made up of the managing underwriter's fee, underwriting fee, and seller's concession. SEE: **Managing Underwriter's Fee, Underwriting Fee, Seller's Concession.**

Underwriting, Standby—SEE: **Standby Underwriting.**

Underwriting Agreement—entered into between the company issuing securities and the managing underwriter, who is the lead investment banker and the agent representing the entire underwriting group. In the agreement, the underwriters agree to purchase the securities, and give the proceeds to the issuer by a stated settlement date. The issuer agrees to make all required SEC filings, comply with all laws, and use the proceeds as stated in the prospectus. The underwriting agreement also states the final public offering price and the spread the underwriters will make from the sale of securities to the public. COMPARE: **Agreement Among Underwriters.**

Underwriting Fee—part of the underwriter's spread paid to the syndicate members to compensate them for the risk they undertook by buying the issue. This is typically **20–30%** of the spread *regardless of who sells the securities.* ALSO SEE: **Managing Underwriter's Fee, Takedown.**

Undivided Account—type of syndicated account where each member has an undivided interest in all bonds and an undivided interest in, and liability for, all issues that remain unsold after the initial sale period. Also called an **Eastern account.** COMPARE: **Divided Account.**

Unearned Income—SEE: **Investment Income.** COMPARE: **Earned Income.**

Uniform Gift to Minors Act (UGMA)—Act provides a simple way for property to be transferred to minors without a formal trust account and without an official guardianship having to be established. Instead, a single custodian is appointed, who acts as trustee of the account in charge of affairs for the minor. ALSO SEE: **Uniform Transfer to Minors Act.**

Uniform Practice Code—a set of rules set up by NASD to establish standard methods and procedures for transactions between members. These rules have to do with how trades are executed and settled, such as establishment of regular way transaction settlement as T+3 for corporate and municipal securities, good delivery rules, confirmation procedures, and ex-date assignment, among other things.

Uniform Transfer to Minors Act (UTMA)—Act adopted by all 50 states, mirroring the UGMA with two exceptions: the kind of gifts that may be given to a minor's account are expanded beyond cash and securities to include real estate, and other assets, and the age at which minors can take control of the account was raised to 21 or 25, depending on the state. ALSO SEE: **Uniform Gift to Minors Act.**

Unissued Stock—stock that has been authorized, but not yet issued.

Unit Investment Trust (UIT)—a non-management investment company that invests in a fixed portfolio of securities. (The UIT will dissolve when the bonds mature, or on a specified date if the UIT is holding other securities.)

Units—SEE: **Accumulation Units, Annuity Units.**

Unqualified Legal Opinion—a legal opinion issued by a bond attorney that says that after thoroughly researching the bond issue, the municipality has the legal authority to issue the bonds. If the bonds qualify for tax exempt status, that will also be stated in the legal opinion. COMPARE: **Qualified Legal Opinion, Ex-Legal.**

Unqualified Retirement Plan—an employer-sponsored retirement account paid for with after-tax dollars. This allows it to have a cost basis so that only a portion of the withdrawal amount (interest portion) is subject to taxation. (Plan can treat employees differently, does not need IRS approval since contributions are not tax deductible, and no need to comply with ERISA.) COMPARE: **Qualified Retirement Plan.**

Uptick—SEE: **Plus Tick.**

Uptrend—SEE: **Trend Lines.**

Value, Current Market—SEE: **Long Market Value.**

Value, Intrinsic—SEE: **Intrinsic Value.**

Value, Loan—SEE: **Loan Value.**

Value, Long Market—SEE: **Long Market Value.**

Value, Par—SEE: **Par Value.**

Value, Short Market—SEE: **Short Market Value.**

Value, Time—SEE: **Time Value.**

Value Line (VL)—Value Line Investment Survey (VL) is a weekly subscription advisory service that ranks hundreds of investment debt securities for safety of principal and timeliness of repayment. It estimates which will have the best or worst price performance in the coming year, and assigns each corporate debt issuer a risk rating based on stock price movements compared to market averages. (Other information on companies is also available through its various research reports and analyses.)

Variable Annuities—packaged securities, often put together by insurance companies, who are responsible for managing the funds in the investment portfolio. A variable annuity contract makes payments to the holder that vary based on value of underlying investments. COMPARE: **Fixed Annuity Contract.**

Visible Supply—an index that shows all bonds that are scheduled to be offered within a 30-day period. (Published in *The Bond Buyer.*)

Voting, Cumulative—SEE: **Cumulative Voting.**

Voting, Statutory—SEE: **Statutory Voting.**

Waiver of Premium—annuity clause that states if the investor becomes disabled and unable to make the required payments, the payments will be suspended but the benefits will remain in force.

Warrants—an additional security offered along with the sale of another security, which allows the warrant holder to buy shares of common stock at some point in the future at a pre-determined price. (These are a **sweetener.**)

Wash Sale—1. when the same securities (or substantially similar securities) are bought and sold simultaneously or within a short period of time. (Wash sales that occur 30 days before or 30 days after a transaction are not capital losses per IRS rules.). 2. buying and selling the same stock to show trading activity. (NASD rules prohibit this.)

Weak Dollar—when the dollar can be exchanged for less of a foreign currency. This makes foreign imports expensive, but encourages other countries to buy more U.S. goods. COMPARE: **Strong Dollar.**

Western Account— SEE: **Divided Account.**

When Issued—a security that has been authorized, but not officially issued yet. The shares are still tradeable, although the official settlement date may not be known (NASD's Uniform Practices Committee decides the final settlement date; settlement is Issue + 3 days.)

Wilshire 5000—index measures the performance of all U.S.-based exchange-traded stock companies. Bulletin board traded companies are excluded because there is no readily available price data. The index is adjusted on a regular basis, with over 6,500 capitalization-weighted stock returns.

Withdrawal Plans—a means of mutual fund redemption where the investor can receive fixed payments on a regular basis. Also referred to as **payout.** (Not designed to guarantee lifetime income like an annuity.)

Withholding—when a broker-dealer holds back part of a new issue so that it can be kept in the broker-dealer's own account, or sold to family members, employees, or other insiders. (This practice is prohibited by NASD rules.) ALSO SEE: **Free Riding.**

Working Capital—amount of cash a company has readily accessible, such as in its bank accounts. Working capital is the money a company lives off of while it is waiting to manufacture more goods, waiting for more sales, or waiting to collect accounts receivable payments from its customers. Working capital is figured as current assets minus current liabilities. COMPARE: **Total Capital.**

Workout Quotes—a price that is approximate because it depends on size of the order or market activity; not firm. ALSO SEE: **Subject Quotes.** COMPARE: **Firm Quotes.**

Writer—one who opens a position in a stock, option, etc. when an investor sells it. You can also say that the investor is the **seller** of the option, or is **short** the option. (These terms are synonymous: **seller = writer = short.**) COMPARE: **Long.**

Writing the Scale—the process the underwriter goes through to figure out how much the bonds can be sold for in the marketplace. The computation will consider the other issues in the marketplace, but will also consider when the bonds will mature, the interest rate, and what the firm can charge for the bonds (the spread). ALSO SEE: **Scale.**

Yellow Sheets—the name of the daily publication of the National Quotation Bureau showing wholesale interdealer listing bid and ask prices of OTC **bonds** not listed on the NASDAQ. (The pink sheets get their name from the color of paper they are printed on.) COMPARE: **Pink Sheets.**

Yield—the rate of return earned on an investment.

Yield, Current—SEE: **Current Yield.**

Yield, Discount—SEE: **Discount Yield.**

Yield, Equivalent—SEE: **Taxable Equivalent Yield.**

Yield, Taxable Equivalent—SEE: **Taxable Equivalent Yield.**

Yield-Based Options—options that trade based on changes in yield instead of changes in price, thus they have a positive relationship with interest rates. COMPARE: **Debt Options.**

Yield Curve—a line on a graph that shows the relationship between yields and maturity dates for a set of similar bonds, by plotting the yields of all bonds from the shortest maturity to the longest maturity. (The yield curve graph shows if short-term rates are higher or lower than long-term rates.) ALSO SEE: **Normal Yield Curve, Inverted Yield Curve, Flat Yield Curve.**

Yield Spread—the differences in return on investment between various issues of securities. (Yield spread usually reflects the markets' expectations of future monetary policy and credit demand.)

Yield-to-Call (YTC)—the total rate of return that an investor will receive by holding a bond until it is called by the issuer, assuming the call is made at the first opportunity.

Yield-to-Maturity (YTM)—the total rate of return that an investor will receive by holding a bond to maturity.

Zero Coupons—bonds that are sold at a deep discount from par because they do not make periodic interest payments, but instead pay the full face amount at maturity.

Zero Downtick—SEE: **Zero-Minus Tick.**

Zero-Minus Tick—term for when the previous trade occurred at the same price as the one before it, but at a price lower than the last different price. The price of the security is stable, but it is still showing a downward trend. This is also referred to as a **zero downtick.** ALSO SEE: **Minus Tick,**

Short Sale. COMPARE: **Zero-Plus Tick.**

Zero-Plus Tick—term for when the previous trade occurred at the same price as the one before it, and at a higher than the last different price. The price of the security is stable, but still in an upward trend. This is also referred to as a **zero uptick.** ALSO SEE: **Plus Tick, Short Sale.** COMPARE: **Zero-Minus Tick.**

Zero Uptick—SEE: **Zero-Plus Tick.**

Index

Page numbers in *italics* indicate charts.

P

Q

R

T

Appendix 1: Answer Keys

Answers to Chapter Quizzes

Chapter 1 Seeking Business for the Broker-Dealer

1. D	5. B
2. C	6. B
3. C	7. A
4. B	

Chapter 3 Providing Customers with Investment Information

1. B	31. D
2. C	32. A
3. D	33. B
4. B	34. C
5. B	35. A
6. D	36. D
7. A	37. D
8. D	38. B
9. B	39. C
10. D	40. D
11. C	41. B
12. B	42. D
13. C	43. C
14. A	44. B
15. D	45. D
16. C	46. D
17. A	47. A
18. A	48. B
19. C	49. D
20. D	50. A
21. B	51. C
22. C	52. B
23. A	53. B
24. C	54. D
25. B	55. C
26. C	56. B
27. B	57. A
28. B	58. A
29. A	59. D
30. B	60. D

Chapter 2 Evaluating Customers' Needs and Investment Objectives

1. D	6. C
2. C	7. D
3. B	8. B
4. A	9. C
5. D	

Chapter 4 Managing Customer Accounts and Records

1. C	8. A
2. A	9. D
3. C	10. D
4. A	11. C
5. D	12. A
6. B	13. A
7. C	

Chapter 5 Explaining Various Securities Markets

1. A	21. B
2. D	22. B
3. D	23. A
4. B	24. C
5. C	25. A
6. C	26. D
7. D	27. D
8. B	28. A
9. D	29. C
10. B	30. B
11. B	31. C
12. C	32. A
13. A	33. D
14. B	34. B
15. C	35. A
16. B	36. A
17. B	37. B
18. C	38. D
19. C	39. A
20. D	40. D

Chapter 6 Processing a Customer's Instructions

1. A
2. C
3. D
4. C
5. B
6. A
7. C
8. C

Chapter 7 Monitoring a Customer's Portfolio

1. B
2. D
3. A
4. D
5. C
6. B
7. D
8. C
9. B
10. A
11. B
12. D
13. C
14. B
15. D
16. A

Answers to Practice Exam #1

1. **B** Share prices for mutual funds are calculated every day after the close of business. The actual share price is called NAV for Net Asset Value. (Page 135)

2. **B** Common stock is ownership, or equity position in a company. Bonds are a debt security, or debt position in a company. (Page 52, 3.3.2)

3. **B** The authorized amount may be exceeded only by shareholder vote. (Page 49, 3.3.1)

4. **B** Normal taxation for an annuity is LIFO, since earnings would be "last in." (Page 140, 3.5.3.7)

5. **C** Zero coupon bonds are the only investment that has no reinvestment risk, since no income is actually paid out. The bonds compound within and accrete in value to mature at par. (Page 107)

6. **B** An inverted yield curve means an investor will not be rewarded for investing long term. As an example, a two-year bond would have a higher yield than a 5-year bond. (Page 274, 5.4.1.3)

7. **A** S&P investment quality, or bank grade, ratings are BBB, A, AA and AAA. (Pages 40, 93)

8. **D** S&P speculative ratings are BB, or lower. Examples: BB, B, C, and D. (Pages 82, 265, 5.3.8.1)

9. **D** Unequal ownership is a feature of JTIC accounts. As an example: 80/20 versus 50/50, which is the case for JTROS. (Page 190)

10. **A** The term SLD means a sale was not reported within the 90 second requirement.(Page 341, 7.3.1)

11. **A** The exercise price and strike price have the same definition. Since options are contracts, the price is locked in during the option, or contract period. Therefore, market price is used to compare against the contract, or option price, to see if the option may be exercised at a profit. (Pages 41, 143)

12. **D** All the choices refer to market fluctuations and are factors to determine what is happening to a stock at any moment in time. (Page 215, 4.3.4.2)

13. **C** An underwriter is also an investment banker. When a company needs assistance in issuing new or additional securities, it would first call an investment banker. After a review of the company's situation, if the investment banker did agree to help the company take the issue to market, the investment banker would become the "underwriter" of the issue. (Page 233, 5.2.1.1)

14. **B** Regulation T refers to the trade date plus five working days. This is commonly referred to as "T+5." In most instances, T+5 is one calendar week. (Page 306, 6.2.2)

15. **A** Both statements are true. Common stock is also referred to as the "junior" security, while bonds are referred to as the "senior" security. (Pages 52, 72, 3.4)

16. **C** As mentioned in the previous question, common stock is "junior," meaning if the company were to be liquidated, common stock is at the bottom of the priority list. (Page 54, 3.3.2)

17. **C** Current yield is always calculated by using "annual interest" and current, or market, price. If semi-annual interest is given, convert to annual interest by multiplying semi-annual interest times two. (Page 76, 3.4.1.3)

18. **C** CUSIP numbers should be viewed as identification numbers for both stocks and bonds. (Page 303, 6.1.6)

19. **C** Straight preferred stock will provide the highest quarterly dividend. If a dividend is missed, the company has no obligation to make up the missed dividend. (Page 49)

20. **B** Limited liability refers to the amount of money invested in relation to potential loss. If a common stock lost all of its value, the stock price would be zero and, therefore, worthless. Common stock values cannot go below zero. (Page 52, 3.3.2)

21. **A** Participating preferred stock allows the owner of the stock to participate in company profits —if agreed to— by the company. That is to say, owners of participating preferred stock *may* participate in profits. (Page 56, 3.3.3)

22. **C** Preferred stock is, in most instances, purchased for its dividend. Therefore, voting rights are normally a secondary issue with the investor. (Page 56, 3.3.3)

23. **D** Buying a premium bond for its higher coupon rate may place the investor in a position of losing money. This situation could occur if the maturity is near and the premium cannot be amortized. (Page 95)

24. **D** MBIA is private bond insurance associated with municipal bonds. (Page 341, 7.2.5.5)

25. **D** Bonds are normally issued at par, therefore the price is set at issue. If a bond is sold prior to maturity, it must be sold on the secondary, or resale market, and may sell for more, or less, than par value. (Page 101)

26. **A** Remember, call up, put down— viewed from ownership (long) position of the option. (Page 143)

27. **C** In-the-money and intrinsic value are indicators of value. This contract is also at the "break-even" point, which means no profit can be made if the option is exercised. (Page 145)

28. **C** Since GO bonds are backed by the taxing authority of the municipality, they are generally very popular with investors. (Page 103, 3.4.8.2)

29. **C** Time value is also a measure of worth for an options contract. A contract with six months remaining at a time value of "5" would be of more value than a contract with one week left and a time value of "5." (Page 145)

30. **D** An option contract depends upon an "underlying security" for its value. Non-equity, means something other than stock—in this instance, an index has been chosen for the underlying security. (Page 150)

31. **C** Both market risk and systematic risk mean essentially the same thing and are used as synonymous terms. (Page 151)

32. **B** SMA, or excess equity, is a line of credit considered to have "buying power." (Page 212)

33. **C** Securities not sold in state would be "blue skyed" by the other state(s) involved. (Page 236)

34. **B** "Standby" for an underwriter, under these circumstances, means exactly as outlined. The underwriter will become involved with the issue if there are shares remaining after the issue is made available to current stockholders. (Page 59)

35. **B** Review consolidated tapes. (Page 341, 7.3.1)

36. **D** DPP's, or limited partnerships, contain all three items as concerns for the investor. In addition, DPP programs will not be effective in sheltering ordinary income—only passive income. (Page 65, 3.3.6; Page 71, 3.3.6.5)

37. **D** Two main reasons for investment companies are to pool funds together toward an objective. This allows the average investor to invest a smaller amount of money and be a part of a large portfolio. (Page 120, 3.5.2)

38. **B** Since many firms have investment banking departments, nonpublic, or inside information, could become common knowledge if safeguards were not in place. (Page 254, 5.3.1.2)

39. **C** The bond year for both corporate and muni bonds is 360 days, containing twelve 30-day months. (Page 90, 3.4.4.5; Page 112)

40. **C** Closed-end companies, sometimes referred to as publicly traded and ETF (exchange traded funds), trade and operate similarly to a stock. Redemption is made by selling shares in the secondary market. (Page 121, 3.5.2.1)

41. **B** Purchasing an option, a call in this instance, places the investor "in charge." Therefore, worst case will be the investor cannot exercise the option, the contract expires worthless, and the premium is lost. (Page 144)

42. **C** NASD rules are 8½% max. (Page 127)

43. **D** Back-end loads are also called contingent deferred charges. This means a client does not see a "front-end load" charge on her statements. The charge is encountered if funds are withdrawn during the existence of the back end load. These funds can never be referred to as "no-load" funds. (Page 127)

44. **D** Money market funds are highly liquid and usually considered to be a place to "park" money on a short-term basis, or until it is needed. (Page 124; Page 98, 3.4.7)

45. **D** ERISA refers to regulations and safeguards in place for nongovernmental retirement income plans. (Page 166, 3.7.3)

46. **B** Defined benefit plans, sometimes called annuity purchase plans, tend to favor older employees, while defined contribution plans tend to favor younger employees. (Page 165)

47. **D** Limited partnerships require suitability statements be signed by the investor and must be structured to produce a profit. Their structure tends to favor higher income individuals. (Page 65)

48. **C** Leading indicators are used to predict trends—either up or down. They are a also sometimes referred to as "spot check" of business activity. (Page 273, 5.4.1.2)

49. **A** The order of occurrence is important to know. (Page 271, 5.4.1)

50. **B** This act refers to the people who must register and identifies those who are charging for advice. (Page 8, 1.1.2)

51. **B** $500,000 is the maximum amount per customer, of which up to $100,000 may be in cash. A customer is defined as one entity, such as John Doe cash and margin account. John & Mary Doe JTROS —a second customer. (Page 257, 5.3.3)

52. **C** To be in control the investor must buy the option. Under these circumstances, the market is expected to move in a direction, therefore the gain is unlimited while loss, if any, will be limited to the sum of both premiums paid. (Page 148)

53. **D** The strategy is acceptable because the investor owns the HTM stock and is writing the call on a "covered call" basis. This strategy is sometimes referred to as option income, due to the premium received for writing the call. The downside of the stock position is protected by the purchase of the HTM 35 put. (Page 155)

54. **C** Registered Options Principal–ROP. (Page 190)

55. **D** Options contracts would be adjusted for all of the items listed. Options contracts are not adjusted for *cash dividends*. (Page 149, 3.6.1.2)

56. **D** Individuals in the lower tax rates may not benefit from municipal bonds, since they may find taxable issues that pay a higher tax equivalent rate. Be sure you know how to calculate the "taxable equivalent yield" for any tax rate given. (Page 116)

57. **B** Serial maturity means issues will mature over a period of years, rather than the whole issue coming due at one time. These issues are usually priced as a "yield to maturity" rather than on a "dollar" basis. (Page 102)

58. **D** What the question really describes is the real meaning for a "firm commitment" made by an underwriting syndicate. A loss due to a new issue not selling could happen and there are very few things that can be done

to prevent this type loss. (Page 238, 5.2.1.5; Page 255)

59. **B** An account may be listed by number if there is a letter on file from the client authorizing the new designation. (Page 192)

60. **C** $100 dollars is the limit. Mutual funds have a lower limit. (Page 229)

61. **B** The order and wire room define one location—the order entry point. (Page 296)

62. **B** The term separate account is used in two products, variable annuities and variable universal life insurance policies. Separate Account indicates where the investments are located. Since the investments generally are "funds," systematic, or market risk, is encountered. (Page 134, 3.5.3.3)

63. **A** Completion of a transaction means payment. The regulation means the client must be advised of exactly what he bought, what charges apply and how much is due. (Page 303, 6.1.6)

64. **C** SMA is equity in excess of the Regulation T requirement. It is considered to be "buying power" and is a line of credit. (Pages 188, 200)

65. **A** The position is uncovered, or naked, which means the maximum gain can be only the premium received for writing the call. The maximum loss will be unlimited, since the call writer must provide the stock at whatever price she can obtain it, if the option is exercised. (Page 147)

66. **A** The client's tax rate is a suitability issue. The issuer's credit rating will relate directly to the overall rating of the bond issue. (Page 100)

67. **B** The question refers to a bond being purchased at a discount, such as 95. With a bond purchase price of $950 and a price at maturity of $1,000, or par, a gain of $50 will be realized—even though the bond is "tax exempt." (Page 114)

68. **C** DPP's are limited partnerships. A popular structure is a Sub, S Corporation. (Page 65)

69. **A** The "Paper Act," or Act of 1933, created the prospectus, which is also known as "full and fair disclosure." (Page 240)

70. **C** Nonqualified plans are commonly used for "key persons" and do not receive the same favorable tax treatment as qualified plans. (Page 164, 3.7.2)

71. **B** These are the four basic option positions. Be sure to know all four! (Page 154)

72. **B** A presale order is allowed in new issues of municipal bonds. A presale order is not allowed for new stock issues. (Page 251)

73. **B** DK stands for "don't know." This procedure is of particular importance to an order, such as the GTC order, which has been in the system for some time. Order verification is another way of saying DK procedure. (Page 309, 6.2.2.7)

74. **D** SRO stands for Self Regulatory Organization. (Page 224, 5.1)

75. **C** The question describes property taxes. Property taxes are paid on a percentage of market value, which is usually called a property's assessed value. (Pages 337, 338)

76. **A** A variable annuity is considered to be an open end company, which means an open ended amount of shares (units) may be issued. (Page 121)

77. **C** Earned surplus is another word for retained earnings, and losses do carry over. (Page 327)

78. **B** While it is true the customer's signature will be required over a period of time, the customer's signature is not required to "open an account" over the telephone to do a transaction such as buying or selling a stock. (Page 188, 4.1)

79. **D** The question is asking you to calculate the tax equivalent yield. To do so, subtract 100 from the tax rate of 37%. The remainder is .63. Using a calculator, enter the bond rate of 4% as .04, then divide by the remainder of .63. The result is .06349, or 6.35%.

You must know how to do this calculation! (Page 119)

80. **C** Class refers to an entire class of an issuer (corporation), e.g., all calls or all puts. (Page 144)

81. **C** Territorial bonds and bonds issued within the investor's state of residence may be triple tax exempt—free from federal, state and local taxes. (Page 100, 3.4.8)

82. **C** An advantage is clear for donations to charity—the value being given is the current market value and not cost basis. (Pages 63, 64)

83. **A** General Partner, the one who calls the shots, and limited partner, the investor are the two types of partners. (Page 67)

84. **B** Breakeven for a call is strike (exercise) price plus the premium paid. (Page 147)

85. **C** Breakeven for a put is strike (exercise) price minus the premium paid. (Page 147)

86. **D** All of the above! Remember, short selling is not suitable for every client. (Page 214, 4.3.4)

87. **A** Almost all new account forms contain the pre-dispute arbitration agreement. (Page 230, 5.1.4)

88. **B** Bonds are senior securities. View the trust indenture as protection for client. (Page 246, 5.2.2.10)

89. **D** A secondary offering is often used when coordination is needed to handle a large amount of company stock a stockholder may have. For example, let's assume it is the CEO who owns the stock. Since the CEO, the stockholder, owns the shares, the proceeds go to that person when they have been sold. (Page 233)

90. **D** The two trade confirmations mentioned refer to the acknowledgment that the client will get the new bond and the second confirmation being when, and how much, money is due. (Pages 62, 306)

91. **B** Regulation T, or Reg. T, sets the loan value for most securities at 50%. That is to say $10,000 in value of securities will produce $5,000 in equity in a margin account—assuming no other debt or holdings in the account. (Page 192)

92. **A** Our clients, often referred as retail purchasers, will buy at the asking price and sell at the bid price. (Page 259; Page 260, 5.3.4.2)

93. **D** Ex-legal means no legal opinion for the tax exempt status of the muni bond. This is normally not a consideration for a public school issue, as an example. However, if the issue involves an industrial park, we need to know the opinion about the tax exempt status of the issue, which would be given by the bond counsel. (Page 248)

94. **D** CUSIP number relates to all of the choices and is critical to have when you need to know exactly what the client holds. (Page 304)

95. **D** Depreciation allowances refer to assets which will wear out. Land will not "wear out" and is not subject to any depreciation schedule. (Page 286)

96. **B** NYSE does require registration of all salespersons and the exchange does retain the right to deny registration. (Page 225, 5.1.1)

97. **B** Due to the convenience of buying mutual funds in fractional shares, dollar cost averaging is an effective strategy. (Page 126)

98. **A** U.S. territorial bonds refer to Guam, Puerto Rico and the U.S. Virgin Islands. These bonds are triple tax exempt in all 50 states. (Page 100, 3.4.8.1)

99. **D** From the choices presented in the question, all of which are true, the desirability of a 2 for 1 split centers around future performance of the company. If the future market price goes up the split will be considered worthwhile. (Page 56)

100. **A** In the western account a certain percentage of risk, or shares of stock, for each syndicate member is assigned. When that allocation is

sold, there is no further obligation to the other syndicate members. (Page 249)

101. **A** The distinct advantage of the Roth IRA is the ability to receive tax exempt income in retirement. (Page 163, 3.7.1.1)

102. **D** All of the information discussed in the question applies to the subscription agreement, which must be signed by all limited partnership investors. (Page 67)

103. **B** Definition of "current"—12 months or less. (Page 329)

104. **D** As discussed in an earlier question, only assets that can be "worn out" may be depreciated. (Page 326)

105. **D** Money market, as outlined in these choices, indicates its value in proper management of cash assets. Money market is also sometimes called a "cash equivalent." (Page 124)

106. **D** Long-term income is the overall goal for a bond fund. Suitability would also include a discussion on the type(s) of funds which may be chosen. (Page 124)

107. **C** The index fund is the best choice, since an index such as S&P will mirror the market without having to make a large number of trades within the portfolio. Therefore, realized gains will be kept to a minimum. (Page 124)

108. **D** Both parties to the information received are liable. The best policy for registered representatives to follow is one of not discussing anything not known to be public knowledge. (Page 254, 5.3.1.2)

109. **D** The spokesperson must be knowledgeable in the subject discussed and must be identified as being paid for the testimonial. (Page 15)

110. **B** As in other options positions, the writer (seller) of an option has the obligation to perform, if the contract is exercised. That means, without owning the underlying stock, the maximum profit can be only the premiums received—$800 in this example. The maximum loss is truly unlimited, since the underlying stock (JKL) will be supplied regardless of cost to the option writer. (Page 155)

111. **D** All choices describe penny stock. Client suitability is major concern. (Page 256, 5.3.2; Page 343)

112. **B** A market order would be the proper order, since it will be executed immediately—if the stock is trading. (Page 299, 6.1.1)

113. **B** The recommendation for the client should be to purchase the stock after the ex-dividend date. To recommend purchase of the stock immediately before the dividend is a compliance issue called "selling dividends." The reason is a purchase before the dividend is at a slightly higher price (the amount of the dividend) and subjects the client to slightly higher taxes—not to mention the slightly higher commissions which will be earned by the Registered Representative. (Page 229, 5.1.3)

114. **C** The investor is bearish, since he is "mostly" *buying* a put—debit of 5 versus credit of 3. The position is a debit put spread because the debit of 5 out weighs the credit of 3 received. It is a put spread because a put is being purchased (DR) and a put is being sold (CR). (Page 157)

115. **C** The traditional IRA differs from the ROTH IRA in these two areas. But the traditional IRA may still be suitable for some investors. (Page 162, 3.7.1)

116. **D** An IPO cannot be purchased on margin (borrowed money). (Page 202)

117. **D** A price above 100 indicates a premium. The pricing structure of dollars versus YTM (yield to maturity) indicates a dollar bond. (Page 203)

118. **D** In an adjustable rate bond, the coupon will change in relation to an index. The result will be the price for this type bond in the resale market will be relatively stable. (Page 102)

119. **D** There are many types of zero coupon bonds. The zero muni bond can provide tax exempt growth, since it is a municipal issue. All zeros operate in the same manner, which means the bond will be purchased at a deep discount (also called OID—original issue discount). (Page 107)

120. **B** The trade may be done, but the order ticket must be marked "unsolicited." If the ticket is not marked, it will be assumed you recommended the trade. (Page 196)

121. **A** CBOE—Chicago Board Options Exchange is the correct answer. (Page 262, 5.3.5)

122. **D** Since preferred stock is normally purchased for the dividend, the amount of the dividend is of prime importance—not voting on issues. Preferred stock may or may not have a par value; if it has a par value it will be $100. (Page 56, 3.3.3)

123. **A** A premium bond will have a YTC (yield to call) lower than CY (current yield). Also, YTM (yield to maturity) will also be lower than CY. (Page 91, 3.4.4.6)

124. **A** The default position for the order is for the day. If the order is to be good beyond the day, it must be marked GTC (good till canceled). (Page 299, 6.1.1)

125. **A** The "tombstone ad" is the only ad which may be placed before a new issue comes to market. (Page 239)

End of first half of the practice exam #1.

126. **A** Both IPO and primary offering are correct. Secondary offering and additional issues occur only after a company has outstanding shares. (Page 233)

127. **D** $700 gain. Selling the call for 5 creates incoming cash (CR) of $500. Closing the position is doing the opposite, or buying a call (DR), for 5 ($500). A "round lot" of shares is 100 shares and 100 shares of XYZ have been purchased for $45 (cost basis). Selling 100 shares of XYZ at $52 closes the long position. Difference is $700 gain. (Page 146)

128. **B** Minimum maintenance requirement is described as 25% of the LMV (long market value). (Page 202)

129. **D** The official statement is used for muni bonds. The prospectus is used for corporate stocks and bonds. In both instances, the preliminary document is called the "red herring." (Page 248)

130. **B** "Open end" fund does mean an unlimited number of shares may be issued. For an open end fund, a secondary market for shares does not exist. Shares are redeemed—then destroyed. (Page 121)

131. **D** A new option has a life of nine months and expires on Saturday 11:59 p.m. following the third Friday of the expiration month. (Page 149)

132. **C** Growth is usually denoted by lack of cash for dividends to stockholders. Growth companies usually reinvest cash in the company. (Page 123)

133. **A** "Selling away" is a serious compliance issue and involves selling a "security" outside your broker-dealer's normal business activities. To do so, without prior approval, can expose you to personal liability and also create liability for your broker-dealer. (Page 229, 5.1.3)

134. **A** Regular way settlement refers to trade date (T) plus 3 working days. The intent is to give 2 days to correct any problem in regard to cash, or securities certificates enroute to a

customer's account. (Page 306, 6.2.2.2)

135. **A** *The Bond Buyer* concentrates on the primary market for municipal bonds. Published every business day, the Thursday edition contains information about muni issues expected to reach the market within the next 30 days. (Page 343, 7.3.4)

136. **C** Variable annuities are investment products and will accept money in many different ways, since there is no "premium" requirement to meet. An "immediate deferred annuity" does not exist, since an immediate annuity is purchased for its immediate income—not tax deferral. (Page 132, 3.5.3)

137. **A** Disintermediation is moving money from the banks to investments outside the bank that are earning a higher return. (Page 273)

138. **B** Since no one knows who will see and/or read an ad, advertising is considered to be not targeted (untargeted) to its audience. (Page 9, 1.2)

139. **B** Revenue bonds do exist and are used for many revenue producing projects, such as toll roads, water, sewer and many other similar projects. (Page 104)

140. **B** For this question the items of importance are the coupon at 6% ($60 annual) and the current market price of 91 ($910). To calculate the current yield (CY) divide the coupon payment (60) by the current market price (910) equals 6.6%. (Page 76, 3.4.1.3)

141. **D** Options can do an effective job for each of the choices mentioned in this question. Limited loss is included because the client will be *long* (own) the position. Remember, in a long options position, loss is limited to the amount of premium paid. (Page 142)

142. **D** Currency risk is the additional risk taken, when a foreign stock is purchased. Excellent performance can be "wiped out" by an unfavorable exchange rate. (Page 44)

143. **A** All of the items listed refer to municipal anticipation notes. The term "anticipation" means anticipation of funds from such areas as taxes, future revenues and bonds. (Page 105)

144. **D** Of the items listed, forward pricing refers to mutual funds. It means pricing of a fund is "forwarded" to the end of the trading day. (Page 129)

145. **D** Client sold a call for 4½ and received $450 (CR). Client is exercised at CMV of 42. The obligation upon our client is to furnish the stock at the call's contract price of 35. The loss is $4,200 minus strike price of $3,500, offset by the premium received of $450—or a net loss of $250. (Page 147)

cash paid DR	cash received CR
	4 1/2
42	35
42	39 1/2
Loss ($250)	

146. **D** Full power of attorney means almost complete authority over the account, including the ability to make deposits or withdrawals from the account. Trading decisions only are described as a "limited power of attorney." (Page 192)

147. **D** Rights enable an existing stockholder to maintain her current level of ownership, if she chooses to do so. A right is normally issued at a price below current market to give current stockholders an incentive to buy more stock. (Page 53)

148. **C** Both the price of a dollar bond (95 as an example) and the lowest potential yield, sometimes called "yield to worst," must be disclosed on the trade confirmation. (Page 102)

149. **D** When broker-dealers act as brokers, they arrange trades and charge commissions. (Page 228)

150. **A** After registration there is a mandatory "cooling off" period. The duration of this period is described as "20 days," even though it quite often is longer than 20 days. (Page 241, 5.2.2.3)

151. **B** "Special situations" are defined as investing in companies with the prospects to "turnaround." Possible takeovers and new management teams are examples of the type of investments included in these funds. (Page 55)

152. **B** Directors and other insiders of a company may not sell stock in their own companies short. An "insider" is anyone with 10%, or more, not 5% as the question suggests. (Page 254, 5.3.1.2)

153. **C** Support level is the bottom of the trading range. (Page 323)

154. **D** All are correct. (Page 65, 3.3.6)

155. **C** IRA accounts may contain many different types of investments, but life insurance is not one of those choices. (Page 163)

156. **A** 100 minus tax rate. Using your calculator, enter .04/.85 = 4.7%. (Pages 116, 119)

157. **B** A person in the lower tax bracket, such as 15%, would not be suitable for a tax exempt municipal bond. (Pages 116, 119)

158. **A** The client "holds" the call, therefore, he owns the position. To make money, the market *must move,* or widen. (Page 153, 3.6.1.3)

159. **B** 6% is correct. To calculate determine the POP (public offering price), $10, and the past 12 months' dividend, $.60. Current yield is annual dividend divided by POP. (Pages 91, 119)

160. **D** The correct answer is OID, which stands for Original Issue Discount. (Pages 106–107)

161. **B** Market discounts are taxable as "ordinary income." (Page 95)

162. **B** A control person is anyone having 10%, or more stock in any company. A control person is considered an "insider" and this information must be notated on new account forms. (Page 244)

163. **C** All listed securities have a trading location or exchange. OTC is a negotiated market, with no actual location to trade. OTC securities are referred to as unlisted. (Page 258, 5.3.4.1)

164. **A** The trade is binding and action must be taken immediately to correct the situation.(Page 303)

165. **A** Two puts, at $400 each, are owned by the client for a total of $800 paid in premium. In a long position, the maximum loss is the premium paid, or $800. (Page 154)

166. **B** Bearish, because buying puts is trying to limit downside losses. (Page 154)

167. **D** Options Clearing Corporation (OCC) is the correct answer. (Page 143)

168. **C** Debentures are debt obligations, but are not secured by specific assets, such as equipment. Therefore, an owner of a debenture is considered to be a general creditor of the company. (Page 192)

169. **D** The Nine Bond Rule provides protection for the small bond order. (Page 266)

170. **C** The time value is the premium ($4.50) minus the intrinsic value (65 minus 63). The remainder is "time value," or $2.50. (Page 146)

171. **A** Life annuity is the highest payout, because of no guarantee to the annuitant's beneficiaries. This is followed by period certain, a guarantee for a certain number of years (10 years, as for example) and then joint life, which takes into consideration two life expectancies. (Page 139)

172. **D** The NASD/NASD minimum maintenance requirement for a short position is 30% of the short market value (SMV). (Page 206)

173. **B** Revenue bonds are intended to be self supporting. Therefore, if revenues are not adequate to meet obligations, bondholders do have risk of default. (Page 104)

174. **D** Think of the graphics in the book regarding how the bond market works. With the call feature at par,

the yield to call will be the "best," or highest. (Page 102)

175. **A** A broker-dealer operating as a "dealer" may do all of the items listed, and would be in a principal capacity. (Page 204)

176. **C** Proper procedure is freeze the account, cancel open orders, await instructions. (Page 196)

177. **D** UGMA accounts are designed to benefit a minor—only one owner and one custodian is allowed. Ownership of the account reverts to the child at the age of majority (age 18 in most states). (Page 168)

178. **B** Since the investor must provide the stock owned at a cost basis of 43 at 45, if exercised ($200 gain), and cash was received (CR) for writing the call in the amount of $300. The positions will be closed out; the result will be a total of $500 maximum gain. (Page 155)

cash paid DR	cash received CR
	3
43	45
43	48
	5 ($500 profit)

179. **B** The best choice for this circumstance is the blue chip (well established larger companies) fund. Mutual funds also have the advantage of investing in a pool of similar securities, thereby reducing overall risk. (Page 124)

180. **C** A buy stop order is used to protect a profit, or limit a loss in a *short position.* It must be viewed from this perspective in order to make sense. Normally, a buy order would be entered below current market—not above. (Page 299)

181. **D** Writing (selling) a straddle will provide two premiums for the client. As always, you point out to the client the position provides premium income, but also contains *the potential for unlimited loss.* (Page 155)

182. **B** The act of 1934 is referred to as the people act, since it governs people involved in trading securities. The prospectus came from The Securities Act of 1933. (Page 253, 5.3.1.1)

183. **D** Stockholders are owners of the company and have claim to company assets after all of a company's creditor's have been paid. (Page 325)

184. **D** The exercise of an option is best viewed from the long options position. The exercise sets up the acquisition—then the subsequent sale creates the gain. (Page 161, 3.6.1.4)

185. **A** New housing authority bonds are a direct obligation of the government and are considered to be the most secure of all muni bonds. (Page 105)

186. **B** Recruitment advertising for new employees would be the only exception to the rule of always identifying the source of the ad. (Page 12)

187. **A** Overbought is correct. Oversold is the opposite market condition, and correction is the term for the decline—not the market condition. (Page 325)

188. **D** All are key considerations to determine suitability of a limited partnership (DPP). If all factors look satisfactory, the experience level of the GP (general partner) may be a reason for caution. (Page 71, 3.3.6.5)

189. **C** NAV, or net asset value of the fund. Open-end funds are never redeemed at the market price. Only closed-end funds use market price as a liquidation price. (Page 130)

190. **B** Share certificates must be able to be broken into even round lots of 100 shares. (Page 306)

191. **A** For a call, the lower the strike price, the higher the premium for the option. In other words, the lower strike price is closer to being in the money. (Page 145)

192. **B** A bond is selling at par, on a yield to maturity basis, if the resale price and the coupon are the same; that is to say, 4½% on the resale market versus a coupon rate of 4½% equals par value. (Page 100)

193. **D** Under these choices, the coupon rate will not vary and is set at the time of issue. (Page 102)

194. **B** The trade confirmation is used as the proof of ownership because it contains all of the details of the transaction. (Page 303, 6.1.6)

195. **A** A non-equity option refers to the underlying security. Equity options, have as the underlying security, stock, or equity. Non-equity options have, as the basis of their contract, an index, currency, or even an interest rate. (Pages 149–152)

196. **C** The exchange markets (NYSE, AMEX, Regional) operate as auction, or double auction, markets, where buyers and sellers are brought together. (Page 258, 5.3.4.1)

197. **C** Cash settlement is defined as trade date. This question points out the need for you and the client to know on what basis the bond is being purchased. (Page 308, 6.2.2.6)

198. **D** The transfer agent normally is the final authority on these type matters. (Page 52)

199. **C** A total of three calls have been sold at $4.00 per share. Since each option is for a round lot (100 shares), the maximum gain is $400 × 3, or $1,200. (Pages 146–148)

200. **B** Simplified arbitration is available, by agreement, to our clients for amounts in dispute of $25,000, or less. It involves one arbitrator who, after reviewing all of the evidence, renders a binding decision within 30 business days. (Page 230)

201. **D** To analyze this situation, match the transactions: Long 2 LMN Jun 70 calls at 6 vs. Short 2 LMN Jun calls at 4. Short 2 LMN Aug calls at 5 vs. Long 2 LMN Aug calls at 3. Set up the chart like so: (Page 143)

cash paid DR	cash received CR
12	8
6	10
18	18
	0

202. **D** The account may be opened if the Registered Principal believes the client has the financial resources required to support the account. (Page 188, 4.1)

203. **A** To simply "transfer" between two broker-dealers is not permitted. You must resign from your present broker-dealer and obtain the U5 form from it. You then reapply to the new broker-dealer, using the U5 form obtained from your previous broker-dealer, and complete a new U4 with new fingerprints. (Page 7)

204. **C** The statement is true. Corporations do receive a 70% exclusion for dividends received from other company securities they own. (Page 61, 3.3.5; Page 98)

205. **C** Index options consist of a broad based index, such as S&P 500, or an index for a particular market segment. Hedging is one of their uses. (Page 150)

206. **A** A control person is anyone with 10% or more of a company's common stock. Also, of course, directors and officers are also included. The overall group would be classified as "insiders." (Page 244)

207. **B** GO bonds are general obligation bonds, which means revenues are not a part of the concern for safety. The concern for safety for a GO bond rests with the remaining three areas, which relate to the quality of the tax base. (Page 103, 3.4.8.2)

208. **C** NASD can't impose a jail sentence, but the SEC can! (Page 231, 5.1.5)

209. **D** Selling a call and writing a call are exactly the same thing and would be used to generate "option income." Writing (selling) a call is considered to be a conservative strategy, since the option is covered. (Pages 155, 156)

210. **A** Money market is where we would find both of these securities. Both have a maturity of 270 days or less, and are of high quality. (Page 98, 3.4.7)

211. **C** Take indications of interest for the issue. For those clients and prospects who have indicated an interest in the issue, you must send the red herring, or preliminary prospectus. (Page 235)

212. **B** The exchange markets refer to an auction process. In an auction, buyers, sellers and the person in the middle—called a specialist—in this instance come together to complete the transaction. (Page 258, 5.3.4.1)

213. **D** The term "stock ahead" simply means the execution of the limit order depends upon whether or not other orders, such as market orders or older limit orders are on file. If so, those orders will take precedence over our client's limit order and will execute first. (Pages 298–300)

214. **A** Options cannot be used to increase the holding period for a stock. In other words, an option cannot make a short term gain into a long term gain.

215. **B** Government bond funds, high grade corporate bond funds and corporate bond UIT's all have high grade bonds as the underlying securities. Therefore, all of these choices would provide income with a good degree of safety of principal. (Page 93)

216. **D** We know the CY will be below the coupon rate of 6.5% because the bond is selling at a premium. The call feature has no relevance to the current yield (CY). Therefore, our calculation is $65 divided by the current market price of $1030—or 6.31% current yield. (Page 91, 3.4.4.6)

217. **B** Maximum loss for an uncovered put will not be unlimited, since zero is as far as the stock will drop. Since the stock could go to zero and a premium has been received for writing the put, the maximum loss is the strike price minus the premium received. (Pages 146–148)

218. **B** The company is the issuer of a security. All other choices listed assist in bringing the security to market. (Page 108)

219. **A** The owner of a option is "in charge" of the option and has the right to do any of the three alternatives listed. (Page 142, 3.6)

220. **A** Market arbitrage involves a specialized trader taking advantage of temporary differences in the market price of a security between two listed exchanges. It is a legal activity. (Page 215)

221. **D** Registered principals are in charge of supervisory activities. These activities include both approval of accounts and orders on a daily basis. (Page 188)

222. **B** Depletion allowance refers to "using up" natural resources, such as oil and gas. Oil and gas DPP's will use the depletion allowance if the partnership is generating income. (Page 70)

223. **C** NAV (net asset value) is the price used to redeem shares from an open end fund. There is no secondary market for these shares, so they are destroyed and are never reissued. (Pages 129, 130)

224. **A** The double barreled municipal bond is normally issued as a revenue bond, but contains the backing of an additional source, such as the tax base of the community. The "double" backing means additional safety for the investor. (Page 106)

225. **B** The options position is a debit put spread because the investor is more predominate, on the cash paid (debit) side. Set up your chart by following the question. (Page 155)

cash paid DR	cash received CR
5	3
5	3
2	

226. **D** A broker-dealer may act as either "broker" or "dealer," but may not be on both sides of the trade and receive both a commission and a markup. (Page 254)

227. **A** A put will have value if the CMV (current market price) is lower than the strike price. There a 50 put will have $4 in intrinsic value at a CMV of 46. Time value will be $1. (Page 145)

228. **A** The specialist views the book from the investor (retail) point of view. Our clients always buy at the best asking price and sell at the best available bid price. (Page 258)

229. **C** The question describes an uncovered (naked) call. Under these circumstances, the maximum gain is always the premium received (3 × $400) and the maximum loss is unlimited, since the stock value could rise indefinitely. (Pages 147, 148)

230. **B** The areas listed are lagging indicators and are used to confirm a new trend. (Page 274)

231. **D** As you can see from the question, suitability is a major concern; stocks—NYSE; municipal bonds—MSRB; options—CBOE. (Page 24)

232. **A** In short, if the materials you plan to use for a sales presentation are not approved—DON'T USE THEM! (Page 12)

233. **D** Beta is a measure for a stock's movement, as compared to the overall market, and both statements are true. In addition, if beta is exactly 1, the stock would be expected to be perform exactly like the market. (Page 319, 7.1.3.4)

234. **D** To have complete protection, you must be "in charge," or own (long) the contract. Partial protection refers to the premium received for writing (short) the contract. The protection in the short position is only the premium received—partial protection. (Pages 154, 155)

235. **B** MSRB (municipal securities rulemaking board) requires an examination of all broker-dealers who deal in the municipal market every 24 months. This examination is to ensure the broker-dealers are in compliance with MSRB regulations, SEC regulations and 1934 Securities Exchange Act. (Page 226)

236. **B** The premium bond callable at par will have, as its lowest rate, YTC (Yield to call). If the call feature for the premium bond stated "callable at a premium," it is possible the YTM (yield to maturity) would be the lowest yield. (Pages 91, 92)

237. **A** Issued stock means the stock is within the amount authorized for the company and it has been sold to an investor. It is not the same as "outstanding stock," since some of the issued stock may no longer be in investors' hands; it could have been repurchased by the company. (Page 49)

238. **D** The new issue must first come to market as an IPO (initial purchase offering), have all inventory be immediately purchased, and begin to rise in price on the secondary (resale) market. (Page 238, 5.2.1.5)

239. **C** The answer is $1,050 loss. Set up your chart as follows:

cash paid DR	cash received CR
	4
85	70.50
85	74.50
(10.5)	

The 10.5 relates to a round lot of 100 and the loss is 10.5 × 100, or $1,050. (Page 143)

240. **D** Rule 144 regulates the sale of control and restricted stock by "insiders." An insider is defined as a director, officer, or any person with 10% or more of a company's outstanding stock. (Page 244)

241. **C** Odd lot purchases and sales cost our clients more in commission, which is disclosed on the trade confirmation under "odd lot differential." (Page 306)

242. **D** Both government assisted housing and historic rehabilitation can offer tax credits to a limited partner. An example of a tax credit would be a credit for energy conservation. (Page 71, 3.3.6.5)

243. **B** The position is called a short straddle. The maximum gain on these contracts will be the sum of premi-

ums received ($1,100) and the maximum loss will be unlimited. (Pages 148, 155)

244. **A** A person wanting to be placed on the do-not-call-list will be on the list for a 10-year period. This list must be kept up-to-date by the broker-dealer, and written procedures must be on file for its maintenance. (Page 10, 1.2.1)

245. **B** Making a "tender offer" for the bonds on the secondary (resale) market is the only choice the issuer will have, since the bonds have already been issued without call features. (Pages 89, 110)

246. **C** If a broker has discretion over an account, it must be in writing and on file with the broker-dealer. In addition, only the activity (to buy or sell), the asset (which security) and the amount (how many) are matters of discretion. The ability to deposit, or withdraw, cash from the account is not a part of having discretion. (Pages 193, 194)

247. **A** Restricted stock is stock placed with a private investor, institution or insider and must be bought for investment purposes—not speculation. There is a mandatory holding period of 12 months for restricted stock before it may be sold. (Page 244)

248. **A** Lack of liquidity is the principal disadvantage for a DPP. Therefore, ease of selling, short term objectives and suitability for low income investors are not discussion points for many investors. (Page 71, 3.3.6.5)

249. **D** Corporate bond issues of $5,000,000 or larger and a maturity of 12 months or longer are regulated by the trust indenture act. The act provides for a trust indenture to be on file and for it to cover promises made to safeguard assets; for example, property and casualty insurance for assets covered by the bond issue. (Page 246, 5.2.2.10)

250. **A** Customer statements must be provided at least quarterly for all accounts. For active accounts, most companies send monthly statements. (Page 195)

END OF FINAL EXAM # 1

Answers to Practice Exam #2

1. **D** The definition is price (vertical) spread. The client is long in one option position (KAT Jan 40 call) and short the opposite side (short KAT Jan 50 call) with the expiration months being the same. To visualize this position consider using the following chart: (Pages 159, 160)

	Oct	Nov	Dec	Jan	Feb	Mar
50				X		
45						
40				X		
35						

Vertical (price) spread

2. **B** Brokers' brokers are used to assist in placing unsold portions of new muni issues with institutional customers. They protect the identity of their customers. (Page 264, 5.3.6.2)

3. **A** Book value does represent the liquidation value, or net worth, of a company. It's found by taking the company's assets minus its liabilities. (Page 331)

4. **C** Reg T sets loan value for securities at 50%. If equity in a margin account falls below this minimum, the account is "restricted." (Page 205)

5. **D** The proper hours for cold calls is between 8:00 a.m. and 9:00 p.m. (Page 10, 1.2.1)

6. **C** The separate account, with the investment choices available for most annuities, can do an effective job in providing good diversification. Depending upon market performance and allocation of funds in the separate account, a variable annuity may keep pace with inflation. (Page 134, 3.5.3.3)

7. **C** Both II and IV say the same thing and both are true. Expense ratios are a measure of a fund's efficiency; stock fund will usually dictate more trading within the fund and higher expenses. (Page 129)

8. **D** Depending upon the circumstances, the specialist may have all of the orders listed (market, limit and stop orders) in the order book. (Page 258)

9. **A** Since the company's stock is expected to remain in a tight trading range, selling a straddle will give the client two option premiums. The downside is the option position has unlimited risk. (Page 155)

10. **C** As a principal, either a mark-up or mark-down will be used. (Page 228)

11. **D** JTIC, or tenants in common, does not have a survivorship provision. The portion of the account owned by the deceased person will remain in her estate until probated. (Page 190)

12. **B** Coterminous debt describes the situation, since it is "overlapping debt." (Page 104)

13. **A** Price changes over a period of time are an important consideration in determining the buying power of a dollar today versus some years ago. Adjusting the value of the dollar to reflect price changes is called "constant dollars." (Pages 271, 272)

14. **B** Churning is an abusive activity and is monitored by turnover of capital in a customer's account. Broker profits versus customer profits and frequency of trades are also considerations in determining this activity. (Page 229, 5.1.3)

15. **D** Our client has written the put and will receive the premium of 5 ($5 per share × 100 shares = $500 in premiums). Possible loss for this short put position is not unlimited, since the stock can go only from the strike price minus the premium to zero, or in this instance—$50 – $5 × 100 = $4,500 maximum loss. (Page 154)

16. **A** A 360-day year consisting of twelve 30-day months is used for both municipal and corporate bond accrued interest calculations. (Page 90, 3.4.4.5)

17. **D** View restricted stock as having "restrictions" on trading for a 12-month period. Therefore, it must be purchased to hold—not for short-term speculation. (Page 244)

18. **B** Preferred stock is usually purchased for its quarterly dividend. Cumulative stock is one type of preferred stock and refers to how "missed" dividends are paid out. (Page 56, 3.3.3)

19. **D** The proper procedure is to discuss why you believe the trade is not suitable for the client: if the client insists in making the trade, mark the order ticket unsolicited. (Page 25)

20. **D** Full power of attorney does give the authority for deposits to and/or cash withdrawals from the account. (Page 192)

21. **D** The client has purchased a ZOR Oct 40 call and sold a ZOR Feb 40 call, the overall definition of a spread. As to the type of the spread, the only difference is the time (Oct and Feb). Therefore, the position is a time or calendar spread. Shown as follows: (Page 160)

	Oct	Nov	Dec	Jan	Feb	Mar
50						
45						
40	X	—	—	—	X	
35						

Time or calendar spread

22. **A** The correct answer is 70 days. The M&S bond will pay out interest on March 1 and September 1. The trade date is listed as May 8, which means settlement date will be May 11 (regular way). Interest is paid up to, but not including, settlement date (May 10). Interest will be due based upon 30 days in March, 30 days in April and 10 days in May, or 70 days in total. (Page 90, 3.4.4.5)

23. **B** The subscription agreement is the correct choice. It is the agreement every limited partner must sign. Among the detail of this agreement is the appointment of the GP (General Partner) to act on behalf of the limited partners. (Pages 66, 70)

24. **D** A KEOGH plan is a qualified retirement plan used for unincorporated business structures. (Page 164, 3.7.1.2)

25. **B** The firm element refers to the annual compliance meeting that you will be required to attend. If you do not attend, your license will be suspended until you do attend a makeup meeting. (Page 226)

26. **C** The Blue List is devoted almost entirely to the municipal secondary market. (Page 343, 7.3.4)

27. **A** The premium for a call option will be higher the closer, or lower, the strike price is to the current market price. (Page 159)

28. **B** Minimum maintenance for a short position in a margin account is 30% of the short market value. (Page 206)

29. **C** Breakpoints are used by many mutual funds to offer lower commission rates for a larger amount of money being placed into the fund. (Page 129)

30. **B** Intangible drilling costs (IDCs) are being described by the question. If the IDC write-off applies, it's usually 100% in the first year. (Page 69)

31. **C** The Registered Representative has the responsibility to do "due diligence" to determine if customer information given is accurate. (Page 25)

32. **B** An insured municipal bond will be insured by private bond insurance, such as MBIA, CGIC, FGIC or AMBAC. This type insurance provides for payment of both interest and principal should a bond default. (Page 341, 7.2.5.5)

33. **D** Insurance usually makes the bond AAA (S & P) or Aaa (Moody's) in rating. (Page 341, 7.2.5.5)

34. **D** The highest degree of safety for a security is a direct obligation of the U.S. Government due to its unlimited taxing authority. GNMA is one of those direct obligations. (Pages 73, 79)

35. **A** Actual settlement date determines when the exchange of securities and funds is required. This procedure is set up by the Uniform Practice Code (UPC). Page 306, 6.2.2)

36. **D** All three answers are correct. UITs do not have active management of securities within the trust. Therefore, they do not need a board of directors or an investment advisor. (Page 131, 3.5.2.2)

37. **D** Legislative risk can have negative consequences for investments a client already owns. As an example, consider the negative impact upon limited partnerships due to tax law changes made in the mid-1980s. (Page 43)

38. **A** Reinvestment risk is a concern as discussed in the question. Also, remember there is only one investment which has no reinvestment risk and that is zero coupon bonds. (Page 41, 3.1)

39. **C** Cumulative voting can favor the small investors if a voting issue is of particular importance to them. In effect, the small investors could allocate their votes to one issue and not vote on remaining issues. (Page 53)

40. **C** This position is called a diagonal spread as the chart below denotes. Both the duration (time) of the option and price (strike price) vary. (Page 160)

	Oct	Nov	Dec	Jan	Feb	Mar
50					X	
45						
40						
35	X					

Diagonal spread (differs in time and price)

41. **B** The description "variable rate" defines the bond. Its coupon does change in relation to some other interest rate that has been specified. Since the interest can change, the resale price will be relatively stable. (Page 105)

42. **A** The company will usually need the assistance of an investment banker to determine what securities should be issued. (Page 233, 5.2.1.1)

43. **D** Mutual funds offer all of the choices listed. (Page 333, 7.2.4.1)

44. **D** In this case the question is asking for the *lowest* monthly income. The answer is joint life, since payments will be calculated over two lifetimes, not one, as in the other choices. (Page 139)

45. **A** An allied member refers to NYSE rules and uses 5% as the tracking percentage for key persons within a member firm. (Page 225)

46. **D** Market value and equity are factors in determining both the Regulation T and maintenance requirements within a margin account. (Page 206)

47. **B** Calculate by using the coupon ($62.50) divided by the bond year (360 days): the answer is .1736 cents per day. (Page 90)

48. **C** The options agreement must be signed, and returned to the broker-dealer in 15 days, or less. (Page 189)

49. **A** The traditional IRA does have a mandatory distribution requirement at age 70½. If the distribution is not made by then, there's a tax penalty of 50% on what should have been taken from the account. (Page 162)

50. **A** In many instances issuers must pay for the bond rating. Sometimes (e.g., for a small county school) the cost of the rating may not be justified in relation to the overall quality of the bond. (Page 108)

51. **C** The usual minimum margin requirement is $2,000 in cash, unless the total amount of the initial purchase is less than $2,000. Under that circumstance, 100% of the purchase amount is required. (Page 189)

52. **B** The primary market refers to the initial sale of a security, such as the IPO for a stock. The proceeds go to the issuer and, of course, not to the underwriter. "Resale" is a general reference to the secondary market. (Page 232, 5.2)

53. **A** All choices are correct. Open orders may be canceled and options may be exercised. New orders and open orders remaining on file may not be filled until the halt has been lifted. Remember, a security may trade in more than one market and the trading halt may apply only to the market where it was issued. (Page 260)

54. **C** The choice of the record date, and the amount of the dividend, is the responsibility of the Board of Directors (BOD). The holders of the security on the record date will receive the dividend declared. (Page 306, 6.2.2.2)

55. **A** The client is attempting to trade the settlement period and the account will be frozen for 90 days. The client must pay for ZORG before the sale of the same stock is made. (Page 196)

56. **B** The dated date (DTD) is the date interest begins to accrue and will usually differ from the settlement date. The buyer will not begin receiving interest from the bond until settlement is made. The interest calculation, for the purposes of bond settlement, will not include the settlement date for the bond. (Page 112)

57. **D** An option listed on an exchange is known as a "listed option" and has standardized exercise (strike) prices and expiration dates. (Pages 143, 262)

58. **D** A fiduciary account in most states will have a listing, or legal list, of approved securities. Speculation in this type account is not normally permitted and a court certification may be required to open the account. (Page 198, 4.2.2)

59. **A** A recourse loan does increase an investor's liability, since the lender may revert to both the general and limited partners for payment. (Page 67)

60. **D** The preemptive rights are in place to offer existing stockholders first chance to buy additional stock from the company, if they choose to do so. The rights are short term offers to allow purchase of the issue below current market price. (Page 53)

61. **B** The transfer agent is responsible for cancellation and reissue of certificates. (Page 52)

62. **A** The trough precedes an expansion in business activity, followed by a peak, then contraction in activity. (Page 271, 5.4.1)

63. **B** An NHA bond is a New Housing Authority bond and is a direct obligation of the government. A low tax rate, such as 15%, will normally exclude the purchase of municipal bonds as being "unsuitable." (Page 105)

64. **A** This option is for experienced investors, so it's considered speculation, or high risk. (Page 153)

65. **B** Capital loss is the very real possibility for loss of the original investment. As a Registered Representative you may not offer any type of account guarantee and may not take discretion over an account unless you have written approval to do so from the client. (Page 61, 3.3.5.1)

66. **D** "Churning" is excessive trading to generate commissions, and is usually spotted by an increase in trading activity after an account becomes discretionary. (Page 230)

67. **D** The breakeven for a long call is always the strike price (65) plus the premium (5), so total break-even for this position is $70 per share. (Page 147)

68. **A** The correct answer is 7.4% and is calculated by taking 100% minus the tax rate (46%). the remainder is 54 (.54). Enter the interest rate for the bond into your calculator as .04 divided by the remainder (.54) and the result is 7.4%. (Page 116)

69. **D** The breakeven points for this straddle will be the sum of the premiums (9) plus and minus the strike price of 55. Therefore, the breakeven points are 55 + 9 = 64 and 55 – 9 = 46. (Page 155)

70. **C** Arbitration is the securities industry's way of solving disputes. However, a

class action suit is not included in an arbitration agreement. (Pages 196, 230, 5.1.4)

71. **B** Reinvestment risk is the concern for GNMA agency backed securities. GNMA (Government National Mortgage Association) is a direct obligation of the government and is backed its taxing authority. (Page 79, 3.4.2.3)

72. **A** Unrealized versus realized gains in mutual funds invested in a cash account is a discussion that must be made prior to the client receiving the 1099. Since an investor in a mutual fund is an owner of the assets of the fund, the investor will receive taxable gains if they are realized. (Page 61, 3.3.5.1)

73. **C** The term convertible (convertible bonds, convertible preferred stock) means the security may be changed into a certain number of shares of common stock. (Page 56, 3.3.3; Page 86, 3.4.4.3)

74. **A** Dilution refers to a reduction in percent of ownership if additional stock is issued and the stockholder does not purchase additional shares. Nonvoting shares will not "dilute" ownership, since voting privileges do not exist, and management will remain intact. (Page 53)

75. **B** A Registered Principal's approval for a new account will take into consideration risk tolerance and other key factors listed on the new account forms. In addition, an "address of record" is required to satisfy the need for specific mailing instructions. (Page 188, 4.1)

76. **D** The regional exchanges do not include either AMEX or NYSE. OTC is, of course, not an exchange. (Page 258, 5.3.4.1)

77. **C** The term "DR" is used for the amount owed the broker-dealer in a customer's margin account. (Page 203, 4.3.3.1)

78. **B** All choices are correct. Also, a closed-end fund may sell above, or below, its NAV. (Page 121)

79. **C** An example of a defensive industry would be food and tobacco. Defensive industry stocks have lower returns, are more stable, and are more suitable for an investor wanting less risk. (Page 55)

80. **D** The LIFO (last in first out) approach is used for taxation of variable annuities. This means the "last in"—interest—is the "first out"—first to be taxed. An increase in the value of an annuity is taxed as *ordinary income.* (Page 139, 3.5.3.7)

81. **D** Cash settlement refers to settlement (payment) on the trade date, and not to bond ratings and/or regular way settlement (T+3). (Page 308, 6.2.2.6)

82. **B** Maximum gain for the position will be the short sale price of $62 per share minus the cost of the long call ($5 per share)—or $57 × 100 shares $5,700. (Pages 214, 215)

83. **C** Maximum loss is limited in this short position by the strike price of the long call ($65). The maximum loss will be the strike price ($65) minus the short sale price ($62)—or $3 per share. Add to the $3 loss plus the price paid for the call ($5) and you have the maximum loss of $8 per share × 100 shares—or $800. You may want to use a T chart like the one here to assist in understanding. (Pages 144, 213, 214)

cash paid DR	cash received CR
65	62
5	
70	62
Loss (800)	

84. **A** The term "exchange" refers to an auction (sometimes called double auction) market, where buyers and sellers come together. "Exchange" also refers to marketplace or location. (Page 258, 5.3.4.1)

85. **D** In a deferred compensation plan the employee does become a general creditor of the firm and, upon retirement, the money is paid out as ordinary income. An additional concern for someone planning to go into the

plan described in the question is the lower credit rating. In other words, will the company still be in business when the employee is ready to retire? (Page 165)

86. **A** The equity in the account will be $65,000. To calculate, use the market value of $110,000 minus the debt owed ($45,000). The remaining amount ($65,000) is equity in the account. (Page 203)

87. **C** The difference between the two prices is called the spread. (Page 237)

88. **A** Over the counter (OTC) is the interdealer market. Here, prices are negotiated. (Page 260, 5.3.4.2)

89. **B** In a limited partnership (DPP) the General Partner has "disproportionate sharing," meaning the GP shares a relatively small portion of expenses, but usually gets a major portion of revenues. (Page 71)

90. **A** As in any security trading without a certificate, the trade confirmation is the proof of ownership. (Page 303, 6.1.6)

91. **C** The syndicate management fee is based upon a charge per bond and is paid out before other charges. The syndicate manager receives this fee based upon efforts required to bring the new issue to market. (Page 237)

92. **A** The investor has downside protection to cover the long position of BAT for the duration of the put. (Page 154)

93. **D** The Official Statement for municipal bonds is the document that must be provided. The Official Statement is the equivalent of the corporate prospectus. (Page 248)

94. **B** The proper procedure is to buy the stock, but mark the order "unsolicited." It is true the stock may not be in the client's best interest, but it is also the client's decision. (Pages 196, 256)

95. **D** Stock ahead does refer to orders in the system that will execute ahead of a new limit order you have just entered for the client. (Pages 299, 300)

96. **D** The current market price of the stock divided by the annual earnings will provide the earnings per share (EPS). As an example, current market value of $27 per share and earnings of $1.50 will produce an EPS of 18. (Page 331)

97. **A** The Firm Element meeting is the annual meeting all Registered Representatives must attend, or they cannot continue in production! (Page 226)

98. **B** The yield to maturity (YTM) for a premium bond will always be lower than the coupon. For your information, the terms coupon rate, interest rate and nominal rate have the same meaning. (Page 91, 3.4.4.6)

99. **C** Options transactions are regulated by the Chicago Board Options Exchange (CBOE). CBOE is a Self Regulatory Organization (SRO). (Page 4)

100. **D** An initial purchase offering (IPO) may never be purchased with "borrowed money," or margin. (Page 202)

101. **A** Buying a put or a call for a stock will defer a decision and lock in a future selling price (put) or a future buy price (call). (Page 153, 3.6.1.3, 154)

102. **B** The employing broker-dealer must always be notified of any new account opened for an employee. This procedure is mandatory and no exception may be made. (Page 194)

103. **A** Almost all options we have to offer are "American-style," which means they may be exercised at any time prior to the option expiration date. "European-style" refers to an option that may be exercised only on the day preceding the expiration date. (Page 308, 6.2.2.4)

104. **B** Ease of transfer is a feature of both individual stocks and bonds. The secondary (resale) market makes

the transfer process smooth and a matter of convenience. (Page 258, 5.3.4)

105. **D** A market order is placed for an immediate execution if the security is trading. The market order does take precedence over all other orders. All orders, unless otherwise marked, are considered to be "day orders" and a "day order" will be canceled at the end of the day, not at the end of the week. (Page 299, 6.1.1)

106. **A** An initial public offering (IPO) must be sold initially at the public offering price (POP). If your firm is involved with the underwriting and/or sale of the IPO you may not, nor may any immediate family member, participate in the initial offering. (Page 238, 5.2.1.5)

107. **B** Most mutual funds do offer many fund choices—often called a family. Using the various fund choices to set up—and revise—an allocation, a change in investment strategy may be easily made. One caution, any change in a fund family may create a taxable event, especially in a regular "cash" investment account. (Pages 129, 294)

108. **A** Trust Indenture Act of 1939 is primarily concerned with corporate debt (bond) issues of 5 million dollars, or larger. (Page 246, 5.2.2.10)

109. **A** The correct answer is do not use the report. Reports must be current, indicate their source and be approved for use by your broker-dealer. Never use a report not approved by your broker-dealer. (Page 15)

110. **D** The act covers using nonpublic (insider) information for profit in making trades—or avoiding losses. It applies to all parties, not just to insiders, and may be "non-financial in nature." (Page 254)

111. **D** Tax credits are a feature of some real estate limited partnership programs and, if available, would offer a dollar for dollar reduction in taxes due for the investor. (Page 65, 3.3.6.1)

112. **D** The pledge of payment for this revenue bond is called the gross revenue pledge and it means debt service will be paid ahead of operations and maintenance costs. (Page 105)

113. **A** A general obligation (GO) bond always publishes a debt statement, since a GO bond is based on the taxing authority of the community. The revenue pledge is normally only for revenue bonds. (Page 103)

114. **B** Discretion, or limited POA, means almost every activity *except* making a deposit or withdrawing money from the account. Full power of attorney is required for those activities. (Pages 194, 195)

115. **D** The correct procedure is outlined in the question. You must freeze the account and cancel open orders to limit future activity. Awaiting further instructions means awaiting instructions from the executor. (Page 197)

116. **A** The general statement, which applies to insider trading, is 300% of profits made, or losses prevented, and up to 10 years in jail. (Page 229)

117. **B** The tax equivalent yield is the driving force for suitability of a municipal issue. The lower tax rate, such as 15%, will not generate sufficient tax advantage as compared to a fully taxable investment. Remember the tax equivalent yield is 100% minus the tax rate (15%) = 85%. Enter the bond rate as .035 divided by the remainder .85 = the tax equivalent yield of 4.1%. (Pages 116, 119)

118. **D** The call is at 45 and the market is 48, therefore, the call has intrinsic value of 48 minus 45, or 3. The remaining amount of the premium is "time," or 1. (Page 144)

119. **A** All order tickets must be approved by a Registered Principal no later than the end of the trading day.

The ROP would approve options transactions. (Page 301)

120. **D** The hypothecation agreement is needed in a margin account before securities may be pledged as collateral. The loan agreement is needed only if the account is to be approved for "short selling." (Page 199)

121. **C** The indicators given are coincident indicators and confirm where the economy is. (Page 273)

122. **D** Options contracts settle the next business day. If stock is delivered against an options contract, as in a call, the settlement for the stock is regular way (T + 3). (Page 307)

123. **B** A sell-stop order is placed below the current market value (CMV) to protect a profit, or to limit a loss. (Page 301)

124. **C** The correct order is secured creditors, general creditors, limited partners and general partner(s). (Page 67)

125. **B** Specialized traders are involved in risk arbitrage. This type activity would not be suitable for the vast majority of our clients. (Pages 214, 215)

End of first half of the practice exam # 2.

126. **D** Since the stock is predicted to remain stable over the option period, writing (selling) a call, for the purpose of retaining the premium would be the proper course of action. (Page 155)

127. **C** The selling concession is the largest portion of the underwriting spread. It is the amount received by a syndicate member for shares sold. (Page 238)

128. **D** JTIC, or Joint Tenants in Common, would be used when unequal ownership and *no right of survivorship* is needed in an account.(Page 190)

129. **A** The breakeven for a long put is the strike price (35) minus the premium (4), or 31. (Page 147)

130. **A** Life insurance may not placed into an IRA. An IRA is a qualified plan. (Page 163)

131. **B** As in any short sale, the short market value (SMV) must go down for the client to profit. (Pages 203, 204, 214)

132. **C** The customer's signature placed on a certificate must be guaranteed (verification the proper person signed the certificate) and may be done by either a commercial bank or broker-dealer. (Page 51)

133. **B** Records must be kept for a period of six years and must be easily accessible for the latest two of those six years. (Page 196)

134. **C** Of the choices listed, the GNMA is the most suitable, since the underlying securities of the fund are direct obligations of the U.S. Government. (Page 29)

135. **B** Growth companies are generally newer companies who are investing in their own future (investing in research and development as an example) and do not have the cash to pay a cash dividend. Based upon the probability the growth company will grow, investors may be very happy with a stock dividend instead of cash. (Pages 53, 55)

136. **A** After-tax dollars are used for cash dividends and all cash dividends are taxable to the stockholder as income. (Page 97)

137. **B** There are orders which may be executed without the specialist's personal involvement. However, all transactions must take place in front of the specialist. (Pages 255, 258, 259)

138. **A** The "inside market," as viewed by the retail client, is the best (highest) bid and best (lowest) asking price. (Page 259)

139. **B** The maximum gain on a debit spread is the difference between the strike price (10) minus the net debit (4 – 3 = 1), or 9 ($900). The maximum loss would occur if neither option were exercised, or net debit (4 – 3 = 1) $100. See the chart below. (Pages 157–160)

cash paid DR	cash received CR
4	3
40	50
44	53
	9 = $900 Gain

140. **A** The top of the trading range is the resistance level—resisting an upward movement. If the stock did go through the resistance level, this would be known as a bullish breakout. (Page 323)

141. **D** The act of 1934, or "people act," regulates the secondary market and trading activities. (Page 253, 5.3.1.1)

142. **B** Funds placed into a UGMA account are considered to be non-returnable to the donor. Upon reaching the age of majority, the adult child may use the funds for any purpose without the custodian's consent. (Pages 168, 191)

143. **D** A special situation mutual fund does contain higher risk companies and would not be suitable for conservative investors. Turnaround candidates, takeovers and other similar corporate situations may be a part of this type fund. (Page 55)

144. **D** All sales must be reported within 90 seconds after the execution of a trade. (Pages 261, 341)

145. **C** Within a variable annuity exchanges between funds are not a taxable consideration. Only when money is withdrawn from the annuity would taxes be a concern. (Page 139, 3.5.3.7)

146. **A** Options are called "derivative" securities since the underlying security—stock, index, etc.—would be the basis for their value. (Page 142, 3.6)

147. **B** Eurodollars are U.S. dollars on deposit outside the United States. They do remain denominated in U.S. dollars, instead of the local currency. (Pages 99, 267, 5.3.8.5)

148. **A** All treasuries are direct obligations of the government and the full amount ($650,000) will be covered by the "full faith and taxing authority" of the U.S. Government. (Page 73, 3.4.1)

149. **D** The definition of an accredited investor is all of the choices listed. Also, annual income may be joint income of at least $300,000 or more, instead of the $200,000 individual income. (Pages 71, 243)

150. **B** Zero coupon bonds "accrete" in value each year and, if in a taxable situation, the accreted amount is the taxable amount. (Pages 95, 107)

151. **C** 50 basis points equal 1/2%. Said another way, 100 basis points equal 1% and every 10 basis points equal one tenth of a percent. (Page 39, 117)

152. **A** Current liabilities are debts due in 12 months or less. (Page 329)

153. **B** Calculate the sales charge by subtracting the public offering price ($12.60) from the net asset value ($12.15). Enter the difference (.45) into your calculator divided by the public offering price ($12.60); the result is 3.57%—or 3.6%. (Page 128)

154. **A** The long call - short put indicates being bullish and a long put – short call indicates being bearish on the market. (Pages 154, 155)

155. **D** The seller's option contract allows a delayed settlement, if the delay in settlement is agreed to in advance of the sale. (Page 307, 6.2.2.3)

156. **B** As discussed in the answers to this question, a put will delay the sale of the stock, but will not make a short-term gain into a long-term gain. Since the intent to sell the stock was short term (10 mos.), the gain is also short term. (Page 161, 3.6.1.4)

157. **A** The syndicate letter, sometimes called the syndicate agreement, is the document which outlines a member's commitments. (Page 249)

158. **D** If a premium bond is being considered, there must be sufficient time remaining until either maturity or call to amortize the additional money paid (premium). If sufficient time is not available, the client will incur a loss. (Page 114)

159. **A** As a member of the syndicate, the purchase price for bonds is the public offering price (POP) minus "total takedown." Total takedown consists of a selling concession plus an additional takedown (discount) available to them as a syndicate member. (Page 249)

160. **D** A private placement may be made to any of the groups listed. However, the purpose for not going public must be investment and not speculation, since there will be a mandatory holding period for the securities. (Pages 243, 247)

161. **D** An overall rating for a bond must take into consideration those areas which may be quantified, such as debt and debt ratios, plus those that may be more subjective. The community's attitude toward paying debt could be one of those more subjective factors. (Pages 109, 110)

162. **B** Supervising and managing are activities of a Registered Principal. A Registered Principal has passed the appropriate Principal license exam(s). (Page 226)

163. **A** Protection for consumers from broker-dealer insolvency is the main mission of SIPC. (Page 257, 5.3.3)

164. **A** Overall, the spread will take the outlook of the more costly option. In this case, the more costly of the two options will be the KAT Feb 60 Call, which was purchased. Since the lower strike price is more expensive for a call and a purchase of the call was made, the position is bullish. (Page 159)

165. **A** Redemptions from a closed end fund are not made by the fund. Liquidation of shares comes directly from selling off the desired number of shares in the secondary market. This is one reason why these funds are called publicly traded funds. (Pages 121, 122)

166. **B** Approval by your employing broker-dealer is required for outside activities. (Page 7)

167. **D** ERISA regulations are used for qualified private retirement plans, such as 401K, KEOGH, SEP IRA, etc. (Page 166)

168. **D** All of the choices are correct. The key words in this question are "could charge" 8½%. Most funds are considerably below 8½% for sales charges. (Pages 126, 335)

169. **C** All order tickets must be marked either long or short. "Long" meaning the client owns the security to be sold and "short" meaning the client does not own the security at the time of the order. (Page 301)

170. **D** The only bond listed that could not be suitable is the income (adjustment) bond. This security is for bankrupt companies being reorganized. (Pages 86, 93)

171. **A** The tax equivalent yield is 8.33%. Calculate by taking 1.00 minus the tax rate .46 = .54. Enter the bond rate into your calculator as .045 and divide by the remainder, .54. The result is the tax equivalent yield of 8.33%. (Page 119)

172. **D** Municipal bonds are sold over the counter (OTC). (Page 263, 5.3.6)

173. **B** The maximum loss for this position is $600. Determine this position by subtracting the strike price for the call (35) from the short sale price (33) = 2. Add the cost of the long call (4) for a total potential loss of $600. See the chart on the next page. (Page 144)

cash paid DR	cash received CR
35	33
4	
39	33
Loss ($600)	

174. **B** A stop limit order goes through a two-step process. The first step in the process is to be "triggered" at the stop price. After the stop price has been attained the order will become a limit order. (Page 300)

175. **B** The assumption for the annuitization payment is called the assumed interest rate (AIR). Once the assumption is made it is compared to actual performance on a monthly basis. The result is the monthly payment for a variable annuity may vary up or down, according to investment performance. (Pages 135, 136)

176. **D** For mutual funds FIFO is the default method for determining cost basis. It will also generally be the option with the largest tax consequence, since the older shares will normally be the least expensive. (Page 64)

177. **A** The investor sold 7 calls and received a premium of 4 for each contract. Since each contract is for 100 shares, the maximum gain will be the premium received or 7 × 4 × 100 = $2,800. (Page 155)

178. **A** The maximum loss for a short position is unlimited. (Page 155)

179. **B** SLD means the latest transaction was delayed. (Page 342)

180. **B** Market breadth is used for a relative indication of market strength, not for volume. (Page 320, 7.2.1)

181. **D** All of the people listed would be considered as immediate family. (Pages 229, 238, 5.2.1.5)

182. **A** When an investor purchases an option the market must be volatile and move away from its present level for the option to be exercised. The term for this type market activity: the market will "widen." (Pages 157–160)

183. **B** The seller of an option receives the "premium." Therefore, this situation is the reverse of the previous question. The investor has received the premium and wants very little movement in the market. The term for this type market activity: the market will "narrow." (Pages 157–160)

184. **D** The specialist performs all of the activities listed. When performing as a principal, the specialist is expected to buy and sell for his own account, not to compete but to assist in maintaining an orderly market. (Pages 255, 258, 259)

185. **C** Book entry bonds do not have certificates to offer, even upon request. The trade confirmation is the client's "proof of ownership." (Page 85)

186. **D** The General Partner (GP) may not do any of the activities listed. In reference to the fiduciary responsibility, even outside a limited partnership, fiduciary responsibility may not be transferred. (Page 67)

187. **B** Arbitration does not cover a "deceptive practice" and the client could bring suit. The period of time (statute of limitations) is three years. (Page 230)

188. **D** The correct time period is 8:00 a.m.–9:00 p.m. These rules do not apply to a client. Also, a client may not be available during this time frame and can request you call her at some other time. (Page 10)

189. **A** The "capital asset pricing" theory does exist, and does analyze the relationship between risk and return. Choices "B" and "D" are too broad and too absolute to be correct. (Page 319)

190. **B** NASD and the MSRB rules both state you may not receive a gift of more than $100 per year from another broker-dealer. In addition, gifts may not be received conditional upon the sale of the broker-dealer's product(s).

191. **A** The Blue List is published every business day and contains the most

complete information available for the municipal bond secondary market. (Page 343, 7.3.4)

192. **D** Zero coupon bonds are the most volatile and are used to speculate on interest rate movements. (Page 45)

193. **D** The correct order is as the question is listed. Unpaid wages, unpaid taxes, secured debt, unsecured debt (debentures), general creditors, subordinated debt (subordinated debentures), preferred stock and last, common stock. (Page 54)

194. **D** Cumulative preferred stock will pay a quarterly dividend. If a dividend is missed, it must be made up (paid in arrears) before current dividends may be paid to stockholders. (Page 56)

195. **B** The overall position is a credit spread and is bearish, since the investor is "mostly" selling calls. Consider the chart below. (Page 157)

cash paid DR	cash received CR
5	7
5	7
	+2

196. **A** The trade date is the date for execution of the order. Settlement is determined to be from that date, such as T+3 for regular way settlement. ("T" is meant to be trade date.) (Page 303)

197. **D** Since the account is not tax sheltered, both gains and dividends are taxable in the current tax year. (Pages 131, 132)

198. **D** A limited partner is "limited" in the scope of any direct participation in the partnership. Therefore, a limited partner may not have management responsibility in the partnership. (Page 67)

199. **C** A territorial bond is a municipal bond that is triple tax exempt in all 50 states. The origin of territorial bonds may be Puerto Rico, Guam and the U.S. Virgin Islands. (Page 100)

200. **A** As you would expect, the two general types are both stock—common and preferred. (Equity refers to ownership = stock) (Page 52, 3.3.2; Page 56, 3.3.3)

201. **A** Limit orders may not be used for over the counter trades. The OTC market is negotiated versus being an "auction" and there is no specialist with which to leave a limit order. (Pages 299, 300)

202. **D** A specialized fund (sector fund) is by definition not a diversified fund, since it will concentrate in one specific area; technology stocks, for example. It does offer both more opportunity for gain—and loss—and is to be considered to be of higher risk. (Page 124)

203. **C** The spread is known as a vertical (price) spread, since only the price is different. Consider the chart below. (Page 160)

	Oct	Nov	Dec	Jan	Feb	Mar
50						
45		X				
40						
35		X				

Vertical or price spread

204. **D** All of the securities mentioned in the question trade OTC. Of particular importance, municipal bonds, resale government bonds and bank stocks. (Page 342, 7.3.2)

205. **A** Raw land is, of course, considered to be speculative and usually illiquid. This type of investment is not suitable for a conservative investor. (Page 68)

206. **B** Covered calls are a strategy used to gain income from a long stock position. The income is produced by writing the call and the risk is limited, since the underlying stock for the option is long in the client's account. (Page 155)

207. **C** Complaints regarding municipal bonds must be kept on file for six years. (Page 196)

208. **B** The proper procedure is to log in the complaint, indicate what actions have been taken and deliver the MSRB's Investor Brochure to the client. The OS mentioned does not apply here, since it is the equivalent of the prospectus for stock and corporate bonds. (Page 196)

209. **A** Providing information to investors identifies the firm as a dealer in the eyes of the MSRB. (Page 254)

210. **B** Two years is the correct answer. Records must be kept for six years, but only the last two years must be kept reasonably accessible. (Pages 196, 302)

211. **C** The Transfer Agent is the usual place for validation of the certificate. (Page 52)

212. **A** Each of the activities may be accomplished by our client. In the case of trading an option, this action could be done tò make a profit, or limit a loss. Holding the option, instead of trading, could be the only choice, since the option may not have any intrinsic value. (Page 153, 3.6.1.3)

213. **D** The resale market for options contracts is a very active market and may fluctuate as often as daily. When the market value for the underlying stock goes down, keep in mind the value for calls and puts will react. As the question proposes, when the value of the underlying stock goes down, calls will be further out of the money and puts will be further into the money. (Page 153, 3.6.1.3)

214. **A** The option owner is in charge of the contract and could sell the option to close out the position. Of the remaining choices, only rewriting "the option contract" is not possible. (Page 144)

215. **B** The definition of a broker is one who charges commissions and arranges trades. All of the other choices refer to the "dealer." (Page 254)

216. **C** Options contracts on the same side of the market are Long calls—Short puts (bullish) and Long puts—Short calls (bearish). (Page 153, 3.6.1.3)

217. **B** Pricing of a variable rate municipal bond on the secondary (resale) market is very stable, since the interest rate does vary according to an interest rate index. Therefore, when interest rates are going up the coupon, or interest rate, is also going up—and vice versa. (Page 101)

218. **A** The result of a reverse split is the client now has fewer shares than before, which is a major concern for the broker (e.g., how many shares should the sell order be written for?). (Page 56)

219. **D** All of the activities mentioned in the question are functions of the Municipal Principal. (Page 226)

220. **B** The percentage is 10%, or more, and the bond may be considered "private activity." If that is the case, the bond is not automatically granted tax exempt status. (Page 100, 3.4.8)

221. **B** For corporate securities only indications of interest may be taken during the cooling off period. In addition, those prospects who have indicated an interest, must receive the preliminary prospectus (red herring). (Page 242)

222. **A** NASD may not impose a jail sentence, only the SEC or government can. (Page 232)

223. **D** In order for the investor to make money with a short straddle, the market must remain stable, or narrow. Under those circumstances, the premium will remain with our investor and will represent the maximum profit potential. (Page 155)

224. **A** In a short margin account the $2,000 is never waived, as it could be for the long margin account. (Page 202)

225. **B** A nominal quote is an assessment of where a stock might trade in an active market. (Page 261)

226. **B** The pink sheets are where penny stocks ($5.00, or less in value) may be found. (Page 343)

227. **C** The NASD 5% markup policy is a guideline to ensure fair treatment of the investing public. It may be higher than 5% if a security is very thinly traded (inactive). (Page 227)

228. **A** An odd-lot for equity securities is a trade of 99 shares or fewer. This type transaction is more expensive for the client and the preferred quantity to buy or sell is a round lot of 100 shares, or a multiple of 100 shares. (Page 306)

229. **D** All of the items listed, plus many more, are included in the trade confirmation. The trade confirmation may also be used for proof of ownership, which would be the situation for book entry bonds. (Page 303, 6.1.6)

230. **C** UITs may be in several forms, such as stocks, corporate bonds, municipal bonds, etc. In all instances the UIT will contain a pool securities that generally remains the same throughout the life of the UIT. Therefore, there is no need for a fund manager, or a board of directors, since there is nothing to trade or vote on. (Page 131, 3.5.2.2)

231. **D** In addition to the requirements listed, if either 100 investors or $100,000 has not been obtained initially, both must be met within 90 days of registration. (Page 121, 3.5.2.1)

232. **A** A final, or summary prospectus, must be provided to the client, as outlined in the question. In addition, open end investment companies do not have a secondary market for their shares. The secondary market is not needed, since the fund redeems the shares directly from the client. (Page 122)

233. **D** Current liabilities for a company include accounts payable, accrued wages payable and also current long term debt which is due within the next 12 months. (Page 325, 7.2.3.2)

234. **A** Commodities are not considered to be a security and a Registered Representative is not licensed to sell them. (Page 4, 1.1)

235. **D** Either the blue chip stock or the balanced mutual fund would provide moderate growth. Between those two choices, the blue chip stock will have more risk, since it is an individual stock versus the diversity of a mutual fund. (Pages 29, 124)

236. **B** The discount for a municipal bond is treated as ordinary income and is not offset by the coupon payment as would be the case for corporate bonds. (Page 115)

237. **C** The informer may receive an informer bounty, which is up to 10% of the amounts recovered. (Page 254, 5.3.1.2)

238. **C** The inside market is best viewed from the client's point of view. Our client's purchase price is the best asking price and our client's selling price is the best bid price. The "best price" is the lowest asking price and the highest bid price—which is known as the inside market. (Page 258)

239. **D** Margin accounts offer all of the possibilities discussed in the question. However, it must be pointed out to the client losses will be more pronounced due to the use of borrowed money for purchases within the margin account. (Page 189)

240. **A** The owner is in control, but loses the premium if the option is not exercised, while the seller is obligated to buy or sell according to the contract. If the option is not exercised, the seller keeps the premium. (Page 142, 3.6.1)

241. **B** The investor purchased an OEX call with a strike price of 450. OEX is now at 470, or up 20 points, or $2,000 ($100 per point). The cost of the call is 5 x 100, or $500. Therefore, the profit for the purchase of this call is $2,000 – $500 = $1,500. (Page 150)

242. **A** The proxy is an absentee ballot intended for the stockholder who

will not be attending the annual shareholders' meeting, but wants to vote on the issues. It is considered to be a form of limited power of attorney, since another person is directed to vote on the shareholder's behalf. (Page 254, 5.3.1.3)

243. **C** Moral obligation bonds are revenue bonds, which may not have enough revenue to pay the debt service. Under certain conditions the state legislature may go on record to provide backing if needed for this type bond. If this is done the state has not passed a law to back the bond issue, but has indicated it has a "moral obligation" to do so. (Page 106)

244. **A** All of the areas listed in the question are important considerations. This includes the existence of any presale orders. Remember, municipal bond issues do have authorization to accept pre-sale orders and to set up an order priority. This differs from corporate issues. (Pages 249, 250)

245. **D** Again, all of the areas mentioned in the question are important for record keeping that will be in compliance. In addition to those listed, a list of all transactions must be kept up to date by the Registered Representative. (Page 309)

246. **D** The blue sky laws cover securities activities with a certain state. This is the reason for a security, a registered representative or a broker-dealer to be blue-skyed in a state in which they intend to do business. (Pages 236, 245)

247. **C** The loss for this position is $1,700. Calculate this position by subtracting the put strike price (65) from the sale price of the stock (42) = $2,300. In this instance the $2,300 is a loss, since the purchase price for the BAT is from the exercise of the put (65) and the sale price is current market value (42). The gross loss is ($2,300). A premium was received for writing the put (6). Subtract the gross loss (minus $2,300) from the put premium ($600) and the net loss is $1,700. Consider this chart. (Page 154)

cash paid DR	cash received CR
	6
65	42
65	48
Loss ($1,700)	

248. **A** An aggressive growth fund could have a turnover of 100% and not be "churning" the account. However, the expenses for the fund may be very high and should be examined. (Page 336)

249. **B** A defined contribution plan will favor younger employees, since they have a longer time period for the accumulation of money. (Page 165)

250. **C** The zero coupon bond is the only bond that does not have reinvestment risk. (Pages 44, 107)